A Resource Guide to the Golden Age of Radio

Special Collections, Bibliography and the Internet

Other Books From Book Hunter Press

Golden Age of Radio Books

The Witch's Tale by Alonzo Deen Cole, edited by David S. Siegel
Flashgun Casey, Crime Photographer: From the Pulps to Radio and Beyond
  by J. Randolph Cox and David S. Siegel

Trade paperbacks available from www.bookhunterpress.com/radio

The Used Book Lover's Guide Series

By David S. and Susan Siegel
Used Book Lover's Guide to New England
Used Book Lover's Guide to the Mid-Atlantic States
Used Book Lover's Guide to the South Atlantic States
Used Book Lover's Guide to the Midwest
Used Book Lover's Guide to the Central/Western States
Used Book Lover's Guide to the Pacific Coast States
Used Book Lover's Guide to Canada

Available in print and online by subscription from www.bookhunterpress.com

A Resource Guide to the Golden Age of Radio

Special Collections, Bibliography and the Internet

By
Susan and David S. Siegel

Book Hunter Press
Yorktown Heights, New York

Printed and bound in the United States of America

Library of Congress Control Number: 2005909420

ISBN: 1-891379-04-6
978-1-891379-04-8

Book Hunter Press
PO Box 193 • Yorktown Heights, NY 10598
(914) 245-6608 • Fax: (914) 245-2630
www.bookhunterpress.com/radio • bookhunterpress@verizon.net

Dedication

This book is dedicated to the thousands of men and women who wrote, performed, directed, produced, engineered or otherwise contributed to both network and local radio from the mid–1920s to the mid–1960s and whose efforts brought comfort, entertainment and vital information to millions of Americans during the dark days of the Depression and the uncertain days of World War II and its aftermath.

Acknowledgments

The authors wish to express their sincere thanks to Barbara Watkins for her tireless efforts proof reading this manuscript.

We would also like to acknowledge the following old time radio authors and researchers who unselfishly provided us with leads on the whereabouts of possible special collections: Howard Blue, Read G. Burgan, Jim Cox, Jack French, J. David Goldin, Chris Lembasis, Terry Salomonson, Karl Schadow, Stewart Wright and Jim Widner.

Last but by no means least, we would like to express our thanks to the countless number of curators and archivists in repositories throughout the United States who helped make this book possible by submitting information about their collections, patiently answering our questions and follow up requests and generously offering suggestions where we might find additional relevant special collections.

Table of Contents

Introduction

Recapturing the Golden Age of Radio

The mid–1920s to the mid–1960s, roughly 40 years, is generally recognized as representing the Golden Age of Radio in the United States.

Today, some four decades after the last of the Golden Age of Radio broadcasts went off the air, dozens of new books are being published annually analyzing and celebrating radio and the immense influence it had on virtually all aspects of American society and culture. In fact, we would venture to guess that at least as many, if not more, books have been written about radio's Golden Age since its passing then were published during the 40 years of its glory.

This interest is, we believe, a belated and long overdue recognition of the powerful role radio played as a social, cultural and economic force that influenced the daily lives of four generations of Americans. From the time they woke up and turned on the radio for the morning news to the mid-day soap operas, late afternoon children's shows and array of programs that entertained the entire family during the evening hours, most Americans were never far from a radio.

Where do modern historians get information about programs that aired a half a century or more ago? Most of the writers, directors and performers responsible for creating the programs never imagined that they would ever be heard again, let alone written about.

There are sources; some relatively easy to find and others much less so. Sound recordings of many of the old time radio broadcasts have survived into the 21st century thanks to the efforts of several archives, the entrepreneurial instincts of certain pioneering collectors and a network of old time radio enthusiasts. And with the advent of the Internet, many of these recordings are now available to a world wide audience for pleasure as well as scholarship. Also thanks to the Internet, long out-of-print books about the Golden Age of Radio can be located on the shelves of used book dealers and in libraries across the country.

Another valuable source of information are the interviews of radio veterans and members of their families, many of which were taped more than 20 years ago by radio historians such as John Dunning, Chuck Schaden, Dick Bertel, Richard Lamparski and others in an effort to keep the memory of radio alive for future generations.

It is ironic, though, that one of the richest sources of information, the actual personal and professional papers of the thousands of people who were associated with radio during its Golden Age and who had the foresight to donate their memorabilia to various institutions, can also be among the most difficult sources to locate — mainly because up until now, there was no single comprehensive listing of primary source material devoted exclusively to the Golden Age of Radio.

While several of the repositories included in the pages of this Guide have long standing and well deserved reputations as specializing in radio, the collections in these institutions represent only "the tip of the iceberg"; it was only during the course of doing the research for this book that the authors discovered the full extent of the primary source material quietly sitting on the shelves of repositories spread across the United States waiting to be discovered.

Indeed, we learned of just such a "discovery" — and what it can lead to — when we added a new title to our ever growing collection of books dealing with the Golden Age of Radio. In the Introduction and Acknowledgment to his 2005 biography of Agnes Moorehead, a frequent guest star on *Suspense*, ("I Love the Illusion: The Life and Career of Agnes Moorehead," Bear Manor Media, 2005), author Charles Tranberg shares the following note of serendipity with his readers:

> I stumbled upon the subject of this book by accident. While visiting the Wisconsin State Historical Society archives in Madison, Wisconsin, doing research on another subject, I discovered that the archives held the papers of Agnes Moorehead — in fact, 159 boxes of papers, scrapbooks, reviews, scripts and other memorabilia. I almost immediately ordered some boxes to review, and I was hooked. I found the subject of the book I always wanted to write. And a fascinating subject she turned out to be.

It is the authors' sincere hope that the publication of this Resource Guide and the new-found awareness of these primary source materials will encourage radio historians, popular culture scholars and old time radio enthusiasts to conduct additional research into aspects of the Golden Age of Radio not previously written about and perhaps share their findings in articles and/or books. It is also our hope that this book will lead to the discovery of additional archival material gathering dust on the shelves of institutions not listed in these pages.

And finally, we hope that those fortunate enough to discover such treasures will contact the authors so that this information may be included in a future volume and made available to other researchers and lovers of old time radio.

Susan and David S. Siegel
December, 2005

Chapter 1: Researching the Golden Age of Radio

How to Use This Guide

What follows is a general introduction that applies to all three sections of this Guide. However, given the different nature of the material in the three sections, each section has its own specialized introduction. In addition, this chapter includes some general suggestions on conducting research involving radio's Golden Age.

What this book is about

The overriding objective of the Guide is to assist researchers locate primary and secondary sources of information about the people and programs associated with the Golden Age of Radio as well as radio station history, the history of radio broadcasting and the impact radio had on American society and culture from the mid-1920s to the mid-1960s.

Unlike encyclopedic type Golden Age of Radio reference books such as John Dunning's "On the Air: The Encyclopedia of Old-Time Radio" or Luther Sies's "Encyclopedia of American Radio" that provide comprehensive listings of programs and radio personalities, the Guide includes people and programs *if and when* the authors have been able to identify a primary or secondary source of information about them.

The Guide is limited to radio programming in the United States, including the Armed Forces Radio Service, but *does not* include the technical aspects of radio or U.S. radio programming for overseas audiences such as *Radio Free Europe* or the *Voice of America*. It also does not include World War II propaganda broadcasts that originated overseas such as those of Tokyo Rose, Lord Haw Haw and Axis Sally.

While this volume is the most comprehensive reference guide of its type published to date, the authors recognize that regardless of how extensive our efforts may have been, repositories are continually acquiring and processing new special collections, new books about the Golden Age of Radio are being published every year and Internet sites come and go. The authors also note that there are additional primary and secondary sources that could possibly prove helpful (see below). With that in mind, the authors welcome any information concerning a resource that may not be in the Guide for inclusion (we hope) in a future volume.

How to use this book

The authors assume that researchers will be using this Guide in conjunction with other reference material and will be coming to it with some prior knowledge of the Golden Age of Radio and the specific subject area that they are investigating. The authors also suggest that researchers will be able to make the most effective use of the Guide by starting with the Index that combines the entries in all three sections under the same subject headings and sets out a road map for future investigation.

For example, a person's name may not be listed in the Index — but information about the person might be found by checking the Index under the names of programs the person was associated with, with the stations that aired those programs, the program genre, or possibly the general subject heading.

This point is best illustrated by the following sample listings; two special collections in two repositories and one bibliographic entry.

Special Collection listings

555. Edward M. Kirby Collection, 1923-1983, bulk 1938-1959. Contains correspondence, scrapbooks, transcription discs, photographs, speeches, scripts, awards and magazine and newspaper articles documenting Kirby's early career in broadcasting, including his work at WSM, as Director of Public Relations for the National Association of Broadcasters and at Broadcast Music, Inc. and as the chief of the radio branch of the War Department during World War II. Also includes material relating to *The Army Hour*. Ten related transcription discs from the collection of Major Glenn Miller and the American Band of the Allied Expeditionary Forces Program have been transferred to the Library's audio collection.

2112. Edward Montague Kirby Reminiscences, 1964. Reminiscences concerning radio broadcasting during World War II by a chief of the Radio Branch of the War Department's Public Relations Bureau, 1941--1945. The recollections encompass mobilization, the Armed Forces Radio Service and a review of programs produced by the commercial networks under army auspices.

Bibliographic listing (World War II Section)

3617. Kirby, Edward M. and Jack W. Harris. Star-Spangled Radio: Radio's Part in World War II. Chicago, Ziff-Davis, 1948.

In the Index, the special collections are listed under the following subject headings: Kirby, Edward M., station history-WSM, National Association of Broadcasters, Broadcast Music, Inc., World War II-government agencies, *Army Hour*, Armed Forces Radio Service (AFRS), Music-big bands and Miller, Glenn. The book is indexed under Kirby, Edward M., World War II-government agencies and AFRS.

Researchers may be interested in either special collection or the book for several different reasons and may "flag" the entries in the Index as a potential source of information either because they are specifically looking for material about Edward Kirby, or without knowing his name and his contribution to the Golden Age of Radio, they may be looking for material relating to at least eight other subject areas: WSM history, radio during World War II, the Armed Forced Radio Service, a specific AFRS program, the National Association of Broadcasters, Broadcast Music, Inc., big bands or specifically the band leader Glenn Miller.

A note about program titles

When specific programs are noted in the Special Collections and Internet sections, the beginning articles "The" and "A" are generally included in the title. However, in order to facilitate searches, the articles are either dropped in the Index or, in the case of "A," is placed at the end of the title. Program titles are in italics as distinct from the titles of individual scripts or episodes which are in quotation marks.

It should be noted that the titles of many long running programs changed over the years as the programs' sponsors changed. For example, *The Eddie Cantor Show* was also known as *The Chase and Sanborn Hour*, *The Camel Caravan* and *Time to Smile* when it was sponsored by Bristol Myers and Sal Hepatica. Similarly, *The Jack Benny Program* was, over the years, also known by several different titles, including *The General Tire Show*, *The Jell-O Program*, *The Grape Nuts and Grape Nuts Flakes Program*, *The Lucky Strike Program* and *The Canada Dry Program*. Researchers are advised, therefore, to check the Index under both the program title and the performer's name.

And sometimes, the program title stayed the same but the performers changed. For example, *The Chase and Sanborn Hour* cited above was an alternate name for *The Eddie Cantor Show*, 1931–1934 — but it was also an alternate title for *The Charlie McCarthy Show* (a.k.a. *The Edgar Bergen-Charlie McCarthy Show*), 1937–1948. A second alternate title for *The Eddie Cantor Show*, *The Camel Caravan*, 1938–1939, was also an alternate title for *The Vaughn Monroe Show*, 1946–1954.

Also, some programs were known by both the sponsor's name as well as by the program title, e.g., *The Theatre Guild on the Air* a.k.a. *The United States Steel Hour*.

Even when the program title remained unchanged, the program may be listed with more than one spelling. Perhaps the best example of alternative spellings is the *Amos 'n' Andy* program which has been listed as: *Amos and Andy, Amos & Andy, Amos 'n Andy* and *Amos 'n' Andy*. Also, there may be differences as to whether a program title ends with the word "Show" or "Program" and whether or not it begins with the article "The."

The "title" issue is further complicated by the fact that some of the materials archivists had to catalog were incomplete and they may not always have had adequate references to properly identify all the material, check spelling or list the variations in titles. And, simple mistakes can and do happen; in the online finding aid for one collection, *Bold Venture* was incorrectly listed as *Bold Adventure* in the "Scripts" portion but listed correctly in the "Production Files" section.

As a general rule, the program titles shown in the Special Collections section of the Guide are the ones used in the repository's catalog, modified at times to correct spelling errors. In the Index, when sufficient information was available to confirm that different titles were indeed the same program, the multiple titles have been cross referenced. In cases where there were similar but slightly different titles across multiple listings but where the authors could not be certain that the different titles referred to the same program, for example, the *Hedda Hopper Show* and *Hedda Hopper's Hollywood* or *Radio Round Up* and *Radio Roundup*, both titles are listed in the Index.

Although every effort has been made to verify program titles and spelling, for some of the lesser known programs, the authors were unable to verify the repository's notation in any available reference materials. It should also be noted that it is not unusual to see variations in program titles and/or spelling for the same program in different reference books.

Given the above, the authors strongly suggest that researchers adopt a broad outlook when checking the Index for specific programs.

Program logs

Researchers new to the Golden Age of Radio will want to familiarize themselves with the concept of the "program log," an important research tool for anyone studying the history of a particular program or genre.

Compiled by old time radio researchers from collections of existing scripts, audio recordings, surviving papers from radio stations and syndication companies and daily radio listings in newspapers and radio magazines, program logs vary in their level of detail and format but all share the same basic characteristics.

1) Name of the program or series
   As noted above, it was not unusual during the Golden Age of Radio for programs which were associated with one personality or character to undergo name changes during the length of its run, sometimes because of a change in sponsorship such as *The Jack Benny Program* example cited above or other times simply because the network was trying to find a more "catchy" title such as *Flash-Gun Casey, Press Photographer* which was changed to *Casey, Press Photographer, Crime Photographer* and *Casey, Crime Photographer* and eventually reverted back to *Crime Photographer*.

2) Dates
   The log generally identifies every date the program was broadcast, from the very first to the final broadcast of the series, including reruns, along with any changes in time slot, program name, network, sponsor, day of the week, etc. The individual programs are generally numbered in broadcast sequence.

3) Episode title
   A specific title is assigned to each episode. For certain types of programs such as detective, drama or adventure series, the title is usually noted in the script's introduction. For non episode programs such as comedy, music, variety and quiz shows, the episode titles are most often shown by the guest stars, comedy routine, theme, first musical number or first question asked.

4) Additional information
Logs may also identify cast members, sponsors, the musical director, director, producer, script writers, etc. Some logs also identify which specific programs in the series are "in circulation," i.e., sound recordings are available.

When using logs, researchers should note that in the case of syndicated programs (see below for more information about syndicated programs) that were broadcast on different dates, in different time slots and in different markets, the key identifier is the episode number.

Abbreviations
Commonly used abbreviations found in the Guide include:

ABC: American Broadcasting Company
AFRS: Armed Forces Radio Service
AFRTS: Armed Forces Radio and Television Service
CBS: Columbia Broadcasting System
FCC: Federal Communications Commission
FTC: Federal Trade Commission
MBS: Mutual Broadcasting System
NAB: National Association of Broadcasters
NBC: National Broadcasting Company
OTR: Old Time Radio

Some definitions
Transcription discs (or disks). An electrical recording, a.k.a. an "ET," generally, but not always, 16" in diameter and running approximately 15 minutes at the speed of $33^{1}/_3$ rpm. Transcription discs were the most common way of preserving radio broadcasts during the Golden Age.

Beginning with the mid–1930s, the discs were made of aluminum and coated with a black lacquer, hence the alternative name, "acetate discs." Between 1942–1945 when aluminum was in short supply because of the war, glass was the mostly frequently used substitute.

The machines used to make the transcription discs were used by both radio stations and individuals who were able to record broadcasts directly from the radio (off-air recordings).

Repositories fortunate enough to own or have access to the 16" turntables needed to play these discs have and are continuing to transfer the discs in their collections to reel-to-reel tape, cassettes and/or CDs in order to preserve them and make them available to researchers and for the listening pleasure of the general public. Less fortunate repositories have either outsourced the transfer task to audio consultants or the network of old time radio enthusiasts or have simply kept the discs in storage with no immediate plans to transfer them to newer formats.

It should be noted that in some special collections, the term "transcription" can sometimes have two meanings. Some archivists use the term "transcription" instead of "transcript" to describe a written version of audio material, e.g., transcriptions of an oral history interview. The more common use of the term, however, relates to a type of audio format, e.g., the 16" transcription discs that were used by studios to record programs.

Instantaneous discs were discs that could be played immediately after the recording was made without the need for the lengthy processes required for mass produced discs.

Syndication. Programs that were produced by an independent organization which marketed the series in the form of transcription discs to radio stations throughout the country for airing at their own convenience. Examples of syndicated programs include *The Lone Ranger, Vic & Sade,* and *Easy Aces.*

Oral Histories
Beginning in the mid–1960s and continuing into the present, several radio historians and organizations have conducted interviews with the performers, writers, directors, technicians and business executives who were part of radio's Golden Age. While these oral history interviews are included in different sections of the Resource Guide, given their research value, they are listed below with a notation where they can be found in the Guide.

1. Dick Bertel interviews. Eighty seven interviews conducted over seven years beginning in 1970 that were broadcast over WTIC, Hartford, CT. A complete list of the interviews is available at www.goldenage-wtic.info. (3694)

2. John Dunning interviews. A Denver based radio historian and author of "On the Air: The Encyclopedia of Old-Time Radio." Tapes of these 50+ interviews are available from the Radio Historical Association of Colorado (3766) and in the collections of many private old time radio collectors.

3. Richard Lamparski interviews. Tapes of many of the interviews are available from collectors and several are included in Lamparski's series of "Whatever Became Of" books. (2618, 2619)

4. Pacific Pioneer Broadcasters interviews. An ongoing collection of interviews with members of the organization who worked in radio. (1086)

5. Radio Pioneers interviews. Conducted by the Oral History Office of Columbia University. (193)

6. Chuck Schaden interviews. A Chicago based radio historian and host of the weekly radio program *Those Were the Days.* Forty six of the interviews are available in book form, "Speaking of Radio," and others are available in audio format from collectors. (3302)

7. SPERDVAC interviews. An extensive collection of past and ongoing interviews. (1219)

Additional primary and secondary sources
To locate additional information about the Golden Age of Radio, the authors suggest the following possible sources:

1. Other people associated with the program, including performers, writers, producers and directors.
2. Friends and relatives of the personality.
3. Radio magazines (see list in the Bibliography section) and newspapers.
4. Specific radio stations.
5. The Internet.
6. Books in the appropriate genre for additional bibliographic references.

7. Educational institutions that the person may have attended.

8. Program sponsors and advertising agencies.

9. Local, regional and state historical societies.

10. Fan clubs for specific performers such as the International Jack Benny Fan Club, www.jackbenny.org, the Eddie Cantor Appreciation Society, www.eddiecantor.com, the Friends of Vic and Sade or the National Lum and Abner Society. Check the Internet for additional clubs.

11. Unions and other social organizations of people associated with the performing arts.

12. Retirement homes for people who were once associated with show business.

Chapter 2: Special Collections

Researching Special Collections

This section includes special collections that can be found in academic libraries, public libraries, historical societies, museums, corporations and non profit organizations. It also includes privately held collections that are available to researchers.

Special collections are defined as collections of archival print and/or audio materials that may contain manuscripts, correspondence, newspaper clippings, scrapbooks, photographs, audio recordings in various formats, memorabilia, program scripts, publicity materials and other printed material. For the purposes of this Guide, the special collections section also includes Ph.D. theses.

How the collections were researched

For the most part, the listings were identified by searching the web sites and/or online catalogs of repositories in the United States, supplemented with follow up emails and phone calls. To insure the broadest possible results, the online search was by keyword using the term "radio."

Information from corporations and other repositories not likely to have online catalogs of their holdings was obtained by email and phone.

It should be noted that primary sources of information about United States radio programs and/or personalities may also be located in some overseas repositories. This is particularly true for print and audio material related to the Armed Forces Radio Service where archival materials not available in the United States may be found in repositories in England, Germany and Japan.

Additionally, the online catalog of the National Union Catalog of Manuscript Collections (NUCMC) maintained by the Library of Congress (www.loc.gov/coll/nucmc) was researched, also using the keyword "radio." The NUCMC includes special collections cataloged by the 41,000 worldwide repositories that are members of the OCLC (Online Computer Library Center) and the 160 universities, national libraries, archives, historical societies and other institutions that are members of the RLG (Research Libraries Group).

The authors also posted messages soliciting collection submissions on online mailing lists subscribed to by archivists, audio collectors, special libraries and old time radio enthusiasts. Additionally, over a dozen organizations involved in the Golden Age of Radio were contacted as were well known authors, researchers and historians in the field of old time radio.

Prior to assembling the data for publication, a preliminary list of collections was sent to each repository asking if they had any additional collections that should be included in the Guide and to correct any errors on the list.

Based on the authors' previous experience with mail questionnaires and the likelihood that special collections's staff would not have the time or resources to respond to a questionnaire, the authors determined during the initial planning phase of the project that the likely response rate to a questionnaire would not be sufficient to justify the time and expense of such a mailing. The validity of this approach became even more apparent when it was determined that even some of the repositories that did submit online submission forms did not always include all the possible collections that the authors later identified when they searched the repositories' web sites. (See below for some additional comments on researching special collections.)

How the section is organized

The section is organized alphabetically by repository, without regard for the geographic location of the repository or the type of repository. Collections that are privately held and are identified by the owner's name are alphabetized under the owner's last name. Within each repository, the collections are listed alphabetically by title; collections that are the names of individuals are alphabetized by first name. In cases where the collections are located within different libraries or centers within a repository, the individual libraries or centers are listed separately in alphabetical order.

In the few instances where major repositories of radio material may be known by both the name of the parent institution and the repository, e.g., the American Heritage Center at the University of Wyoming, one name is cross referenced to the other.

Each collection has a unique entry number, beginning with the number "1" and numbered consecutively throughout the book. The collection number is used in the Index to identify the collections.

Information about collections that was received too late to be included in the main section of this chapter is included in an Addendum at the end of the chapter.

What types of collections are included and excluded

In keeping with the general guidelines of the book as previously discussed, the collections focus on the people and programs associated with the Golden Age of Radio in the United States as well as radio history and station history in the United States.

Not included are collections that deal with the technical aspects of radio such as transmission and radio equipment, or

---

* Although collections including material about Radio Free Europe and similar programs may be found in many repositories, the authors note that the Hoover Institution at Stanford University is particularly strong in this area.

United States programming broadcast *outside* the United States such as Radio Free Europe and Radio Liberty.*

Without a crystal ball, it is impossible to know in advance all the possible subject areas, programs or people future researchers will be interested in investigating. Some subjects are fairly obvious, e.g., anything to do with popular nationally broadcast programs such as *Amos 'n' Andy, Our Miss Brooks,* or *The Lux Radio Theatre*, or well known radio performers such as Jack Benny and Fred Allen, or writers such as Norman Corwin or Arch Oboler. But what about lesser known national, regional and local programs such as *Grandpappy and Pals* or *Hoosier Hop,* or regional personalities such as Walter "Salty" Brine, a fixture on Rhode Island radio for over 50 years, or programs dealing with issues of concern to farmers in the 1940s or the peaceful uses of atomic energy. Indeed, a case could be made that as it is generally easier to find the "popular stuff," the main contribution of a resource such as this is in identifying where to find information on the less popular or more obscure aspects of the Golden Age of Radio.

As a general rule, this section includes any special collection that contains any material about any local, regional or national radio program, including the program's writers, directors, producers, actors, etc., as well as anything related to station history, the history of radio, including laws and regulations governing broadcasting, and audio collections of radio broadcasts.

Also included are the personal collections of performers who appeared on radio although they may have been known primarily for their non radio careers. Examples of such collections include the singer Ella Fitzgerald, talk show host Johnny Carson and the actor Vincent Price.

This section also includes collections with material on single programs relating to special local or regional events or historical programs such as the sesquicentennial observance of the Louisiana Purchase or a series of broadcasts dealing with the history of taverns in Maine as well as collections of prominent writers such as Clifford Odets and Cornell Woolrich if the collections include plays that were written for radio.

The decision as to whether to include collections of non radio personalities who gave talks on radio presented the authors with a challenge as it was not always clear from the catalog listing whether the talks were occasional addresses or part of regularly scheduled programs. Depending on the degree of detail in the catalog listing, some of these collections have been included while others have been omitted.

Important historical addresses such as Winston Churchill's "Iron Curtain Speech" as well as regularly scheduled programs by political figures to their constituents are included in this section. Political talks and campaign speeches are generally excluded.

With a few exceptions, this section also does not include ephemera. Researchers are advised, however, that when contacting repositories about their special collections, they should also inquire about any ephemera materials that may be cataloged separately.

Oral history interviews that were included in the search results for "special collections" are listed in this section. However, it should be noted that there may be many more interviews of people who were involved with radio during the Golden Age, or of people reminiscing about early radio broadcasting, that are not included.

Content of each listing

While the authors have made every effort to provide as much detail as possible about the radio related contents of each collection, in some instances the information available online or supplied by the repository was limited, sometimes *very* limited, resulting in a very brief description of the collection's contents.

With allowances for editorial consistency and the goal of focusing primarily on the radio material in the collection, the text for each listing has been taken directly from the online finding aid (see below for a discussion of finding aids) or the repository's online catalog listing. Collection titles are generally shown as they are listed in the repository's catalog, except where they have been modified for editorial consistency. As a general rule, non radio related material in the collection is not described.

Within each listing, the names of regularly scheduled programs are italicized and the titles of individual programs, episodes or plays as well as names of publications are in quotation marks. When the distinction between the two was not clear based on the limited information in the catalog listing, the authors used their best judgement in applying either italics or quotation marks.

Where appropriate, the listing directs the reader to either an online or unpublished finding aid for more detailed information about the collection.

When a collection includes audio material, the distinction is not always made as to the type of audio format, e.g., transcription disc, reel-to-reel tape, cassette, CD or phonograph record; in some cases the catalog listing or finding aid does not indicate the format. It should also be noted that in some instances, repositories with transcription discs do not have the necessary equipment to play the discs.

Where available, the web site for the repository's Special Collections home page has been included at the beginning of each institutional listing. Most listings also contain email addresses although some sites prefer email messages be sent directly from the web page. Note that some email addresses are generic, e.g., "archives@" and should remain valid regardless of future staff changes. Other email addresses, as well as the names of individuals to contact for additional information, are subject to change.

Also, because this Guide is only about radio, the word "radio" is often omitted in the content descriptions or in the subject headings in the Index, e.g., when the description just says "scripts," it means radio scripts. Similarly, radio station call letters, e.g., WXYZ , are not prefaced by the words "radio station," and "history" refers to radio history.

In some catalog listings, it was not always clear which radio program/s the materials related to or if the material fell within the time frame of this volume. Also, when collections contained both radio and television material, it was not always clear whether specific items in the collection, such as scripts, related to radio *or* television. The online listing for the Ilka Chase papers, for example, says "bound scripts of her program." But, as Ms. Chase was associated with more than one radio program, it was not clear which program the scripts were for. And in the Laraine Day collection, the catalog notes that her papers include material about her radio program but it does not mention the name of the program.

Missing information

One of the more frustrating aspects of describing the contents of some collections was deciding how to treat unidentified script and other program material, such as the following listing:

> **Frona Wait Colburn Collection, 1900–1942.** Includes some scripts, n.d., for an unidentified half hour radio program that Colburn hosted for ten months.

While staff at some repositories were extremely helpful in filling in some of these information gaps, particularly when the information being requested was readily available in an in-house database or card catalog, in general, the authors fully understood that it was not practical to expect archival staff to drop everything they were doing in order to retrieve multiple collections from storage and go through countless boxes and folders searching for program names or dates that may or may not have been in any of the papers to begin with.

As a possible way around this information gap, the authors suggest that researchers check the Index for the names of other people who may have been associated with the program that they are researching, including writers, producers and directors, and, if they have the information, the station the program was broadcast on.

Audio collections

While individual audio recordings listed in a repository's online catalog are generally not included in the definition of "special collection," this section does include several "large" audio collections with, if available, a brief description of the scope of the contents, e.g., the types of programs and/or date range. In the Index these collections are listed under "Audio collections." If the contents of the collection have been cataloged (not all collections have been) and can be searched online, an appropriate link is shown. In other instances, the researcher is advised to contact the repository for more information.

In addition to contacting these repositories for access to audio copies of specific programs not listed in the Index, researchers may also want to extend their search to the online network of old time radio collectors and dealers who may have copies of the same programs that are in the repositories but which may be easier to acquire.

Script collections

Several special collections contain scripts for a large number of different programs. In the Index, these collections are listed under the heading "Script collections." With the exception of the script collections at Duke University, The Broadcast ARTS Library and the Ziv collection at Media Heritage, Inc., the program titles in large assorted script collections are generally not included in the collection's description but, depending on the size of the collection and number of program titles, the individual programs may be listed separately in the Index. Where appropriate, the reader may be directed to an online link that contains a list of the scripts, a notation that there is an unpublished finding aid listing the scripts, or the suggestion to contact the repository for more information.

In some personal collections such as those of a writer or producer, when the description identifies specific scripts in the collection, it was not always clear if the list was a definitive one of just a sampling. Based on the other information in the listing and the researcher's knowledge of the person, a follow up call to the repository may be appropriate.

Photograph collections

Some special collections consist exclusively or primarily of photographs. In some cases, the radio related material, e.g., photographs of a station, may be part of a collection that includes the records of a commercial studio. In other cases, the collection may include photographs of an assortment of entertainers, including people who performed on radio. These collections are shown in the Index under the heading "Photograph collections." Collections that include photographs *in addition to* other print material are indexed under the name of the relevant person, program or station and are not indexed as "photograph collections."

Accessing the collections

Each repository has its own procedures for accessing special collections. In most cases, these procedures are detailed on the repository's "Special Collections" page. In the case of some corporate archives, some very specific access restrictions are noted.

Note also that each repository has its own policy regarding copying materials in special collections and that even with the same repository, these policies may vary from collection to collection depending on restrictions placed by the original holder of the materials.

Conducting Additional Research

Limitations of online searches

To a large degree, archivists are playing "catch up" to the world of computers and in many cases only a portion of a repository's special collections are listed online. What that portion is is usually not shared with visitors to the web page. While some repositories have 100% of their processed collections listed on their web site, at the other extreme, there are some repositories that have not put any collection information online. Most repositories are somewhere in between these two extremes with the exact percentage of the collection information available online constantly changing — and growing.

Additionally, some repositories list their unprocessed collections online, noting that the collections have not yet been processed, while others prefer not to release publicly *any* information on collections in their possession not yet processed.

In general, it is best to assume that a repository listed in this Resource Guide *may* have additional collections and to ASK. Of course, asking only helps if the researcher is following a lead that took him or her to the repository in the first place — or if the researcher decides to make a "cold call" to a repository not already listed in the Guide. At a minimum, staff may be able to check an in-house computerized catalog, a card catalog (which often includes valuable ephemera type material) or a listing of unpublished finding aids. Some repositories may charge for this service.

The above comments notwithstanding, even when collection information is available online, it may not always be in a format that is useful to researchers.

On some web sites, special collections are listed alphabetically by name, e.g., Jane Doe, John Smith, etc., with no additional descriptive information. These alphabetical listings are helpful *if* the researcher is looking for the papers of a specific person. However, if the researcher is looking for collections dealing with a subject, e.g., radio, and is not familiar with the names Jane Doe or John Smith, then there is no way of knowing if those collection should be investigated further.

Some institutions go one step beyond an alphabetical listing of names and group their collections under subject headings, e.g., local history, family papers, entertainment, business, etc. Needless to say, the more subject headings available, the greater the likelihood of identifying relevant collections. However, it should be noted that some key radio related information, such as station history, may be found in collections listed under "Family papers" or "Business papers" as Jane Doe may have been a prominent citizen of the county — who also owned the local radio station.

Sketchy or incomplete listings can also be a problem, especially if the researcher is doing a general keyword search. For example, the catalog entry for the Kate Smith collection at one academic library did not contain the word "radio" in its description so it did not come up in response to a keyword search using the word "radio."

Researchers should also be aware of the lack of standardization of terms when searching for certain types of radio material; plays are sometimes referred to as "radio dramas" and the difference between a play and a script is not always apparent. Spelling differences can alter search results, such as "playscript" or "play script."

Finding aids

Finding aids (FAs) which provide more detailed information about the contents of a collection are a researcher's first and best tool in deciding whether a collection contains relevant information. Finding aids may be either online or in an unpublished format in the repository. If the finding aid is available online, a direct link to the FA will be shown. Some repositories have separate web pages for collections with searchable FAs. Not all collections listed online have FAs.

While all FAs follow the same general format, their levels

of detail and usefulness to researchers vary considerably. In cases where the radio material is limited or represents only a minor part of the overall collection, information may be even more limited.

A "typical" finding aid will have a brief Administrative Summary (name and location of the collection) followed by a brief Description of the contents, a Biographical section with information about the person or organization (this section can be especially helpful in instances where the person or organization is not immediately recognizable as being "radio related") and a Scope of Contents section that highlights the types of materials in the collection, e.g., manuscripts, sound recordings, scripts, correspondence, etc.

The most helpful part of the FA is the "Container List" which, depending on its level of detail, lists the contents of each series, folder or box within the collection. Whereas the Scope and Content section might say "contains radio scripts," the Container List might show that the scripts are in Series II and Series II, in turn, might contain a list of scripts by program name and date.

In some instances, the biographical and/or descriptive summaries may discuss a radio connection, but no radio information is included in the Scope of Contents. In these cases, the collection may either not contain radio material, or the Scope of Contents may be too brief or superficial to list any radio material. In these cases, it is best to contact the repository for more information.

In particularly long FAs, it may be helpful to use the "Find" button at the top of the browser window to search for the word "radio" within the FA.

Some suggestions for conducting online searches

Anyone familiar with computer searches knows that the output results are determined, in part, by how the search criteria are inputted; the slightest change in the search criteria can generate vastly different results.

While there are countless variations on catalog sites, what follows are some general searching tips. For best results, however, and because of the different ways special collections are listed online, it is always best to check with the repository's web page and/or special collections's staff.

1. **Determine which libraries to search**

    Within some repositories, particularly universities, special collections may be located in more than one library, e.g., the Rare Books and Manuscripts Library, a Music Library and a University Archives. Additionally, some universities have different research centers and/or institutes, each with its own library and online catalog. As the university's "general" online catalog may or may not include special collections in all libraries and institutes, it is advisable to check each relevant library's unique home page. (See below on "setting limits.")

2. **Special collections page**

    Once the appropriate library or center has been identified, look for a link to a "Special Collections" page. In general, these links are more helpful than going through the repository's general catalog, but in many cases both should be checked as the "Special Collections Page" may only contain a partial listing of the repository's collections.

3. Searching the general online catalog

a. Advanced search

If available, use the "Advanced Search" option that allows you to "set limits." This will help focus the search by separating "special collections" from books and other types of materials. The two most useful "limits" are:

1) "Search Where." This allows the researcher to select ALL libraries within the repository or limit the search to only certain libraries within the repository. On some sites, the researcher can widen the search to other libraries in the region or state or different branches of the university.

2) "Type of Materials." This allows the researcher to narrow the focus of the search to books, or audio or maps or archival materials, etc. Unfortunately, there is no standardization of terms among repositories and "archival materials" may be found under "archival material," "mixed materials" and sometimes under "manuscripts."

b. Catalog icons

If the online catalog does not include a "set limits" option, or if the researcher prefers to search the entire catalog (which might bring up promising books not included in the Bibliography section of this Guide, especially radio related books with a more regional focus), some catalog sites contain icons that distinguish books from manuscripts or audio material. The icons can be especially helpful when there are many pages of listings to scroll through and the researcher is only interested in archival materials.

c. Keyword searches

For the broadest possible reach, the authors recommend doing a general keyword search across all fields using the word "radio" with the limits described above. While such a search will bring up some irrelevant material, e.g., RKO **Radio** movie studio, the United Electrical **Radio** and Machine Workers of America Union, **radio** astronomy, or even a short story by John Cheever with the word **radio** in the title, it has been the authors' experience that these extraneous listings are relatively few.

d. Finding aids

Check with the special collections staff about the availability of any online finding aids that might not be highlighted on a web page.

List of Repositories

Spertus Institute of Jewish Studies	1228	University of New Orleans	1669
Sports Museum of New England	1229	University of North Carolina at Chapel Hill	1670–1706
Stanford University	1230–1277	University of North Carolina at Greensboro	1707
State Historical Society of Iowa	1278–1279, 3782–3786	University of North Texas	1708–1712
State Historical Society of North Dakota	1280–1289	University of Notre Dame	1713–1717
State University of New York at Buffalo	1290	University of Oklahoma	1718
State University of New York at Potsdam	1291	University of Oregon	1719–1742
Staten Island Institute of Arts and Sciences	1292	University of Pennsylvania	1743–1747
Charles Stumpf	1293	University of Pennsylvania Museum of Archaeology and Anthropology, Education Dept.	1748
Syracuse University	1294–1314	University of Pittsburgh	1749–1763
Temple University	1315–1325	University of Rochester	1764–1785
Tennessee State Library and Archives	1326–1331	University of South Carolina	1786–1789
Texas A & M University	1332–1334	University of Southern California	1790–1804
Texas State Library and Archives Commission	1335	University of Texas-Austin	1805–1840
Texas Tech University	1336–1341	University of Texas-El Paso	1841–1844
Thousand Oaks Library (*American Radio Archives*)	1342–1365	University of Texas-San Antonio	1845–1847
Tufts University	1366	University of the Pacific	1848–1849
Tulane University	1367	University of Utah	1850–1860
Union College	1368	University of Vermont	1861–1863
University of Alaska Anchorage	1369–1371	University of Virginia	1864–1885
University of California at Berkeley	1372–1384	University of Washington	1886–1895
University of California at Davis	3787	University of West Virginia	1896–1904
University of California at Los Angeles (UCLA)	1385–1503	University of Wisconsin-Milwaukee	1905–1908
University of California at San Diego	1504	University of Wyoming	1909–1984
University of California at Santa Barbara	1505–1507	(*American Heritage Center*)	
University of California at Santa Cruz	1508	Utah State Historical Society	1985–1989
University of Chicago	1509–1512	Robert VanDeventer	1990
University of Connecticut	1513	Vermont Historical Society	1991–1993
University of Delaware	1514–1517	Virginia Commonwealth University	1994
University of Florida	3788–3789	Virginia Historical Society	1995–2003
University of Georgia	1518–1527	Walt Disney Archives	2004
University of Houston	1528	Washington State Archives	2005–2006
University of Idaho	1529–1530	Washington State Historical Society	2007
University of Illinois, Urbana-Champaign	1531–1546	Washington State University	2008–2036
University of Iowa	1547–1558	Wayne State University	2037–2045
University of Kansas	1559–1570	West Virginia Division of Culture and History	2046–2048
University of Kentucky	1571–1572	Western Reserve Historical Society	2049–2062
University of Louisville	1573–1576	Western Washington University	2063–2067
University of Maine	1578–1587	WGBH Education Foundation	2069–2070
University of Maryland	1588–1590	Wheaton College	2071–2072
University of Memphis	1591	Wichita State University	2073
University of Michigan	1592–1617	Will Rogers Memorial Museum	2074
University of Minnesota	1618–1646	Williams College	2075
University of Mississippi	1647	Wisconsin Historical Society	2076–2231
University of Missouri-Columbia	1648–1649	WNYC Radio Archives	2232
University of Missouri-Kansas City	1650–1654	Yale University	2233–2248, 3790–3797
University of Missouri-St. Louis	1655–1663	Yiddish Radio Project	2249
University of Montana	1664–1665	YIVO Institute for Jewish Research	2250–2251
University of Nebraska/Lincoln	1666	Youngstown State University	2252–2256
University of Nevada	1667–1668		

Special Collections

Academy of Motion Picture Arts and Sciences
Margaret Herrick Library, Dept. of Special Collections
333 S. La Cienega Boulevard, Beverly Hills, CA 90211
(310) 247-3036, Ext. 218
specialcollections@oscars.org; Contact: Barbara Hall
www.oscars.org/mhl/sc/index.html

General comments: The library has additional special collections of many people associated primarily with the world of movies but who may also have appeared on radio. However, these special collections are not part of the library's online catalog nor can they be searched using the keyword "radio." A partial list of the collections can, however, be searched by name. Detailed contents of each collection is not available online.

1. Anne Seymour Collection, bulk 1960s–1970s. Does not appear to include material about Seymour's radio career.

2. Edit Angold Collection, 1935–1970, bulk 1940s–1950s. Deals primarily with Angold's theater, television and radio work and consists of scripts, programs and contracts.

3. Edith Head Papers, bulk 1950–1982. Contains correspondence, biographical data, contracts, general files, scrapbooks, magazine and newspaper clippings. Also includes audio tapes of her program, *Fashion Notes*, aired on CBS, 1963–1965.

4. Hattie McDaniel Collection. Includes more than 400 transcription discs for *The Beulah Show* starring Hattie McDaniel as Beulah in 15-minute radio serializations. A script for the March 10, 1948 episode features Hattie and her brother Sam McDaniel. Also includes photographs and material on Sam from his vaudeville days and some scripts from films, television and other radio programs.

5. Hedda Hopper Collection, bulk late 1940s to mid–1960s. Consists primarily of Hopper's personal files relates almost exclusively to her work as a columnist and to her social life but also contains documentation about her radio appearances.

6. Howard W. Koch Collection, 1953–1959. Contains production and general files relating to his work in the movies. Koch also worked with Orson Welles at the Mercury Theater.

7. Jean Hersholt Collection, 1916–1956, bulk 1920s–1940. Contains primarily scrapbooks with reviews, news items and articles relating to his film career as well as the *Dr. Christian* radio series.

8. Louella Parsons Collection, 1915–1961. Consists of scrapbooks containing thousands of columns she wrote over six decades. Also contains biographical clippings on Parsons and coverage of her various radio programs.

9. *Lux Radio Theatre* Collection, 1936–1955. Consists primarily of disc recordings and scripts.

10. Sidney Skolsky Collection, 1928–1982. Consists primarily of material on various personalities utilized by Skolsky in the preparation of his tintypes. Additional items include miscellaneous television and radio scripts.

Adriance Memorial Library
93 Market Street, Poughkeepsie, NY, 12601
(845) 485-3445
localhistory@poklib.org; www.poklib.org

11. Poughkeepsie Radio Stations Scrapbooks, 1938–1953. Photograph album and scrapbook of clippings concerning WGNY, 1938–1940, and scrapbooks of clippings concerning WHVA, 1947, and WKIP, 1940–1953.

Alabama Department of Archives & History
624 Washington Avenue, Montgomery, AL 36130-0100
(334) 242-4435; debbie.pendleton@archives.alabama.gov
http://archives.state.al.us; Contact: Debbie Pendleton

12. Clifford J. Durr Papers, 1899–1976. Includes papers relating to Durr's appointment to the Federal Communications Commission in the 1940s.

13. Hank Williams Collection, ca. 1950–1978. Bulk of collection consists of photographs, with the remainder consisting of clippings concerning Williams's career as a country singer and his personal life as well as original sheet music and programs containing copies of his songs and audio tapes of his speeches.

14. *Letters From Home* Collection, 1943–1945. Consists of examples of *Letters From Home* program and correspondence from military personnel regarding changes of address, thank yous and comments regarding the program. Broadcast on WSFA, Montgomery, AL for the Montgomery County men and women in the Armed Forces during World War II.

Allentown Symphony Orchestra
Library, 23 North Sixth Street, Allentown, PA 18101   (610) 432-6715; Fax: (610) 432-6735
info@allentownsymphony.org; allentownsymphony.org

15. Donald Voorhees Collection, 1940s–1960s. Programs and musical scores used by Voorhees for the *Bell Telephone Hour* radio and television programs. A sound recording of a special May 16, 1955 program, the "Birthday Broadcast," is also available in a separate collection.

American Bible Society
1865 Broadway, New York, NY 10023
(212) 408-1200; Fax: (212) 408-1526
info@americanbible.org; www.americanbible.org
Contact: Matthew Kern

16. American Bible Society Records, 1922–1953. Contains transcripts of radio and television scripts, 1939–1958, including those of Francis C. Stifler, texts of radio broadcasts, 1921–1943, relating to the church's missionary work and public relations material including samples of radio broadcasts, 1923–1924. Note: Additional collections may also contain radio material.

American Federation of Television & Radio Artists
5757 Wilshire Blvd., 9th Fl., Los Angeles, CA 90036
(323) 634-8131; Contact: Meredith Snow

losangeles@aftra.com

17. Archives. The Los Angeles local of AFTRA houses the union's archives. For more information about the contents and access contact the local.

American Heritage Center
(See University of Wyoming)

American Institute of Physics
Center for History of Physics, Niels Bohr Library
One Physics Ellipse, College Park, MD 20740
(301) 209-3177
nbl@aip.org; www.aip.org

18. *Everybody's Mountain*, 1958. A sound recording of a series created by Robert Lewis Shayon based on significant accomplishments in education during a period of concern for the quality of science education in the United States. This segment in the series was an in depth report on the accomplishments of the Frontiers of Science Foundation of Oklahoma.

American Legion
700 North Pennsylvania Street, Indianapolis, IN 46204
(317) 630-1366; Contact: Joe Hovish
jhovish@legion.org

19. Archives. Contains recordings and some scripts for the *This Is Our Duty* and *Decision Now* series which were 15 minute public service type messages dealing with national security, veteran's welfare, child welfare and patriotism.

American Radio Archives
(See Thousand Oaks Library)

American University
Library, Special Collections
4400 Massachusetts Ave. NW, Washington, DC 20016-8046
(202) 885-3256; Fax: (202) 885-3226
archives@american.edu; Contact: Susan McElrath
www.library.american.edu/about/archives/special.html

20. John R. Hickman Audio Collection. Consists of over 10,000 broadcast quality audio recordings of vintage radio news and entertainment programming, 1920s–1961, on reel-to-reel tapes, metal and vinyl discs and electronic transcriptions from studio masters. Includes episodes from most of the major radio series of that era as well as historic radio news broadcasts. An inventory for a portion of the collection can be made available to researchers.

Antique Wireless Museum
2 South Avenue, Bloomfield, NY 14469
(585) 567-6280; Contact: Edward Gable
egable@rochester.rr.com; www.antiquewireless.org;

21. Amateur Radio Call Books, 1913–1970. Collection of radio call books, 1913–1970, and handbooks, 1926–1970.

22. WHAM, Rochester, NY Records and Photographs. Collection of records, scrapbooks and photographs.

Arizona Historical Society/Southern Division
Library & Archives
949 East 2nd Street, Tucson, AZ 85719
(520) 617-1157; Fax: (520) 629-8966
ahsref@vms.arizona.edu
http://lista.azhist.arizona.edu/libinfo.html

23. Bacil B. Warren Papers, 1948–1952. Includes 11 scripts and a program list for the KVOA series *Tales of Tucson*, 1950–1951, with two additional scripts produced by Batten, Batten, Durstine and Osborn, Inc. Series concerns personalities, places and events in Tucson, including Preston N. Jacobus, Charles H. Meyer, Geronimo, the 1887 earthquake and the 1881 Halley's comet.

24. McClintock Papers, 1889–1931. Contains correspondence and manuscripts, mostly dealing with Arizona history covering exploration, settlement, Native Americans, Rough Riders and journalism, and some material about Spanish-American War veterans and their organization.

25. Pete Kitchen Biographical Materials, 1870–1948. Primarily one scrapbook created by Kitchen's granddaughter concerning Kitchen and his son-in-law, T.D. Casanega. Includes a transcript for a 1948 radio program about Kitchen.

26. Rosemary Drachman Taylor Papers, 1931–1949. Consists mostly of manuscripts and notes chiefly for the 1930s program *Cheerio* broadcast to cheer shut-ins.

27. Van Valkenburgh Papers, 1868–1950, bulk 1928–1950. Includes typescripts from Van Valkenburgh's program, *Sheriff's Story*, a weekly program produced by KTUC, 1948–1951, concerning law enforcement, crime and criminals in Pima County.

Arizona State University
Library, Box 871006, Tempe, AZ 85287-1006
(480) 965-6164; www.asu.edu/lib

28. Performing Arts Scrapbook Collection, 1898–1946. Includes 38 scrapbooks of newspaper clippings about theatre, radio and film personalities, 1898–1946. Radio material covers 1932–1945.

29. Radio Broadcasts from KTGM, Window Rock, 1938. Collection of scripts of broadcasts held on successive Tuesdays from October 18–December 20, 1938 covering topics concerning the Navajo Indians and the Navajo Reservation.

Atlanta History Center
Kenan Research Center
130 West Paces Ferry Road, NW, Atlanta, GA 30305
(404) 814-4000; Fax: (404) 814-2041
reference@atlantahistorycenter.com
www.atlantahistorycenter.com

30. Graham Washington Jackson Papers, 1923–1983. Contains correspondence, advertisements and public relations materials, lyrics, sheet music, comedy material, programs and scripts, music catalogs, biographical material, autograph books, clippings and other papers relating to Jackson's career as a musician and entertainer who appeared on WERD.

31. Taylor Flanagan Papers. Contains newspaper clippings relating to Flanagan's career as an African American performer who appeared on WSB, Atlanta, GA.

Auburn University
Ralph B. Draughon Library, Auburn, AL 36849-5606
(334) 844-1707; Fax: (334) 844-4424
coxdway@auburn.edu; www.lib.auburn.edu/archive
Contact: Dwayne Cox

32. Alabama Cooperative Extension System Records. Includes radio related material.

33. *Alabama's Heritage.* Contains notes about the 33 week dramatic series based on the lives of Alabamians produced by the Birmingham Public Schools and broadcast over WAPI and WAFM, 1947–1948. (In Dobbins Collection.)

34. Auburn Knights Orchestra Records, 1928–1992. Includes scrapbooks, photos, correspondence and other memorabilia for the band which was organized in 1928 as a studio band to play for the campus radio station, WAPI.

35. *Health by Radio.* A series of radio lectures on personal and public health presented over WAPI by J.D. Dowling, 1931.

36. Highlander Folk School Audio Collection. Includes audio recordings of labor and civil rights conferences, workshops and panel discussions held under the auspices of the Highlander Folk School, 1953–1963.

37. John Herbert Orr Papers, 1940–1984. Contains correspondence, legal and financial documents, business records, copies of patents, scientific journal articles, recording equipment and blueprints, pamphlets, scrapbooks, church records, tape recorded sermons and speeches. Includes Orr's work at WAPI, his founding of WJHO, Opelika, AL and his role as a pioneer in the "electronic church" of the 1950s advocating the use of radio and television by Methodists.

38. Luther Patrick Papers, 1937–1957. A Congressman, author and poet, Patrick was also a radio personality for WAPI and WBRC. Collection includes unidentified radio scripts, 1932–1946, and five recordings, n.d., of the program *Coffee With Congress.*

39. Posey Oliver (P.O.) Davis Papers, 1917–1971. May include papers relating to Davis's work with the Alabama Cooperative Extension Service and broadcasts on WAPI. Check finding aid in the repository.

40. "Rocky Mountain Rangers Hillbilly Song Parade," **1940s.** A song book (lyrics only) of Smiling Jack Baggett and The Rocky Mountain Rangers who performed on WAPI, Birmingham, AL. (In Alabama Collection.)

41. WAPI Programs and Press Announcements. Covers period February 18, 1926–April, 1931. Library has other WAPI related information. (In Auburn University Collection.)

Augustana College
The Center For Western Studies
Box 727, Sioux Falls, SD 57197
(605) 274-4008; Contact: Dr. Harry Thompson
cws@augie.edu; www.augie.edu/cws/index.html

42. Ray Loftesness Papers. Includes orchestral arrangements, sheet music, playbills, programs, personal papers, correspondence, photographs and memorabilia. Loftesness was an announcer and musicologist at KSOO, Sioux Falls, IA and did publicity for Fred Waring.

43. *South Dakota Speaks: A Centennial Portrait.* A series of 52 radio features on seven audio tapes dealing with aspects of change in South Dakota during its first hundred years.

Austin History Center
Austin Public Library

PO Box 2287, Austin, TX 78768-2287
(512) 974-7480; ahc_reference@ci.austin.tx.us
www.cityofaustin.org/library/ahc/collect.htm

44. Archives. The center maintains a collection of oral histories, photographs and manuscripts related to Austin personalities, history and business. To check whether any of the collections include material relating to radio, users can submit an online query.

Balch Institute
(See Historical Society of Pennsylvania)

Berea College
Hutchins Library, Berea, KY 40404
(859) 985-3272; Fax: (859) 985-3912
steve_gowler@berea.edu; Contact: Steve Gowler
www.berea.edu/hutchinslibrary/specialcollections

45. Bradley Kincaid Papers, 1861–1989, bulk 1920s– **1970s.** Contains correspondence, photographs, newsclippings, songbooks and sheet music from Kincaid's career as the radio ballad singer, the "Kentucky Mountain Boy," who broadcast on WLS. Kincaid also appeared on stations in Cincinnati, Pittsburgh, Boston and on WHAM, Rochester, NY and from 1942–1947 with WSM's Grand Ole Opry in Nashville.

46. Doc Roberts Papers, 1910–1938, bulk 1924–1935. Roberts appeared on the *National Barn Dance* on WLS, on stations in Council Bluffs, IA, 1932, on WLAP, Lexington, KY, 1934, and after 1935 made guest appearances on WLW and WHAS.

47. John Lair Papers, 1930–1984. A music broadcaster, music collector and community historian, Lair's papers consist of business correspondence, mail from listeners, photographs, program scripts, newsclippings, promotional material and 50 sound recordings, including *National Barn Dance* and *Renfro Valley Barn Dance* and *Renfro Valley Gatherin'* which Lair created while working for WLW, Cincinnati, OH and which were also heard on WHAS, Louisville, KY. In addition to appearing on the *National Barn Dance*, Lair was a producer and music librarian at WLS.

48. John Lair *Renfro Valley Barn Dance* Oral History Collection 1994–1999. A series of 46 audio recordings of interviews with performers and others who were associated with the *Renfro Valley Barn Dance* and other programs produced by Lair during the 1940s and 1950s.

49. John S. Phillips Papers, 1944–1966. Contains clippings, scrapbooks, short stories, poetry and photographs that document Phillips's work as a West Virginia newspaper columnist, radio personality and station manager.

50. Lily May Ledford Collection, 1936–1985. Includes autobiographical writings, articles, clippings and photographs documenting her career as a Kentucky country music performer.

51. Reuben Powell Early Country Music Collection, 1910– **1982.** Contains correspondence, clippings and audio recordings of music and interviews that reflect Powell's efforts at documenting early country music performers, mainly 1930 – 1950, with a focus on performers from Kentucky and those associated with programs such as the *National Barn Dance* and the *Renfro Valley Barn Dance.*

52. Southern Music and Radio Photographic Collection. Contains photographs relating to early country music performers, traditional musicians, radio personalities and events.

53. WHAS Radio Historical Collection, 1936–1967. Audio collection of broadcasts, including commercials, from WHAS, Louisville, KY. Includes a wide range of Kentucky and national political figures, news events, entertainment programs, soap operas, musical variety shows, country music and sporting events such as the Kentucky Derby. Names, events and subjects are searchable via an in-house database.

Bob Jones University
Audio Services Department
Greenville, SC 29614
(864) 242-5100, ext. 5790
audio@bju.edu; www.bju.edu

54. Radio Audio Collection. Includes sound recordings of *Dr. Bob Jones Says* from the 1950s and *Miracles* and *Hymn History* from the 1950s and 1960s. Most of the last two programs are on tape and some are on 16" transcription discs.

J.S. Mack Library
1700 Wade Hampton Blvd., Greenville, SC 29614
(864) 242-5100, ext. 6050; Fax: (864) 232-1729
library@bju.edu; www.bju.edu

55. Radio Print Collection, 1920s–1960s. Consists of 10 scripts for *Miracles* plus some miscellaneous other scripts, text of Dr. Bob Jones Sr. radio messages and material relating to the history of WMUU.

Boise State University
Albertsons Library
1910 University Drive, Boise ID 83725
(208) 426-3958; Contact: Alan Virta
avirta@boisestate.edu; http://library.boisestate.edu/Special/

56. Barry Shipman Collection, 1911–1997. Includes two radio plays, n.d. The bulk of the collection is related to Shipman's film career.

57. Helen M. Olsen Papers, 1943–1990. Consists chiefly of correspondence, poems, short stories, scripts and plays.

58. Nell Shipman Collection, 1892–1971, bulk 1925–1971. Includes a few radio plays plus correspondence, 1938, with Amerigo Serrao about placing Shipman's plays with the networks and two preview recordings, 1945, on 16" discs for potential radio shows. The bulk of the collection relates to Shipman's film career but there are a few items about radio.

Boston College
140 Commonwealth Avenue, Chestnut Hill, MA 02467
(617) 552-4861; Fax: (617) 552-2465
burnsref@bc.edu; www.bc.edu/libraries

59. Eleanor Early Papers, 1917–1969, bulk 1937–1969. Contains a variety of material relating to Early's work, including reviews, clippings, transcripts of radio broadcasts, photographs and copies of articles and manuscripts.

Boston Public Library
Research Library, 700 Boylston Street, Boston MA 02134
(617) 536-5400 ext. 4236; Fax: (617) 536-7758
Contact: Roberta Zinghi

speccoll@bpl.org; www.bpl.org/research/special

General comments: Special collections are located in more than one department in the library, including Music, Rare Books and Theater. Also, access to the library's online finding aids, "Archival Resources," is available through the "Electronic Resources" link at www.bpl.org/research/special/index.htm. Out-of-town researchers can request a "log in" identification to use the site. See the Addendum section of this chapter for additional collections.

60. Fred Allen Collection. Includes correspondence, scripts, records, tapes and photographs.

61. Jack Benny Letters and Clippings. Includes letters, mostly written by Benny to Frank Remley, the left-handed guitarist who played on the Benny radio shows. The letters are almost all comments on "Ripley's Believe It or Not!" articles.

62. Joseph Rines Collection, 1925–1954. Consists of song lyrics, song and dance band music, radio scripts, newspaper clippings and scrapbooks covering Rines's career as composer, arranger, radio music director and producer. Also includes correspondence and photographs.

63. William B. Jackson Jr. Theater Collection. Includes programs, playbills and clippings for virtually every theater in Boston operating from the 1920s–1950s. May contain information about actors who also appeared on radio.

Boston Symphony Orchestra
Symphony Hall, Boston, MA 02115
(617) 638-9434; Contact: Archives
bcarr@bso.org

64. Archives. Contains 8,000-9,000 audio recordings dating from the 1940s and print material including scrapbooks and biographical information about the artists. Collection is searchable via an in-house catalog. Note: Additional BSO recordings may be in the NBC Collection in the Library of Congress.

Boston University
Howard Gotlieb Archival Research Center
771 Commonwealth Avenue, Boston, MA 02215
(617) 353-3696; Fax: (617) 353-2838
archives@bu.edu; www.bu.edu/archives
Contact: Karen Hook

General comments: At the time the Boston University collections were researched online, the site listed its special collections by name but no additional information was available. However, the collections are in the National Union Catalog of Manuscript Collections (NUCMC) and can be searched online by name at www.loc.gov/coll/nucmc. Also, the Center has a set of brochures listing all of its collections by subject, e.g., Literary, Theatre and Film, Journalism, etc. What follows are highlights of some of the collections the authors were able to identify by name as being radio related and for which records were found on the NUCMC web page. In most cases, there was little or no information in the listings indicating what, if any, radio related information might be in the collections. For more specific information, contact the Center where detailed finding aids are generally available. In late 2005, the University is planning to add biographical information and "scope and content" notes to the online listings for several collections. Finding aids will, however, still not be available online.

65. Albert Spalding Collection. Contains correspondence, printed material, memorabilia, photographs, scrapbooks, sheet music, miscellany and audio tapes of his music career.

66. Alexander Kipnis Collection, 1918–1983. Contains correspondence, financial records, clippings, scrapbooks, programs, musical scores and photographs.

67. Arthur Fiedler Collection, 1856–1979, bulk 1927–1979. Includes musical scores, correspondence, financial and personal documents, photographs and sound recordings.

68. Basil Rathbone Collection, 1924–1950. Contains production materials, poems, scrapbooks, 1936–1939, photographs with Hollywood celebrities, scripts by Rathbone and his wife, Ouida Bergere Rathbone, and correspondence.

69. Billie Burke Collection, 1910–1957. Contains correspondence and photographs.

70. Boston Symphony Orchestra Collection. Contains musical scores.

71. Carl de Suze Collection. Includes several items regarding WBZ, Boston and de Suze's career as a local radio figure.

72. Charles Munch Collection, 1935–1966. Contains manuscripts, photographs and printed material.

73. Clifton Webb Collection, 1929–1961. Contains mostly photographs of stage performances of films, family and friends, publicity photos, a movie script and some correspondence.

74. Dorothy Kirsten Collection, 1938–1951. Contains scrapbooks, newspaper clippings, reviews, programs and some video materials.

75. Douglas Fairbanks, Jr. Collection, 1888–1980. Contains manuscripts of articles, books, poems, screenplays, speeches, movie scripts, printed articles by and about Fairbanks, scrapbooks, film reels, memorabilia and correspondence.

76. Ernest Truex Collection, 1895–1985, bulk 1895–1973. Contains photographs from various film and stage performances, playbills and scrapbooks documenting Truex's career and personal and professional correspondence.

77. Fred Astaire Collection, 1932–1993. Contains correspondence, scrapbooks, costumes, reviews, videotapes, other printed material and clippings.

78. Hans Conried Collection, 1934–1982. Contains manuscripts, artwork, awards, correspondence, subject files, photographs, printed material, scrapbooks, audio tapes and miscellany.

79. Janet Gaynor Collection, 1920–1982. Contains scrapbooks, audio cassettes, correspondence, photographs and other materials.

80. Jessie Royce Landis Collection, 1930–1962. Contains mostly photographs, scrapbooks, playbills, programs, awards, newspaper clippings and theater posters.

81. Joey Adams Collection, 1950–197? Contains manuscripts, printed material, photographs, clippings, audio tapes and memorabilia.

82. Joseph Liss Collection. Contains several scripts by Liss

including *The Human Adventure, We Care, Warriors of Peace, The Eternal Light, Report to the Nation, Charlie Wild Private Detective, You Are There, The Story of Our Time* and others. Also includes several letters, research files and other documents regarding his work in radio.

83. Kate Smith Collection, 1930–1976. Contains correspondence, scrapbooks, 1930–1960, photographs of Smith and other celebrities, home movies, film reels of television appearances and sound recordings.

84. Madeleine Carroll Collection. Contains photographs and printed material.

85. Marc Connelly Collection, 1915–1980. Contains manuscripts, including scripts by Connelly and by others which he produced, correspondence, financial material, printed material, scrapbooks, photographs, subject files, notebooks and memorabilia.

86. Myrna Loy Collection, 1915–1998. Contains correspondence, financial and business records, publicity materials, scripts, personal memorabilia, diaries, photographs and other papers.

87. Norman Corwin Collection. Contains several manuscripts of Corwin's radio work, including the scripts for "The Plot to Overthrow Christmas" and "They Fly Through the Air With the Greatest of Ease." Also includes several recordings of original broadcasts and letters from several notable figures in broadcasting.

88. Orson Welles Collection. Contains manuscripts, correspondence and printed material.

89. Patrick Hamilton Collection, 1937–1939. Contains manuscripts.

90. Ralph Bellamy Collection, 1926–1988. Contains manuscripts, printed materials, photographs, correspondence and miscellany.

91. Rex Harrison Collection, 1914–1991, bulk 1960–1990. Contains diaries, notes, performance materials and scripts, scrapbooks, photographs and other memorabilia.

92. Robert Benchley Collection. Contains manuscripts, notes, diaries, research material, printed material, correspondence, memorabilia and photographs.

93. Robert H. Newman Collection. Contains scripts for several series, including *City Hospital*, 1951–1958, *Inner Sanctum*, 1941–1952, *Mystery in the Air*, 1945, *NBC Radio Theatre, Adventures of the Thin Man, Theatre Five, The Man From G-2, Adventure Theatre* and other shows. Also includes a draft of a confidential report Newman wrote in 1943, probably for the government, and other documents regarding radio broadcasting.

94. Robert Hardy Andrews Collection, 1925–1985. Contains correspondence, manuscripts, including radio scripts, photographs, printed material, film reels, audio tapes, scrapbooks, professional material, printed material, financial material and research papers relating to his career as a producer.

95. Robert Lawrence Collection, 1926–1972. Contains correspondence, manuscripts, photographs, programs and other papers relating to Lawrence's career as a conductor, musicologist and critic.

96. Robert Lewis Shayon Collection. Contains numerous manuscripts, letters and other documents about the history of radio broadcasting. Includes scripts and recordings of *You Are There, The Eagle's Brood*, 1947, and many other programs. Also includes correspondence from Edward R. Murrow and other notable broadcasting figures.

97. Robert Preston Collection, 1920–1991. Contains correspondence, photographs, assorted scripts, scrapbooks and personal memorabilia.

98. Saul Levitt Collection, 1933–1976. Contains manuscripts, printed material, correspondence and miscellany.

99. Sir Cedric Hardwicke Collection, 1935–1939. Contains correspondence.

100. W. Gordon Swan Collection. Contains scrapbooks, various documents and audio recordings regarding the history of WBZ, Boston where Swan was Program Director for many years.

101. William Bennett Lewis Collection. Contains numerous manuscripts, letters and other documents regarding the history of radio and broadcasting. Includes many items related to Lewis's work for the Office of Facts and Figures and the Office of War Information during World War II.

102. Zino Francescatti Collection, 1936–1997, bulk 1936–1991. Contains mostly correspondence and some photographs, programs and posters.

School of Theology Library
745 Commonwealth Avenue, Boston, MA 02215
(617) 353-3034; Fax: (617) 358-0699
sthlib@bu.edu; www.bu.edu/sth/sthlibrary

103. James R. Houghton Papers, 1931–1964. Contains papers collected from his various activities, including sermons from Dr. William L. Stidger's program, *Getting the Most Out of Life*, sponsored by Fleischmann's Yeast, 1937–1939, annotated with hymns and fan letters. Houghton also provided the music for the program.

Bowling Green State University
Center for Archival Collections
Jerome Library, 5th Fl., Bowling Green, OH 43403
(419) 372-2411; Fax: (419) 372-0155
scharte@bgnet.bgsu.edu; Contact: Steve Charter
www.bgsu.edu/colleges/library/cac/cac.html

104. Peter C. Cavanaugh Interview. A 1989 interview with Cavanaugh, Executive Vice President and Chief Operating Officer of Reams Broadcasting Corporation, Toledo, OH. Cavanaugh worked as a rock 'n' roll radio personality on the air from 1957 to 1978, the majority of the time in Flint, MI at WTAC-AM. Collection also includes newsclippings.

105. World Government Reports, 1949. Scripts, prepared by J. Wesley Littlefield for the Toledo Chapter of United World Federalists and presented over WTOL between May and August, 1949.

Music Library and Sound Recordings Archives
Jerome Library, 3rd Floor
(419) 372-2307; Fax: (419) 372-2499
wschurk@bgnet.bgsu.edu; Contact: William Schurk
www.bgsu.edu/colleges/library/music/music.html

106. "Citizen Sounds" Sound Recording. A recording that features 16 different 30-second voiced spot announcements using sound effects to show the value of radio. One side repeats the same sound effects without voice so local announcers can use the copy with a local call letter insertion.

107. Audio collection. Listings can be searched in the online catalog.

108. "W. C. Fields On Radio," 1940s. A recording of comedy sketches Fields did on radio shows, including sketches with Edgar Bergen, Charlie McCarthy and Don Ameche.

109. "Years to Remember" Sound Recording. Great moments in radio broadcast history selections narrated by Jack Benny and Frank Knight. Includes day time radio programs and commercials, introduction to soap operas, commercials, news, sports, comedy, adventure and mystery.

Brandeis University
University Archives & Special Collections
415 South Street, Waltham, MA 02454
(781)736-4701; kabramso@brandeis.edu
http://lts.brandeis.edu/research/archives-speccoll

110. Stephen S. Wise Collection, 1896-1949. Includes unidentified material relating to CBS, 1947, to the debates Wise had with Clarence Darrow, 1927-1930, Father Lonegran, 1927-1928, Betrand Russell, 1931-1932 and Ben Lindsey, 1927-1928. Also material relating to *Town Meeting of the Air*, 1945, and *Martha Deane*, 1947-1948.

Brigham Young University
Harold B. Lee Library, L. Tom Perry Special Collections
Provo, UT 84602
(801) 422-3175; Fax: (801) 422-0461
specialcollections@byu.edu; http://sc.lib.byu.edu
Contact: James D'Arc

111. Andy Devine Papers. Includes scrapbooks and approximately 20 radio transcription discs of his appearances, 1937–1947, on *The Andy Devine Radio Show, Screen Guild, Jell-O Program, Symphonies of Sage* and *Texaco Star Theatre*.

112. Bosley Crowther Papers, 1924–1978. The radio and television portion of the collection documents Crowther's participation on several radio and television programs, including a *CBS Reports* on censorship, *Movie Memories with Bosley Crowther*, WQXR, New York and Crowther's radio and TV movie reviews during "The New York Times" strike of 1963. Includes scripts and research material pertaining to the shows.

113. Cecil B. DeMille Papers. Includes papers relating to *Lux Radio Theatre*, 1936–1945.

114. Dean Jagger Papers, 1920–1980. Includes scrapbooks, photographs and audio cassettes relating to Jagger's career in the theatre, motion pictures, radio and television.

115. Franklin S. Harris Papers, 1931–1960. Contains miscellaneous correspondence, including typed programs of the KSL series *The Book of Mormon: Messages and Evidences*.

116. James Stewart Papers. Includes a collection of 51 transcriptions of performances from 1939–1953 of shows, including the *Bing Crosby Show, Jack Benny Show, Silver Theatre, The Six Shooter, Hollywood Star Playhouse, Suspense, Jimmy Stewart Show* and *Screen Guild*.

117. KBYU Records, 1940–1960. Includes photographs and some papers related to the history of KBYU, the first radio station at Brigham Young University.

118. KBYU-FM Scripts, 1954. Includes various radio scripts, including "The Challenge, World Series of Basketball—1954," and "Why Do I Love You?"

119. L. H. Curtis Papers, 1934–1976. Includes programming guides, correspondence, newspaper articles, speeches, notes, questionnaires, newsletters, editorials, a video tape and an audio tape relating to Curtis's speeches and editorials on KSL radio and television.

120. Laraine Day Papers. Includes correspondence and audio recordings of her baseball program with her husband Leo Durocher.

121. Mary Astor Papers. Consists of an 80 page scrapbook of newspaper and magazine articles relating to Astor's acting career in film and radio.

122. Owen S. Rich Papers. Includes course information, papers, correspondence and research projects relating to the Communications classes that Rich taught at BYU and an autobiography of his career in broadcast education involving KBYU.

123. Robert Cummings Papers. Contains correspondence, scripts and sound recordings of many of Cummings's roles on radio, including *Screen Guild Players, The Hollywood Theatre, Lux Radio Theatre, Screen Directors' Playhouse, The Four Star Playhouse, Cavalcade of America, Edgar Bergen-Charlie McCarthy Show, Hallmark Playhouse* and *Suspense.*

124. Roscoe A. Grover Papers, 1932–1975. Consists of newspaper clippings, radio broadcast programs, reproductions of paintings, correspondence, diary entries, pamphlets and miscellaneous items related to Grover's career as a broadcaster and as an artist.

125. William M. Timmins Radio Talks, 1959. Collection of 13 talks given by Timmins on KSL in 1959.

Broadcast Pioneers Library
(See Library of American Broadcasting)

Bronx County Historical Society
3309 Bainbridge Avenue, Bronx, NY 10467
(718) 881-8900; www.bronxhistoricalsociety.org

126. Audio Tape Collection, ca. 1960–1985. Contains radio shows, lectures, oral histories and events, all relating to the Bronx. Includes material relating to the Barry Sisters.

Brooklyn College
Special Collections
2900 Bedford Avenue, Brooklyn, NY 11210
(718) 951-5346; Fax: (718) 951-4557
tonyc@brooklyn.cuny.edu; www.Brooklyn.cuny.edu/archives
Contact: Anthony M. Cucchiara

127. Margaret E. Sangster Jr. Collection. Contains scripts, correspondence and other papers relating to her writings for radio and television. Includes scripts for *My True Story,* 1948–1960 and *Whispering Streets,* 1953–1960. Also includes outlines and storylines for future scripts, possible plots and audition scripts that Sangster wrote and correspondence she

received from ABC and NBC. Little personal information is included in collection.

128. Morton Wishengrad Scripts, 1940–1959. Contains radio and television scripts, 1940s–1950s, some published, some typescript versions written by Wishengrad for *The Eternal Light.* Also includes a few scripts for *I Have Seen the Light,* WQXR, 1947, *Birthday of the World,* 1950s, for ABC, and the NBC *Inter-American University of the Air,* 1944.

129. Sam Levenson Papers, 1949–1980. Contains books, articles, scripts, including radio scripts, monologues and jokes written by Levenson. Also includes material written about him, as well as phonograph recordings, audio tapes, films, correspondence and memorabilia.

Brown University
John Hay Library
20 Prospect Street, Box A, Providence, RI 02912
(401) 863-3723; Fax: (401) 863-2093
hay@brown.edu; www.brown.edu/Facilities/
University_Library/collections/index.html

130. Harris Collection of American Poetry and Plays. Approximately 250,000 volumes of American and Canadian poetry, plays and vocal music dating from 1609 to the present day. Includes radio scripts.

131. "Lights Out?: A Saga of World War II," 1945. Script for program broadcast November 11, 1945 on WQXR, New York City.

132. Miller Collection of Wit and Humor. An extensive collection dealing with humor in many genres. Includes the works of many humorists and comedians who performed on radio such as Fred Allen, George Burns, Gracie Allen and others.

133. Robert J. Tierney Jr. Entertainment Memorabilia Collection, ca. 1945–1995. Consists of 350 radio and television scripts representing musical variety, science fiction, drama, mystery, westerns and comedies of the 1950s and 1960s and related correspondence, promotional and program material. A list of scripts is available.

134. "Roots of Radio's Rebirth: Audiences, aesthetics, economics and technologies of American broadcasting." A Ph.D. thesis by Alexander Todd Russo, Brown University, 2004. (In Brown University Archives.)

135. Sheet Music Collection, bulk 1800–1950. Contains approximately 500,000 pieces of sheet music, largely American, including about 35,000 pieces representing songs from the musical theatre, films, radio and television shows. Many of the pieces, primarily 1930s and 1940s, include photographs of the individuals or groups (bands, orchestras etc.) who are identified as radio performers. Also includes a large collection of band and orchestra arrangements that were used by WEEI's orchestra until it was disbanded. Note: Because the sheet music, only some of which is listed in the online catalog, is filed by title, a researcher would have to see the actual cover to determine if it included a photograph of a radio personality.

136. "The Spell of the Yukon," 1937. Script for the August 3, 1937 program broadcast on WFIL, Philadelphia. Written by John L. Clark.

137. *William and Mary* Scripts. Approximately 350 *William* *and Mary* scripts written as skits for the *Dinah Shore Show*, 1943–1944, with Cornelia Otis Skinner as Mary and Roland Young as William.

Buffalo & Erie County Public Library
Grosvenor Room
1 Lafayette Square, Buffalo, NY 14203
(716) 858-8900;
ddspc@buffalolib.org; www.buffalolib.org

138. Zona Gale Papers, 1923–1933. Twelve scripts for *Neighbors: A Story of the Air*, an adaptation for radio by Zona Gale and Marian de Forest of Zona Gale's "Friendship Village" that were aired over WEAF (NBC), between February 24 and May 29, 1933. Also includes correspondence between Gale and de Forest about the *Neighbors* series and an outline of the series.

California State Library
914 Capitol Mall
PO Box 942837, Sacramento, CA 95814
(916) 654-0261; Fax: (916) 654-0241
cslsirc@library.ca.gov; www.library.ca.gov

139. Alameda City Schools Radio Scripts, 1938–1940. Scripts of radio plays broadcast for Northern California school children in the late 1930s and early 1940s.

140. Frona Wait Colburn Collection, 1900–1942. Includes some scripts, n.d., for an unidentified half hour radio program that Colburn conducted for ten months.

141. James A. Hayes Oral History Interviews, 1990. Includes a discussion of Hayes's early employment in radio broadcasting at KLX, Oakland, CA. Note: Copies of the interview are also available at UC/Berkeley and UCLA.

142. W. H. (William Henry) Hutchinson Papers, 1951–1990. Includes radio scripts, 1947–1954 and 1980–1981, for programs written, narrated and produced by Hutchinson relating to California history.

California State University, Northridge
Oviatt Library, Room 265
18111 Nordhoff Street, Northridge, CA 91330
(818) 677-2832; Fax: (818) 677-2589
tony.gardner@csun.edu; Contact: Tony Gardner
http://library.csun.edu/spcoll/hpsc.html

143. Armed Forces Radio Service Record Albums, 1942–1945. Approximately 25 recordings.

144. Milton Geiger Papers. Includes papers and scripts from 1939 relating to Geiger's work in radio. As of 2005, the collection was being processed.

145. Violet Atkins Klein Papers, 1942–1967. Contains finished scripts, unproduced manuscripts, legal documents, correspondence and research materials, including undated radio scripts for *The Treasury Star Parade, Camel Caravan,* and *The Camel Hour.*

CBS Archives-Sales
524 West 57th Street, New York, NY 10019
(212) 975-4321; Contact: Toni Gavini

146. CBS Audio Archives. Includes recordings of news broadcasts, 1933 to present. Some tapes have been donated to the National Archives and to the Milo Ryan History in Sound: KIRO-CBS Collection, formerly at the University of Washington, Seattle, WA and now at the National Archives. Access to tapes is available on a "for sale" basis. Archives may also contain some recordings of general programs but no listing is available and access may not be possible due to legal issues.

147. CBS Print Archives. All requests must be submitted in writing. Only requests from publishing authors will be answered. Print materials dating back to the Golden Age of Radio are "hit and miss."

Chemung County Historical Society
Booth Library, 415 East Water Street, Elmira, NY 14901
(607) 734-4167; Fax: (607) 734-1565
Archivist@chemungvalleymuseum.org
chemungvalleymuseum.org; Contact: Kim Richards

148. Communications Collection. Contains newspaper clippings, pamphlets and miscellaneous papers dealing with radio in Central New York State, 1925–1970.

Chicago Historical Society
Clark Street at North Avenue, Chicago, IL 60614
(312) 642-4600; Fax: (312) 266-2077
www.chicagohs.org/collections/archives.html

149. Harry R. Booth Papers, 1930-1974. Includes documents relating to lawsuits involving Chicago stations WFMT and WEFM.

Chicago Symphony Orchestra
Rosenthal Archives
220 South Michigan Avenue, Chicago, IL 60604
(312) 294-3055; Fax: (312) 294-3450
www.cso.org

150. Archives. Contains sound recordings of radio broadcasts. See online search form.

Cleveland Orchestra
Severance Hall
11001 Euclid Avenue, Cleveland, OH 44106
(216) 231-7356; Contact: Carol Jacobs
cjacobs@clevelandorchestra.com

151. Cleveland Orchestra Broadcasts. Contains a few off-air audio recordings from the 1940s and 1950s and a more significant collection of pre-1960s print material about the broadcasts, including scrapbooks and some biographical information about performers. For more information about the audio recordings contact the archives. Audio recordings beginning with mid-1960s are more generally available.

City College
Morris R. Cohen Library, North Academic Center
Convent Avenue & 138th Street, New York, NY 10031
(212) 650-7609; Fax: (212) 650-7604
archives@ccny.cuny.edu; www.ccny.cuny.edu/library/divisions/archives

152. Art Stillman Tape, ca. 1950, Memorabilia Collection. An audio tape of lyricist Art Stillman from the *California Radio Show.*

Cobleskill Public Library
Historical Cabinets
Union Street, Box 219, Cobleskill, NY 12043

(518) 234-7897
http://www2.telenet.net/community/mvla/cobl/

153. Ray F. Pollard Papers, 1931–1943. Scripts for the program *Farming and Country Life.*

Colgate University

Everett Needham Case Library
13 Oak Drive, Hamilton, NY 13346
(315) 228-7305; Fax: (315) 228-7934
cpeterson@mail.colgate.edu; Contact: Carl Peterson
http://exlibris.colgate.edu/services/departments/speccoll/

154. Orrin E. Dunlap Collection of Radio and Television. Contains manuscripts, correspondence, including letters from Guglielmo Marconi, Lee De Forest and Vladimir Zworykin, and memorabilia dealing with the early history of radio and wireless telegraphy.

Colorado Historical Society

Stephen H. Hart Library
1300 Broadway, Denver, CO 80203
(303) 866-4602; Contact: Keith Schrum
research@chss.state.co.us; www.coloradohistory.org

155. 1940s Radio Scripts. Collection contains scripts, ca. 1940–1949, including *Sketches in American Melody.*

156. "Bright Destiny" Recording. An hour long program on the history and future of Denver broadcast by KOA.

157. George R. Eichler Collection, 1957–1958. Writer for *This Is Denver* and *Westward America.* Collection includes some scripts.

158. Harry E. Huffman Papers, 1883–1969. Includes records of the Aladdin Radio and Television Company.

159. Hugh B. Terry Oral History Interview, 1974. Terry discusses his 41 year career in radio and television in Denver.

160. Jesse A. Slusser Oral History Interview. Slusser recounts his career as an engineer with KOA, Denver.

161. KFML Program Guide, 1955. A program guide.

162. KOA Collection, 1934–1988. Assorted papers. As of 2005, collection is unprocessed.

163. Pete Smythe Collection, 1860–1964. Consists of correspondence, drawings, clippings and other material relating to Smythe's broadcasting career.

164. Ralph Freese Collection, 1920–1929. Papers, including scrapbooks and press releases, relating to Freese's employment with NBC and KOA, Denver. Collection unprocessed as of 2005.

165. Reynolds Radio/KLZ Collection, bulk 1915–1935. Contains station history papers and audio for KLZ, Denver.

166. Socialist Labor Party of Colorado Collection, 1898–1972. Contains correspondence and other papers about the organization, including radio scripts. As of 2005, collection is partially processed.

167. Sounds of Colorado. Assorted off-air recordings with Colorado related subject matter. Each recording is listed separately. Many are undated.

Columbia University

Butler Library, Rare Books & Manuscripts Library
535 West 114th Street, New York, NY 10027
(212) 854-5153; Fax: (212) 854-1365
rbml@libraries.cul.columbia.edu; Contact: Jennifer B. Lee
www.columbia.edu/cu/lweb/indiv/rbml/

168. Algernon D. Black Papers, ca. 1932–1979. Consists of correspondence, speeches, memoranda, minutes and publications, including radio talks and platform addresses given at the Ethnical Culture Society, and other papers.

169. Ben Grauer Papers, 1915–1977. Includes correspondence, scripts, notes, subject files, documents, financial records, photographs, memorabilia, clippings and printed materials relating to Grauer's radio career. Also includes a tape of an off-air recording of *Salute to Ben Grauer*, November 15, 1950.

170. Bennett Cerf Papers, ca. 1898–1977. Contains correspondence, manuscripts, memorabilia, photographs, phonograph and tape recordings and printed files.

171. Cornell Woolrich Papers, 1958–1964. Includes copy of 1958 radio play, "Wardrobe Trunk."

172. Elliott Maxwell Sanger Papers. Contains personal diaries of Sanger, founder of WQXR, New York, business papers relating to the station, including daily schedules, market surveys and photographs, audio tapes of 1973 interviews with Sanger and cassettes celebrating WQXR's 50th Anniversary.

173. Erik Barnouw Papers, 1920–1990. Contains correspondence, scripts, manuscripts and reports regarding his activities in the American radio and film industries. Included are papers regarding projects about various television and radio networks and private ventures. Also includes material regarding the Center for Mass Communications of Columbia University in which Barnouw figured prominently and files for the books he has written dealing with radio history. The online catalog listing for the *Papers* includes the names of more than a dozen radio related people referenced in the collection. The Radio Pioneers Oral History project also contains a transcript of a Barnouw interview.

174. George Ephraim Sokolsky Papers, 1919–1962. Includes approximately 1,800 transcriptions of Sokolsky's radio broadcasts, 1948–1961.

175. Gilbert Highet Papers, 1929–1978. Consists of correspondence, manuscripts, typescripts, notes, photographs and printed materials relating to his research, writing and teaching. Also includes correspondence concerning his syndicated radio talks.

176. Giles Cooper Papers, ca. 1945–1984. Includes playscripts, correspondence about his scripts, poems, notebooks and other manuscripts, including drafts, typescripts, notes, photographs, mimeographed scripts and printed materials relating to Cooper's plays, radio and television scripts, short stories and novels.

177. Harry James Carman Papers. Includes editorial broadcasts on WMCA, 1958–1959.

178. Herbert Lionel Matthews Papers, 1943–1982. Includes some unidentified radio material, possibly relating to the fall of Batista's Cuba, the rise of Fidel Castro and the Spanish Civil War.

179. James Lawrence Fly Papers, 1920–1977. Correspondence, manuscripts, drafts, notes, reports, legal briefs and other documents, books, clippings and other printed materials dealing with Fly's professional activities and relationships in all phases of his career. Fly was chairman of the FCC, 1939–1944, and a frequent lecturer about radio, television and freedom of speech.

180. Jerome Moross Papers. Includes papers and music scores for some radio plays.

181. John C. Hall Papers, 1950–1997. Contains correspondence and manuscripts, including drafts, typescripts, notes, photographs, mimeographed scripts and printed materials relating to Hall's plays, radio and television scripts, short stories and novels.

182. Leah Salisbury Papers, 1925–1975. Includes radio scripts written by Salisbury.

183. Letters on the Marconi Memorial Medal, 1938–1939. Letters about the formation of the Committee on Award of the Marconi Memorial Medal. The medal was to have been awarded annually for contributions to radio and David Sarnoff had been chosen as the first recipient but the Committee was dissolved as a result of a disagreement with the policies of the Italian government and the medal was never awarded.

184. Mark Van Doren Papers, ca. 1917–1976. Contains correspondence and manuscripts consisting of letters, poems, short stories, novels, plays, broadcast transcripts for *Invitation to Learning* and other papers.

185. Rose Franken Papers, 1925–1982. Includes 501 scripts for the *Claudia* series plus sound recordings of some of the programs, scrapbook clippings and an audio tape interview of Franken (with typescript transcripts) conducted by her grand-nephew, David Korr, in October, 1977.

186. Rose Nadler Franzblau Papers, ca. 1930–1978. Contains correspondence, manuscripts, notes, radio scripts, letters asking Franzblau's advice, clippings, memoranda, announcements, photographs, tape recordings, records, books, pamphlets and memorabilia.

187. Samson Raphaelson Papers, 1916–1982. Includes some radio scripts.

188. Samuel and Bella Spewack Papers, 1920–1980. Consists chiefly of correspondence and production files relating to the creation, production and performance of their works for stage, screen, radio and television.

189. Society for the Prevention of Crime Records, 1878–1973. Contains scripts for programs on criminal behavior, 1946–1948, including *I Was A Convict* and *Criminal Casebook.*

190. Ted Berkman Papers, 1942–1948. Includes radio dispatches from wartime Yugoslavia and Greece, 1944, when Berkman (a.k.a. Edward O. Berkman) was a correspondent for ABC.

191. Theodore Roscoe Papers, ca. 1850–1980. Includes some unidentified radio scripts.

192. Virgil Thomson Papers, ca. 1920–1971. Includes manuscripts, related correspondence, notes, printed material and audio tapes. Note: Online catalog lists 125 reels of tapes of Thomson's program on WNCN, New York, 1969-1970.

Oral History Research Office
Butler Library, 535 West 114th Street, New York, NY 10027
(212) 854-7083; oralhist@libraries.cul.columbia.edu
www.columbia.edu/cu/lweb/indiv/oral/

General comments: The Columbia University Oral History Research Office contains nearly 8,000 taped memoirs. A list of the individuals is available online. Most of the interviews related to the Golden Age of Radio are part of the Radio Pioneers Project which includes dozens of engineers, station and network executives, government officials, writers, directors and performers. In addition to checking the online alphabetical listing of participants, the Office has a separate list of the people who are included in the Radio Pioneers Project. Listed below is a sampling of some of the interviews and the diversity of the material covered. Although not shown below, the project also includes an interview with radio historian Erik Barnouw.

193. Oral History Research Papers, ca. 1900–1998. In addition to the transcripts of the individual interviews, this collection consists of miscellaneous papers relating to the memoirists who were interviewed by the Oral History Office. Includes original papers, printed materials and microfilm copies of materials not retained by Columbia. One half of the collection consists of original notes, draft transcriptions, related correspondence and documents related to the Radio Pioneer Project. Of those papers only available on microfilm, about one-third have a list of contents.

194. Arthur Judson Reminiscences. Covers Judson's career as agent for many musical artists.

195. Donald G. Little Reminiscences, 1951. Little discusses his career with KDKA, broadcasting the 1920 election, short wave and FM broadcasting and studio techniques.

196. Dorothy Lerner Gordon Reminiscences. Gordon discusses her early experience in radio, including the *Children's Corner,* 1930, *Yesterday's Children* and *Youth Forums* for "The New York Times," 1943.

197. Frank Atkinson Arnold Reminiscences, 1951. Arnold discusses his early advertising experiences, first contacts with radio, broadcasting and advertising, his role as Director of Development for NBC, pre-recorded programs and early radio advertisers.

198. Frank Ernest Hill Reminiscences. Hill discusses his involvement with adult education programs at CBS.

199. Frank Stanton Reminiscences, 1968. Stanton discusses his early radio research and his years as president of CBS, 1946–1948.

200. George R. Brown Reminiscences, 1981. Brown discusses format changes at WOR after World War II, the relationship between WOR and the Mutual Network, union work rules and their effect on network news coverage, the philosophy and practice of news coverage at WOR, the move from writer to manager of news operations, the organization of network personnel, radio personalities, including Bob and Ray and Marianne Taylor-Young, program innovations, programming cutbacks and remote reporting.

201. HansVon Kaltenborn Reminiscences, 1950. Discusses his broadcast career with CBS and NBC, 1921–1950, the Association of Radio News Analysts and his views on past and future roles of radio.

202. Howard Barlow Reminiscences. Barlow discusses his work on *Neighborhood Playhouse, Voice of Firestone* and other programs.

203. James Albert Pike Reminiscences, 1961. Pike discusses his role in religious broadcasting.

204. Lyman Lloyd Bryson Reminiscences, 1951. Bryson discusses his career at CBS, educational broadcasting, the relationships between networks and local stations, fiscal issues and his impressions of academic and broadcasting personalities.

205. Mark Woods Reminiscences, 1951. Woods discusses his early days at Broadcasting Corporation of America and NBC, an administrative view of broadcasting, commercials, the division of NBC into two networks and the formation of ABC.

206. Norman Corwin Reminiscences, 1966. Corwin discusses his career as a writer, director and producer, his early days in radio, WQXR, the *Twenty-Six by Corwin* program, advertising agencies, and "Red Channels."

207. Phillips Carlin Reminiscences, 1951. Carlin discusses his career as an announcer with WEAF, 1923–1926, as program manager with NBC, 1926–1940, Vice President in charge of programs with ABC, 1941–1944, and talent agent with MBS.

208. Ruth Ashton Taylor Reminiscences, 1990. Part of the Washington Press Club Project, this interview contains material relating to Taylor's radio career, including CBS Radio News during World War II and late 1940s, her reflections on major figures at CBS Radio News, a description of staff and programming, production of news story on atomic energy, women in broadcasting, as a radio broadcaster in Los Angeles during 1950s and 1960s and on *Firing Line*, 1964–1966.

209. William Robert Yates Reminiscences. Yates was a story editor for CBS, 1956–1959, and worked in program development for ABC, 1960–1961.

210. William S. Paley Reminiscences, 1960. Paley discusses the use of radio in advertising and his involvement with CBS from 1928.

211. WOR Oral History Project, 1981–1982. Participants discuss the creation and development of WOR from several viewpoints. Accounts deal with broadcast news, trade unions, program innovations, music, technical developments and the effects of blacklisting. Includes portions of individual interviews with George Brown, Morton Gould, Henry Morgan and Jack Poppele.

Concord Free Public Library
129 Main Street, Concord, MA 01742
(978) 318-3342; Fax: (978) 318-3344
LWilson@minlib.net; Contact: Leslie Perrin Wilson

212. *Nature in New England* **Broadcasts, 1940–1946.** Transcripts of the program, written by Richard C. Potter and presented over WTAG, Worcester, MA.

Connecticut Historical Society
1 Elizabeth Street at Asylum Avenue, Hartford, CT 06105
(860) 236-5621; Fax: (860) 236-2664
barbara_austen@chs.org; www.chs.org
Contact: Barbara Austen

213. Florence Piccolo Volpe Scrapbooks, 1938. Clippings from the "Hartford Courant" and "Boston Post" describing the hurricane of September 22, 1938, including accounts of a group of amateur radio enthusiasts who relayed vital orders to mobilize national guardsmen, open roads to isolated communities and sent messages to worried relatives of victims.

214. John Harper Trumbull Scrapbooks, 1919–1945. Includes material related to WTIC, Hartford, CT.

Consumers Union Archives
101 Truman Avenue, Yonkers, NY 10703
(914) 378-2000; www.consumersunion.org

215. Persia Crawford Campbell Papers, 1931–1974. Contains radio scripts and other papers related to Campbell's career as a government advisor, consumer advocate, economics professor, representative of international organizations to the United Nations and author.

Cornell University
Division of Rare and Manuscript Collections
2B Carl A. Kroch Library, Ithaca, NY 14853
(607) 255-3530; Fax: (607) 255-9524
rareref@cornell.edu; http://rmc.library.cornell.edu

216. Bristow Adams Papers, 1853–1970. Includes scripts for unidentified radio programs regularly broadcast on WGY, Schenectady, NY and WHCU, Ithaca, NY.

217. Carl E. Ladd Director of Extension Papers, 1924–1930. Includes correspondence, reports and other records, including those relating to radio, during Ladd's tenure as Director of Extension at the New York State College of Agriculture.

218. Carolynne Cline Papers, 1933–1984. Collection consists of correspondence, scrapbooks and two tapes of *Carol's Corner* interviews with Cornell-affiliated people, 1960.

219. Clesson Nathan Turner Papers, ca. 1926–1987. Includes material relating to farming issues broadcast on WGY.

220. Cooperative Extension Association of Tompkins County Records, 1914–1987. General files relate to county extension work, including 4-H scripts, 1955–1956.

221. Cornell University Cooperative Extension Records, 1915–1992. Contains files of Lincoln Kelsey, primarily relating to Cornell United Religious Work (CURW) and to the Christian Rural Fellowship movement, including radio scripts, 1932–1941.

222. Cornell University Cooperative Extension, Teaching and Information Dept. Recordings, ca. 1937–1955. Includes the inaugural program for WENY, Elmira, NY.

223. Cornell University Debate Association Records, 1924–1966. Includes radio and television debates and other records of the Cornell Debate Association.

224. Cornell University Department of Natural Resources Records, 1909–1983. Includes material on radio talks, ca.

1930–late 1940s, of the Cornell University Department of Natural Resources, formerly the Conservation Department.

225. David Lee Hanselman Recording, 1954–1957. Recording of "Symphony of the Birds," an 11 minute tape of bird songs recorded and produced in 1955 and 1956 by Peter Paul Kellogg and Jim Facett who hosted a CBS radio symphony orchestra program at the Cornell University Laboratory of Ornithology. Also includes a recording of Arthur Augustus Allen talking about the hummingbird and taped excerpts of a program Hanselman produced for the *Farm and Home Radio Show,* Christmas, 1957. The program includes a 1954 recording of Bristow Adams telling the story of the Christmas bells.

226. Edward Roe Eastman Papers, 1923–1970. Contains correspondence, pamphlets and clippings concerning or authored by Eastman on agricultural issues. Also includes speeches, radio talks, notes, scrapbooks, reports and surveys.

227. Edward Sewall Guthrie Papers, ca. 1907–1962. Includes texts of various broadcasts Guthrie gave, 1929–1934, for the *Cornell Agricultural Hour* on WEAI and WESG.

228. Ethel Letitia Cornell Papers, 1906–1964. Includes "Plan for the Evaluation of the *Empire State FM School of the Air* program."

229. Festival of Contemporary Arts Records, 1945–1959. Contains programs for the Festival held at Cornell, 1945–1963, including tape recordings from the Festival aired on WHCU, 1957.

230. Frank Ernest Gannett Papers, ca. 1859–1958. Contains papers, tape recordings and 25 unidentified radio transcriptions.

231. Frank K. Singiser Papers, 1923–1981. Contains scripts for radio broadcasts, including five minute newscasts and MBS programs, including *Wall Street Reports, Plain Table* and other shows.

232. From the Sexologists to Sexual Liberation: Nonfiction in the Human Sexuality Collection, 1880–1973. Includes transcript of a two part radio program on homosexuality, *Homosexual in Our Society,* aired on KPFA, 1959.

233. Harry H. Love Papers, 1907–1964. Include radio talks relating to agriculture given by Love.

234. Helen Powell Smith Papers, 1941–1995. Includes photocopies and memorabilia reflecting on Smith's career on WHCU on *Let's Make a Dress* and *Education on the Air.*

235. Hendrik Willem Van Loon Papers, 1884–1972. Contains papers documenting Van Loon's career in radio beginning in 1929, including his time at NBC starting in 1932 and for WRVL, 1939–1940. Also includes manuscripts for broadcasts, 1935–1942.

236. Hugh Anderson Moran Papers, 1919–1947. Contains correspondence, memoranda, reports, minutes and other items concerning Cornell University Religious Work (CURW) and its predecessor, the Cornell University Christian Association (CUCA), including radio scripts.

237. John M. Young Papers, 1937–1965. Contains mostly radio scripts for *The Right to Happiness.* Also includes radio and television scripts for *Doctor Eve, Days of Our Lives,* *Attorney at Law, Road of Life, From These Roots, Date with Life, The Verdict is Yours, Golden Windows, The Second Mrs. Burton, Woman in White, Zenith, There Was a Woman, The Wheels of Time, The Rising Tides, Return of Constance Curtis, Four Corners, U.S.A.* and the *Doris Blake Show.* Also includes correspondence, plot synopses, notes, research for some of the scripts and some fan mail.

238. Justin S. Morrill Papers, 1814–1937, 1982. Includes a folder on the *Land Grant College Radio Hour,* August 19, 1936.

239. Mack Buckley Swearingen Papers, 1920–1969. Contains personal and professional correspondence, course schedules, rosters, student letters and other material related to Swearingen's career as a professor of history. Also includes unidentified radio broadcasts.

240. Margaret Morse Nice Papers, 1917–1968. Includes personal correspondence and manuscripts for articles, lectures and radio broadcasts on ornithology.

241. Myron G. Fincher Papers, 1908–1993. Contains personal and professional files of the Chair of the Department of Veterinary Medicine and Obstetrics at the New York State College of Veterinary Medicine, including papers relating to radio programs.

242. National Grange of the Patrons of Husbandry Records, 1842–1994. Includes material relating to the work of the National Association of Television and Radio Farm Directors, mostly 1950s, and other radio addresses.

243. Ralph Sheldon Hosmer Papers, 1885–1941. Contains papers and articles by Hosmer, including manuscripts of radio talks.

244. Romeyn Berry Papers, ca. 1898–1956. Contains personal and business correspondence and other papers, clippings, manuscripts of articles and radio broadcasts, photographs, scrapbooks, pamphlets and other printed matter reflecting Berry's varied talents and interests.

245. Steven Muller Interview by Astrid M. Eckert, 2003. A recording of an interview with Muller in which he discusses his career as a child actor in Hollywood and as a contestant in radio quiz shows, including *The Hollywood Smarty Party* and also his appearances on other radio shows such as *I Was There* and the *Mercury Theater of the Air.*

246. Student Raid of WVBR Records, 1952. A phonograph record and transcript of the May 28, 1952 student raid on WVBR and the broadcasting of music and a false news report concerning Russian bombings of London and Marseilles.

247. WBBF, Rochester, NY, Civil Rights and Race Relations Events, 1960–1966. Thirty five tape recordings of meetings, interviews and other events relating to civil rights and race relations in Rochester, NY recorded by WBBF.

248. WEAI Miscellany, 1930–1947. Contains two pamphlets entitled "Farm Radio Programs: WEAI, 1930," published by the New York State College of Agriculture at Cornell University, and "Twenty Years of Broadcasting, 1925-1945, 1947," by Charles L. Taylor, a transcript of "Radio Station Development, Cornell University" by Elmer S. Phillips and bound volumes of *Farm Radio Program* quarterly issues, 1930-1944.

249. WHCU Records, 1955–1958. Accounting records.

250. Widmer Wine Cellars Records, 1906–1963. Includes 1930s radio advertising material.

251. WVBR Records, 1946–1976. Contains reports, letters, station logs, 1948–1951, and other records.

School of Industrial and Labor Relations
M.P. Catherwood Library, Kheel Center
521 Ives Hall, Ithaca, NY 14853
(607) 255-3182; Fax: (607) 255-9641
kheel_center@cornell.edu; Contact: Patrizia Sione
www.ilr.cornell.edu/library/catherwood

252. Collection of Labor Play Scripts, 1915–1943. Collection of 50 plays and radio scripts (published and unpublished) relating to patriotic themes or labor issues. Most of the scripts date from the 1930s or the World War II period.

253. Frederick F. Umhey Executive Secretary Correspondence (ILGWU), 1934–1955. Includes material on the Unity Broadcasting Corporation which owned a number of radio stations across the country.

254. Gus Tyler Additional Records, 1959–1996, bulk 1975–1995. Includes correspondence, subject files, articles, transcripts of broadcasts, photographs and other materials dating from the end of the 1950s to 1996. Series III contains publications, writings and transcripts of broadcasts Tyler hosted on WEVD, New York. See also: Gus Tyler Assistant President Records, 1952–1980, bulk 1960–1975.

255. Inter-University Labor Education Committee Files, 1951–1957. Includes proposal for the expansion of union public service radio programs in New Jersey.

256. International Ladies Garment Workers Union. Research Department. Files, 1890–1971. Includes books, journals, reports, pamphlets, advertisements, radio campaigns and correspondence. Note: The library has additional ILGWU collections with materials relating to radio programming.

257. Irving Robert Feinberg Arbitration Papers, 1946–1975. Consists of documentation of cases arbitrated by Feinberg, including CBS vs. Radio Writers Guild and Directors' Guild of America, 1953, 1974, on issues of contract interpretation, position classification, overtime and plant rules.

258. Morris Sigman Presidential Records, ILGWU, 1923–1928. Includes some material related to WEVD, New York.

259. National Broadcasting Company, Inc. Selected Radio Broadcasts, 1935–1950. Thirty tape reels with recordings of speeches, debates, discussions, reports and analyses aired on NBC radio, all related to labor issues.

260. National Policy Committee Reports and Memoranda, 1943–1945. Contains memoranda concerning National Policy Committee dinners and reports of meetings at which were discussed political and economic issues confronting the postwar world, including the press and radio in wartime.

261. New York Teachers Guild Records, 1923–1957. Includes undated material relating to radio programs.

262. Robert Louis Aronson. Associated Actors and Artists of America Merger. Consists primarily of reports and supporting research materials collected for a study on the proposed merger of several performers' unions affiliated with the Associated Actors and Artists of America. The unions were:

Actors' Equity Association (AEA), American Guild of Radio Artists (AGRA), American Federation of Variety Artists (AGVA), Television Authority (TVA), American Guild of Musical Artists (AGMA) and Chorus Equity Association (CEA).

263. Teachers' Union of the City of New York Papers, 1916–1964. Includes correspondence, articles, publications, radio broadcasts from the 1940s and speeches of the Teachers' Union of the City of New York.

264. Workers' Education Bureau of America Records, 1921–1951. Consists of governance and financial documents, reports, correspondence, memoranda and notes pertaining to radio programs, courses and programs to promote workers' education, adult and vocational schools and educational programs, 1921–1951.

Country Music Hall of Fame and Museum

222 Fifth Avenue South, Nashville, TN 37203
(615) 416-2001; Fax: (615) 255-2245
Contact Reference Librarian
astoker@countrymusichalloffame.com
www.countrymusichalloffame.com

General comments: The Museum maintains collections devoted to oral histories, sound recordings and photographs. The collections cannot be searched online but the library can search an internal database upon request.

265. Bob Pinson Recorded Sound Collection, 1939–Present. Contains over 14, 000 transcription discs focusing on country music, including syndicated radio shows. Also includes a large collection of AFRS transcription discs. Programs represented in the collection include: *Grand Ole Opry, Prince Albert Show, Eddie Arnold Show, Checkerboard Jamboree, Ralph Emory Show, American Country Countdown, Radio Ozark* and other syndicated shows.

Lou Curtiss

Folk Arts Rare Records
2881 Adams Avenue, San Diego, CA 92116
(619) 282-7833; lou_curtiss@cox.net

266. Private Audio Collection. A privately held collection of 90,000 hours of programs, mostly on reel-to-reel tape. Although the collection includes all programming genres, it is particularly strong in music, especially jazz, blues, county and western, including *Renfro Valley Barn Dance, Midwestern Hayride, Louisiana Hayride, Hollywood Barn Dance and Town Hall Party.*

Dallas Symphony Orchestra

231 Flora Street, Dallas, TX 75201
(214) 692-0203; Contact: Media Relations
www.dallassymphony.com

267. Archives. May have some material relating to radio broadcasts from the early 1960s. For more information contact the Symphony.

Dartmouth University

Rauner Special Collections Library
6065 Webster Hall, Hanover, NH 03755
(603) 646-2037; Fax: (603) 646-0447
rauner.reference@dartmouth.edu; Contact: Jay Satterfield
www.Dartmouth.edu/~speccoll

268. Aldous Huxley Papers, 1923–1971. Includes a copy of a Christmas radio play and related correspondence.

269. *Author Meets the Critics.* A news release for the program relating to literary awards of 1949. Includes remarks of Edgar T. Rigg on the presentation of the award to Robert Frost.

270. Charles Albert Palmer Papers, 1925–1990. Contains papers relating to his career, including his work as a radio and television script writer.

271. F. E. (Frank Eugene) Austin Papers, ca. 1938. Papers relating to his studies of ants as pets and his invention of the ant farm. Some of the papers are radio scripts for broadcasts over NBC, March–June, 1938.

272. Radio Scripts, 1936–1955. Contains scripts for radio plays and dramatic readings, 1936–1938, and news broadcasts, 1949–1955, by noted journalists and writers, including Stephen Vincent Benét, Norman Lewis Corwin, Cedric Foster, Fulton Lewis, Edward R. Murrow, and William N. Robson.

273. Robert Frost Radio Play. Robert S. Newdick's introduction to his radio arrangement of a Robert Frost poem, possibly "The Generations of Men," broadcast ca. 1938.

274. Walter Amos Morgan Papers, 1925–1954. Includes texts of radio broadcasts, poetry, essays, fiction and plays written by a Congregational and later Presbyterian minister.

David Sarnoff Library
201 Washington Road, CN 5300, Princeton, NJ 08543
(609) 734-2636; Contact: Alex Masgoun
amagoun@davidsarnoff.org; www.davidsarnoff.org

275. Library. The library contains a museum, archives and a web site. In addition to the Sarnoff papers and memorabilia, the library's holdings include 25,000 photographs and thousands of notebooks, reports, publications and artifacts related to the history of RCA Laboratories and RCA.

Detroit Federation of Musicians, Local 5
20833 Southfield Road, Southfield, MI 48075
(248) 569-5400; Fax: (248) 569-1393

276. Detroit Symphony Orchestra Collection. Includes more than 1,000 DSO recordings back to 1950 of radio broadcasts. For more information contact the Local.

Detroit Public Library
5201 Woodward Avenue, Detroit, MI 48202
(313) 833-1480; Contact: David Poremba
dporemba@detroit.lib.mi.us; www.detroit.lib.mi.us

Burton Historical Collection

277. Brace Beemer Papers. Includes correspondence, scripts, fan mail and other papers relating to his role as the Lone Ranger.

278. "Cruising with the Michigan State Police." Reprints of a series of 18 radio talks on the organization and activities of the Michigan State Police broadcast on WKAR, ca. 193?

279. Donald J. Sublette Papers, 1925–1976. Contains correspondence, autobiography, reports, radio scripts and other papers relating to Sublette's career with the Detroit Civil Service Commission and his outside interests.

280. George Trendle Papers. Includes manuscripts, contracts, correspondence, scripts and other papers relating to *The Lone Ranger, The Green Hornet* and *Sergeant Preston.*

281. Jan Marian Kreutz Papers. Contains material relating to Kreutz's Polish daily radio commentary program. Materials are in English and Polish.

282. Ralph H. Pino Papers, 1911–1975. Includes material on radio talks, 1931–1953. See finding aid for more information.

283. Raymond Meurer Papers. Contains correspondence, legal papers, photographs, scrapbooks and some scripts relating to Meurer's work with George Trendle on *The Lone Ranger, The Green Hornet* and *Sergeant Preston.*

284. Richard Osgood Papers. Contains papers relating to interviews Osgood conducted over WXYZ, 1935–1971.

285. Stanislaw Wachtel Papers, 1907–1959. Contains scripts by Wachtel and other authors, sound recordings of radio dramatizations and other materials related to Polish themes.

286. WWJ Station Logs, 1922–1925. Contains daily logs.

287. Zofia Habrowska Papers, 1904–1983. Contains correspondence, poems, radio presentations, teaching aids, illustrations, theater programs, yearbooks, songbooks, scrapbooks, certificates of merit, clippings, postcards and photos relating to her activities with the Polish theater and radio in Detroit.

Main Library Music & Performing Arts

288. WJR, Detroit, MI. A sound recording commemorating 35 years of broadcasting, 1922–1957, on WJR, the "Goodwill Station."

Diocese of Rochester (New York)
1150 Buffalo Road, Rochester, NY 14624
(585) 328-3210; Contact: Sister Connie Derby
derby@dor.org

289. Archbishop Fulton J. Sheen Archives. Includes a complete set of scripts for *The Catholic Hour,* 1930-1950s.

Duke University
John W. Hartman Center for Sales, Advertising and Marketing History
PO Box 90185, Durham, NC 27708
(919) 660-5827; Fax: (919) 660-5934
hartman-center@duke.edu
http://scriptorium.lib.duke.edu/hartman/

290. Ad Access Project. Digital images, with searchable database, for over 7,000 advertisements printed in U.S. and Canadian newspapers and magazines between 1911 and 1955. Radio programs can be searched separately at http://scriptorium.lib.duke.edu/adaccess/.

291. Advertising Council Records, 1935–1999 and n.d. Includes sample radio spots in the Campaigns Series.

292. Carroll Carroll Papers, 1937–1956. Contains personal and professional papers of Carroll who was associated with the J. Walter Thompson Co. (JWT) and the development, writing and production of many radio programs, including *Kraft Music Hall.* Also contains material relating to his work as a ghost writer for Bob Hope and with the Office of War Information.

293. Colin Dawkins Papers, bulk 1920–1981. A former Vice President of JWT, the majority of the collection focuses on JWT through short company histories and the establishment and growth of departments such as Broadcast and Radio. Also of interest is the Oral Interview Series.

294. D'Arcy Masius Benton & Bowles Archives, 1929–1989, bulk 1950s–mid-1980s. Includes material that documents three advertising agencies: D'Arcy Masius Benton & Bowles (DMB&B), Benton & Bowles (B&B), and D'Arcy-MacManus & Masius (D-MM). Most of the radio related material is in the "Clients Series, 1931–1985, n.d., bulk 1970–1980s, n.d." Includes material about the *Maxwell House Radio Showboat*, May, 1933, and six scripts about great composers broadcast on Prudential's *The Family Hour*, 1943.

295. Dan Seymour Papers, 1951–1974, bulk 1955–1960s. As an executive with JWT, Seymour's papers deal primarily with television but he was involved with the company's reorganization of its radio and television operations into a single Radio-Television Department as television emerged as the leading media in the United States in the 1950s.

296. Edgar Hatcher Papers, 1952–1992. Includes papers and audio recordings of radio commercials for several companies. Hatcher was a copywriter and creative director for several major advertising agencies, including G.M. Basford Co., Benton & Bowles, Ogilvy, Benson, & Mather, Kenyon & Eckhardt, Batten, Barton, Durstine, & Osborn's San Francisco office, McCann-Erickson and J. Walter Thompson.

297. Howard Henderson Papers, 1867–1978. The "General Cigar Co. Folder (1941–1969)" contains information on sponsorship of radio commentators Raymond Swing and Raymond Clapper.

298. J. Walter Thompson Co. (JWT) Archives. The Archives are organized into more than 45 separate collections, each with its own online finding aid that describes in very general terms the types of documents in the collection and which may or may not include radio related material. For example, the "Quaker Oats Account Files, 1945-1965, 1977" collection contains 31 Aunt Jemima reports, 1945-1965, 1977 but does not indicate whether radio is discussed in any of the reports. A complete list of the JWT finding aids is available at: http://scriptorium.lib.duke.edu/dynaweb/findaids/

299. JWT Archives: Account Files Collection, 1885–1987, n.d., bulk 1920–1979. An artificially created collection of information about client accounts held by JWT that provides information about the agency's management of client advertising campaigns. The collection includes account histories, research reports, memoranda, correspondence, printed material, clippings, brochures and pamphlets, product labels and packaging designs. Additionally, the files document deliberations about such topics as media selection, markets and target audience for individual advertising campaigns. The largest account files are those relating to Chesebrough-Pond's, Inc., the General Cigar Company, the Andrew Jergens Company, Oneida Limited, Pan American World Airways, Standard Brands, Inc. and the United States Playing Card Company. The online finding aid lists other clients.

The only radio program specifically mentioned in the finding aid is the *Chase and Sanborn Hour*, 1929–1943, although radio material could be included in other client history materials.

300. Kensinger Jones Papers, 1934–2001. Papers document Jones's primary career as an executive for several major advertising agencies, including the Leo Burnett Company, Campbell-Ewald Company, D.P. Brother and Company, Wilding Advertising and William R. Biggs/Gilmore Associates. Materials consist primarily of correspondence, memoranda, notes, reports, scripts and audio visual materials that document the development of print, radio and television advertising campaigns for a wide variety of clients. The bulk of the materials appear to deal with television.

301. Radio Programs, 1953–1961 and n.d. Fifteen reels of audio tape containing radio commercials, programs for Won's Frozen Chinese Foods and Schlitz beer, the radio show *Ford Startime* and some unidentified radio programs.

302. Script File. The Center maintains a file listing all the scripts in the collection. (The scripts are not searchable online.) The listing is organized by show title or star. What follows is a partial list of scripts. For more information contact the Center directly. All scripts are on microfilm and print copies can be ordered.

A Saga of Aviation, 1938–1939
Abbot and Costello Show, 1941–1942
Alec Templeton Time, 1946–1947
All Colored Show, Apr–Jun, 1937
Angelo Patri, 1931–1935
Around the World with Libby, 1929–1930
Aunt Hannah's Kiddy Show, Jan–Apr, 1949
Aunt Jemima, 1929–1932
Aunt Jenny Hitchhikes, Jan–Apr, 1949
A Battle of Music with Raymond Paige, Dec 2–30, 1945
Bob Crosby Show, Jan–Jul, 1946
Broadway Matinee, Jan–Aug, 1944
Buck Rogers, 1936
Burns and Allen, n.d.
California Carry On, Sep–Dec. 1943
Camel Comedy Caravan, Jun, 1943
Canadian Marconi Program, Sep–Dec, 1930
Ceco Manufacturing Co. Dealer Program, May–Oct, 1930
The Circle, 1935–1939
Davey Tree Hour, 1930–1932
Devils, Drugs and Doctors, 1931–1932
Dione Lucas Cooking School, Feb–Dec, 1949
Do You Want To Be An Actor? 1936–1937
Don Ameche, 1942–1943
Dr. Howard W. Haggard, 1932–1933
Dr. West Celebrity Night, Apr–May, 1936
Dr. William L. Stidger, 1937–1939
Earl Wilson, Jan–Jul, 1945
Eddie Cantor Show, 1931–1934
Eddie Dooley-Football & Sports Review, 1932–1935
Eleanor Roosevelt, 1933–1937
Elgin National Watch Company, Recording of 75th anniversary celebration at World's Fair, Aug 18, 1939
Fair Meadows USA, Nov–Dec, 1951
The Family Man, 1939–1940
Five Dollar Fact Show, 1940–1941
Fleischmann's Baking Industry Program, Oct, 1931

Fleischmann's Food Talks, Jan–Apr, 1929
Floyd Gibbons, 1933–1935
The Ford Show, 1946–1947
Four Corners USA, Feb–Aug, 1941
Frances Greer, Apr–Jun, 1945
Frank Fay, Apr–Aug, 1936
Frank Sinatra Program, Jan–Dec, 1944
Fred Allen, 1945–1949
Fred Waring, Sep–Dec, 1944
Fresh Up Show, 1945–1946
The Garden Hour, 1931–1932
Gene Autry's Melody Ranch, 1941–1943
General Cigar World's Fair Exhibit Bldg. Recording,
   May 2, 1940
General Electric Radio Program, 1941
George Jessel, Feb–Mar, 1932
Georgie Price, Jun–Dec, 1932
Gliding Swing Program, 1938–1940
Good Will Court, Sep–Dec, 1936
Goodrich Silver Fleet/Defiance Tire Radio Program, 1930
Gracie Fields, Jun–Aug, 1944
Granlund & His Girls, 1935–1936
Great Moments in History, 1932–1933
Gruen Guild Radio Program, 1930–1931
Hammond Organ Hour, Sep–Dec, 1937
Happy Ramblers, 1932–1934
Harry Richman, May–Sep, 1932
Herbert Marshall, Nov–Dec, 1941
His Honor the Barber, Jan–Apr, 1946
Homefront Matinee, Nov–Dec, 1943
Horlick's Picture House, 1937–1938
Husbands & Wines, Jul–Sep, 1936
Husbands & Wives, 1936–1937
I Love A Mystery, 1939–1941
Ida Bailey Allen, 1930–1931
Information Please, Oct–Dec, 1946
Iowa Barn Dance Frolic, Aug–Nov, 1943
James Melton, Jan–Oct, 1937
The Jergens Program with Ray Perkins, 1931–1932
The Jergens Program with Cornelia Otis Skinner,
   Jun–Aug, 1935
The Jergens Program with Walter Winchell, 1933–1936
Jimmy Durante, 1933–1934
Joe Cook, Jan–Jun, 1937
Joe Penner, 1933–1935
Jolly Bill & Jane, 1929–1933
Kaltenborn Edits the News, n.d.
Kodak Mid-Week Hour/Kodak Week-End Hour, 1930–1932
Kraft Music Hall, 1933–1955
La Geradine Program, 1931–1933
The Libby Grocer, Sep–Dec, 1930
Life and Love of Dr. Susan, Aug–Dec, 1939
Life for the Wounded, Mar 24, 1943
Lux Radio Theatre, 1934–1955
Lux Toilet Soap Movie Club, 1938
Magic Baking Powder (Canada) (Commercials), 1934–1938
Major Bowes, 1935–1936
Marionette Show, 1937–1948
Martha Deane, 1936–1937
Mary Martin, 1943–1945
Mary Pickford, 1935
Maurice Chevalier, Feb–Jun, 1931

Mentholatum Mountaineers, 1944–1946
Marjorie Mills Participation Program, 1941–1943
The Music America Loves Best, 1944–1948
Musical Pictures, Nov 13–28, 1942
My True Story, 1945
National Spelling Bee, 1936–1937
Nelson Eddy, 1942–1943
Nemo-Flex Broadcast, Mar–May, 1931
Nero Wolfe, Apr–Sep, 1943
The Nestle's Chocolateers, 1931–1937
The Odorona Cutex Program, Apr–Oct, 1931
Old Witch Radio Program, 1929–1930
One Man's Family, n.d.
Opera Series, 1934–1935
Paul Whiteman, Jun–Aug, 1943
"Pearls"-Homemaker's Hour, Jan 9–22 ,1930
Peggy Winthrop, 1930–1931
Pertussin Play Boys, 1930–1931
Peter's Milk Cocoa, Jan–Jun, 1929
Placidan, 1934
Ray Perkins, 1930–1931
Raymond Clapper, Sep–Dec, 1942
Raymond Gram Swing, 1939–1942
Republican Campaign, Sep–Nov, 1940
Richman Brothers Program, Mar–Jun, 1932
Rinso Radio Revue, 1937
Robert Ripley, 1935–1937
Roses & Drums, 1932–1935
Royal Baking Powder Talks, 1928–1938
Royal Gelatin Audition, Sep–Dec, 1931
Sammy Kaye, 1943–1944
Rex Saunders, May–Jun, 1951
Sealtest Village Store Program, Jul 8, Aug 5, Nov 25, 1943
The Robert Shaw Chorale, Jun–Sep, 1948
Rudy Vallee, 1930–1936
Shell Chateau, 1935–1936
Shell Comes to the Party, Aug 7–21, 1941
The Shell Road Reporter, 1932–1933
Shell Show, 1934–1935
Sims & Baily, Apr–Sep, 1933
Springtime and Harvest, 1939–1940
Stars of the Future, Jan–Dec, 1945
Stebbins Boys, 1931–1932
Swift Hour, 1934–1935
Tennessee Jed, 1945–1947
This is Helen Hayes, Feb–Jul, 1945
Textron Theatre, 1945–1946
Those We Love, 1938–1940
Three Bakers, 1931–1932
Three Ring Time/Three Ring Round Up, 1941–1943
Tommy Dorsey, 1945–1946
Tommy Riggs, Apr–Oct, 1941
Town Crier, 1933–1935
True and False Program with Dr. Harry Hagen, 1938–1943
Uncle Abe and David, 1930–1931
*United Nations Information Bureau-Eight Legal Govern-
   ments of Invaded Europe, What they are doing to defeat
   Hitler and Establish Peace*, 1943 (Norway, Yugoslavia)
United States Marine Corps., Mar 12, 1943
US Industrial Alcohol, 1931, 1933–Audition Script
V.E. Meadows Beauty School, Aug–Sep, 1931
Vermont Lumberjack, 1931–1932

Vogue Fashion Program, Apr–Oct, 1931
Vox Pop, Jul–Sep, 1935
Wartime Conference, 1943
Washington Merry-Go-Round, Jul–Sep, 1940
Werner-Jannsen, Jul–Sep, 1937
What's New, Sep–Dec, 1943
Who's for Who in America, Nov 18, 1947
Womanpower, Mar 25–26, 1943
Women's National Republican Club, 1947–1948
Writer's War Board, 1943
You and Your Dog (Defense Dog), Jun, 1943,
Zenith Foundation, 1938

Special Collections
PO Box 90185, Durham, NC 27708
(919) 660-5822; Fax: (919) 660-5934
special-collections@duke.edu
http://scriptorium.lib.duke.edu/

303. Alliance for the Guidance of Rural Youth, 1887–1963. Includes scripts of Alliance broadcasts, 1925–1939 and 1945. The programs were broadcast from Richmond, New York, and Washington, DC and gave information on specific occupations and discussed vocational guidance issues. Additional records for the Alliance from 1947 to 1963 can be found in the Amber Arthur Warburton papers also located in the Manuscript Department.

304. Basil Lee Whitener Papers, 1889–1968. Contains papers relating to Congressman Whitener's private and unofficial affairs, including press releases concerning the topics of his weekly radio programs, schedules of when programs were to be aired and some information about pay TV.

305. Bobbye S. Ortiz Papers, 1919–1993 and n.d., bulk 1950–1990. The Audio Tape Series includes recordings of radio programs, interviews and readings related to Ortiz's activism. (In the Sallie Bingham Center for Women's History & Culture.)

306. David H. H. Felix Papers, 1929–1946. Includes speeches broadcast on *Debating the News,* WPEN, 1929–1940, and other radio talks, 1935–1942.

307. Douglas MacKinnon Papers, 1916–1983. Contains diaries, correspondence, financial papers, photographs, printed materials and newsclippings related to MacKinnon's radio broadcasting and business career as well as his personal life. Some materials pertain to his work in New York where he founded WQXR, Armed Forces Master Records, Inc., the Armed Forces Radio Service and Radio Free Europe. Note: As of 2005, the collection may be unprocessed. Contact library for more information.

308. Graham Arthur Barden Papers, 1934–1960. Contains some unidentified papers relating to the Beaufort Radio Station, NC, 1954.

309. Josiah William Bailey Papers, 1833–1967. Includes correspondence and printed material presenting the station's attempts to get favorable ratings and more power from the Federal Radio Commission for WPTF, the station owned by Durham Life.

310. Liggett and Myers Tobacco Company Records, 1908–1980s. Consists primarily of advertisements for various Liggett & Myers tobacco products such as Chesterfield, Fatima and Piedmont cigarettes, ca. 1910–1950s, as well as advertisements for competitors during the 1970s. Also includes scripts for radio and television commercials, 1949–1961.

311. Lois A. Gaeta Papers, 1956–1961. Contains scripts written by Gaeta for television and radio commercials during the 1950s, especially for Mentholatum, but also for other products advertised by JWT.

312. Paris Cleveland Gardner Papers, 1834–1976. By far the bulk of the papers are Federal Trade Commission files. As an attorney-examiner with the FTC between 1941 and 1962, Gardner worked with cases involving alleged deceptive advertising practices in the print media and radio. Collection includes worksheets for 1948–1951 from the Division of Radio and Periodical Advertising.

University Archives
PO Box 90202, Durham, NC, 27708
(919) 684-5637; Fax: (919) 660-5987
uarchives@notes.duke.edu
http://www.lib.duke.edu/archives/

313. Joseph C. Wetherby papers, 1930–1976. Papers include the development of WDBS at Duke University.

East Stroudsburg University
Vintage Radio Center
200 Prospect Street, East Stroudsburg, PA 18301
(570) 422-3204; Contact: Sarah Reilly
vintageradioproject@po-box.esu.edu

314. Audio Collection. Collection of 3,000 recordings of broadcasts, 1920s–1950s. Contact Center to identify specific programs in the collection.

Eastern Washington University
JFK Library, 816 F Street, 100 LIB, Cheney, WA 99004
(509) 359-2475; cmutschler@ewu.edu; www.ewu.edu

315. Byron Opendack Papers, 1959–1988, bulk 1983–1988. Collection of literary manuscripts, including, poetry, novels and radio plays.

Emory University
Pitts Theology Library
505 Kilgo Circle, Atlanta, GA 30322
(404) 727-1223; kira.homo@emory.edu
www.pitts.emory.edu/SpecColl/archives.html

316. Arthur Edwin Shelton Sermons, 1954–1965. Includes copies of devotional messages presented twice daily on WEER, Warrenton, VA from November 1958 through June 1959.

Woodruff Library
540 Asbury Circle, Atlanta, GA 30322
(404) 727-4885; Contact: Stephen Enniss
librse@emory.edu
http://specialcollections.library.emory.edu/index.html

317. Duncan MacDougald Papers, 1936–1965. (In Hansard-MacDougald Memorial Collection.) Includes radio scripts and other writings about food, cooking and travel, primarily in Europe, linguistics and other topics and other papers.

318. Elmo Israel Ellis Papers, 1947–1981. Consists of papers relating to Ellis's career as a broadcast executive and journalist, including editorials, book manuscripts, radio scripts, speeches and sound recordings of programs, 1965–1981, broadcast over WSB.

319. Emily Woodward Papers, 1918–1966. Includes transcripts of her radio broadcasts.

320. Ernest Rogers Papers, 1918–1967. Includes papers relating to Rogers's career as a broadcaster with WSB beginning in 1922. Also includes sound recordings of his 1952 radio show on WSB.

321. Joyce Blackburn Papers, 1965–1978. Includes drafts of manuscripts about Blackburn's Suki books that were aired on WMBI in 1945.

322. Lucy M. Stanton Collection, 1910–1981. Includes a sound recording of a radio interview of the artist.

323. Oliver Franklin Reeves Papers, 1936–1961. Bulk of the collection consists of manuscripts of Reeves's writings, including program materials for WAGA, Atlanta, GA.

324. Reminiscences of Radio Pioneers. Transcripts, on microform, of the Radio Pioneers Oral History Project from Columbia University. (See full listing under Columbia University Collections.)

325. Ted Hughes Papers, 1958–1992. Consists of Hughes's personal and literary papers, including radio scripts.

326. *Will the Circle Be Unbroken* Program Files and Sound Recordings, 1957–1997. An award winning documentary produced by the Southern Regional Council that chronicles the struggle to end segregation in the South. Collection is organized into five series: Interview transcripts, Audio visual materials, Scripts, Program research files and Production files

327. William H. Charlton Papers, 1933–1942. Papers document Charlton's role in promoting the programs of the National Recovery Administration and include bulletins, news releases, reports, radio scripts, speeches and stories chronicling the Depression.

328. WSB, Atlanta Collection, 1955–1980. Contains papers and sound recordings of news and other programming, 1950–1970s. Includes a celebration of the station's 50th anniversary. Also includes photographs.

Evangelical Lutheran Church in America
321 Bonnie Lane, Elk Grove Village, IL 60007
(847) 690-9410; Fax: (847) 690-9502
archives@elch.org; www.elch.org

329. *Church At Work*, late 1950s–1966. Includes some sound recordings, correspondence and reports.

330. *Lutheran Vespers*, 1950s–. Includes sound recordings (beginning in 1961) and some scripts.

331. *March of Faith*, 1942–1948. Includes scripts of the program produced at St. Olaf College, Northfield, MN and at WCAL.

332. National Lutheran Council, Division of Public Relations, Department of Radio and Television: Correspondence Files, 1943–1964. Contains correspondence, reports, articles, program scripts, contracts, copyright certificates,

program listings, publicity materials and form letters relating to the Department's involvement in administering its radio programs, including *Children's Chapel* and *Invitation for Tomorrow*, its television program *Light Time* and its participation in the CBS radio program *Church of the Air.* See related file with Department minutes and agendas, 1941–1964.

Family Theater Productions
7201 Sunset Boulevard, Hollywood, CA 90046
(323) 874-6633; Fax: (323) 874-1168
droverato@familytheater.org; www.familytheater.org
Contact: Dennis Roverato

333. *Family Theater.* Recordings of the program from 1947 to the early 1960s.

Fiorello H. LaGuardia Community College
LaGuardia and Wagner Archives
31-10 Thomson Ave., Room E-238
Long Island City, NY 11101
(718) 482-5065; Fax: (718) 482-5069
www.laguardiawagnerarchive.lagcc.cuny.edu

334. Fiorello H. LaGuardia Papers, 1882–1983, bulk 1922–1947. Includes transcriptions of LaGuardia's radio broadcasts, 1942–1947. Also sound recordings of broadcasts.

Florida State University
Claude Pepper Library
636 West Call Street, Tallahassee, FL 32306-1123
(850) 644-9305; Fax: (850) 644-9303
baltman@mailer.fsu.edu; Contact: Claude Pepper Librarian
www.claudepeppercenter.fsu.edu/pepperlibrary.htm

335. Claude Pepper Collection, 1915–1993. Contains official and personal papers and extensive audio holdings of Pepper's broadcasts during World War II and the post war period, 1945–1950, covering a wide range of domestic and international issues. See online finding aid for details.

Special Collections Department
105 Dogwood Way
Tallahassee, FL 32306-2047
(850) 644-3271; Fax: (850) 644-1221
spc@reserves.lib.fsu.edu; www.fsu.edu/~speccoll/

336. Bertie Badger Moyers Papers, 1916–1964. Includes stories, radio rights and scripts, 1928–1946, written by Moyers.

337. Cinema Promotional Papers, 1957–1976. Contains advertising materials, including radio commercials, used to promote a variety of motion picture studio films.

338. Fuller Warren Papers. Contains papers, correspondence, scrapbooks, radio speeches and spots, 1948–1956, of the former Governor of Florida and a 1948 recording of *The Voice of Florida* broadcast on WRUF.

339. Radio Scripts, 1942–1955. The majority of the scripts are from the Writers War Board which produced radio plays and pageants on such subjects as general morale, salvage, rationing, etc. as well as other scripts by the Mutual Life Insurance Company of New York, Broadcast Music Inc., RCA Victor Records *Thesaurus* Program Continuity Service and an episode of *Mr. Sycamore*, a 30 minute radio comedy-drama produced during the 1940s. There are also program brochures prepared by the Educational Department of MBS about programs for young people and public interest programs. Also includes a pageant script written by Roger M. Busfield entitled, "Land of Plenty," regarding a program at Michigan State University.

340. Spessard Lindsey Holland Papers, 1892–1971. Papers of Florida's 28th Governor, 1941–1945, including a 1971 broadcast of "Spessard L. Holland Day."

341. Stephen Graham Papers, 1908–1975. Includes transcripts of radio shows from World War II and other papers relating to Graham's career as an author and world traveler.

342. Thomas LeRoy Collins Papers, 1903–1991. Most of the collection covers his post gubernatorial career, 1961–1991, but it does include some radio material from 1958–1959 when he was Governor.

Flower Pentecostal Heritage Center

1445 North Boonville Avenue, Springfield, MO 65802
(417) 862-1447; Contact: Joyce Lee
Archives@ag.org; www.agheritage.org

343. *Gospel Rocket*, 1948–1949. Contains story scripts for most of the 15 minute programs which were for children plus sample opening and closing scripts for each of the 52 programs, buttons and blank certificates of membership and possibly some unprocessed 16" transcription discs.

344. *Revivaltime*, 1950–1996. Includes extensive correspondence, brochures, sermon scripts, choir recordings, choir tour itineraries and 16" transcription discs. The first year's programs featuring C.M. Ward and Dan Betzer are available on CD. Reel-to-reel tapes of the broadcasts are also available.

345. *Sermons in Song*, 1946–1950. Includes only articles about the program in "The Pentecostal Evangel" and a few historical articles about the program and possibly some unprocessed 16" transcription discs. Featured on the 15 minute program which received the "Best All-around Religion Broadcast" from the National Religious Broadcasters in 1947 were E.S. Williams and Wesley R. Steelberg.

Franciscan Friars of the Atonement–Graymoor

PO Box 300, Garrison, NY 10524
(845) 424-2120; Fax: (845) 424-2129
wgagne@atonementfriars.org; Contact: Father Walter Gagne
www.atonementfriars.org

346. *Ave Maria Hour*, 1935–1969. Includes scripts and audio for the program broadcast on WMCA and the Inter City Network. Most, but not all, of the audio is on 16" transcription discs.

347. Father Paul James Francis Wattson Papers, 1884–1963. Includes transcripts of Wattson's radio broadcasts.

348. *St. Anthony's Hour* Collection. Includes scripts of the program.

Franciscan Provincial Archives, Prov. of Santa Barbara

2201 Laguna Street, Santa Barbara, CA 93105
(805) 682-4713; Contact: Brother Timothy Arthur
friartim@aol.com

349. *Hour of St. Francis*. Includes print and audio material in mixed formats relating to the program.

Franklin D. Roosevelt Library and Museum

511 Albany Post Road, Hyde Park, NY 12538

(845) 486-7755; Fax: (845) 229-0872
robert.parks@nara.gov; www.fdrlibrary.marist.edu
Contact: Robert H. Parks

General comment: See the online catalog for a fuller listing of radio related material. The Library is one of several Presidential Libraries operated by the National Archives.

350. Correspondence on Radio Shows, 1937–1940. Contains correspondence generated by two radio shows which Eleanor Roosevelt hosted, 1937 and 1940.

351. Eleanor Roosevelt Sound Recordings, 1939–1962. Includes three radio series, 1940–1941, 1948–1949 and 1950–1951, which featured guests interviewed by Mrs. Roosevelt or her daughter Anna and discussions.

352. Franklin D. Roosevelt Sound Recordings, 1923–1945. Collection includes recordings of speeches of the President, political speeches and radio appearances by administration spokesmen, radio dramatizations produced by government agencies and political and nonpolitical radio addresses by associates and members of the President's family, including his wife, Eleanor and mother Sara Delano Roosevelt. Note: Radio related material produced during Roosevelt's years in office may be in more than one collection.

353. Republican National Committee (U.S.). Research Division Records, 1929–1948, bulk 1933–1945. Includes typewritten copies of public statements and copies of broadcasts by President Roosevelt and printed materials about Roosevelt and his policies, chiefly relating to his years in the White House with some material pertaining to him as Governor of New York and as a Presidential candidate.

General Mills Archives

One General Mills Blvd., Golden Valley, MN 55426
(763) 764-2679
katie.dishman@genmills.com; Contact Katie Dishman

354. General Mills Archives. Contains various, but limited, material about some of the radio shows sponsored by General Mills, 1930s–1950s. The partially processed collection includes some scripts (the program titles are listed individually in the Index), audio recordings, photographs and newsletter articles. Note: Researchers must contact archivist directly for information. The Archives is accessible only to serious outside researchers. Like most corporate archives, the main function of this department is serving company employees.

George Mason University

Fenwick Library, Fairfax, VA 22030
(703) 993- 2220; Fax: (703) 993-2669
speccoll@gmu.edu; www.gmu.edu/library/specialcollections

355. Federal Theatre Project Playscript and Radioscript Collection. Contains over 200 playscripts and radioscripts, written and performed between 1936–1939 for the Federal Theatre Project. Many of the scripts have been annotated with additional theatrical instructions, corrections and textual changes. Also includes copies of 62 programs and handbills.

356. Sophocles Papas Papers. Contains music scores, manuscript scores, phonograph records, correspondence, music journals, photographs and guitar music manuals. Papas performed live on WCAP.

357. "The Voice of the Listener: Americans and the Radio Industry, 1920–1950." A Ph.D. thesis by Elena Razlogova, George Mason University, 2003.

George Washington University

Melvin Gelman Library
2130 H Street, NW, Washington, DC 20052
(202) 994-0628; speccoll@gwu.edu
www.gwu.edu/gelman/spec

358. Murray Frank Papers, 1945–1977. Chiefly articles and lecture notes, mostly in English with a few in cursive Yiddish, and some printed press releases. Does not appear to contain any information related to Frank's employment as an announcer for *The Voice of Israel,* 1958–1961. See finding aid for more information.

Georgetown University

37th and N Streets, NW, Washington, DC 20057
(202) 687-7631;   Contact: Lynn Conway
conwayl@Georgetown.edu
www.library.georgetown.edu/dept/speccoll

359. Lawrence Gilman Papers. Includes Gilman's Program Notes and correspondence relating to his broadcasts of New York Philharmonic concerts, 1933 and 1936.

360. Lisa Sergio Papers, 1937–1988. Includes correspondence, manuscripts of books and articles, transcripts for lectures, addresses and radio broadcasts, including some sound recordings. Her career in radio included *The Magic Key, Let's Talk It Over, Tales of Great Rivers, Column of Air* and *Prayers Through the Ages.* Sergio was a news commentator on WQXR, NY and ABC.

361. Paul Hume Papers. Includes papers related to *The Catholic Hour.*

362. Paul Sullivan Papers. Contains papers relating to Sullivan's involvement with the production of *Blue and Gray,* Fall, 1946–May 26, 1951 and *Radio Forum* from its origins in 1946. Includes scripts and correspondence. Both programs were coordinated by the campus radio station WGTB and WARL, Arlington, VA.

363. Rev. Daniel Lord, SJ Papers. Includes transcripts of *Hour of Faith,* 1940s.

364. Rev. John Courtney Murray SJ Papers. Includes transcripts of *Hour of Faith.*

365. Rev. Wilfrid Parsons, SJ Papers. Contains papers relating to Parsons's involvement with *The Catholic Hour,* including a list of past and prospective speakers.

Georgia State University

Special Collections Department, Popular Music Collection
100 Decatur Street, Atlanta, GA 30303
(404) 651-2477; Fax: (404) 651-4314
libphd@langate.gsu.edu;   www.library.gsu.edu/spcoll/
Contact: Laura Botts

366. Country Music Collection. See online list of individual performers who may have performed on radio during the Golden Age.

367. Don Naylor Papers, 1934–1970. Includes scrapbooks relating to his life and career and scripts for radio programs that he wrote, produced and performed, 1934–1950. Most of the scripts were written during his tenure at WGST although some of them, dating from 1934 and 1935, were written for use on KTAT and KFJZ, Fort Worth, TX. Many of the folders of scripts also include listener correspondence relating to the programs and some contain background material that Naylor used when creating the shows. Also includes open reel audio tape copies of recordings of WGST shows and papers relating to Naylor's work on WAGA.

368. Ephemera Files. Contains materials on a variety of musical topics, including files on Johnny Mercer and his contemporaries, country music, various aspects of radio and television and several miscellaneous topics relating to twentieth century music and/or the music business. For list of items see: www.library.gsu.edu/spcoll/Collections/Music/ephemera.htm.

369. Frances L. Wallace Papers, 1903–1995, n.d., bulk 1940–1991. Contains annotated scripts and performance notes for programs aired on WSB and WCON, most of which date from the late 1940s. Series III contains several kinds of music, including a significant portion of the music library of WSB, mainly printed dance arrangements and manuscript band and orchestra arrangements of popular songs. Also includes Wallace's personal papers documenting her career as a musician, including playing the organ for many radio programs.

370. Johnny and Ginger Mercer Papers, 1925–1992. Contains papers of Johnny and Ginger Mercer and related materials, including audio recordings, sheet music, scripts, scrapbooks, correspondence, photographs, business records, lyrics, clippings and autobiographical materials. (See Johnny Mercer Papers below.)

371. Johnny Carter Collection, 1948. Eighteen transcriptions of *The Happy Two* broadcast over WAGA, Atlanta, GA from May–September of 1948. The program featured performers Shorty Bradford and Lee Roy Abernathy.

372. Johnny Mercer Papers, 1885–1991. Includes biographical information, correspondence, manuscripts, scrapbooks, some sound recordings and other papers focusing primarily on Mercer's career in film, radio and theater. Note: Other special collections include material relating to Johnny Mercer.

373. Lane Brothers Commercial Photographers Collection, bulk 1939–1975. Includes photographs of Georgia radio stations, including WGBE, WBML and WPLO.

374. Ray Avery Collection of Johnny Mercer Recordings, 1932–ca. 1974. Consists of commercial and non-commercial sound recordings of tunes, songs, music, radio shows and dictated letters by Mercer and his friends, colleagues, collaborators and fans. Some recordings contain interviews, dictated letters, and other non-musical material.

375. Wayne W. Daniel Collection. Contains books, periodicals such as "Rural Radio" (1939), "Radio Romance" and "Movie-Radio Guide" and research files dealing with country, bluegrass and Southern gospel music, including papers relating to radio broadcasts.

376. WSB Radio Records, 1922–1985, bulk 1960–1980. Contains correspondence, memos, newsclippings, publicity materials, program log books, photographs, artifacts and sound recordings dating from 1922 through approximately 1984 and covering such topics as the history of WSB, performers and programs offered over the air and radio's response to the advent of television. Also includes approximately 300 transcription discs, primarily of political programs, speeches and events, photographs and artifacts.

Gonzaga University

Foley Center Library
Special Collections Department, Spokane, WA 99258
(509) 323-3814; Fax: (509) 323-5904
kingma@gonzaga.edu; www.gonzaga.edu
Contact: David Kingma

377. Bing Crosby Collection. Contains correspondence, photographs, memorabilia, secondary material about Crosby, materials from Crosby societies and fan clubs and an extensive collection of sound recordings of Crosby radio programs, including *The Bing Crosby Show*, 1949–1954, *Kraft Music Hall*, 1943–1946, *Minute Maid Fresh Squeezed Orange Juice*, 1949–1950, *Philco Radio Time*, 1946–1949 and miscellaneous programs, 1936–1960.

Graduate Theological Union

Flora Lamson Hewlett Library
2400 Ridge Road, Berkeley, CA 94709
(510) 649-2506; Fax: (510) 649-2508
lglenn@gtu.edu; http://grace.gtu.edu/

378. "Broadcasting and the Protestant Pulpit: An examination of certain emphases in broadcasting important to pulpit effectiveness." A Ph.D. thesis by Henry Babcock Adams, 1957, San Francisco Theological Seminary.

379. Harry Emerson Fosdick Radio Sermons Collection, 1941–1946. Contains sermon transcripts broadcast on *National Vespers,* New York. Each transcript includes title, date, and preacher.

380. "Lectures on Ephesians," 1937. A series of messages delivered over KMPC, Beverly Hills, CA, by Louis T. Talbot, pastor, Church of the Open Door, Los Angeles, CA.

Grand Rapids Public Library

111 Library Street NE, Grand Rapids, MI 49503
(619) 988-5402; www.grpl.org
Contact: Rebecca Mayne

381. Delbert W. Blumenshine Collection, 1949–1975. Contains papers relating to Blumenshine's career with WOOD-AM and FM during the 1960s. Also includes details of WOTV policy, procedures and staff and examples of both audio and audio visual tapes used in broadcasting.

Greenwich Public Library

10 West Putnam Avenue, Greenwich, CT 06830
(203) 622-7900; www.greenwichlibrary.org

382. NBC Symphony Orchestra. Near complete collection of recordings of *NBC Symphony Orchestra* broadcasts plus some recordings of radio programs of Toscanini conducting the New York Philharmonic.

Hagley Museum and Library

PO Box 3630, Wilmington, DE 19807
(302) 658-2400; Fax: (302) 658-0545
mmcninch@hagley.org; www.hagley.lib.de.us
Contacts: Marge McNinch, ext. 330 (Soda House, Manuscripts and Archives)
John Williams, ext. 276 (Pictorial Collections Department)

383. *Cavalcade of America* Ephemera, 1937–1945. (Soda House, Manuscripts & Archives.) Mostly flyers for individual programs giving show title, cast of characters and text of DuPont advertisements run during the show. Some programs list featured players or contain plot summaries.

384. *Cavalcade of America* Photograph Collection, 1939–1953. (Pictorial Collections Department.) Consists of a complete run of the scripts, and sound recordings for a majority of the programs (a list of the shows is available). Also includes 697 photographs relating to the program. The majority are views of live performances and include photos of actors and actresses, the DuPont Chorus, live audiences and the production staff. Other miscellaneous photographs include DuPont Company exhibits advertising the show, of awards being presented to the DuPont Company and of tours of DuPont plants being given to actors and actresses.

385. E.I. du Pont de Nemours & Company. Advertising Dept General files, 1807–1971, bulk 1917-1965. (Soda House, Manuscripts & Archives.) Files of the Radio (Subseries V) and Television (Subseries VI) sections describe in detail the several shows sponsored by the company, particularly *Cavalcade of America* and the *DuPont Show of the Month.*

386. E.I. du Pont de Nemours & Company, Yerkes Plant. Contains a scrapbook documenting a live broadcast of an installment of *Cavalcade of America* from Buffalo in 1947. Titled "The Oath," the broadcast was based on the life of Buffalo native Millard Fillmore and starred William Powell. Includes historical photos relating to Fillmore, his family and career as well as contemporary ones of Powell and the live broadcast before a theater audience.

387. *Stark County Story.* Scripts of the *Good Neighbor Broadcasts* conducted by the Stark County Historical Society in cooperation with the Ohio Broadcasting Corporation over WHBC-WHBC-FM, May 11, 1947–October 12, 1959.

Harry S. Truman Library & Museum

500 W. US Highway 24, Independence, MO 64050
(816) 268-8200; Fax: (816) 268-8295
truman.library@nara.gov; www.trumanlibrary.org

388. Archives. For a more detailed listing of radio material relating to Truman and other members of his administration, check online catalog. The Library is one of several Presidential Libraries operated by of the National Archives.

Harvard University

Andover-Harvard Theological Library
45 Francis Avenue, Cambridge, MA 02138
(617) 496-2485
reference@hds.harvard.edu; www.hds.harvard.edu/library

389. Algernon D. Black Papers, 1932–1981. Includes radio talks by Black, 1934–1935.

390. Unitarian Universalist Association Audio Tapes. Contains assorted audio tapes, including radio spots. For more information see unpublished finding aid.

391. Unitarian Universalist Association Radio Programs with Dr. Harold Scott. Includes audio tapes of programs on religion with Dr. Harold Scott from the Unitarian Society of Salt Lake City, UT. For more information see unpublished finding aid.

Harvard Business School, Baker Library
(617) 495-6411
histcollref@hbs.edu; www.library.hbs.edu/

392. Boston Evening Transcript Records, 1841–1941, bulk 1867–1941. Includes records relating to WBET which was owned by the newspaper.

393. Vertical File Collection on Labor Unions, 1923–1950. Includes material on the American Federation of Radio Artists, 1940. For more information see unpublished finding aid.

Houghton Library
(617) 495-2449; houghref@fas.harvard.edu
http://hcl.harvard.edu/houghton/

394. Alexander Woollcott Correspondence, ca. 1856–1943, bulk 1920–1943. Check online finding aid to determine if any of the correspondence relates to Woollcott's radio program, *The Town Crier.*

395. Papers By Or About B. Traven, 1950–1977. Bulk of the collection is correspondence concerning rights to a Traven story adapted for radio and television by Ted Allan, a playwright who worked for the Canadian Broadcasting Corporation.

Houghton Library, Harvard Theatre Collection
(617) 495-2445; htc@harvard.edu
http://hcl.harvard.edu/libraries/houghton/collections/htc.html

396. Paul Muni Collection, 1908–1980, bulk 1932–1959. Includes manuscripts, cassette tapes and transcripts of interviews of Muni, photographs, programs, clippings, letters (mostly copies), scripts and articles relating to Muni's life and career. For collection details relating to radio check preliminary list in repository.

Pusey Library, Harvard University Archives
(617) 495-2461; Fax: (617) 495-8011
http://hul.harvard.edu/huarc/

397. WHRB Comment Books, 1940–1990. Comment Books reflect student life and student culture, including politics, musical trends and campus controversies. WHRB is a student run radio station that previously operated under the call letters WHCN and WHRV.

Hebrew Union College
American Jewish Archives
3101 Clifton Avenue, Cincinnati, OH 45220
(513) 221-1875; Fax: (513) 221-7812
kproffitt@huc.edu; Contact: Kevin Profitt
www.americanjewisharchives.org

General comments: The online catalog listings for some of the collections listed below did not include specific information identifying the names or dates of the radio programs. For more information contact the Archives.

398. Abraham Jehiel Feldman Papers. Includes some radio material, 1930–1940.

399. Abraham L. Feinberg Papers. Contains papers relating to Rabbi Feinberg's radio career, 1932–1972, including *Message of Israel*, 1937–1969, *Brotherhood Hour* (broadcast in Canada), 1947, *Grey Lib*, 1972, and his career as the singer Anthony Frome on the *Poet Prince* on NBC, 1932–1935. Note: A second Feinberg collection includes material on radio messages he delivered in 1942.

400. Board of Jewish Education of Greater New York Records. Includes scripts for *Hadassah's Story Teller Playhouse*, 1950.

401. David Lefkowitz, Jr. Papers. Includes Rabbi Lefkowitz's radio addresses, 1937–1949.

402. Edgar E. Siskin Papers. Includes papers relating to Rabbi Siskin's involvement in the New Haven, CT Interfaith Broadcasts, 1938–1942.

403. Ferdinand M. Isserman Papers. Includes radio sermons delivered by Rabbi Isserman, 1932–1963.

404. Hebrew Union College Records. Includes material about *Message of Israel*, 1945, broadcast on WSAI.

405. Herman E. Snyder Papers. Includes papers and sermons of Rabbi Snyder, including his talks on *Today's Forum*, 1938–1942.

406. Iphigene Bettman Papers. Includes papers relating to Bettman's career as the moderator for the radio forum, *What's on Your Mind?* Also includes radio addresses Bettman delivered in 1944.

407. Jerome D. Folkman Papers. Includes radio sermons.

408. Joseph L. Fink Papers. Includes sermons broadcast on *The Humanitarian Hour,* 1930–1956. Some sermons from the 1930s discuss the evils of Nazism.

409. Levi A. Olan Papers. Includes material relating to WFAA, 1952–1955, 1968–1970.

410. Maurice Samuel Papers. Includes transcripts, tape recordings and correspondence pertaining to *The Words We Live By*, a series of conversations on the Bible between Samuel and Mark Van Doren that were part of *The Eternal Light*. Also includes scripts and notes for other programs by and about Samuel that were broadcast on *The Eternal Light.*

411. Morris S. Lazaron Papers. Includes correspondence and transcripts of Lazaron's sermons on many programs, 1926–1946, including *Church of the Air*, 1931–1939, *Message of Israel*, 1934–1946, *Town Hall Meeting of the Air*, 1938–1954, and *Wheel of Life.*

412. Raphael Lemkin Papers. Includes scripts of radio programs, 1947–1956.

413. Roland B. Gittelsohn Papers. Includes radio sermons delivered by Rabbi Gittelsohn, 1956–1962, possibly on *My Honor Roll.*

414. Samuel H. Goldenson Papers. Includes radio addresses given by Rabbi Goldenson, 1931–1944.

415. Stephen S. Wise Collection. Includes sound recordings of radio talks given by Wise on WJZ and WOR.

416. Union of American Hebrew Congregations Records. Includes material relating to radio broadcasting, 1927–1932.

417. Women of Reform Judaism Records. Includes records relating to a 1937 radio project.

The Henry Ford
Benson Ford Research Center
PO Box 1970, Dearborn, MI 48121
(313) 982-6070; Fax: (313) 982-6244
www.thehenryford.org/collections

418. Ford Motor Company: Advertising Department. Records 1921–1953. Includes papers relating to the Ford Company's radio advertising.

419. *Ford Sunday Evening Hour* Collection, 1934–1946. Includes a complete bound set of William Cameron's talks, 1934–1942, and printed music programs, 1934–1942 and 1945–1946. Also contains two reel-to-reel audio recordings of Cameron's talks, September 1941–1942.

420. William John Cameron Records, 1915–1950, bulk 1936–1945. Includes his talks for the *Ford Sunday Evening Hour,* 1936–1937, in both rough and final draft. See also separate *Ford Sunday Evening Hour Collection.*

History Center of Tompkins County
Clinton House
401 East State Street, Ithaca, NY 14850
(607) 273-8284; Fax: (607) 273-6107
archives@thehistorycenter.net; www.thehistorycenter.net
Contact: Donna Eschenbrenner

421. Charles Chatfield Papers, 1949–1976. Includes scripts delivered over WHCU, Ithaca, NY, dealing with national, state and local issues.

Historical Society of Pennsylvania (Balch Institute)
1300 Locust Street, Philadelphia, PA 19107
(215) 732-6200; Fax: (215) 732-2680
webmaster@hsp.org; www.hsp.org

General comments: The Balch Institute, which became part of the Historical Society in 2002, is a source for information on many ethnic groups. The online site can be searched by ethnic group.

422. Albert M. Greenfield Papers, 1921–1967, bulk 1930–1939. Papers include Greenfield's ownership of WFIL, Philadelphia, PA. Note: See also Lit Brothers Collection and WFIL Collection below.

423. Charles Belohlavek Papers, 1903–1983, bulk post 1945. Belohlavek founded the *Slovak Radio Circle* aired on WJBK and later WJLB in Detroit, MI in the 1940s and hosted a half hour program sponsored by the General Stefanik Society. Papers contain a limited amount of material on the *Slovak Radio Circle,* including meeting minutes, membership lists, reports and correspondence. Included is a 1947 letter informing the of the cancellation of programs such as theirs that bought time from the station and then sold portions of it to individual advertisers. There are also angry letters and a petition denouncing the discontinuance of foreign language programming by the *Circle's* subsequent broadcasting station, WJLB, in 1948. Approximately 90% of the collection is in Slovak with the majority of documents in English being newsclippings.

424. Electric and Radio Shows 1933–1936. Contains photographs of exhibitions. sponsored by groups like the Philadelphia Electric Co. and the Electrical Association of Philadelphia that displayed a variety of electrical appliances including model homes, lighting, radios and phonographs. The collection includes documents relating to radio broadcasts.

425. Fiorani Radio Productions, 1931–1975. Contains materials documenting Rose and Angelo Fiorani's 42 years in radio broadcasting, including correspondence, advertisements, program schedules and scripts, savings passbooks, bills and receipts, tax returns, fan mail and souvenir programs of special events. Personal letters, some business correspondence and a majority of the advertisements are in Italian. However, many of the advertisements have English translations and most of the business correspondence is in English. The programming schedules and sketches in Series IV span the years 1935–1951 and depict the early orientation toward Italian-Americans. At their peak, the Fioranis had programs on three stations: WARM and WGBI, Scranton, PA and WAZL, Hazelton, PA. In 1953 they founded Midway Broadcasting Company, Inc. and operated WPTS known as "The Family Station of Northeast Pennsylvania" and the "Golden Oldie" station. Specific programs cited in the online finding aid include the *Italian-American Variety Program, The Voice of Italy* and *The Italian Hour.*

426. Lit Brothers Papers, 1928–1966. Contains papers relating to their ownership of WFIL, Philadelphia, PA. Note: See also Albert M. Greenfield Papers and WFIL Collection for additional papers relating to WFIL.

427. Lithuanian Radio Programs. Three separate collections include papers relating to the Lithuanian Radio Clubs in Rochester, NY, Boston, MA and Philadelphia, PA. See library records for contents of each collection.

428. Owen B. Hunt Papers, 1975. (In Robin O'Brien Hiteshew Collection. See Below.) Includes transcripts from a series of programs concerning Irish and Irish-American history presented by broadcaster Hunt on WIBF, Philadelphia.

429. Patrick Stanton Papers, 1927–1976, bulk 1930s–1976. Papers document Stanton's private life and radio and film activities as they relate to Ireland and the Irish-American community, including his career as an announcer at WIAD where he created the *Irish Hour* and his later ownership of WJMJ. Includes correspondence, speeches, radio scripts, newspaper clippings, scrapbooks, certificates, photographs and a large amount of material on Irish history and culture. Note: A separate Stanton collection includes 261 photographs, many of which are of radio personalities.

430. Philadelphia Fellowship Commission Programs, ca. 1940–1955. Includes over 750 recordings, most of which are 16" transcription discs, of programs aired on WFIL and WIP, Philadelphia, PA including *Within Our Gates, Philadelphia Award, Valor Knows No Creed, Lest We Forget These Great Americans* and other programs produced by the Fellowship Commission, a community service organization dedicated to promoting better relations among diverse ethnic and religious groups. Also includes miscellaneous commercially recorded broadcast discs and standard pressings. Scripts for *Within Our Gates* are held at Temple University's Urban Archives. Note: As of 2005, the Society does not have equipment for listening to the discs although plans for digital transfer are in process.

431. Robin O'Brien Hiteshew Collection. An assemblage of materials collected by Hiteshew which document Irish music in Philadelphia. The materials include the personal papers of area musicians and broadcasters such as Thomas Caulfield, Seamus McGill, Owen B. Hunt and William Regan as well as scripts, sheet music, scrap books and phonograph records. The collection also contains a quantity of printed ephemera such as flyers, posters and programs from events sponsored by area musical organizations, including the Irish Musician's Union and fraternal organizations such as the Donegal Society, the Ancient Order of Hibernians and the Galway Society. Within the Hiteshew Collection, personal papers are grouped under individuals' names. See separate listings.

432. S. Carl Mark Papers, 1947–1952. Includes correspondence, clippings and program schedules concerning WTTM, part of the Trent Broadcasting Co.

433. Tommy Caulfield Papers, 1911–1968. (Robin O'Brien Hiteshew Collection). Contains papers relating to Caulfield's involvement in Irish music, including programs aired on WHAT, WTEL and WCEM, including the *Irish Hour.*

434. WCAU (Philadelphia, PA.) Papers, 1942–1961, bulk 1942–1952. Includes papers relating to the operation of the station. See also Albert M. Greenfield Papers above.

435. WFIL Papers, 1935–1964. Contains papers relating to the operation of the station. Note: See also Lit Brothers Papers and Albert M. Greenfield Papers for additional material about WFIL.

436. Will Regan Papers, 1937–1990. (Robin O'Brien Hiteshew Collection.) Contains papers related to Regan's career as a broadcaster in Philadelphia, including correspondence, clippings, printed materials, a scrapbook, uncataloged photographs and sound recordings

437. WPEN (Philadelphia, PA) Papers, 1947–1950. Includes papers relating to the operation of the station. See also Albert M. Greenfield Papers.

Hofstra University
West Campus Library, University Archives
619 Fulton Avenue, Hempstead, NY 11550
(516) 463-6407
geri.solomon@hofstra.edu; Contact: Prof. Geri Solomon
www.hofstra.edu/Libraries/WestCampus/SpecialCollections/

438. Broadus Mitchell Collection, 1926–1975. Contains personal and professional papers, including scripts for *Radio Talk*, a program he hosted in 1933.

439. Harvey Joshua Levin Papers, 1947–1992, bulk 1954–1991. Consists of Levin's professional and research papers, professional correspondence and background material for the courses he taught. The research papers include talks, presentations and lectures on issues as they related to, or impacted on, media broadcast regulations.

440. Matthew N. Chappell Papers, 1909–1964, bulk 1930–1945. Contains papers and correspondence documenting various aspects of Chappell's radio career, including scripts for *Logic In Science*, 1934, WLTH, *For Worriers Only*, 1937, WMCA and *Psychological Forum of the Air*, 1937–1938, WNEW. Also includes proposed scripts for other programs, audience measurement papers, 1945–1946, testimony before the FCC, 1943, and material relating to advertising.

Hope College
Joint Archives of Holland
PO Box 9000, Holland, MI 49422
(616) 395-7798; Fax: (616) 395-7197
archives@hope.edu; www.hope.edu/resources/arc/
Contact: Geoffrey Reynolds

441. Centennial of Holland, Michigan, 1947. Sound recordings of *Echoes of a Century*, a series of programs broadcast on 150 stations throughout the United States illustrating the story of Holland, MI from the origins of the Dutch settlers' decision to immigrate to the New World to the then present-day.

442. Garret A. Wilterdink Papers, 1946–1990. Contains correspondence, sermons, radio broadcast transcripts and other papers.

443. Harry James Hager Papers, 1917-1977. Contains sermon outlines, correspondence and other papers and audio tapes of the *America for God* broadcasts. The program originated at WCFL and was carried by other midwest stations. All of the extant numbered programs (1-436) have been retained in the collection.

444. Henry Bast Papers, 1906–1983. Includes sermons of Dr. Henry Bast on the *Temple Time Radio Broadcast*, 1952-1973 and other papers.

445. Henry Ernest Schoon Papers, 1918–1962. Contains correspondence, sermons, meditations, radio messages, 1938–1952, WHTC, and other papers.

446. Jacob Prins Papers, 1925–1975. Includes his entire sermon collection. Prins broadcast on WASH and WHTC between 1939–1968.

447. John A. Dykstra Papers, 1886–1968. Includes sermons, prayers, radio messages, articles and correspondence.

448. Martin R. De Haan Papers, 1891–1965. Includes sermons for *Radio Bible Class*, 1938–1965.

449. Norman Vincent Peale Papers, 1940–1970. Contains writings about Peale in articles, clippings and publications, along with writings by Peale, including articles, booklets, radio addresses, 1936–1945, a handbook and sermons.

450. Theodore Schaap Papers, 1945–1951. Includes sermons broadcast over Chicago stations WMBI and WDLM.

451. *Western Seminary Hour* Records, 1930–1959. Includes program scripts.

Howard University
Library, 500 Howard Place, NW, Washington, DC 20059
(202) 806-7234; www.howard.edu/library

452. *Sleepy Joe*, Sound Recording, 1948. An audition recording for the children's program *Sleepy Joe* meant to explain and justify the show to potential sponsors. Also includes Program #4 of *These Are Americans*, February 19, 1944, hosted by Chet Huntley, and a *Blue Coal Minstrels* program, n.d.

453. Sound Recordings. Check online catalog for listings of individual programs featuring or about African American performers or themes. Includes several episodes of *Destination*

Freedom and a few *Chicago Roundtable of the Air* broadcasts.

454. W.C. Handy interview. Sound recording of an interview of Paul Robeson, including a Robeson performance on *The Shell Chateau* program in the fall of 1936.

Idaho State Historical Society

Historical Library
450 North 4th Street, Boise, ID 83702
(208) 334-2441; Fax: (208) 334-3198
cbowler@ishs.state.id.us; www.ishs.state.id.us
Contact: Carolyn Bowler

455. Gene and May-Floyd Shumate Papers, 1935–1986. Contains biographical information and papers pertaining to their professional careers in broadcasting, particularly KRXK, Rexburg, ID which they owned from the 1950s to the 1970s.

456. Henry Westerman Whillock Papers, 1918–1985. Records of Whillock's business, political, military and civic career, including correspondence, scrapbooks, photographs and subject files relating to KDSH.

457. KFAU Papers, 1908–1927. Contains newspaper clippings, licenses and photographs pertaining to the operation of KFAU, Boise High School, Boise, ID. (See also the Gladdon W. Hull Collection for additional clippings related to KFAU.)

458. KIDO Records, 1927–1960. Contains correspondence, several scrapbooks, newspaper clippings and photographs pertaining to KIDO and its operations. See also a separate KIDO Correspondence, 1942–1943, Collection that contains letters regarding acquisition of equipment and personnel changes under wartime regulations and a collection that includes an ad for the "Turkey A Day" contest sponsored by the station, 1954–1955.

Indiana Historical Society

Manuscripts and Visual Collections Department
William Henry Smith Memorial Library
450 West Ohio Street, Indianapolis, IN 46202
(317) 234-0321
www.indianahistory.org/library

459. Indiana Broadcasters Pioneers: Oral History Project. Consists of interviews of Indiana's early broadcasters and papers relating to the preparation of a book-length manuscript on the state's broadcast pioneers. Includes tapes and transcripts of 26 Indiana pioneer broadcasters, covering topics in Hoosier broadcasting from 1926–mid-1990s.

460. John K. Mackenzie Collection, 1887–1976. While the bulk of the collection deals with Mackenzie's involvement in the recording industry, there is some material on his career producing sound effects for radio and the movie industry.

461. *The Negro in America: The Last Citizen*, 1958. Sound recordings of the series broadcast on WBAA, Purdue University. The interviews examine local and national social issues, including crime, religion, intimidation, protest, African American journalism and art, housing and the National Urban League.

462. Ole Olsen Papers, 1910–1999. Contains personal and professional papers, including materials and photographs relating to the comedy team of Olsen and Johnson and their shows. Materials range from their vaudeville days beginning in the 1920s through their success on Broadway and radio in the

1930s and 1940s to their later years performing in smaller venues in the 1950s. Includes radio scripts from 1930s and 1950s.

463. Woman's Press Club of Indiana Records, 1913–1988. Records of the organization which included women in radio and television broadcasting.

Indiana University/Bloomington

Archives of African American Music and Culture
Smith Research Center, Suite 180, Bloomington, IN 47408
(812) 855-8547; Contact: Brenda Nelson-Strauss
aaamc@indiana.edu; www.indiana.edu/~aaamc/index.html

464. *Black Radio: Telling It Like It Was*, 1996. A 13-part series on the role of radio in transforming the African American community in the twentieth century produced by Jacquie Webb for Smithsonian Productions. Collection contains research and production materials, including photographs, articles, transcripts and over 400 hours of historical air-checks and interviews with over 150 disc jockeys, radio professionals, record company executives, journalists and scholars.

465. Other Black Radio Collections. The Archives contains several collections of black radio personalties, including Ed Castleberry, George Nelson and Rick Roberts, and a collection of photographs of black radio performers. Check with library to determine if any of the collections include material dating back to the Golden Age of Radio.

466. William Barlow Collection. Includes recorded interviews, interview transcripts, newspaper articles and other materials relating to black radio. Check with library regarding dates of materials.

Archives of Traditional Music
Morrison Hall 117 & 120, Bloomington, IN 47405
(812) 855-4679; Fax: (812) 856-0193
atmusic@indiana.edu; www.indiana.edu/~libarchm/

467. Donald E. Lake Collection. Contains 69 transcription discs, 1941, 1947 and 1950, of the *Hoosier Hop* broadcast on WOWO, Ft. Wayne, IN. Also contains photographs, publicity materials and songbooks.

468. Hoagy Carmichael Collection, 1899–1981. Contains papers, including scripts for the *Hoagy Carmichael Show*, 1945, and *Columbia Broadcasting System Presents Hoagy Carmichael*, 1947–1948, memorabilia and sound recordings.

Lilly Library
1200 East 7th Street, Bloomington, IN 47405
(812) 855-2452; Fax: (812) 855-3143
liblilly@Indiana.edu; www.indiana.edu/~liblilly
Contact: Becky Cape

469. American Literature Mss. (Manuscript), 1806–1969. Includes two 1947 radio scripts written by Ernest Hemingway for the English section of the series, *Radioteatro de America.*

470. Clifford Odets Papers. Includes two radio plays, "Night Music," 1941, and "The Show Must Go On," n.d.

471. McGreevey Mss., ca. 1942–19–. Contains correspondence and writings of John McGreevey. Includes scripts for *Armstrong Theatre of Today, Cavalcade of America, Dr. Christian, Suspense, Arizona Adventures, Poe Presents,* and *Nick Carter, Master Detective.* McGreevey was a writer and announcer for KTAR, Phoenix, AZ, 1948–1952.

472. Weissberger Mss., 1938–1949. Consists primarily of correspondence and legal papers relating to the financial affairs of Orson Welles and the Mercury Theatre as handled by Welles's personal attorney, L. Arnold Weissberger. Includes copies of contracts and agreements between Welles and ColumbiaArtists as his representative, between Welles and RKO, other legal documents relating to Mercury Theatre insurance policies for both Orson and Virginia Welles and photographs, mostly of theatre productions and performers.

473. Welles Mss., 1930–1959. Consists of the correspondence, papers and memorabilia relating to the career of Orson Welles. Includes 142 bound scripts and more than 140 sound recordings for most of the programs and series in which Welles appeared after 1937, including *Mercury Theatre on the Air, Campbell Playhouse, Orson Welles Almanac (Lady Esther), Ceiling Unlimited, Hello Americans, This Is My Best* and *Mercury Summer Theatre.* See detailed online finding aid at www.indiana.edu/~liblilly/lilly/mss/html/welles.html. See also Weissberger Mss. Collection for additional Welles radio related material and additional Welles collection covering his film career.

474. White Mss. 1932–1969. Consists of correspondence, writings and memorabilia of William Anthony Parker White, critic, editor and writer most widely known by the pseudonym Anthony Boucher. Includes scripts and extensive files for the series *Adventures of Ellery Queen, The Casebook of Gregory Hood* and *Sherlock Holmes,* all dating from the mid-1940s.

475. Wokoun Mss., 1941–1953. Consists mostly of scripts for NBC affiliated, Chicago based programs collected by William Wokoun. Includes *The Guiding Light, Captain Midnight, Lone Journey, Ma Perkins, Masquerade, The Road of Life, Today's Children, Vic and Sade* and *Woman in White.* Also includes emcee scripts for music and variety shows and commercial scripts for various products and companies. See online finding aid for complete list.

University Archives
Bryan Hall 201, Bloomington, IN 47405
(812) 855-1127; Fax: (812) 855-8104
archives@indiana.edu; www.libraries.iub.edu/archives

476. Radio and Television Department, Chairman's Office Records, 1937–1967, bulk 1945–1960. Includes annual reports, budgetary material on guest radio speakers, correspondence to and from the Indiana Broadcasters Association, radio department course and curriculum material, files on radio shows and I.U. spots, correspondence with radio station personnel around the country and files on television programming.

Indiana University of Pennsylvania
Stapleton Library, Special Collections & University Archives
431 South Eleventh Street, Indiana, PA 15705
(724) 357-3039; Fax: (724) 357-4891
mcdevitt@iup.edu; www.lib.iup.edu
Contact: Theresa McDevitt

477. Elizabeth Bain Collection, 1959–1988. Includes speeches and articles written by Bain, American Women in Radio and Television reports and convention proceedings, TV show ratings and movie reviews and miscellaneous other articles. Bain worked as a music librarian for KFI-KECA in Los Angeles in 1941 and as a traffic director for WCFL.

478. Indiana Art Association Collection, 1944–1991. Contains yearbooks, newsletters, minutes and other materials from the association, including a radio script from March 16, 1953.

479. Stephenson Collection. Contains materials gathered by Dr. Dale Landon and used in the class, History of Indiana University of Pennsylvania, including scripts for the program *Keystone of Democracy,* 1942.

International Lutheran Layman's League & Lutheran Hour Ministries
Lutheran Hour Ministries Research Center Archives
660 Mason Ridge Center Drive, St. Louis, MO 63141
(800) 944-3450; Contact: Gerald Perschbacher
gerald.perschbacher.lhm.org; www.lhm.org

480. *Day By Day With Jesus* Collection, 1940s–1960s. Includes scripts, background program material, biographical information on speakers and sound recordings.

481. *Family Worship Hour* Collection, 1940s–1960s. Includes scripts, background program material, biographical information on speakers and sound recordings.

482. *Lutheran Hour* Collection, 1930–, bulk from 1935. Includes scripts, background program material, biographical information on speakers, sound recordings and films.

Iowa State University
Special Collections Department and University Archives
403 Parks Library, Ames, IA 50011
(515) 294-6672; Fax: (515) 294-5525
archives@iastate.edu; www.lib.iastate.edu/spcl/index.html
Contact: Tanya Zanish-Belcher

General comments: See Addendum for additional collections.

483. Ada Hayden Papers, 1864–1989. Contains biographical information, correspondence, photographs, articles and radio talks, 1946–1955, promoting Iowa parks and other papers.

484. Adrian L. Bowers Papers, 1934–1936. Contains radio talks, taped oral history interviews and newspaper clippings dealing with farm related issues.

485. Edith M. Sunderlin Papers, 1930–1983. Includes biographical material, scripts of *Homemaker's Half-Hour,* 1945–1964, and other papers. Sunderlin was also the host of the children's program, *Storybook Lady,* later changed to *The Children's Corner,* broadcast on WOI, 1940–1958. She was also associated with the *Radio Child Study Club* program.

486. Edmund Groomes Papers, 1938–1973. Contains biographical information, radio scripts, correspondence and other papers.

487. Elizabeth (Bess) Storm Ferguson Papers, 1897–1983. Contains biographical materials, scripts and correspondence for radio programs and other papers of hers and her husband, Fred E. Ferguson.

488. Harold DeMott Papers, 1925–1968. Includes biographical materials, correspondence, scripts for his talks on WOI, news clippings and other papers, all relating to agriculture.

489. Herb Plambeck Papers, 1920–2001. Contains correspondence, addresses, reports, newspaper clippings, printed material and other papers relating to his career as head of the Farm Department of WHO, Des Moines, 1936–1970.

490. Louise Jenison Peet Papers, 1925–1995 and n.d. Contains biographical information, correspondence, research materials, radio talks, 1942–1953, photographs and other papers.

491. Martin L. Mosher Papers, 1899–1979. Consists of manuscripts, clippings, correspondence, diaries, transcripts of radio discussions, scrapbooks and photographs relating to his work in agriculture.

492. Radio Scripts, 1940–1951. Contains scripts from programs, mostly *Homemaker's Half Hour,* which were broadcast over WOI and sponsored by the University's Textiles and Clothing Dept. (Program titles for the other scripts are not indicated.) The programs focused on dressmaking, general fabric care and laundry tips. Most of the bound scripts come with a title page listing the author/speaker and title(s) of the speech. (In University Archives.)

493. Ralph Kenneth Bliss Papers, 1904–1971. Includes correspondence, reports, radio talks, 1948–1971, memoranda, minutes, teaching notes, lectures, biographical information, photographs and other papers. Bulk of material relates to agricultural and home economics extension work in Iowa and food production during World Wars I and II.

494. Raymond F. Baker Papers, 1924–2000, bulk 1927–1967. Includes correspondence, reports, speeches, transcripts of radio broadcasts and other papers relating to agriculture.

495. Records of Iowa State University Cooperative Extension Service, 1918–1967, bulk 1933–1967. Includes annual reports, correspondence, publications, surveys, photographs, maps, newspaper clippings, radio and television scripts and other papers.

496. Ronald C. Bentley Papers, 1926–1963. Consists of correspondence, printed matter, farm market related news broadcasts, market research data, surveys and related papers involving his broadcasts on WOI which were heard on 26 additional stations.

497. WOI Radio and Television Records, 1925–1985. Contains reports, administrative files, programming records and photographs.

Ithaca College
1201 Gannett Center, Ithaca, NY 14850
(607)274-3096
archives@ithaca.edu; Contact: Bridget Bower
www.ithaca.edu/library/archives/

498. Gustave Haenschen Collection, 1925–1952. Extensive collection of scores, orchestrations, and program notes accumulated by Haenschen for radio musical programming, 1925–1952. While the name of the program is usually identified on the score, in general, the collection cannot be searched by program name. Note: The collection is stored off-site and is not easy or inexpensive to access.

499. Milton Cross Collection. Contains notes and scripts for the *Metropolitan Opera Broadcasts,* 1931–1975, scripts for *The Chamber Music Society of Lower Basin Street,* 1942–1944, WJZ's *Piano House,* 1949–1950, *General Motors Concerts,* 1934–1936, and ABC's *Festival,* 1955–1957. Also includes handwritten stories for *The Children's Hour* plus correspondence, clippings and sound recordings.

500. Rod Serling Papers. May contain some papers related to Serling's early career writing for a Cincinnati radio station. Check with repository for more information.

James Madison University
Carrier Library, Harrisonburg, VA 22807
(540) 568-3612; www.lib.jmu.edu/special

501. Mary A. Thompson Papers. Primarily family and personal papers, but Folder 6 includes schedules and list of staff for WSVA, Harrisonburg, VA, 1940 and 1950–1951.

Jewish Museum
National Jewish Archive of Broadcasting
1109 Fifth Avenue, New York, NY 10128
(212) 423-3200; aingall@thejm.org; www.thejm.org
Contact: Andrew Ingall

502. Audio and Video Tapes and Records, ca. 1930–1985. An assorted collection of sound recordings of programs dealing with Jewish culture and history, including entertainment, news, religious programs and public affairs. Recordings can be listened to in the Museum.

Jewish Theological Seminary
Ratner Center, 3080 Broadway, New York, NY 10027
(212) 280-6011; Contact: Ellen Kastel
elkastel@jtsa.edu; www.jtsa.edu/research/ratner

503. David J. Putterman/Park Avenue Synagogue Collection. Contains broadcast recordings done during World War II for Jewish troops. Includes Cantor Putterman officiating at High Holiday services and Rabbi Phillip S. Bernstein and Governor Herbert Lehman addressing troops. Also includes recordings, some scripts and music scores for *The Eternal Light,* 1945–1948.

504. Marjorie Wyler Papers, 1938–1993. Consists of Wyler's files as head of the Seminary's Office of Public Information which became the Communications Department which was involved with the Seminary's radio programs. See also Record Group 8, Radio and Television Department, and Record Group 11, Communications Department.

505. Morton Wishengrad Papers, ca. 1944–1962. Contains mostly correspondence but also includes drafts of scripts, contracts, clippings and a few photographs, including material related to *The Eternal Light.* Note: The bulk of *The Eternal Light* records remain unprocessed.

506. Moshe Davis Papers. Includes scripts for *Original Pantomimes,* 1942, n.d., *The Eternal Light,* 1956, and some unidentified scripts and other papers. Davis was the program editor for *The Eternal Light.*

507. Philip L. Lipis Papers. Includes a group of Lipis's radio scripts, ca. 1950s–1960s.

508. Record Group: 11, Communications Department Records, 1930s–1980s. Includes material related to *The Eternal Light.* Note: Contact the Seminary regarding audio recordings of *The Eternal Light,* 1952–1980s. Additional paper materials relating to *The Eternal Light* program are found in several other collections.

John Brown University
University Archives
2000 West University Street, Siloam Springs, AR 72761

(479) 524-7207; Contact: Heather Crain
Hcrain@jbu.edu; www.jbu.edu

509. KUOA Collection. Contains records of KUOA, including articles detailing the station's history, FCC records beginning from 1933, financial records, press releases, printed promotional materials, programming transcripts and radio programs on 16" transcription discs, reel-to-reel tape and cassettes. The audio recordings form the largest part of the collection and include many sermons by John E. Brown Sr., owner of the station and founder of the University, as well as national radio program releases, advertising spots and other programming related to local interests. The earliest audio recording inventoried as of Spring, 2005 was from July 1, 1946.

John Rivers Communications Museum

58 George Street, Charleston, SC 29424
(843) 953-5810; Fax: (843) 953-5915
zenderr@cofc.edu; www.cofc.edu/~jrmuseum
Contact: Rick Zender

510. Audio Collection. Contains about 100 16" transcription discs of a wide range of programs, mostly from the mid-1940s, and hundreds of additional programs on cassette, reel-to-reel tape and 8 track formats. The Rivers Family were the former owners of WSCS, Charleston, SC. As of 2005, the collection was in the process of being catalogued. Researchers looking for specific programs should contact the Museum.

Juilliard School Library

60 Lincoln Center Plaza, New York, NY 10023
(212) 799-5000; Fax: (212) 769-6421
jdahmus@juilliard.edu; www.juilliard.edu
Contact: Jennie Dahmus

511. Scrapbooks, 1947–1952. Contains press clippings, including reviews of concerts, operas and dance and radio broadcasts by the school.

Kansas State Historical Society

6425 SW 6th Avenue, Topeka, KS 66615
(785) 272-8681; Fax: (785) 272-8682
www.kshs.org

General comments: Although finding aids are generally available for most manuscript collections, for the most part, the collections cannot be searched online. The reference staff will, however, conduct a limited search upon request. The following information comes from the Society's card catalog based on a keyword search for "radio."

512. D. D. Murphy Papers, n.d. Contains correspondence with radio stations, including Ekko stamps and other listener verification materials. Also includes some promotional materials for radio stations or specific programs.

513. Fond Memories of WIBW Radio, 1977. Reminiscences of Don Hopkins who worked for WIBW, Topeka, KS, 1942–1955.

514. Jess C. Denious Papers, 1879–1953. Includes papers dealing with KGNO, Dodge City, KS and the Dodge City Broadcasting Company owned by Denious.

515. John R. Brinkley Papers, 1885–1942. Contains business and personal papers, including information on the operation of various radio stations owned by Brinkley.

Kent State University

Main Library
Box 5190, 1 Eastway Drive, Kent, OH 44242
(330) 672-1678; Contact: Kathleen S. Medicus
http://speccoll.library.kent.edu

516. Cid Corman, Papers, 1942–1976. A highly prolific poet, translator and prose writer, Corman hosted *This Is Poetry*, a 15 minute program aired on WMEX, 1949–1951, on which noted poets read their works.

517. Dorothy Fuldheim Papers, 1968–1990, bulk 1972–1980. Although Fuldheim's career dates back to the 1940s and her work on WTAM and WEWS, this collection of her papers does not appear to cover that period. The finding aid indicates that the collection includes "many of the commentaries that she became famous for in her broadcasting career" but does not note the dates.

518. Walton D. Clarke Papers, 1940–1975. Includes papers relating to WKSU, Kent, OH.

Kurt Weill Foundation for Music

Weill-Lenya Research Center
7 East 20th Street, New York, NY 10003
(212) 505-5240; Fax: (212) 353-9663
kwfinfo@kwf.org; www.kwf.org/pages/wlrc/intro.html
Contact: Dave Stein

519. Kurt Weill and Lotte Lenya Works Including Radio Broadcasts. Includes print material and sound recordings of radio interviews of Weill and Lenya as well as programs about their works and plans for a series of radio operas.

Lake Hopatcong Historical Museum

Hopatcong State Park, Lakeside Boulevard
PO Box 668, Landing, NJ 07850
(973) 398-2616; Fax: (973) 316-6466
llhistory@att.net; www.hopatcong.org/museum
Contact: M. Kane

520. Joe Cook Collection. Includes photos, articles, programs, sheet music, advertisements, sound recordings of radio programs, including the *Shell Chateau*, 1930s, and other memorabilia relating to Cook's career as a vaudevillian, on Broadway in musical comedies and on radio.

Lake Placid Historical Society/Elba Historical Museum

PO Box 189, 242 Station Street, Lake Placid, NY 12946
(518) 523-1608

521. Kate Smith Collection. Contact the Society regarding collection details.

Latah County Historical Society

327 East Second Street, Moscow, ID 83843
(208) 883-7208; Fax: (208) 882-0759
lchlibrary@moscow.com; http://users.moscow.com/lchs/
Contact: Marilyn Sandmeyer

522. "Tribute to Genesee." Script written by Elston Wyckoff and broadcast on KHQ, Spokane, WA , February 6, 1934.

Library of American Broadcasting

University of Maryland
3210 Hornbake Library, College Park, MD 20742
(301) 405-0397; Fax: (301) 314-2634

labcast@umd.edu; www.lib.umd.edu/LAB/
Contact: Chuck Howell

General comments: The LAB holds a wide-ranging collection of audio and video recordings, books, pamphlets, periodicals, personal collections, oral histories, photographs, scripts and vertical files devoted to the history of broadcasting. Much of the Library's holdings can be searched online. However, as material is continually being added to the collection, researchers are advised to contact the Library directly if they do not find what they are looking for online. Listed below is a brief summary of the collections by type of material followed by a list of individual special collections.

The LAB is housed with the National Public Broadcasting Archives. For information about NPBA, see the University of Maryland listing.

523. Audio Collections. Includes thousands of recordings covering all genre. In addition to large collections associated with specific programs or performers such as the *Vox Pop* and *Arthur Godfrey* collections (see below), the Library has several special audio collections enumerated below as collections 524–532.

524. Broadcast Music Incorporated Collection. Consists of over 500 tape recordings of broadcast programming conferences held from 1951–1957. These one-day conferences, or "clinics," were presented throughout the United States and Canada. With the advent of television, radio broadcasters during the 1950s were forced to re-define their roles in serving their audiences. These clinics addressed a wide range of issues affecting broadcasters, including programming strategy, advertising sales, station promotion, public service, news and specialized audience programs. This recording collection reflects many of the trends affecting U.S. commercial radio during that decade.

525. Edwin B. Dooley Collection. Consists of several thousand discs containing a wide variety of material, including acetate recordings dating from the 1930s when WLW broadcast commercially at 500,000 watts and could be heard over most of the U.S. Dooley saved hundreds of field recordings made by WLW engineers during this period as part of an effort to counter complaints from other stations which claimed that this early superstation was blasting them off the air.

526. Miscellaneous Collection. Highlights include ten glass discs recorded by the BBC featuring Glenn Miller and Dinah Shore from August, 1944, a complete set of original pressings of early transatlantic broadcasts from 1925 and 1926 and *NBC Stands By,* a D-Day coverage test/preview recording from May, 1944. Also includes several examples of syndicated programming as well, including episodes of *The Cliff "Ukulele Ike" Edwards Show, Joseph Cotten & Co., Columbia Workshop,* and a special three disc set of *The Jack Frost Sugar Program,* a musical review series from 1934.

527. Radio Advertising Bureau Collection, 1954–1968, bulk 1958–1964. Consists of over 2,000 discs containing radio commercials for products representing the entire scope of American industry in the 1950s and 1960s and illustrating the work of dozens of advertising agencies. The discs are sorted into product categories ranging from Airlines to Wine. Items of special interest include commercials written by and featuring Stan Freberg and his troupe and some Piel's Beer advertisements with comedians Bob and Ray.

528. Subscription Service Discs. The LAB has a growing collection of discs from various radio syndication and subscription services prevalent in the industry from the 1930s–1960s. Each of these companies provided a basic library of radio programming, including a library of musical selections, complete in itself except for local commercial tie-ins. The service included periodic issues of new discs and replacements. The discs were leased for on-air use as long as the station paid the necessary fees. The overall collection includes individual collections numbered 529–531 below.

529. The Standard Program Library. Comprised of 450 discs sent to subscribing stations regularly as supplemental programming in the 1940s and 1950s. The emphasis is on musical selections, including performances by Bing Crosby, Doris Day and Tommy Dorsey.

530. The World Broadcasting Service. Comprised primarily of 225 transcribed musical programs dating from the early 1930s, including a run of *Rubinoff's Musical Moments* featuring the famous violinist.

531. RCA Thesaurus. Includes a number of dramatic offerings plus programs for holidays and other special occasions.

532. Westinghouse/Group W Collection, 1957–1982. The audio tape morgue of the Westinghouse/Group W Washington News Bureau consisting of 2,300 tapes providing a comprehensive look at worldwide events delivered over the radio, 1957–1982. The collection focuses on many of the most important issues of the period.

533. Books. Nearly 4,000 volumes, including books published in the 1920s and 1930s that trace the evolution of broadcasting from its earliest days, histories of the industry and individual stations, biographies of broadcasting notables, engineering texts and vintage children's series like *The Radio Boys.* The books can be found in the catalog of the University of Maryland Libraries, http://catalog.umd.edu/. The Library is also the home to the National Association of Broadcasters Library Collection which consists of over 7,000 broadcasting-related books, reports, pamphlets, journals and subject files.

534. Oral History Collection. Nearly 1,100 oral histories, interviews, and speeches conducted under the auspices of the Library, often in conjunction with other organizations such as the University of Maryland and the American Women in Radio and Television (AWRT). The interviews cover the careers of individuals involved in every facet of the broadcasting industry. Many of the taped interviews have been transcribed.

535. Pamphlet Collection. An extensive collection of over 7,000 titles, ranging from 1920s vintage Bell Laboratories radio engineering bulletins to promotional materials and internal studies generated by the broadcast networks. Also includes government documents and Congressional reports and hearings.

536. Periodicals and Journals. Over 300 periodical titles, including runs of trade press publications such as "Broadcast Weekly," 1930–1936, the "Heinl Radio Business Letter," 1930–1950, "Radio and Television News," 1919–1958, "Radio Guide," 1931–1943, "Ross Reports/Television Index," 1949–present, "Sponsor," 1946–1964, "Broadcasting," 1931–present and "Wireless Age," 1913–1925. The Library also has a large number of academic journals, including "The Journal of Broadcasting and Electronic Media," "The NAEB Journal," "The Journal of Popular Film and Television" and "Education By Radio". See complete list of titles online.

537. Photograph Collections. Contains over 225,000 photos, slides and negatives dating from the 1920s to the present and covering a wide variety of subjects, including individuals involved in every facet of the broadcasting industry. The collection chronicles those on radio and television programs as well as the studios, facilities, community activities of local stations and the activities of organizations related to broadcasting, such as the National Association of Broadcasters and Broadcast Music Incorporated. The overall collection includes individual photograph collections 538–541 below.

538. Alois Havrilla (Photograph) Collection. Consists of the almost 500 photos compiled by Havrilla, Jack Benny's first announcer in 1932, to accompany his unpublished manuscript, "Radio's Golden Age of Adventure," which related his experiences during the medium's formative years.

539. Donald V. West Broadcasting & Cable Photo Archives. Represents the photo morgue of "Broadcasting & Cable" magazine, for 73 years one of the leading publications of its kind. The 200,000+ images represent almost the entire history of the medium and is likely to include anyone who was prominent or influential in radio and television over the past seven decades.

540. Library Of American Broadcasting On-Line Photo Archive. Over 8,000 images are now available online in both thumbnails and full scans at www.lib.umd.edu/LAB/photos.html.

541. St. Louis Post Dispatch Collection. Represents the pre-1970 photo morgue of the "Post-Dispatch's" radio and television section and is heavily weighted towards publicity photos of performers and programs. Photos range from the earliest days of network radio to more contemporary figures such as Sonny and Cher and Mister Rogers.

542. Scripts and News Transcripts. Contains over 5,000 radio and television scripts representing almost every example of programming including dramas, comedies, variety programs, music programs, soap operas, children's programs and quiz programs among others. *A Broadcast Novelty* is the oldest item in the collection, dating from 1926. Others programs of note include early *Amos 'n' Andy* scripts from 1929, *Bob Hope, Jack Benny* and *Bergen and McCarthy*, a large number of radio and television soap operas and 106 scripts of the horror program *Quiet Please*.

543. Station history files. Contains a range of materials, including clippings, promotional brochures, pamphlets and market data. Stations with extensive or unique items have their own folder. See online listings.

544. Subject Files. Includes a collection of biographical and vertical files arranged by subject as well as by program genre.

545. Transcripts Collection. Contains transcripts for many of its audio recordings, particularly oral histories, interviews and speeches. Conducted under the auspices of the Library,

often in conjunction with other organizations such as the University of Maryland and the American Women in Radio and Television (AWRT), the taped interviews number in the hundreds and cover the careers of individuals involved in every facet of the broadcasting industry.

Individual Special Collections

546. Allan Gray Collection (Housewives Protective League). Contains scripts, correspondence and promotional materials relating to *The Housewives Protective League* (HPL), a women-oriented consumer advice program aired on CBS, 1951–1962, created by Gray who used the on-air name Fletcher Wiley.

547. Almanacco Dell'Aria Records, 1941–1942. Consists of daily scripts and commercials, correspondence and daily spots for the sponsor, Pastene & Co. A majority of the documents are in Italian. The 15 minute program was broadcast in Italian on WEVD, New York

548. American Women in Radio and Television (AWRT) Collection. Contains more than 100 oral histories done in the late 1970s and early 1980s under the auspices of the AWRT in which women broadcasters talk candidly about the often uphill road they traveled in a male-dominated industry. The interviews, which include audio cassettes, audio reels and print transcriptions, have been transcribed and cataloged and, as of 2005, are being indexed. The collection also includes scrapbooks, photographs, correspondence, memos, business and meeting records, reports, convention materials, audio tape, 16mm film, video, slides, newspaper clippings, magazine articles and publicity kits.

549. Carl Haverlin Collection. A collection of tapes, 1951–1957, donated by Haverlin, the first president of Broadcast Music, Inc., along with photos and documents that chronicle the founding of BMI. Collection was unprocessed as of 2005.

550. Charles H. Crutchfield Papers, 1951–1973, bulk 1972. Contains correspondence, speeches and articles written by Crutchfield, including some material from Crutchfield's 44 year career with the Jefferson Standard/Jefferson Pilot Broadcasting Company (WBT, NC). Also includes an oral history interview on tape completed in 1977.

551. Committee to Preserve Radio Verifications QSL Collection. A collection of over 30,000 radio verifications, a.k.a. "QSL's," (from the Morse code symbol "Q-S-L" for "I acknowledge receipt"). The cards and letters were sent to radio hobbyists by radio stations to confirm the listener's reception of a distant or hard-to-receive station.

552. Dick Dorrance Papers, 1940–1945, bulk 1940–1944. Papers document the work Dorrance did for FM Broadcasters, Inc. (FMBI), the Office of War Information (OWI) and the Broadcasters' Victory Council (BVC). Collection includes FMBI newsletters, BVC newsletters, Radio Background Material, an Information Guide published by the OWI and various speeches and memos written by Dorrance. The bulk of the material relates to the rise of FM broadcasting and the role broadcasters and radio could play in the war effort.

553. Donald H. Kirkley, Jr. Collection, 1931–1991, bulk 1945–1951. Collection consists largely of audio tapes, books, records, videotapes and pamphlets, including 206 reel-to-reel tapes of speeches of Franklin D. Roosevelt and Harry S. Truman plus the "Iron Curtain" speech by Winston Churchill and radio programs, including *Columbia Workshop, Hear It Now* and some quiz shows and soap operas. Also includes some unidentified oral history cassette tapes and non radio related photographs.

554. Dr. Herman S. Hettinger Papers, 1941–1956, bulk 1950–1956. Contains correspondence, memoranda, legal papers, handwritten notes and tables and charts relating to two legal cases involving radio for which Hettinger served as an advisor. The first involved the extent of cross-ownership between radio stations and newspapers. The second involved the Agricultural Broadcasting Company, owners of WLS, Chicago, among others, which sought tax relief under Section 722 of the Internal Revenue Code. Handwritten notes include data on WLS broadcast revenue and an outline of points to be made and legal strategy in this case. Also contains information comparing WLS to other comparable stations.

555. Edward M. Kirby Collection, 1923–1983, bulk 1938–1959. Contains correspondence, scrapbooks, discs, photographs, speeches, scripts, awards and magazine and newspapers articles documenting Kirby's early career in broadcasting, including his work with WSM, as Director of Public Relations for the National Association of Broadcasters , as a founder of Broadcast Music, Inc. and as the chief of the radio branch of the War Department during World War II. Also includes material relating to *The Army Hour.* Ten related transcription discs from the collection of Major Glenn Miller and the American Band of the Allied Expeditionary Forces Program have been transferred to the Library's audio collection.

556. Edythe J. Meserand Collection. Includes scrapbooks, photographs, American Women in Radio and Television (AWRT) publications, press releases, magazine articles, newspaper clippings, correspondence, speeches on discs, AWRT minutes and reports, WOR related materials (scripts, etc.), books, correspondences, certificates, posters and audio tapes.

557. Elmo N. Pickerill Collection. Papers documenting Pickerill's work as an engineer with Lee DeForest and later for RCA. Materials include correspondence with Guglielmo Marconi, David Sarnoff, and DeForest as well as scrapbooks, photographs and early publications on wireless telegraphy. Collection was unprocessed as of 2005.

558. Helen J. Sioussat Papers, 1928–1995, bulk 1937–1958. Contains a variety of material from every aspect of her career, including scripts, memoranda, press releases, scrapbooks, a complete run of "Talks Magazine," a manuscript for her book, "Mike's Don't Bite," photographs and an interview of Sioussat recorded on October 3, 1979. Also contains materials pertaining to her work with Phillips H. Lord and the program *G-Men*, including lists of artists, correspondence, scripts and a *Seth Parker* scrapbook. Much of correspondence and other papers relates to her time at CBS, including her tenure as Director of the Talks and Public Affairs Department.

559. Henry L. Miller and Anne Lorentz Miller Papers, 1942–1971, bulk 1942–1954. Includes scripts, correspondence, background material used to develop scripts, broadcast tapes and photographs covering work the Millers did for commercial radio as well as the Voice of America. The scripts

for commercial radio, 1942–1953, are not identified. Correspondence discusses scripts Lorentz wrote for the National Council of the Churches of Christ. Documents also include information on WABC and WCBS and the program *Wickbur House* developed by Lorentz for WTAG in 1942. Also includes 57 "V" discs, produced for the Armed Forces Radio Service and recordings of Voice of America.

560. Irene Beasley Collection, 1908–1978, bulk 1930–1953. Contains photographs, scripts for *Grand Slam*, business records, correspondence, publicity and promotional material, a commemorative issue of "Grand Slam News" for the sixth anniversary show, 1952, sheet music and some miscellaneous material. Also includes scripts, records and music from *Aunt Zelena*.

561. Institute for Public Interest Representation (INSPIRE) Collection. Documents relating to a 1976 study of the FTC and the FCC, including how appointments to the agencies were made, 1949–1974. Includes correspondence, manuscript notes, written interviews, maps, graphs, photographs, charts, transcripts of 39 oral interviews and cassettes.

562. Jerry (Tucker) Schatz Papers, 1931–1987, bulk 1931–1943. Contains scripts, 1930–1942, including one for *Twenty Grand Salutes Your Happy Birthday* that is autographed by Babe Ruth, Jimmy Dorsey, Buddy Shuts and Gene Tierney. Also includes photographs, a scrapbook, a magazine article and two videotapes containing biographical information about Schatz's radio and film career.

563. Julie Stevens Collection. Contains over 100 photographs, contracts, newspaper clippings, fan mail, scripts, awards, telegrams, theatre programs and periodicals relating to her acting career, including her role as Helen Trent in *The Romance of Helen Trent*, 1944–1960. Stevens's real name was Harriet Foote Underhill.

564. Justin Meacham Collection, 1922–1976, bulk 1922–1955. Contains information related to WGAZ and WSBT, South Bend, IN, including logbooks, historical notes, publicity material and correspondence.

565. Louis J. Hazam Papers, 1937–1971. Consists of scripts from Hazam's career as a writer and producer for radio and television, five photographs and a single transcription disc from the program *An American Prayer*. Includes scripts for commercials for Fleischmann's Yeast and Lux Flakes for *Lux Radio Theatre*, scripts for the series *America Grows Up*, 1938, *Home Is What You Make It*, 1945–1948, and *Living*, 1948–1952, and scripts for plays and other programs, including *Let There Be Light*, 1947, *Flag Day 52*, 1952, *Cuba, Pearl of the Antilles*, 1942, *Johnny 100,000*, n.d., and *Reba Resolves, or Girl Meets Culture*, n.d. *Living*, which ran from 1948–1952, was the successor to *Home Is What You Make It* and was a weekly documentary series. Ben Grauer was the narrator of many episodes, and some scripts, were co-authored with Wade Arnold.

566. Martha Brooks Collection. Contains photos, correspondence, newspaper clippings, scripts, certificates, publicity materials, speeches, manuscripts, broadcasting themed jewelry, plaques, audio tape, film, telegrams, framed citations, scrapbooks and other ephemera related to the career of Irma Lempke Kroman who broadcast on WGY, Schenectady, NY using different names, including Alice Lee Underwood,

Joan Davis, and most prominently, Martha Brooks. As "Brooks," she hosted *Market Basket* which evolved from the typical women's program into a more stimulating discussion-oriented format which, though still aimed at the housewife, dealt with such formerly taboo subjects as gynecological problems and marital strife.

567. Mildred Funnell Collection. Includes scrapbooks, correspondence, scripts, photos, memoranda, notes and newspaper clippings and magazine articles relating to Funnell's career as co-host with Gloria Brown of *The Mildred and Gloria Program* and *The Idea Shop* on WTAM radio and on television. Also contains material covering the first years of Funnell's career as a stage and radio actress, including a stint in the early 1930s on *Lum and Abner* as Lum's fiance Evalena.

568. Mona Kent Collection. Consists of more than 3,500 scripts for *Portia Faces Life* dating from the mid–1940s onward as well as some biographical material.

569. National Association of Broadcasters Library Collection, 1923–1990s. Contains NAB publications and memos, meeting minutes, photographs, convention programs and public service campaigns for use by member stations to promote radio and television. The association's library of broadcast-related books is now part of the LAB library.

570. Norman R. Glenn Papers, 1933–1998, bulk 1940s–1960s. Glenn's career was in the field of trade publications relating to radio. The collection contains two scrapbooks, correspondence and publications, including bound volumes of "Sponsor" magazine, 1946–1964, and three bound volumes of "US Radio," 1957–1961, that are shelved in the Library's periodicals section.

571. Norman Sweetser Papers, 1913–1971, bulk 1913–1941. Contains an assortment of materials documenting Sweetser's career in the New York theater and radio broadcasting worlds. Includes 127 portrait sketches done by Sweetser on the backs of radio show scripts of the people he worked with, 1937–1941, and two scrapbooks containing smaller portrait sketches and photographs covering the period from Sweetser's college days through his radio career. Also includes theater programs, newspaper and magazine clippings, correspondence and miscellaneous items such as membership cards.

572. Pegeen Fitzgerald Collection. Contains photo albums, magazines, brochures, newspaper clippings, charcoal drawings, correspondence and audio tapes relating to *The Fitzgeralds,* the long running husband and wife breakfast show that aired for 42 years, beginning in 1940.

573. Philip James Papers, 1929–1960, bulk 1929–1936. Contains correspondence, a catalog of James's musical works, two bound books of program notes from the *Bamberger Little Symphony Orchestra* programs and 10 volumes of printed sheets of music used by James in the broadcasts. Business correspondence includes communications with WOR, NBC and CBS.

574. Robert L. Coe Collection, 1902–1975. Includes biographical materials, radio licenses, correspondence, photographs, writings, teaching notes and awards, the unfinished manuscript for the book Coe was writing, "A Saga of American Broadcasting," based on his own experiences, the log book for Coe's first radio station, 9AON and 9ZV, audio tapes of *Day Is Done, Madam & Eve* and other programs with which Coe was associated and tapes of an interview with Coe.

575. Roger Bower Collection, 1927–1979, bulk 1940s–1960s. Contains correspondence, newspaper and magazine clippings, programs and invitations, photographs, books, audio recordings, scrapbooks, promotional material and other papers. Contents are particularly strong in material pertaining to WOR and cover the wide number and variety of programs Bower was involved with, including *Can You Top This?* which is especially well documented with clippings of cast interviews, photographs, audio recordings and a cartoon. The photographs document Bower's association with such well-known personalities as Milton Berle, Richard Wright, W.C. Handy, Paul Robeson, Canada Lee, Bill Robinson and Erskine Butterfield. Collection also contains eight audio reels and cassettes consisting mainly of oral history interviews with Bower and other figures, including Col. Jacob Ruppert (owner of the New York Yankees) and John Bagwell, a colleague of Bower's in Saigon. Also includes a documentary on the history of the Nigerian Television Service and excerpts from some of Bower's WOR programs, especially *Can You Top This?*

576. Sol Taishoff Papers, 1962–1982. Contains mostly business correspondence and financial information from the latter part of Taishoff's career as editor-in-chief of "Broadcasting" magazine. Also included in the collection are personal letters, information relating to Taishoff's professional activities and a small accumulation of books, magazines, pamphlets, photographs, awards and other objects from his office.

577. Thad Holt Collection, 1936–1982. Includes business records, business and personal correspondence, financial records and other documents relating to Holt's involvement with WAPI, WAPI-FM and television. The WAPI documents include original leases, contracts and applications for radio licensing to the FCC, the spread of FM radio and the rise of television. Also contains papers relating to Holt's contributions to the Murrow Symposia which he helped organize in memory of his friend Edward R. Murrow.

578. Tom Kelly Collection. As of 2005, an unprocessed collection chronicling Kelly's 20 year career as a disc jockey for WBIG, Rockville MD and other stations in Colorado and New York.

579. Tom O'Connor Collection, 1919–1990. Consists primarily of materials relating to Baltimore, MD broadcasting, including WBAL-AM, WFBR and WCAO. Includes newspaper and magazine clippings, research notes for a book about Baltimore radio, photographs and photocopies of photographs, two phonograph discs, business records and correspondence, scripts and promotional materials.

580. *Vox Pop* Collection, 1932–1966, bulk 1932–1948. Contains correspondence, scripts, newspaper clippings, magazines, promotional materials, notebooks, scrapbooks, tickets to the broadcasts, awards, certificates, photographs, artifacts and a collection of interview questions, both on cards and paper. Over 400 broadcasts of *Vox Pop* were recorded on transcription discs, many of which are in poor condition and are awaiting conservation. As of early 2005, 10 discs have been transcribed and are available to researchers.

581. WENR-KYW Station Collection, 1921–1971, bulk

1927–1933. Papers document the personnel and broadcasting history of two Chicago stations, KYW and WENR, and include photographs, correspondence, pamphlets, notes, reports and newspaper articles. Also contains materials pertaining to a survey of 18 broadcasting stations outside Chicago conducted by Paul McCluer for The Great Lakes Broadcasting Company and WENR that inquired about internal operations, salary scales, union policies, rate structures, local programming services, operating expenses and profits. The collection includes surveys of 17 stations, including, WJR, Detroit, MI, WHAM, Rochester, NY, WGY, Schenectady, NY, WEEI, Boston, MA, WTIC, Hartford, CT, WEAF, New York, NY, WJZ, New York, NY, WCAU, Philadelphia, PA, WBAL, Baltimore, MD, KDKA, Pittsburgh, PA, WFBM, Indianapolis, IN, WDAF, Kansas City, MO, WHO, Des Moines, IA, WOC, Davenport, IA, WCCO, Minneapolis, MN, KSTP, St. Paul, MN and WTMJ, Milwaukee, WI.

582. WHB Station Collection, 1922–1953, bulk 1930s–1940s. Includes scrapbooks of John T. Schilling containing newspaper clippings, correspondence, advertisements and photographs relating to publicity for WHB, Kansas City, MO.

583. William S. Hedges Papers, 1917–1976, bulk 1917–1918, 1966–1976. Contains correspondence, clippings, diaries, financial statements, logs, memoranda, newsletters, pamphlets, photographs, biographical information, publications and speeches relating to Hedges's pioneering career in broadcasting, including the Broadcast Pioneers History Project, the Broadcast Pioneers Educational Fund and the Broadcast Pioneers Library. Also included are sporadic issues of the publication, "Broadcast Pioneer," 1966–1974.

584. WNET/Thirteen Arthur Godfrey Collection. Contains hundreds of kinescopes of Godfrey television programs, more than 4,000 audio tapes and wire recordings of his various radio shows as well as other video tapes and transcription discs. Also contains Godfrey's voluminous personal papers and business records over a period of more than 50 years. The collection is of major importance, not only because of the insight it allows into the career of Godfrey, but also for the background it provides on the business of radio and television from the 1930s until Godfrey's death in 1983. As of 2005, only parts of the collection are open for research.

Library of Congress

101 Independence Ave. SE, Washington, DC 20540
www.loc.gov

General comments: Listing all the radio related material in the Library of Congress is an impossible task. That said, what follows is a select list of Special Collections, primarily in the Library's Manuscript Division (MSS) and the Motion Picture, Broadcasting and Recorded Sound Division (MBRS), but also in other divisions that were identified in the Library's online catalog as having some radio related material.

For people, programs or topics not included in these listings, researchers should do a more in depth search of the Library's online catalogs and also contact the appropriate division within the LOC as even in the LOC, not everything is searchable online.

American Folklife Center
Mail: 101 Independence Avenue, SE, Washington, DC 20540

Location: Thomas Jefferson Building, Room G53
(202) 707-5510; Fax: (202) 707-2076
folklife@loc.gov

585. Charles Bailey Photograph and Autograph Collection. Includes autographs and photographs of Bailey, a country music and bluegrass performer on WSM's *Grand Ole Opry* and other radio programs in Tennessee, North Carolina and West Virginia.

586. Duncan Emrich Autograph Album Collection, 1843–1923. Consists of autograph albums with material created in response to Emrich's appearance on *NBC Weekend*. No transcript or recording of the broadcast has been located.

587. Fahnestock South Sea Collection, 1939–1994, bulk 1940-1941. Consists of sound recordings, film footage, photographs and accompanying manuscript documentation on two widely publicized expeditions to Oceania and Indonesia in 1940 and 1941 that documented music and dance in the South Sea islands. Includes a copy of the NBC Blue Network program broadcast live from Suva, Fiji by the Fahnestock expedition on August 19, 1940.

Manuscript Division
Location: James Madison Memorial Building, Room LM101
(202) 707-5387; Fax: (202) 707-6336
www.loc.gov/rr/mss

General comments: For an alphabetical list of online collection finding aids see: www.loc.gov/rr/mss/f-aids/mssfa.html. Catalog listings and finding aids do not always provide detailed information about the radio material in the collections. Also, some radio script collections are located in the Recorded Sound Division.

588. Albert Payson Terhune, 1890–1957, bulk 1919–1940. Contains correspondence, literary manuscripts, articles, addresses, radio scripts, clippings, scrapbooks and other papers consisting primarily of manuscripts for Terhune's short stories and articles which relate chiefly to dogs.

589. *Amateur Hour* and *Major Bowes' Original Amateur Hour* Collection, 1934–1948. Contains program scripts.

590. *Amos 'n' Andy* Scripts, 1928–1937. Scripts are on microfilm. (See also Copyright Deposit Drama Collection for additional scripts.)

591. Angelo Patri Papers, 1904–1962, bulk 1924–1962. Professional and some personal correspondence, radio scripts, 1928–1943, and other papers relating to Patri's writings on children and education.

592. Archibald MacLeish Papers. Includes notebooks containing drafts of poetry and prose, manuscripts, drafts of plays, speeches and radio broadcasts.

593. Arthur Sweetser Papers, 1926–1968. Correspondence, radio broadcast transcripts and obituaries chiefly concerning Sweetser's interest in psychoanalysis and his efforts to secure funding for the psychoanalytic movement from the Rockefeller Foundation.

594. Bryson B. Rash Papers, 1918–1992. Correspondence, speeches, broadcast scripts, book draft, biographical material, newsclippings and photographs documenting Rash's career in broadcast journalism.

595. Clifton Fadiman Papers, 1952–1964. Drafts and proofs of his books and articles and correspondence.

596. Columbia Broadcasting System Radio Scripts, 1929–1960. Primarily entertainment programs of the 1930s and 1940s with a few news programs and documentaries. Programs include: *Adventures of Ellery Queen, Brave New World, City Hospital, Doorway to Life, Haunted House, Lux Summer Theater, Open Hearing, Pursuit of Happiness, Report to the Nation* and *Showboat.*

597. Copyright Deposit Dramas Collection. Contains some 250,000 play scripts, including many little known radio scripts, some of which are being microfilmed. Scripts that have been retained in paper form include: *The Goldbergs, Lone Ranger, Marx Brothers, Tarzan, Five Star Theatre, Amos 'n' Andy* (1940s) and others.

598. Dan Golenpaul Papers, 1934–1981, bulk 1934–1977. Correspondence, writings, scripts, contracts, clippings and guest lists relating particularly to *Information Please* produced by Golenpaul for radio and television and to his subsequent publication, "Information Please Almanac."

599. Daughters of the American Revolution Dramatic Scripts, 1938–1940. Scripts of historical broadcasts sponsored by the Daniel Newcomb Chapter (South Dakota) of the Daughters of the American Revolution.

600. Edgar Kobak Papers, 1916–1966, bulk 1949–1962. Correspondence, autobiographical memoir, speeches and writings, business papers, clippings and scrapbooks relating primarily to Kobak's work with McGraw-Hill Publishing Company, NBC and MBS, the early years of radio and television broadcasting and to his expertise in the field of public relations and communications.

601. Edward L. Bernays Papers, bulk 1920–1990. Correspondence, publicity material, scrapbooks, memoranda, research notes, speeches, articles, drafts of books, lists, surveys, reports, printed matter, photographs and other material documenting Bernays's career as a pioneer in the field of public relations and the development of that profession and its influence on American society. Includes material on Bernay's work for the radio broadcasting industry.

602. Elmer Holmes Davis Papers, 1893–1957, bulk 1946–1957. Contains correspondence, radio scripts, 1940, 1945–1955, and other papers.

603. Emily Post Scripts, 1930–1931. Transcripts of weekly radio talks on etiquette.

604. Eric Sevareid Papers, 1930–1992. Includes correspondence, fan mail, radio and television scripts, news analyses, lectures, speeches, writings, book and subject files, awards, newspaper clippings, printed matter, photographs and other papers but primarily consisting of scripts of Sevareid's radio and television news broadcasts and analyses documenting his career with CBS from World War II until his retirement from CBS News in 1977.

605. Francis W. Reichelderfer Papers, 1918–1983, bulk 1939–1967. Correspondence, transcripts of radio broadcasts and other papers pertaining primarily to Reichelderfer's career in meteorology as chief of the U.S. Weather Bureau, 1938–1963.

606. Frank Farrell Papers, 1897–1988, bulk 1945–1975. Correspondence, memoranda, speeches, magazine articles, poetry, reports, radio broadcast transcripts and other papers chiefly documenting Farrell's career from 1945–1975, including his career as a commentator for various stations and networks from 1948–1969.

607. Fred Allen Original Radio and Television Scripts, 1932–1951. Available on microfilm.

608. Fred Allen Papers, 1932-1951. Radio scripts and broadcasts for *Town Hall Tonight, The Chesterfield Supper Club, Jack Benny Show, Bing Crosby Show, Bob Hope Show, Henry Morgan Show* and *The Big Show.*

609. Frederic William Wile Papers, 1898–1941. Scrapbooks chiefly containing clippings of news stories, dispatches and columns written during Wile's career in journalism and as a radio commentator.

610. Frederick Lewis Allen Papers, 1890–1954, bulk 1933–1954. Correspondence, articles, biographies, date books, diaries, radio scripts, histories and speeches documenting Allen's career as editor of "Harper's Magazine," director of the Foreign Policy Association, author of many popular works on American social history and an overseer of Harvard University.

611. General Foods Corporation Radio Script Collection. Scripts span the years 1932–1949 and include: *The Adventures of the Thin Man,* 1944–1945, *The Adventures of Topper,* 1945, *As the Twig Is Bent,* 1941–1942, *Don Winslow,* 1941–1942, *House of Mystery,* September 1945–March 1949, July–August 1949, *Juvenile Jury* 1947–1949, *Kate Hopkins, Angel of Mercy,* October, 1940–January, 1942, February, 1942, *Maxwell House Show Boat,* October, 1932– January, 1935, May, 1935–September, 1937, *Portia Faces Life,* 1940–1944, *The Raymond Scott Show,* n.d., *The Second Mrs. Burton,* 1941–1942, *We Love and Learn,* 1944, *When A Girl Marries,* 1941–1942, *A Woman of America,* 1944, and *Young Dr. Malone,* December, 1939–October,1940, February, 1941–March, 1942. Scripts include commericals and occasionally production records, including cast lists, plot synopses, sound effects, music clearances, rehearsal sheets and the script editing circuit.

612. George Fielding Eliot Papers, 1939–1971, bulk 1950–1971. Correspondence, diary, biographical material, writings, drafts of various articles, notes, speeches and radio broadcasts, newspaper clippings and printed matter relating mainly to Eliot's career as a contributor to magazines.

613. George Vernon Denny Papers, 1930–1959. Correspondence, memoranda, reports, speeches, writings, financial records, research notes, awards, printed matter and photographs documenting Denny's career. Part II of the collection documents Denny's role as moderator, 1935–1952, of *America's Town Meeting of the Air.*

614. Goodman Ace Papers, 1931–1972, bulk 1931–1967. Bound volumes containing approximately 2,000 scripts and related correspondence for radio and television programs for which Ace wrote. Most of the radio scripts are for *Easy Aces,* 1928–1945. Also includes radio scripts for the *Danny Kaye Show.* As of 2005, an additional unprocessed collection of glass recordings is being transferred to the MBRS Division.

615. Hedrick Smith Papers, 1923–1992, bulk 1965–1990. Includes correspondence, memoranda, interview transcripts, drafts of speeches, articles, books, notes, radio broadcasts, legal material, research material, family papers, press releases, printed material, posters, maps and other papers relating primarily to Smith's career.

616. Hume Cronyn and Jessica Tandy Papers, 1885–1994, bulk 1935–1993. Includes family papers and productions and projects file documenting Cronyn and Tandy's stage, screen and television performances together and separately and Cronyn's directorial and theatrical production activities. Does not contain any radio material.

617. Irving R. Levine Papers, 1930–1995, bulk 1949–1964 and 1971–1994. Correspondence, memoranda, notebooks and notes, transcripts of interviews, radio and television scripts and other papers documenting Levine's career as a broadcast journalist and news commentator.

618. Jacob A. Riis, 1870–1990, bulk 1887–1913. Correspondence, scrapbooks, radio scripts, clippings and other papers relating chiefly to Riis's work as a journalist documenting the plight of urban slum dwellers in New York City.

619. Jan Papánek Papers, 1917–1967, bulk 1939–1948. Correspondence, transcripts of radio broadcasts and other papers relating to Papánek's years in the U.S. as representative of the Czechoslovak government in exile during World War II and to his service in the United Nations, 1945–1948.

620. Joe Lester Norris Collection of Midwestern Political Material, 1924–1936. Includes Republican Party radio broadcasts, 1932.

621. John Kieran Papers, 1917–1981. Correspondence and papers and a photograph pertaining to his career as a sports columnist and as a panelist on the radio and television show, *Information Please.*

622. John L. Balderston Papers, 1915–1950. Correspondence, speeches, radio scripts, clippings of Balderston's newspaper articles and photograph of Balderston relating to his career as journalist and playwright.

623. Johnny Carson Papers. Papers deal exclusively with the *Tonight Show* on television.

624. Lawrence E. Spivak Papers, 1917–1994, bulk 1945–1983. Chiefly material relating to *Meet the Press,* including letters, 1957–1968, from viewers, radio and television scripts, 1945–1970, newspaper clippings, 1945–1973, and lists of program broadcasts, 1945–1969. See listing in Recorded Sound section for audio recordings of the programs.

625. Lyman Bryson Papers, 1893–1977, bulk 1917–1959. Correspondence, diaries, memoranda, articles, lectures, writings, transcripts of broadcasts, subject files, business and financial records, biographical material, appointment books, newspaper clippings and other papers documenting Bryson's public relations career and his role in developing educational radio and television programs for CBS. Includes material on Department X, a committee organized by Bryson at the request of CBS president William S. Paley to examine issues relating to global changes in politics, economics, science, technology, public opinion and social and government policy in the future.

626. MacKinlay Kantor, 1885–1977, bulk 1920–1970. Correspondence, diaries, drafts and galleys of playscripts for radio, screen and stage, poems, songs and fiction and nonfiction books and other papers relating chiefly to Kantor's literary career.

627. Margaret Halliwell Hale Papers, 1932–1945. Scripts used in *First Nighter* and *Talkie Picture Time* programs. Written under Hale's maiden name, Margaret Halliwell, in collaboration with Dorothy de Jagers, Beatrice M. Gottlieb, Hilda Gottlieb, Jeanette I. Helm, Hal Field Leslie and Marion Waldman.

628. Marquis James Papers, 1914–1955, bulk 1930–1949. Correspondence, literary and biographical articles, radio scripts and plays, legal and financial papers, clippings, printed material, photographs and other papers.

629. Martin Agronsky Papers, 1907–1999, bulk 1940–1990. Correspondence, radio, television and film scripts, writings, speeches, research material, notes, clippings, printed material, photographs and other papers concerning Agronsky's career as a radio and television journalist.

630. Mary Margaret McBride Papers, 1926–1975. Correspondence, articles, clippings, printed material, photographs and other papers pertaining chiefly to McBride's career in journalism and radio. See separate collection of her radio broadcasts in the listings of Recorded Sound Division collections.

631. Mary Marvin Breckinridge Patterson Papers, 1939–1940. Transcripts of Patterson's broadcasts as a correspondent for CBS in Western Europe during World War II.

632. Maude Adams Papers, 1925–1956. Annotated typescripts and mimeographed copies of Adams's unpublished autobiography, other writings and notes for a proposed radio program with Homer Saint-Gaudens.

633. Moral Re-armament Records, 1812–1991, bulk 1873–1966. Correspondence, subject files, financial records, play and film scripts, radio and television broadcasting files, press releases, clippings, print and near-print material, scrapbooks and other records, chiefly 1924–1977, documenting the policies, organization, programs, activities and membership of the organization. Includes papers of MRA founder Frank Nathan Daniel Buchman.

634. National Association for the Advancement of Colored People (NAACP) Records, 1842–1999, bulk 1919–1991. Includes material on racial stereotyping in film, television and radio.

635. National Committee on Atomic Information Records, 1945–1948. Includes the committee's attempts to use radio to promote understanding of the implications of atomic energy in a nontechnical, easily understood form.

636. National Urban League Records, 1910–1986, bulk 1930–1979. Includes transcripts of radio broadcasts, 1941–1945, by Langston Hughes and prominent African American entertainers in support of the war effort.

637. Norman Lewis Corwin Papers, 1941–1942. Autographed draft and corrected typescripts of Corwin's 1941 broadcast *We Hold These Truths.* Also includes *An American in England*, a series of plays given over the CBS network from

New York City in December 1942.

638. Owen Lattimore Papers, 1907–1997, bulk 1950–1989. Includes correspondence, journals, writings, reviews, speeches, research notes, interviews, reports, transcripts of hearings and other papers.

639. Paul Rhymer Radio Scripts, 1934–1937. Scripts for the *Vic and Sade* program.

640. Perriton Maxwell Collection, 1931–1932. Papers relating to the symposium *Is Radio a Blessing or a Menace?* Contributors include George Ade, Brooks Atkinson, M. H. Aylesworth, Gutzon Borglum, Ellis Parker Butler, James Branch Cabell, Sen. Arthur Capper, Irvin S. Cobb, Walter Damrosch, Benjamin De Casseres, Lee DeForest, Clarence C. Dill, W. N. Doak, James Montgomery Flagg, Daniel Frohman, Fannie Hurst, Joseph Jastrow, H. L. Mencken, George Jean Nathan, Eugene O'Neill, Gov. Gifford Pinchot, Charles Edward Russell, Upton Sinclair, Harry B. Smith, Sigmund Spaeth, Ernest Milmore Stires, Booth Tarkington, Samuel Untermyer, Carolyn Wells, William Allen White, Brand Whitlock, Owen Wister and Adolph Zukor.

641. Raymond Clapper Papers, 1908–1960, bulk 1913–1444. Correspondence, memoranda, diaries, speeches, manuscripts of articles and books, notebooks, dispatches, releases, radio scripts, reports, reference files, pamphlets, promotional material, scrapbooks, clippings, memorabilia and photographs. Chiefly reference material pertaining to the Franklin D. Roosevelt administration and World War II.

642. Raymond Swing Papers, 1935–1963. Primarily scripts of Swing's radio broadcasts, including those presented on the Voice of America. Also includes correspondence, lectures, addresses, articles and other papers. See Recorded Sound section below for audio recordings of Swing's broadcasts.

643. Ruth Hetzel Harshaw Papers, 1947–1967. Correspondence, scripts, program listings and other material concerning Harshaw's programs *Battle of Books, Carnival of Books* and *The Hobby Horse Presents*.

644. Selman A. Waksman Papers, 1915–1960. Correspondence, speeches, articles and radio scripts pertaining to Waksman's career in the field of microbiology.

645. Theodore (Ted) Granik Papers, 1930–1970, bulk 1941–1967. Correspondence, legal proceedings, printed transcripts of radio and television broadcasts, scripts, memoranda, production inventories, office and business papers and newspaper clippings, chiefly 1941–1967. The radio papers relate primarily to *American Forum of the Air, Youth Wants To Know,* and *All America Wants To Know.*

646. Theodore Stark Wilkinson Papers, 1942–1945. Personal and official correspondence, diary, orders to duty, awards, citations, transcripts of radio broadcasts, memoranda and clippings relating to Wilkinson's duties as deputy commander, South Pacific area.

647. Vincent Price Papers, 1883–1992, bulk 1932–1992. Contains correspondence, speeches and writings, lectures, business records, family papers, scripts, programs, playbills, publicity material, photographs and other papers relating to Price's career and other interests.

Performing Arts Reading Room (Music Division)
Location: James Madison Memorial Building, LM113
(202) 707-5507; Fax: (202) 707-0621
www.loc.gov/rr/perform/general.info.html

648. Federal Theatre Project Collection, 1932–1943, bulk 1935–1939. An extensive collection that includes material on the Radio Division. For more specific information see http://memory.loc.gov/ammem/fedtp/fthome.html and for finding aid, http://hdl.loc.gov/loc.music/eadmus.mu995001.

649. Nicolas Slonimsky Collection. Materials collected by Slonimsky that document his life and work as musicologist, composer, conductor, lecturer and author. Includes radio broadcasts.

Recorded Sound Section
Location: James Madison Memorial Building, Room LM 113
(Performing Arts Reading Room)
(202) 707-7833; Fax: (202) 707-8464
http://www.loc.gov/rr/record/

General comments: For radio script collections, see also the Manuscripts Division above. The Library's recorded sound collection includes over 2 million items encompassing audio formats from cylinders to CDs. For general information about the Recorded Sound Division see: http://memory.loc.gov/ammem/awhhtml/awrs9/using_coll.html

As of 2005, the Library's sound recordings are roughly 50% cataloged.

The SONIC (Sound Online Inventory and Catalog) database which includes the Library's radio broadcast holdings is comprised of some 350,000 bibliographic records representing roughly 25% of the Library's entire sound recording holdings. A complete listing of SONIC Contents by general categories and collections is available at: http://star1.loc.gov/cgi-bin/starfinder/0?path=sonic.txt&id=webber&pass=webb1&OK=OK

Additionally, bibliographic records for approximately 20% of the collection, primarily data describing commercial LPs and CDs, can be found at the Library's main online catalog at: http://catalog.loc.gov.

A chart of cataloged Recorded Sound materials and their appropriate bibliographic databases is included in a Recorded Sound Collection Bibliographic Location Matrix at: http://www.loc.gov/rr/record/matrices.html.

The Library also maintains a Recorded Sound Reference Center Card Catalog Supplement that contains information about recordings inventoried by the Library between 1951 and 1990. These recordings are held in the Library and include mostly archival recordings plus all types of music, the spoken word and radio broadcasts. The card catalog supplement is searchable by name, title, and subject at: http://memory.loc.gov/ammem/awhhtml/awrs9/reference_center.html.

Also of interest to researchers is the Library's Radio Form/Genre Terms Guide page, http://www.loc.gov/rr/record/frmgen.html, which includes a thesaurus of terms used to describe various types of radio programs, reconciles variant terms, establishes relationships between terms and guides users in the application of terms.

Listed below are the highlights of the collections of NBC and

WOR recordings and other sound collections listed by name on the SONIC home page.

650. Arch Oboler Collection. Unprocessed as of 2005.

651. AFRTS (AFRS) Radio Series. Contains 300,000 16" and 12" transcription discs, 1942-1998 with a variety of programming. A partial inventory of pre-1959 16" discs is available. The 12" discs are cataloged in the LC online catalog where they are searchable by program title, genre, and in many cases performer name and song title.

652. Andre Kostelanetz Collection. Contains 1,136 records, including records for his radio shows, *Chesterfield Presents* and *Tune-up Time,* primarily from the 1930s.

653. Bob Frank Collection. Contains 108 records, including radio programs featuring Andre Kostelanetz.

654. Brander Matthews Dramatic Museum Collection. A series of private, experimental and radio broadcast recordings made at Columbia University, principally during the 1930s. The Collection comprises a wide range of spoken arts, including documentaries, speeches, interviews and prose and poetry readings.

655. Carlton E. Morse Copyright Script Collection, 1939–1952, n.d. Includes 47 *I Love A Mystery* scripts, 1939–1944, 1949–1952, four *Adventures by Morse* scripts, 1944, and 13 *I Love Adventure* scripts, 1948.

656. Columbia Broadcasting System Collection. Includes the complete 24-hour programming for two full weeks, May 13-26, 1957, from Washington, DC, affiliate station WTOP.

657. Cynthia Lowry/Mary Margaret McBride Collection. Includes more than 1,200 hours of interview programs and related broadcasts documenting all phases of McBride's radio career, 1935–1970s. See also separate collection of McBride's papers in the Manuscript Division.

658. Danny Kaye/Sylvia Fine Kaye Audio Materials. Contains 218 records, 1944–1964.

659. *Freedom Sings.* Contains 161 records of radio broadcasts featuring the U.S. Marine Band, 1950s–1970s. See a second U.S. Marine Band collection below.

660. George Gershwin. Contains six records, including Gershwin radio broadcasts.

661. Irving R. Levine Collection, 1950s and n.d. Contains 12 records, including some radio/television broadcast material.

662. Jim Walsh Collection. Includes sound recordings and papers related to Walsh's career collecting, researching and writing about early popular recordings and recording artists. Includes correspondence with prominent artists and collectors, research notes, photographs of performers, scripts for Walsh's radio shows, drafts of his columns and articles, clippings, bound journals, advertisements, scrapbooks and ephemera. Series III of the collection includes scripts for Walsh's regular broadcasts on WDBJ and WSLS, Roanoke, VA. The majority of the scripts date from 1943–1949 and are for *Walsh's Wax Works.* Many of the scripts include separate playlists. Many of the programs showcased a particular recording artist or composer and an index to these shows is attached to the end of the finding aid. Also contains a few scripts for Walsh's

Sunlight and Shadows show, 1947, 1948, and a folder of unidentified and partial scripts.

663. John Peter Collection. Includes sound recordings of Peter's radio interviews dealing with the history of modern architecture.

664. *Meet the Press* Collection. Contains 2,027 records of the radio program and audio from the television program, 1945–1984. See Manuscript Division for scripts of the program.

665. Manfred Frank DeMartino Collection of Radio Scripts, 1943–1945. Scripts (some autographed by performers) and a photograph acquired by DeMartino while working backstage at CBS during the mid-1940s. Includes scripts for *The Frank Sinatra Show*, April 26 and December 4, 1944, *Philip Morris Playhouse*, January 27, February 11 and February 18, 1944, and *Your Hit Parade*, October 16, 1943, April 8, 1944 and August 25, 1945. The scripts include advertisements for sponsors.

666. National Broadcasting Company (NBC) Radio Collection. For an overview of the NBC collection, with links to specific parts of the collection see: www.loc.gov/rr/record/recnbc.html. Summarized below are the contents of the "History" file, followed by a list of the other files in the collection.

667. NBC/Company History Files, 1922–1986. Collection includes memoranda, correspondence, speeches, reports, policy statements and pamphlets covering the creation of the network, its growth in the field of radio and its subsequent expansion into television broadcasting. The materials span 1922–1986, but most date from the mid-1920s through the late 1940s.

Additional files include
Topical folders, 1922–1986, (649 folders)
Advertisers, 1927–1961, (38 folders)
Personnel and organizations, 1926–1980 (88 folders)
Committees, councils, and internal organizations, 1923–1973, (122 folders)
Board of directors, 1926–1956, (100 folders)
Network affiliates, 1923–1983, (44 folders)
General reports, 1930–1936, (67 folders)
Annual reports, 1932–1959, (6 folders)
Programs, subject lists, schedules, samples, 1931–1972, (126 folders)
Speeches, 1923–1990, (63 folders)
Programs, schedules, transcripts, and masterbooks, 1922–1979, (28 folders)
Election news, 1962–1988, (55 folders)
Consultant reports, 1947–1957, (14 folders)
Pamphlets, (566 folders)

668. NBC/Radio and Television Program Schedules, 1949–1958. Daily schedules that give the radio and television programming between 5:00pm–12:00am for the MBS, ABC, CBS, and NBC networks. Gives ratings for each program and sponsors when applicable. Includes weekly daytime programming schedules beginning in May, 1950. Includes both network and local programs. These schedules were used by NBC sales staff for the purpose of selling NBC network airtime to advertisers and sponsors. Beginning in December, 1952 the back pages of the schedules feature interesting tidbits of information on NBC programs to entice potential sponsors. Some schedules have handwritten corrections.

669. NBC/Sound Recordings: Contains approximately 150,000 discs from the early 1930s to the late 1960s, including comedy, drama, public affairs, musical variety, sports, news, information and international shortwave broadcasts. Everything recorded through 1953, plus a selection of programs after 1953, has been preserved and is cataloged on SONIC. Also check the publication "Radio Broadcasts in the Library of Congress, 1924–1941," (LOC, 1982).

670. Office of War Information (OWI). Contains over 8,000 records with OWI news, information, entertainment and propaganda broadcasts, 1942–1945. Primarily in English.

671. Raymond Gram Swing Collection. Contains 1,298 records of news and commentary by Swing, 1938–1947. Some of the records have brief summaries. See Manuscript Division for collection of Swing scripts.

672. RCA Victor *Thesaurus* Transcription Discs. Contains 54 discs made for radio broadcast. Includes music, auditions and other programs.

673. UCLA Collection. Contains 115 miscellaneous records of radio programs from instantaneous discs.

674. U.S. Marine Band Concerts. Contains 54 records of radio broadcasts featuring the U.S. Marine Band, 1959–1960. See a second U.S. Marine Band collection.

675. WOR Collection/Radio and Television Records, 1937–1970. Contains approximately 15,000 discs including news, documentaries, musical variety, dramas, comedies, soap operas, quiz shows and information. Collection also includes print materials, including scripts and papers relating to writer and producer Phillips H. Lord's programs, *Gang Busters*, 1937–1953, *Counterspy* and *Policewoman*, 1946–1947, and scripts for many of the radio adaptations of books by Kathleen Norris. The audio portion of the collection is searchable by program title in a published finding aid available in the Recorded Sound Reference Center.

Library of Virginia
800 E. Broad Street, Richmond, VA 23060
(804) 692-3919; Contact: Jay Gaidmore
jgaidmore@lva.lib.va.us;   www.lva.lib.va.us

676. WRVA Radio Collection, 1925–2000. Consists of papers and sound recordings that document the history of WRVA, Richmond, VA, the role the station played in Virginia and Richmond for over half-a-century and the development of radio in Virginia and the United States. Includes applause letters, minutes, anniversary booklets, program scripts, program guides, newsletters, histories, interviews, employee questionnaires, sales manuals, audience and sales promotions, rate cards, listener surveys, posters, newspaper clippings, scrapbooks, FCC applications and reports, drawings, photographs and sound recordings, 1925–1999. All programs included in the collection are listed in the Index.

Living Traditions
45 East 33rd Street, Level B, New York, NY 10016
(212) 532-8202; Fax: (212) 532-8238
info@livingtraditions.org;   www.livingtraditions.org

Contact: Henry Sapoznik

677. Yiddish Radio Collection. Contains print and audio material dating back to the 1930s. Print material includes scripts, correspondence, newspaper clippings, FBI and FCC files, advertising and posters. Sound recordings encompass 197 separate shows broadcast on 28 stations, mostly in New York on WEVD, WLTH, WBBC, WHN and other stations, on WCOP, Boston and on WDAS, Philadelphia. As of 2005, 85% of the 1,300+ discs have been cataloged.

Louisiana State University
Baton Rouge
Hill Memorial Library, Baton Rouge, LA 70803
(225) 578-6547; Contact: Elaine Smyth
esmyth@lsu.edu; www.lib.lsu.edu/special/location.html

Shreveport
Noel Memorial Library, 1 University Pl, Shreveport 71115
(318) 797-5378; Fax: (318) 797-5156
Contact: Laura Lyons McLemore;   LMcLemore@lsus.edu

678. Bob Hill Shreveport Music Collection, 1930–1976. Contains recordings of country, western and spiritual music, including recordings of KWKH programs. (Shreveport)

679. Brooks Read Brer Rabbit Collection, 1950-1991, bulk 1950-1959. Comprised mostly of reel-to-reel audio tape and scripts (about 500) of Read's recordings of both original "Brer Rabbi"t stories and stories he wrote based on the characters. The recordings were broadcast by radio stations nationwide. Subject files contain correspondence, contracts, marketing materials, artwork and newspaper articles related to the broadcasts. Also includes phonograph records of background music and sound effects used in the shows.

680. Don Devol Oral History Interview, 1982. Devol discusses Huey Long's radio addresses and his relationship with the news media. An abstract of the interview is available.

681. Frank Page Collection, 1935–1998. Page was stage announcer for KWKH's *Louisiana Hayride*. Collection includes photographs but mostly newspaper clippings of the program's artists. (Shreveport)

682. Frans Ferdinand Blom Papers, 1919–1941. Includes scripts for unidentified radio and film programs, engravings, photographs and clippings.

683. J. Thomas (James Thomas) Tanner Papers, 1869–1980. Diary entries include information about Huey Long's radio programs, 1929–1935.

684. Lloyd Lenard Papers, 1961–1962. Lenard was moderator of the KWKH program *Party Line*, 1961–1962. Collection includes correspondence from listeners and notes about the broadcasts. (Shreveport)

685. Paul L. Carriger Correspondence and Records, 1928–1975. Contains photographs, broadcast notes, news articles from the 1930s, a few items on KWKH and some material on W5XA and W5CBU (Southern Television and Broadcasting Co.) and W9XX. an experimental radio station W9XX. Carriger, was the chief announcer and engineer for KWKH, KRMD and KWEA in Shreveport. (Shreveport)

686. Ralph Sims Oral History Interview, 1997. Transcript includes a discussion of Sims's work at WJBO, Baton Rouge,

LA before and after World War II and his association with station owner Charles Manship, Sr.

687. *Register* **Records, 1948–1980.** Includes scrapbooks, 1948–1965, with photographs, newspaper clippings, correspondence and ephemera related to *The Register*, the radio and television broadcasts hosted by the paper's publisher, Orene Muse (Mrs. Elton Huckabay) in the 1940s–1950s.

688. Scripts, 1953–1954. Includes radio scripts and cover letters signed by Wade O. Martin relating to the sesquicentennial observance and history of the Louisiana Purchase. The scripts include manuscript annotations by Martin.

689. Walter Coquille Papers, 1917–1959. Contains correspondence related to Coquille's work as an entertainer on radio and stage, including notes and scripts, 1936–1956, and audio cassettes. Also contains newspaper clippings, programs, advertisements and other papers. Access restricted until 2024.

Lyndon B. Johnson Presidential Library & Museum
2313 Red River Street, Austin, TX 78705
(512) 721-0212; johnson.library@nara.gov
www.lbjlib.utexas.edu/

General comments: See the online list of other personal collections at the library for possible radio related materials.

690. Drew Pearson Papers. Contains materials created or collected by Pearson during his career as a newspaper columnist, television and radio broadcaster and lecturer.

Mahoning Valley Historical Society
Business & Media Archives of the Mahoning Valley
648 Wick Avenue, Youngstown, OH 44502
(330) 744-7621; Fax: (330) 744-8391
business_media@mahoninghistory.org
www.mahoninghistory.org; Contact: Constance L. Jones

691. WKBN Broadcasting Corp. Records. Includes phonograph records from WKBN's record library, corporate records and photographs. The corporation, founded in 1926, owned AM and FM stations in the Mahoning Valley that encompasses eastern Ohio and western Pennsylvania.

Maine Historical Society
489 Congress Street, Portland, ME 04101
(207) 774-1822; Fax: (207) 775-4301
rdesk@mainehistory.org
www.mainehistory.org/library_search.shtml

692. Horace A. Hildreth Papers, 1906–1987. Contains material relating to Hildreth's career as a broadcast executive, including his position as founder and executive of the Hildreth Network which included WABI, WPOR and the Aroostook Broadcasting Company.

693. Maine Council of Churches Records, 1924–1974. Contains radio scripts, including scripts for *Book of Books* and *Church School of the Air* programs.

694. Phillips Haynes Lord Collection, 1929–1932. Includes fan letters, request letters to "Seth Parker," order forms, articles, clippings, miscellaneous receipts and other papers pertaining to *Seth Parker.*

Marquette University
Raynor Memorial Libraries

Department of Special Collections and University Archives
1355 W. Wisconsin Avenue, Milwaukee, WI 53233
(414) 288-5903; Fax: (414) 288-6709
Phil.Runkel@marquette.edu; Contact: Phil Runkel
www.marquette.edu/library/collections/archives

695. Arthur L. Olszyk Papers, 1946–1996, bulk 1965–1980. Contains papers dealing with Olszyk's broadcast journalism career with WTMJ-AM and WTMJ-TV.

696. Catholic Broadcasters Association Records, 1947, 1955–1972, n.d. Records of a network of Catholic communications professionals which established the Gabriel Awards to recognize programs that "uplift and nourish the human spirit," including correspondence, newsletters, pamphlets, photographs, press releases and proceedings of general assemblies and awards banquets. Includes radio scripts and some recordings.

697. Donald (Don) T. McNeill Collection, 1928–1969. Contains records of *The Breakfast Club,* 1933–1968, and *Don McNeill's TV Club,* 1950–1951, and related personal papers of McNeill. Includes program scripts and outlines, publicity and advertising material, photographs, clippings and scrapbooks, films of *Breakfast Club* simulcasts, *TV Club* programs and other television programs featuring McNeill. Also includes sound recordings of several *Breakfast Club* programs from the 1940s and 1950s and master audiotapes for the last seven months of *The Breakfast Club*, May–December, 1968.

698. Hildegarde Papers, 1921–1982. Contains correspondence, photographs, press clippings, programs and ephemera documenting the career of the singer/pianist Hildegarde Loretta Sell known professionally as "The Incomparable Hildegarde."

Maryland Historical Society Library
Manuscripts Department
201 West Monument Street, Baltimore, MD 21201
(410) 685-3750; Fax: (410) 385-2105
library@mdhs.org
www.mdhs.org/explore/library/collections.html

699. Vincent Godfrey Burns Papers, 1918–1979. The bulk of collection is comprised of Burns's plays, novels, short stories and poetry and includes radio scripts for *Voice of Chiropractic, The Chiropractor's Broadcast* and *The Keep Smiling Program,* 1937–1938.

Massachusetts Historical Society
1154 Boylston Street, Boston, MA 02215
(617) 536-1608; Fax: (617) 859-0074
http://www.masshist.org/library/abigail.cfm

700. New England Committee to Defend America by Aiding the Allies Records, 1940–1942. Records, including radio programs, of the chapters in Connecticut, Maine, Massachusetts, Rhode Island and New Hampshire.

Media Heritage, Inc.
8070 Tylersville Road, West Chester, OH 45069
(513) 777-7891; Contact: Mike Martini
mmartini@radiocincy.com; www.mediaheritage.com

701. Eugene Patterson Collection. Includes several hundred photographs, mainly from WLW, Cincinnati, OH, 1934–1936, taken by Patterson who was an engineer at WLW. Also includes two dozen recordings from World War II era relating to Patterson's work for the Office of War Information.

702. Frederic W. Ziv Archive, 1938–1961. Contains over 11,000 transcription discs, both masters and pressings, of Ziv Company programs, 1940–1960. Includes some out-take reel-to-reel tapes and 34 boxes of contracts, scripts, Ziv-created advertising kits and other related items. Ziv was a syndicator of radio and television shows. The programs included in the collection are listed below. Note: The number of episodes indicates the total number of episodes that were originally created based on company files. The "**" indicates that the collection includes only a few episodes from the series or none at all.

Barry Wood, 182 episodes
Bold Venture (Bogart and Bacall), 78 episodes
Boston Blackie, 218 episodes
Bright Star (Dunne and McMurray), 52 episodes
Calling All Girls, 270 episodes**
The Career of Alice Blair, 130 episodes**
Cisco Kid, 885 episodes
Dearest Mother (soap opera), 143 episodes**
Dorothy and Dick, 120 episodes**
Easy Aces (repackaged network), 763 episodes
Eddie Cantor Show, 259 episodes
Eye Witness News (news analysis), 160 episodes**
Favorite Story (Coleman), 118 episodes
Forbidden Diary (soap), 130 episodes**
Fred Waring (music), 156 episodes
Freedom USA (with Tyrone Power), 52 episodes
Guy Lombardo Show, 92 episodes
Hour of Stars, 260 episodes**
I Was a Communist for the FBI, 78 episodes
Korn Kobblers (country/western), 376 episodes
Lightning Jim, 98 episodes
Manhunt (crime), 39 episodes**
Meet the Menjous (talk, Menjous), 520 episodes
Mr. District Attorney (repackaged), 52 episodes
Movietown Radio Theater, 52 episodes**
Old Corral (western), 143 episodes
Parents Magazine of the Air, 52 episodes
Philo Vance (detective), 104 episodes
Pleasure Parade, 138 episodes**
Red Skelton (repackaged network), 260 episodes
Sam Balter—One for the Book, 192 episodes**
Secret Diary (soap), 117 episodes**
Showtime from Hollywood, 78 episodes**
Sincerely, Kenny Baker (music), 130 episodes
Songs of Good Cheer, 117 episodes
Sparky and Dud, 66 episodes
This is America, 26 episodes
War Correspondent, 78 episodes
Washington Views and Interviews, 120 episodes
Wayne King (music), 78 episodes
World's Greatest Mysteries, 260 episodes

703. Henry Thies Collection. Includes two photo scrapbooks, ca. 1935, that belonged to Thies, a Midwest band leader and WLW music director.

704. Minabelle Abbott Collection. Contains 51 transcription discs of programs broadcast on WLW, 1935–1936, and about a dozen photographs from the same era.

705. Ohio (Cincinnati-Related) Stations Collection, 1930–1960. Contains scripts, photographs, publicity material and about 2,000 hours of recordings from WKW, WKRC, WCKY,

WSAI, WFBE and WCPO. Although there are no long "runs" of any particular series, the collection does include a "decent" supply of *Moon River*, WLW, and *Canal Days*, WSAI. Also includes personal items related to the career of Ruth Lyons and some material relating to Cleveland radio history.

Mercer University
Tarver Library Special Collections
1300 Edgewood Avenue, Macon GA 31207
(478) 301-2968; Contact: Arlette Copeland
copeland_a@mercer.edu; http://tarver.mercer.edu/archives

706. WMAZ Station Records. Station records for WMAZ, including scripts, correspondence and responses to a 1929 survey about the college's experience operating a radio station.

Metropolitan Museum of Art
11 West 53rd Street, New York, NY 10019
(212) 708-9400; www.moma.org/research/archives/index.html

707. Carl Lerner Papers, 1929–1972, bulk 1940–1972. Includes material about proposed radio projects.

708. Early Museum History: Administrative Records. Includes papers relating to the *Art in America* program.

Metropolitan Opera Archives
Lincoln Center, New York, NY 10023
(212) 799-3100; Contact: John Pennino
jpennino@mail.metopera.org; www.metopera.org

709. Archives. See searchable online database for complete information on all performers, operas and ballets at the Met since 1883. The database also includes photos, designs, reviews, statistics, and chapters on great events in Met history. Contact organization regarding access to print archives.

Michigan State University
University Archives & Historical Collections
101 Conrad Hall, East Lansing, MI 48824
(517) 355-2330; Fax: (517) 353-9319
millerwh@msu.edu; www.msu.edu/unit/msuarhc/
Contact: Whitney A. Miller

710. "A Public Service Program History of Radio Station WFAA–820." A Ph.D. thesis by George Mitchell Stokes, Northwestern University, 1954.

711. "Development of Network Religious Broadcasting in the United States, 1923–1948." A Ph.D. thesis by Stanley F. Knock, American University, 1959.

712. "Life and Times of Frances Alvord Harris: Michigan's First Woman Newscaster." A Ph.D. thesis by Carole Mary Eberly, Michigan State University Department of English, Program in American Studies, 1995.

713. Radio Broadcasting Records (WKAR), 1935-1970. Records include production logs, 1945–1946, radio scripts, 1942–1952 and n.d., radio scrapbook poems, 1948–1953, and miscellaneous reports, news releases, surveys and other materials.

714. Radio Club Records, 1924–1992, bulk 1948–1989. Includes minutes of meetings, financial transactions, correspondence and station and contest logs. One bound volume contains early logs for WKAR, 1924, and W8SH, 1927–1931, as well as minutes of meetings, 1932–1936, a list of operators, 1927–1936, treasurer's reports, 1933, and vibration experiment notes, 1925. The records also include two boxes of QSL or "Radio Contact Cards," 1927–1950, arranged alphabetically by state and city. Certificates and commemorative QSL cards, 1929–1986, are filed separately.

Vincent Voice Library
100 Library, East Lansing, MI 48824
(517) 432-6123; Contact: John Shaw
shawj@lib.msu.edu; http://vvl.lib.msu.edu/index.cfm

General comments: The G. Robert Vincent Voice Library is one of the largest academic voice libraries in the nation and houses taped utterances (speeches, performances, lectures, interviews, broadcasts, etc.) by over 50,000 persons from all walks of life recorded over the past 100 years. In addition to searching the online database, the site has a listing of online finding aids broken down by category, http://vvl.lib.msu.edu/findingaids.cfm, including 22 radio related finding aids. Summarized below are collections related to the Golden Age of Radio. See the finding aids for more details.

715. Audio Biography of Radio. Six sound recordings of various historic persons and news events from Thomas Edison to Al Jolson.

716. Carlos Hagen Collected Radio Broadcasts, n.d. Recordings of four programs of Carlos Hagen. Note: Online finding aid lists subjects but not dates.

717. *University of Chicago Roundtable of the Air*, **1940s–1950s.** Includes 203 recordings of the program.

718. Don McLaughlin Interview, 1974. A sound recording of an interview with McLaughlin in which he talks about his career in radio.

719. George M. (George Michael) Cohan, 1878-1942. Collected speeches of Cohan on five recordings.

720. Institute for Democratic Education, 1940. Collected broadcasts of nine *Lest We Forget These Great Americans* programs. Note: In catalog, the program is listed as *Lest We Forget These Famous Americans*.

721. Norman Ernest Brokenshire. A 1946 recording of *The Minstrel and the Story Man*, a program for children.

722. Radio Programs. Recordings of 188 programs, plays and serials. See online finding aid for list of programs.

723. Sidney Mosely. A speech, February 16, 1945.

724. Steve Smith Collection Radio Programs, n.d. Two recordings offering a radio history of World War II.

Middle Tennessee State University

Center for Popular Music
Bragg Mass Communications, Room 140
PO Box 41, Murfreesboro, TN 37132
(615) 898-2449; Fax: (615) 898-5829
ctrpopmu@mtsu.edu; http://popmusic.mtsu.edu

General comments: The Center for Popular Music is an archive and research center devoted to the study of American popular music from the pre-Revolutionary War era to the present. The archive includes text and sound material as well as sheet music that can be searched online.

The following list of collections is based on a "radio" keyword search; other collections may include performers who also appeared on radio but because the word "radio" did not appear in the online finding aid, the collections were not brought up in the search. It should also be noted that some of the collections included copies of recordings originally made between the 1920s–early 1960s and that it was not always clear if those recordings included radio broadcasts. The collections also include post 1970 interviews of performers that may include discussions of earlier work on radio.

725. "A Basie Dozen," 1938–1947. A tape from WMOT, Memphis, TN that includes 25 minute public radio modules of Count Basie memorabilia. See online finding aid for a list of the songs and performers.

726. Bill Monroe Radio Broadcasts, ca. 1949. Copies of off-air discs made by Tut Taylor, ca. 1949, from radio broadcasts by Bill Monroe and the Blue Grass Boys and by other traditional string band performers who appeared on the same programs, including Flatt and Scruggs, the Smokey Mountaineers, Jack [Thompson?], Lonnie Glasson, Little Ray Wiggins, Curly Fox, Lonzo and Oscar, Hank Williams and Howdy Forrester.

727. Bronzemen Quartet Radio Transcription Discs. Three undated transcription discs made by Standard Radio, Hollywood, CA for distribution to radio stations.

728. C. L. (Les) Haney. A recording, probably from WLBJ, Bowling Green, KY, January 6, 1948, documenting a radio show featuring some of Haney's songs and comedy routines. Also includes photographs.

729. Deford Bailey Historic Marker Dedication, 1991. Sound recording and photographs commemorating harmonica player Deford Bailey who performed on the *Grand Ole Opry,* 1925–1941.

730. Dewey *Red, Hot and Blue* **Phillips.** The audio tape consists of air-checks used to send samples of Phillips's program, *Red Hot and Blue,* to other radio stations from WHBQ, Memphis, TN, April 18, 1952. Note: The online catalog lists the show as *Red White and Blue* while the description lists it as *Red Hot and Blue.*

731. Evelyn Overstake Collection, 1932–1952. Consists of scrapbooks, personal papers and recordings documenting the history of The Three Little Maids featured on the *National Barn Dance, Round-Up, Dinnerbell, Musical Journey with Miss Evelyn, Dreamers Bay* and *Hilltoppers.* Also includes scripts, advertisements, fan letters, photographs of WLS performers and binders of songbooks. Sound recordings include home recordings, radio air-checks, instantaneous discs and 78rpms.

732. Gorden Henderson Orchestra Scrapbooks, 1928–1939. Scrapbooks document the engagements of the orchestra with clippings providing a chronology of the orchestra's performances. Also includes photographs, programs and other materials. The orchestra was heard on various radio stations, including KPO and KFWB and other stations affiliated with NBC and CBS.

733. John Wesley Work III. Copies of audio tapes of black music and related photographs gathered by Work from 1935 to 1942 that were used for a radio program *Roots of American Popular Music* which aired over National Public Radio in February 1989.

734. Master Tapes of Negro Quartet Singing. Copies of commercial discs, test and unissued discs and radio transcription discs, ca. 1920s–1950s, accumulated from various sources by Nashville gospel music researcher Doug Seroff. Tapes consist of harmony selections, primarily religious songs, by a wide variety of Negro quartets.

735. "The Other Music City" Interview. Interview with P.J. Broome and Clay Tucker on WGNS, Murfreesboro TN, January 19, 1991, which describes the big band jazz scene in the Nashville area, 1920–1960.

736. *Southern Songbirds*, 1920s–1980s. Copies of a 13 part radio series developed by Appalshop, Whitesburg, KY and broadcast over public radio, 1989–1990. The series, *Southern Songbirds: The Women of Early Country Music and Old-Time Music,* was developed to document women's role in the development of country music. The broadcasts focus on the life stories of the Powers Family, Phyllis Marks, Jean Ritchie, Ola Belle Reed, Patsy Montana, Girls of the Golden West (Dolly and Millie Good), Martha Carson, Etta Baker, Ramona Jones, Wilma Lee Cooper, Matokie Slaughter, the Carter Family and Hazel Dickens.

737. WLS *National Barn Dance*. Although not categorized as a "special collection," the Center does have a variety of materials relating to the program.

Miley Collection, Inc.
441 Scenic Drive, Evansville, IN 47715
(812) 479-9143
jmindiana@aol.com; Contact: John Miley

738. Audio Collection. A private collection of broadcasts of sporting events, including many regular season and World Series baseball games dating back to 1933, regular season and Bowl football games dating back to around 1935, basketball games, auto racing, including a few Indy 500s, many boxing matches dating back to 1936, a limited pre-1960 golf collection and some event highlights such as horse racing, mainly Kentucky Derbys dating back to the mid-1930s, and several NHL hockey games and highlights dating back to 1945.

Minnesota Historical Society
345 W. Kellogg Boulevard, St. Paul, MN 55102
(651) 296-6980; Fax: (651) 296-9961
michael.fox@mnhs.org; www.mnhs.org/library/index.html
Contact: Michael Fox

739. 3M Historical Corporate Records, 1902–1995. Includes sound recordings of radio commercials advertising the company's products.

740. 4-H History. A sound recording of T. A. Erickson, a 4-H leader, being interviewed on WCCO by Larry Haeg on the history of the 4-H in Minnesota, March 4, 1952.

741. Alice Gortner Johnson Papers, 1928–1938, 1942–1953. Includes scripts for a series of programs, 1933, produced by KSTP, to celebrate the 22nd anniversary of the founding of the Camp Fire Girls. A folder list with additional information about this collection is available in the repository.

742. Allen J. Furlow Congressional Papers, 1924–1929. Includes papers relating to Furlow's work in the field of broadcast regulation during his terms in Congress, 1925–1929.

743. *American School of the Air*, 1939. Transcript of program broadcast March 16, 1936, possibly dealing with Minnesota history.

744. B. W. Harris Manufacturing Co., Advertising and Promotional Materials. Contains sound recordings of Zero King radio commercials, including re-recordings of a series of 1947 radio spots.

745. Brenda Ueland Papers, 1860–1985. Includes scripts Ueland wrote for the following radio shows: the *Anne Herrold Program,* a radio news program broadcast in Minneapolis, March 11–May 28, 1936, *Tell Me More,* a program that featured Ueland's answers to listeners' personal problems, June–July, 1942, and *Stories for Girl Heroes,* a children's program that profiled notable women.

746. Charles Fremont Dight Papers, 1883–1984. Includes typed copies of talks on heredity and eugenics presented over various radio stations, 1928 and 1933, and correspondence regarding talks on WRHM, 1933–1934.

747. Charles Lindbergh Speech. Sound recording of a speech Lindbergh delivered to the National Press Club, June 11, 1927.

748. Chester-Kent Corporate Records, 1905–1959. Includes material on radio advertising, possibly for Adlerika, a laxative and a treatment for appendicitis, Adla tablets for stomach ailments, Daru liver pills and Vinol, a vitamin tonic. An inventory that provides additional information about these materials is available in the repository.

749. *The CIO Marches On*, 194? A possible Hennepin County, MN CIO sponsored radio series. Check with repository for more information.

750. *Don Leary's Open House*. A sound recording of the program aired on WDGY, Minneapolis, MN. Broadcast live from Don Leary's Record and Radio Store in Minneapolis, the show featured records produced on the Continental label.

751. Dr. Chesley on the *Bee Baxter Show*. A sound recording of an interview with Dr. Albert J. Chesley, secretary and executive officer of the Minnesota State Board of Health on *Public Health Is People* broadcast on KSTP, May 19, 1955.

752. Edward Marx Franey Papers, 1940–1986, bulk 1950–1970. Includes papers relating to Franey's involvement with the WLOL radio and WTCN television show *Sportsmen's Roundtable,* 1947–1959, and other papers documenting his career as a journalist, conservationist and leader of the Izaak Walton League of America (IWLA).

753. Eleanor Freemantle Scrapbooks and Related Papers, 1906–1996, bulk 1923–1934. Two dismantled scrapbooks, 1906–1942 and n.d., containing correspondence, programs and newspaper clippings relating to her career as a pianist and her work as an accompanist on WCCO, 1923–1925.

754. Esther Jerabek and Family Papers, 1914–1979. Includes talks Jerabek gave on WCAL, 1949, dealing with Czech and Slovak history and culture.

755. *The First Forty.* An air-check recording of a program broadcast Oct 2, 1964 on the occasion of the fortieth anniversary of WCCO.

756. Frances Howe Satterlee Papers, 1892–1968. Contains correspondence, reports, minutes, clippings, financial records and radio and television scripts relating to Satterlee's life and work, mainly 1941–1961, with women's clubs and dealing with consumer affairs.

757. Gordon Mikkelson Papers, 1929–1990. Includes papers related to Mikkelson's work in public relations and special projects with WCCO, 1957–1988.

758. Governor Harold Stassen Broadcast Recordings, 1939–1943. Includes several 16" transcription discs of radio broadcasts.

759. Grain Terminal Association Corporate Records, 1923–1991, bulk 1938–1976. Includes radio scripts of GTA *Food for Freedom* broadcasts, 1943–1946.

760. H.P.L. (*Housewives Protective League*), **1956.** Sound recording of the *Housewives Protective League* program broadcast on July 11, 1956 on WCCO featuring Juergen Nash and Tom Swain, Executive Director of the Minnesota Statehood Centennial Commission, discussing the goals and plans for the centennial celebration, including the roles of women in the celebration.

761. History of the Minneapolis Symphony and Associated Organizations, 1956–1958. Includes material about the orchestra's radio performances.

762. *Ice Follies* **Collection, 1949–1967.** A collection of sound recordings that includes music from several Ice Follies shows and interviews with Oscar Johnson.

763. Isabel Hilgedick Reminiscences, 1964. Typescript of "Radio Forty Two Years Ago" written by the spouse of Rudy Hilgedick who was instrumental in building Duluth's first radio station, WJAP. The reminiscence is centered on the first broadcast of a Christmas midnight mass, December 25, 1922. Topics include a description of the studio, the station's range, listening devices used at the time and the use of volunteer performers and staff. Several excerpts from cards and letters received from listeners throughout the U.S. after the broadcast are also included.

764. Kingsley H. Murphy and Family Papers, 1886–1986. Includes papers relating to the Murphy family's ownership of radio stations, possibly the Murphy Broadcasting Company. Check inventory in repository for additional information.

765. League of Minnesota Poets Records, 1928–1990. A microfilm edition of earlier scrapbooks, 1928–1952, containing biographical sketches, photographs and poems of members of the League compiled in 1952. Included on the microfilm is a volume entitled "Minnesota Centennial Poetry: History with Music on Radio" consisting of scripts for a series of 13 radio programs presented in 1949.

766. "Let's Talk About Brucellosis," 1949. Script for a June 13, 1949 program written by Dr. Robert N. Barr.

767. "Life as a Third Banana." Sound recording produced by Robert C. Bruce in 1991 in which he chronicles his 50 years as an actor, writer, producer and director in radio, television and motion pictures.

768. Lydia Paulson Papers, ca. 1902–1975, bulk 1922–1975. Includes material relating to Paulson's radio career.

769. Mac Martin Advertising Agency, Client Scrapbooks, 1905–1980, bulk 1920–1960. Advertising proofs, brochures, booklets, catalogs and photographs documenting work done for more than 130 different companies headquartered mainly in Minneapolis and St. Paul, MN that were clients of this Minneapolis advertising agency. An inventory with additional information is available in the repository.

770. *March of Minnesota*: **Hibbing, 1937.** Script of a radio play broadcast in 1937 about the history of Hibbing, MN. The script appears to be incomplete.

771. Marianne Hamilton Papers, 1945, 1964–1975. Includes radio scripts and other items regarding the GI Wives Club of Minneapolis organized in 1945.

772. Minnesota Citizens Defense Corps, Director's General Correspondence and Miscellaneous Records, 1941–1945. Includes information about the group's emergency radio service.

773. Minnesota Library Association Records, 1891–1998. Includes radio scripts, 1938 and 1940, for an unidentified program/s.

774. *Minnesota Milestones,* **1958.** Sound recording and scripts, written by Charles Sarjeant, of the official Minnesota statehood centennial radio broadcasts dramatizing 100 years of Minnesota progress and the future aired on WCCO in 1958.

775. Minnesota Statehood Centennial Commission Audio Materials, 1958. Tapes of programs documenting Minnesota's Centennial celebration as recorded by WCCO, May 11, 1958.

776. Minnesota War History Committee Administrative Files, 1942–1945. Includes radio scripts for unidentified program/s.

777. Newspaper Guild of the Twin Cities Records, 1926–1982. Includes files on organizing efforts in radio and television stations WTCN and WCCO.

778. Oscar Christgau Papers, 1900–1978. Papers, including radio addresses, of temperance lecturer and Anti-Saloon League of America official Oscar Christgau.

779. Political Personalities (Assorted). The Library contains several individual collections of Minnesota political figures, many of which include some print and audio material relating to radio addresses delivered by the individuals. Check online catalog by name.

780. Radio Scrapbook, ca. 1929–ca. 1931. Scrapbook (compiler unknown) of clippings concerning Twin Cities radio stations and personalities including both network and local stations. Contains programming information for WCCO and KSTP. Annotations sometimes give information on subsequent careers of persons pictured.

781. Radio Script for Minneapolis United, 1937. Script for broadcast over KSTP on December 15, 1937 for Minneapolis United, an organization of Minneapolis businessmen, discussing the problems of businesses in Minneapolis in 1937.

782. Rae Druck Papers, 1917–1956. Includes papers and radio scripts relating to the *Child Psychology Study Circle.*

783. Rainbow Club Records, 1945–1995. Includes an audio tape of *Twin City Roundtable*, January 16, 1955, featuring the club which was established in 1947 to foster friendship and understanding among individuals of different racial, cultural and religious backgrounds.

784. *Rainy Lake Legends*, 1941–1947. Includes scripts for the CKFI, Fort Frances, Ontario program *Rainy Lake Legends* based on stories by I.W. Hinckley and other authors about the Rainy Lake region and Fort Frances, ON.

785. Robert C. Sermon Papers, 1911–1964. Includes radio scripts, 1949–1950, prepared by the City and County Public Service Union Local No. 66 giving information on Duluth municipal finances.

786. Rufus W. Hitchcock Speeches, 1935. Transcripts of Hitchcock's radio speeches on the progress and problems of the 1935 Minnesota legislative session of which he was a member from St. Louis County.

787. Ruth Easton Edelstein Papers, 1925–1935. Copies of newspaper clippings containing reviews, notices and related items documenting Edelstein's theatrical and radio career.

788. Sylvester McGovern Papers, 1918–1977. Contains correspondence, newspaper clippings, speeches, news releases and unpublished manuscripts relating to McGovern's career on KSTP as a journalist and public relations manager.

789. Thomas D. Rishworth Papers, 1847–1979. Contains correspondence, speeches, newspaper clippings, genealogical materials and audio material relating to Rishworth's career in radio education and broadcasting and as the first educational director of a commercial radio station in the U.S. Rishworth also appeared as Uncle Tom on KSTP in the 1930s and worked in radio in Texas and Oregon in the 1950s.

790. Victor J. Tedesco Papers. Contains papers relating to Tedesco's ownership and management of 12 radio stations, including KCHY, Cheyenne, WY and the Northern States Broadcasting Corporation of the Black Hills, Rapid City, SD.

791. War Production Board Scrapbook. Disassembled scrapbook of a Minneapolis metal dealer and junk yard operator who served as a special assistant in the Minneapolis regional office of the War Production Board during World War II. The scrapbook contains letters, press releases, scripts of radio spot announcements, clippings, speeches, advertisements and other material documenting publicity for a 1943 salvage campaign in Minnesota and the Dakotas known as the Farm Scrap Program.

792. William Moritz Papers, 1930–1978. Includes radio scripts, outlines and other notes for Moritz's weekly Christian program, *Good News Broadcast,* which was broadcast over KMHL, Marshall, MN during the 1950s plus information on other radio broadcasting, 1949–1956.

793. WPA Statewide Library Project Records, 1926–1944. Includes nine scripts for a promotional radio series about the library system.

794. WPA War Information Service Records, 1942–1943. Includes radio scripts.

Aaron Mintz Audio Collection
2 Bloody Brook Drive, South Deerfield, MA 01373
(413) 773-2183; ahmintz@housing.umass.edu
www-unix.oit.umass.edu/~ahmintz/index.htm

795. Audio Collection. A privately held collection available to researchers. The collection is strong in sports broadcasts from 1930s–1970s, especially baseball, basketball and football. Also disc jockey air-checks from 1955–1972, radio newscasts, interviews, documentaries and specialty shows and other programs. The entire collection can be searched online.

Mississippi Department of Archives and History
200 North Street, PO Box 571, Jackson, MS 39205
(601) 576-6850; Fax: (601) 576-6964
refdesk@mdah.state.ms.us;
www.mdah.state.ms.us/arlib/find.html

796. Boyd Family Papers. Includes script for a 1941 WJDX Memorial Day radio broadcast, "A Page from the Past," that was presented by the W. D. Holder Chapter of the United Daughters of the Confederacy.

797. Elms Papers. Includes a transcript of NBC's *Town Meeting of the Air* entitled "What Kind of Peace Must We Have?" n.d. but likely mid-1940s.

798. Eugene Octave Sykes Papers, 1885–1975. Consists of correspondence, printed materials, social papers, a scrapbook of photographs, newspaper clippings and other papers relating to his career which included his role as chairman of the Federal Radio Commission and the first chairman of the FCC.

799. Harris Dickson Collection, 1939–1942. Consists of bound volumes of scripts, both rough drafts and typescripts of actual broadcasts, for *Magnolia Sketches* broadcast over WJDX, Jackson prepared under the WPA Federal Writers' Project. The topics covered include historical sketches of towns in Mississippi, famous personalities in the state, anecdotes, stories of industry and business from early days to the time of the broadcasts and other historical material. The material was prepared and delivered by Dickson.

800. John P. Harkins Papers. Includes scripts for *Orchids to You* written by Harkins, a Jackson florist. Each script contains biographical information on a citizen of Jackson or the surrounding territory.

801. Lamar Life Insurance Company Records, 1906–1988. Contains papers relating to the company's early involvement in radio and television broadcasting in Mississippi, including the establishment of Mississippi's first network radio station, WJDX, in 1929.

802. Lindsey-Orr Family Papers, 1840–1958 and n.d. Includes freelance papers of Mary Mason Lindsey, including unidentified and undated radio advertising scripts.

803. Mississippi Broadcasters' Association Records, 1924–1975. Includes a list of the first licensed stations in Mississippi, a list of the existing AM and FM stations in Mississippi showing location, date first licensed and changes in call letters, 1924-1936, program logs of WPFB, March 17 and September 2, 1932, and WROB, October 18, 1947, and studio log and meter readings for station WRBJ, 1931.

804. Natchez Garden Club Records, 1929–1982 and n.d. The Publicity and Promotional Series includes unidentified material relating to radio broadcasts.

805. Paul Howard Pittman Collection, 1900s–1980s, bulk 1950s–1980s. Contains a variety of materials, including compositions, correspondence, military records, newsclippings, oral history transcripts, photographs, political campaign ephemera and memorabilia, printed material, public relations material, scrapbooks, slides, sound recordings, speeches, subject files and miscellany. May contain information relating to Pittman's role as president of Tylertown Broadcasting Company and general manager of WTYL AM-FM.

806. William Grant Still Papers, 1947–1965. Miscellaneous papers, consisting primarily of programs and articles written by and concerning Still, an African American composer. Includes a copy of Still's own manuscript of the song "Mississippi" composed for the *Sound Off* program and first presented on that program over the ABC network, July 26, 1948.

807. WONA Records, 1960–1969. Records for WONA, Winona, Montgomery County.

Missouri Historical Society/Missouri History Museum
PO Box 11940, St. Louis, MO 63112-0040
(314) 746-4513; Fax: (314) 746-4548
klf@mohistory.org; www.mohistory.org
Contact: Klara Foeller

808. Charles Meyerson Collection. Contains 747 recordings, mostly on reel-to-reel tape, of off-air recordings of popular radio programs. Mixed genres. Program titles and some broadcast dates and performer information is available in an in-house catalog.

809. Kensinger Jones Collection. Contains scripts, research documentation and correspondence relating to *The Land We Live In.*

810. KMOX Radio Recordings, 1939–1943. Contains 449 transcription discs featuring local St. Louis productions and CBS network feed programming, including *CBS News Analysis, Columbia Country Journal, Hedda Hopper's Hollywood, Marvels Cigarettes-Viewing the News, News of Europe, People's Platform, Goldbergs* and *World Today.*

811. Union Electric *The Land We Live In* Collection. Contains 576 transcription discs of the program that aired 1938–1952, first on KMOX and then on KSD.

Montana Historical Society
PO Box 201201, 225 North Roberts, Helena, MT 59620
(406) 444-2681
MHSLibrary@mt.gov; www.his.state.mt.us

812. Barclay Craighead Papers, 1924–1949. Includes papers relating to Craighead's association with the Great Falls Broadcasting Company.

813. Chet Huntley Interview, 1975. A tape of a one hour interview.

814. Edmund B. Craney Papers, 1916–1979. Includes correspondence, financial records, subject files, printed materials, yearbooks, clippings and legal documents relating to Craney's career as a pioneer in Montana radio broadcasting, founder of the Pacific Northwest Broadcasting and owner of the radio stations with the "XL" call letters in Spokane, Portland, Butte, Bozeman and Missoula and the Z Bar network.

815. *Land of the Shining Mountains.* Scripts for a radio series possibly sponsored by the Missoula Woman's Club in the late 1950s.

816. Myrna Loy Papers, 1903–1978. Consists of personal items and some photographs.

817. Perry S. Melton Papers 1935–1987. Covers Melton's career as a union leader and includes some material about his role as a radio commentator for the union in North Carolina.

Mount Holyoke College
8 Dwight Hall, 50 College St, South Hadley, MA 01075
(413) 538-3079; Fax: (413) 538-3029
archives@mtholyoke.edu
www.mtholyoke.edu/lits/library/arch/index.shtml

818. Edward R. and Janet Brewster Murrow Papers. Correspondence, published and unpublished writings, subject files, financial and legal records, biographical material, memorabilia and Brewster and Murrow family papers and photographs chiefly dating from 1929–1965. Of particular note are letters written by and to the Murrows while they were in Great Britain during World War II which reflect his work as director of European broadcasting for CBS, Inc. and her duties as executive director of the London Committee of Bundles for Britain, Inc.

Museum of Broadcast Communications
400 North State Street, Suite 240, Chicago, IL 60610
(Relocating in 2006 to State Street & Kinzie)
(312) 245-8200; Fax: (312) 245-8207
archives@museum.tv; Contact: Madeline Mancini
www.museum.tv

819. Audio Collection. The Museum has a collection of 85,000 hours of television and radio programming, including 4,000 radio programs. The web site maintains an online searchable database and the staff of the Museum's archives also responds to research requests. Note: The Museum is closed to the public until Summer, 2006 although the research staff can respond to requests.

Museum of Fine Arts, Houston
Hirsch Library
1001 Bissonnet Street, Houston, TX 77265
(713) 639-733
archives@mfah.org; www.mfah.org/library

820. James H. Chillman, Jr. Correspondence and Miscellaneous Subjects, 1924–1970. Includes correspondence documenting Chillman's active role in the Museum's weekly radio programs and public service radio spot announcements regarding museum events.

821. James H. Chillman, Jr. Radio Spot Announcements and Programs, 1938–1950. Contains scripts for spot announcements and programs broadcast on KTRH, KPRC and KTHT, 1938–1947. The announcements provided information about the Museum and its collection, new acquisitions, exhibitions, demonstrations, films, gallery talks, concerts and the Museum's hours. Scripts are included for the following programs: *Look and Listen*, 1939–1944, *Art and Music*, 1944, *Art is Fun*, 1943–1950, and *Art Techniques*, 1943–1944. Note: Some scripts are undated or approximately dated. An unpublished finding aid is available in the repository.

Museum of Television & Radio

25 West 52nd Street, New York, NY 10019, (212) 621-6600
465 N. Beverly Dr, Beverly Hills, CA 90210, (310) 786-1000
www.mtr.org

822. Audio Collection. The Museum maintains a large audio collection of radio programs that can be listened to on site. Program holdings cannot be searched online but the research staff will respond to individual queries. The New York City location maintains the main archive. If a program is not available in the Beverly Hills site, a researcher can request that it be dubbed in New York and sent to California. See the Addendum for an additional collection dealing with broadcasts of boxing matches.

Museum of the City of New York

1220 Fifth Avenue, New York, NY 10029
(212) 534-1672; Fax: (212) 534-5974
research@mcny.org; www.mcny.org
Contact: Eileen Morales

823. "Look Magazine" Photographs, 1941–1958. Includes photographs of radio programs and personalities. Contact the Museum for information about specific programs or people included in the collection.

824. Personality Files, ca. 1800–1986, bulk 1900–1986. An extensive collection containing a diverse range of material about thousands of theatrical and musical personalities who appeared in New York City during the 18th– 20th centuries. Collection covers both important and many lesser known personalities and includes personal correspondence, portrait engravings or lithographs, photographs, biographical data, clippings, articles, programs, playbills, original sheet music and sheet music covers. Also includes drawings, playscripts, scrapbooks, fan letters, manuscripts of biographies, sketches, texts of speeches and personal items. Check with Museum for specific personalities included in the collection.

825. Yiddish Theater Collection, ca. 1900–1986. Includes some internal records of WEVD.

National Archives and Records Administration

700 Pennsylvania Avenue, NW, Washington, DC 20408
(866) 272-6272; www.archives.gov

General comments: The National Archives and Records Administration (NARA) is the repository for the permanently valuable records of the United States Federal Government as well as Presidential papers and commercially produced materials of historic significance. Materials are located in Washington, DC and at satellite locations around the United States.

For information about collections in the Presidential Libraries check www.archives.gov/presidential-libraries/index.html.

For information about commercial recordings, including radio programs, see below.

Motion Picture, Sound, and Video Unit
Special Media Archives Services Division
8601 Adelphi Road, College Park, MD 20740
(301) 837-3540 (General); Fax: (301) 837-3620
(301) 837-1649 (Ask a Librarian)
mopix@nara.gov; www.archives.gov/facilities/md/archives_2.html

Approximately 40%–50% of the sound collection is listed in the automated online database (ARC). For a more comprehensive search of the holdings relating to the Golden Age of Radio, the following in-house resources should be checked. Researchers unable to check the card catalogs in person can request a librarian at the archive to search for a specific program. See phone number above.

826. Main Sound Catalog. Briefly describes both government and privately produced sound recordings from a variety of sources, including radio broadcasts, speeches, interviews, documentaries, oral history and public information programs. The earliest recording is from 1896 but most recordings fall in the 1935–present time span. Titles are described numerically and by personal name reference.

827. Milo Ryan Phonoarchive Collection Catalog. Describes 5,000 recordings, primarily of CBS-KIRO broadcasts, 1931–1977, which were originally maintained at the University of Washington. The collection consists of news and public affairs programs, actualities, speeches, interviews, wartime dramas and daily World War II news programs. Two finding aids are available: History in Sound: A Descriptive Listing of KIRO-CBS Collection of Broadcasts of the World War II Years (1963) and History in Sound: Part II (1972). Catalog cards contain brief content summaries and are more detailed than the published guides. Most entries are available on reel-to-reel reference tapes.

828. ABC Radio Collection Catalog. Describes 27,000 broadcasts of news and public affairs programs, 1943–1971. The catalog is arranged chronologically by date of broadcast and thereunder by program series, title, keyword or personal name reference.

National Baseball Hall of Fame

Library, 25 Main Street, Cooperstown, NY 13326
(607) 547-0330; Fax: (607) 547-4094
http://abner.baseballhalloffame.org/search/

829. Audio Collection. Includes broadcasts of World Series and All Star games, primarily from 1930s and 1940s with some 1950s and some general games from the 1960s. Also has radio interviews with players and radio re-enactments.

830. "Baseless Fears: Professional Baseball's Wary Relationship With Radio, 1921–1934." A Ph.D. thesis by Lowell D. Smith, University of Nebraska, Lincoln, NE, 1955.

831. Broadcaster Files. The Photo and Player Files include material relating to the baseball career and personal lives of many players who became broadcasters after retiring from the game. For more information check the online catalog.

832. Clipping File. Includes biographical information on announcers.

833. Commercial Schedule, Yankee Baseball, 1959. An inning-by-inning script of sponsored advertisements for broadcast during Yankee games. (Camel cigarettes and Ballantine beer.)

The National Broadcasters Hall of Fame

2201 Marconi Road, Wall, NJ 07719
(732) 280-3000; Contact: Fred Carl
nbhf@infoage.org; www.infoage.org/NBHF.htm

834. Archive. Includes artifacts, exhibits, displays, recordings, film and memorabilia on radio and biographical material on the radio personalities inducted into the Hall of Fame.

National Cowboy & Western Heritage Museum
Donald C. and Elizabeth M. Dickinson Research Center
1700 NE 63rd Street, Oklahoma City, OK 73111
(405) 478-2250
www.nationalcowboymuseum.org

835. John Rao Jr. Western Entertainers Collection, 1900–1972. Contains sound recordings and other print materials and memorabilia of western cowboys, including Gene Autry, Smiley Burnette, Jimmie Rodgers, Eddie Dean, Roy Rogers, Tom Mix, Allan "Rocky" Lane, Fuzzy Knight, Tex Ritter and others.

836. *The World is Yours.* Undated scripts for the program broadcast on NBC.

National Public Broadcasting Archives
(See University of Maryland)

National Shrine of the Little Flower Catholic Church
2123 Roseland Avenue, Royal Oak, MI 48073
(248) 541-4122; Contact: Jack Hoolehan
jhoolehan@shrinechurch.com; www.shrinechurch.com

837. Father Charles Coughlin Collection. Contains bound and unbound transcripts of radio sermons, mostly from the 1930s, some sound recordings, personal papers, correspondence, issues of "Social Justice" and other papers by and about Coughlin.

Nebraska Historical Society
PO Box 82554, 1500 R Street, Lincoln, NE 68501
(402) 471-4751; lanshs@nebraskahistory.org
www.nebraskahistory.org/databases/nhprc/index.shtml

838. Al Bates/KFAB, Omaha, NE Radio Collection. Includes Bates's log book, 1925–1927, various KFAB publications, photographs and an operations scrapbook, 1946–1954. Bates was an engineer with the station.

839. Barney (Arthur Barney) Oldfield Papers. Oldfield hosted a program on KFOR, Lincoln, NE in the late 1930s. Papers relate to his career in print and broadcast journalism and document his later involvement with the Radio-Television News Directors Association and the Radio-Television News Directors Foundation.

840. Camp Fire, ca.1910–ca.1994 and n.d., bulk 1950s–1980s. Collection relates to the activities, membership and administration of the Lincoln, NE chapter of the youth group Camp Fire (formerly known as Camp Fire Girls) and includes photographs, scrapbooks, moving images and approximately 40 sound recordings. Check with repository for more information about radio related material in the collection.

841. George Kister Papers, 1900–. Includes scrapbooks, correspondence, clippings and station programs for KMMJ, Clay Center and Grand Island, NE covering Kister's 41 years at the station as Program Director, Farm Director and Public Service Director.

842. George Nate Bragg Papers, 1897–1975. Includes correspondence, broadcasting materials, certificates, newsletters and a photograph documenting Bragg's activities as an operator of an amateur radio station in Blue Springs, Liberty, Peru and Trenton, NE and in Concordia, KS.

843. Karl Stefan Papers, 1884–1951. Papers include radio talks and programs during Stefan's congressional career, 1935–1951. Stefan helped build WJAG, the station of the Norfolk, NE "Daily News." He was chief announcer and newscaster of WJAG, 1922–1934, when he was elected to Congress.

844. KFMQ Radio Lincoln, NE Papers, 1951–1969. Papers, photographs and 69 sound recordings relating to KFMQ-FM, Lincoln, NE. Much of the collection contains information about Herbert William Burton who owned and operated the station from 1958–1966.

845. Louis Francis Leuck, ca. 1897–1953. Consists of a scrapbook, 1918–1943, relating to Leuck's career as a radio operator and electrical engineer in Lincoln, NE.

846. Nebraska Radio Collection. Correspondence, news items, pamphlets, sound recordings and recollections relating to Nebraska radio stations, programs, broadcasting, personalities, etc.

847. Radio Related Photographs, 1930s–1940. Collection of approximately 125 photographs, many of which show radio characters from the 1930s in costumes depicting their radio personas. There are also interior shots of the radio stations showing studios equipped with grand pianos and showing the sound effects man with various instruments to create sound effects. Also included are photographs of broadcasting equipment and station transmitters. Photos may include WOW, Omaha and KOIL, Lincoln, NE.

848. Richard Jerome Tanner Papers, 1902–1943, bulk 1920s–1930s. Contains correspondence, printed materials, manuscripts, records and scrapbooks relating to frontier life, including information about well known figures and events. Also includes some manuscripts used in radio shows at KMMJ, Norfolk, NE, 1934–1935.

849. Robert Beecher Howell Papers, 1923–1933. Contains correspondence, legislative bill files, committee files and appointment and subject files relating to Howell's service in the U.S. Senate. Topics include agriculture, farm relief, public utilities, public power and radio broadcasting.

850. Robert R. Jensen Papers, 1920–1979, bulk mostly 1933–1936. Contains papers and photographs relating to Nebraska stations KFAB and KOLN in Lincoln for which Jensen worked and also KFOR.

851. Roland A. Anderson Papers, 1920–1951, mostly 1920s. Contains papers, photographs and sound recordings related to the Anderson Radio Station of Wahoo, NE. The station was one of the first broadcast stations in the U.S. and the first radio sending station in the Midwest. Collection, which includes photographs and nine sound recordings, relates to Anderson's broadcasts and the history of radio. May also include material about Eddie Killan's Harmony Five.

852. Roman L. (Lee) Hruska Papers. Papers of a former U.S. Senator and Congressman. Included in the audio recordings are radio programs on which Hruska appeared, including *Capitol Cloakroom* and *The Leading Question.*

853. *Tribute to Nebraska* **Radio Program.** Contains materials relating to the General Motors's show, *The Parade of the States: A Tribute to Nebraska*, broadcast on April 25, 1932 over the NBC network.

854. Women's Christian Temperance Union (NE), 1889–1957, 1969, bulk 1889–1939. In addition to papers relating to the group's history, the collection includes five audio discs of *Americans to the Rescue*, a national Women's Christian Temperance Union radio program.

New England Conservatory of Music
Spaudling Library
290 Huntington Avenue, Boston, MA 02115
(617) 585-1250; Contact: Jean Morrow
jmorrow@newenglandconservatory.edu
www.newenglandconservatory.edu/libraries/index.html

855. New England Conservatory of Music Concerts. Sound recordings of concerts from the early 1950s broadcast on WGBH.

856. *Vaughn Monroe Show* Collection. Contains sound recordings for a complete run of the program, 1940–1952, and scrapbooks. Note: The program was also known as. *The Camel Caravan.*

857. *Voice of Firestone* Collection. Audio recordings (78rpm and cassettes) of some *Voice of Firestone* specials and kinescopes of the 1949–1964 programs (with a gap from 1961–1964) which were simulcast on radio and television. Also includes some transcription discs of speeches of Harvey Firestone from late 1920s–1930s talking about political issues. Note: Library does not have equipment for playing back or transferring the kinescopes.

New Jersey Historical Society
52 Park Place, Newark, NJ 07102
(973) 596-8500, ext. 249; Fax; (973) 596-6957
library@jerseyhistory.org
www.jerseyhistory.org/archivesmain.html

858. Mandolin Club of Newark Records, 1932–1972. Includes correspondence, newspaper clippings, photographs, concert programs, 1945–1966, and other memorabilia of the Mandolin Club of Newark. The group performed on WOR-AM, 1932–1933, and later on WGCP. Much of material is in German.

New Mexico State University
Library, Rio Grande Historical Collections
PO Box 30006, Las Cruces, NM 88003
(505) 646-3839; Fax: (505) 646-7477
archives@lib.nmsu.edu;   http://archives.nmsu.edu

859. Ralph Willis Goddard Papers, 1893–1968, bulk 1904–1929. Personal and professional papers of Goddard who was the Dean of Engineering at the New Mexico College of Agriculture and Mechanic Arts. Goddard was the founder of KOB.

New York City Municipal Archives
Dept. of Records and Information Services
31 Chambers Street, Room 103, New York, NY 10007
(212) 639-9675; Contact: Leonora Gidlund, Director
www.nyc.gov/html/records/html/about/archives.shtml

General comments: For additional WNYC material, see also separate repository listing for WNYC.

860. History of WNYC Records, 1933–1942, bulk 1939–1940. Includes manuscripts, notes, programs, schedules, correspondence and reports. The records document efforts to assemble information needed for a history of the station and a critique of its programming as part of the Federal Writers' Project. There is no evidence that the draft manuscript was ever published.

861. "New York Learns" Records, 1939–1942, bulk 1939. Includes a discussion on the use of media, such as radio and motion pictures, in education.

862. WNYC Collection of Broadcast Recordings, 1938–1970. More than 20,000 tapes of programs representing the full range of programming offered at the station over the years. The most complete holdings are programs dealing with local historical and political events. A finding aid is available in the repository. Note: Materials pertaining to Fiorello LaGuardia are cataloged separately.

863. WNYC Phonograph Records, 1939–1967. Consists of approximately 14,000 phonograph records of broadcasts, including event reports, interviews and speeches with mayors, city officials and other dignitaries as well as programs of drama and music. Note: Some records have been transferred to magnetic tape and are housed at the Rodgers and Hammerstein Archives in the New York City Public Library for the Performing Arts.

864. WNYC Speeches, 1930–1937. Transcripts of radio speeches given over WNYC pertaining to the history and government of the City of New York starting on January 13, 1930 through June 24, 1937.

865. WNYC Subject Files, Phonodisks, Awards, Scrapbooks, 1935–1981. Contains several types of records documenting the activities of WNYC, including administrative files, 1948–1981, public relations files, 1967–1983, publications, 1938–1984, awards and plaques, 1949–1979, LaGuardia broadcasts, 1944–1945, and six phonodisks and scrapbooks, 1926–1971.

New York Historical Society
170 Central Park West, New York, NY 10024
(212) 873-3400; Fax: (212) 875-1591
www.nyhistory.org/collections.html

866. The Radio Entertainers and Announcers Collection, 1937–1945, bulk 1942–1943. Photographs depicting popular radio performers during World War II, often engaged in war conservation efforts. Approximately 1,500 photographs. ABC, CBS, MBS, NBC, WOR and WEVD are among the networks and stations represented. Also includes a series of photographs showing radio employees picking up short wave communications at the "listening posts," which were then transmitted to the News Room. Overall, this collection documents the impact not only of radio on troop morale but also of the war itself on home front entertainment. A complete list of entertainers is available in the Department of Prints, Photographs, and Architectural Collections.

New York Philharmonic
Avery Fisher Hall
10 Lincoln Center Plaza, New York, NY 10023
(212) 875-5900; Fax: (212) 875-5717
www.newyorkphilharmonic.org; Contact: Barbara Haws

867. Broadcasting and Recording Records, 1930s–Present. Includes audio recordings and scripts for New York Philharmonic radio programs, 1940s–ca. 1980, letters from listeners, 1951–1956, program notes, press releases and other papers relating to fund raising, radio membership and the radio programs.

New York Public Library

General comments: The radio related special collections in the New York Public Library are located in four distinct divisions of the Library and at three separate sites. The four divisions are listed below in alphabetical order.

1. Humanities & Social Sciences Library for collections of people, organizations or events generally *not* associated with the performing arts.

2. Performing Arts Library, Billy Rose Theatre Collection for print materials.

3. Performing Arts Library, Rodgers and Hammerstein Archives of Recorded Sound for sound recordings.

4. Schomburg Center for Research in Black Culture for collections relating to African American personalities and/or themes.

Humanities & Social Sciences Library
Room 328, Manuscripts and Archives Division
Fifth Avenue and 42nd Street, New York, NY 10018
(212) 930-0801; Fax: (212) 302-4815
mssref@nypl.org; Contact: Ben Alexander
www.nypl.org/research/chss/spe/rbk/mss.html

868. American Association for Adult Education Records, 1939–1940. Records focus on a survey concerning radio listeners who used radio for educational purposes. The results were used to promote better education by radio. The *America's Town Meeting of the Air* program took part in the survey.

869. Bryan Hannon Papers, 1932–1961. Includes a script, "The Trolley Bible of the Broadway Line," 1944.

870. Cathrine Curtis Papers, ca. 1930–ca. 1955. Consists of correspondence, memoranda, reports, speeches, radio talks, press releases and other papers of Cathrine Curtis who was a radio commentator during the 1930s.

871. Clark M. Eichelberger Papers, 1920–1991. Consists of personal papers and sound recordings of his radio broadcasts about the United Nations.

872. Dorothy Schiff Papers, 1904–1989, bulk 1950s–1970s. Contains papers related to the "New York Post's" ownership of several radio stations in New York City, Los Angeles and San Francisco, including WLIB, WMCA, WLAC and WKYA.

873. Earle McGill Papers, 1935–1947. Consists of correspondence relating to radio programs during McGill's career as a producer and director for CBS.

874. Florence Nightingale Levy Papers, 1890–1947. Consists of correspondence, manuscripts of Levy's lectures, radio scripts, magazine articles and other writings.

875. Jane Cowl Papers, 1907–1949, bulk 1927–1945. Consists of correspondence, financial papers, diary and biographi-

cal materials collected by Cowl who hosted a radio program in the 1940s.

876. *Jewish Book Week* **Radio Broadcast, 1939.** Transcript of the May 10, 1939 program broadcast on WBZ.

877. Mark Hawley Papers, 1935–1940. A news announcer for MBS, the collection contains Hawley's fan mail consisting of complimentary letters and suggestions and corrections of errors in pronunciation. Also includes comments on current events, products advertised and other matters.

878. National Advisory Council on Radio in Education Records, 1929–1941. Consists of correspondence, memoranda, reports, minutes and printed matter. Materials include general correspondence with members of NACRE, organizations and corporations, applications for membership and approvals and correspondence with radio stations throughout the U.S.

879. *The New World*, **1956.** A series of ten programs about the peacetime uses of atomic energy, produced by WUOA with the cooperation of the Oak Ridge Institute of Nuclear Studies.

880. New York World's Fair 1939–1940 Records, 1935–1945, bulk 1939–1940. Includes radio programs about the Fair.

881. Randall B. Smith Collection of Spanish Civil War Materials. Consists of materials relating to the Spanish Civil War and the Veterans of the Abraham Lincoln Brigade, including 73 audiotapes, ca. 1975–1985, some of which include radio programs.

882. Town Hall, Inc. Records, 1895–1955, bulk 1940–1955. Contains records of *America's Town Meeting of the Air*, 1935–1956, including general correspondence, letters from listeners, office memoranda, audience mail reports, speakers aid materials, correspondence of the director of radio and television operations, publicity materials, photographs and newsclippings.

883. Walter Damrosch Presentation Volume, 1928. Contains transcripts of letters of appreciation and sketches sent to Damrosch by high school students in Des Moines, IA regarding his radio programs.

884. *Western Business Round-Up*, **1958–1966.** Selected transcripts, lists of each season's programs and lists of participating panelists.

885. Yankee Baseball Collection, 1913–1950. Includes papers dealing with broadcasting negotiations.

Performing Arts Library, Billy Rose Theatre Collection
40 Lincoln Center Plaza, New York, NY 10023
(212) 870-1639; Fax: (212) 870-1868
theatrediv@nypl.org; Contact: Robert Taylor
www.nypl.org/research/lpa/the/the.html

General comments: Only a small portion of the Billy Rose holdings can be searched online. However, additional finding aids are available in the library. For out-of-town researchers, the library will respond to queries by phone, email or regular mail asking what material may be available on specific individuals or programs. As of 2005, the library also has many additional unprocessed collections. The library also has special collections that include information about many actors who appeared on stage and film and who may also have appeared on radio.

Card Catalog. In addition to the special collections, the library maintains an extensive card catalog documenting the library's other radio related holdings, including books and ephemera.

886. Abe Burrows Papers, 1904–1993. Contains personal and professional papers, correspondence, production files, radio scripts, autobiographical writings, interviews, speeches, articles, songs, business files, clippings, photographs and other visual materials. Includes bound and unbound scripts for *Duffy's Tavern*, 1941–1945, *Hollywood and Company,* 1946, *The Ford Show,* 1946, *Abe Burrows Show,* 1947, *Breakfast with Burrows,* 1949, *We Take Your Word,* 1950–1951, *The Bing Crosby Show*, 1949, and other scripts. Also includes an article by Burrows about Ed Gardner, correspondence, contracts and other documents relating to productions he was involved in, photographs and some records of his radio appearances. Note: Sound recordings of his programs are listed separately in the Rodgers and Hammerstein Archives of Recorded Sound section listed below.

887. Anne Nichols Papers, 1873–1965. Contains correspondence, some personal papers and photographs and writings documenting a portion of Nichols's career. The materials are mostly about the play *Abie's Irish Rose* and its various productions as well as its film and radio versions.

888. Beatrice Lillie Papers, 1911–1995. Consists of correspondence, scripts, personal and business papers, photographs and scrapbooks. The only radio related material appears to be a script for an undated appearance on *Radio Round Up*. Note: There are two Beatrice Lillie Collections.

889. Bert Bertram Scrapbooks, 1915–1984. The scrapbooks contain photographs and clippings documenting his acting career. Bertram created and directed a radio acting company, Theater of the Air. During World War II he produced, directed and played a leading role in "Civilians in Action," a radio play in Augusta, GA and managed and played in USO companies in Europe. In 1950 he was in France as a correspondent for New England radio stations.

Billie Burke Papers. *See Flo Ziegfeld-Billie Burke Papers.*

890. Billy Rose (William Samuel Rosenberg) Collection, 1932–1964. Includes correspondence, contracts, photographs and other papers.

891. Brooks Atkinson Papers. Includes a folder of correspondence relating to *Breakfast With Dorothy and Dick*, 1958.

892. Charles Pierce Papers, 1954–1998. Includes letters, 1992–1994, from Bob Mowers ("Uncle Bob") to Pierce. Mowers was the radio announcer who worked with Pierce in Watertown in the 1940s on WWNY. The letters include many reminiscences of Mowers's radio days and of recordings from his collection of 78rpms.

893. Cheryl Crawford Papers, 1920–1986. Contains correspondence, production files, scripts, photographs, ephemera, ledgers, financial materials and scrapbooks documenting her career as a producer and director, including one undated

folder marked "Radio Interests."

894. Clifford Odets Papers, 1926–1963. Contains diaries, scripts, screenplays, personal and professional notes, research materials, clippings, photographs and scrapbooks. Radio related material includes a script for "Waiting For Lefty" adapted by Victor E. Smith, 1938, Odets's acting script for a radio show entitled "At The Water Line," 1926, and a pamphlet Odets used for research for the program *American Justice and the Negro*, 1949.

895. Daily Paskman Papers, 1904–1939. Contains correspondence, professional and personal papers, WGBS materials, publicity materials, ephemera, synopses, scripts and one scrapbook. Contains extensive information about the beginnings of WGBS and *The Radio Minstrels,* including invitations, program notes, lists of guests and participants, drafts of scripts, applause cards and proof of reception cards. Also includes royalty statements and correspondence documenting many of the songs Paskman co-wrote.

896. Dorothy Kilgallen Papers and Scrapbooks, 1930–1965. Consists of personal papers, photographs and scrapbooks documenting her versatile career as newswoman, actress, TV personality, radio hostess, wife and mother from 1930 to her death in 1965.

897. Edith Meiser Papers, 1902–1985. Bulk of collection consists of radio scripts written by Meiser, including complete runs for *Island Boat Club,* 1932, *Judge Priest,* n.d., *The New Penny,* 1935–1936, and *Alias Edward Taylor,* 1930, as well as a large collection of scripts for other programs including, *Dr. Susan,* 1939, *The Adventures of Bill Baker,* 1937, *The Adventures of Polly Preston,* 1929–1930, *Mysteries in Paris,* 1932, *Barbara Wayne,* 1931, *Hollinger Stories,* 1941, *A Case for Mr. Fortune,* 1937–1938, *O. Henry Stories,* 1932, *Old Gold Program,* 1940, *Rudyard Kipling Stories,* 1932, *Sherlock Holmes,* 1932–1936, *Welcome Valley,* 1936–1937 and scripts for adaptations. Many of the scripts have handwritten notes and corrections. Also contains various business letters, including separate folders for *A Case for Mr. Fortune* and *Sherlock Holmes* programs, and contracts, some personal papers, photos and mementos. The collection does not include much information on her career in vaudeville, Broadway or the movies before 1930 or after the 1940s. Note: Additional Meiser scripts for *Sherlock Holmes* are located in the Sherlock Holmes Collection at the University of Minnesota.

898. Eileen Burns Papers, 1928–1994. Contains papers documenting Burns's career as a stage actress, radio performer, writer and, later on in her life, a teacher. Papers, both business and personal, include contracts, correspondence, journals, writings, photographs, calendars and ephemera.

899. Elaine Carrington Papers, 1903–1959. Bulk of collection consists of bound radio scripts for Carrington's popular daytime serials, including *Pepper Young's Family,* 1936–1959, *When a Girl Marries,* 1939–1957, and *Rosemary,* 1944–1955. Also includes bound scripts for a few short radio serials as well as her Carrington Playhouse in which she produced original plays by new playwrights and an extensive collection of her unbound scripts and stories for radio, magazines, the theater and television arranged alphabetically by title, plus personal papers, clippings, correspondence and speeches and interviews. Some material deals with her involvement with issues of radio censorship and the effect of daytime radio soap operas on national morale during World War II.

900. Elisabeth Fraser Papers, 1920–1999. The only radio related material are scripts for an interview Fraser did with Montgomery Clift in 1941 in Memphis to promote a play they were appearing in and a 1943 script from the program *Five O'Clock Follies* on WEEI, Boston concerning the play "Winged Victory" by Moss Hart.

901. Eunice Stoddard Papers, 1913–1938. Consists of correspondence, opening night messages, photographs, programs, scripts, sides and clippings from productions in which she participated. Does not appear to include any material related to her radio career.

902. Flo Ziegfeld–Billie Burke Papers, 1907–1984. Papers covers Burke's career approximately from the time when she first went on the stage in the early years of the twentieth century until her retirement and superficially covers that portion of Ziegfeld's career and life after Burke and he were married. Radio related material includes scripts for *Fashions in Rations,* 1943–1944, and scripts for guest spots, 1943–1948, on numerous programs, including *The Milton Berle Show, The Eddie Cantor Show, The Rudy Vallee Show* and others plus some unidentified scripts. See detailed list in online finding aid. Also includes clippings about *The Ziegfeld Follies of the Air,* photographs and business and financial papers.

903. Florida Friebus Papers, 1926–1988. Contains personal and professional papers, correspondence, photographs, scrapbooks and writings documenting Friebus's career. The only radio related material relates to her work on *Theatre Guild on the Air,* 1951.

904. Francis Wilson Papers, 1875–1958. Includes typescript of suggested speeches, not verbatim quotes, for *The Eveready Hour,* September 28, 1926.

905. Georgia Johnstone Papers Regarding Agnes Moorehead, 1930–1974. Primarily correspondence between Moorehead and her personal secretary, Georgia Johnstone. Also includes their correspondence with third parties relating to Moorehead's career, two speeches by Moorehead and text material she used or considered using. Also contains press releases rich in biographical information and clippings and scrapbooks about Moorehead.

906. Gypsy Rose Lee Papers, 1910–1970. The only radio related material falling within the time frame of this volume includes five partial scripts from an unidentified program and/or possibly USO shows, one with ventriloquist Edgar Bergen, and a 1946 photograph of Lee with radio host Frederic Babcock on the program *Game of Books* broadcast on WGN, Chicago.

907. Hallie Flanagan Papers. Contains papers from the production files of the Radio Division of the Federal Theatre Project, 1935–1939, and information about the radio campaigns to keep the project alive, 1938–1940.

908. Harriet Lundgaard Papers, 1923–1958. Consists primarily of scripts from *The Ted Malone Show* (a.k.a. *Between the Bookends* and *A Broadcast*), 1946–1948, 1951–1958, as well as correspondence relating to both Lundgaard and Malone and some personal correspondence.

909. Helen Gates Struble Theater Ephemera, 1922–1963. Includes publicity photographs of radio news events, 1933, 1941, and n.d.

910. Ilka Chase Papers, 1850–1977, bulk 1916–1977. Consists of correspondence, photographs, newspaper clippings, scripts, scrapbooks and other material related to Chase's career. Includes the entire run of scripts from an unnamed radio program hosted by Chase, January, 1951–October, 1951.

911. J. Edward Bromberg Papers, 1924–1951. Contains business papers, scripts, playbills, programs, correspondence and clippings relating to his work as an actor and director. Includes a transcribed radio interview Bromberg gave in 1947 on *Personality Time,* 1947.

912. Jack Pearl Papers, 1899–1973. Consists of correspondence, contracts, scripts, programs and photographs, primarily of his professional life and career.

913. James Elson Papers, 1950–1970. Contains correspondence, production materials and scripts relating to Elson's career as a director and producer of theater, radio and television. Collection does not appear to include any radio related material.

914. Jennie Moscowitz Papers, 1907–1943. The papers, though sketchy, document Moscowitz's life and career as an actress of the stage and radio. Contains some radio scripts, including one of a sketch with Al Jolson.

915. Julia Sanderson Papers, 1913–1935. Consists of scrapbooks documenting Sanderson's career in musical comedy, 1913–1928, and some correspondence. The scrapbooks also include information about her husband Frank Crumit's career. Does not appear to contain any information about the couple's radio career from 1930s–1943.

916. Lawrence (Jerome) and Lee (Robert E.) Papers, 1917–1970. Contains correspondence, scripts, drafts of scripts and rewrites, production files, production notes, programs, clippings and personal papers that document their careers from 1942–1966. Contains correspondence and bound volumes of scripts for *Flash-Back,* 1940–1942 and *Gulf Screen Guild Theatre,* 1940, an extensive file relating to Armed Forces Radio Service, 1942–1945, photographs of broadcasts and correspondence between Lawrence and Lee regarding guidelines, budgets, ideas for programming and program lists. Also includes scripts written, directed or adapted by Lawrence and Lee for *Hallmark Playhouse,* 1950–1953, *The Railroad Hour,* 1948–1954, *Request Performance,* 1945–1946, *The World We're Fighting For,* 1943, and *Young Love,* 1949–1950. Also scripts and other papers relating to *Adventure in Good Radio,* 1944, *Halls of Ivy,* 1950–1951, *Mr. & Mrs. Blandings,* 1950, *No Laughing Matter,* 1950, *Presenting Charles Boyer,* n.d., and single scripts for other programs, including *Suspense, The Saint, Escape,* and others. Also includes scrapbooks, financial papers and scripts by others, some for consideration for radio. See separate listing below for the Lawrence & Lee (Sound Recordings) Collection, 1939–1966, in the Rodgers and Hammerstein Archives of Recorded Sound.

917. Lillian Gish Papers, 1909–1992. Includes publicity book with outline of program concept and scripts for the *Famous Sisters of History,* n.d. and an undated script for a Red Cross radio broadcast.

918. Lucille Kallen Papers, 1938–1999. Contains correspondence, personal papers, financial papers, scripts, book drafts, publication materials, clippings, scrapbooks and some photographs concerning her professional life as a writer of radio, theater, television and novels. Radio related materials, 1945–1976, include scripts and related papers for *Those Halliday Girls*, 1945, an audition script for *The Helen Hayes Show*, 1946, *Talent Unlimited*, 1946, co-written with Sylvia Page, *Buckingham Theatre*, 1946, *Wherefor Art Thou Romeo?*, 1946, and several unproduced scripts and undated and untitled material.

919. Mark Linder Papers, 1933–1950. Includes script Linder wrote for *American Presidents On Parade*, 1938.

920. Maurice Evans Papers, 1934–1970. Contains correspondence, financial records, scrapbooks and scripts primarily documenting his American career as an actor and producer. Includes a script for a radio adaptation of "The Browning Version," 1949, and some 1934 production notes for an unidentified radio program.

921. Montgomery Clift Papers, 1933–1966. Contains correspondence, writings, scripts, scrapbooks and clippings. The only radio related material is an annotated script for "The Glass Menagerie." Note: The Elisabeth Fraser Collection (see above) includes the script for a radio interview Clift did with Fraser in 1941 during the national tour of the play "There Shall Be No Night."

922. Nila Mack Papers, 1910–1953. Contains personal and professional correspondence, papers, press releases for *Let's Pretend*, clippings, scrapbooks, radio programming lists, 1930–1949, which list the scripts used on radio programs, a five page obituary, a handwritten play entitled "Western Farmer and Hero Tramp," scripts for the National Advisory Council on Radio in Education concerning vocational guidance, 1932, and *The Adventures of Helen and Mary*, 1930.

923. Olive Reeves-Smith Papers, 1879–1964. Consists of personal papers, writings, correspondence, contracts, photographs, programs, clippings, scrapbooks and sheet music. Does not appear to include any material related to her radio career.

924. Parker Fennelly Papers, 1915–1980. Consists of clippings, correspondence, photographs, programs and scripts documenting his career as an actor of stage, screen, television and radio.

925. Paul Lovett Papers, 1943–1967. Contains scripts Lovett wrote, mostly from the period of World War II, including a script from his Army radio show, *Let's Linger*, an undated typescript in various versions for a radio show that was a tribute to President Franklin Delano Roosevelt after his death and a script for "The Sabbath Candle" set in a displaced persons camp after World War II.

926. Paul Muni Papers, ca. 1920–1967. Consists of correspondence, photographs, clippings, scrapbooks, personal papers and writings documenting his career as an actor of stage and screen. Does not appear to contain any radio related material except for an undated radio speech he wrote and gave for Hadassah.

927. Phyllis Merrill Papers, 1932–1956. Contains materials from her writing career at the J. Walter Thompson Co. and includes memos, correspondence, notes, press and other promotional materials for radio programs, writings and scripts. Includes scripts for *The Charlie McCarthy Show (Chase and Sanborn)*, 1947, *Ford Sunday Evening Hour* (and precursor, *Stars of the Future*), 1944–1950, *Lux Video Theatre*, 1940–1951, *NBC University of the Air*, 1944–1948, *Old Gold Show*, 1943–1944, *Alec Templeton Time (Chase and Sanborn)*, 1946–1947, *Owens Glass*, 1943–1944, *Robert Shaw Chorale*, 1948, *Textron Theater*, 1945–1946, and miscellaneous scripts, 1932–1955. Other programs covered in the collection include religious radio programs, *The Dreft Star Playhouse* and commercials for RCA Victor.

928. Radio Writers Guild Records, 1930–1958. Consists of correspondence, contracts and minutes, 1930–1958. Material is limited to the Guild as a national organization and to the activities of the Eastern Region. While there are some contracts between the Western Region and local radio stations, there is little correspondence for the Western Region and almost none for the Mid Region.

929. Robert Benchley Papers, 1920–1956. Consists of correspondence, photographs, clippings, scrapbooks, programs and reviews relating to the careers of both Benchley and his son Nathaniel.

930. Robert Benney Research Materials, 1926–1978, bulk 1926–1947. Includes photographs, clippings, posters, playbills and ephemera relating to his career as an illustrator of the stars of stage and screen. Also includes photographs and clippings of some radio personalities. (See online finding aid for a list.) Also includes information about radio stations WNBC, WEAF and WJZ.

931. Ruth and Augustus Goetz Papers, 1900–1996. Includes correspondence, agreements and royalty statements, 1950–1992. Includes material relating to the radio adaptation of "The Heiress."

932. *Second Mrs. Burton* Scripts, 1952–1960. Scripts consist of daily episodes of the soap opera written by Hector Chevigny.

933. Suzanne Caubaye Papers, 1919–1979. Includes a scrapbook containing clippings, programs and photographs documenting Caubaye's stage career. Although Caubaye appeared on several radio shows, including *The Fat Man, Fred Allen,* and *Ma Perkins,* it is not clear if any of the scrapbook material covers her radio work.

934. USO Camp Shows Publicity Records, 1941–1955. Includes photographs of the *Radio Roundup* troupe.

935. Vincent J. Donehue Papers, 1946–1965. Papers document the director's professional career bringing plays to the stage and the television screen in the 1950s and early 1960s and does not appear to contain any information related to his earlier radio career. See also separate Vincent J. Donehue Correspondence and Ephemera Collection, 1930–1973, and Vincent J. Donehue Designs Collection, 1950–1963.

936. Vladimir Selinsky Scripts, 1941–1975. Contains annotated scripts for broadcasts for which he composed and conducted music, including *CBS Textron Theatre, The Electric Theatre, Helen Hayes Theatre, Kaiser Aluminum Hour* and *Down in the Valley,* some audition scripts, annotated scripts for *The Jeffersonian Heritage,* 1953, and *People Under Communism,* n.d., sponsored by the National Association of Educational Broadcasters and some *Voice of America* programs. Also includes material related to his work in television.

937. Walter Abel Papers, 1900–1976. Consists primarily of correspondence, contracts, speeches and clippings documenting his work as an actor and includes some correspondence and clippings relating to his radio career.

938. Walter Winchell Papers, 1920–1967. Contains correspondence, annotated radio scripts, 1930–1959, miscellaneous scripts for stage and film, thematic news articles, scrapbooks and clippings. The largest portion of the collection are the radio scripts, including annotated typewritten copies of his broadcasts, 1930–1959. Because of their fragile condition, these scripts are available only on microfilm. The most numerous letters and clippings in the collection are in the Billy Rose folders which contain significant information about Rose as well as about his relationship with Winchell.

939. Worthington Miner–*Studio One* Production Files, 1948–1955. Includes the shooting script for the *Studio One* production of "Beyond Reason" adapted from the radio script of the same name by Devery Freeman.

940. WPA Radio Scripts, 1936–1940. Contains final drafts of radio plays and other texts produced by the *Federal Theatre of the Air.* Most scripts are from either the New York or Los Angeles offices of the Federal Theatre Project. In some instances copies of scripts for the same program but from different jurisdictions are included in the same series. Finding aid includes detailed list of individual programs and dates.

941. Zero and Kate Mostel Papers, 1915–1986. Contains personal papers, writings and a limited amount of material relating to Mostel's radio appearances, including some comedy sketches that could be radio, television or nightclub material, 1942–1976, and one radio script for *Chamber Music Society of Lower Basin Street,* 1942.

Rodgers and Hammerstein Archives of Recorded Sound
40 Lincoln Center Plaza, New York, NY 10023
(212) 870-870-1663 *; Fax: (212) 870-1720
rha@nypl.org; www.nypl.org/research/lpa/rha/rha.html

* Phone is only answered during library hours.

General comments. Online finding aids are available for only a portion of the library's sound recording collections but additional printed finding aids are available in the library. For information on LPs and tapes cataloged through 1979, check the library's free standing card catalog. A bound version of this catalog, published by G. K. Hall and Company, is located on-site and in reference libraries throughout the world. For recordings cataloged after 1979, check the Atlas database, an in-house computer database located at the reference librarian's desk. An additional special database is also searchable by librarians but not the general public. Also, a growing amount of material is cataloged in CATNYP, the online catalog of The New York Public Library. Researchers are also advised to check the Rigler Deutsch Index to 78rpm records that is available at the library and other select locations. For researchers located outside New York City, library staff will answer brief reference queries by phone.

942. Abe Burrows Collection, 1946–1972. Contains recordings of the complete runs of both *The Abe Burrows Show* and *Breakfast with Burrows.* There are also recordings of many of the numerous guest appearances Burrows made on other radio and television programs and some home and private recordings of the Burrows family. For print material about Burrows, see the Abe Burrows Collection in the Billy Rose Theatre Collection.

943. *Adventures of Frank Merriwell* Collection, 1946–1947. Consists of 51 episodes, 1946–1947. Most items are off-air recordings from WEAF, New York. Episode titles are unknown unless specified.

944. Armed Forces Radio Service Collection of Broadcast Recordings, 1942–1949. Collection of 750 discs representing a variety of AFRS programs, including *Yarns for Yanks, Command Performance, Mail Call, Globe Theater, Words With Music, Music From America* and weekly broadcasts of concerts of many major American symphony orchestras, including the Boston Symphony, NBC Symphony, New York Philharmonic and other groups, 1943–1945. See also separate listings for specific AFRS programs.

945. *Bell Telephone Hour* Recordings, 1941–1968. Consists of 1,414 discs. See finding aid for details.

946. *Command Performance* Sound Recordings. Collection of 23 discs, including numbers: 17, 98, 104, 122, 123, 134, 135, 144, 145, 165, "Christmas Command Performance", 1944, "Victory Extra" and "Dick Tracy."

947. Deems Taylor Collection, 1935–1954. Contains transcription disc recordings primarily of Taylor's spoken word radio programs, 1935–1954, including *Information Please, Coronet* and *Swift's Studio Party* as well as special radio shows such as the ASCAP *Cavalcade of Music* and memorial tributes to Stephen Vincent Benet and Jerome Kern.

948. Franklin Delano Roosevelt Radio Broadcast Speeches.

949. Henry Cowell Collection. Includes recordings of *American Musical Festival.*

950. Irving Berlin Collection of Noncommercial Sound Recordings, 1933–1989. Includes recordings from radio broadcasts, live performances and private recordings.

951. Joan Crawford Collection. Unprocessed as of 2005.

952. Kirsten Flagstad Collection of Radio Broadcasts and Live Performances, 1923–1963.

953. Lanny Ross Collection of Radio Broadcasts, 1938–1946. Check with library catalog for more information.

954. Lawrence & Lee Collection, 1939–1966. Includes the complete run for *The Railroad Hour, Favorite Story* and *Young Love* as well as representative holdings for *Request Performance, Hallmark Playhouse, A Date with Judy* and numerous other programs. All programs that Lawrence and Lee wrote or produced for the Armed Forces Radio Service are cataloged separately as part of the Armed Forces Radio Service Collection. See online finding aid for details of recordings and separate listing above for the Lawrence (Jerome) and Lee (Robert E.) Papers, 1917–1970, collection in the Billy Rose Theatre Collection.

955. Lee Tracy Collection, 1934–1964. Consists primarily of Tracy's performances on radio, including *Hall of Fame, Hollywood Hotel, Kraft Music Hall, Lux Radio Theatre, Rudy Vallee Hour, Shell Chateau* and *Silver Theater.*

956. Lennie Hayton Collection of Recorded Broadcasts, 1933–1959. Check with library catalog for more information.

957. Leo Reisman Recordings, 1932–1948. Contains primarily private acetate disc recordings of Reisman's radio performances of the 1930s, including extensive holdings of his Philip Morris radio program (the specific name of which is unclear but possibly *Philip Morris Presents*) and *Schaefer Beer Nine O'Clock Revue* appearances. Also includes less complete holdings for *Your Hit Parade* and a program sponsored by the Ponds company for which the name is unknown.

958. *Let's Go To The Opera* Radio Broadcast Collection, 1946. Seventy seven recordings of the program.

959. Luther Sies Collection of Radio Broadcasts, 1920s–1970s. Unprocessed as of 2005.

960. *Mail Call* Sound Recordings. Collection of 23 programs.

961. *March of Time*, 1935–1943.

962. Mary Howe Sound Recording Collection, 1938–1960. Includes recordings of interviews broadcast on WNBC and WNYC.

963. *Metropolitan Opera* Broadcasts. Recordings of the Saturday afternoon *Metropolitan Opera Radio Broadcasts*, 1932–present.

964. National Orchestral Association Collection of Broadcast Rehearsals and Concerts, 1938–1968.

965. New York Philharmonic Orchestra Radio Broadcasts, 1934–1955.

966. Patricia Kurland Collection of Radio Interviews, 1961–1979.

967. *Railroad Hour* Sound Recordings, 1948–1954. Collection includes 490 transcription discs and 42 tapes of the broadcasts which presented excerpts of famous musical comedies as well as original stories. Note: The collection is part of the larger Lawrence and Lee Collection of Broadcast Recordings.

968. Richard Rodgers Collection of Musicals and Interviews Sound Recordings, 1926–1980. Contains commercial discs and noncommercial recordings of performances of his music by contemporary performers as well as radio and television programs that used Rodgers's music. The noncommercial items in the collection include excerpts from radio and television series and a number of interviews of Rodgers, including the complete interviews made for the BBC program *The Life and Music of Richard Rodgers*. Includes the following radio programs: *Andre Kostelanetz Show, Best of All, Coca-Cola Program, Fred Allen Show, Fred Waring and His Orchestra, March of Time, Million Dollar Band, Prudential Hour, RCA Victor Show, Railroad Hour, Singing Lady, Tex and Jinx Show, Theatre Guild on the Air, Today, Tune up Time, Rudy Vallee Program, Batte un Cuore Genovese per Richard Rodgers, War Savings Program, Invasion Day, Life and Mu-*

sic of Richard Rodgers, Millions for Defense and *Tribute to Lorenz Hart*. Recordings are part of the Richard Rodgers Papers.

969. Robert Bowman Collection of Music Recordings From Radio, 1952–1963. Includes 390 tape reels of noncommercial recordings of radio broadcasts of primarily classical music. Broadcasts by the New York Philharmonic are the most numerous in the collection with selected concerts from 1952–1963. Orchestras with a smaller representation include the Boston Symphony, the NBC Symphony and the Concertgebouw Orchestra. Also includes selected *Voice of Firestone* programs, 1952–1956, containing opera, operetta, and orchestral selections as well as popular songs.

970. Rosa Ponselle Collection, 1926–1987. Includes recordings of Ponselle on *Magic Key*, 1937.

971. Sophie Tucker Private Recordings Collection, 1925–1953. Contains Tucker's appearances on radio programs, interviews, live night club performances and various unissued studio recordings. Some of the radio programs represented in the collection are *Blue Ribbon Town, Frank Sinatra Show, It's Time for Pabst* and the *Philco Hour*. Other performers represented in the collection include Ben Bernie, Judy Garland, Frank Sinatra, and Orson Welles.

972. Sound Recordings Collection, 1941–1963. Recordings of violinist Joseph Szigeti that may have been broadcast on the *Concerto* series, WOR, Washington, DC.

973. Toscanini Legacy Collection of Sound Recordings, 1926–1968, bulk 1940–1957. Includes some recordings with the NBC Symphony.

974. Vincent Persichetti Collection, 1945–1987. Includes recordings of radio broadcasts with Persichetti performing and also interviews with Persichetti.

975. Vito Marcantonio Collection of Political Speeches, Late 1930s.

976. WNYC Recordings, 1938–1970. Collection of selected broadcast tapes. Includes recordings of *New World A-Comin'*.

Schomburg Center for Research in Black Culture
515 Malcolm X Boulevard, New York, NY 10037
(212) 491-2224; scmarbref@nypl.org
www.nypl.org/research/sc/scm/marb.html

977. Alberta Hunter Papers, 1919–1986. Consists of personal and professional papers documenting Hunter's singing and nursing careers. Professional papers include contracts for performances, recordings, publication of her songs, television and radio royalties, copyright registration, scrapbooks that contain information about her radio program in the 1930s and other papers.

978. Alma John Papers, 1955–1980. As Executive Director of the National Association of Colored Graduate Nurses, John hosted and wrote the scripts for *Brown Women in White*. In 1952 she got her first radio program on WWRL covering everything from religion to teenagers.

979. American Negro Theatre Scrapbooks, 1945–1948. Includes material about the American Negro Theatre's radio broadcasts of plays and operas, its School of Drama and other clippings relating to ANT activities.

980. Barbara M. Watson Papers, 1929–1984. Contains personal and professional papers, including papers relating to her program, *I'm Your Next Door Neighbor*, n.d.

981. Bob Howard Papers, 1927–1986. Consists of personal and professional papers, biographical information and miscellaneous radio, television and performance material.

982. Canada Lee Papers, 1912–1999, bulk 1941–1952. Contains personal and professional papers, including correspondence, speeches, contracts, newsclippings, financial records, memorabilia and scripts for *New World A-Comin'*.

983. Cleo Sims Collection, 1944–2002. Consists of biographical information and papers relating to her fashion shows. May include information about her radio programs.

984. Don Redman Papers, 1906–1980. Consists principally of music and some personal and professional papers. In 1932, Redman's band was the first black orchestra to play for a sponsored radio series, *Chipso*.

985. Elliot Carpenter Papers, 1922–1979. Consists of personal and professional correspondence, handwritten music, programs, lyrics, scripts and newsclippings. The series "Miscellaneous Writings, 1946–ca. 1970," consists primarily of scripts intended for performances on stage or radio.

986. Eusebia Cosme Papers, 1927–1973. Includes scripts for the *Eusebia Cosme Show* broadcast on CBS, n.d., but probably 1940s.

987. Frederick O'Neal Papers, 1941-1973. Consists of three scrapbooks of newsclippings, 1941–1958, in addition to a small amount of correspondence and other materials documenting O'Neal's theatrical career. Includes newsclippings discussing the Coordinating Council for Negro Performers and integration and discrimination of African Americans on radio, television and in movies.

988. Fredi Washington Papers, 1922–1941, 1981, n.d. Includes a summary of material presented at a conference held under the auspices of the National Negro Congress to survey the position of blacks in the theater, radio, screen, music and advertising, March 16, 1947. Also includes radio scripts performed by Washington.

989. Harry E. Jones Papers, 1941–1968. Consists primarily of papers relating to Jones's role as a Boy Scout leader for African American boys in New Jersey and some material relating to his career as a musician. May not contain any material related to his 1930s weekly radio program.

990. Hilda Simms Papers, 1937–1994. Consists of correspondence, printed matter, play scripts and clippings documenting Simms's acting career in film, television and radio.

991. *I Remember When* Recordings Collection. Sound recordings of the program hosted by Etta Moten Barnett and produced in the 1950s by WMAQ, Chicago.

992. John Marriott Papers, 1933–1977. Includes radio scripts, playbills, programs, correspondence, certificates and newsclippings pertaining to Marriott's career.

993. Julian Mayfield Papers, 1949–1984. Includes some unidentified and undated radio scripts related to Mayfield's career as a writer, educator and actor and his activities as a political expatriate in West Africa and Guyana.

994. Katharine Handy Lewis Papers, 1925–1983. Contains personal and professional papers, including biographical information, correspondence, printed material and financial records concerning her musical career.

995. Langston Hughes Collection, 1926–1967. Contains papers relating to programs, activities and events in which Hughes participated or was the subject, including memorial tributes, personal appearances, radio broadcasts, recordings, speeches and television broadcasts.

996. Milton A. Galamison Papers, 1947-1987. Includes transcripts of his series *Faith in Our Time*, aired on CBS, 1952–1953.

997. Negro Actors Guild of America Records, 1904–1982, bulk 1937–1982. Records document the functions and activities of the organization and includes material related to blacks in radio.

998. Radio Scripts Collection, 1937–1966. Consists of transcripts of radio programs, both serials and single broadcasts, that show the contributions of African Americans to the social, economic, political and historical development of the United States. Many of the scripts were created for public service programs during the 1940s to foster national unity and better race relations. Included are *Freedom's People*, 1941–1942, *Give Me Liberty*, 1939, *Native Sons*, 1941–1951, *Unity at Home Victory Abroad*, 1943, *New World A-Comin'*, 1944–1966, and *Within Our Gates*, 1945–1948, broadcast on WMCA, directed by Mitchell Grayson and narrated by Canada Lee. There are also several single scripts, including "Speech of Paul Robeson," "Hampton Institute Forum of the Air," 1944, "Lincoln, Douglas and the Honor Roll In the Race Relations" and "Wings Over Jordan."

999. Ralph J. Bunche Papers, 1922–1988. Includes sound recordings of Bunche appearing on a variety of radio programs.

1000. Rose McClendon Scrapbooks, 1919–1935. Includes material related to her radio appearances.

1001. Virginia Girvin Papers, 1902–1975. Consists of biographical information of her acting career on stage, film and radio, drafts of her memoirs, letters primarily acknowledging her volunteer efforts and a letter from Orson Welles offering his advice on her acting career.

New York State Historical Association

Research Library
PO Box 800, Cooperstown, NY 13326
(607) 547-1470; Fax: (607) 547-1405
library@nysha.org; www.nysha.org/library/entry_list.asp
Contact: Wayne Wright

1002. Jared Van Wagenen Papers, 1959–1962. Includes four scripts for broadcasts by Van Wagenen over WGY, Schenectady, 1959.

1003. "Radio and Rural Life: A Case Study of WGY and Otsego County." A Ph.D. thesis by Jean Hanavan, State University of New York at Oneonta, 1989.

1004. *York State Yarns*, New York State Radio Bureau, 1948–1951. Mimeographed series of 103 six minute scripts for stand-by programs on New York State folklore issued between November, 1948 and December, 1951. A second similar collection includes 10 scripts of folklore stories.

New York University
Taminent Library, 10th Floor of Elmer Holmes Bobst Library
70 Washington Square South, New York, NY 10012
(212) 998-2639
peter.filardo@nyu.edu; Contact: Peter Filardo
www.nyu.edu/library/bobst/research/tam/collections.html

1005. International Brotherhood of Electrical Workers Local 1212 Records, 1940–ca. 1979, bulk ca. 1960–1979. Records involving CBS form a major portion of the collection. (In Robert F. Wagner Labor Archives.)

1006. John Lyons Papers, 1906–1957. Includes notes from Lyon's program, *Social Democratic Radio Forum,* broadcast on WEVD.

1007. National Association of Broadcast Employees and Technicians, Local 11 Records, 1947–1984, bulk 1955–1984. Local 11 represents NBC on a vertical basis and includes radio, television and satellite technicians, engineers, desk assistants, news writers, maintenance workers and all other employees. Records also cover ABC. (In Robert F. Wagner Labor Archives.)

1008. Paris Morris Papers, 1934–1968. Includes manuscripts of *Review of the Week*, 1943–1946, a news commentary program on WEVD.

University Archives
10th Floor, Elmer Holmes Bobst Library
(212) 998-2646; Fax: (212) 995-4070
nancy.cricco@nyu.edu; http://dlib.nyu.edu/divlib/bobst/
archives/findingaids/archives.html

1009. WNYU Station Records, 1949–1969. Records of the college radio station.

North Dakota State University
Institute for Regional Studies
PO Box 5599, Fargo, ND 58105
(701) 231-8914; Fax: (701) 231-5632
archives@www.lib.ndsu.nodak.edu; www.lib.ndsu.nodak.edu

1010. Diamond C Ranch History, 1952. Historical sketch of the Diamond C Ranch located near Killdeer, ND in Dunn County. The sketch was used as a radio broadcast.

1011. Earl C. and Marie E. Reineke Papers, 1929–1965. Contains letters, clippings, programs and pamphlets relating to WDAY which was founded by Reineke.

1012. Fargo Diamond Jubilee Corporation Records, 1949–1950. Includes a file on Johnny Olson, host of *Ladies Be Seated,* including photos and press releases.

1013. Frank and Audrey Scott Papers, 1901–1996. Includes scrapbooks documenting Audrey Scott's career from 1930–1940 when she performed on WDAY.

1014. Frank Scott Photograph Collection, 1930s–1995. Includes portraits of Scott, his various bands and his work and other entertainers at WDAY. Includes photographs of Lawrence Welk, Pat Kelly, Laura Campbell and Don Roseland.

1015. Gordon MacGregor Family Papers, 1933–1954. Includes several letters to and from the Ripley's *Believe It or Not*

program, 1937, concerning an appearance by Chief White Bull on the show.

1016. Harlow L. Walster Papers, 1883–1957. Includes scripts for the series *Looking South* discussing Walster's trip to Latin America as guest of the Carnegie Endowment for International Peace and describing agriculture and other subjects.

1017. Henry Luke Bolley Papers, 1890–1946. Includes scripts of radio addresses given by Bolley concerning his trips to Argentina and Brazil, 1930, on behalf of the flax industry and to Russia pursuant to the study of flax.

1018. *I Call It Adventure*/Irene Turli, 195? Reminiscence concerning her father, Henry Plummer, a Norwegian immigrant from Aurland, Norway, including early radio programs in Montana.

1019. Martin J. Connolly Collection, 1939–1954. Includes script for "Historical Sketch of North Dakota" broadcast in observance of North Dakota's fiftieth year of statehood.

1020. Orestes Brownson Study Club No. 3 Records, 1933–1977. Records of a women's group organized to study Catholic literature, including manuscripts of several radio programs.

1021. Rainier Schickele Papers, 1931–1975. Includes manuscripts for radio talks given at Iowa State on agriculture.

Northeastern University
Archives and Special Collections, 92 Snell Library
360 Huntington Avenue, Boston, MA 02115
(617) 373- 2351; archives@neu.edu
www.lib.neu.edu/archives/collect/acoll.htm

1022. Arthur Batcheller Papers, 1888–1977, bulk 1913–1955. Papers deal primarily with regulatory issues. Also includes photographs of radio personalities

1023. Glen Gray and the Casa Loma Orchestra Records, 1915–1979. Contains original musical scores and arrangements, photographs of Glen Gray and the Casa Loma Orchestra at all stages of the band's career, newspaper clippings and scrapbooks documenting the band's performance history and reception by both critics and the public over time. Also includes audio tapes of CLO recordings and interviews with band associates, phonograph records of original CLO recordings and other recordings of big band music.

1024. Lowell Institute School Records, 1883–1996. Includes records relating to the establishment of the Lowell Institute Cooperative Broadcasting Council, 1946, which pioneered the use of radio as a vehicle for adult education programming.

1025. Young Men's Christian Association of Greater Boston, West Roxbury/Roslindale Branch Records, 1948–1995, bulk 1951–1970. Includes YMCA ads on local radio and television stations.

Northern Arizona University
Cline Library, Special Collections & Archives Department
PO Box 6022, Flagstaff, AZ 86011
(928) 523-5551; Fax: (928) 523-3770
www.nau.edu/library

1026. Buzz Holmstrom Interviews, 1909–1946. Transcripts of radio interviews of Holmstrom after his solo river trip down the Green and Colorado Rivers in 1937.

Northern Kentucky University

Schlachter Family Archives
W. Frank Steely Library, Highland Heights, KY 41099
(859) 572-6158
archives@nku.edu;   http://library.nku.edu/arc/

1027. Jennifer Gregory Taliaferro Collection. Includes 50 announcer's scripts from the Radio Division, Bureau of Public Relations, National Recovery Administration. Although the scripts are undated, they are probably from 1933–1936. It is likely that Southgate Haynie, a journalist and writer who did work for radio, wrote some or all of the scripts.

Oberlin College

Archives, 420 Mudd Center
148 West College Street, Oberlin, OH 44074
(440) 775-8014;   Fax: (440) 775-8016
www.oberlin.edu/archive/

1028. Florence Mary Fitch Papers, 1875–1959. Includes material on radio broadcasts from Cleveland, New York and South Bend, IN stations, 1945–1947.

Ohio Historical Society

982 Velma Avenue, Columbus, OH 43211
(614) 297-2300
occ@ohiohistory.org;   www.ohiohistory.org

1029. Columbus Town Meeting Association Records, 1939–1970. Contains transcripts of the Association's weekly radio and television program, *Columbus Town Meeting*, including opening statements for some of the broadcasts and other papers.

1030. National Communications, Inc. Papers relating to the history of WNCI-FM and WRFD-AM, including correspondence, public affairs and religious programming files, newscast scripts, editorials, radio logbooks, log analyses, advertising copy and reference files. Access to this collection may be restricted. Contact repository for more information.

Ohio State University

Jerome Lawrence & Robert E. Lee Theatre Research Institute
1430 Lincoln Tower, 1800 Cannon Dr., Columbus OH 43210
(614) 292-6614;   Fax: (614) 688-8417
Couch.1@osu.edu;   Contact: Nena Couch
http://library.osu.edu/sites/tri/abtri/location.html

1031. Harriett Mortimore Toomey Scrapbooks, 1922–1979. Includes biographical clippings, programs, press notices and personal memorabilia concerning Toomey's life and career as a soprano known for her work in light opera, oratorio, concerts, radio and television.

1032. International Al Jolson Society Collection, 1912–1994. Includes programs, original music scores with Jolson's songs, membership forms for the Al Jolson International Society, photographic copy prints of Jolson, a few audio and video cassettes and other Jolson papers and memorabilia.

1033. Jerome Lawrence–Robert E. Lee Collection, 1939–. Contains radio and television scripts, script development notes, production files, correspondence, teaching materials, photographs, clippings, journal and magazine issues, artifacts, audio visual materials, original art, autographs, playbills, souvenir booklets, theatre and writer organizations materials, brochures and conference materials and posters. Includes scripts for *Armed Forces Radio Service, Favorite Story, The Railroad*

Hour, Hallmark Playhouse, Young Love, The World We're Fighting For, Man About Hollywood, Songs by Sinatra, Lady Esther's Album, I Was There, Meet Mr. Music, Saturday Morning, CBS Shows, The Little Show, Call For Music, Request Performance, The Unexpected and others. For a detailed list of radio scripts by program title and date check finding aid at: http://library.osu.edu/sites/speccoll/finding/LandL.html#series2.

1034. Joseph G. Bernhard Theatre, TV, Radio, Movies Scrapbook, 1928–1950. Scrapbook of clippings collected by Bernhard covering multiple personalities.

1035. Paulette Goddard/Burgess Meredith Collection, 1937–1949. Contains mainly personal correspondence between Goddard and her husband, Burgess Meredith, along with a biography of Goddard, obituaries, telegrams, postcards (original and transcribed), photographs and other material. Does not appear to contain any radio specific material.

Rare Books and Manuscripts
327 Main Library
1858 Neil Avenue Mall, Columbus, OH 43210
(614) 292-5938;   Fax (614) 292-7859
librar@osu.edu;   http://library.osu.edu/sites/rarebooks/

1036. Channing Pollack Letters, 1942–1945. Includes text of debate with Oswald Garrison Villard, "Just What Is Democracy?" broadcast on *Wake Up America!* January 4, 1942.

1037. Film and Playscript Collection, 1932–1981. Includes scripts for films, plays and radio dating from 1932–1981. List of titles is available in the library.

1038. "Leviathon '99," n.d. An undated script by Ray Bradbury.

1039. Norman Cazden Papers, ca. 1923–1980. Includes material relating to Cazden's radio programs, 1940–1953, and other papers relating to his music career.

1040. W.C. Handy Papers, 1944–1952. Includes letters relating to some of his songs, an article about Handy and a radio schedule for WGAR, Cleveland for September 24–30, 1944 featuring Handy on the cover.

University Archives
2700 Kenny Road, Columbus, Ohio 43210
(614) 292-2409;   Fax: (614) 688-4150
chute.6@osu.edu;   Contact: Tamar Chute
http://library.osu.edu/sites/archives/

1041. Albert Belmont Graham Papers, 1885–1958. Includes radio talks, 1931–1953 dealing with agricultural issues.

1042. Edgar Dale Papers, 1933–1984. Includes Dale's research, correspondence and reports on communication media and radio.

1043. Erwin F. Frey Papers, ca. 1930–1960. Includes correspondence, photographs of his works, unidentified radio scripts, gallery catalogs and scrapbooks.

1044. Hans Sperber Papers, 1911–1963. Includes radio talks (in German) on the German language, 1927–1928.

1045. Howard L. Bevis Papers, ca. 1937–ca 1957. Includes papers relating to WOSU.

1046. I. Keith Tyler Papers, 1932–1969. Includes papers relating to the *Ohio School of the Air*, WOSU and educational broadcasting.

1047. Institute for Education by Radio and Television Papers, 1960. Includes program bulletins, correspondence, reports and studies on radio instruction.

1048. James Lewis Morrill Papers, 1928–1941. Includes papers relating to WOSU.

1049. *Ohio School of the Air*, 1925–1969. Includes publications, annual reports, bulletins, audio recordings and scrapbooks. Also contains scripts for some broadcasts, including *Economic Detective, Once Upon a Time in Ohio* and *Story Time.*

1050. Ralph Currier Davis Papers, 1939–1967. Papers include WOSU organizational manual.

1051. Richard E. Byrd Papers. Includes information about radio broadcasts Byrd made from Antarctica to the United States. The actual broadcasts are not part of the collection.

1052. Richard Parker Goldthwait Papers, 1924–1977. Includes information about radio programs on which Goldthwait appeared, most likely discussing subjects related to geology.

1053. Robert S. Newdick Papers, 1934. Includes lectures on English literature by Newdick on WOSU, 1934.

1054. Telecommunications Center Records (WOSU), 1946–Present. Includes materials on Ohio educational radio, including *Ohio School of the Air* and WEAO.

1055. *Three Witnesses to Our Crisis* Transcripts, 194?–1955. Transcripts of a series of radio talks delivered over WOSU by Oskar Seidlin relating to the 20th century German authors Franz Kafka, Rainer Maria Rilke and Thomas Mann

1056. WOSU Collections, 1922–Present. Includes office files, audio tapes, administration and project files as well as information on radio in Ohio and the U.S. A second WOSU collection includes over 2,000 phonograph records of broadcasts, 1930s–1940s.

Oklahoma Historical Society
2100 N. Lincoln Boulevard, Oklahoma City, OK 73105
(405) 521-2491; www.ok-history.mus.ok.us

1057. Oklahoma Association of Broadcasters Records, n.d. Microfilmed copies of memorabilia pertaining to KVOO, KRAV, KAKC, KADA and KOMA. Includes scrapbooks, photographs, history of stations and promotional items.

Onondaga Historical Association Research Center
321 Montgomery Street, Syracuse, NY 13202
(315) 428-1862; Fax: (315) 471-2133
ohaarchivist@yahoo.com
www.cnyhistory.org/research.html

1058. Syracuse Historical Radio Collection, 1941–1949. Includes sound recordings and transcripts of broadcasts of historical programs, mostly on WFBL, including the *Caravan of Industry* which focused on the history of a particular industry each week. Also recordings of historical programs relating to the Syracuse Centennial, streetcars, the Village of Manlius and the Syracuse Republican Party.

1059. WFBL Radio Scripts, 1946. Includes scripts for *Kaylan Cutlery Historical Showcase* relating to Syracuse his-

torical events and narratives.

1060. White Family Papers, 1829–1983. Includes scripts for *The Social Shopper,* 1934–1940, hosted by Katharine Cook.

Oral Roberts University
Holy Spirit Research Center
7777 South Lewis Avenue, Tulsa, OK 74171
(918) 495-6898; Fax: (918) 495-6662
hsrc@oru.edu; www.oru.edu/university/library/holyspirit/

1061. Pentecostal Collection. Contains sound recordings and printed material documenting the Pentecostal faith. Mostly from early 1960s. Contact the Center for collection details.

Oregon Historical Society Research Library
1200 SW Park Avenue, Portland, OR 97205
(503) 306-5240; Fax: (503) 219-2040
libreference@ohs.org; www.ohs.org/collections/index.cfm

<u>Audio Collections</u>

General comments: The following individual audio collections are part of the Meyer Sound Recordings Collection of 1,700 recordings, 1940–1970, with the bulk dating from World War II and the following decade. The recordings have been transferred from transcription discs to cassettes.

1062. Commercial Advertising Radio Disc Collection, 1950–1978, bulk 1950–1960. Compilation of 31 cassettes of numerous short advertisements for local, regional and national companies which aired on Portland area stations. Includes spots for the Oregon Shakespearean Festival, 1959, Blitz-Weinhard Brewing Co. and the U.S. National Bank.

1063. KAST Radio Disc Collection, 1955–1970. Twenty-eight cassettes of different programs, including a promotional spot for a performance by the United States Air Force Band at the Astoria Armory, the *Douglas Grader Show* broadcast from the Clatsop County Fair and a number of commercials for various Astoria area merchants, including Garcia Ford, Bjorklund's and the Owl Drug Store.

1064. KBPS Radio Disc Collection, 1938–ca. 1955. Compilation of 50 discs containing educational programs produced under the auspices of the Portland Public Schools as well as programming produced by KGW or released from other affiliates. Programs include *The American Challenge*, a U.S. history series, *Their Name was Courage*, historical dramas about Washington state, *Bill Scott, Forest Ranger*, a conservation program sponsored by the U.S. Forest Service, live coverage of the 1941 Benson High School dance and a drama from Reed College, 1939.

1065. KEX Radio Disc Collection, 1939–1985, bulk 1941–1955. Collection of 25 recordings containing local and national news programs (NBC and ABC), including World War II and Korean War news and the historical series *Mr. President*. Local programs include the sports news program *Radio Box Score* and the country music program *Neath Western Skies*.

1066. KGW Radio Disc Collection. Collection of 150 discs containing local and national programs on World War II and the early Cold War. Highlights include: D-Day invasion news, a translation of a Hitler speech from Danzig, live coverage of an atomic bomb detonation, speeches by presidents Franklin Roosevelt, Harry Truman and Dwight Eisenhower, British prime minister Winston Churchill and New York governor

Thomas Dewey. National entertainment programs include soap operas such as *Lora Lawton* and musical variety shows. Local highlights include Roosevelt's speech from Bremerton, WA, local news programs, Mayor Earl Riley's blackout order for Portland following the Japanese attack on Pearl Harbor, coverage of the last run of the Spokane, Portland & Seattle Railway's train to Seaside, OR, educational programs such as *Reading is Fun* and the local variety show, *Grandpappy and Pals.*

1067. KOIN Radio Disc Collection, 1939–1960, bulk 1941–1955. Collection of 400 discs containing local and national news programs (CBS), including reports on World War II, the Korean War and the Cold War as well as the speeches of Franklin Roosevelt, Harry Truman, Winston Churchill and others. Local programs include documentaries on the Tillamook Burn, 1943 and 1953, live reports on Kaiser shipyard launchings, 1941–1945, reports on the Vanport Flood, 1948, the *Northwest Neighbors* talk show, the historical drama "Song of the Columbia," the award-winning documentary on African-American physician Dr. Charles Drew entitled "Who Killed Dr. Drew," *Kid Critics*, featuring Portland area grade school children reviewing books, Pacific Power and Light and Northwest Electric commercials, 1941–1947, and a live concert with Jane Powell from Portland's South Park Blocks.

1068. Miscellaneous Radio Disc Collection, 1943–1968, bulk 1945–1955. Compilation of 37 miscellaneous national programs.

1069. Public Service Advertising Radio Disc Collection, 1955–1970. Three audio cassettes of numerous short public service announcements which aired on Portland area stations. Includes spots for the Oregon Junior Symphony, 1958, the Odd Fellows, 1970, and the Oregon State Game Commission.

1070. Songs and Sounds of Oregon Radio Disc Collection, 1943–ca.1985. Compilation of 37 musical and spoken pieces which aired on Portland area stations.

1071. United States Navy Recruiting Radio Disc Collection, ca. 1955. Four audio recordings of advertisements promoting Navy recruitment aired on Portland area stations.

1072. United States Savings Bonds Radio Disc Collection, 1956–1960. Compilation of 40 recordings of advertisements promoting the purchase of U.S. savings bonds which aired on Portland area stations. The spots often featured celebrity guest stars, including Mel Torme, Maureen O'Hara, "Tennessee" Ernie Ford and others.

Print Collections

1073. Amos Burg Papers ca. 1917–1985. Includes transcript of radio interview of Burg.

1074. Marshall Newport Dana Papers, 1869–1969, bulk 1910–1966. Covers all aspects of Dana's professional activities and includes some radio addresses and material on a radio project about Dana.

Oregon State Library
250 Winter Street NE, Salem, OR 97301
(503) 378-4243; Fax: (503) 585-8059
jim.b.scheppke@state.or.us; http://arcweb.sos.state.or.us/

1075. Oregon State Library Radio Program Records 1928–1954, bulk 1942–1954. Contains correspondence, program schedules and scripts that document library radio programs, including *Ask Your State Library*, 1942–1943, and *Library Hour*, 1949.

Oregon State University
University Archives
121 The Valley Library, Corvallis, OR 97331
(541) 737-2165; archives@oregonstate.edu
http://osulibrary.oregonstate.edu/archives

1076. Ava Milam Clark Papers, 1884–1976. Includes transcripts of Clark's radio talks, 1933–1954, on homemaking issues.

1077. Buena Maris Mockmore Papers, 1916–1969. Include speeches, radio program materials, publications and teaching materials prepared in her role as an extension specialist in child development and family life at Oregon State College and Iowa State University.

1078. Edwin Russell Jackman Papers, 1917–1968. Includes transcripts of radio talks delivered by Jackman.

1079. E. E. Wilson Papers, 1838–1961, bulk 1850–1961. Contains Wilson's personal and professional papers and includes scripts for the 15 minute radio spots prepared by the Oregon State Game Commission which Wilson headed. The programs were broadcast bi-monthly over KOAC, 1940–1944.

1080. Guide to the Extension and Experiment Station Communications Records, 1949–1995. Includes news releases, sound recordings of radio programs and public service announcements by University Extension programs in agriculture, home economics, marine resources and 4-H.

1081. Guide to the KOAC Records, 1923–1965. Records document the establishment and functioning of the KOAC public radio and television stations at Oregon Agricultural College (Oregon State University). Includes administrative records, radio scripts and programs and sound recordings.

1082. J. Kenneth Munford Collection, 1866–2000, bulk 1930–2000. Includes scripts and related notes, correspondence and documentation pertaining to several radio productions on Oregon history and geography that Munford created in the mid 1930s and early 1940s. Also includes records relating to KOAC, School of the Air and other radio programs.

1083. Wallace L. Kadderly Papers, 1931–1963. Papers consist of agriculture related materials produced or collected by Kadderly during his work overseas as a farm broadcaster on the radio and newsclippings announcing his departure from KOAC in 1933.

Other Minds' Internet Archive Station
333 Valencia Street, Suite 303, San Francisco, CA 94103
(415) 934-8134; Fax: (415) 934-8136
berhanrd@otherminds.org; www.otherminds.org
Contact: Bernard Francis Kyle

1084. KPFA Music Archive, 1953–1992. Approximately 4,000 recordings, including interviews, concerts, other music programs and poetry originally aired 1949–1992. Also includes recordings of 20th century music festivals and concerts. For specific programs, check with in-house database.

Pace University Archives
1 Pace Plaza, New York, NY 10038
(212) 346-1787; Fax: (212) 346-1701

ESowchek@Pace.Edu; http://appserv.pace.edu/library/
Contact: Ellen Sowchek

1085. Miscellaneous Records, 1927–1985. Records of the Office of University Information, including transcripts of radio shows, some of which were broadcast on WNYC on various educational topics, 1960s–1970s, including the *Let's Go To Class* series.

Pacific Pioneer Broadcasters

PO Box 4866, North Hollywood, CA 91617
(323) 461-2121
www.pacificpioneerbroadcasters.org/archive.html

1086. Archives. Collection includes sound recordings of network comedy, mystery, music, Armed Forces Radio Service, music libraries, news programs, including World War II news broadcasts, CBS and standard library of recorded sound effects as well as many manual sound effects, oral histories, scripts, including *Fibber McGee and Molly* and *The Dennis Day Show*, photographs, publications, including trade magazines, equipment and other radio memorabilia. In the future, the PPB archives will be combined with the American Radio Archives at the Thousand Oaks Library in Thousand Oaks, CA. The Pacific Pioneers is a membership organization comprised of men and women with at least 20 years professional employment in the field of radio and television broadcasting or allied fields.

Pacifica Radio Archives

3729 Cahuenga Blvd West, N. Hollywood, CA 91604
(818) 506-1077; Fax: (818) 506-1084
Bdeshazor@pacificaradioarchives.org
www.pacificaradioarchives.org
Contact: Brian De Shazor

1087. Pacifica Radio Archives Collection. The archives maintains an online database with information on more than 40,000 recordings broadcast by the four Pacifica stations: KPFA, Berkeley, CA, KPFK, Los Angeles, CA, WBAI, New York and KPFT, Houston, TX.

Penn State University

313 Pattee Library, University Park, PA 16802
(814) 863-2911; Fax: (814) 863-5318
fredwaring@psulias.psu.edu; Contact: Peter Kiefer
www.libraries.psu.edu/waring/

1088. Fred Waring Collection. A 98% complete collection of all radio broadcasts by Fred Waring and the Pennsylvanians, 1933–1949. Collection includes audio tapes, scripts, production notes, promotional items, scrapbooks, photographs and posters. As of 2005, the archive is processing a list of celebrity personalities who were guests on the programs plus noted musicians who performed as part of the organization.

Phil Harris/Alice Faye Museum

Regions Bank, PO Box 560, Linton, IN 47441
(812) 847-4635; Contact: Reginia Kramer

1089. Phil Harris/Alice Faye Collection. Includes memorabilia, scripts, sound recordings and photographs. Most of the material is about the *Phil Harris/Alice Faye Show* with a limited amount of material, mostly in the scrapbooks, about their appearances on other radio programs such as the *Jack Benny Show*. As of 2005, the transcription discs were being transferred to CDs. Special note: The collection is maintained by volunteers and is housed in the basement of a local bank.

Presbyterian Church in America Historical Center

12330 Conway Road, St. Louis, MO 63141
(314) 469- 9077; Contact: Wayne Sparkman
wsparkman@pcanet.org; www.pcanet.org

1090. D. James Kennedy Papers. Includes sound recordings and printed material for *Truths That Transform*.

Presbyterian Historical Society

PO Box 849, Montreat, NC 28757
(828) 669-7061; Fax: (828) 669-5369
refdesk@history.pcusa.org; www.history.pcusa.org

1091. United Presbyterian Church in the USA, Division of Mass Media Records, 1926–1971. Consists of office files of individuals, correspondence, minutes, reports, photographs, scripts of radio programs and spots, sermons preached on the air, articles, addresses and staff papers about religious broadcasting. Includes papers relating to *The Protestant Hour*.

Princeton University

Library, Rare Books and Special Collections
One Washington Road, Princeton, NJ 08544
(609) 258-3174; Fax: (609) 258-2324
msrich@princeton.edu; www.princeton.edu/~rbsc/
Contact: Margaret Sherry Rich

1092. Alexander Woollcott Manuscripts. Includes two radio essays, 1929.

1093. Booth Tarkington Papers, bulk 1899–1946. Includes unidentified radio scripts by Tarkington.

1094. Carl Van Doren Papers, 1900–1950. Includes scripts for *Words At War*.

1095. Council on Books in Wartime Archives, 1942–1947. Includes scripts for radio book dramatizations on *Words at War* and author interviews on *Fighting Words* and *Books are Bullets*.

1096. David Lawrence Papers, 1901–1973, bulk 1915–1970. Includes transcripts, 1927–1951, of his broadcasts, including the weekly series *Our Government*.

1097. Edward Le Roy Rice Papers, 1892-1940. Contains material on Rice's interests in radio, including material dealing with his varied business enterprises in minstrel shows for the major radio networks.

1098. F. Scott Fitzgerald Papers, 1897–1944. Includes four radio scripts by Fitzgerald.

1099. *The Free Company Presents*, 194? Consists of manuscripts of three plays and an introduction compiled by James Boyd. The scripts were written as American propaganda plays and presented over CBS in the spring of 1941. Includes Boyd's "One More Free Man" (final title) and a mimeographed copy of Orson Welles's "His Honor, the Mayor" (annotated, probably by Boyd). The third play, "Above Suspicion," is ascribed to Sherwood Anderson although the play was not completed at his death. Anderson's idea was developed by the company and the play was presented in tribute to him.

1100. Freedom House Archives, 1936–1997. Contains radio scripts designed to sway public opinion during World War II and the post World War II era, including *Our Secret Weapon* with Rex Stout as the "lie detective" debunking Axis propaganda, *Freedom House Forum* and *Pride and Prejudice*, a forum for representatives of different races and religions to discuss issues of prejudice.

1101. Herbert S. Gorman Papers, 1909–1960. Includes Gorman's adaptations of novels for radio, including "Pere Goriot" and "Don Quixote."

1102. Joseph D. Bennett Papers, 1951–1973. Includes transcripts of unidentified radio broadcasts.

1103. Leonard L. Milberg Autograph Collection, 1962–1978. Includes a 1962 radio play by Brendan Behan, "An Evening with Brendan Behan."

1104. Miriam Y. Holden Collection, 1930–1969. Includes copies of 34 scripts for the 1939–1940 series *The Gallant American Women* written by Jane Ashman.

1105. Molly Shenstone Collection on Thomas Mann, 1939–1969. Includes text of two radio broadcasts made by Thomas Mann, December, 1940.

1106. Radio Broadcasting Collection, 1938–1959. Consists of scripts for *Cavalcade of America*, 1945–1948, *World Peaceways*, scripts #422–479, and *The Bookman*, scripts #170–184, 202–233. Also includes promotional material for the major radio networks, including ABC, CBS, NBC, MBS and the Municipal Broadcasting System (WNYC), material regarding the coverage of news during the latter years of World War II and copies of clippings about the Orson Welles broadcast of *The War of the Worlds* in 1938.

1107. Radio Scripts Collection, 1938–1947. Contains an assortment of scripts, including *Cavalcade of America*, 1940–1944 (originals and revised versions; scripts are numbered), *Cavalcade of America Announcement of Broadcasts, Pepper Young's Family, When A Girl Marries, To The President, What's New in Books, Beyond Victory, Party Line-Prairie Folks, The Eternal Light* (an incomplete script by Arch Oboler), December 24, 1944, *A Woman Looks At the World of Books*, n.d., *Books and Authors*, n.d., *The Goldbergs*, 1930, 1943, *For This We Fight*, n.d., *The Bookman*, n.d., *The Treasury Star Parade*, n.d., *Plays For Americans, Writers' War Board Publications* and several miscellaneous scripts. A detailed list is available at: http://libweb.princeton.edu/libraries/firestone/rbsc/aids/tc059.html. Note: While some scripts do not contain dates, script numbers are available.

University Archives
Seeley G. Mudd Manuscript Library
65 Olden Street, Princeton, NJ 08544
(609) 258-6345; Fax: (609) 258-3385
mudd@princeton..edu; Contact: Dan Linke
www.princeton.edu/~mudd/finding_aids/archives.html

1108. Records of the Princeton Listening Center, 1939–1941. Contains transcripts of Axis and Allied propaganda broadcasts monitored by the Listening Center staff from November, 1939 through May, 1941. Also includes subject and research files of the organization.

Procter & Gamble
One P&G Plaza, Cincinnati, OH 45202
rider.em@pg.com; Contact: Ed Rider

1109. Corporate Archives. According to the Archives Department, almost no records of the company's sponsorship of radio soap operas have been preserved. However, the department does have a listing of the programs that were sponsored by the company, including *The Puddle Family* which was replaced by *Ma Perkins, 'O'Neill's*, 1935, *Vic and Sade, Guiding Light* and *Pepper Young's Family* and a few scripts for *Ma Perkins* and photographs of some of the show casts.

Prudential Life Insurance Company
751 Broad Street, Newark, NJ 07102
(973) 802 7779; Contact: Gabrielle Shanin
gabrielle.shanin@prudential.com

1110. Prudential Sponsored Programs, 1939–1950. Papers covering an overview of the company's sponsorship of several programs, including *When A Girl Marries*, 1939–1941, *The Prudential Family Hour*, 1945–1948, *The Prudential Family Hour of Stars*, 1948–1950 and *The Jack Berch Program*, 1945–1950?. Also includes scripts of the company's commercials for the programs.

Radcliff College
Schlesinger Library
3 James Street, Cambridge, MA 02138
(617) 495-8647; www.radcliffe.edu/schles/

General comments: In addition to the collections listed below, the library has papers of other women who gave talks on radio on specific subjects. Check the online catalog.

1111. Adelaide Fish Hawley Cumming Papers, 1922–1967. Contains correspondence, speeches, program scripts, publicity photos and articles primarily concerning her career which included narrating *The Woman Reporter* and *Woman's Page of the Air*. Cumming played the role of Betty Crocker, an advertising agent for General Mills, on radio and television. Papers concerning her Betty Crocker role consist mainly of promotional literature and speeches.

1112. Alice Bradley Papers, 1893–1980. Consists primarily of brochures and clippings from Miss Farmer's School of Cookery and biographies of Alice Bradley by her sister, Marion Bradley Atwood. Note: Bradley taught cooking on the radio.

1113. Clara Savage Littledale Papers, 1903–1982, bulk 1903–1956. Contains diaries, manuscripts, radio talks, speeches, personal and professional correspondence, photos and clippings. See online finding aid for list of radio talks.

1114. Dorothy Dunbar Bromley Papers, 1897–1986. Consists of photographs, correspondence, published articles by and about Bromley and background material for her articles and book. Check preliminary finding aid for any material related to her unidentified radio program, 1952–1958.

1115. Ella Fitzgerald Papers. Contains mostly publicity photographs of Fitzgerald.

1116. Eva Elise vom Baur Hansl Papers, 1939–1954. Includes scripts of *Women in the Making of America*, 1939–1940, broadcast in cooperation with the WPA's Federal Theatre Radio Division, and *Gallery of Women*, a series produced by the University of Michigan, 1954, and broadcast in cooperation with the U.S. Office of Education. Also includes program outlines, posters and clippings.

1117. Federal Theatre Project Records, 1939–1976. Includes clippings about Jane Ashman's two radio programs, *Americans All, Immigrants All*, 1938, and *Women in the Making of America*, 1939, for which historian Mary Beard was a consultant.

1118. Helen Brewster Owens Papers, 1867–1948. Contains papers relating to Owens's involvement with the *Gallant American Women* series, 1940–1941.

1119. Izetta Jewel Kenney Brown Miller Papers. Contains diaries of Miller's mother, family correspondence and photographs, radio scripts, fan letters, etc. Note: As of early 2005, the collection was unprocessed and closed.

1120. Jane Barton Papers, 1938–1984. Contains scrapbooks concerning her work with the WAVES, correspondence, press books, clips, photographs, etc. Barton was program director of the New York State Radio-TV Bureau. Note: As of 2005, the collection was unprocessed.

1121. Lydia E. Pinkham Medicine Company Records, 1776–1968, bulk 1859–1968. A large collection that includes audio tapes of radio ads.

1122. Marjorie Child Husted Papers, 1946–1954. Contains biographical material, speeches and pamphlets relating to women in business. Husted was an advertising executive, home economist and, as director of the Home Service Department of General Mills, she planned and implemented the *Betty Crocker* program, 1926–1946.

1123. Mary Anderson Radio Broadcast, 1942. Sound recording of three radio speeches broadcast on February 22, 1942 by Anderson for the working women of the Allied nations. Anderson describes the changing nature of employment for women before and during World War II, the history of sex discrimination in employment and forecasts how the employment climate for women may change after the war.

1124. Mildred Levine Albert Papers, 1910–1991. Albert was an international fashion consultant, educator, lecturer, columnist, producer of fashion shows and radio/TV personality. Check unpublished finding aid for possible radio related papers.

1125. Mrs. William Lowell Putnam Papers, 1887–1935. Contains correspondence, speeches, articles, letters to the editor, reports, bulletins, notes, radio broadcasts and clippings documenting Putnam's work in maternal and infant health care and conservative politics.

1126. Ruth Cowan Nash Papers, 1905–1990. Includes transcripts of her news broadcasts from Europe, 1943–1945, and other radio appearances.

1127. "The Women Who Won," 1960. Script for a program on the women's suffrage movement aired on WEEI, Boston, MA August 25, 1960.

1128. Women's Orchestras Collection, 1943. Consists of brochures advertising Phil Spitalny's All Girl Orchestra, the *General Electric Hour of Charm*, 1943, and two photographs of an unidentified women's band, n.d.

Radio & Television Museum
2608 Mitchellville Road, Bowie, MD 20716
(301) 390-1020; Fax: (301) 3338
bcbelanger@aol.com; www.radiohistory.org
Contact: Brian Belanger

1129. Library. Contains about 3,000 books. Although the emphasis of the collection is on technical material relating to radio and television hardware, there is a considerable amount of material on radio and television programs and performers. Also houses a collection of audio cassettes of radio programs. Holdings are listed online.

Record-Rama Sound Archives
1130 Perry Highway, Pittsburgh, PA 15237
(412) 367-7330; Fax: (412) 367-7388
www.recordrama.com; Contact: Paul C. Mawhinney

1130. Record Sound Archives. A collection of three million phonograph records, including radio programs and radio personalities. The archives maintains a database. Note: This is a commercial archive that charges for searches.

Rensselaer Polytechnic Institute
Folsom Library, Troy, NY 12180
(518) 276-8340
lib-archives@rpi.edu; www.rpi.edu

1131. WRPI Records, 1947–1972. Records of the college station.

Rhode Island Historical Society
Research Library, 121 Hope Street, Providence, RI 02906
(401) 273-8107; Fax: (401) 751-7930
www.rihs.org

1132. Walter "Salty" Brine Papers, 1937–1998. Consists of correspondence, biographical newspaper articles, broadcast scripts and advertisements, award certificates, travel itineraries and miscellaneous materials documenting Brine's 50 year career in broadcasting on WPRO, beginning as an announcer for *Time, News and Temperature* and later as the host of *Salty's Shack*, 1955–1968.

1133. Warren Walden Papers, 1907–1987. Majority of collection consists of newspaper clippings compiled about various sporting events covered by Walden during his career as sports commentator for WEAN and WJAR. Also includes radio scripts which include odd sports stories and trivia.

Rice University
Fondren Library, Woodson Research Center
6100 Main Street, Houston, TX 77251
(713) 348-2124; Fax: (713) 348-6172
afocke@rice.edu; www.rice.edu/fondren/woodson
Contact: Amanda York Focke

1134. Oveta Culp Hobby Papers, 1817–1995. Includes personal and business papers. Papers relating to KPRC are in Hobby's personal office files and range from early architectural drawings to licenses to instructions on how to run the switchboard. Also includes files from FCC hearings, 1955–1959, and a history of the station.

1135. Waggaman Family Collection Papers, 1841–1977, bulk 1932–1963. Consists largely of photographs and newspaper articles but also includes some personal correspondence and memorabilia. The bulk of the material relates to Camille Brown Waggaman and focuses on her radio career, 1932–1963, and the years after her retirement. Waggaman hosted a radio talk show in Alabama, *Around the Town*, for 31 years.

Roanoke Public Libraries
Virginia Room
706 South Jefferson Street, Roanoke, VA 24016
(540) 853-2073; Fax: (540) 853-1781
varoom@roanokeva.gov; Contact: Laura S. Wickstead

1136. Hayden Huddleston Records. Contains 402 reel-to-reel tapes (226 original reels and 176 duplicates) of music tracks and original programming broadcast by Huddleston and the Hayden Huddleston Advertising Agency, 1924–1981, on over 350 stations across the United States and Canada. Programs represented on the tapes include *Lazy Bill Huggin, Breakfast at the Ponce, Let's Go to Church, What's the Answer, The Hayden Huddleston Show, Claim to Fame, Klub Kwiz, Kiddie Kollege* and *Klassroom Kuiz*. Also includes approximately 500 index cards containing questions used on the quiz shows, 1962–1981.

Rochester Museum & Science Center
Collections and Research Department
657 East Avenue, Rochester, NY 14607
(585) 271-4552
Lea_Kemp@rmsc.org; Contact: Lea Kemp
www.rmsc.org/museum/museumframeset.htm

1137. Howard W. Coles Papers, 1839–1996. Papers of Rochester's first African American radio personality broadcasting on WSAY, including scripts for *The Vignettes, The Gospel Hour, The Bronze Trombones, The King Coles Show* and other programs, 1946–1974, and related material. Collection also includes tapes of the programs.

Rosenberg Library
2310 Sealy Avenue, Galveston, TX 77570
(409) 763-8854; www.rosenberg-library.org

1138. Hurricane Carla Records, 1961–1964. Transcripts of KGBC, Galveston, TX announcements during Hurricane Carla, 1961, including records from various agencies describing the storm and its aftermath and letters to station manager Steve Cowan from grateful listeners.

Roy Rogers Museum
3950 Green Mountain Drive, Branson, MO 65616
(417) 339-1900; Contact: Dick Cook
administrator@royrogers.com; www.royrogers.com

1139. Audio Collection. Recordings of the *Roy Rogers Show* from the 1940s. No additional material about the programs is available.

Rutgers University
Archibald S. Alexander Library
Special Collections and University Archives
169 College Avenue, New Brunswick, NJ 08901
(732) 932-7006, ext 360; Fax: (732) 932-7012
www.libraries.rutgers.edu/rul/libs/scua/scua.shtml
Contact: Nancy Martin

1140. Harold Richard Segoine Papers, 1863–1968. Includes 1952 publicity literature of Chanticleer Broadcasting Company. Note: Radio material may only be a small part of the collection.

Sacred Heart Program, Inc.
3900 Westminster Place, St. Louis, MO 63108
(314) 533-0320; Fax: (314) 533-0335
gkolarcik@sacredheartprogram.org
www.sacredheartprogram.org; Contact: Gary Kolarcik

1141. Sacred Heart Collection, 1942–. Contains a large volume of scripts and other papers relating to the *Scared Heart Program* dating back to about 1942. Also includes sound recordings (in different formats), some from 1940s, then from 1960s to the present and material on the television version of the program.

St. Louis Public Library
St. Louis Media Archives
1301 Olive Street, St. Louis, MO 63103
(314) 539-0399; Fax: (314) 539-0393
jgosebrink@slpl.org; Contact: Jean E. Meeh Gosebrink
www.slpl.lib.mo.us/libsrc/stlmediaarchive.htm

1142. Alfred Fleishman Papers. Contains personal papers and business records of the co-founder of the Fleishman-Hillard public relations firm, including material on his KMOX radio program.

1143. At Your Service, 1960. The first *At Your Service* program aired February 29, 1960 on KMOX with Paul Wills, announcer, Bob Holt, character voices, and Jack Buck, host. Other recordings include the first anniversary program, February 28, 1961, its twentieth anniversary show, February 29, 1980 and the 28th anniversary show in 1989.

1144. Bob Hardy Interviews on KMOX, 1960s–1992. Interviews with local and national politicians and personalities.

1145. Brad Holiday Radio Features, 1960s–1970s. Contains 20 audio tapes of Holiday's interviews and other programs on KFUO. Also includes biographical information about Holiday.

1146. Crusin', 1958. Sound recording features Jack Carney's WIL radio show. The tape was released as part of the series *Crusin' the Fifties and the Sixties.*

1147. Dizzy Dean Show, 1948. Two recordings of the show broadcast on KSD. Includes 13 episodes.

1148. Early Ralston Purina Radio Shows, 1940s–1960s. Includes *Ask Your Vet* and a *Tom Mix* air-check from 1945.

1149. Frank (John Francis) Eschen, 1942–1960. Contains scripts, speeches, notes, correspondence and other material related to Eschen's career as Director of Special News Events, an announcer and reporter on KSD. Also includes audio tapes and photographs.

1150. Gene Chase Interviews on WIL, 1960s. Includes 31 interviews with celebrities such as Cab Calloway, Andy Devine, Ginger Rogers, Carol Channing, Arthur Godfrey and others.

1151. Harry Fender. Contains photographs, books, theater programs, clippings, correspondence, audio and videotapes and memorabilia covering Fender's various careers. Includes correspondence from well-known entertainers, including Florenz Ziegfeld, Eddie Cantor and Max Morath, some 500 photographs of Fender with celebrities he interviewed for KXOK and KMOX and an autograph book with hundreds of signatures from celebrities. Fender hosted an interview show on KXOX and KMOK from 1947 to the 1970s.

1152. Jesse "Spider" Burks Papers, 1922–1975. Includes photographs, clippings, awards and certificates and memorabilia covering Burks's radio disc jockey career beginning in 1947 at KXLW and later with KSTL, KATZ and KADI. Also includes material on his TV career.

1153. John Roedel. Rodel was a staff announcer and newsman at KSD, 1947–1975. Collection includes five recordings of his auditions, ca. 1947, and additional post-1960 radio and television material.

1154. "Johnny Rabbit" on KXOK. Audio tapes, photographs and newspaper articles of KXOK disc jockeys Ron Elz and Don Pietromonaco who used the on-air name "Johnny Rabbit."

1155. KMOX Collections. Contains recordings of programs, 1930s–1940s, including *Barnyard Follies*, newscasts, interviews, sports and other programming with station favorites such as France Laux, Jack Buck, Harry Caray, Bob Hardy, Rex Davis, John McCormick, Jack Carney, Anne Keefe and others. Also includes publications, reports, advertisements, clippings and a variety of other material.

1156. KMOX-Muny Opera. Thirteen recordings of the St. Louis Municipal Opera broadcast on KMOX, 1946–1948.

1157. *KMOX Radio–70 Years in the Making*, **1995.** Program aired December 24, 1995 with Jack Buck and Jim White as hosts. Features Jack Carney with Bob Starr and Rex Davis.

1158. *KMOX Radio–75 Years in the Making.* Videocassette that captures the history of the station from its sign-on on December 24, 1925 through recordings and historic photographs.

1159. KSD Collection, 1920s–1970s, bulk 1960s–1970s. Contains over 200 audio tapes of KSD local programming, newscasts and specials. Includes more than 100 photographs showing scenes from KSD studios and KSD/NBC personalities, scripts, public relations releases, pamphlets, clippings and other printed materials. Also includes recordings of Russ David's program, *St. Louis Serenade*, that was fed to NBC.

1160. KXOK 1960s Reunion Program. A roundtable discussion by 1960s KXOK staffers recorded September 29, 2001.

1161. KXOK Sports. Interviews with the Soldan High School basketball team taped before a game, 1940. Includes Harry Caray's broadcast on the sale of the St. Louis Cardinals, 1947.

1162. *The Land We Live In*, **1937–1952.** Scripts of 380 shows sponsored by the Union Electric Company of Missouri and broadcast first on KSD and later on KMOX. The shows present the history of the St. Louis area. Also includes photographs and recordings.

1163. Louise Munsch/Alva N. Dopking. Includes biographical information on Munsch who hosted *Just For Women* on WEW, 1940s–1950s, and Alva Dopking who was chief of the St. Louis bureau of the Associated Press. See additional audio collection below.

1164. Louise Munsch/Dopking. Recording of *Just for Women* on WEW, January 22, 1953, with interview of Dr. Lillian Gilbreth, efficiency engineer and author of "Cheaper By the Dozen" on "Managing Minutes in Your Kitchen." Also interviews with Betty Furness, CBS television personality and home economist Nancy Haven as well as other programs, 1955–1956.

1165. Nick Charles Papers. KXOX disc jockey, 1962–1982. In addition to personal information, the papers cover labor/management issues and AFTRA representation.

1166. Oral History Interviews With Persons Associated

with St. Louis Radio. Includes interviews of Ed Bench, KSTL, KATZ and KCFM; Joan Colegrove; Don Corey, KSHE, KADI-FM and KIRL; John Craddock; Rex Davis, KMOX; Harry Eidelman, KCFM; Harry Fender, KXOK and KMOX; Dick and Nancy Friedman, KRCH; Robert Hille, KXOK; Gene Hirsch, WIL; Tim Lyons; Kay Morton; Chuck Norman; Ellie Ohrn; Roy Queen, KMOX; Ollie Raymand, KMOX; Sibley Smith, KCFM.

1167. Radio and Entertainment In and Around St. Louis, v. 1-3, 1931–1933. Includes a variety of promotional items from St. Louis radio stations, including coffee mugs, T-shirts, bags, bumper stickers, posters, pens and pencils, postcards, buttons, patches, frisbees, visors, key chains, magnets, balloons, coupons, posters and more. Among the more unusual items is a KATZ license plate.

1168. Radio Programming. A collection of more than 200 sound recordings, including programs, interviews, air-checks, promotional spots and similar materials. For details see department finding aid.

1169. Radio Scripts, Manuscripts, Publications, Photographs, Etc. Includes pamphlets, promotional material, magazines and clippings related to St. Louis radio stations and radio personalties. Clippings, dated from the 1920s, have been copied from the library's extensive collections. Collections for KMOX, KSD and KXOK are particularly strong. Other items include *The Community Forum* scripts broadcast on KSD, June 21, 1942, *Inquiring Girl Reporter* scripts, KWK, 1942–1943, *News Events in Social Work* scripts for the weekly WIL program, chiefly January–May, 1942, and *Down Memory Lane* scripts, 1949–1954 (possibly *Down Memory Lane with Kathryn Kane* broadcast on KIDO).

1170. Reed Farrell. Includes 30 photographs showing Farrell and guests on his television show and videocassette interviews of celebrities. Collection may not have material on Farrell's earlier career in radio in the mid–1950s on KWK, WIL, KSD and KMOX.

1171. Rex Davis Collection. Contains biographical information, scripts, promotional and advertising materials for Davis's broadcasts and 160 photographs of Davis and other KMOX personnel. Also includes Davis's interviews and other audio of his broadcasts. Davis began his career at KMOX in 1946 and served as newscaster, news director and director of community relations.

1172. Roy Queen. Includes letters of congratulations, proclamations, photographs and biographical information of the country music star who had a program on KMOX from 1929 to early 1950s and later on other St. Louis stations.

1173. *The Sacred Heart Program*, **1946, 1957, 1958, 1970, and 1988.** Recordings of the program broadcast on WEW.

1174. *Saturday at the Chase*, **1947–1953.** Includes broadcasts featuring nationally known musicians such as the Tommy Dorsey Orchestra, Eddie Duchin and Spike Jones as well as St. Louis bands.

1175. *The St. Louis Story*, **1952.** Two transcription discs of the Boatmen's National Bank's recording of the broadcast November 2, 1952 on KMOX about the St. Louis Public Library.

Salvation Army, USA

PO Box 269, Alexandria, VA 22313
(703) 684-5500; Contact: Col. John Falin

1176. *Heartbeat Theater* Collection. Sound recordings of the program, 1940s–1950s. Note: Recordings are on transcription discs and the archive does not have equipment for listening to them. No print material about the program is available.

San Francisco Performing Arts Library & Museum

401 Van Ness Avenue, Room 402, San Francisco, CA 94102
(415) 255-4800, ext. 14; Fax: (415) 255-1913
info@sfpalm.org; www.sfpalm.org
Contact: Kirsten Tanaka

General comments: The library maintains a biographical clippings file on performers who appeared in productions in San Francisco or who were passing through the city and were written about in the local papers.

1177. Adrian Michaelis Papers. As of 2005, the recently acquired collection has not been processed. However, it does contain a large volume of print material, including photographs, relating to the *Chevron Standard Hour* which Michaelis produced. Also includes some transcription discs for the *NBC University Theater*.

1178. *Chevron Standard Hour* Collection, 1940–1952. Transcription discs of the program. As of 2005, about 300+ programs have been transferred and plans are to transfer the remaining discs. Also see Adrian Michaelis Collection above.

1179. Commonwealth Club of California Collection, 1931–1941. Includes copy of a program broadcast on NBC's *America's Town Meeting of the Air* entitled, "Is War With Japan Inevitable?" Note: The catalog does not specify whether the material is a print transcript or an audio recording.

1180. Radio Stations Collection, ca. 1924–. Contains clippings, photographs and program and publicity materials on San Francisco Bay Area radio stations.

SC Johnson Company

1525 Howe Street, Racine, WI 53403
(262) 260-2000; gewolfe@scj.com
Contact: Gary Wolfe

1181. Corporate Archives. Some print material dealing with the company's sponsorship of radio programs may be available on a limited basis to qualified researchers. All sound recordings have been donated to the Museum of Broadcasting in Chicago.

Schenectady City History Center

City Hall, Jay Street, Schenectady, NY 12305
(518) 382-5088

1182. Charles H. Huntley Papers, 1942–1945. Includes scripts of *Our Home Town* written and delivered by Huntley (a.k.a. "Old Mr. Citizen") about Schenectady on WGY.

1183. William B. Efner Collection. Contains miscellaneous items involving the history of Schenectady, including items about the General Electric Company which sponsored radio programs.

Schenectady Museum

Nott Terrace Heights, Schenectady, NY 12308
(518) 382-7890; Contact: Chris Hunter
schdymuse@schenectadymuseum.org
www.schenectadymuseum.org

General comments: See Addendum for additional collections.

1184. WGY Collections. The "Papers" portion of the collection contains promotional items, including program schedules, advertisements, newsletters, promotional booklets, cookbooks and press releases. The "Recordings" portion contains more than 20 programs, including the 50th anniversary special in 1972 and a recording of a Bobsled Ride in 1941. The "Photograph" collection contains 5,000 images of the station, 1925–1955.

Niel Shell

632 Smith Street, Franklin Square, NY 11010
(212 650-5116; nsxcc@cunyvm.cuyn.edu

1185. Nathaniel Shilkret Archives. Clippings, papers and 2,000 recordings, including air-checks and transcription discs of the Orchestra's appearance on many programs, including the *Eveready Hour*. Collection is privately held.

Shubert Archive

Lyceum Theatre
149 West 45th Street, New York, NY 10036
(212) 944-3895; Fax: (212) 944-4139
Maryannc@shubertarchive.org; www.shubertarchive.org
Contact: Maryann Chach

1186. Radio Scripts, 1946. A collection of proposed scripts prepared by Young & Shubert, Inc. designed to sell radio shows to agencies and sponsors. Includes multiple copies of scripts for proposed radio series; sometimes there are several episodes. It is not clear whether or not any of the proposed shows actually made it to the air. Some of the proposals include budgets for the radio episodes. A list of the scripts is available from the repository.

1187. Sound Recordings, 1945–1946. Transcription discs of Shubert productions, mostly operettas, broadcast on WGN, Chicago, 1944–1954, for *Chicago Theatre of the Air*, *The Railroad Hour*, *The Celanese Hour* and *Texaco Star Theatre*. Collection also includes cassettes of productions of "The Student Prince" (remastered from discs) that aired on the *Texaco Star Theatre*, July 21, 1946 and *The Celanese Hour*, May 24, 1945. Also radio commercials advertising Broadway shows in Shubert houses. Note: Equipment is not available to listen to the discs.

David S. Siegel Radio Archives

PO Box 193, Yorktown Heights, NY 10598
(914) 962-3680; Fax: (914) 245-2630
otrdsiegel@verizon.net

1188. Audio and Print Collection. A privately held audio collection of approximately 85,000 hours of programs representing all genres. Also contains an extensive collection of print broadcast history materials, including books, scripts, program logs, magazines, ephemera and looseleaf binders containing mostly clippings from old radio magazines that are organized by program and/or performer.

Smithsonian Institution

Archives Of American Art
750 9th Street, NW, Suite 2200, Washington, DC
Mailing address: PO Box 37012, Washington, DC 20013-7012
(202) 275-1961; www.aaa.si.edu/catalog.htm

1189. Amy Freeman Lee Papers, 1934–1980. Includes 12 bound volumes of scripts from Lee's program, *Call Board*, 1947–1951, correspondence, scrapbooks and other material.

1190. *The Artist Reviews Art* Records, 1943–1944. Eighteen transcripts of the weekly program *The Artist Reviews Art* featuring Fernando Puma and Helen Waren, including scripts #15-23, October 1, 1943–February 18, 1944, broadcast on WEVD and WABF, New York City.

1191. Edith Bry Papers, 1922–1970. Contains correspondence, scrapbooks, financial papers and other papers, including a script for *Art in a Democracy*, a symposium presented by the Federal Theatre Project in New York City, and three 7" untranscribed tapes of an interview of Bry and Philip Evergood for an *Art in a Democracy* broadcast on WQXR, New York City, April 29, 1938.

1192. Lena Gurr Papers, 1908–1979. Includes correspondence, notes, scrapbooks about the artist and a phonograph record of an interview of Gurr conducted by Jan Gelb on *Of Interest to Women*, 1950.

1193. Nickolas Muray Papers, 1911–1978. Includes biographical material, letters, subject files, transcript of an interview of Muray's appearance on the *Fleischmann's Yeast Hour*, 1929, notes, writings, art works, photographs and other printed material.

1194. René d'Harnoncourt Papers, 1920–1983. Includes correspondence, biographical material, printed material, scrapbooks, personal files and material related to d'Harnoncourt's work on *Art and America*.

1195. Sacramento Art Center Records, 1937–1941. A community art center funded by the Federal Art Project. Collection includes an unidentified radio script.

National Museum of American History
14th & Constitution Ave., NW, Washington, DC 20013
(202) 633-3270; Fax: (202) 786-2453
archivescenter@si.edu
http://americanhistory.si.edu/archives/home.htm

Advertising, Marketing & Commercial Imagery Collections
1196. Breck Girls Collection, ca. 1936–1995. Includes radio scripts for *American Girl Philharmonic*, 1946.

1197. Campbell Soup Advertising Collection, 1904–1989. Includes oral history interviews.

1198. The Eskimo Pie Corporation Records, 1921–1996. Includes scripts for radio announcements and advertisements, 1930–1985. Also includes sheet music for the radio jingles, "I Scream, You Scream, We All Scream for Ice Cream," "Oh My, Eskimo Pie," and "New Eskimo Pie on a Stick" and a photograph of Don Ameche.

1199. Maidenform Collection, 1922–1997. Includes transcripts of radio ads from 1950.

1200. Marlboro Advertising Oral History and Documentation Project, ca. 1926–1986. Includes radio commercials, 1956–1957 and 1986, and radio spots, 1956–1957.

1201. Procter & Gamble Company, Ivory Soap Advertising Collection, 1883–1998. Includes a print ad with a reference to *Crestfallen Manor* and a second ad with a reference to a Lowell Thomas CBS radio program at the bottom of the page.

1202. Sam DeVincent Collection of Illustrated American Sheet Music, ca. 1790–1987. Contains a collection of automobile and petroleum industry advertisements, ca. 1920–1949, that include sheet music and other material from radio programs sponsored by gasoline, oil or automobile companies. Also includes photographs of the radio personalities appearing on the covers.

1203. The Sandra & Gary Baden Collection of Celebrity Endorsements in Advertising, ca. 1897–1979. A wide-ranging collection of over 1,000 celebrity advertising endorsements culled from high-end magazines. Includes radio personalities such as Jack Benny, Bing Crosby, Fred Allen, Jack Webb, Bob Hope and others as well as advertisements that involve radios or radio stations. See online finding aid for list of personalities and products.

1204. Simmons Company Records, 1892–2000. Includes transcripts for radio ads for Simmons products, some on *Simmons Radio Hour,* including some 1930s and some n.d., and a May 25, 1936 script for the *Home Hour* with L.L. Murray.

Archives Center
1205. *Adventures in Science* Programs, 1955–1956. Nineteen original audio tapes produced for the CBS public affairs program *Adventures in Science* hosted by Watson Davis, director of Science Service and editor of "Science News Letter." On the program, Davis interviewed guests ranging from psychologists to an engineer from an air conditioner manufacturing company.

1206. Don Brown Collection of Duke Ellington Recordings, 1925–1973. Collection of 928 recordings by Duke Ellington's orchestra, including 132 unissued recordings, some of which were done for radio. Check repository for a preliminary inventory.

1207. Duke Ellington Collection, 1934–1974. Contains sound recordings, original music manuscripts and published sheet music, handwritten notes, correspondence, business records, photographs, scrapbooks, newsclippings, concert programs, posters, pamphlets, books and other ephemera. See online finding aid for list of radio broadcast material.

1208. Duke Ellington Collection Music Manuscripts (Series 1), ca. 1930–1981. Includes an air-check of the program broadcast January 4, 1961 featuring Arthur Godfrey performing "Passion Flower."

1209. Ed Dodd (*Mark Trail*) Collection, before 1985. Sound recordings of *Outdoors With Ed Dodd,* weekly 15-minute programs that focused on conservation and human interaction with the natural world and included camping tips. The tone of the program is informal, usually consisting of a brief conversation between the show's host, Peter Roberts, and Ed Dodd, the creator of the *Mark Trail* comic strip. Occasionally there are identified guests. Also includes video taped interview with Dodd and a copy of a television program.

1210. Franklin Delano Roosevelt Exhibition Records, ca. 1981–1982. Records of a major 1982 exhibition mounted by the National Museum of American History recounting Roosevelt's relationship with the American people through mass media, particularly radio broadcasting. Includes exhibition scripts documenting the early political years of Roosevelt and his presidency, especially emphasizing his skillful use of radio and the fireside chats during the 1930s and 1940s.

1211. George H. Clark Radioana Collection, ca. 1880–1950. Includes materials that span the entire history of the growth of the radio industry. While most of the materials document technical aspects of radio, Series 109 and 134 contain considerable information on broadcasting history.

1212. Science Service Records, ca.1910–1963. Science Service was a news service designed to popularize science and disseminate scientific knowledge. The collection includes materials about the CBS program, *Advances in Science*, 1935–1939. Check repository for partial contents.

1213. Smithsonian Institution. Editorial and Publications Division Records, 1906–1965. Contains records, 1936–1942, including scripts and related promotional literature for *The World Is Yours* and a file of collected information on other contemporary educational radio programs. Check repository for additional information.

1214. Smithsonian Productions. Production Records, 1876, 1963–2002. Includes records documenting the many film, video and radio production activities of the Smithsonian. See online listing for names of specific projects.

1215. Smithsonian Productions, 1938–2001. Consists of master audio tapes for *Radio Smithsonian* programs #750–1098, 1984–1989.

1216. Stan Freberg Advertising Collection, 1958–1991. Commercially available recordings of Freberg's radio series *The Best of the Stan Freberg Shows*, 1958, his satire, *Stan Freberg Presents the United States of America*, 1961, and the *New Stan Freberg Show*, 1991.

1217. United States National Museum. Department of Engineering and Industries, Radio Program Records, 1936–1940. Includes an incomplete set of scripts and programs, scrapbooks, correspondence and newsclippings concerning radio programs on technology and science aired on *The World Is Yours*.

1218. WANN Records, 1946–1997. Contains documents chronicling the station's business and regulatory history, including correspondence with fans, business records, publicity materials, advertising, certificates and awards, sales reports, photographs, printed material, posters and tape recordings. WANN, MD was one of the first radio stations with a black-oriented format.

Society to Preserve and Encourage Radio Drama, Variety and Comedy (SPERDVAC)
PO Box 7177, Van Nuys, CA 91409
(877) 251-5771 or (310) 219-0053
sperdvac@aol.com; www.sperdvac.org

1219. Mixed Collections. The non profit group maintains a large lending library of sound recordings of programs and interviews with radio pioneers as well as printed materials, including scripts, logs, photographs,. videotapes of meetings with old time radio actors and personnel talking about their careers in radio and radio magazines. A portion of the group's varied holdings are listed online at www.sperdvac.org/index_listing_info.htm. Contact the organization for information about additional resources.

South Carolina Historical Society
The Fireproof Building
100 Meeting Street, Charleston, SC 29401
(843) 723-3225; Fax: (843) 723-8584
karen.stokes@schistory.org; www.schistory.org/archives.htm

1220. Anne King Gregorie Papers. Includes scripts for talks she gave about South Carolina history on WIS, 1940, that were part of the University of South Carolina's *School of the Air.*

1221. Charles Ministerial Union Records, 1941-1944. Includes a schedule of radio services, 1941, and a "List of Transcribed Religious Music in the WCSC Library," 1941.

1222. Charles Oil Co. Records, 1891–1988, bulk 1959–1981. Advertising material includes sketches of ad ideas, advertising copy and scripts for radio commercials.

1223. McLeod Family Papers, 1873–1990, bulk 1900–1965. Includes a poster, 1930s, for radio broadcasts of Walter Wells Collins known as "The Pee Dee Philosopher."

South Dakota State University
H.M. Briggs Library Archives, Room 241
Box 2115, Brookings, SD 57007
(605) 688-5094; Fax: (605) 688-6133
stephen_vanburen@sdstate.edu; Contact: Stephen VanBuren
http://lib.sdstate.edu/archives/index.html

1224. George C. Biggar Papers, 1920–1988, bulk 1943–1944. Includes scripts, interviews, clippings, photographs and other material related to Biggar's career in radio. The collection offers some insight into the formative years of radio, especially the material related to the *National Barn Dance* and WLS, Chicago. Papers also cover Biggar's work at WLW, Cincinnati and WLBK, DeKalb, IL. Also includes other papers. Note: The audio cassettes, photographs and slides in the collection have been removed for preservation purposes. Check with staff regarding their availability.

Southern Baptist Historical Library
Southern Baptist Convention Building
901 Commerce Street, Nashville, TN 37203
(615) 244-0344; Contact: Taffey Hall
taffey@sbhla.org; www.sbhla.org/info.htm

1225. *Baptist Hour* Sermons, 1942–1978, bulk 1968–1978. Contains copies of sermons from the *Baptist Hour*, a weekly broadcast produced by the Southern Baptist Convention Radio and Television Commission.

Southern California Library for Social Studies and Research
6120 South Vermont Avenue, Los Angeles, CA 90044
(323) 759-6063; Fax: (323) 759-2252
archives@socallib.org; www.socallib.org

1226. Robert Shaw Papers, 1916?–1996. Consists primarily of scripts written by members of the Hollywood Writers Mobilization during World War II and political speeches and spots written for the California Democratic Party in 1946 and for Henry Wallace's 1948 Progressive Party presidential campaign. See online finding aid for list of scripts.

1227. Union Files Collection, 1920s–1980s. Collection of materials from over 150 unions spanning the decades from the 1920s through the 1980s. The majority of the material comes from unions active in the Southern California area, including the Radio Writers Guild, Screen Writers Guild and AFTRA.

Spertus Institute of Jewish Studies

Asher Library
618 South Michigan Avenue, Chicago, IL 60605
(312) 322-1749; asherlib@spertus.edu
http://norman.spertus.edu:4505/ALEPH

1228. Mixed Materials. A variety of print and audio collections related to the culture of the Jewish people. Also the home of the Chicago Jewish Archives. Check online catalog for specific radio related material.

Sports Museum of New England

1175 Soldiers Field Road, Boston, MA 02134
(617) 624-1236; Contact: Richard Johnson
rajcurator@aol.com

1229. Audio Collection. Includes sound recordings of baseball and basketball games from 1940s to present.

Stanford University

Archive of Recorded Sound
Braun Music Center
541 Lasuen Mall, Stanford, CA 94305
(650) 725-1146; Fax: (650) 725-1145
soundarchive@stanford.edu; Contact: Jerry McBride
www-sul.stanford.edu/depts/ars/

General comments: Check with Archive for additional Golden Age of Radio audio material.

1230. Pryor Collection, 1940–1942. Houses over 1,000 transcription discs covering a wide range of subject matter. The discs were made directly from local and network broadcasts between 1940–1942 and provide a snapshot of day-to-day life at the time, particularly wartime attitudes toward local and world politics, the economy and social issues. Includes entertainment shows and commercials. Note: A second Pryor sound collection with recordings related to World War II is included below in the Hoover Institution listings.

Hoover Institution
Archives, Stanford, CA 94305-6010
(650) 723-3563; Fax: (650) 725-3445
danielson@hoover.stanford.edu; Contact: Elena S. Danielson
www-hoover.stanford.edu/hila/collectionsp.htm

General comments: Because the titles of the collections listed below are the titles used in the online catalog, some of the collections are shown generically as "Interview," "Miscellany" or "Radio Broadcast" followed by a date.

1231. *A Reporter Remembers*, Vol 1, The War Years, n.d. Two sound recordings with a compilation of Edward R. Murrow's radio broadcasts from Europe, 1939–1946, relating to military activities in Europe and the home front in Great Britain during World War II.

1232. *Americans All, Immigrants All*, 1939 and n.d. Sound recording of broadcasts relating to the immigration of various national and ethnic groups to the United States. Also includes recordings of *Treasury Star Parade*, n.d.

1233. *America's Town Meeting of the Air*, 1945. Two sound recordings of the program relating to the founding of the United Nations and its prospective role in ensuring world peace.

1234. Christopher Temple Emmet Papers, 1913–1974. Contains correspondence, memoranda, reports, press releases, writings, transcripts and recordings of radio broadcasts, 1939–1973, and photographs relating to anti-Nazi and anti communist movements in the United States, American foreign policy during the Cold War and American-German relations.

1235. Commonwealth Club of California. Includes thousands of radio broadcasts dating back to 1944. Programs featured prominent guests in national politics, science, sports and the humanities. Also includes papers and photographs relating to the Club.

1236. December 7, 1941 Sound Recording, 1966 Compilation. A sound recording representing a compilation by Bud Greenspan of speeches, radio addresses and radio news broadcasts, 1940–1945, relating to the Japanese attack on Pearl Harbor, the events leading up to it and its aftermath. Includes facsimiles of pages from "The New York Times," December 6–9, 1941.

1237. Edmund Albert Chester Papers, 1933–1947. Includes photographs, clippings, correspondence, press releases and memorabilia relating to Latin American politics and to CBS radio broadcasting in Latin America.

1238. Ethel G. Phillips Collection, 1933–1941. Clippings from American newspapers relating to American foreign and domestic policy during the New Deal and reflecting conservative criticism of that policy. Includes pamphlets issued by the American Liberty League, 1935–1936, and texts of broadcasts of the *Ford Sunday Evening Hour*, 1936–1940.

1239. George Alexander Hill Papers, n.d. Includes broadcast transcripts for *Go Spy the Land* relating to British intelligence activities in Russia, Turkey and the Balkans, 1917–1918.

1240. George E. Sokolsky Papers, 1916–1962. Contains writings, broadcast transcripts, correspondence, printed matter, phonorecords and photographs relating to politics, communism, internal security and anti communist movements in the United States and to politics and communism in China and elsewhere.

1241. "Greece As I Saw It," n.d. Recording of a broadcast by Oscar Theodore Broneer relating to conditions in Greece at the end of World War II as recorded by NBC. In English and Greek.

1242. "How the U.S. Heard About Pearl Harbor," 1961. Relates to the dissemination of information to the American public by radio commentators about the Pearl Harbor attack, December 7, 1941.

1243. Inez Richardson Papers, 1922–1963. Includes correspondence, memoranda, reports, minutes, speeches, writings and other printed matter relating to international relations, international education and the role of radio and television in education.

1244. Interview, 1949. A recording of an interview of Herbert Vere Evatt conducted by Clark M. Eichelberger, director of the American Assn. for the United Nations, that was broadcast on NBC relating to the activities of the United Nations.

1245. Julius Klein Papers, 1928–1933. Contains transcripts of broadcasts and speeches relating to American economic conditions, foreign trade and economic policy during the administration of President Herbert Hoover.

1246. Leland T. Chapin Papers, 1941–1944. Includes writings, minutes of meetings, radio transcripts and serial issues relating to the promotion of patriotism in Hawaiian schools and within the Asian community in Hawaii and to military government in the Marshall Islands during World War II.

1247. Lester Ziffren Papers, 1933–1989. Includes news dispatches, broadcast transcripts, pamphlets, clippings, serial issues and other printed matter relating to political and social conditions in Spain and to the Spanish Civil War.

1248. Miscellany, 1942, 1944. Contains correspondence and miscellanea relating to the broadcast of *Salute to the War Mothers*, 1942, and the publication of a pamphlet "Salute to the Gold Star Mothers," 1943, by the American Legion, San Francisco Post No. 1.

1249. "On a Note of Triumph," 1945. Sound recording of Norman Corwin's broadcast relating to the surrender of Germany in World War II broadcast May 8, 1945.

1250. Peter Stansky Miscellaneous Papers, 1937–1987. Includes correspondence with Harry Milton and others, broadcast transcripts, clippings, photographs and miscellany relating to the acquaintanceship of Milton with the British writer George Orwell in Spain during the Spanish Civil War.

1251. Princeton Listening Post Transcripts, 1939–1941. Includes transcripts of news broadcasts from London, Paris, Rome, Berlin and Moscow relating to war news, December, 1939–May, 1941.

1252. Radio Broadcast, 1945. Recording of appeals by Nicholas Kalmer to Greek-Americans to contribute medical and food relief to Greece through the Greek War Relief Association at the end of World War II. In Greek.

1253. Radio Broadcast, 1945. A recording of a U.S. Army Infantry Christmas radio broadcast from Tokyo.

1254. Radio Broadcast, 1952. A recording of addresses by Dwight D. Eisenhower and Adlai Stevenson, Republican and Democratic candidates for president of the United States, broadcast over CBS as part of a program sponsored by the National Citizens' Committee for United Nations Day.

1255. Radio Broadcast Series, ca. 1942. Three sound recordings of *United Press Is On The Air* relating to news-gathering activities of the United Press during World War II.

1256. Radio Broadcasts, 1941–1942. A collection of 57 sound recordings of broadcasts relating to American neutrality in World War II, the Japanese attacks on Pearl Harbor and the Philippines and the first weeks of American participation in the war. Includes speeches by President Franklin D. Roosevelt and Prime Minister Winston Churchill of Great Britain and newscasts. Collection was compiled by Roy Pryor.

1257. Radio Broadcasts, 1957. Thirteen recordings of *Tower of Peace* relating to the facilities, history, purpose and activities of the Hoover Institution on War, Revolution and Peace. Includes interviews with Herbert Hoover and with staff members and researchers at the Hoover Institution. The program was sponsored by the Hoover Institution.

1258. Radio News Broadcast, 1945. Sound recording of a broadcast from Chungking, China recorded by the MBS relating to the reopening of the Burma Road.

1259. Radio News Broadcast, Nuremberg, Germany, 1946. Sound recording of Arthur Gaeth from Nuremberg, Germany broadcast over MBS relating to the execution of leading Nazis convicted of war crimes.

1260. Radio News Broadcast, Stockton, CA, 1948. Sound recording of a broadcast over KCVN, College of the Pacific, Stockton, CA relating to controversies regarding the city government of Stockton.

1261. Records (America First Committee), 1940–1942. Includes radio scripts used by the private organization to promote U.S. nonintervention in World War II.

1262. Sound Recordings, 1948. Two recordings of Voice of Democracy Committee promotional announcements and model radio broadcasts relating to a contest for high school students for radio broadcast scripts on democracy in the United States. The contest was sponsored by the United States Junior Chamber of Commerce, the National Association of Broadcasters and the Radio Manufacturers Association.

1263. Templeton Peck Papers, 1944–1988. Includes memoirs, broadcast transcripts, memoranda and reports, 1944–1945, relating to the activities of the Office of War Information during World War II and especially to its radio broadcasts of news and commentary in various languages to Europe from its London station.

1264. *Then Came War*, 1939. Sound recordings with Elmer Holmes Davis relating to the outbreak of World War II. Includes recordings of radio addresses by leaders of the belligerent nations.

1265. William Hard Radio Broadcast Transcript, 1929. Transcript of radio broadcast in which Hard discusses the Kellogg-Briand Pact and American intervention in Latin America.

1266. William M. Mandel Papers, 1953–1994. Includes broadcast transcripts, other writings and sound recordings relating to American opinion regarding the Soviet Union and the development of the Cold War, 1945–1948.

<u>Special Collections and University Archives</u>
557 Escondido Mall, Stanford, CA 94305
(650) 725-1026; Contact: Polly Armstrong
speccollref@stanford.edu; www-sul.stanford.edu/depts/spc/

1267. Carlton E. Morse Oral History Interview and Related Correspondence and Reference Material, 1936–1981. Forty oral history interviews (tapes and transcripts) conducted between 1970 and 1975. Also contains address and cast lists for *One Man's Family*, original scripts for August 16 and 19, 1936, and program ephemera. Also newsclippings, "Random Reflections," written by Morse, 1972–1974, photographs of Morse and his family and a video "Good Old Days of Radio," narrated by Steve Allen, n.d.

1268. Carlton E. Morse Papers, 1932–1982. Contains radio and television scripts for *One Man's Family*, including radio scripts for 1932–1949, correspondence, newsclippings, publicity materials, photographs, 90 reels of television film and sound recordings. For detailed information see online finding aid at www.oac.cdlib.org/findaid/ark:/13030/tf62900550.

1269. Cole Porter Papers, 1943–1971. Contains correspondence, radio scripts, manuscripts, notes, tapes, reviews of productions, photographs, periodicals and clippings. Although online finding aid lists a box of radio scripts, the contents of the box are not shown.

1270. Coolidge Family Papers, 1979–1948. Includes a collection of religious writings and radio talks of Harriett Brown Coolidge, 1936–1944.

1271. "Cooptation: A History of a Radio Station." A Ph.D. thesis by Susan Krieger on the history of the music station KMPX, San Francisco, Stanford University, 1976.

1272. "Fifty Years on Wheels," 1946. Text of a CBS broadcast commemorating the 50th anniversary of the automobile industry of America.

1273. J. E. (John Ewart) Wallace Sterling Photographs, ca. 1945. Includes publicity photographs taken during a CBS radio series *Citizens Forum*, ca. 1945.

1274. *Jack Benny Program* #13, 1953. Contains corrected script for the half-hour program broadcast December 6, 1953. Includes two 15-minute segments with an introductory and midway script for Lucky Strike advertisements.

1275. Pacifica Foundation Publicity Brochures and Papers, 1949–1984. Documents on the Pacifica Foundation, with emphasis on KPFA, Berkeley, CA. Consists primarily of printed articles about KPFA, programming schedules, information flyers and publicity materials.

1276. William ("Buster") Collier Papers, 1948–1950. Consists of two volumes of scripts by Bob Burns for the *Bob Burns Show*, 1944–1945, and 13 scripts written by Joel Malone, possibly for *The Whistler*, 1948–1950.

1277. William Saroyan Notebooks, 1932–1939. Entries document the apprenticeship and early success of Saroyan. Includes Saroyan's notes about radio shows.

State Historical Society of Iowa
Centennial Building
402 Iowa Avenue, Iowa City, IA 52240
(319) 335-3916; Contact: Mary Bennett
Mary.Bennett@uiowa.gov
www.iowahistory.org/library/index.html

General comments: See Addendum for additional collections at the Society's Des Moines location.

1278. Cummins Family Papers, 1869–1998. Includes articles, scripts and photographs of Tait Cummins, a sports writer and broadcaster in Cedar Rapids. His second wife, Dorothy Ireland Cummins, also worked at WMT.

1279. Henry Field Papers, 1946-1955. Contains transcripts of Field's program, the *Letter Basket*, broadcast on KFNF, station publications, programming schedules, postcards and photographs of radio personalities. The collection provides an account of the development of commercial radio. Note: Library has additional ephemera relating to Field and KFNF.

State Historical Society of North Dakota
State Archives and Historical Research Library

612 East Boulevard Avenue, Bismarck, ND 58505
(701) 328-328-2091; Fax: (701) 328-2650
archives@state.nd.us; www.state.nd.us/hist/sal.htm

1280. Bismarck High School Radio Scripts, ca. 1937. Scripts of dramatic radio re-enactments of significant events in North Dakota history.

1281. Harry Roberts Papers, ca. 1960s. Includes KDIX scripts concerning James Foley, Chateau de Mores, pioneer ranchers located along the Little Missouri River and a list of cowboy songs and dance music popular in early Medora.

1282. John W. and Constance (Blackstead) Boler Collection, 1936–199? Papers relating to broadcasting outlets (radio and television), mostly in North Dakota, but also in South Dakota and Virgin Islands owned by Boler and his other business and political activities.

1283. KBOM. Records, 1961–1962. Station history items.

1284. KVHF Radio Logs, n.d. Station radio logs.

1285. Leo D. Harris Manuscript, ca. 1930. Includes two typescripts describing the efforts at rabbit eradication and *Signal Rock*. Note: While the catalog listing does not identify *Signal Rock* as a radio program, "radio broadcasting" is listed as a subject heading and the words are italicized.

1286. M. J. Connolly Manuscript, June 15, 1939. A radio play script focusing on 50 years of North Dakota statehood entitled "Historical Sketch of North Dakota."

1287. North Dakota National Defense Welfare Service Records, 1941–1942. Includes radio scripts relating to the USO and the North Dakota National Defense Welfare Service.

1288. Robert (Bob) McLeod Audio/Visual Collections. 1945, and n.d. Includes interviews and visual items from McLeod's career as a radio broadcaster on KYFR.

1289. United States Navy Recruiting Station Records, 1943. Radio script describing battleships and the U.S.S. North Dakota.

State University of New York at Buffalo
University Archives
420 Capen Hall, Buffalo, NY 14260
(716) 645-2916; Fax: (716) 645-3714
lib-archives@buffalo.edu; Contact: John Edens
http://ublib.buffalo.edu/libraries/units/archives/

1290. Francis Hamilton Striker Papers, 1929–1986. Contains bound scripts for serial radio programs, 1929–1941, including 44 volumes of *The Lone Ranger*, 1932–1937, 63 volumes of *The Green Hornet*, 1936–1941, and *The Crimson Fang*. Also includes a case history of the filming of *The Lone Ranger* for Republic Studios and taped interviews with Lee Trent, 1970, and Paul Harris, 1973, regarding radio performances of *The Lone Ranger* and other serials for WEBR in the 1930s.

State University of New York at Potsdam
F. W. Crumb Memorial Library
44 Pierrepont Avenue, Potsdam, NY 13676
(315) 267-3326; Fax: (315) 267-2744
library@potsdam.edu; www.Potsdam.edu
Contact: Jane Subramanian

1291. Student Societies Records, 1874–1982. Includes

records for campus radio station WNTC that was run by the Inter College Radio Network.

Staten Island Institute of Arts and Sciences

Archives/Library
75 Stuyvesant Place, Staten Island, NY 10301
(718) 727-1135; Fax: (718) 273-5683
salmonf@aol.com; www.statenislandmuseum.org
Contact: Patricia Salmon

1292. Staten Island Institute of Arts and Sciences Proceedings. Includes program notes and transcripts for *Staten Island Today*, a weekly program produced by the Institute and aired on WNYC, New York, 1949–1950.

Charles Stumpf

803 Hazelwood Apartments, Hazelton, PA 18202
(570) 454-4261

1293. Walter Tetley Papers. A privately held collection of the actor's papers. Tetley appeared on *The Great Gildersleeve,* the *Phil Harris/Alice Faye Show* and many other programs.

Syracuse University

Belfer Audio Laboratory and Archive
222 Waverly Avenue, Syracuse, NY 13244
(315) 443-3477; Fax: (315) 443-4866
ststinso@syr.edu
http://libwww.syr.edu/information/belfer/

1294. General Audio Collection. Collection is cataloged but cannot be accessed online. Staff will respond to phone or email inquiries. Highlights of collection include recordings of Norman Corwin dramas and historical network broadcasts.

Special Collections Research Center
E. S. Bird Library, Room 600, Syracuse, NY 13244
(315) 443-2697; Fax: (315) 443-2671
scrc@syr.edu; http://libwww.syr.edu/information/spcollections/index.html

1295. Bob Considine Papers, 1921–1968, bulk 1945–1966. Includes correspondence, newspaper columns, articles by and about and photographs of Considine who was a radio journalist and war correspondent.

1296. Dorothy Thompson Papers, 1914–1961, bulk 1940–1961. Includes personal and professional papers and some radio scripts.

1297. Ed Begley Papers, 1943–1965. Consists of predominantly scripts for stage, radio, television and film plus correspondence, photographs and printed material, including playbills, theatre programs and a small amount of personal records and memorabilia.

1298. Eva Elsie vom Baur Hansl Papers, 1918–1968, bulk 1935–1948. Contains correspondence, radio scripts and speeches and research material related to Hansl's career as program supervisor, 1939–1940, for the series *Women in the Making of America* broadcast in cooperation with the WPA's Federal Theatre Radio Division, *Gallant American Women,* and *Womanpower,* 1943–1944.

1299. Fulton Lewis Papers, 1920–1966. Includes research files for broadcasts, 1937–1966, and sound recordings used in broadcasts and other professional and personal papers. A second collection includes post 1966 correspondence and other material.

1300. Gertrude Berg Papers, 1930–1962. Contains correspondence, radio and television scripts, clippings and other material in scrapbooks. Includes materials relating to *The Goldbergs, House of Glass* and *Mrs. G Goes to College.* See unpublished finding aid for more information.

1301. Hamilton Cochran Papers, 1932–1977. Papers include unidentified radio scripts.

1302. Hugo Gernsback Papers, 1908–1965. Contains correspondence, manuscripts of Gernsback's articles, editorials, speeches and printed material, including runs of periodicals published by Gernsback and amateurs' manuals relating to electronics and radio.

1303. Jack Douglas Papers, 1938–1955. Includes scripts for radio and television comedies and talk shows, 1938–1955.

1304. Long John Nebel Papers, 1926–1969, bulk 1964–1969. Contains correspondence, book manuscript and audio tapes of interview and talk radio shows.

1305. Mike Wallace Papers, 1958–1962. Papers relate to Wallace's television work only.

1306. Norman Lewis Corwin Papers, 1931–1967, bulk 1937–1967. Contains production material, including scripts and phonograph recordings, relating to Corwin's work as a writer for stage, screen and radio, 1937–1967.

1307. Norman Vincent Peale Papers, 1920–1965. Contains correspondence, manuscripts and personal files, including material relating to *Art of Living.*

1308. Office of Student Affairs and Services, Athletics, Department of Crew, James A. Ten Eyck Records, ca. 1881–ca. 1964. Includes radio talks by Ten Eyck about rowing.

1309. Peter Lipman-Wulf Papers, 1945–1975. Includes unidentified radio scripts, 1950–1955. Note: Although no finding aid is listed, based on other information in the catalog listing, the radio material may deal with art.

1310. Ralph W. Sockman Papers, 1903–1970, bulk 1935–1960. Includes correspondence, manuscripts of addresses, articles, books, lectures, radio scripts and sermons.

1311. Robert Lee Sherrod Papers, 1910–1963. Papers include radio scripts. For more information check unpublished finding aid.

1312. School of Speech and Dramatic Art, Radio and Television Center Records, 1938–1960. Includes scripts of daily student broadcasts, 1942–1948.

1313. Street and Smith Records. Contains internal records, manuscripts, radio scripts, books and periodicals of the publishing company. Includes scripts for *The Avenger,* 1941 and n.d., *Doc Savage,* 1943, *Chick Carter-Boy Detective,* 1943–1945, *Nick Carter, Master Detective,* 1943–1955, and *The Shadow* (including Australian scripts and South American scripts in Portuguese), 1937–1954. See online list at http://libwww.syr.edu/digital/guides/s/StreetAndSmith/.

1314. Vincent Sheean Papers, 1940–1965. Includes material on unidentified radio broadcasts. For more information see unpublished finding aid.

Temple University

Paley Library
1210 West Berks Street, Philadelphia, PA 19122
(215) 204-8230; Fax: (215) 204-5201
whitetm@temple.edu; Contact: Thomas M. Whitehead
http://library.temple.edu/collections/special_collections/

Special Collections Department

1315. Arnold Snyder Papers, 1953–1964. Contains correspondence, papers and typescripts of the news show *It Looks To Me* that aired on WTTM, Trenton, NJ.

1316. *Gang Busters* Scripts, 1937–1944. Nine original scripts for the series in various drafts. The scripts belonged to the real-life criminologist Dr. Carleton Simon who was a character in the episodes and who sometimes also played the part in the actual broadcast. Also includes a letter from the show's producer requesting Simon's permission to use his name.

1317. Leslie Reade Radio Scripts, 1948–1950. Scripts adapted by Reade from Terence Rattigan's "The Winslow Boy" and Robert Louis Stevenson's "Dr. Jekyll and Mr. Hyde" for the *Theatre Guild on the Air*. Collection includes two drafts of each script, including the final broadcast version.

1318. *Lux Radio Theatre* Scripts, 1934–1955. Includes 132 bound volumes of scripts (with stage directions), 1930s–1950s.

1319. Ownership Characteristics of Broadcasting Stations and Newspapers Report, 1971. An historical analysis of the broadcast and print media ownership in the top 100 U.S. markets between 1922 and 1967 prepared by Christopher H. Sterling for the National Association of Broadcasters.

1320. Radio and Television Scripts of Carlton E. Morse, 1929–1965. Contains 80 volumes of scripts for *One Man's Family* and sound recordings of the shows. Also includes scripts for *I Love a Mystery*, 1939–1952, *His Honor the Barber*, *Adventures by Morse*, *Family Skeleton*, 1953–1954, *Slice of Life*, 1949, and *Chinatown Tales* (a.k.a. *Chinatown Squad?*), 1929, and 44 sound recordings of other shows.

1321. Radio-Television Scripts (NBC Mixed Shows), 1936–1950. Collection of scripts for the *Abbott and Costello Show* and the *Oscar & Elmer Show*.

1322. Ruth Wilson Papers, 1917–1963. Includes manuscripts for mystery stories written by Wilson as well as scripts for radio shows she did on WHYY, Philadelphia, including *Story Teller's Holiday, Poet's Place* and other papers.

1323. *The Stark County Story*, n.d. The first 76 scripts of the *Good Neighbor Broadcasts* written by Edward Thornton and broadcast over WHFC. The program was a joint venture of the Stark County Historical Society in cooperation with the Ohio Broadcasting Corporation.

Urban Archives
(215) 204-1639; Contact: Brenda Galloway-Wright
brenda.galloway-wright@temple.edu
http://library.temple.edu/collections/urbana/

1324. Fellowship Commission Records. Includes 23 bound volumes of scripts for *Within Our Gates*, January, 1945–March, 1951. Located in boxes 44-46.

1325. Philadelphia Labor Market Studies, 1936. Includes a survey of 686 radio workers.

Tennessee State Library and Archives

403 Seventh Avenue North, Nashville, TN 37243
(615) 741-2764; Fax: (615) 741-6471
www.state.tn.us/sos/statelib/

1326. *Building for Peace*, 1945. Text for several broadcasts in the series related to World War II. Note: Each program is listed in the catalog as a separate collection.

1327. *Radio Talks*, 1936–1949. A quarterly digest of addresses presented in the public interest by CBS. Includes an April, 1937 talk, "Special Supreme Court Edition."

1328. *Stories of American Industry*, 1938. A series of Saturday afternoon talks by Harry Randolph Daniel of the U.S. Department of Commerce broadcast by CBS. Library has first and second series of the broadcasts.

1329. *Tar Heel Tales*, 1957. Text for the programs broadcast weekly during March and April, 1938 by WPTF, Raleigh, NC.

1330. "The War and Human Freedom," 1942. Text of a radio address by Secretary of State Cordell Hull over all national networks, July 23, 1942.

1331. *Weep No More, My Lady*, 1950. An enlargement on a series of two broadcasts over the Smith-Douglass radio network, February 8 and 9, 1950, in answer to comments on the South by Mrs. Eleanor Roosevelt in her column, "My Day."

Texas A & M University

Cushing Memorial Library, College Station, TX 77843
(979) 845-1951; Fax: (979) 845-1441
cushing-library@tamu.edu
http://library.tamu.edu/

1332. Ide Peebles Trotter Papers, 1922–1964. Includes text of radio talks, 1939–1941, 1948–1949 and 1952, usually on agricultural topics.

1333. Jack T. Kent Radio Scripts, 1945–1950. Contains manuscripts of radio lectures on mathematics, mathematicians and the solar system by Kent and others which were aired on WTAW, College Station, TX, 1945–1950.

1334. Texas Battleship Papers, 1948. Papers include the order of events for the radio program that covered the ceremony decommissioning and recommissioning the battleship into the Texas Navy, April 11–June 11, 1948, and transcripts of speeches.

Texas State Library and Archives Commission

PO Box 12927, Austin, TX 78711-2927
(512) 463-5480; Fax: (512) 463-5430
archinfo@tsl.state.tx.us; www.tsl.state.tx.us
Contact: Tonia Wood

1335. Governor W. Lee O'Daniel Records. Contains 135 transcripts of broadcasts made by the Governor, 1939–1941, most of which were regular weekly Sunday morning half hour programs and some special events. Weekly programs were usually religion based and family oriented although he also discussed legislative and social issues. Also includes some papers relating to the broadcasts.

Texas Tech University

Special Collections Library/Southwest Collection
PO Box 41041, Lubbock, Texas 79409
(806) 742-9070; Fax: (806) 742-0496

Patricia.Perry@ttu.edu; www.swco.ttu.edu/
Contact: Patricia Perry

1336. Amy Freeman Lee Papers, 1909–1997 and n.d. Papers document Lee's activities as an artist and include scripts for *Call Board*, 1949–1951 and n.d., broadcast over KONO.

1337. Athletic Council Records, 1925–1994 and n.d. Includes records relating to radio broadcasts, 1948–1953.

1338. Don Belding Papers, 1897–1969. Contains personal and business records. Belding was the founder of Foote, Cone and Belding Advertising Agency. Includes some unidentified radio scripts and other radio related material.

1339. Gordon Barton McLendon Papers, 1917–1978. Includes editorials, political files, political campaign materials, movie promotions, business correspondence and radio station policy books. Also includes sound recordings of programs, jingles, soundtracks, music, historical recordings, interviews, editorials, soundtracks, movie promotions, easy listening music, documentaries and advertisements. McLendon started KLIF, Dallas and began the Liberty Broadcasting System, an independent affiliation that encompassed over 400 radio stations during its five years of operation He was also the voice of the "Old Scotsman" broadcasting sports events and during the 1950s he developed the top 40 format.

1340. Indian Schools Collection, 1929–1945. Includes papers relating to the *Window Rock* broadcasts, 1938.

1341. Marshall Clinton Formby Papers, 1911–1984. Includes papers relating to Formby's ownership of numerous radio stations in Texas, including KPAN in Hereford, KFLD in Floydada, KTVE in Tulia, KSML in Seminole, KACT in Andrews and KLVT in Levelland.

Thousand Oaks Library
American Radio Archives
1401 East Janss Road, Thousand Oaks, CA 91362
(805) 449-2660; Fax: (805) 449-2675
Specoll@mx.tol.lib.ca.us; Contact: Jeanette Berard
www.tol.lib.ca.us

General comments: In addition to the special collections listed below, the Archives includes extensive pamphlet files, a collection of books dealing with radio and additional scripts and audio materials. A book cataloging the scripts in the collection is scheduled for publication in 2006 and is included in the Bibliography section under the heading "Scripts."

1342. Allin Slate Collection. Contains over 400 recordings of Slate's broadcasts, including his programs with co-hosts Leo Durocher and Jimmy Piersall as well as recordings of post-game interviews and press conferences with athletes and luncheons of the Southern California Sports Broadcasters Association. Also includes typescripts used in his broadcasts, photographs and publicity material related to his shows. As of 2005, the collection was partially processed.

1343. Arthur F. Wertheim Collection. Contains research material used by Wertheim in the writing of his book "Radio Comedy." Includes notes, photocopies of script pages, newspaper and magazine clippings and various drafts of his manuscript as well as 95 recordings of programs that he collected for his research.

1344. Austin Peterson Collection, 1942–1945. Contains papers related to Peterson's service with the Armed Forces Radio Service, including reports, photos, memoranda, AFRS spots, scripts for *Command Performance*, 1942–1943, and other miscellaneous scripts.

1345. Bob Crosby Collection. A collection of scripts for the *Jack Benny Show*, 1953–1954.

1346. Bob Gordon Collection. A collection of scripts for radio and television series, 1945–1946, 1949, including the *Abbott and Costello Show* and one script for *Birds Eye Open House*.

1347. C.A.R.T. Collection. Contains sound recordings, beginning in 1989, from a Hollywood repertory company that performs plays and theater pieces written or adapted for radio, including some productions written and directed by Norman Corwin.

1348. Carlton E. Morse Collection. Contains scripts for radio and television series, 1930–1954, including *Captain Post: Crime Specialist*, 1930–1931, *Chinatown Squad*, 1932, *Barbary Coast Nights*, 1933, *I Love a Mystery*, 1943–1944, 1949–1952, *Adventures by Morse*, 1944–1945, *His Honor the Barber*, 1945–1946, *I Love Adventure*, 1948, *Slice of Life*, 1949, *Mixed Doubles*, 1949, *One Man's Family*, 1949, 1951–1952, and *Family Skeleton*, 1953–1954. Also contains some memorabilia on Morse's career (awards, clippings, etc.) and production documents related to particular series.

1349. CBS-KNX Script Collection, 1940–1960. Contains over 9,300 individual scripts, 1940–1960, from what was the radio script archive at KNX, Los Angeles, a CBS affiliate station. Included in the collection are long series runs of *I Was There*, 1940–1942, 1944–1945, *Amos 'n' Andy*, 1944–1951, *Romance*, 1944–1946, 1948–1951, *The Story of Sandra Martin*, 1944–1945, *Suspense*, 1945–1959, *The Whistler*, 1945–1951, 1954–1955, *Escape*, 1947-1954, *My Friend Irma*, 1947-1954, *My Favorite Husband*, 1948-1951, *Our Miss Brooks*, 1948–1957, *Yours Truly, Johnny Dollar*, 1949–1960, *The Lineup*, 1950–1953, *Meet Millie*, 1951–1954, *Junior Miss*, 1952–1954, *Hallmark Hall of Fame*, 1953–1955 and *Have Gun–Will Travel*, 1958–1960. In addition to scripts, the collection also contains scattered production notes and memoranda related to the broadcast of specific series. Note: See "General Comments" above relating to the publication of a book cataloging the scripts.

1350. Fletcher Markle Collection. Contains scripts for radio and television, including *Studio One*, 1947–1948, *Ford Theater*, 1948–1949, *Life With Father*, 1954, *Sears Radio Theater*, 1979–1980 and *Mutual Radio Theater*, 1980–1981. Also includes documents, photos, press clippings and most correspondence related to these series.

1351. Frank Bresee Collection. Consists of about 3,900 tapes, mostly of Bresee's program *Golden Days of Radio* as it was broadcast on the Armed Forces Radio and Television Service, 1967–1995, as well as source material for his program, including complete episodes of many radio series from the 1940s and 1950s. As of 2005, the collection is partially processed and papers are being added to the collection on an ongoing basis.

1352. Hilliard Marks Collection. Consists of scripts for the *Jack Benny Show* on radio, 1950–1957, and one script for the television series, 1954.

1353. John Pickard and Frank Provo Collection, ca. 1928–1976. Consists largely of radio scripts written by Pickard and Provo for radio and television, including *Wendy Warren and the News*, 1947–1958, and occasional episodes for *Young Dr. Malone*. Also includes scripts from Australian Broadcasting Company programs that Pickard either wrote, directed or acted in (ca. 1932–1935) for the Australian Broadcasting Company prior to his emigration to the United States as well as presentation scripts for proposed television and radio series, manuscripts of plays and novels and correspondence.

1354. Marvin E. Miller Collection, 1931–1985, bulk 1935–1965. Contains papers, including scripts, correspondence and scrapbooks and 135 reel-to-reel tapes covering Miller's acting and announcing career.

1355. Milt Josefsberg Collection, 1930–1980, bulk 1960–1978. Contains papers relating to his career as a television producer and writer and as the author of a biography of Jack Benny and a book on comedy writing. Includes correspondence, radio and television scripts, book manuscripts, sound recordings, press clippings, research notes and other materials.

1356. Milton and Barbara Merlin Collection, 1923–1997, bulk 1940–1965. Contains scripts for *Mr. President, Boston Blackie, The Ginny Simms Show, Everything for the Boys, The Man Called X* and *Halls of Ivy* plus correspondence, including Milton Merlin's involvement with various writers' organizations such as the Hollywood Writers Mobilization during World War II and the Radio Writers Guild in which he served as national president in the early 1950s.

1357. Monty Masters Collection, 1941–1960, bulk 1946––1951. Contains scripts of *Spotlight Playhouse*, 1946, *The Eddy King Show*, 1947–1948, *Ready for Brady*, 1948–1949, *The Monty Masters Show*, 1948–1949, and *Candy Matson*, 1949–1951. In addition to these series, the collection contains story treatments and sample scripts for proposed television and radio series from the early 1950s as well as single copies of scripts from various radio programs.

1358. Morris Freedman Collection, 1946–1958. Contains scripts for radio and television series, including *Duffy's Tavern*, 1946–1949, *Jimmy Durante Show*, 1950, *That's Rich*, 1954, *Ray Milland Show*, 1954–1955, *Meet Millie*, 1955–1956, *Professional Father*, 1955 and *How to Marry a Millionaire*, 1957–1958. Collection also includes series treatments, story outlines, sketches and jokes. Some items include production notes.

1359. Norman Corwin Collection, 1910– , bulk 1938–1990. Currently contains materials selected and organized by Corwin for inclusion during his lifetime, including correspondence, scrapbooks, radio and television scripts, motion picture screenplays, sound recordings, video recordings, photographs, business records and contracts, press clippings and ephemera. The bulk of the accessible materials documents Corwin's career in radio and television broadcasting, motion pictures, the theater and as an author and teacher, 1935–1990. As of 2005, the collection is partly arranged and described.

Pacific Pioneer Broadcasters
(See Pacific Pioneer Broadcasters)

1360. Ralph French Collection, 1935–1955. Consists primarily of black and white photographs of Rudy Vallee, his friends and associates and locations where he performed. Also includes one color photograph of Vallee and his wife Eleanor (ca. 1980), one letter from Vallee, several greeting cards and a small file of press clippings. Note: French was a friend and associate of Vallee and was his business manager during the 1940s and early 1950s. See also separate Rudy Vallee Collection below.

1361. Robert Q. Lewis Collection, 1940–1960, bulk 1947–1956. Contains material for Lewis's television and radio programs, including complete scripts as well as jokes and monologues written for use on these programs, correspondence, newsclippings, music scores and photographs that document his entertainment career between the mid-1940s and 1960. Radio programs that are represented in this collection include *Arthur Godfrey Time* and both the radio and television versions of the *Robert Q. Lewis Show.*

1362. Rudy Vallee Collection, 1901–1986, bulk 1925–1975. Contains personal documents in Vallee's possession at the time of his death, including correspondence, scrapbooks, radio and television scripts, sound recordings, musical scores, photographs, business records, press clippings and ephemera. The bulk of accessible materials document Vallee's career in radio broadcasting and entertainment, 1925–1975. See also Ralph French Collection above that includes photographs of Vallee.

1363. Sportsmen Collection. Contains musical scores and arrangements prepared and used by the members of the Sportsmen Quartet during their performing career, 1943–ca. 1970. The group is most closely associated with the Jack Benny radio and television programs.

1364. Tom Koch Collection, 1959–1976, bulk ca. 1974–1976. Contains 1,061 scripts for five-minute sketches used on the *Bob and Ray Show*, ca. 1974–1976.

1365. Tom Price Collection, ca. 1935–ca. 1975. Contains over 11,000 recordings of radio programs, 1930–1960, as well as documentary recordings from later years plus papers that include extensive research files largely concentrating on *Fibber McGee and Molly* and its stars Jim and Marian Jordan. Only those sound recordings that have been transferred to cassette are available for use.

Tufts University
Fletcher School of Law and Diplomacy
160 Packard Avenue, Medford, MA 02155
(617) 627-3700
fletcherweb@tufts.edu; http://library.tufts.edu/

1366. Edward R. Murrow Papers, 1927–1965. The collection has been transferred to 50 microfilm reels. A 38 page "Guide" to the collection is available in the library.

Tulane University
Howard-Tilton Memorial Library
7001 Freret Street, New Orleans, LA 70118
(504) 865-5605; www.tulane.edu

1367. Countee Cullen Papers, 1903–1946. Includes an unidentified radio serial plus correspondence, records, other writings, scrapbooks and clippings.

Union College

Schaffer Library
Special Collections Schenectady, NY 12308
(518) 388-6616; Contact: Ellen Fladger
specialcollections@union.edu
www.union.edu/PUBLIC/LIBRARY/about/speccoll.htm

1368. John Galsworthy Papers. Includes a script with hand-written notes for a *The March of Time* program, 1933.

University of Alaska Anchorage

Consortium Library, Archives & Manuscripts Department
3211 Providence Drive, Anchorage, AK 99508
(907) 786-1849; Fax: (907) 786-1845
ayarch@uaa.alaska.edu; Contact: Dennis F. Walle
www.lib.uaa.alaska.edu/archives/

1369. Armed Forces Radio in Sitka and Kodiak, AK during World War II. Transcripts of interviews for an oral history project, 1981–1984, of Armed Forces Radio in Sitka and Kodiak, AK during World War II.

1370. Ruben Gaines Papers, 1952–1983. Contains papers, published works and story illustrations dealing with life in Alaska. Includes scripts and audio recordings for *Conversations Unlimited, Pop* and *Beluga Bugle.*

1371. U.S. Army: "Story of the Alaska Communications System 1900–1943." Consists of a copy of an unpublished official Army history (author unknown) containing over 50 appendices including route maps, magazine and newspaper articles, list of radio stations and other information.

University of California

The listings below for the University of California are organized by campus. Although each campus maintains its own online catalog, a single web site can be accessed to search the online holdings of all UC libraries, as well as some additional California libraries. Check: http://melvyl.cdlib.org/

University of California at Berkeley

Bancroft Library, Berkeley, CA 94720
(510) 642-1839; Fax: (510) 642-7589
abliss@library.berkeley.edu; Contact: Anthony Bliss
www.berkeley.edu/libraries/index.html#search

1372. Anna Blake Mezquida Papers, 1888–1975, bulk 1898–1965. Professional and personal correspondence concerning Mezquida's activities and writing. See online finding aid. Note: Finding aid shows one folder of scripts, labeled "KYA, 1936." The other folders may not be radio related.

1373. "Bernard Herrmann's Radio Music for the *Columbia Workshop*." A microform version of a Ph.D. thesis by Robert Kosovsky, City University of New York, 2000.

1374. Charles Augustus Keeler Papers, 1889–1979, bulk 1911–1933. Includes miscellaneous letters and notes, plays, radio dramas, short stories and poems.

1375. *Cross Cuts* Materials, n.d. Copies of scripts for a radio program with Laurence L. Cross, in the form of minstrel shows.

1376. Eloise Keeler Papers, 1938–1986. Contains writings in many different media, including short stories, newspaper and magazine articles, plays, screenplays, radio and television scripts, poetry and a biography on her brother Leonard

Keeler. Note: The catalog listing does not describe the radio material.

1377. Elsa Knight Thompson Papers, 1935–1987. Consists of personal papers documenting Knight's broadcasting from World War II through the 1970s. Contains family and personal correspondence, business files, legal files related to litigation with KPFA, including transcripts, a draft autobiography, calendars, photographs and ephemera.

1378. George Sumner Albee Papers, ca. 1929–1958. Mainly correspondence and manuscripts of his novels and short stories and some financial papers. Includes some unidentified radio scripts. Albee also worked for an advertising agency and wrote commercials for *Cavalcade of America.*

1379. Grayson-Rosser Productions Papers, 1931–1932, n.d. Consists of internal corporate and production files and radio scripts of the electronic transcriptions that Grayson-Rosser Productions produced. The radio plays were written by King Hamilton Grayson and Winifred Rosser and were first copyrighted to Radio Programs, Limited and later to King Hamilton Grayson and Winifred Rosser and Associates. The subjects of the plays include mysteries, comedies, dramas and one murder mystery set in Oakland, CA. The scripts and catalogs contain annotations regarding actors and sounds.

1380. KPFA History Miscellany. Draft history of the station, 1946–1960, "KPFA History," by Eleanor McKinney, January 1960, with annotations in an unknown hand. Also, "The Beginnings of Pacifica Foundation" by Gene R. Stebbins, 1969.

1381. Pacifica Radio Sampler. Photocopies of papers selected from KPFA, Berkeley files by Vera S. Hopkins, a retired staff member, to document the founding, development and problems of listener sponsored radio, 1946–1984. Emphasis is on the early history of Pacifica and on KPFA.

1382. Tarea Hall Pittman Papers, ca. 1951–1970. Consists of photographs commemorating activities and events involving Pittman and the NAACP Regional Office, 1951–1970. May not contain information about Pittman's radio program *Negroes in the News.*

1383. *This is San Francisco* Scripts, 1951, 1957. Scripts for the program broadcast on KCBS, San Francisco, November 28, 1951 and May 6, 1957.

1384. William I. Gardner and Mercedes P. Gardner Family Papers, 1900–1991. Chiefly writings by Mercedes P. Gardner, including scripts for *Scooter,* 1940s–1950s, broadcast in Sacramento, CA.

University of California at Los Angeles (UCLA)

General comments: Most of the special collections with radio related material are located in two libraries: the Special Collections unit of the Arts Library (located on the second floor of the Charles E. Young Research Library) and the Department of Special Collections of the Charles E. Young Research Library. Researchers are advised to check both locations. As a general rule, "older" collections, i.e., those donated prior to 1993, are located in the Department of Special Collections of the Charles E. Young Research Library. Additional collections located in other libraries are noted below.

Arts Library, Special Collections
Charles E. Young Research Library, Room 22478
PO Box 951575, Los Angeles, CA 90095
(310) 825-7253; Fax: (310) 825-1210
www.library.ucla.edu/libraries/arts/
Online finding aids: www.oac.cdlib.org/institutions/ark

General comments. In addition to the online finding aids (see above link), additional unpublished finding aids are available in the repository for some collections. In the library's online catalog, the "title" for some collections of scripts for specific programs are sometimes shown as "Collection of scripts for ....." For the purpose of the listings below, however, the collection title has been changed to reflect the name of the program. Also, additional material relating to the same person or program may be located in separate collections in the Department of Special Collections, Charles E. Young Research Library.

1385. Al Lewis Radio and Television Scripts, 1943–1954. Collection consists primarily of radio scripts related to Lewis's career as a writer and director. Includes scripts for *The Camel Program*, 1944, *Command Performance*, 1944, *The Danny Kaye Show*, 1945–1946, *GI Journal*, n.d., *Jubilee*, 1944, *Mail Call*, 1943–1945, *Only Yesterday*, 1943, *Our Miss Brooks*, 1948–1954, *Philco Radio Time*, 1946–1947, *Request Performance*, 1945, and *Sweeney and March*, 1946–1948. See online finding aid.

1386. Albert McCleery Papers, 1935–1971. Includes scripts for the *Inheritance* radio program, April–September, 1954. Most of the collection consists of television scripts and personal and business papers.

1387. *Amos 'n' Andy* **Radio Scripts, 1943–1953.** Consists of scripts for 222 episodes, October 8, 1943–May 24, 1953.

1388. Ann Sothern Papers, 1954–1961. Includes scripts and production information for Sothern's television show and other papers. Check unpublished finding aid for any possible radio related material.

1389. Axel Gruenberg Interview. Transcript of interviews with Gruenberg by Irene Kahn Atkins, November 28, 1979–January 16, 1980. Part of the Directors' Guild of America Oral History series.

1390. *Baby Snooks* **Radio Scripts.** Consists primarily of scripts for episodes featuring Fanny Brice. Includes scripts from *Maxwell House Presents Good News*, November 4, 1937–July 25, 1940, *Maxwell House Coffee Time*, September 5, 1940–May 28, 1942 and October 8, 1942–May 31, 1945, with no episodes December 4, 1941–March 5, 1942 and no Baby Snooks spots September 7, 1944–May 31, 1945, *Maxwell House Iced Coffee Time*, June 16–August 31, 1944, *Post Toasties Time*, June 4–August 6, 1942, and *Toasties Time*, September 11, 1944–June 10, 1945. Also includes Frank Morgan spots and annotated scripts.

1391. Ben Norman Collection of Radio Scripts, 1953. Consists of 41 scripts for *Mike Malloy* and nine scripts for *Starr of Space*. Also includes several television story treatments.

1392. Charles Isaacs Television and Radio Series Scripts, 1941–1973. Consists primarily of television and radio series scripts. Also includes photographs and correspondence relating to Isaacs's career. Radio materials include *Kraft Music*

Hall, 1947–1949, *The Bob Burns Show*, 1946–1947, *The Rudy Vallee Show*, 1941, and *The Martin and Lewis Show*, 1949–1950. Includes some bound volumes.

1393. Collection of Radio Series Scripts, ca. 1933–1980, ca. 1940–1959. Consists of miscellaneous scripts including over 143 titles. The bulk of the collection dates from the 1940s through the 1950s and includes series titles such as *Burns and Allen, Duffy's Tavern, Jimmy Durante Show, Errand of Mercy, The Fred Allen Show, The Henry Morgan Show, Hollywood Star Preview, Mutual Radio Theater, Sears Radio Theater* and others.

1394. David Freedman Collection of Scripts for Radio Programs, 193?–1946. Includes scripts for the *Chase and Sanborn Coffee Hour, Elmer Everett Yess, The Big Show, The Red Skelton Show, Joe Cook's Patent Office, The Fire Chief, Ziegfeld Follies of the Air* and other programs. Also includes Eddie Cantor sketches and some material related to other programs and treatments for screenplays. See online finding aid for complete list of programs with dates. See also a separate Freedman collection, also with scripts, in the Department of Special Collections, Charles E. Young Research Library. Note: As some of the above program titles could not be verified with standard references, they may be either misspelled in the catalog listing or simply lesser known programs.

1395. Eddie Quillan Collection of Scripts for Radio Programs, 1938–1950. Majority of the scripts are from *The Eddie Cantor Show*, 1944–1949, *Time to Smile*, 1942–1944 with gaps, and *Wednesday With You*, 1945. Most scripts are annotated by Quillan. Note: Some of the same scripts may be in the Manning Ostroff Collection.

1396. Edward Jurist Collection of Radio and Television Scripts. Consists of a series of scripts related to Jurist's career as a writer and producer, including the *Aldrich Family* and *The Jonathan Winters Show*.

1397. Ellwood Ullman Collection of Scripts for Motion Pictures, Television and Radio, 1930s–1960s. Includes a number of unidentified radio scripts.

1398. Eugene Rodney Collection of Scripts and Production Material, ca. 1950–ca. 1963. Consists of radio, television and motion picture scripts and production material. Includes radio scripts for *Father Knows Best*, 1950–1954. Also includes correspondence and stills, some of which are related to the Robert Young-Eugene Rodney Production Co.

1399. Gene Stone Papers, 1947–1989. Consists of scripts and ephemera related to Stone's career and scripts for *The Great Gildersleeve* and other unidentified plays.

1400. Hal Collins Papers, 1946–1964. Includes scripts for *Camel Caravan*, 1939, *Hank McCune Show*, 1947, *Lew Parker*, 1945, *Philip Morris Playhouse*, 1942, *Sammy Kaye*, 1943, and *Time to Smile*, 1939–1942. See online finding aid.

1401. *Hallmark Hall of Fame* **Collection of Scripts for Television and Radio Productions, 1951–1984.** Includes radio scripts for *Hallmark Playhouse* (a.k.a. *Hallmark Radio Hall of Fame*), January, 1952–March 1955, and production material, property procurement and releases, 1948–1952.

1402. Harry Crane Papers, 1939–1998. Consists of script material, notes, humor topicals, gag files, general files, photographs and personal papers. Includes material related to Crane's long association with renowned comedians and represents his prolific career writing for radio, television, motion pictures and live performance projects. Although a detailed finding aid identifying specific radio programs is not available online, the online abstract does list the following entertainers that Crane wrote for and befriended: Bud Abbott and Lou Costello, Milton Berle, Abe Burrows, Perry Como, Joan Davis, Jimmy Durante, Jackie Gleason, Alan King, Steve Lawrence and Eydie Gorme, Dean Martin and Jerry Lewis, Groucho Marx, Jan Murray, Frank Sinatra, Danny Thomas and Andy Williams.

1403. Herbert Baker Papers, 1939–1978. Includes some unidentified radio material along with script materials for television shows, awards shows and specials and some motion picture and stage productions.

1404. Himan Brown Interview. Transcript of interviews by Irene Kahn Atkins, February 6–May 22, 1979. Part of the Directors' Guild of America Oral History series.

1405. Hollywood Entertainment Museum Collection, 1900–1968. Includes radio scripts, stills, scrapbooks, books, magazines and sheet music. Parts of the collection are on deposit with the Academy of Motion Picture Arts and Science, the American Film Institute and the University of Southern California, Cinema Studies Library.

1406. Irve Tunick Collection of Radio Scripts, 1936–1958. Consists of radio scripts related to Tunick's career as a writer. Includes scripts for *American School of the Air*, 1944–1948, *Cavalcade of America*, 1949–1953, *Towards a Better World*, 1943–1944, and *The World Is Yours*, 1937–1941.

1407. Jack Hines Papers, 1925–1962. Consists of manuscripts, galley proofs, correspondence, a scrapbook, photographs, clippings and books.

1408. Jack Webb Collection of Scripts for Radio and Television, 1949–1975. Includes scripts for *Dragnet* and *Pat Novak, for Hire*. See online finding aid.

1409. James Sheldon Collection of Television Series Scripts, 1946–1986. Consists primarily of television scripts but also includes scripts for the radio series *Crimes of Carelessness*, 1946–1947, which Sheldon directed.

1410. Jean Renoir Papers, 1915–1927. Consists of material related to Renoir's career as a director and screenwriter and includes scripts, correspondence and photographs relating to his radio productions in the 1940s. See online finding aid and additional material in Department of Special Collections, Charles E. Young Research Library.

1411. John Dunkel Collection of Scripts for Radio Programs, 1954–1958. Includes scripts for *Suspense, Gunsmoke*, 1956–1959, *Romance*, 1954–1955, *Have Gun–Will Travel*, 1958, *Hallmark Hall of Fame, Escape, Fort Laramie*, 1956, and radio spots for *I Was There*, 1941–1944.

1412. Joseph G. Catanich Papers, 1935–1964. Contains transcription discs of radio shows for the Los Angeles Community Chest, 1940–1942, and script material for the series *Heartbeats of the City* and other radio programs. Also includes Campaign Radio Plays and transcripts of commercials, publicity material for the *Joey Bishop Show*, 1961–1964,

and approximately 100 photographs.

1413. Ken Englund Papers, 1933–1972. Consists primarily of scripts for motion pictures (produced and unproduced), television, stage and radio, including *The Armour Hour*, 1933–1935, *Joe Penner*, 1937, *National Biscuit Show*, 1937, and *The Ken Murray Show*, 1937. Also includes personal papers and project files including treatments and story ideas written by Englund and his collaborators. See online finding aid and a second collection in Department of Special Collections, Charles E. Young Research Library that includes scripts for many additional programs.

1414. Larry Gelbart Papers. Includes scripts and other material for the following radio programs: *The Bob Hope Show, Command Performance, Duffy's Tavern, The Ginny Simms Radio Show, The Jack Parr Show, The Joan Davis Show, The Kenny Kaye Baker Show, Junior Ad Club Spotlight on Achievement, Mastergate* and the *Sealtest Village Store*. See online finding aid.

1415. Larry Williams Collection of Scripts for Medical and Health Related Television Programs, 1952–1969. Does not contain material related to Williams's writing career for radio.

1416. Lloyd Bochner Collection of Scripts for Television, 1960–1992. Consists primarily of television scripts related to Bochner's acting career but also contains scripts for several radio programs, including *CBS Radio Mystery Theater, Mutual Radio Theater: The Adventure Show, Mutual Radio Theater: The Love Show, Sears Radio Theater* and *Sears Radio Theater: The Adventure Show*. See online finding aid and additional information in Department of Special Collections, Charles E. Young Research Library.

1417. Lou Derman Papers, 1944–1975. Collection consists of 81 bound volumes of various radio and television scripts including the following radio programs: *Life With Luigi*, 1948–1953, *Our Miss Brooks*, December, 1953–June, 1954, *Happy Island* starring Ed Wynn, September, 1944–February, 1945, *Let Yourself Go* starring Milton Berle, March–June, 1945, *The Eddie Cantor Show*, 1945, 1947, *The Jim Backus Show*, 1948, *Kiss and Make Up*, 1946, *Lefty*, 1946, *The Mighty Casey*, 1947, Robert Q. Lewis's *Little Show*, 1947, and *That's Rich*, 1954. See online finding aid.

1418. Louis Pollock Papers, 1940–1964. Consists of material related to Pollock's career as a writer and includes various drafts of teleplays, screenplays, radio scripts, outlines and treatments for productions and correspondence files. Pollock was mistakenly blacklisted and later cleared.

1419. Manning Ostroff Collection of Scripts for Radio and Television, 1943–1954. Includes radio scripts for *The Eddie Cantor Show*, 1944–1949, *Time to Smile*, 1943–1944, and *Wednesday With You*, 1945. Note: Some of the same scripts may be in the Eddie Quillan Collection.

1420. Marcia Wolf Collection of Scripts for Radio and Television Programs, 1945–1951. Includes radio scripts for *Mark Trail*, 1950–1952, *Tom Corbett, Space Cadet*, 1952, *One Foot in Heaven*, 1945, *Adventures of Topper*, 1945, and *Fighting Heroes of the U.S. Navy*, n.d. Note: The same collection is also listed below as the Stanley J. Wolf Collection of Radio and Television Series Scripts.

1421. Margarite Wallace Scripts, 1945–ca. 1957. Includes scripts and some production information for the *Ozzie and Harriet Show*, 1946–1952, *Suspense*, 1946–1951, and television shows. Also includes a small amount of advertising spots and other radio, television and motion picture scripts. Additionally there is script material for an unproduced Orson Welles project.

1422. Martin Berkeley Collection of Television and Motion Picture Scripts, ca. 1940–ca. 1960. Consists primarily of scripts and screenplays, including several undated scripts for *Assignment U.S.A.* that Berkeley did in collaboration with Stanley Roberts and Clark E. Reynolds.

1423. Milton Berle Radio and Television Scripts, 1947–1953. Consists of scripts from the radio series, *The Milton Berle Show,* programs #1-58, March 1947–April 1948, and television scripts. See online finding aid.

1424. Norman Lessing Papers, 1943–1982. Includes script and production materials for approximately 80 television series, 20 radio programs, and 10 motion pictures and teleplays. Unpublished finding aid.

1425. *Our Miss Brooks* Scripts, 1950–1956. Consists of radio and television scripts, including radio scripts for April, 1950–April, 1956, #82-336 with some gaps, and television scripts for February, 1952–April, 1955, #1-100. See online finding aid.

1426. Paul and Margaret Schneider Collection of Script Material for Television, 1953–1983. Consists primarily of material written by Paul and/or Margaret Schneider for a variety of television productions, including *The Eddie Cantor Comedy Theatre* (television) but also some unspecified material dealing with radio. Unpublished finding aid.

1427. Pinky Herman Collection of Columns Written for Television Industry Newspapers, 1942–1971. Contains columns published in the entertainment trade papers, including "Television Today," "Motion Picture Daily" and "Radio/TV Daily." The columns cover projects and industry professionals from 1943–1950 and 1954–1971.

1428. Renata Vanni Scripts 1955–1988. Consists of scripts related to Vanni's acting career which, in the early years, included work on Italian radio in New York.

1429. Rosalind Russell Papers, 1930–1970. Consists of scripts, clippings, pressbooks, scrapbooks, programs, photographs, awards, records, correspondence and miscellaneous material related to Russell's career. Also includes papers related to Russell's husband, Frederick Brisson, who served as chief of radio propaganda and special consultant to the Secretary of War during World War II. Includes radio sketches on which Russell appeared for the Special Services Division, A.S.F. and also material related to the Office of Radio Production. See additional collection in Department of Special Collections, Charles E. Young Research Library.

1430. Stanley Wolf Collection of Radio and Television Series Scripts. Consists of radio and television series scripts, including radio scripts for *Adventures of Topper,* June–September, 1945, *Fighting Heroes of the U.S. Navy,* n.d., *Mark Trail,* Series 1–4, January, 1950–June, 1952, *One Foot In Heaven, January–November,* 1945, and *Tom Corbett, Space Cadet,* January–June, 1952. Note: The same collection is listed above as the Marcia Wolf Collection.

1431. Tony Barrett Papers, 1916–1974. Contains scripts, production materials and correspondence for television series and radio programs, 1952–1973.

1432. True Boardman Papers, 1934–1977. Collection includes scripts and treatments for various radio programs, including *Silver Theatre,* 1937–1946, *Cassandra,* 1937, *Lux Radio Theatre* and television programs.

1433. Vincent Bogert Radio and Television Scripts, 1946–1964. Consists of scripts and production information related to his work on *Duffy's Tavern, The Eddie Cantor Show* and other projects. See the online finding aid for specific program dates.

1434. Virginia Brown Faire Papers, 1918–1977, bulk 1918–1929. Consists of photographs and scrapbooks related to Faire's career and includes a 1977 interview transcript with Faire. The actress did some radio work in Chicago.

1435. William Froug Collection of Scripts From Radio Programs and Television Series, 1950s–1981. Includes 10 episodes of *Romance* and audio tapes and transcripts of interviews conducted by Froug for his book "The Screenwriter Looks at the Screenwriter."

1436. *Yale Reports* Radio Program Transcripts 1958–1971. Includes transcripts of the weekly program presented by Yale University and broadcast on WTIC, Hartford, CT. Includes over 400 issues spanning 1958–1971. Not all years are complete.

Department of Special Collections
Charles E. Young Research Library
PO Box 951575, Los Angeles, CA 90095
(310) 825-4988; spec-coll@library.ucla.edu;
www.library.ucla.edu/libraries/special/scweb/
Online finding aids: www.oac.cdlib.org/institutions/ark

General comments: In addition to the online finding aids (see link above), additional unpublished finding aids are available in the library. Also, additional material relating to the same person or program may be located in separate collections in the Arts Library, Special Collections.

1437. Alan Reed Papers, ca. 1931–1972. Consists of correspondence, manuscripts, typescripts, photographs, sheet music and scrapbooks from Reed's career as a character actor in radio, television and film.

1438. Baruch Lumet Papers, 1955–1983. Consists of Lumet's personal papers relating to his career in the theater as an actor and writer. Includes photographs, manuscripts, clippings, scripts and videotapes. Papers do not cover Lumet's radio career, 1932–1942.

1439. Ben Blue Papers. Consists of radio scripts for comedy shows, including those for the *Jack Benny Show, Burns and Allen, Milton Berle Show, Eddie Cantor Show* and others.

1440. Ben Starr Scripts, 1948–1968. Consists of scripts by Starr and various collaborators for television, radio, film and a play.

1441. Charles Laughton Papers, 1930–1962. Consists of

materials related to Laughton's career in all areas of show business, including screen, stage, radio and television productions. Includes radio scripts for *Corwin Presents.*

1442. Clifford E. Clinton Papers, 1934–1969. A restaurateur active in Los Angeles politics and civic reform movements, the collection includes papers and scripts of Clinton's program *The People's Voice*, 1940–1945, heard on various Los Angeles stations. See online finding aid.

1443. Collection of Material about Prejudices, 1950–1976. Consists of anti-semitic, anti-Afro American and extreme right-wing political and religious booklets, pamphlets, and periodicals. Includes material by Southern religious fundamentalist radio preachers and other groups.

1444. Collection of Miscellaneous Phonograph Records, ca. 1940–1971. Collection of records and occasionally album notes and photographs featuring music, news, interviews, speeches, poetry and stories. Some records are of radio programs, including *The Fred Allen Show* and *Burns and Allen.*

1445. David Freedman Papers, 1930–1940. Collection contains scripts for radio programs in which Al Jolson, Bert Lahr, Fanny Brice, Eddie Cantor, Red Skelton, Tommy Dorsey and others starred, including *Whose Baby Are You, Chase and Sanborn Hour, Baby Snooks, Circus Night in Town, Kraft Music Hall* and *Lifebuoy Soap.* See online finding aid for list of programs and dates. See also separate Freedman collection that includes scripts in the Arts Library, Special Collections.

1446. Dorothy Healey Broadcast, 1973. Transcript of Healey's broadcast on KPTK, Santa Monica, on the occasion of her resignation from the Communist Party, July 9, 1973. Healey broadcast on KPTK for 20 years. Duplicate transcript is available at UC/Berkeley.

1447. Dorothy Warenskjold Oral History Transcript, 1992. Warenskjold discusses her radio performances.

1448. Ed Wynn Papers, 1920–1938, bulk 1931–1938. Consists of scrapbooks, clippings, ephemera and sheet music documenting Wynn's career in the Broadway theater and radio productions.

1449. Eddie Cantor Papers, 1915–1964. Consists of materials related to Cantor's career, including radio and television scripts, sheet music, orchestrations, photographs, awards, tributes, correspondence, sound recordings and scrapbooks. Includes radio scripts for *The Eddie Cantor Show, Show Business Old and New, Eddie Cantor Comedy Theatre* and March of Dimes scripts.

1450. Ernie Kovacs Papers, 1940–1962. Consists of scripts and recordings of Kovacs's television shows. Also includes manuscripts of his novel as well as personal papers, contracts, financial papers and scrapbooks. Collection may not include any material related to Kovacs's early radio career.

1451. Federal Theatre Project Scripts and Publications, 1936–1939. Consists of plays, synopses of plays, lists of plays, radio scripts and three volumes of folk songs and ballads. Also includes copies of scripts from the Project archives at George Mason University and videotaped interviews with Gene Stone and Jeff Corey. A list of the radio scripts is available online.

1452. George Brandt Papers, 1925–1950. Consists of plays, screenplays, television and unnamed radio plays, scrapbooks, magazines and photographs documenting Brandt's writing career.

1453. George Larkin Papers, ca. 1915–1946. Consists of manuscripts jointly written by Hollywood actors George and Olive Kirby Larkin, mostly mystery scripts for radio, stage and film. Personal material includes a book, clippings, other printed material, photographs, postcards and prints. Includes an undated script, "Bulldog Courage," and some unidentified radio audition material.

1454. George Spaulding Papers, 1913–1940. Consists of theater programs, mementos and a scrapbook relating to Spaulding's acting career on screen, stage, radio and television.

1455. Gerald Heard Papers, 1935–1971. Consists of Heard's manuscripts of published and unpublished books, correspondence, 16 boxes of tape recordings of his lectures, lecture notes, articles and other papers. Includes transcripts of lectures aired over CBS and CBS-KNXT, 1956–1957.

1456. Hale Sparks: "The University Explorer" Oral History Transcript, 1966. Sparks discusses the history of radio programming at the University and his activities with the Office of War Information during World War II. Includes a discussion of the *University Explorer, Science Editor* and *Master Storytellers in the Modern World* programs.

1457. Jack Benny Papers, 1930–1974. Includes radio and television scripts, photographs and production stills, personal and business records for the years 1935–1955, magazines containing Benny articles, memorabilia and awards. Includes radio scripts for the *Jack Benny Show*, which, depending on the sponsor, was also known as *The Canada Dry Ginger Ale Program, The Chevrolet Program, The General Tire Program, The Jell-O Program, The Grape Nuts Program* and other names. Also includes tapes of Benny radio broadcasts.

1458. Jackson Stanley Papers. Includes scripts and other material related to the following radio programs: *The Great Gildersleeve* (outlines), *Paging the Judge, Jackie Coogan Show, Let's Broadcast, Duffy's Tavern* and other materials.

1459. James Poe Papers, 1940–. Consists of radio, television and film scripts, correspondence, ephemera, stills and tapes. Radio scripts are identified by name and sometimes date but not the program on which they were aired.

1460. Jim Tully Papers, 1920–1947. Consists of book and article manuscripts (published and unpublished), galley proofs, movie scripts, unidentified radio scripts and tear sheets from magazines.

1461. John Houseman Papers, 1930–1989. Consists of correspondence, scripts for stage, movies, radio and television, newspaper clippings, ephemera and videotapes of television interviews, commercials and television performances.

1462. Joseph Edward Shaw Papers, ca. 1887–1963, bulk 1933–1941. Consists of correspondence, manuscripts, business papers, tape recordings, photographs, phonograph records, clippings and printed material related to Los Angeles politics when Shaw served as secretary to his brother, Los Angeles Mayor Frank Shaw. Includes radio speeches and material related to radio campaigns.

1463. Ken Englund Papers, 1933–1972. Consists of materials related to Englund's career as a television and screen writer. Includes scripts, correspondence, clippings, a list of Englund's screen, radio and stage credits, n.d., and ephemera. See online finding aid for a detailed list of scripts for *America Marches On, The Big Broadcast of 1938, Blue Ribbon Town, The Armour Hour, Joe Penner, Ken Murray Theater Guild, The Marx Brothers, Mickey's Hollywood Premiere, National Biscuit Show, The Packard Hour, Laugh With Ken Murray* and *Twin Stars.* See also separate collection of Englund scripts in the Arts Library. Note: Check with repository to determine if any of the scripts in the two collections are duplicates.

1464. Kenneth Gamet Papers, 1940–1970. Consists of story outlines, treatments, production notes, memoranda, correspondence, radio and television scripts, original screenplays and supporting materials. Includes radio scripts for *Growin' Up,* Episodes 1-125, *Barnacle Bill* and additional radio plays. See online finding aid for detailed list.

1465. Kurt Louis Flatau Papers, ca. 1940–1950. Consists of Flatau's radio scripts broadcast on KMTR, KLAC and KMPC, 1942–1946, and clippings of his regular newspaper columns.

1466. Larry McCormick Oral History Transcript, 1998–1999. McCormick discusses his early broadcast career in Kansas City in 1957 and move to Los Angeles in 1958 where he worked for KGFJ, KDAY, KFWB, KLAC and KMPC before switching to television.

1467. Leroy E. Hurte Central Avenue Sounds Oral History Transcript, 1995. Hurte discusses his early life and musical training and his later career as a record producer, conductor, magazine publisher, radio station owner and champion of classical music in Los Angeles's African-American community. Major topics covered include independent record labels in Los Angeles during the 1930s and 1940s.

1468. Milt Gross Papers, 1928–1948. Collection consists of materials by and relating to cartoonist and writer Gross. Includes scripts, legal papers and correspondence, 1950–1952, for *That's My Pop* plus scrapbooks containing clippings of his cartoons and newspaper columns, original drawings, manuscripts, photographs, correspondence, including fan letters, and ephemera.

1469. Mimi Perloff Oral History Transcript, 1991. Perloff discusses her career as a pianist, music teacher, freelance composer and radio performer.

1470. Mort Fine Papers, 1950–1968. Contains radio, motion picture and television scripts written by Fine and David Friedkin. Also contains business records of Friedkin & Fine, including contracts, production reports, story ideas and business and personal correspondence that are organized by production title. Includes scripts for the following radio programs: *Adventures of Robin Hood, Bold Venture, Broadway is My Beat, Cathy and Elliot Lewis On Stage, Front Page, Journey Into Adventure, Michael Flagg, M.D., Pursuit, Suspense,* and *Yours Truly, Johnny Dollar.* Also includes a phonograph record that includes *Suspense, Broadway is My Beat* and *Philip Morris Playhouse.* Online finding aid lists program name but not dates for scripts and production titles, e.g, *Bold Venture* for business papers.

1471. Norman Corwin Collection: Material By and About, 1952–1959. Consists of scripts, programs and clippings. Includes scripts for "The World of Carl Sandberg," "The Charter in the Saucer," "Lust for Life," and "The Golden Door." Also includes a hardbound copy of the "The Plot to Overthrow Christmas" and an acting edition of "The Rivalry."

1472. Norman Cousins Papers, 1924–1991, bulk 1944–1990. Collection covers the range of Cousins's career as a magazine editor, author and professor and includes material on some of his radio broadcasts.

1473. Peggy Hamilton Adams Papers, 1911–1976. Consists of materials related to Hamilton's career as a designer, fashion editor, socialite and host for local radio programs, 1929–1933, on KHJ that dealt with fashion concerns of the modern woman. Includes paste-ups, scrapbooks, photographs, newspaper clippings, printed ads, radio scripts and ephemera.

1474. Philip Pearce Kerby Papers, 1949–1984. Consists of correspondence, speeches, writings by Kerby and printed materials relating to his editorship of "Frontier" magazine. Also includes manuscripts of speeches, n.d., and broadcasts on KPFK, Los Angeles.

1475. Ray Bradbury Papers, 1950–1960. Consists of manuscripts, correspondence and ephemera by and related to Bradbury. Includes a radio script for the August 31, 1958 broadcast of *Suspense* titled, "The Whole Town's Sleeping."

1476. Richard Alan Wilson Papers, ca. 1945–1967. Consists of production files for film, radio and stage productions, correspondence, photographs, press clippings, screenplays, shooting scripts, material on research, budget and publicity materials, interviews, articles and addresses by Wilson. Also includes material relating to Orson Welles and the Mercury Theater production of "Macbeth" and material chronicling Wilson's efforts to transfer the 1948 CBS radio series, *Doorway to Life* to other media.

1477. Rob Wagner Papers. Includes papers relating to Wagner's radio program for the birthday of "Script," the magazine he published.

1478. Robert Bellem Papers, 1931–1968. Consists of short stories, novels, movie scenarios, radio scripts and television plays written by Bellem. Radio scripts are for *Creeps By Night.* Collection also includes research materials, synopses and scripts for the television version of *Death Valley Days.*

1479. Robert Hardy Andrews Papers, 1945–1966. Consists of literary manuscripts, movie and television scripts, newspaper columns and ephemera related to Andrews's career. Does not appear to include material related to his work in radio.

1480. Rod Serling Papers, 1945–1969. Consists mostly of scripts for films and television, but also includes radio scripts he wrote for WLW, Cincinnati, OH, 1950–1951, and some unidentified radio scripts, 1947–1950. Also includes correspondence and business records, primarily 1966–1968.

1481. Sam Ross Papers, 1941–1992. Consists of literary manuscripts, correspondence, cassette tapes and other printed material. Includes the radio play "40-40" co-written with Studs Terkel for a WPA broadcast with related correspondence and a second play, "Columbus," for an unidentified program.

Neither play script is dated.

1482. Sidney Forrester Mashbir Papers, 1942–1960. Contains mimeographed summaries of radio broadcasts, newspaper accounts, various special reports and publications in Japanese prepared by the Allied Translator and Interpreter Section of the Intelligence Office during the occupation of Japan, 1945–1947. Audio discs of Mashbir's Japanese broadcasts have been transferred to the UCLA Film and Television Archive.

1483. Sleepy Lagoon Defense Committee Records, 1942–1945. Contains correspondence, publications, publicity materials, radio scripts, office records, petitions and research materials of the Sleepy Lagoon Defense Committee.

1484. Stanley Kurnik Papers, 1945–1986. Consists of manuscripts, teaching, research and personal materials, theater programs, memorabilia, correspondence, clippings, photocopies, photographs, reel-to-reel tape recordings, including some of his productions for KPFK, n.d., magazines, posters and ephemera. Online finding aid does not include details of the KPFK productions.

1485. Todd Hunter Papers, ca. 1940–1961. Consists of unidentified radio and television plays.

1486. Tryout Theatre Collection of Radio Plays, 1948–1949. Consists of scripts of radio plays and introductions with corrections and additions and three programs of the Tryout Theatre.

1487. Violet Schram Papers, 1914–1963. Consists of photographs (mostly film stills), newspaper clippings, ephemera and a poster relating to Schram's theatrical, radio and movie career.

1488. William A. Bacher Papers, 1930–1960. Consists of radio scripts of series produced by Bacher, sound recordings of *Treasury Star Parade* and various screenplays and treatments sent to Bacher but never produced. Also includes materials on *Palmolive Beauty Box Theatre, Texaco Star Theatre, Maltine Story Hour, Maxwell House Showboat* and *Camel Caravan*. See online finding aid.

1489. Yoneo Sakai Papers, 1848–1979. After World War II, Sakai hosted the radio program *Amerika Dayori* (*News from America*). The collection consists of Sakai's correspondence, manuscripts, published works, notebooks and diaries.

Film and Television Archive
Archive Research and Study Center
46 Powell Library
(310) 206-5388; Fax: (310) 206-5392
arsc@ucla.edu; Contact: Mark Quigley

1490. Archive Research and Study Center Audio Collection. Consists of contemporary syndicated rebroadcasts of classic radio programs, including *Amos 'n' Andy, Burns and Allen, The Jack Benny Show, Dragnet, Suspense, CBS Radio Mystery Theater, Your Hit Parade* and other programs.

Music Library, Special Collections
Room B425, Schoenberg Hall
Box 951490
Los Angeles, CA 90095
(310) 825-1665; Fax: (310) 206-7322
music-spec@library.ucla.edu

www.library.ucla.edu/libraries/music
Online finding aids: www.oac.cdlib.org/institutions/ark

1491. Bernard Herrmann Collection of Music for Film, Television, and Radio Productions, 1935-1969. Consists of manuscripts, scores and parts of radio, television and film music. Includes arrangements used in *Crime Classics* and *Christmas Carol*. See online finding aid for list of programs.

1492. Bert Shefter Motion Picture and Television Collection, ca. 1930–1980. Collection does not contain material relating to Shefter's tenure as music director for WINS or his other radio related work.

1493. BMI (Broadcast Music, Inc.) Orchestral Library, ca. 1940. Scores and parts of orchestral arrangements published by Broadcast Music, Inc. for live radio broadcasts.

1494. Collection of Big Band Photographs, 1930–1945. Consists of commercial publicity photographs of American dance bands, combo bands and singers.

1495. Dennis Day Collection of Music for Radio. Consists of scores and manuscripts for the radio programs on which he appeared. Online finding aid does not include description, title or date of material.

1496. Jeff Alexander Television, Radio, and Motion Picture Music Collection, 1943–1970. Consists of manuscripts and copies of musical sketches for radio programs, most notably *Amos 'n' Andy*, TV commercials and television shows.

1497. Jimmy Durante Collection of Sound Recordings and Manuscripts. Includes sound and video recordings, clippings, scrapbooks, sheet music, orchestrations and other papers. As of 2005, the collection is being processed but is likely to contain radio material.

1498. Jimmy Van Heusen Collection of Musical Works and Papers. Consists of published sheet music and manuscripts, sound recordings, personal papers, correspondence with Johnny Burke, Sammy Cahn, Bing Crosby and Frank Sinatra, business documents and works lists, programs, clippings, biographies and professionally assembled scrapbooks.

1499. John Nathaniel Vincent Collection of Musical Manuscripts, Correspondence, Documents, Memorabilia, and Sound Recordings, 1940–1976. Material relating to radio is located in boxes 57-59 but contents were not available online.

1500. National Retail Radio Spots, Inc. Collection, n.d. Transcription discs of radio advertising and related material created by National Retail Radio Spots, Inc.

1501. Transcriptions of radio programs and other recordings from the archives of the Pacifica Radio Station, KPFK, Los Angeles. Includes programs hosted by Leonid Hambro, David Cloud and William Malloch. See unpublished finding aid for additional information.

Oral History Program
A253 Bunche Hall, Box 951575, Los Angeles, CA 90095
(310) 825-4932; Fax: (310) 206-2796
oral-history@library.ucla.edu

1502. Oral History Program. Additional oral histories with radio related information may be included under the subject headings "Motion Pictures and Television," "Theatre" and "Music." There is no separate "Radio" subject category. For more information, contact the Program office.

University Archive

21560 Young Research Library

(310) 825-4068

univ-archives@library.ucla.edu

www.library.ucla.edu/libraries/special/scweb/archives.htm

1503. University of California Radio Service Texts of Radio Broadcasts, 1932–1936. For more information see unpublished finding aid.

University of California at San Diego

Library

9500 Gilman Drive #0175, La Jolla, CA 92093

(858) 534-3336; http://libraries.ucsd.edu

1504. "Democracy, Power, and Equal Rights: The AFL vs. CIO Battle to Unionize U.S. Broadcast Technicians, 1926–1940." A Ph.D. thesis by Dennis William Mazzocco, 1996, University of California, San Diego.

University of California at Santa Barbara

Donald C. Davidson Library, Performing Arts Collections

Santa Barbara, CA 93106

(805) 893-5444; Contact: David Seubert

seubert@library.ucsb.edu; www.library.ucsb.edu/speccoll/pa/pamss03.html

1505. Bernard Herrmann Papers, 1927–1977. Includes manuscripts, personal and professional papers, photographs and recordings, including recordings of Herrmann conducting the CBS Symphony from late 1930s–1940s.

1506. John Hilly Collection. Includes recordings of several radio shows featuring Hilly as a guest, including one episode of *Hi Jinx* and seven *Gang Busters* programs.

1507. Screen Guild Players Recordings Collection, 1942–1948. Ninety seven recordings of *Screen Guild Theater* programs used as a fundraising effort for the Motion Picture Relief Fund. Note: The name of the program changed depending on the sponsor, e.g., Gulf, Lady Esther Cosmetics and Camel Cigarettes.

University of California at Santa Cruz

University Library

1156 High Street, Santa Cruz, CA 95064

(831) 459-2547

specoll@library.ucsc.edu; http://library.ucsc.edu/speccoll

1508. Hulda Hoover (McLean) Papers 1956–1963. Includes correspondence, speeches, minutes, memoranda, reports, studies, newspaper clippings, reference material and scripts for *Your County Government Report* documenting McLean's civil service activities during her terms on the Santa Cruz County Board of Supervisors, 1956–1963.

University of Chicago

Library, Special Collections Research Center

1100 East 57th Street, Chicago, IL 60637

(773) 702-8705; specialcollections@lib.uchicago.edu

www.lib.uchicago.edu/e/spcl/

1509. Ernest Watson Burgess Papers, 1886–1966. Contains correspondence, research notes, manuscripts, reports, administrative files, subject files, bibliographies, essays, memoranda, research proposals, questionnaires, charts, graphs, maps, typescripts and books. Subseries 7, Radio Study, deals with a 1933 study that involved radio and children.

1510. Fight for Freedom Committee Records, 1941–1947. Contains correspondence, press releases, informational material, broadsides, radio scripts, lists of supporters and contributors, clippings and scrapbooks with memorabilia. Material relates to the Committee's efforts to involve the United States in World War II.

1511. "Organization and Collective Bargaining by Radio Artists." A Ph.D. thesis by Jewel G. Maher, 1951, University of Chicago.

1512. Percy Boynton Papers, 1925–1936. Consists of correspondence and three scrapbooks and includes material related to *Book Talk* aired during the 1920s.

University of Connecticut

Thomas J. Dodd Research Center

Archives & Special Collections

405 Babbidge Road, Unit 1205, Storrs, CT 06269

(860) 486-2993; Contact: Heidi N. Abbey

www.lib.uconn.edu/online/research/speclib/ASC/

1513. Andre Schenker Papers, 1918–1972. Includes transcripts of radio broadcasts, 1935–1949, reflecting Schenker's activities as a commentator at WTIC, Hartford, CT chiefly concerning events leading up to and during World War II and its aftermath, including D-Day, Pearl Harbor and the death of Franklin D. Roosevelt.

University of Delaware

Library, Special Collections

181 South College Avenue, Newark, DE 19717

(302) 831-2229; Fax: (302) 831-6003

LRJM@udel.edu; www.lib.udel.edu/ud/spec

Contact: Rebecca Johnson Melvin

1514. Charlotte Shedd Tapes and Papers. As of 2005, a partially processed collection that includes material relating to the four programs Shedd hosted on WDEL.

1515. Julian Symons Papers, 1944–1994, bulk 1970–1990. Consists of manuscripts, correspondence and reviews of movies, television and radio programs and theater productions, most relating to Symons's work in the field of crime literature.

1516. Papers of Senator J. Allen Frear, Jr. Includes 200 recordings of *The Week in Congress*, Senator Frear's weekly radio address to the people of Delaware which was delivered on WDOV, Dover, DE, 1953–1959, reflecting topics such as the Korean War, the spread of communism and domestic affairs.

1517. World War II Maps and Radio Broadcasts. Includes transcripts of daily radio news broadcasts from WOR and WDEL.

University of Georgia

Hargrett Rare Book and Manuscript Library

Jackson Street, Athens, GA 30602

(706) 542-7123; Fax: (706) 542-0672

hargrett@uga.edu; www.libs.uga.edu/hargrett

Contact: Chuck Barber

1518. Charles Coburn Papers, 1892–1959. Includes scrapbooks, scripts, photographs and interviews dealing with Coburn's film, theater, radio and television career.

1519. Emily Woodward Papers, 1916–1957. Consists of correspondence, programs, invitations, speeches, radio scripts, newspaper clippings and scrapbooks.

1520. George B. Storer Scrapbooks, 1947–1971. Scrapbooks document Storer's career in the communications industry, 1947–1971, and include some newspaper clippings, photographs, correspondence and memorabilia relating to the Storer Broadcasting Company, 1953–1971.

1521. Gilbert Maxwell Papers, 1931–1979. Contains published and unpublished manuscripts, including an unpublished biography of Tallulah Bankhead, correspondence, reviews, poetry, literary contracts and photographs relating to Maxwell's activities as an author, editor and educator. Correspondence discusses Maxwell's writings, publication and readings of his works, his production of radio programs and his involvement with the Federal Writers' and Federal Theatre Projects.

1522. Olin Downes Collection and Olin Downes Lectures and Papers, 1932–1953. Two collections that contain lectures, including handwritten manuscripts, typed drafts with corrections and final copies. Many of the lectures were broadcast on the *CBS Music Hour*. Papers also includes talks for *CBS Symphony Broadcasts*.

Walter J. Brown Media Archives
Ilah Dunlap Little Memorial Library
(706) 542-4757; Contact: Ruta Abolins
abolins@uga.edu; www.libs.uga.edu/media/

1523. Arnold Michaelis Library of Living History. Consists of hundreds of hours of Michaelis's audio, film and video interviews recorded since 1958 with leading political and cultural personalities. Michaelis served as host-writer-producer of *Music Magazine* aired on WQXR, New York and produced *Invitation To Learning* and *Of Men and Books*.

1524. Atlanta Gas Light Company Collection. Contains films, videos and radio spots produced by the Atlanta Gas Light Company, 1950s–1970s.

1525. General Audio Collections. The Archive has duplicate collections of material held at The Museum of Television and Radio Collection (approximately 11,000 radio transcription discs from the 1930s, 1940s and 1950s), the Broadcasting Foundation of America Collection (approximately 3,000 audio reels of radio news programs from the early 1970s) and the UCLA Radio Collection (approximately 1,300 radio transcription discs, primarily, 1930s–1950s). Contact the Archive for information about specific programs.

1526. Himan Brown Collection. Contains transcription discs of programs Brown produced or directed plus other CBS programs. Collection includes: *You Are There* (a.k.a. *CBS Is There*), *The Thin Man, Flash Gordon, Inner Sanctum, Suspense, Mystery Theatre, CBS Radio Workshop, Backstage Wife, Mr. Chameleon, Inspector Brooks, Young Widder Brown, Stella Dallas* and *Inspector Hawkes and Son*. An inventory of the collection is available in the Media Department.

1527. Peabody Awards Collection. Collection holds over 40,000 titles, with radio programs dating from 1940 and television from 1948, of news, documentary, entertainment, educational, children's and public service programming.

University of Houston
Special Collections
114 University Libraries, Houston, TX 77204

(713) 743-9750; Fax: (713) 743-9893
speccol@lib.uh.edu; www.lib.uh.edu

1528. Floyd Glass Navy Recruiting Literature Collection, 1941–1949. U. S. Navy recruiting literature, including a radio play for WAVES recruiting, n.d.

University of Idaho
PO Box 442350, Moscow, ID 83844
(208) 885-6584; www.lib.uidaho.edu

1529. Frank Bruce Robinson Papers, 1929–1951. Includes brief radio advertisements for a free copy of Robinson's 6,000 word lecture on Psychiana which was available from the radio station carrying the advertisement and a radio address broadcast over KEX, May 17, 1934.

1530. University of Idaho Presents. Scripts 1-4 and 6 of a thirteen part series, *University of Idaho Presents*, written by Ross Alm of the Department of Speech, possibly in the 1950s, and designed to acquaint the citizens of Idaho with the operation of the university.

University of Illinois, Urbana-Champaign
1408 West Gregory Drive, Urbana, IL 61801
Rare Book & Special Collections Library
(217) 333-3777; Fax: (217) 333-2214
j-somera@uiuc.edu; www.library.uiuc.edu/rbx/index.html
Contact: Jane Somera

1531. Ad Council: Campaign Bulletins and other Collections, 1946–. Reports and clippings relating to the Council's use of radio. Also contains Radio/TV Fact Sheets, 1946–1971, with background information on major Ad Council campaigns. Material is located in more than one collection.

1532. Carl Sandburg Papers, 1898–1962. Includes recordings and transcriptions of Sandburg's radio broadcasts.

1533. Gloria Parker Papers. Includes unidentified radio scripts, ca. 1951–1952, some for ABC.

1534. "History of Black Oriented Radio in Chicago 1929–1963." Ph.D. Thesis by Norman W. Spaulding, 1981.

1535. *One Man's Family.* Script for Chapter 64, Book Four (26th week). Includes dialogue and action with cast and set lists.

1536. *The Whistler.* Script for December 31, 1947.

University Archives
(217) 333-0798 Fax: (217) 333-2868
illiarch@uiuc.edu; http://web.library.uiuc.edu/ahx/

1537. Charles H. Sandage Papers, 1910–1993. Papers document Sandage's work in advertising as it related to radio, including the radio/TV diary method of survey research. Also includes research surveys in Ohio and Illinois.

1538. Claude Gordon Personal Papers and Music Instrument Collection, 1888–1992. Includes sound recordings of Gordon's band performing at the Hollywood Palladium and for local California radio shows during the 1950s plus scrapbooks, reviews, business records and other papers.

1539. Harry J. Skornia Papers, 1937–1991. Papers detail Skornia's career in educational broadcasting.

1540. *Library Presents* **File, 1945–1957.** Includes correspondence, lists of programs and guests, scripts, booklists and published programs aired on WILL and WIUC.

1541. Listener Surveys, 1949. Printed and duplicated reports on surveys of radio listeners, including a study on teenage listening habits and a "diary of radio listening" for a Radio Research project.

1542. Radio Station WPGU File, 1958–1979. Includes correspondence, audit reports, financial statements, minutes, newspaper clippings, photographs, press releases, publications, rosters, schedules, constitutions and bylaws and other papers.

1543. *Radio Talks* **File, 1937–1938.** Includes schedules and scripts of talks for December, 1937, January–May 1938, November–December, 1938 and January–May, 1939. The talks most likely dealt with health and medical issues.

1544. Ralph T. Fisher Papers, 1954–1998. Includes transcriptions of broadcasts of the Radio Liberation series *Our Youth*, 1955–1956.

1545. Research Reports, 1949–1977. Contains research reports done by members of the faculty and staff concerning educational radio and TV, content analysis, psychological effects of mass media and music broadcasting.

1546. WILL Collections 1935–1997. Several individual collections that include scripts, sound recordings, scrapbooks, special program announcements, annual reports and a subject file that contains general correspondence, reports, studies, publications, personnel files and legal documents.

University of Iowa
Iowa Women's Archives
100 Main Library, Iowa City, IA 52242
(319) 335-5068; Fax: (319) 335-5900
lib-women@uiowa.edu; www.lib.uiowa.edu/iwa/info.html
Contact: Karen Mason

1547. Betty Jean Clark Papers, 1935–2000. Papers include some presentations Clark made on radio, 1948–1950, possibly on a program called *Matin*.

1548. Edith Reed Atkinson Papers, 1935–1997, bulk 1986–1997. Contains biographical information in the form of newspaper clippings and feature articles about Atkinson. Also includes letters and cards of thanks she received following her performances and lectures, several performance programs and announcements and materials pertaining to her 1997 Woman of the Year Award. Beginning in 1943, Atkinson had a radio show on WMT during which she sang songs in response to listener requests. In 1952 she began serving as a typist and Spanish translator in the editing department of Collins Radio (now part of Rockwell International) and later became a production scheduler. For additional information about material related to her radio career check the finding aid.

1549. Edythe Stirlen Papers, 1930–1981. Papers primarily document Stirlen's life work as a radio minister on KFNF and KMA, Shenandoah, IA, including over three decades of transcripts of sermons. Also includes the prayers and announcements she read on the radio during her program, printed prayer pamphlets, postcards, calendars and copies of the magazine she sent out to keep in touch with her listeners.

1550. Elizabeth Wherry Papers, 1904–1960. A farm magazine writer, Wherry also wrote scripts for radio in the 1930s and 1940s. Collection includes manuscripts for the WSUI program *Country Landscape* that aired between 1940–1941.

1551. Evelyn Birkby Collection of Radio Homemaker Materials, 1948–1994. Collection is divided into several series. The Birkby series contains clippings about Birkby, including a 1991 "New Yorker" article by Jane and Michael Stern that relates the history of KMA and KFNF and the radio homemakers and includes an interview with Evelyn and Robert Birkby. The KFNF and KMA series, 1926–1987, contains primarily newsletters and recipe books, some taken from the homemakers' programs. Among the homemakers featured are Jessie S. Young, Edith Hansen, Florence Falk, Evelyn Birkby and Billie Oakley. The KMA Radio series also includes a small collection of photographs. The Miscellaneous Radio Homemaker materials includes books by radio homemakers from South Dakota and Oklahoma. The Photographs series, 1948–1965 and n.d., consists of photographs of Birkby and other radio homemakers. The Audiovisual series includes a video documentary about the radio homemakers and audio tapes of radio homemaker programs.

1552. Julie Englander Papers. Includes interviews and radio programs about women and sports conducted and produced by Englander for WSUI, n.d. As of 2005, the collection is unprocessed.

1553. Leanna Driftmier Papers, 1954–1991. Includes letters written in support of Driftmier's candidacy for the Iowa Mother of the Year Award, newspaper clippings about her career, family sketches taken from a scrapbook and a published memoir by Driftmier's daughter, Lucile Verness. A radio broadcaster, Driftmier was the founder of *Kitchen-Klatter* on KFNF, Shenandoah, IA.

1554. Mary Jane Odell Papers, 1936–2002. Odell was the host of radio and television programs, 1950s–1970s, in Des Moines and Chicago. Collection includes some newspaper clippings relating to her radio work in the 1950s.

1555. Rose Claire Huth Papers, 1950–1997, bulk 1950–1953. Consists of biographical material, correspondence, manuscripts of Huth's radio scripts for *Dr. Christian* and one photograph.

Special Collections
100 Main Library, 3rd Floor, Iowa City, IA 52242
(319) 335-5921; Fax: (319) 335-5900
sid-huttner@uiowa.edu; www.lib.uiowa.edu/spec-coll
Contact: Sidney F. Huttner

1556. Arthur Ross Papers, 1943–1965. Includes scripts by Ross for *Mr. & Mrs. Blandings* and *Suspense*, three recordings of *Suspense* and other papers related to his television and film career. See online finding aid for list of other scripts which are not identified as being radio or television.

1557. Radio Television News Directors Association Records, 1947–1995. Includes correspondence, minutes of the board of directors, convention reports, financial records and committee and membership files. Also includes copies of the organization's publications such as the "Commentator" and "RTNDA Bulletin." Correspondents include Edward R. Murrow. As of 2005, much of the collection remains in a semi-processed and/or unprocessed state although there is an online finding aid.

1558. W. Earl Hall Papers, 1917–1969. Includes several boxes of scripts of his weekly column *One Man's Opinions,* n.d

University of Kansas

Spencer Library, Special Collections Department
Lawrence, KS 66045
(785) 864-4334; Fax: (785) 864-5803
rclement@ku.edu; Contact: Richard W. Clement
http://spencer.lib.ku.edu/sc/additional.shtml

General comments: The library's online listings contained very limited information about the contents of the collections listed below. Some of the collections may consist primarily of ephemera as distinct from collections with personal and business papers. They are, however, included because of their uniqueness.

Kansas Collection

1559. Hurst B. Amyx Ephemeral Materials. Includes transcripts of radio broadcasts dealing with sex education. Papers form part of the Wilcox Collection of Contemporary Political Movements.

1560. "Kansas City Star." Contains profiles of the various people who worked for the newspaper, including WDAF Radio and WDAF-TV owned by the paper.

1561. Kansas Radio Audience, 1937–1939. Kansas radio facts and radio listeners' survey.

1562. Story of the "Kansas City Star," 1948. A souvenir booklet prepared to explain the operations of a metropolitan newspaper. Also includes information about the newspaper's paper mill and radio station.

1563. Studio and Broadcasting Station KFNF: The Friendly Farmer Station. A booklet describing the station.

1564. Transcripts and Broadcast Sound Recordings of Alfred M. Landon. Includes 44 transcripts and broadcast recordings of speeches and interviews by and about Alfred M. Landon probably broadcast on WREN, Topeka, KS. For a fuller description of collection, see the Manuscripts Inventory in the Kansas Collection.

1565. "Victory's Victims? The Negro's Future." Transcript of a radio discussion by A. Philip Randolph and Norman Thomas

1566. "The Voice of the Nazi." Eight broadcast talks given between December, 1939 and May, 1944.

1567. Weekly Broadcast. Text of weekly radio program of Dean Clarence E. Manion, possibly titled *Manion Forum* or *Manion Forum of Opinion.* Includes March 6, 1955 broadcast and possibly others.

Other Special Collections

1568. Katzman Collection. Includes arrangements of popular music, primarily for George Gershwin's radio show, 1933–1935. Katzman was an arranger, organist and pianist for Gershwin.

1569. Reminiscences, 1970. Two letters from Henry Manners Katzman to George Griffin of Broadcast Music Inc., San Francisco, March 5 and 10, 1970, reminiscing about the New York popular music and radio scene, 1932–1935. Katzman describes George Gershwin's radio show in detail with anecdotes.

1570. *Seth Parker's Hymnal.* Includes some biographical information about Phillips Hayes Lord and material from *Seth Parker's Hymnal.*

University of Kentucky

Special Collections and Archives
King Library South, Lexington, KY 40506
(859) 257-8611; Fax: (859) 257-8379
crmcca00@uky.edu; www.uky.edu/Libraries/Special/
Contact: Claire McCann

1571. Gilbert W. Kingsbury Papers, 1952–1964. Contains papers associated with Kingsbury's career as a journalist, including his broadcast career with WLW, Cincinnati, OH and later as a vice president for WLW's parent company, Crosley Broadcasting. Includes scripts for *Personalities in Government,* a program that profiled important Kentuckians and national figures.

1572. Ruth Fox Newborg Papers. Newborg was program director for WBKY, Beattyville, KY from 1940–1941. The station was created as an experiment in bringing educational radio broadcasts to the remote Appalachian regions of eastern Kentucky.

University of Louisville

Dwight Anderson Music Library
(502) 852-5659; Fax: (502) 852-7701
krlitt01@gwise.louisville.edu; Contact: Karen Little
http://library.louisville.edu/music/coll/special.html

1573. WHAS Sheet Music Collection, 1920s–1950s. Consists of originals and adaptations of songs and small combo arrangements from the 1920s–1950s performed by musicians during the broadcasts. Index cards in a large filing cabinet acquired from WHAS serve as the finding aid. The collection is indexed by title, composer and subject.

Photographic Archives
Ekstrom Library, Louisville, KY 40292
(502) 852-6752; Fax: (502) 852-8734
susan.marie@louisville.edu; Contact: Susan M. Knoer
http://library.louisville.edu/library/ekstrom/special/
pa_info.html

1574. Caufield and Shook Studio Photographs, 1903–1978. Includes an image of the Ballard Chefs who had a program on WHAS.

1575. Jean Thomas Collection, 1920–ca. 1969. Contains photographs of country music performers, including some who appeared on the radio.

1576. R.G. Potter Collection, ca. 1880–1970. Includes photographs of early WHAS performers and other radio related subjects. Collection can be searched online by keyword.

University Archives
Ekstrom Library, Louisville, KY 40292
(502) 852-8731; Fax: (502) 852-8734
jemana01@louisville.edu; http://library.Louisville.edu
Contact: James Manasco

1577. Louise Weiller Papers, 1897-1994. Papers document Weiller's radio career beginning in 1945 with WINN and include scripts for her program *Lady Lookout,* 1949–1953, a radio talk show log for 1946 and scripts for *A Woman's Way* aired on WAVE, 1956–1971.

University of Maine
Maine Folklife Center
Northeast Archives of Folklore and Oral History
5773 South Stevens Hall, Orono, ME 04469
(207) 581-1891; Fax: (207) 581-1823
folklife@maine.edu; www.umaine.edu/folklife

General comments: The Folklife Center has many oral history interviews of performers associated with country and western music, including Raymond "Slim" Clark, Eva Littlefield, Ann and Ray Little, the Lone Pine Mountaineer, Horace Dinsmore, Norm Lambert and many others. Additional oral interviews discuss the early days of radio. Listed below are two of the many collections within the oral history archive.

1578. Interviews About Early Radio and Country Music, 1975. Interviews with Irving Hunter about early radio and country western music in Bangor in the 1930s. Includes an interview with musician Watie Akins about his employment with WLBZ, ca. 1930. Subjects covered include local and national programming, equipment used by the station, affiliations with different networks, technological advancements in radio and equipment, remote and delayed broadcasts, a discussion of performers, the process of making radio logs and more.

1579. Oral History Interview With Glenice Beaulieu, 1975. Interview about country and western music in the 1920s and 1930s, including broadcasts on WLBZ.

Raymond H. Fogler Library
Special Collections
Orono, ME 04469
(207) 581-1661; Fax: (207) 581-1653
spc@umit.maine.edu; www.library.umaine.edu/speccoll
Contact: Richard Hollinger

1580. "A Rhetorical Study: The Radio Speaking of Edward R. Murrow." A Ph.D. thesis by Thomas Russell Woolley, Northwestern University, 1957.

1581. Floyd Phillips Gibbons Papers, 1900–1940. Papers contain radio scripts, correspondence, columns, comic strips, manuscripts of his writings, recordings, newsclippings, photographs and Gibbons family memorabilia.

1582. Henry Ives Baldwin Papers, 1900–1950. Contains radio scripts dealing with conservation, forestry, wood utilization and other papers relating to Baldwin's career as a research forester for the New Hampshire Forestry and Recreation Commission and president of the Northern Wood Utilization Council.

1583. "Radio Programs in Secondary School Classrooms of the State of Maine, 1940–1941." A Ph.D. thesis by Herbert L. Prescott, University of Maine, 1941.

1584. Rudy Vallee Papers and Memorabilia, 1917–1984. Includes correspondence from 1917–1984, newspaper clippings, scores, photographs, scrapbooks, phonograph records, a megaphone and other memorabilia.

1585. Sanford Phippen Literary Papers 1954–. Papers of a Maine author, poet, high school teacher and alumnus of the University of Maine. Collection includes radio scripts.

1586. Station Records, WLBZ, 1931–1973. Consists mostly of station logs, 1931–1956, plus some audio tapes and materials concerning licensing and operations.

1587. Taverns and Inns in Maine, 1932–1974. The history of taverns and inns in Maine was prepared by the chapters of the Daughters of the American Revolution for radio broadcasts in 1932 and 1933. Collection includes text of the broadcast aired February 12, 1932 on WCSH, Portland, ME.

University of Maryland
Hombake Library
College Park, MD 20742

General comments: The University's library is home to the Library of American Broadcasting (listed separately under "L") and the National Public Broadcasting Archives (see below). In addition, based on a search of the library's online catalog, at least one special collection with radio related material was identified in the library's general catalog.

Maryland Room Archives, Historical Manuscripts
(301) 314-2712; Fax: (301) 314-2709
www.lib.umd.edu/ARCV/histmss/

1588. Jacob Elry Metzger Papers, 1915–1938. Includes transcripts of radio talks on agricultural issues.

National Public Broadcasting Archives
(301) 405-9160; Fax: (301) 314-2634
tconnors@mail.umd.edu; www.lib.umd.edu/NPBA
Contact: Thomas Connors

General comments: Check the NPBA web site, www.lib.umd.edu/NPBA, for additional collections. Although most of these collections contain post–1960s material, some of the collections may contain some earlier information. The site also has links to other repositories in the fields of educational and public broadcasting.

1589. KBPS Records, 1923–1995. Papers documenting the history and programming of KBPS, Portland, OR. Includes correspondence, reports, financial documents, scripts, speeches and sound recordings.

1590. Morris S. Novik Papers, 1940–1992. Contains documents relating to Novik's career in public broadcasting, including correspondence, reports, hearings, clippings, conference materials, press releases and other papers. Novik was associated with WNYC, New York, and was executive secretary of the National Association of Educational Broadcasters. Papers also include correspondence with the FCC and the Institute for Education by Radio-Television.

University of Memphis
Periodicals/Non Print Collections
126 R. McWherter Library
Memphis, TN 38152
(901) 678-2204; Contact: Marvin R. Bensman
mbensman@Memphis.edu
https://umdrive.memphis.edu/mbensman/public/

1591. The Bensman Radio Program Archive. An extensive audio collection of old time radio programs that provides a representative sampling of most shows and series. An online catalog is available and copies of individual programs can be purchased on cassette.

University of Michigan
Bentley Historical Library
1150 Beal Avenue, Ann Arbor, MI 48109
(734) 764-3482; Fax: (734) 936-1333

tepowers@umich.edu;   www.umich.edu/~bhl/
Contact: Thomas E. Powers

1592. Allmendinger Family Papers, 1890–1974. Includes papers related to Helene Allmendinger's radio show and the Ann Arbor Organ Company.

1593. Arthur H. Vandenberg Sound Recordings. Includes sound recordings of radio speeches and other addresses on politics and public issues.

1594. Arthur Pound Papers, 1928–1968. Includes research materials on the RCA Corporation and radio broadcasting.

1595. Blair Moody Sound Recordings. Includes recordings of *This is Washington*, radio reports to his constituents on his senatorial activities, 1951, and *Meet Your Congress*, 1951, 1953–1954, containing discussions of politics, domestic and foreign policy during the Eisenhower administration and other issues of then current interest. Also includes recordings of additional radio programs and 1940 campaign broadcasts.

1596. "Broadcasting by the Newspaper-owned Stations in Detroit, 1920–1927." A Ph.D. thesis on the broadcasting stations owned by newspapers in Detroit, MI, 1920–1927 by Maryland Waller Wilson, University of Michigan, 1952.

1597. Campus Broadcasting Network (University of Michigan) Records, 1953–1989. Records documenting the history of campus radio broadcasting stations at the University of Michigan.

1598. Catherine Baker Sound Recording. An undated recording of the program *This Is Bay City* aired on WBCM.

1599. *Echoes of Heaven* Collection. Reprints of the weekly broadcasts by ministers from the Burns Avenue Baptist Church, Detroit, MI.

1600. Edgar A. Guest Papers, 1898–1950. Includes manuscripts of radio talks and other papers.

1601. Edward F. Baughn Papers, 1936–1986. Includes papers relating to Baughn's ownership of WPAG radio and television stations in Ann Arbor, MI.

1602. Ethel B. Sutton Papers, ca. 1956–1965. Includes scripts of the inspirational series *Today's Good Word* and clippings concerning the United Church Women of Flint and religious broadcasting.

1603. *Ford Sunday Evening Hour*, 1934–1942. Bound copies of the talks from the program.

1604. Garnet R. Garrison Papers, 1928–1990. Papers related to Garrison's career in broadcasting, including his published writings, speeches, scripts and audio visual materials.

1605. George Cushing Papers, 1942–1955. Includes correspondence, radio transcripts, scrapbooks and recordings of broadcasts. Cushing was a news editor and vice president of WJR, Detroit, MI and moderator of *In Our Opinion*.

1606. Gordon Webber Papers, 1938–1986. A writer for radio and television and an advertising executive, the papers include scripts for *I Remember Mama, The Firefighters* and *Reflections*. Also includes materials relating to his other work. Note: It is not clear from catalog listing if scripts are for radio or television.

1607. Interlochen Center for the Arts Records, ca.1880–. Includes documentation of the dispute between Interlochen and James C. Petrillo, head of the American Federation of Musicians, over the use of non-union amateur musicians in the radio broadcasts of Interlochen performances.

1608. Karl William Detzer Papers, 1916–1981. Contains papers relating to Detzer's work as a writer and editor for "Reader's Digest," including scripts and other papers concerning his activities as a script writer for radio, television and motion picture production.

1609. Kenneth H. MacDonald Papers, 1932–1989. Includes scrapbooks, advertisements and other materials relating to WSAM, one of a network of Michigan stations owned by MacDonald, and other papers detailing MacDonald's involvement with the National Association of Broadcasters.

1610. Lawrence K. Rosinger Papers, 1937–1973, bulk 1937–1953. Contains transcripts of radio broadcasts, 1941–1945, and other papers relating to his trips to China and transcripts of interviews with Chinese leaders.

1611. Leo J. Fitzpatrick Papers, 1894–1971. Contains correspondence, financial material and printed miscellanea largely concerning the operation of WJR, Detroit, MI and the history of radio broadcasting in general, including a transcript of an oral history interview and John F. Patt's remembrances of radio pioneer George A. Richards. Also includes a letter from Father Charles Coughlin, 1929, containing brief comments on religious broadcasting.

1612. Preston W. Slosson Papers, 1918–1952. Collection includes transcripts of radio addresses on world politics, 1940–1947.

1613. Ross Johnston Wilhelm Papers, 1925–1982. Includes copies of Wilhelm's commentaries on *Business Review*, 1960–1981, plus other papers. Note: A second collection, Ross Johnston Wilhelm Photograph Series, contains photographs of Wilhelm broadcasting on WUOM.

1614. Washtenaw Broadcasting Company Historical Sketch, 1945. Includes an historical sketch and attached program schedules for WPAG and WGUN.

1615. William Bender Papers, 1949–1956, 1962–1965. Contains correspondence and other materials relating to his career with the hospital, including radio scripts on Michigan topics prepared for the broadcasting service of the university.

1616. WUOM Records, 1914–1982, 1940s–1950s. Contains administrative records documenting the development of radio broadcasting at the University of Michigan, Ann Arbor, including scripts, transcripts of talks given by faculty, publicity, scrapbooks, photographs and sound recordings of programs produced and broadcast by WUOM.

1617. John Zoller Papers. Collection most likely includes sermons from the *America Back to God* program.

University of Minnesota
Children's Literature Research Collection
113 Andersen Library
222 – 21st Avenue South, Minneapolis, MN 55455
(612) 624-4576; Fax: (612) 626-0377
clrc@umn.edu; http://special.lib.umn.edu/clrc

1618. Caddie Woodlawn Production Material. Includes material for a Caddie Woodlawn memorial program broadcast in February, 1940 on the Idaho State University radio station dealing with the adventures of growing up on the Wisconsin frontier in the 1860s.

1619. Edythe Warner Papers, 1958–1964. Includes some radio script material.

1620 . Jean Lee Latham Papers, 1948–1965. Includes some radio plays.

1621. Margaret Hodges Papers, 1958–1989. Includes some radio scripts.

Immigration History Research Center
311 Andersen Library
222 – 21st Avenue South, Minneapolis, MN 55455
(612) 625-4800; Fax: (612) 626-0018
ihrc@umn.edu; www.ihrc.umn.edu
Contact: Joel Wurl

1622. Alexander W. Yaremko Papers, 1924–1969. Contains biographical information, personal correspondence, materials pertaining to Ukrainian American organizations and cultural activities and historical material on Ukraine and Ukrainians in America, including a program booklet of the Third Annual Ukrainian Radio Day held on August 29, 1948 in Pittsburgh, PA.

1623. American Council for Nationalities Service Records, 1918–1986. Papers include the group's use of radio to further its programs covering all aspects of immigration and resettlement.

1624. Anthony Nurczynski Papers, 1929-1951. Nurczynski arranged music for the Shep Nolan Band and Krakowiaki who played live on the *Echoes of Poland.* Papers consist primarily of published and mimeographed sheet music. Mainly in Polish with some English material. See also Walter and Valeria Nurczynski Collection below.

1625. Antonio Consiglio Papers, 1928–1959. Includes a publicity kit issued by American Relief for Italy, Inc. in 1947 containing radio spots, proclamations, editorial announcements and a fact sheet about the organization's activities.

1626. Erik A. Dundurs Papers, 1949–1982. Contains correspondence, memorabilia, newspaper clippings, speeches, scrapbooks and files on various organizations to which Dundurs belonged, including those related to the Latvian American community. Some time after 1951, Dundurs worked as a radio talk show host. Check with repository to determine if papers cover his radio career.

1627. Father Bertrand Kotnik Papers, ca. 1895–1966. Contains personal and church related papers and sheet music, including concert leaflets and programs commemorating the *Slovenian Radio Hour* in Pueblo City, CO. Some of the materials are in Slovenian.

1628. George Graff Papers, 1931–1947. Consists of correspondence, minutes, newspaper clippings, reports, newsletters and miscellany pertaining to the Service Bureau for Intercultural Education, including materials related to *Americans All, Immigrants All.*

1629. George L. Quilici Papers, 1934–1969. Clippings in the collection pertain to Quilici's anti-fascist radio work and to the movemenet to erase General Italio Balbo's name from Chicago streets and parks.

1630. Girolamo Valenti Papers, 1904–1960. Contains correspondence and published items, newspaper clippings on fascism, socialism and World War I, photographs, pamphlets, cartoons and caricatures by Fort Velona and materials pertaining to Arturo Giovannitti and New York politicians. Valenti also worked for the Italian American station WHAY in Connecticut. Check with repository to determine if papers cover his radio career.

1631. Joseph Gorassi Order Sons of Italy in America Collection, 1926–1973. Includes transcripts of radio speeches, 1939, 1941–1942.

1632. Karol T. Jaskolski Papers. Papers reflect Jaskolski's involvement with the *Polish Variety Hour* and *Voice of America.* Also includes materials pertaining to many Polish American organizations in the Boston area.

1633. Maurice R. Marchello Papers, 1922–1972. Contains biographical material, personal correspondence, materials relating to his legal and literary careers and civic and political activities, miscellany, photographs, newspaper clippings, ephemera, scripts of radio broadcasts, speeches, lectures, short stories and book manuscripts.

1634. Michael Komichak Papers, 1938. Komichak worked as engineer and assistant manager for WPIT-AM and FM, Pittsburgh, PA and was director of Ukrainian radio programming. Papers are in Ukranian and English. Note: The finding aid does not describe the contents of the collection.

1635. Nikolajs Rasins Papers, 1954–1979. Contains tape recordings, slides, newspaper clippings, correspondence and financial records relating to Rasins's Latvian American broadcasting and other Latvian American community activities in Colorado Springs, CO and the Twin Cities, MN.

1636. Pasquale Cajano Papers. Includes transcripts of radio programs, sheet music and playbills. Materials are in Italian and English.

1637. Polish American Congress Records, 1935–1974. Records of a national organization composed of many Polish American fraternal, social, cultural, professional, veteran and other similar organizations. Collection includes many press releases, papers relating to a special commission dealing with radio and television issues and a radio address commemorating the fifth anniversary of the invasion of Poland.

1638. Rachel Davis DuBois Papers, ca. 1917–1973. Contains both personal papers and organizational records and includes correspondence, minutes, reports, publications, scripts, newspaper clippings, listener aids, research files and phonograph records from *Americans All, Immigrants All* for which DuBois served as consultant, 1938–1939.

1639. Walter and Valeria Nurczynski Papers, 1936–1968. Consists of correspondence, newspaper clippings, sheet music (mostly of songs sung by Valeria), radio scripts, and financial reports of the Polish War Relief Committee of Boston, ca. 1944. From 1937–1944 Nurczynski produced *Echoes of Poland.* Also includes correspondence and photographs of Alexandra J. Jaskolski and papers of Karol Jaskolski.

1640. Wasyl Halich Papers, ca. 1921–1971. Contain biographical information, postcards, newspaper clippings and correspondence, much relating to the Ukrainian community and including material on the *Ukrainian Family on Radio* and other radio announcements.

1641. *Yugoslav (Slovenian ?) Radio Hour* **Collection, ca. 1942–1953.** Includes scripts used for radio programs that were broadcast from Milwaukee, WI.

Special Collections and Rare Books
222 – 21st Avenue South, Minneapolis, MN 55455
(612) 624-7526; Contact: Tim Johnson
johns976@umn.edu
http://special.lib.umn.edu/rare/

1642. Universal Sherlock Holmes Collection. Contains materials relating to all aspects of Sherlock Holmes in different media, including a log of Sherlock Holmes on radio, 316 Edith Meiser radio scripts, 154 sound recordings of the broadcasts on 33¹/₃rpm and 16" transcription discs and much more. A print guide to the collection, "Edith Meiser and Her Adventures with Sherlock Holmes: A Guide to the Edith Meiser Collection at the University of Minnesota," is available from the Department of Special Collections for $10.

University Archives
222 – 21st Avenue South, Minneapolis, MN 55455
(612) 624-0562; Fax: (612) 625-5525
uar@tc.umn.edu; http://special.lib.umn.edu/uarch

1643. Frederick J. Wulling Papers, 1884–1948. Includes correspondence, articles, radio talks, speeches and other papers relating to Wulling's work in the field of pharmaceuticals

1644. Helen Parker Mudgett Papers, 1945–1964. Includes a series of KUOM scripts, November, 1950–March, 1953, probably related to the Minnesota Chippewa or Ojibwa Indians, and other papers relating to Mudgett's work dealing with the Chippewa Indian culture.

1645. Truman Raymond Nodland Papers, 1940–1967. Includes transcripts of radio talks delivered by Nodland, 1940–1967, on agricultural issues.

1646. William A. O'Brien Papers, 194?–1947? Consists of a series of scripts on various aspects of public health. Also includes outline notes for the scripts.

University of Mississippi
J. D. Williams Library, Blues Archive
PO Box 1848, University, MS 38677
(662) 915-7753; Fax: (662) 915-5734
gj1@olemiss.edu; Contact: Greg Johnson
www.olemiss.edu/depts/general_library/files/archives/blues

1647. John Richbourg Collection, ca. 1942–1986. Contains papers, sound recordings, photographs and memorabilia relating to Richbourg's career as a disk jockey for WLAC, Nashville, TN, 1942–1973. Includes tapes of air-checks, primarily from the 1960s. Papers include clippings, articles and a brief handwritten memoir documenting his career as a broadcaster, record producer and as an educator who founded a school of broadcasting for black students in the 1950s.

University of Missouri-Columbia
University Archives
703 Lewis Hall, Columbia, MO 65211
(573) 882-3727; Fax: (573) 884-0027
coxgd@missouri.edu; http://muarchives.missouri.edu/
Contact: Gary Cox

1648. James E. Smith Papers, 1939–1981. Includes scripts for radio talks given by Smith on floriculture.

1649. *On The Waterfront.* Sound recordings and scripts for 16 radio programs dealing with local issues. Possibly aired post-1960s.

Western Historical Manuscript Collection
Ellis Library, Columbia, MO 65201
(573) 882-6028; Fax: (573) 884-0345
WHMC@umsystem.edu; www.umsystem.edu/whmc/

General comments: The collection is divided into subject categories and the web site lists the names of the collections within each category but does not provide a description of the collection. Check with library to determine if any of the collections include any radio related information.

University of Missouri-Kansas City
Department of Special Collections
Miller Nicholas Library
Street address: 5100 Rockhill Road
Mailing address: 800 E. 51 Street, Kansas City, MO 64110
(816) 235-1532; Fax: (816) 333-5584
www.umkc.edu/lib/spec-col/index.html

1650. Arthur B. Church KMBC Radio Collection. Documents Church's 30 years in radio and television, including as owner and operator of KMBC radio and television in Kansas City, MO from the 1920s–late 1950s. Church was the creative force behind several syndicated shows, including *The Brush Creek Follies, The Texas Rangers* and *Phenomenon.* Collection includes photos, published sheet music, scripts, scrapbooks, promotional material, contracts, telegrams, station newsletters and broadcast recordings. Recordings are in the Marr Sound Archives (see below).

1651. Wilder Wylie Collection, 1922–1958. Consists of scripts for KIDO-NBC, including *KIDO Showcase, Fashion Club, Down Memory Lane with Kathryn Kane, The Bob Hope Show* and various other NBC programs.

Marr Sound Archives
A unit of the Department of Special Collections
(816) 235-2798
Contact: Chuck Haddix

General comments: The Archives has nearly 250,000 recordings from the 1890s–1980. A portion of the collection includes vintage radio programs. For more information on specific programs in the Archives, check first with the library's general catalog. However, as not all recordings are cataloged, information on specific programs may be available from the following additional sources: indexes in the Archives and Music/Media Library, discographies, the OCLC catalog available through the NUCMC web site and other finding aids. Listed below are three specific large collections that include radio material.

1652. Armed Forces Radio Service Collection. Approximately 8,000 transcription discs of educational, variety and musical recordings from World War II and the post war era.

1653. Gaylord Marr Collection. Approximately 3,000 transcription discs, 1940–1950, featuring variety and musical shows broadcast over the Armed Forces Radio Service and other government sponsored programs.

1654. J. David Goldin Collection. Approximately 10,000 transcription discs of programs, 1935–1955, with emphasis on programs and events from 1940–1950.

University of Missouri-St. Louis
Thomas Jefferson Library
Western Historical Manuscript Collection
8001 Natural Bridge Road, St. Louis, MO 63121
(314) 516-5143
whmc@umsl.edu; www.umsl.edu/services/library

1655. African American Pioneers in Journalism and Broadcasting. An oral history project. The online listing gives names of the participants without identifying whether they were in radio, and if so, when. Check with library for more information.

1656. American Radio Collection, 1931–1972. Collection of 514 audio tapes with broadcasts from the Golden Age of Radio. Mostly entertainment shows of various genres but also includes some news items and speeches. For a list of the contents check: http://www.umsl.edu/~whmc/guides/whm0256.htm.

1657. Bernard Hayes Papers, 1961–1989. Papers document Hayes's career as a radio broadcaster, 1961–1988, although he began his radio career in the Air Force in 1950 as an announcer for the Armed Forces Radio Service and in 1956 he began work as the black on-air personality and first black news announcer for a station in Alexandria, LA. Includes photocopies of scrapbooks containing publicity literature and photographs reflecting Hayes's radio work from the early to mid–1960s in Chicago, including his work on WMMP, the first black owned station in the Midwest, WSBC, WVON and WGES.

1658. Frank Eschen Collection. Contains correspondence, scripts, newsclippings, and photographs relating to Eschen's radio and television career, including his work on KFRU, WIL and KSD, 1946–1956. Collection also includes an oral interview with Eschen's son about his father.

1659. Gloria Pritchard Papers, 1910–1983. Includes correspondence, press releases and scripts for *World of Women*, 1960–1962, that Pritchard hosted on KATZ beginning in 1957.

1660. Joseph Pulitzer Papers, 1897–1958. Papers deal primarily with Pulitzer's editorship of the "St. Louis Post-Dispatch" and cover nearly every aspect of the operation and production of the newspaper, including radio advertising, 1925–1927.

1661. Pearl Schwartz Papers, 1915-1980. Beginning in 1963, Schwartz hosted *Open Road* on KATZ, St. Louis.

1662. Robert Hyland Papers, 1935–1990. Papers cover Hyland's early career in sales in radio and later as general manager of KMOX, St. Louis. Contains some mostly unspecified recordings, 1958–1964, including "Pass The Biscuits, Mirandi," with the Spike Jones Combo broadcast September 9, 1963.

1663. Thomas A. Dooley Papers, 1932–1986. In addition to papers related to Dooley's career and personal life, the collection includes transcripts and tapes of *That Free Men May Live*, Dooley's weekly program on KMOX. St. Louis.

University of Montana
Maureen and Mike Mansfield Library, Missoula, MT 59812
(406) 243-2053; archives@selway.umt.edu
www.lib.umt.edu/dept/arch/arch.htm

1664. Chet Huntley Papers, 1920–1977. Materials by and about Huntley, including biographical information, personal and professional correspondence, scripts written for his radio and television projects, speaking engagements and news commentary projects and press clippings, primarily spanning his years with NBC. Boxes 2-6 in Series III contain radio scripts. See online finding aid for list of programs, interviews and dates.

1665. Chet Huntley Radio Pieces. Sound recordings of Huntley broadcasts on April 13, 1944 and June 6, 1944 commenting on developments in World War II.

University of Nebraska/Lincoln
Music Library
Westbrook Music Building 30, Lincoln, NE 68588
(402) 472-6300; Fax: (402) 472-1592
abreckbill1@unl.edu; www.unl.edu/libr/libs/music
Contact: Anita S. Breckbill

1666. Ruth Etting Archive, 1900–1990. Contains 357 photographs, scrapbooks, 127 sound recordings, correspondence, memorabilia, videotapes and films documenting Etting's career as a singer.

University of Nevada
University Library, University Archives, Reno, NV 89557
(775) 784-6500; specoll@unr.edu
www.library.unr.edu/specoll/geninfo.html

1667. *College Bowl* Collection, 1963. Includes general correspondence concerning the preparation for the show, photographs, samples of questions, news releases, newsclippings and information on *College Bowl* teams and statistics, 1963/64–1964/65.

1668. *Land-Grant College Radio Hour,* 1938. Contains the script for the July 20, 1938 program, six phonograph recordings of the program, including the sound of the Morrill Hall bell, a scrapbook which contains a second copy of the script, letters of congratulations and other comments and photographs taken during the production.

University of New Orleans
Earl K. Long Library, Room 402, New Orleans, LA 70148
(504) 280-6543
http://library.uno.edu/about/louisiana.html

1669. Evelyn Soule Ford Kennedy Papers, 1919–1980, bulk 1931–1949. Contains manuscripts of writings by or about Kennedy reflecting her life and writing career, including plays, radio scripts, poetry and miscellaneous texts.

University of North Carolina at Chapel Hill
Wilson Library Manuscripts Department
Chapel Hill, NC 27514
(919) 962-1345; Fax: (919) 962-3594
mss@email.unc.edu; www.lib.unc.edu/mss/
Contact: Tanya Fortner or Jan Paris

Southern Folklife Collection

1670. Billy Faier Collection, 1955–2003. Contains reel-to-reel recordings of Faier's disc jockey programs aired on KPFA, Berkeley, CA and WBAI, New York, including *The Midnight*

Special on WBAI and an acetate recording of Dillybean Radio Spots.

1671. David Morton Collection, 1928–2003. Documentation, sound recordings and a videotape relating chiefly to Morton's work with African American harmonica player DeFord Bailey who performed on WSM's *Grand Ole Opry*.

1672. Folklife Section Collection, 1980. Extensive oral history of Dewey "Pigmeat" Markham, an African American performer. The oral history focuses on his career, his early work in medicine shows and carnivals and his later work on Broadway and on radio and television.

1673. Glenn Thompson Collection, 1944–2002. Papers of country singer and guitarist turned band leader Glenn Thompson and his Dixie Playboys. The group appeared on a variety of radio stations, including WGH in Newport News, VA, WDLP, Panama City, FL and on the *WDVA Barn Dance*, WDVA, Danville, VA. Also includes papers and photographs relating to other performers who performed with Thompson on *WDVA Barn Dance* and at other venues. Audio recordings do not appear to be from radio programs.

1674. Guthrie T. Meade Collection. Consists of materials gathered by Meade in his study of traditional country music and Kentucky fiddlers. Contains about 50 radio items, including guides to radio programming, both weekly publications and local newspaper columns. The "Old Time Radio Programs" folder contains Meade's research notes and indicates the dates and times that programs aired on various stations. Finding aid lists specific radio stations.

1675. Highlander Research and Education Center Collection, 1937–1948 and n.d. Contains sound recordings of radio programs on issues related to the work of the Highlander Folk School, including labor issues with the Tennessee Valley Authority (TVA).

1676. Jack Bernhardt Papers, 1943–1993. Papers dealing with Bernhardt's writings relating to country, old-time, bluegrass and gospel music, including Uncle Joe Johnson, a radio personality at WPAQ, Mount Airy, NC. The Uncle Joe Johnson materials include a magazine article written by Bernhardt for "Bluegrass Unlimited" about WPAQ and a number of photographs of Uncle Joe Johnson and others.

1677. Jay Anania Collection, 1973. Includes an interview with Arthur Jackson, commonly known as Peg Leg Sam, an African American blues harmonica player and medicine show performer, about his experiences in show business, medicine shows, radio broadcasting and riding freight trains.

1678. John Edwards Memorial Collection. Includes transcript of a 1971 interview with Art Satherly, talent scout and recording executive for hillbilly and race record labels in the 1920s and 1930s, and interviews with Wilber Ball and Cliff Carlisle, early country musicians from Kentucky, about the early days of radio in Louisville, KY.

1679. Johnson Family Singers Collection, 1943–1997. Includes radio scripts and sound and video recordings documenting the careers of the Johnson Family Singers and Betty Johnson. Includes 158 scripts from WBT shows, Charlotte, NC, 1943–1965, in which the Johnson Family Singers performed and Larry Walker appeared on the *Margaret Ann Show*.

1680. Leland Ledgerwood Collection, 1880–1998. Correspondence dealing with the Ledgerwood's Tennessee Fiddlers, a.k.a. the Ledgerwood-Harmison Old Time String Band, and the group's weekly broadcast on WKBN, Youngstown, OH, 1927–1930. Collection includes some sound recordings that do not appear to be from radio programs.

Southern Historical Collection

1681. Adolph Bregman Papers. Includes scripts written by Bregman for David Dickon's program, *Parade of American Songs,* broadcast weekly over WEVD, New York in the early 1930s. Collection includes other materials relating to folk music and Bregman's personal life.

1682. Ameel Joseph Fisher Papers. Includes correspondence, notes, scripts, films and other items relating to Fisher's career in radio and in television news broadcasting. Online finding aid lists names and dates of scripts but not for what radio program.

1683. Betty Smith Papers, 1909–1971. Included in the large collection of Smith's papers and writings is the radio script for "A Tree Grows in Brooklyn" and material regarding the musical version of the story.

1684. C. Hugh Holman Papers, 1930s–1980s. Contains about 100 items dealing with radio plays, including correspondence, copyright notices, playscripts and other materials, chiefly from the 1930s and 1940s. Some of the radio plays were written by Holman while others were edited by him. Many of the plays were used in the *Forum of the Air* series which aired in the late 1930s.

1685. Chapel Hill Council of Churches Records. Papers include radio broadcasts of the Council, an interdenominational organization established in Chapel Hill, in 1947.

1686. Charles Harvey Crutchfield Papers, 1938-1982. Contains papers relating to Crutchfield's career, including his work at WBT, Charlotte, NC as a radio announcer, program director and general manager, as president of the Jefferson Pilot Broadcasting Company, 1965–1977, and also his career at CBS.

1687. Charles Kuralt Collection. The bulk of the items in the collection pertain to Kuralt's career between the 1970s and the 1990s and include scripts, publicity materials and a small amount of fan mail.

1688. Elmer R. Oettinger, Jr., Papers, 1862–2002. A portion of the papers relate to Oettinger's career with the Tobacco Radio Network and WNAO, Raleigh, NC and contain articles, advertisements and scripts for radio programs, including *The Citizen's Forum of the Air.*

1689. Eugenia Rawls and Donald Seawell Theater Collection, 1916–1988. A portion of the collection includes a large number of radio, television and theatrical scripts for productions in which Rawls appeared.

1690. Gilbert Brooks Radio Broadcasts. Includes sound recordings and related materials chiefly containing radio programs, 1958–1961 and n.d., hosted by Brooks and sponsored by the Hayward, CA chapter of the NAACP. The programs are mostly concerned with the status of African Americans in the mid–20th century.

1691. Hal Kemp Papers, 1918–1992. Contains correspondence, photographs, clippings, legal documents, sheet music and recorded music documenting Kemp's career as a band leader. Also includes sheet music, records and audio cassettes although none of the cassettes appears to be of radio programs. Check online finding aid to determine if any of the print materials relate to Kemp's performances on the *Penzoil Parade* and *Chesterfield* programs.

1692. Isaac Edward Emerson Papers. Emerson was the inventor of Bromo-Seltzer. The papers contain strategies for marketing the product, including sponsoring the *Effervescent Hour* that aired on numerous radio stations in the 1930s.

1693. John Marsden Ehle Papers, 1942–1993. Includes sound recordings of *University Hour* episodes which Ehle either wrote, narrated or appeared in.

1694. John Harden Papers. Includes material related to *Tales of Tar Heelia*, a series broadcast on WPTF for 18 months, 1946–1947, that Harden moderated.

1695. John Minott Rivers, Jr., Papers. Includes papers relating to WCSC-AM and WXTC-FM, Charleston, SC owned by the Rivers family which owned WCSC, Inc. Collection also includes some unidentified sound recordings that were received by WCSC as promotional items. Access to these discs may be restricted. See also the separate listing for the John Rivers Communications Museum in Charleston, SC.

1696. Laurence Housman Papers. Includes an untitled radio script by Housman about "Macbeth."

1697. Lynn Gault Papers, 1937–1998. Primarily documents Gault's work in theater, especially with the Carolina Playmakers in the late 1940s and early 1950s but also includes "An Unknown Land," a radio play by Gault.

1698. Maxwell Anderson Papers, 1888–1959. Includes a letter from Anderson to F. R. Bellamy, 1941, regarding a radio production. File does not identify the name of the program.

1699. Myra Page Papers, 1910–1990. Includes a few radio plays by Dorothy Markey, a writer, union activist and communist who wrote under the name Myra Page in the 1930s–1950s. The radio plays are included in the "Short Writings" folder and are identified by name.

1700. Nelson Benton Papers. Contains subject files, appointment books, assignment notebooks, scripts, official press packs and other papers documenting more than 20 years of Benton's career at various divisions of CBS News.

1701. Paul Green Papers, 1880–1985. Contains radio plays of the Pulitzer prize winning playwright. Collection includes a detailed list of the titles and dates but no indication as to the radio program/s that broadcast the plays.

1702. Sam J. Ervin Papers, 1954–1975. The "Radio Program Files, 1954–1974" portion of the collection includes sound recordings and partial transcripts of Ervin's weekly program and other papers relating to his involvement with specific stations.

1703. WEED Radio Station, Rocky Mount, NC. Includes correspondence and other files of WEED, Rocky Mount, NC and scattered files of WBAR, Bartow, FL, both of which were owned by William Avera Wynne. The WEED files include program logs, channel surveys and communications with the FCC and both the NBC and ABC radio network offices.

1704. Weil Family Papers. Contain business papers relating to the family's many business ventures, including a department store in Goldsboro, NC and promotional materials for the store, including scripts for a 10-episode program *Romance of Goldsboro.*

1705. Wesley Herndon Wallace Papers. Contains personal and professional correspondence, including materials from 1935–1941 relating to WSOC, Charlotte, NC.

University Archives

1706. Records of the Dept. of Radio, Television, and Motion Pictures, 1928–1968, bulk 1946–1968. Contains correspondence and other files, including considerable material pertaining to radio productions at the university during the 1950s and a large number of scripts.

University of North Carolina at Greensboro
Jackson Library
1000 Spring Garden Street, Greensboro, NC 27402
(336) 334-5246; Contact: Carolyn Shankle
Carolyn_Shankle@uncg.edu
http://library.uncg.edu/depts/speccoll/

1707. Joseph M. Bryan Business Papers, bulk 1931–1995. Business papers include Bryan's ownership of WBIG, Greensboro, NC and WBT, Charlotte, NC.

University of North Texas
Music Library
PO Box 305190, Denton, TX 76203
(940) 565-2860; Fax: (940) 565-2599
mmartin@library.unt.edu; www.library.unt.edu/music
Contact: Morris Martin

1708. Don Gillis Collection. Papers and audio tapes relating to Toscanini and the NBC Symphony. Tapes (approximately 500–10"reels) include a complete set of tapes for *Toscanini: The Man Behind the Legend*, including the *Toscanini Centennial Series,* 1961–1967, interview tapes recorded for the show and tapes of a few rehearsals. Papers include guest lists, scripts, correspondence, station lists, publicity materials, etc. Gillis was a producer at NBC during the Toscanini era.

1709. WFAA and WBAP Collections. Contains more than 400,000 items, including sheet music, published orchestrations and original arrangements used by the studio orchestras of the oldest radio stations in Dallas and Fort Worth. Collections are searchable online.

1710. Whit Ozier Sound Archive. Contains 130,000 78rpms, principally jazz and popular music, dating from the earliest days of recorded music to the 1950s. Includes thousands of radio transcription discs. Access to collection is by the Rigler and Deutsch Record Index.

Willis Library Archive
PO Box 305190, Denton, TX 76203
(940) 565-2766; Fax: (940) 565-2599
rhimmel@library.unt.edu

1711. Alfred Bailey Jolley Collection, 1890–1979. Contains correspondence, printed material and photographs relating to Jolley's career as a county agriculture agent, including his work on KRLD, 1953–1967.

1712. John Henry Faulk Oral History. A 1981 interview with Faulk. Includes a discussion of his work for CBS radio and television and his involvement with blacklisting.

University of Notre Dame
607 Hesburgh Library, Notre Dame, IN 46556
(574) 631-6448; Fax: (574) 631-7980
archives@nd.edu; www.library.nd.edu/

General comments: The university also has an extensive collection of audio recordings of radio broadcasts of Notre Dame sporting events. For details, check the Archives, Audio Visual Division at: http://archives.nd.edu/av.htm

1713. A. W. Terminiello Papers, 1939–1962. Papers of the Catholic priest known as the "Father Coughlin of the South" who broadcast on *The Pastor's Fireside* on radio and television. Includes sound recordings and transcripts of Terminiello's memoirs plus letters, sermons, clippings and other papers.

1714. *Family Theater* Scripts, ca. 1950s. More than a dozen scripts for the program written by several authors. Note: Each script is listed as a separate collection in the online catalog although they are included in bound volumes. When searching the online catalog, search for "Family Theater" in either the "title" or "keyword" fields as the words "Family Theater" are in some, but not all collection titles.

1715. John Francis Noll Papers, 1904–1956. Contains correspondence relating to Noll's personal and professional affairs and includes manuscripts of Catholic radio broadcasts, 1940s–1950s.

1716. Richard Sullivan Papers, 1873–1981, bulk 1930–1981. Contains correspondence, financial records, manuscripts, subject files and sound recordings of his programs *Notre Dame Authors* and *The Story of Notre Dame*, ca. 1940s. Check online finding aid for details.

1717. William J. Dunn Papers, 1941–1945. Contains transcripts of radio broadcasts during World War II when Dunn was a CBS correspondent covering the Pacific theater. Includes broadcasts from Batavia, Bandoeng, Melbourne, Sydney, Port Moresby, Hollandia, Leyte, Manila, Yokohama, Luzon and Tokyo.

University of Oklahoma
Library, Western History Collections
630 Parrington Oval, 452, Norman, OK 73019
(405) 325-3641; Fax: (405) 325-2943
http://libraries.ou.edu/info/info.asp?id=22

1718. Fritz Willie Woyna Collection, 1933–1965. Includes radio stories and programs written by Woyna dealing with Oklahoma.

University of Oregon
Knight Library, Special Collections
1501 Kincaid, Eugene, OR 97403
(541) 346-3068; Fax: (541) 346-1882
spcarref@uoregon.edu
http://libweb.uoregon.edu/speccoll/mss

1719. "Active Radio: Pacifica's Brash Experiment." A Ph.D. thesis by Jeffrey Richard Land, University of Oregon, 1994.

1720. Albert M. Ottenheimer Papers, 1935–1980. Consists of investigation files relating to his being blacklisted during the McCarthy era, including a diary he kept during his 30-day jail sentence, correspondence, literary manuscripts and scripts for television, radio and the theater.

1721. Anti-Chain Store League Radio Program Transcripts, 1930. Transcripts of three programs broadcast over KVEP, Portland, OR, March 3–5, 1930, that were sponsored by the Anti-Chain Store League of Portland and delivered by Robert G. Duncan.

1722. Brice P. Disque Papers, 1899–1957. Includes transcripts of radio broadcasts covering commerce, labor, industry, history, military preparedness, poverty, prisons and international trade.

1723. Charles H. Martin Speech, 1937. Galley proof of radio speech given by Governor Martin over KALE and KEX, December 6, 1937. The speech calls for a settlement to the dispute between two opposing labor groups by holding a special election on December 9, 1937.

1724. Doris Gates Papers, 1936–1985. Consists largely of professional correspondence, manuscripts of books, short stories, articles and radio scripts.

1725. Eloise and William McGraw Papers 1923–1991. Contains correspondence, literary manuscripts and book reviews and includes several radio scripts written by Eloise McGraw.

1726. Eugene Lyons Papers, 1929–1964. Consists primarily of book manuscripts, correspondence and an original corrected copy of an interview with Joseph Stalin, November 22, 1930, signed by Stalin. Lyons was a radio commentator. Check unpublished finding aid to determine if collection includes any radio related papers.

1727. George W. Joseph Radio Address, 1928. Copy of radio address given by Senator George W. Joseph over KXL, Sept. 13, 1928. The speech opposes Chief Justice John L. Rand, candidate for re-election to the Oregon Supreme Court.

1728. Janet Marshall Stevenson Papers, 1929–1996. Includes some radio scripts and sound recordings of interviews with Robert W. Kenny, an influential liberal who championed the rights of several of the Hollywood 10 before the House Committee on Un-American Activities (HUAC) and interviews from radio shows when Stevenson and her first husband, Philip Stevenson, were guests.

1729. John T. (John Thomas) Flynn Papers, 1928–1961. Includes scripts for *Behind The Headlines* and other papers.

1730. KOAC *Library Hour* Records, 1951–1952. Typescripts for the program prepared under the direction of Martin Schmitt for the University of Oregon Library. Includes related correspondence, program schedules and short critiques of some of the programs.

1731. Loren Holcombe Milliman Papers, 1922–1975. Consists of professional correspondence, manuscripts of articles, radio scripts and speeches.

1732. Mason Y. Warner Papers, 1859–1954. Contains the papers of Claire Warner Churchill Thompson, including radio scripts she wrote for WPA programs and papers relating to *Soldiers of the Air,* 1941–1942, a series of radio dramas for the Army Recruiting Service that were broadcast on KOIN.

1733. "Norman Corwin: A Study of Selected Radio Plays by the Noted Author and Dramatist." A Ph.D. thesis by Jerrold I. Zinnamon, University of Oregon, 1984.

1734. Peter Bernard Kyne Papers, 1917–1957, bulk 1935–1940. Includes personal and professional correspondence and manuscript copies of novels and short stories. Also includes correspondence about the "Cappy Ricks" radio rights controversy although the "Cappy Ricks" stories are not included in the collection.

1735. Ruth Cornwall Woodman Papers, 1913–1969. Includes scripts and associated material for 204 *Death Valley Days* radio and television programs, an index to the scripts, notebooks from summer research trips and correspondence with *Death Valley* acquaintances.

1736. Ruth Langland Holberg Papers, 1911–1977. Consists of diaries, correspondence, manuscripts of novels, short stories, poetry, radio scripts, research material, financial material and copies of her published works.

1737. Thomas A. Curry, Jr. Papers, 1922–1967. Consists of manuscripts of novels, novelettes, short stories, articles, comic strip treatments, radio scripts and motion picture treatments. The correspondence relates mainly to Curry's professional and business affairs with some personal letters. Online finding aid lists titles of the radio scripts but not dates or the names of the programs.

1738. Virgil MacMickle Papers, 1897–1967. Consists of personal and business correspondence relating to MacMickle's writings, including his radio show on medicine and political subjects.

1739. Wally Butterworth Papers, 1930–1973. Consists of correspondence, radio scripts, writings by Butterworth, sound recordings, photographs and memorabilia. May include material related to *Pages in Time.*

1740. Wayne L. Morse Papers, 1919–1969, bulk 1944–1968. Includes radio material related to his political career.

1741. Willis E. Stone Papers, 1955–1982. Papers deal primarily with Stone's involvement with the issue of tax reform and include his personal papers, research materials for his books, articles, radio broadcasts, newsclippings and published articles.

1742. WPA. Oregon Historical Records Survey Records. Consists of detailed documentation of Oregon history and records and includes scripts of WPA radio programs.

University of Pennsylvania
Rare Book and Manuscript Library
3420 Walnut Street, Philadelphia, PA 19104
(215) 898-7088; shawcros@pobox.upenn.udu
www.library.upenn.edu

1743. Curtis Publishing Company Records, ca. 1887–1960. Includes records of the company's Division of Commercial Research, Advertising Department which conducted early studies into radio.

1744. Eugene Ormandy Papers, 1921–1991. Papers and broadcast recordings of the Philadelphia Orchestra, 1960–1981, broadcast on WFLN.

1745. Leopold Stokowski Papers, 1916–1994. Contains personal and business papers, correspondence, scrapbooks, memorabilia and other printed materials.

1746. Marian Anderson Papers, ca. 1900–1993. Subseries B includes scripts for radio and television performances, personal appearances and proposed films or appearances. See online finding aid for list of radio appearances.

1747. Theodore Dreiser Papers, ca. 1890-1965, bulk 1897–1955. Contains correspondence, writings, including radio scripts, and other papers.

University of Pennsylvania Museum of Archaeology and Anthropology, Education Department
3260 South Street, Philadelphia, PA 19104
(215) 898-4000; Fax: (215) 898 0657
apezzati@sas.upenn.edu; www.museum.upenn.edu

1748. *Once Upon A Time* Radio Scripts, 1943–1952. Seventeen volumes of scripts, some written by Roy LaPlante, and aired on KYW, Philadelphia. Show was a weekly fifteen minute program narrated by school children. Collection also includes sound recordings of the same program, mostly 1944–1945 and one from 1948, and recordings of *The World of Yesterday, The Crow and the Daylight, The Mouse Merchant* and *The Legend of the Willow Plate.*

University of Pittsburgh
Archives Service Center
7500 Thomas Boulevard, Pittsburgh, PA 15260
(412) 244-7091; Contact: Michael Dabrishus
michaeld@pitt.edu
www.library.pitt.edu/libraries/archives/archives.html

General comments: Some additional collections in the ethnic and/or business files in the Archives Center may also contain radio related information. Check with the library for more information.

1749. Charles Owen Rice Papers, 1935–1998. Consists of correspondence, subject files, transcripts of radio broadcasts on KDKA and WWSW, 1937–1969, manuscripts, case files, family papers, audio tapes and a film of the Pittsburgh Catholic priest who was active in labor relations and social causes.

1750. Ernest Hillman Papers, 1928–1969, bulk 1946–1969. Includes papers relating to Hillman's involvement with Republican Party politics in the 1950s and some material related to Fulton Lewis, Jr.'s radio programs. Also, Folder 141 includes what are likely transcripts of Rev. Carl McIntire's program, *Twentieth Century Hour,* 1958–1961 (intermittent).

1751. Harry Phillips Davis Papers, 1915–1944. An engineer and executive for Westinghouse Electric and Manufacturing Company, the collection also includes papers relating to Davis's involvement in the beginnings of KDKA, the first commercial radio station in the United States. Also includes material about WJZ.

1752. James R. Cox Papers, 1904–1950, bulk 1923–1950. Contains Father Cox's diary, scrapbooks of newspaper clippings, photographs and 28 audio cassettes of radio broadcasts, sermons and hymns, 1944–1950.

1753. Lillian A. Friedberg Papers, 1904–1975. Includes scripts of Friedberg's radio program, 1946–1959. Friedberg was active in Pittsburgh area Jewish organizations.

1754. Margaret Hodges Papers. Papers include scripts Hodges wrote for *The Children's Bookshelf* and other materials related to the program and also about her role as a storyteller on *Let's Tell A Story* which became the nationally broadcast television program *Tell Me A Story*.

1755. Pittsburgh Chamber Music Society Papers, 1961–1999. Papers include brochures, programs and reviews, tax forms, posters and papers concerning the taping of concerts by WQED-FM.

1756. Records of the National Association for the Advancement of Colored People, Pittsburgh Branch 1940–1966, 1974. Includes radio broadcasts from the 1950s.

1757. Records of the American Service Institute, ca. 1920–1961. Includes scripts and other material for radio programs during the 1940s, including material for *You Are An American*, 1942–1944. The Institute was concerned about promoting better understanding and appreciation among people of all cultural and national backgrounds.

1758. Records of the Brashear Association, Pittsburgh, PA, 1891–1978. Contains a script, possibly radio, announcing Buhl Planetarium's Regional Convention of Astronomers and Stargazer's Fair in May, 1940. Also undated scripts for 78 broadcasts of *Adventures in Research: Beloved Lens Maker* that was part of the Modern Americans in Science and Invention Series.

1759. Records of the Community Chest of Allegheny County, 1933–1960. Includes radio material on some of the organization's fund raising campaigns.

1760. Records of the Congress of Clubs and Clubwomen of Western Pennsylvania, 1890–1963. Includes material on radio broadcasts, 1928–1950.

1761. Records of the Jewish Community Relations Council, Pittsburgh, PA, 1928-1959. Contains radio material, including material relating to Father Coughlin, *Americans All, Immigrants All* and propaganda in the press and radio.

1762. Thomas Parran Papers, 1916–1962. Includes text of radio addresses on various health issues, 1930s–1940s, during his tenure as Surgeon General of the United States.

Special Collections
363 Hillman Library, Pittsburgh, PA 15260
(412) 648-8190; Fax: (412) 648-8192
cea@pitt.edu
www.library.pitt.edu/libraries/special/special.html

General comments: Check with the library for collections that may have radio related material that are not reflected in the online catalog, e.g., the Curtis Theatre Collection may have material about specific performers who appeared on radio.

1763. Philip Dunning Papers, 1915–1968(?) Primarily Dunning's personal collection of 94 scripts for plays, radio, TV and film and a small amount of related papers, clippings and correspondence. Catalog listing does not include any details about the radio scripts.

University of Rochester
Eastman School of Music
Sibley Library, 26 Gibbs Street, Rochester, NY 14604
(585) 274-1320; sibref@esm.rochester.edu
www.rochester.edu/Eastman

1764. Howard Hanson Collection of Sound Recordings, 1933–1957. Includes recordings of *Milestones in the History of Music,* 1938–1940 and 1950–1953, *NBC University of the Air* and *NBC Orchestras of the Nation* series as well as various special concerts, speeches and lectures by Hanson.

1765. Howard Hanson Papers. Several collections containing correspondence, ephemera and manuscripts. Some contain material relating to his radio broadcasts.

Rush Rhees Library
Department of Rare Books and Special Collections
Rochester, NY 14627
(585) 275-4477; Fax: (585) 273-1032
rarebks@library.rochester.edu
www.lib.rochester.edu/rbk/About.stm

1766. Anne Holahan Papers, 1932–1976. Consists of theater, film, book and radio reviews clipped from newspapers and magazines, correspondence, theater and ballet programs and radio and film scripts.

1767. Arthur Caswell Parker Papers, 1860–1952. Includes 86 scripts Caswell wrote for the Rochester War Council Speakers' Bureau, 1942–1943 and 28 scripts for *The Romance of Old Indian Days* broadcast on WHAM, 1937–1938, sponsored by the Rochester Museum of Arts and Sciences.

1768. David Rhys Williams Papers, 1912–1970. Contains correspondence, manuscript sermon notes, speeches, prayers, meditations and tributes, newspaper clippings and text of radio addresses.

1769. Democrats-for-Wilkie Papers, July–November 1940. Includes material related to the role of radio in the campaign.

1770. Dr. Susan B. Anthony Papers, 1954–1987. Includes some material related to her program *This Woman's World* broadcast in the 1940s and additional suggestions for a radio program.

1771. Elizabeth Hull Gould Papers. Includes papers relating to the radio program for children, *The Little Advocate*.

1772. Ira Solomon Wile Papers, 1894–1943. Includes text for radio speeches delivered in the 1930s, most of which appear related to mental health issues.

1773. John A. Williams Papers. Consists mostly of post–1950 materials related to Williams's personal life and career as a writer, editor and journalist although there are some earlier papers, including correspondence, photographs and some material from 1959 dealing with WOV.

1774. John Edward Hoffmeister Papers. Consists of two volumes of typescripts of Dr. Hoffmeister's speeches, convocation addresses, commencement addresses, radio talks, writings, etc., 1934–1960.

1775. John Gardner Papers. Includes some radio plays written by Gardner. See online finding aid for titles.

1776. Marion Bayard Folsom Papers, 1922–1968. Includes interviews and talks dealing with national economic issues in the 1950s.

1777. Rochester Broadcasting Corporation Papers, 1944–1947. Correspondence, financial material, etc. of the Roches-

Broadcasting Corporation founded in 1944 by a group of Rochester businessmen to operate a radio station in the city. The corporation dissolved in 1947 when it was denied a permit to construct a radio station.

1778. Thomas E. Dewey Papers. Includes material on his radio speeches. For a more detailed listing, contact the library.

University Archives

1779. *Background of the War News* **Papers, 1943.** Scripts and correspondence relating to the 12 radio programs Dr. Arthur J. May of the University of Rochester History Department gave over WHAM in 1943. Note: Script for program #11 is missing.

1780. *Let's Learn Spanish:* **Papers Relating to Radio Program, 1944-1945.** Contains correspondence, publicity, etc. for a 39-week radio series which was prepared by Time Inc., sponsored by the University of Rochester and broadcast over WHAM.

1781. *The World Tomorrow* **Papers, 1942.** Transcripts and other material related to the series of 17 radio discussion programs sponsored by the War Information Center of the University of Rochester in the fall of 1942 and broadcast over WHAM.

1782. *This Atomic World* **Papers, 1946.** Includes correspondence, scripts, and publicity relating to the series of 10 radio programs.

1783. *Understanding the Headlines* **Papers, 1943–1945.** Includes correspondence and scripts relating to the program broadcast over WHAM, 1943–1945.

1784. WRUR News Reports, 1948. Western Union news reports received by campus radio station WRUR during the first months of its operation, February–May, 1948.

1785. WRUR Papers, 1947–1948. A small collection of correspondence and processed material relating to the campus radio station, WRUR, that began broadcasting on February 10, 1948.

University of South Carolina
Manuscripts Division
South Caroliniana Library, Columbia, SC 29208
(803) 777-5183; Fax: (803) 777-5747
fulmerh@gwm.sc.edu; Contact: Henry Fulmer
www.sc.edu/library/socar/mnscrpts/index.html

General comments: As of 2005, approximately one third of the holdings of the Manuscripts Division are described in the online catalog. For more thorough subject access to holdings, contact the library or consult "A Guide to the Manuscript Collection of the South Caroliniana Library" (1982) by Dr. Allen H. Stokes.

1786. Frank Beacham Papers. Collection focuses on two of Beacham's principal media projects, including six audio cassettes entitled "Theatre of the Imagination: The Radio Days of Orson Welles," co-produced by Beacham and the late Richard Wilson in 1988. The cassettes feature tales on tape from the radio career of the young Welles and document Beacham's efforts at restoring more than 160 hours of surviving Welles programming.

1787. Louis DeSaussure Lang Papers, 1925–1977. Contains scripts, correspondence and miscellaneous printed items covering Lang's career at WIS beginning in 1941. Lang wrote public service scripts during World War II, including those for the *Victory Bond* program which were broadcast coast-to-coast and *Let's Go to Town* which were sent to servicemen. Also contains material on WIS history, including a 340-page annotated typescript entitled "So Rich a Heritage: A History of WIS Radio and Television."

1788. Rebecca Dial Papers, 1922–1960. Includes scripts for theater, radio and television. To browse list of scripts, plays and other unpublished works included in this collection, see Dial's autobiography, "My Stream Without a Name."

McKissick Museum
816 Bull Street, Columbia, SC 29208
(803) 777-7251; Fax: (803)777-2829
taylors7@gwm.sc.edu; www.cas.sc.edu/mcks/
Contact: Saddler Taylor

1789. South Carolina Broadcaster's Association Archive. Contains audio and video artifacts, photographs and papers relating to early South Carolina radio, 1930s–1960s, plus several thousand 78rpm records, reel-to-reel tapes and cassettes. Also includes extensive scrapbooks and a substantial amount of administrative materials from several South Carolina radio stations.

University of Southern California
Doheny Memorial Library
3550 Trousdale Parkway, Los Angeles, CA 90089

Cinema-Television Library
(213) 740-8906; Fax: (213) 821-3093
ncomstoc@usc.edu; www.usc.edu/isd/archives/arc/
Contact: Ned Comstock

1790. Andy Devine Collection. Consists of radio and television scripts for *Wild Bill Hickock*, 1951–1957, and other papers related to Devine's career.

1791. Billie Burke Collection, 1907–1950. Consists of 240 production stills from Burke's films, miscellaneous publicity and promotional photographs, 50 radio scripts, three scrapbooks of clippings and personal photographs.

1792. Burns and Allen Collection. Consists of 82 volumes of radio scripts, 1932–1950, television scripts, scrapbooks, clippings, 600 disc recordings and films of the television show.

1793. Charles Bickford Collection, 1925–1967. Consists of scrapbooks, stills, radio transcription discs, clippings, publicity, photographs, correspondence, theatre programs and awards.

1794. Don Defore Collection, 1947–1967. Consists of papers related to Defore's work in film and television, transcription discs of late 1940s radio programs and other professional papers, clippings and personal items.

1795. Gladys Cooper Collection. Consists of scripts, contracts, programs, correspondence, scrapbooks and clippings relating to Cooper's appearance on five radio programs, 1935–1954, films and plays.

1796. Irving Brecher Collection. Consists of 325 audio tapes of *The Life of Riley*, 1944-1951.

1797. Jim and Henny Backus Collection. Consists of screenplays in which either Jim or Henny Backus appeared, 1940–1967. Also includes scripts for *The Jim Backus Show* and recordings of *Jubilee,* 1940s.

1798. John J. Anthony Collection. Consists of transcription discs, tapes, scripts and files from several programs on which Anthony was featured, including the *Goodwill Hour* later renamed the *John J. Anthony Hour.*

Archival Research Center: Rare Books and Manuscripts
(213) 740-4035; Fax: (213) 740-2343
Contacts: John Ahouse; ahouse@usc.edu, or
Claude Zachary, czachary@usc.edu
www.usc.edu/isd/archives/arc/

1799. "An Experimental Study of the Relative Effectiveness of Certain Types of Radio and Television Commercials." A Ph.D. thesis by James Joseph Rue, 1954.

1800. "An Historical Study of the Armed Forces Radio Service to 1946." A Ph.D. thesis by Theodore Stuart DeLay, Jr., University of Southern California, 1951. A separate collection (see below) contains DeLay's research notes.

1801. Armed Forced Radio Service. Research archive gathered by Theodore S. Delay in support of his 1951 USC dissertation, "An Historical Study of the Armed Forces Radio Service to 1946." Consists largely of memoranda and reports of official U.S. Army origin and copies of AFRS "Playback Magazine." See online finding aid for detailed inventory. The period covered is 1944–1945 and the focus is on the Pacific theater of action.

1802. *Greater Than the Bomb.* The text of a radio program by Norman Corwin broadcast internationally in 1950 and repeated many times.

1803. Lawrence Lipton Collection. Includes material on unidentified radio programs, business files, tax records, correspondence, clippings, literary journals, tape recorded interviews, readings and archives for his "Radio Free America" column in the "Los Angeles Free Press."

1804. Minorities in America. Includes sound recording of *Minority Report,* 1957, broadcast on KNX.

University of Texas-Austin
Benson Latin American Collection
Sid Richardson Hall 1.108, Austin, TX 78713
(512) 495-4520; Fax: (512) 495-4568
blac@lib.utexas.edu; www.lib.utexas.edu/benson/

1805. Lalo Astol Collection, 1879–1982, bulk 1910–1972. Papers include information about Astol's involvement in the early days of Spanish-language radio and television in San Antonio, TX on KCOR.

Center For American History
1 University Station, SRH-2.101, Austin, TX 78712
(512) 495-4518; Fax: (512) 495-4542
cahref@uts.cc.utexas.edu; www.cah.utexas.edu

1806. Fred Acree Papers, 1820–1947. Includes some photographs of *Amos 'n' Andy* and other radio personalties, 1933–1939 and n.d.

1807. Ice Manufacturers' Association Records, 1913–1964. Includes broadcast material from 1935.

1808. James Paul Buchanan Papers, 1896–1954. Includes text of Buchanan's radio addresses, 1935–1936.

1809. Jane Y. and Arthur N. McCallum Family Papers, 1894–1982. Contains personal and professional papers, including radio talks, 1930 and n.d.

1810. John Avery Lomax Family Papers, 1842, 1853–1986. Includes correspondence, song lyrics, music, literary productions, diaries and logs, scrapbooks, classified files, financial records, photographs, phonograph recordings, audio tapes, newspaper and magazine clippings, radio scripts, 1941–1945 and n.d., other radio related material and scrapbooks.

Center For American History, Media History Archives
1811. Andy Rooney Papers, 1942–1945, 1957–1991. Papers, including radio and television scripts, 1964–1991, documenting Rooney's career as a journalist and broadcaster with CBS. Also includes papers documenting his work as a journalist covering World War II.

1812. Chester Burger Papers, 1921–Present. Papers documenting Burger's personal life and professional career in radio, television, public relations and consulting through scrapbooks, videotapes, notes and printed materials. Burger worked at CBS, 1941–1954.

1813. Henry Cassirer Papers, 1936–1991. Papers documenting Cassirer's life and career, including his work in the 1940s as an executive with CBS.

1814. John Henry Faulk Papers, 1936–1990. Papers documenting Faulk's career as a folklorist, entertainer, author and target of the blacklist during the McCarthy years. The collection includes extensive files relating to Faulk's blacklisting experience and his legal case that interrupted his burgeoning career in radio and television broadcasting.

1815. Joseph and Shirley Wershba Papers, 1936–1993. Papers, ephemera, audio and video tapes reflecting the Wershbas' careers in radio and television news broadcasting with CBS.

1816. Robert Trout Papers. Papers documenting Trout's career as a radio and television news broadcaster, 1931–1992. The "Broadcasting Files, bulk 1931–1974," include material relating to Trout's career with CBS, NBC, ABC, WSJV, WCBS and National Public Radio. Includes material relating to Franklin D. Roosevelt, political conventions, presidential elections, fireside chats, D-Day, World War II- European theater, United Nations, Dwight D. Eisenhower, King George, Queen Elizabeth and the following programs: *Perspectives, Political Broadcasts, World News Round-Up, Professor Quiz* and *Who Said That?*

1817. Sig Mickelson Papers, 1930–1994. Contains papers, audio and video materials reflecting Mickelson's career as a broadcast executive, including nearly 20 years with CBS beginning in 1943.

1818. Walter Cronkite Papers, 1931–Present. Contains papers documenting Cronkite's career as a United Press wire reporter and war correspondent before joining CBS in 1950. A second collection, "CBS Evening News Archive, 1962–1981," documents Cronkite's television program.

Fine Arts Library, Historical Music Recordings
Doty Fine Arts Building, Austin, TX 78713

(512) 495-4475; Fax: (512) 495-4490
Contact: David Hunter
david.hunter@mail.utexas.edu
www.lib.utexas.edu/fal/hmrc/

1819. Austin Symphony Orchestra. Contains approximately 700 tapes and discs dating from the mid–1940s. Check library's in-house database if any of these are radio broadcasts. An annotated chronological list is available.

1820. Houston Symphony Orchestra. Includes transcription discs of the radio series begun in 1945 and sponsored by Texas Gulf Sulphur. It was on one of these broadcasts that Van Cliburn made his debut at age 12. An annotated chronological list is available.

1821. Irving Feld Collection. Includes approximately 1,700 tapes of the following radio drama series: *The Black Museum, The Detectives, NBC University Theater, Theatre Royal, Suspense, The Queen's Men, The Lives of Harry Lime, Inner Sanctum* and *The Scarlet Pimpernel.* A list of the contents of most of the tapes is available.

1822. Longhorn Broadcasting Network. In addition to being a radio station, KUT was for many years the hub of the Longhorn Broadcasting Network. As a result, the station received tapes of numerous series from producers in the U.S. and abroad, including music, interviews with artists, writers and musicians and comedy. Check in-house database regarding specific programs and dates.

1823. Mary Henrietta Chase Collection. Includes 200 off-air recordings from December, 1948–October, 1956. A typed list gives details of the contents of the discs. Note: The discs are in poor condition.

1824. University of Texas at Austin, School of Music Broadcasts. Includes tapes of KUT broadcasts of *UT Music and Musicians* featuring UT faculty, students and guest artists such as Percy Grainger. A list of the contents of most of the tapes is available.

Harry Ransom Humanities Research Center
PO Box 7219, Austin, TX 78713
(512) 471-8944; Fax: (512) 471-9646
rworkman@mail.utexas.edu
www.hrc.utexas.edu/collections/manuscripts/
Contact: Richard Workman

1825. Arthur Miller Collection. As of spring, 2005, the collection was partially processed. The portion of the collection that can be accessed by researchers does include some radio plays and possibly other radio related material.

1826. Benjamin Appel Papers, 1920–1977. Includes radio script "Ask Anybody in the Neighborhood" that Appel wrote for a war service agency.

1827. Edouard Dujardin Papers, 1861–1951. Papers document Dujardin's career as a novelist, poet, playwright, publicist, journalist and history of religion professor and includes material relating to his radio broadcasts, 1936–1939, and his radio plays.

1828. Gloria Swanson Papers, 1927–1982, bulk 1934–1958. Includes correspondence, scripts (also synopses and story outlines), photographs, music, clippings, legal and financial records and audio recordings which document Swanson's radio appearances, 1927–1981. The types of programs include interviews, radio plays, serials, patriotic appeals during World War II, commercials and talk shows. Includes material on *The Gloria Swanson Show,* 1950–1951, the *Lux Radio Theatre* version of "Sunset Boulevard," 1951, and other programs. See detailed list in finding aid. Note: The papers are divided into separate collections, each with its own finding aid.

1829. Isaac Bashevis Singer Papers. Includes scripts in Yiddish, some of which were broadcast on WEVD.

1830. John Steinbeck Collection, 1926–1977. Includes radio adaptations of 'The Moon Is Down" and 'The Pastures of Heaven."

1831. Laurette Taylor Papers, 1907–1959. Includes recordings, mostly 78rpm, of a 1939 WJZ broadcast of "Peg O' My Heart," and a Rudy Vallee program, 1939.

1832. Leslie Daiken Papers, 1935–1963. Includes manuscripts for two radio plays: "Three Outcasts," which dramatizes the stereotypes found in children's rhyme and "The Circular Road," which explores a child's bereavement in the Jewish-Irish community. Names of programs on which the plays were broadcast is not shown.

1833. Minstrel Show Collection, 1821–1959, bulk 1860–1940. Collection documents individual performers and minstrel show companies, including touring companies and contains material on *Daily Paskman's Radio Minstrels.*

1834. The Musicians Collection. Consists of materials that are primarily visual in nature and portray approximately 1,700 musicians and musical groups, including Billy Carlin, Paul Whiteman, Anne Shirley, the WIOD Orchestra, Rudy Vallee and Eddie Cantor.

1835. Nancy Wilson Ross Papers, 1913–1986. Contains virtually complete documentation of her professional writing career, including radio plays, 1922–1947, and a transcript of a radio talk, 1947. See online finding aid for details.

Miscellaneous Ph.D. Theses
Library, Post Office Box P, Austin, TX 78713
(512) 495-4350; Fax: (512) 495-4347
www.lib.utexas.edu

1836. "A History of the Broadcasting of Daytime Serial Dramas in the United States." A Ph.D. thesis by Raymond William Stedman, University of Southern California, 1959.

1837. "A Study of the Professional Criticism of Broadcasting in the United States, 1920-1955." A Ph.D. thesis by Ralph Lewis Smith, University of Wisconsin.

1838. "Federal Regulation of the Radio and Television Broadcast Industry in the United States, 1927–1959, With Special Reference to the Establishment and Operation of Workable Administrative Standards." A Ph.D. thesis by Robert Sears McMahon, Ohio State University, 1960.

1839. "The Impact of John R. Brinkley on Broadcasting in the United States." A Ph.D. thesis by Ansel Harlan Resler, Northwestern University, 1958.

1840. "The Practices and Policies Regarding Broadcasts of Opinions About Controversial Issues by Radio and Television Stations in the United States." A Ph.D. thesis by

Joseph Marion Ripley, Jr., Ohio State University, 1961.

University of Texas-El Paso
C.L. Sonnichsen Library Special Collections Department
500 W. University, El Paso, TX 79968
(915) 747-5672; Contact: Claudia A. Rivers
crivers@libr.utep.edu
http://libraryweb.utep.edu/special/special.cfm

1841. Conrey Bryson Papers 1938–1988. Bryson was a broadcaster with KTSM, El Paso, TX, 1936–1954, and later a TV news anchor. Collection includes radio scripts for several programs, including *Fort Bliss Centennial, Pathfinders of Medicine, 25th Anniversary, Magoffin, Gifts of the Season, El Paso Pays Tribute, Master of Music, Over SW Trails, Voice of El Paso, Southern Union Gas Co. Industry at the Pass of the North, Men of Vision, Through the Years, Farm Reporter* and other special programs.

1842. The Kohlberg Family Papers. Extensive family files. Includes radio scripts for *Builders of El Paso* broadcast on KTSM, 1939.

1843. KROD Scrapbooks 1940–1957. A CBS affiliate owned by Dorrance Roderick of Roderick Broadcasting.

1844. S.L.A. (Samuel Lyman Atwood, a.k.a. Slam) Marshall Papers, 1900–1979. Personal and professional papers of a military historian and commentator, including transcripts of radio broadcasts, 1940–1942, some 1951 and others after 1965. Program dates are listed but not names of programs.

University of Texas- San Antonio
Library, Special Collections
6900 N. Loop 1604 West, San Antonio, TX 78249
(210) 458-5505; Fax: (210) 458-2386
Archives@utsa.edu
http://lib.utsa.edu/Special_Collections/

1845. Rosita Fernandez Papers, 1925–1997. Papers trace Fernandez's career from her early days in radio to her work in television and movie productions, through to her retirement in 1982 and subsequent activities. The collection consists of scrapbooks, photographs, honors and awards, the bulk of which are in the form of plaques.

1846. Sam and Bess Woolford Papers, 1834–1979. Contains manuscripts, including some unidentified radio scripts, research notes and other materials documenting Texas history and folklore. The Woolfords promoted the Witte Museum in San Antonio through a radio variety show in the 1930s.

1847. San Antonio Area Council of Girl Scouts Records, 1926–2000. Includes radio broadcast material, 1943–1985 and n.d.

University of the Pacific
Library, 3601 Pacific Avenue, Stockton, CA 95211
(209) 946-2945; Contact: Shan Sutton
ssutton@pacific.edu; http://library.pacific.edu/ha/

1848. Elsie Flower Papers, 1886–1968. Includes scripts for *City Journal,* broadcast on KGDM, 1945–1955, plus other papers and correspondence.

1849. Henry Dorris Hubbard Papers, 1889–1970. Papers include radio dramatizations of the history of the San Joaquin County area.

University of Utah
J. Willard Marriott Library, Manuscripts Division
295 S. 1500 East, Salt Lake City, UT 84112
(801) 581-8558; Fax: (801) 585-3464
slarson@library.utah.edu; Contact: Stan Larson
www.lib.utah.edu/spc/mss/spcmss.html

1850. Alvin G. and Lena M. Pack Papers, 1907–1988. Pack was a pioneer in the radio broadcasting industry who worked primarily with KALL and KSL. Included are radio scripts, correspondence, newsclippings and personal and professional papers. Boxes 1-14 contain scripts, 1931–1945, for ongoing feature programs written mainly by Pack, including *Famous Furniture Stories, Organ Stories, Pioneer Stories* and *Spelling Bee* as well as some audition scripts and campaign proposals. A separate collection includes photographs of KSL. See online finding aid for a list of the programs and dates.

1851. B. Floyd Farr Papers. Papers span Farr's career in broadcasting, 1935–1984, including KDYL in Salt Lake City, KPO in San Francisco where he was associated with the *Valley of the Moon* program, and later KEEN, San Jose, CA, the first of a network of radio stations he managed throughout the West and Pacific Coast area.

1852. Frank Carman Papers, 1938–1984. Contains clippings, station logs, correspondence, announcements and histories of stations KLUB and KUTA in Salt Lake City.

1853. G. Bennett Larson Papers, 1929–1987. Contains scripts (an inventory is available upon request), correspondence and other papers. Larson was associated with KDYL, Salt Lake City and the Informountain Broadcasting and Television Corp.

1854. George Snell Papers, 1920s–1978. Includes scripts, sales contracts, newsletters, memos, photos, sound recordings and brochures. Snell was an announcer and script writer for KDYL, Salt Lake City, 1938–1944, a producer for KPO, San Francisco, 1945–1947, and the owner of a chain of radio stations in California and the co-developer of the all-country music radio format.

1855. Jack Paige Papers. Includes publications, reports and correspondence with information centering around WNAX, Yankton, SD, 1940s–1980s.

1856. John M. Baldwin Papers, ca.1930–1979. Contains clippings, scrapbooks, financial works and autobiographical information containing reports on local, national and international radio and television stations Baldwin was involved with, including KDYL, Salt Lake City.

1857. KSUB Records, 1944–1983. Several collections (print and audio) dealing with history of the Cedar City, UT station.

1858. KZN Radio Collection, 1922–1975. Papers relating to the first commercial radio station in Utah that began broadcasting on May 22, 1922 from Salt Lake City.

1859. Sidney S. Fox Papers, 1928–1980. Much of the material focuses on the development of KDYL, Salt Lake City which Fox owned, his financial dealings with the FCC and legal matters concerning the sale of KDYL to Time Life, Inc.

1860. "Utah Women Who Pioneered in Radio," 1985. Photocopy of typescript by Helen B. Gibbons. Includes material relating to KSL, Salt Lake City.

University of Vermont

Bailey/Howe Library, Special Collections
Burlington, VT 05405
(802) 656-2138; Fax: (802) 656-4038
cburns@zoo.uvm.edu; Contact: Chris Burns
http://bailey.uvm.edu/specialcollections

1861. Bundles for Britain Records, 1940–1944. Includes radio scripts of the voluntary organization sending aid to Britain during World War II.

1862. Dorothy Canfield Fisher Collection, 1851–1958. Includes correspondence, articles, speeches, radio broadcasts and other manuscripts.

1863. WDEV Open Day Remarks, 1931. Mimeographed copy of the remarks made by Sir Henry W. Thornton to a gathering of news people celebrating the opening of WDEV in Waterbury, VT, July 16, 1931.

University of Virginia

Law Library
580 Massie Road, Charlottesville, VA 22903
(434) 924-7354; Fax: (434) 924-7536
www.law.virginia.edu

1864. "Federal Control of Defamation by Radio." Legal thesis by Joseph E. Keller, Georgetown University, 1935.

1865. "Federal Regulation and Control of Radio Communication." Legal thesis by John B. O'Brien, Jr., Georgetown University, 1933.

1866. "Freedom of Speech and Radio Broadcasting." Legal thesis by Leonard Bertram Levenson, Georgetown University, 1936.

1867. "Legal Problems Involved in the Dissemination of News by Radio Broadcast." Legal thesis by John W. Kendall, Georgetown University, 1936.

1868. "Program Evaluation by the Federal Communications Commission Does Not Constitute an Abridgment of Free Speech." Legal thesis by Thomas Henry Wall, Georgetown University, 1951.

1869. "Radio-Television Free Forum." Legal thesis by Louis H. Mayo, Yale Law School, 1953.

Special Collections Department
Alderman Memorial Library
PO Box 400110, Charlottesville, VA 22904
(434) 924-3025; Fax: (434) 924-4968
mssbks@virginia.edu; www.lib.virginia.edu/speccol

1870. Atcheson L. Hench Papers, 1935–1974. Contains correspondence and other files, including material relating to Hench's programs *Words, Words, Words* and *What's the Good Word?* Tapes of the programs are also available.

1871. Carter Sisters Photograph, ca. 1946. A glossy print of a publicity photograph of the Carter sisters. Original photograph made by WRVA, Richmond, VA to advertise its *Old Dominion Barn Dance* program. (See also *Old Dominion Barn Dance* collection below.)

1872. "Come Back, Little Sheba" Script, 1951. Uncorrected final rehearsal script adapted for radio by Robert Anderson, produced by The Theatre Guild, Inc. and presented on *The United States Steel Hour.*

1873. Florence Stearns Papers, 1920–1955. Consists chiefly of manuscripts of her works, including poems, essays, articles, plays, speeches and lectures, reviews and an undated radio serial, *The Dark Closet.*

1874. Julius Bartlett Lankes Recordings, ca. 1920s–1981. Includes cassettes of Lankes narrating and commenting on a variety of topics, including jazz bands, vaudeville, other music groups and Fred Allen's *Chase and Sanborn Program.*

1875. League of Women Voters of Charlottesville and Albemarle County Papers, 1944–1975. Includes scripts of WCHV broadcasts, April 21-25, 1947, on the history of Albemarle and Charlottesville with tie-ins to post World War II local issues.

1876. Major Edward Bowes Letter, 1939. A letter to Harriet Lancashire White, May 29, 1939, thanking her for a letter of appreciation that she had sent.

1877. O. Henry Papers from the Doubleday and Company Archive, 1894–1958, bulk 1894–1927. Contains radio adaptations of O. Henry stories by Henry Fisk Carlton, one in collaboration with Robert Winternitz.

1878. *Old Dominion Barn Dance* Picture Album, ca. 1946. Album contains copies of studio photographs of radio personalities who performed on the program broadcast on WRVA. Includes Mother Maybelle Carter and the Carter sisters.

1879. Political Addresses, Music, Educational and Entertainment Programs, 1944–1947. An audio collection of 81 discs that includes political addresses, the June 12, 1945 broadcast of *American Forum of the Air*, the May 17, 24 and June 21, 1945 broadcasts of *Town Meeting of the Air*, transcriptions of many AFRS programs and other programs. See catalog listing for more information.

1880. Roanoke Radio Station WSLS. A brief biography of Roanoke businessman Ferdinand Rorer. Includes information relating to WSLS.

1881. Robert Frost Collection, Miscellaneous Manuscript Ephemera, 1938–1963. Includes text for the August 18, 1946 *Invitation to Learning* program that discussed Frost's poetry.

1882. Scripts for Movies and Radio Shows, 1946–1948. Scripts for *Pursued, Key Largo, Fighter Squadron*, and *Greatest Story Ever Told*. Note: Catalog listing does not identify which scripts are for movies and which for radio.

1883. WCHV News releases, 1951. News releases and spot announcements broadcast on WCHV, Charlottesville, VA.

1884. "When Massachusetts and Georgia Meet," n.d. Text of radio song written by Paul Nixon for the *Pepperell Hour.*

1885. William Faulkner Interviews, n.d. Two interviews with Faulkner for the WCHV program *What's the Good Word?* hosted by Atcheson Laughlin Hench.

University of Washington

Library, Box 352900, Seattle, WA 98195
(206) 543-1929; Fax: (206) 543-1931
jdbolcer@u.washington.edu or speccoll@u.washington.edu
www.lib.Washington.edu/specialcoll/findaids
Contact: John Bolcer

General comments: As of 2005, only a small percentage of the library's finding aids are available online. Check with Reference Services Librarian for additional information. Also, the "Milo Ryan/KIRO-CBS Phonoarchive Collection of Broadcasts of the World War II Years and After" previously located at the University of Washington is now part of the National Archives.

1886. Harvey Manning Papers, 1946–1973. Consists of correspondence, writings and ephemera relating to Manning's work as a writer of conservation publications and wilderness guides and his employment in Seattle with KXA and KISW, 1954–1957.

1887. Howard D. Weiss Papers, 1947–1982. Tape recordings of Sephardic songs, interviews and radio broadcasts, together with research files, indexes and publications relating to the research of Weiss and his assistant, Michelle Shallon, into Sephardic music in Seattle.

1888. Irving M. Clark Papers, 1938–1976. Consists of correspondence, minutes, speeches, writings, case files and campaign materials relating to Clark's career as a lawyer specializing in environmental cases and as a civic leader and radio talk show host.

1889. John L. King Papers, 1954–1966. Consists of correspondence, speeches, writings, clippings and ephemera relating to his support for Nationalist China, his interest in community affairs and his role as a regent of the University of Washington. King was an executive at KIRO, Seattle. Check with repository about any radio related information in the collection.

1890. KCMU Records, 1947–1991. Consists of correspondence, minutes, annual reports, financial records, grant files, newsletters and other papers. As of 2005, collection may only be partially processed.

1891. Personal and Family Papers of the Stimson and Bullitt Families, 1872–1993. Includes papers of Dorothy Stimson Bullitt who managed Stimson family real estate interests and in 1946 acquired a radio station which she expanded into the King Broadcasting Company, a regional radio and television network. Includes records of the King Broadcasting Company, 1933–1993, mainly from Bullitt's office, consisting of correspondence, memoranda, FCC applications and testimony, minutes, program schedules, production notes and scripts, annual reports, financial records, personnel policy documents, press releases, publicity programs, awards, scrapbooks and memorabilia, station logs, blueprints, sound recordings and several films.

1892. Robert L. Nichols Papers, 1960–1964. Contains scripts and advertising copy for Nichols's program, *Prescription for Living*, broadcast on KIRO, Seattle.

1893. Saul Haas Papers, 1917–1973. Papers documenting Hass's broadcasting career beginning in 1935 when he bought an almost defunct radio station, KPCB, and renamed it KIRO. Haas was also president of the Queen City Broadcasting Company and chairman of the board until KIRO was sold in 1964. Papers also cover later years and non radio related aspects of his life.

1894. Spencer G. Shaw Papers, 1949–2001. Shaw was the script writer and narrator of *Story Hour on the Air,* produced

by WHLI, Hempstead, NY and sponsored by the Nassau Library System. Collection includes sound recordings of the program, 1961–1968.

1895. William Earl Millikin Papers, 1912–1942. Includes correspondence, speeches, radio broadcasts, news releases and other records.

University of West Virginia
Wise Library, West Virginia and Regional History Collection
PO Box 6069, Morgantown, WV 26506
(304) 293-3536; Fax: (304) 293-3981
jcuthber@wvu.edu; Contact: John Cuthbert
www.libraries.wvu.edu/wvcollection/manuscripts/

1896. Harry C. Woodyard Papers, ca. 1913–1929. The miscellaneous papers of the Congressman include excerpts from radio addresses delivered during the 1924 national election campaign in Los Angeles, San Francisco, Chicago and Washington, D.C.

1897. Hugh Ike Shott Papers, 1848–1954. Contains personal and business papers and memorabilia of the newspaper publisher who was also the founder and owner of WHIS, Bluefield, WV.

1898. *It's Wheeling Steel* Collection, 1930s–1940s. Includes photographs, scripts, 1937-1944, scrapbooks and transcription discs, 1930s–1940s. As of 2005, about 620 reel-to-reel tape copies of the discs have been made.

1899. Izetta Jewel Brown Miller Clippings and Photographs, ca. 1913-1929. Includes originals and copies of clippings and photographs concerning her life and career in the theater, Women's Suffrage Movement, radio, agriculture, television, and politics.

1900. Jeanette Shulz Oral History, 1980. An interview with the daughter of Scott Phillips conducted by John A. Cuthbert concerning Mrs. Shulz's recollections of her father's musical activity, stringbands, radio performances and recordings.

1901. Morgantown Council of Churches Archives, ca. 1946–1967. Contains correspondence, newsletters, financial reports and records of meetings. Includes material about radio and television ministries.

1902. Thomas Jonathan Jackson Papers, 1845–1862, 1951. Includes a script of a radio broadcast, "Stonewall Jackson," broadcast over WLW, August 21, 1951.

1903. Warren E. Hall Papers, 1916–1969. Contains correspondence, newspaper clippings, sermons, radio addresses and a photograph of Hall, a Presbyterian minister. The radio addresses were made in Michigan and Morgantown, WV.

1904. World War II. West Virginia War History Commission. Records, 1928–1946. Contains correspondence, reports, photographs, posters, maps, clippings, old radio scripts, and printed materials of state and county Civilian Defense offices.

University of Wisconsin-Madison
(See Wisconsin Historical Society)

University of Wisconsin-Milwaukee
Golda Meir Library, Room W250
2311 East Hartford Avenue, Milwaukee, WI 53201
maxyela@uwm.edu; Contact: Max Yela
www.uwm.edu/Libraries/arch/index.html

1905. Anthony Szymczak Papers, 1945–1974. Papers of a prominent Milwaukee Polish announcer for WISN and WRJN and host of *The Kuryer Polski Polish Hour*. Includes scripts describing his visits to Poland, holiday broadcasts and to commemorate the deaths of Franklin D. Roosevelt and John F. and Robert Kennedy. Also includes correspondence, photographs and biographical information and background information on WRJN.

1906. Jack Krueger Papers, 1922–1978. Papers of a Milwaukee pioneer in the field of broadcast journalism, including material relating to WTMJ and national and state organizations such as the National Association of Radio News Directors and the Radio Television News Directors Association.

1907. Mieczyslaw Friedel Papers, 1931–1980. Papers of a journalist, actor, radio program director and World War II army intelligence officer, including a printed version of his army diary and biographical information.

1908. Milwaukee Area Radio Enthusiasts Papers, 1976–1994. Nearly a complete run of newsletters and a flyer from the organization comprised of fans of Old Time Radio. The newsletters contain minutes of their meetings as well as membership lists and information about old time radio in Milwaukee and nationally.

University of Wyoming

American Heritage Center, Department 3924
1000 E. University Avenue, Laramie, WY 82071
(307) 766-3756; Fax: (307) 766-5511
ahcref@uwyo.edu
http://ahc.uwyo.edu/usearchives/default.htm

General comments: For more information about most of the collections listed below, check with the repository for unpublished finding aids.

1909. Al C. Ward Papers, 1940–1968, bulk 1952–1968. Contains mainly scripts written by Ward along with outlines, treatments and miscellaneous other materials for the radio program *Big Town* and other television programs.

1910. Aleen Leslie Papers, 1930–1966, bulk 1930–1952. Contains materials relating to Leslie's work as a journalist and writer, 1930–1966. Collection is mainly comprised of scripts, contracts and production materials for the radio and television versions of *A Date With Judy*, 1942–1952, fan mail and correspondence regarding her newspaper column, 1930–1940, and other non radio scripts.

1911. Alice Reinheart Papers, 1910–1985. Contains personal and professional correspondence, photographs and other papers relating to the actress's career plus sound recordings of *Life Can Be Beautiful* and other unidentified programs, 1939–1977.

1912. Allan Jackson Papers, 1948–1975. Contains professional correspondence, 1952–1975, extensive scripts for various radio programs on the CBS Network, 1948, 1950–1975, and miscellaneous memorabilia.

1913. Andy White Papers, 1935–1979. Contains materials relating to White's production and writing career, including scripts for *The Victor Borge Show*, *Fibber McGee and Molly* which were written by Don Quinn and Phil Leslie (script summaries for 1935–1946 are also included) and *The Great* *Gildersleeve*, 1935–1947. Also includes sound recordings of programs broadcast over KVOA, 1941–1944.

1914. Anne and Frank Hummert Scripts, 1932–1958. Consists of scripts of many of the Hummerts' programs, including *Just Plain Bill, Lorenzo Jones, Easy Aces, Young Widder Brown, Front Page Farrell, Lora Lawton, Mr. Keen, Tracer of Lost Persons, Orphans of Divorce, Backstage Wife, Stella Dallas, David Harum, Romance of Helen Trent, Our Gal Sunday*, and *John's Other Wife*.

1915. Arnold Marquis Papers, 1943–1947. Contains mainly scripts written by Marquis along with 27 reel-to-reel tapes and miscellaneous other materials for the programs *The Fifth Horseman, The Pacific Story* and *Unlimited Horizons*.

1916. Arthur Henley Papers, 1938–1974. Consists mainly of scripts for radio and television programs written or produced by Henley with production files containing correspondence, notes, schedules and outlines. Also includes related reviews, awards, promotional materials, scrapbooks, photographs of Henley, manuscripts of two of his books, phonograph records of radio broadcasts, films and audio tapes of *Make Up Your Mind* and other programs. Also includes material for *Everything Goes, What Makes You Tick, Marry-Go-Round, Phrase That Pays* and *Honeymoon in New York*.

1917. Beatrice Kay Papers, 1909–1980. Consists of papers relating to Kay's acting career and audio recordings of *Gay Nineties Revue* and other programs Kay appeared on, 1939–1956.

1918. Bernard Jacob Reines Papers, 1939–1969. Contains scripts Reines wrote for *Cavalcade of America*. Catalog listing notes that he also wrote radio scripts for the U.S. Treasury Department but collection does not appear to include any of those scripts.

1919. Billy Idelson Papers, ca. 1960–ca. 1979. Contains mostly scripts for television comedy shows of the 1960s but also includes Idelson's research about Paul Rhymer and *Vic and Sade*.

1920. Carroll Carroll Papers, 1936–1977. Consists mainly of radio and television scripts written by Carroll and sheet music for songs written by Carroll or in collaboration with Dick Manning. Contains material on the *Bob Crosby Show, Club 15, Kraft Music Hall* and *Old Gold Show*, including correspondence and manuscripts of various writings. Also includes Carroll's column for "Variety" magazine and books ghost written for Bob Hope, Mike Douglas and others, sound recordings of radio commercials and programs and records, some with music written by Carroll and some performed by the Bob Crosby Orchestra.

1921. Clark Kinnaird Papers, 1858–1977, bulk 1919–1977. Includes papers relating to Kinnaird's career as a syndicated columnist, broadcaster and book reviewer, 1949–1970. Collection includes some unidentified radio scripts.

1922. D.W. Kingsley Radio Scripts, 1938–1939. Contains scripts by Kingsley on water conservation, 1938. Note: The collection is also listed in the catalog as "Papers, 1928–1946" with George N. Carter as the "author."

1923. David E. Lesan Papers, 1937–1973. Collection contains correspondence, 1945–1964, miscellaneous materials related to Lesan's work in radio, 1937–1947, and television scripts.

1924. David Ross Papers, 1920–1975. Contains correspondence, poems, phonograph records, including poetry readings and auditions, scripts for *Words in the Night* and other papers. Ross also did poetry readings on *Poet's Gold*.

1925. Dick Powell Papers, 1904–1963. Includes scripts for *Richard Diamond, Private Detective,* 1949–1950, in which Powell played the title role. (See collection #1980 below.)

1926. Donald S. Frey Radio History Collection, ca. 1920–1978. Contains three audio tapes of a history of radio broadcasting consisting of over 18 hours of programs with accompanying script put together by Frey, one audio cassette of openings for radio programs and an interview with Frey on collecting radio broadcasts.

1927. Dorothy Collins Papers, 1950–1971. Contains mainly materials relating to her work with *Your Hit Parade*, including 20 boxes of musical scores from the radio and television versions of the show.

1928. Dudley Dean McGaughey (McGaughy) Papers, 1932–1985. Contains manuscripts, related correspondence, research files and synopses of many of McGaughey's western novels, including scripts for *Gene Autry's Melody Ranch* and *Hopalong Cassidy*.

1929. Duncan Renaldo Papers, 1924–1980. Contains some personal materials but mainly materials relating to Renaldo's acting and his portrayal of the Cisco Kid. In addition to scripts for the radio and television program, the collection contains memorabilia, promotional material, fan mail, personal and general correspondence with some relating to the Screen Writers and Screen Actors Guilds.

1930. Ed Begley Papers, 1944–1970. Consists mainly of scripts for movies, television programs and a few radio programs in which Begley appeared, including the *Hills Brothers Coffee Show* and *One Man's Family*.

1931. Edward Everett Horton Papers, 1900–1970. Consists of material relating to Horton's acting career, including mainly scripts for plays, motion pictures and radio and television commercials and shows. Also includes photographs, programs, correspondence, broadsides and other promotional materials, personal account books, contracts, scrapbooks, memorabilia, sound recordings of two interviews of Horton, 1969 and 1970, and many phonograph records of performances and interviews.

1932. Episcopal Church, Missionary District of Wyoming Records, 1904–1972, bulk 1904–1927. Includes materials relating to Wyoming's first radio station, KFBU, Laramie which was operated out of St. Matthew's Cathedral in the late 1920s.

1933. F. Hugh Herbert Papers, ca. 1940–ca. 1955. Consists mainly of scripts, 1943–1946, written by Herbert for *Meet Corliss Archer* along with manuscripts of novels, short stories, plays and screenplays and other materials relating to his writing.

1934. Francine Larrimore Papers, 1916–1965. Includes scripts for *Grand Central Station,* 1941, and other papers relating to Larrimore's acting career.

1935. Francis D. Van Hartesveldt Papers, 1941–1963. Consists mainly of Van Hartesveldt's writings, including scripts for many radio shows, story ideas, outlines and a few scripts for television. Also includes a small amount of related correspondence, some contracts and photographs of Van Hartesveldt with celebrities. Van Hartesveldt wrote for the following radio programs: *Your Nutrilite Radio Theatre, Suspense, Sky King, CBS Radio Workshop, The Great Gildersleeve, Romance* and *Roy Rogers*.

1936. Francis Stuart Harmon Papers, 1947–1976. Consists chiefly of materials relating to Harmon's work with the Riverside Church and WRVR, including correspondence, minutes, reports, grant proposals, transcripts of listener mail, transcripts of Harmon's testimony before the FCC in WRVR licensing matters, memorandums, budgets and surveys.

1937. Frank Blair Papers, 1958–1967. Includes speeches and radio scripts from *Frankly Speaking, Focus on the News* and *Emphasis on the News*.

1938. Frank D. Barton Papers, 1932–1977. Contains miscellaneous materials relating to Barton's work as a television and radio announcer, including correspondence, newspaper clippings, photographs of Barton with various bands, an audio tape of a 1947 episode of *One Man's Family,* phonograph records of Barton with the Tom Croakley Orchestra playing on the *Hills Brothers Coffee Show,* 1934–1938, scattered scripts for *One Man's Family*, a video tape of Barton on the *Tomorrow Show* in 1974 upon his retirement from NBC and a scrapbook.

1939. Frank Woodruff Papers, 1939–1961. Contains mainly scripts for radio and motion pictures that Woodruff directed and miscellaneous materials for *This Is Hollywood, Lux Radio Theatre* and the *Camay Show*. Also includes sound recordings of *This Is Hollywood* and the *Camay Show*.

1940. Gene Thompson Papers, ca. 1930–1969, bulk 1965–1969. Consists of an extensive file of jokes typed on 3 x 5 cards, arranged alphabetically by topic, from several radio shows from the 1930s and scripts for television programs.

1941. George Bloom Papers, 1957–1969. Consists mainly of radio and television scripts for variety shows written by Bloom, 1950s–1960s, reel-to-reel tapes of highlights of *The Gold Coast Show* written by Bloom and a few materials relating to Bloom's night club writings.

1942. George L. Rockwell Papers, 1913–1954. Contains miscellaneous biographical information, correspondence with Fred Allen, J. J. Shubert and RKO Corporation, scripts for *The Fred Allen Show, Texaco Star Theater, Dr. Rockwell's Brain Trust,* and *Jack Oakie's College* plus scrapbooks, photographs, clippings and other materials.

1943. George Q. Lewis Papers, 1848–1954. Contains typescripts of jokes used by various comedians on radio shows, 1947, a 3x5 card file of jokes, manuscripts of articles and short stories, humor newsletters and other papers.

1944. Harold Medford Papers, 1940–1973. Contains scripts for *Suspense* and *Calling All Cars,* scripts for television and stills for motion pictures.

1945. Hy Freedman Papers, 1945–1978, bulk 1945–1963. Consists mainly of scripts, 1945–1963, written by Freedman for radio and television. Also includes sound recordings of *You Bet Your Life* and *Seabees Time on the Air*, material relating to *Duffy's Tavern* and photographs of Freedman and radio and television celebrities, including Groucho Marx, and the manuscript of Freedman's 1977 book "Sex Link."

1946. Irene Corbally Kuhn Papers, 1875–1986, bulk 1928–1986. Collection documents Kuhn's career as a radio war correspondent for NBC, 1940–1949, and contains papers and sound recordings, including her broadcasts of the liberation of Shanghai and Manila in 1945 and *The Kuhns* broadcasts she did with her daughter Rene. Papers include financial records, legal files, news releases, newspaper clippings, photographs, subject files, awards, biographic information and miscellaneous other materials.

1947. Jack Hilton Papers, 1964–1979. Includes scripts for *Balance Sheet* and other papers relating to Hilton's work with the J. Walter Thompson Company.

1948. Jay Dratler Papers, 1934–1968. Includes manuscripts of the writer's novels and plays, scripts for motion pictures, television and radio programs written or co-written by Dratler. Also includes related correspondence, outlines, story ideas and legal documents concerning a copyright case.

1949. Jerry Seelen Papers, 1912–1965, bulk 1944–1965. Contains mainly scripts for radio and television written by Seelen, including the radio programs *Birds Eye Open House, The Drene Shampoo Show* and *Toasties Time.* Seelen also wrote for the *Danny Thomas Show.*

1950. John F. Meagher Papers, 1954–1962. Includes professional correspondence, photographs and a scrapbook. Meagher was a radio executive and vice-president of the National Association of Broadcasters, 1954–1964.

1951. John Knox Jessup Papers, 1945–1978. Contains professional correspondence (including letters with Henry Luce), speeches and radio scripts for *Spectrum.*

1952. John M. Anspacher Papers, 1945–1977. Includes miscellaneous correspondence, a scrapbook and 48 audio cassettes of *As Others See Us,* a talk show with foreign correspondents covering the United States.

1953. John Mies Papers, 1953–1978, bulk 1953–1962. Contains mainly scripts for radio programs written by Mies and other materials relating to his work in radio and television, 1953–1978. Includes scripts for *The Gold Coast Show, Concert or Corn, Would You Believe It,* and *Secession Report* (with scripts for commercials), which was a radio news show that reported occurrences in the 1860s and was aired during the centennial of the Civil War, 1953–1962. Also includes one audio cassette with a 1961 episode of the *Secession Report* and a 1955 episode of *The Gold Coast Show.*

1954. John Whedon Papers, 1928–1973. Contains mainly scripts written by Whedon along with outlines and miscellaneous other materials for several radio and television programs, motion pictures and theater, 1935–1973. Includes scripts for *The Great Gildersleeve* and *The Rudy Vallee Hour.*

1955. Laurence Marks Papers, 1901–1988, bulk 1940–

1988. Includes scripts, production materials, outlines, synopses, research notes and treatments for many radio and television programs, 1940–1987, including the following radio programs: *Duffy's Tavern, The Bob Hope Show, General Fuqua's Warcast, The Fred Allen Show,* and *The Joan Davis Show.* Collection also includes other professional correspondence.

1956. Lawrence B. Marcus Scripts, 1948-1967. Includes scripts for two *Suspense* programs plus other television programs and films.

1957. Lawrence Goldtree Blochman Papers, 1921–1975. Contains materials relating to Blochman's writing career with some personal correspondence. Professional materials include correspondence, manuscripts, reviews of his work, a scrapbook, photographs and radio scripts. Blochman wrote for *The Fred Allen Show,* Town *Hall Tonight,* and *Texaco Star Theater.*

1958. Lawrence M. Klee Papers, 1936–1957. Contains materials relating to Klee's writing career and includes mainly scripts along with story lines and research notes for *Backstage Wife, Chaplain Jim, U.S.A.* (completed for Hummert Radio Features during World War II), *The Chase, The Clock, The Fat Man, Front Page Farrell, Mr. & Mrs. North, Mr. Chameleon, Mr. Keen, Tracer of Lost Persons* and *Valiant Lady.* Also includes television and movie scripts.

1959. Lew Lansworth Papers, 1924–1969, bulk 1940–1969. Contains materials relating to Lansworth's career as a radio writer and author, including correspondence, 1943–1969, scripts, research notes, photographs, publicity materials and newspaper clippings for *Murder Will Out* and *Whodunit?,* 1940–1955. Also includes 21 sound recordings of *Murder Will Out* and other materials relating to Lansworth's career.

1960. Lew Pollack Papers, 1922–1945. Includes an audio cassette of *Let's Write a Song,* ca. 1940, that featured Pollack and miscellaneous other papers relating to his career.

1961. Louis M. Heyward Papers, 1944–1974. Consists mainly of scripts for radio and television programs and motion pictures written or produced by Heyward along with miscellaneous related materials, manuscripts of novels and scenery drawings for the *Garry Moore* television show. Includes papers relating to *Personality Time* and *Startime.*

1962. Louis Pelletier, Jr. Scripts, 1936–1969. Contains scripts written by Pelletier for plays, radio and television programs and motion pictures, including *The FBI in Peace and War.*

1963. Maxwell Shane Papers, 1936–1967. Contains materials relating to Shane's work in radio, television and motion pictures and includes radio scripts for *Big Town,* 1939–1940, and the script for the World War II propaganda film "We Refuse to Die" along with a script for the radio adaptation.

1964. Milt Josefsberg Radio Scripts, 1938–1946. Contains scripts for the *Jack Benny Show* and the *Bob Hope Show* written by Josefsberg.

1965. Milton M. Raison Papers, 1937–1971. Contains mainly scripts for motion pictures, radio and television written by Raison along with treatments and outlines, 1937–1963, correspondence, 1944–1971, research notes and a scrapbook. Includes material for the *Chase and Sanborn Hour.*

1966. Morgan Beatty Papers, 1929–1975. Contains correspondence, including letters in German to Hermann Goering, fan mail, subject files used as background materials for radio broadcasts, 1948–1967, three scrapbooks, scripts for *AP Newsfeatures* and *News of the World*, 1937–1967, and other papers. Also contains two sound recordings of Beatty's 10th anniversary broadcast on *News of the World*, 1956, seven recordings of Beatty narrating for AP's *The World in Sound*, sound recordings of *News of the World*, 1959–1967, a 1966 videotape interview with Beatty and a film of a 1959 *News of the World* broadcast.

1967. Mort Reis Lewis Papers, 1939–1985. Consists mainly of scripts, correspondence, notes, story lines and fan mail for many of the radio and television programs for which Lewis wrote. Also includes Lewis's subject files, general correspondence and materials relating to the Writers Guild of America, West. Lewis wrote for the following radio programs: *Sparring Partners, Philco Hall of Fame, Jonathan Trimble, Esq., Behind the Mike* and *The Charlie McCarthy Show.*

1968. Neal Gordon Keehn Papers, 1959–1975. Contains correspondence, two 78rpm records of a KMBC broadcast, Midland Broadcasting Company, Kansas City, MO, n.d., a 78rpm record of an episode of *Police Headquarters*, n.d., and other material relating to film production.

1969. Olive Ewing Clapper Papers, 1933–1961. Contains scripts, 1944, 1948–1950 and 1957, including portions of the 1944 Republican National Convention relating to CARE (Cooperative for American Relief Everywhere), other papers and a sound recording of a personality sketch of Clapper by Mutual Broadcaster Virgil Pinkley, 1958.

1970. Ozzie and Harriet Nelson Papers, 1937–1963. Contains materials relating to the Nelson family, their orchestra and radio and television programs, including *Adventures of Ozzie and Harriet, Red Skelton Show* and *Emmy Lou.* Includes scripts for both the Nelson's radio and television programs and for other radio programs, the Orchestra's sheet music for instrumental parts, photographs of the Nelson family and the television show and phonograph records of radio broadcasts.

1971. Pacific Power and Radio Program Scripts, 1961–1977. Includes scripts of *Stories of Pacific Powerland*, a five-minute program sponsored by Pacific Power and Light Co. All 1,273 programs were narrated by Nelson Olmsted. Each program dealt with Western history, biography or folklore.

1972. Parke Levy Papers, 1933–1965. Consists mainly of scripts for radio and television programs written by Levy, 1933–1965, including the *Ben Bernie Show, Bert Lahr Show, Duffy's Tavern* and *My Friend Irma.*

1973. Paula Stone Papers, 1920–1981. Includes two audio tapes of Stone's radio interviews of 10 producers and actors, including Cecil B. De Mille, Ed Wynne and Eddie Cantor, and other papers relating to her acting and producing careers. Stone was a radio personality in the 1940s. The catalog lists the names of the 10 interviewees but not the dates of the interviews.

1974. Phillips H. Lord Papers, 1929–1967. Contains extensive correspondence, musical scores, newsclippings, advertisements, legal and financial material, photographs, scrapbooks, scripts and phonograph records for *Seth Parker, Seth Parker's Old Fashioned Singing School* and *Sunday Evenings at Seth Parker's.*

1975. Ray Singer Papers, 1944–1969. Contains mainly scripts for radio and television programs written by Singer, 1944–1969. Includes scripts for *The Phil Harris/Alice Faye Show* and *The Sealtest Village Store.*

1976. *Richard Diamond, Private Detective* Scripts, 1949–1950. Scripts for the program in which actor Dick Powell played the title role. Note: Check with library to determine if these are the same scripts that are included in the "Dick Powell Collection" listed above.

1977. Sam J. Slate Papers, 1937–1964. Contains scripts for *Defense for America, Gang Busters, Mr. District Attorney,* and *Your Defense Reporter* written by Slate, 1937–1941, plus scrapbooks and papers relating to his career as a producer with CBS, 1951–1963, and sound recordings of programs he produced for the BBC.

1978. Selena Royle Papers, 1904–1983. Consists of papers related to Royle's career in theater, film and on her own radio show, *Women of Courage.*

1979. Sheldon Stark Papers, 1942–1988. Contains mainly scripts for radio, television, theater and motion pictures written by Stark along with miscellaneous other materials, 1942–1986. Includes scripts for *American School of the Air* and *Straight Arrow.* Stark also wrote for *The Lone Ranger* and *Escape.*

1980. Stanley Niss Papers, 1946–1969. Consists mainly of scripts along with budgets, treatments, correspondence, research materials, contracts, outlines and synopses for many of the radio, television and motion pictures written or produced by Niss, plus professional correspondence, two scrapbooks, 94 phonograph records, an audio tape for *Twenty-first Precinct*, 1954–1955, one phonograph record for *Gang Busters*, 1954, material related to *Charlie Wild, Private Detective* and other television and film related material.

1981. Thomas J. McDermott Papers, 1922–1976. Contains papers related to McDermott's early involvement in radio and television programs and advertising as an executive with N. W. Ayer & Sons.

1982. Tom Anderson Papers, 1924–. Includes reel-to-reel tapes of episodes of *Straight Talk*, n.d.

1983. William (Bill) Stern Papers, 1929–1968. Includes scrapbooks, awards, trophies and certificates, two letters, a bronze bust of Stern, memorabilia, a copy of Stern's book "A Taste of Ashes" and miscellaneous other materials.

1984. William Boyd Papers, 1930–1977. Contains materials concerning Boyd's portrayal of Hopalong Cassidy, including correspondence, fan mail, scripts for *Hopalong Cassidy* on radio and in other productions, press kits, business records and promotional material including broadsides, product labels, toys and clothing.

Utah State Historical Society

300 South Rio Grande Street, Salt Lake City, UT 84101
(801) 533-3535; Fax: (801) 533-3504
historyresearch@utah.gov
http://history.utah.gov/utah_history_research_center

General comments: The library has an Historical Pamphlet Collection that contains radio material, including station history and promotional material regarding a specific broadcast. The pamphlets are listed individually in the Library's online catalog and are not included in the list of special collections below.

1985. "Ballad of Joe Hill." A radio script, n.d., for a program, possibly entitled *Industrial Workers of the World.*

1986. Eugene Jelesnik Papers, 1905–1992. Contains correspondence and files for musical events, radio and television productions, USO performances, newspaper clippings, etc. Also contains an extensive collection of orchestrations, original arrangements, music books, sheet music, music instruction books and individual music parts. The collection also has an extensive audio visual collection as well as studio recordings and commercial phonograph records. Check with library for more information on radio materials. A separate Jelesnik photograph collection, 1930–1999, has some material relating to KDYL and photographs of Ted Mack's 1957 visit to Utah, most likely to audition entertainers for *Ted Mack's Original Amateur Hour.*

1987. "Pioneer Tales." A radio script by Gladys Pinney presented on KSL, October 11, 1944, about Indians of Skull Valley and the early settlers of Grantsville.

1988. Radio Addresses, January, 1936–March, 1938. A series of addresses on KSL by prominent citizens on the subject of smoking.

1989. Radio Scripts for *Arthur Gaeth News*, 1942. Scripts written by Gaeth, mostly concerning issues dealing with Utah during World War II.

Robert VanDeventer

33 Ponderosa Lane, Palmyra, VA 22963
(434) 591-0589

1990. *Twenty Questions*, 1946–1955. Consists of some publicity material, legal papers, other correspondence and sound recordings. Collection is held by the son of the program's creators. Mr. VanDeventer appeared on the program as "Bobby McGuire."

Vermont Historical Society

60 Washington Street, Barre, VT 05641
(802) 479-8500; Fax: (802) 479-8510
vhs@vhs.state.vt.us; http://vermonthistory.org
Contact: Paul Carnahan

1991. Charles S. Doe Interview. Doe talks about his role founding WLAK.

1992. Fairbanks Family Papers, 1798–1953. Multi generation family papers. Includes "Yankee and the Scales," a radio script about Erastus and Thaddeus Fairbanks produced by the DuPont Company, 1952.

1993. Janet King Lyle (Janet Merle) Papers, 1920–1987. Consists of Lyle's manuscripts for radio and stage and other papers. Radio scripts may be for a serial *Paying Ghosts*, n.d.

Virginia Commonwealth University

Library Special Collections and Archives
901 Park Avenue, VCU Box 842033, Richmond, VA 23284
(804) 828-1108; Fax: (804) 828-0151

ulsjbcsc@vcu.edu; Contact: Ray Bonis
www.library.vcu.edu/jbc/speccoll/speccoll.html

1994. Calvin Tompkins Lucy Papers, 1914–1978. Contains papers relating to the founding of WRVA, Richmond in 1925, Virginia's first radio station. Includes daily program logs, 1925–1932, broadcast and publicity material, scrapbooks, photographs and some phonograph records. Lucy was an announcer, writer, producer, performer and general manager of the station during its early years. Also includes papers relating to the Larus & Brother Company, a tobacco firm that owned the station.

Virginia Historical Society

PO Box 731, Richmond, VA 23221
(804) 342-9677; Contact: Shepard L. Lee
lshepard@vahistorical.org; www.vahistorical.org

General comments: The Society's general book collection includes several titles relating to the history of Virginia radio stations as well as other radio related subjects. Also, radio related ephemeral materials are located in the Society's Vertical File, including an *Old Dominion Barn Dance* program and items about radio broadcasting in Virginia and WRVA, Richmond.

1995. Barbara Colquhoun Trigg Brown Papers, 1913–1976. Includes correspondence relating to Brown's program, *Up-to-Date With Barbara Brown*, broadcast on WINA.

1996. Calvin Tompkins Lucy Papers, 1921–1940. Consists mostly of correspondence, a speech and notes, ca. 1932, regarding WMBG and WRVA. Lucy was a manager for WRVA and also worked for the Larus & Brother Company that owned WRVA.

1997. Collection of Historic Radio Broadcasts, 1918–1963. An eclectic collection of 41 cassettes with programs of historic interest, e.g., speeches of Winston Churchill, Adolph Hilter, the invasion of Normandy, the Hindenburg disaster, Charles Lindbergh, *Amos 'n' Andy*, Benny Goodman, etc. A complete list of titles is filed with the collection.

1998. Larus & Brother Company, Richmond, VA Records, 1877–1974. Records include the company's subsidiaries, including WRVA, 1925–1969, and WRVA-FM, 1948–1969.

1999. Maude Howlett Woodfin Papers, 1915–1948. Contains scripts, 1941–1942, of radio interviews of August Dietz, Maude Howlett Woodfin and Louis Booker Wright concerning the publication of books about William Byrd.

2000. Watson Family Papers, 1771–1934. Includes correspondence, 1882–1933, of Anne Watson Archer concerning radio shows.

2001. Woolsey Bruce Shafer Papers, 1933–1950. Includes Shafer's weekly radio broadcasts from Washington, D.C.

2002. WRNL Materials, 1935–1992. Collection documents the history of WRNL and includes copies of newspaper articles, photographs and text tracing the history of the Richmond station founded in 1937. The station was the successor to WPHR, Petersburg, VA.

2003. WRVA 50th Anniversary Sound Recording. A recording, 197?, of the station's 50-year history.

Walt Disney Archives

500 D. Buena Vista Street, Burbank, CA 91521
(818) 560-5151

2004. *Mickey Mouse Theater of the Air.* Includes print and possibly some audio material relating to the 1938 program. Note: Access to the collection is extremely restricted and is generally discouraged. Initial contact with the company should be through the Legal Department.

Washington State Archives

PO Box 40238, Olympia, WA 98504
(360) 586-1492; research@secstate.wa.gov
www.secstate.wa.gov/archives

2005. Guide to the Records of the Washington State Public Broadcasting Commission, 1961–1983. The Commission was established in 1953 to encourage educational and public interest radio and television broadcasting. The records include correspondence, grant applications and meeting files.

2006. Washington State Liquor Control Board Records, 1934–1993. Records include material on radio advertising.

Washington State Historical Society

1911 Pacific Avenue, Tacoma, WA 98402
(888) 238-4373
www.washingtonhistory.org

2007. "Columbia Magazine," Summer 1990. Includes text of a live radio broadcast from the Grand Coulee Dam on its inauguration of power.

Washington State University

Library: Manuscripts, Archives, and Special Collections
Pullman, WA 99164
(509) 335-2185
Contact: Cheryl Gunselman; gunselma@wsu.edu
www.wsulibs.wsu.edu/holland/masc/masc.htm

2008. Edward R. Murrow Speeches, 1941–1961. Text of four addresses on World War II and on radio and television journalism.

2009. Edward R. Murrow Papers, 1928–1932. Chiefly handwritten letters to Hermine Duthie. Includes annotated copy of a theatrical prompt book.

2010. Edward R. Murrow Photographs, 1909–1964. A collection of photographs of Murrow.

2011. Enoch Albert Bryan Papers 1843–1989. Includes text for a program on the history of the Pacific Northwest, 1953.

2012. Guide to the Public Radio Oral History Project Papers, 1977–1978. Transcripts and interviews with pioneers of public radio broadcasting in the United States conducted by Burt Harrison, former manager of KWSU, 1977-1978, under a contract from the Corporation for Public Broadcasting.

2013. Hugh Augustus Rundell Papers, 1938–1983. Correspondence and subject files principally regarding the Department of Communications at Washington State University. Also includes transcripts and working papers from the Pacific Northwest Broadcasting Oral History Project.

2014. Inez Puckett McEwen Papers, 1885–1982. Papers relating to McEwen's career as a newspaper reporter and feature writer, radio reporter and private speech instructor. She wrote scripts for the serial program *Hodgepodge* that was aired on a Twin Falls radio station.

2015. KFAE/KWSU Records, 1922–1984. Records of the Washington State University campus station KFAE which became KWSU. Includes program logs and some audio recordings. Records are located in three separate collections. Additional photos of KWSU are in the separate Hutchinson Studio Photographs Collection.

2016. Knute Hill Papers, 1909–1963. Contains correspondence and printed material relating to several aspects of Hill's activities, including his career as a reporter for the *Radio Farm Program.*

2017. KWSC Broadcast on Steptoe Battle and Retreat, n.d. Script for program dealing with Indians of North America, 1847–1865, prepared by the Washington State Parks and Recreation Commission and broadcast on KWSC, Pullman, WA.

2018. KWSU Radio Station Records, 1916–1977. Contains correspondence, program scripts, Mary Avery's program, *Washington Archives,* and other papers. Scripts cover such items as agricultural extension broadcasts, musical and literary programs, dramatic productions and school broadcasts.

2019. Mary Avery Washington Archives of KWSC Radio Scripts, 1960–1965. Radio scripts of a program on Northwest history based on primary source materials, mostly manuscripts in the WSU Library. Approximately 100 recordings of the program are in the Mary Avery Cassette Collection at the Eastern Washington State Historical Society located in the Joel E. Ferris Research Archives & Library, 2316 West First Avenue, Spokane, WA 99204, (509) 363-5310; contact Larry Schoonover, larrys@northwestmuseum.org.

2020. "Mighty Poorly," ca. 1938. Script for a drama prepared by the U.S. Office of Education about the Civilian Conservation Corps.

2021. "The Northwest Pioneer" Radio Scripts, 1938. Scripts for a series of broadcasts over KWSC. Written by Milo Wesley Goss, the scripts include biographies of John Akins, Lulu Downen, George Draper, Clifford Drury, Garret Kincaid and May Squires.

2022. Office of Indian Affairs of the Department of the Interior Presents, ca. 1935. Scripts for a series of radio programs dealing with the historical background, development and present-day conditions of the American Indian. Program was presented by the Bureau of Indian Affairs.

2023. Pioneer Reminiscences, 1931. Reminiscences of Eastern Washington. The material was submitted for a pioneer contest on KHQ, Spokane, WA.

2024. "Pioneer Trails," 1938. Transcripts of historical talks by Radford Kuykendall broadcast on KWSC, Pullman, WA, March–June, 1938.

2025. "The Strattons in the West," 1934? Script written by Gladys Stratton about overland journeys to the Pacific broadcast on KWSC, Pullman, WA, 1936?

2026. Sybil Warfield Papers, 1951–1957. Contains correspondence, minutes of meetings, project reports, contest entries, radio scripts, photographs and scrapbooks collected or prepared by Warfield, Chairman of the Six Federated Clubs of Clarkston, for the club's entry in the "Build Freedom with

Youth" contest sponsored by the General Federation of Women's Clubs.

2027. Thomas W. Baird Papers, 1924–1932. Contains correspondence, clippings, photographs, licenses, QSL cards and other papers relating to amateur radio stations in Washington state.

2028. "Trails of the Great Northwest," ca. 1930. Scripts for a radio program on frontier and pioneer life broadcast on KHQ, Spokane, WA.

2029. "Tribute to Cities and Towns in the Northwest," 1933. Transcripts of radio broadcasts dealing with cities and towns in the Pacific Northwest written by Elston Wyckoff broadcast on KHQ, Spokane, WA, 1933.

2030. Washington State Association of Broadcasters Records, 1950–1962, 1977–1981. Includes correspondence, financial records and meeting notes.

2031. Yakima Public Schools Radio Education Department, n.d. Includes script of an historical documentary broadcast in tribute to the City-County Health Department of Yakima prepared by the Yakima Public Schools in conjunction with the Business and Professional Women of Yakima. Subject was likely the prevention of typhoid fever.

Special Media Collections (Audio Collections)
Holland/New Library
(509) 335-7664
http://www.wsulibs.wsu.edu/MMR/pitzer.htm

2032. Reel McCoy Old-Time Radio Program Collection. An audio collection of assorted Old Time Radio programs donated by Pat McCoy. As of 2005, the contents of the collection were not available online.

2033. Vintage Radio Program Collection. A tape collection of assorted Old Time Radio programs donated by Paul C. Pitzer. A complete listing of the contents of all 937 reels is available online at http://www.wsulibs.wsu.edu/MMR/speccoll.htm.

Washington University
Olin Library, Department of Special Collections
Campus Box 1061, 1 Brookings Drive, St. Louis, MO 63130
(314) 935-5495; Fax: (314) 935-4045
spec@library.wustl.edu; http://library.wustl.edu/units/spec

2034. Cid Corman Papers. Papers consist almost entirely of correspondence between the author and the book dealer Henry Wenning, 1962–1964, most of which deal with the distribution of Origin Press materials and books and with Corman's life and work in Japan. Does not contain any material about Corman's program *This Is Poetry*, 1948–1951.

2035. Fannie Hurst Papers. Contains transcripts of radio programs for which Hurst was a panelist, including *America's Town Meeting of the Air*, December 26, 1935.

2036. Samuel Beckett Papers, 1946-1981. Includes material relating to Beckett's radio work, including several plays

Wayne State University
Walter P. Reuther Library
Archives of Labor and Urban Affairs
5401 Cass Avenue, Detroit, MI 48202
(313) 577-4024; Contact: William LeFevre

reutherreference@wayne.edu; www.reuther.wayne.edu

2037. Ben Legere Papers, 1906–1970. Contains correspondence, notebooks, diaries, notes, radio scripts and other materials relating to Legere's activities in the American and Canadian labor movements, California politics and the west coast theater.

2038. Brendan Sexton Papers, 1938–1988. Papers relating to Sexton's activities with the United Automobile Workers union. Includes scripts from the UAW program *Eye Opener.*

2039. Joseph Mattson Papers, 1947–1950. Contains correspondence, minutes and other materials relating to Mattson's activities with the United Automobile Workers, including the union's radio stations.

2040. Joseph Pagano Collection. Contains correspondence, petitions, clippings, radio broadcasts, constitutions and by-laws relating to Pagano's activities with the United Automobile Workers. Also includes an oral history transcript.

2041. *Mark Adams* Script Collection, 1948–1951. Contains correspondence and scripts relating to the program that was created and researched by members of the Detroit Employers Association.

2042. Radio Program Notes & News. CIO Publicity Department, 1953–1955. Includes notes for *As Vandercook Sees It.*

2043. Ted Andras Papers, 1947–1956, bulk 1947–1952. Contains correspondence, license applications, construction permits and engineering exhibit applications relating to the construction of the UAW's station WDET-FM. Photographs related to the station are located in the Audio-Visual Department.

2044. UAW Community Relations Records, 1944–1974. Contains correspondence, minutes, notes, radio and television transcripts, reports, clippings, publications and other materials relating to the establishment and promotion of UAW stations WCUO, Cleveland, OH and WDET, Detroit, MI, 1948-1952. Correspondents include Morris Novick, an AFL-CIO radio consultant. Note: Although the online catalog shows the spelling of consultant's name as "Novick," based on two other collections in other repositories, the correct spelling is most likely "Novik."

2045. William Dufty Papers, 1940–1947, bulk 1941. Contains correspondence, clippings and radio scripts relating to Dufty's union and public relations activities.

West Virginia Division of Culture and History
The Cultural Center, Capitol Complex
1900 Kanawha Boulevard East, Charleston, WV 25305
(304) 558-0220; Fax: (304) 558-2779
debra.basham@wvculture.org; Contact: Debra Basham
www.wvculture.org/history/specialcollections.html

2046. *On The Air*, 1940. Record album folder for the NBC program with information about its radio programming, ca. 1940.

2047. Various Radio Pieces. Includes a 1939 program for the WVVA *Jamboree* and a *Doc Williams Border Riders* family album, ca. 1935–1945. Additional collections, listed separately under "publications" in the online catalog include a WWVA 1936 Flood Souvenir program, a WHIS *Freedom for All* broadcast in conjunction with a 1950 *Bluefield Coal Show,* a 1948 WMMN family album program, a 1951 WWVA 25th Anniversary booklet and a WPAR radio bulletin for the *Farm Chat Program*, 1936.

2048. Walter Fredericks Collection. Includes material about WOBU, an early Charleston station, 1928–1932.

Western Reserve Historical Society
10825 East Boulevard, Cleveland, OH 44106
(216) 721-5722, 224
reference@wrhs.org; www.wrhs.org

2049. Anna M. Sotak Papers, 1939–1972. Radio talks from the *Slovak Hour* and other papers dealing with Slovak fraternal organizations and activities and Sotak family business.

2050. Anson F. Hardman Papers, 1947–1960. Hardman was general advertising manager of the Ohio Bell Telephone Company, 1924–1951, and director of the *Ohio Story*. Papers pertain largely to the development of the program, from original idea to final casting, broadcast and publicity. Includes scripts and script drafts, administrative papers, correspondence, story ideas and suggestions, research articles, subject lists, broadcast material, clippings, music scores, photographs and biographical information on Hardman. See also separate collection listing for *Ohio Story* Scripts. Sound recordings and films of the program are located in the Audio-Visual collection.

2051. Bertelle M. Lyttle Papers, 1915–1959. Includes scripts and other papers relating to the series *Movies, Art, and Problems* directed by Lyttle and broadcast over Cleveland stations WHK and WCLE.

2052. Carl C. Byers Papers, 1937–1966. Includes scripts for *Carl C. Byers Presents* which espoused the principle that fun and laughter are important for success and longevity.

2053. Frank Szappanos Papers, 1939–1975. Papers of the Hungarian-American radio announcer, including a Hungarian song book compiled by Szappanos in 1941, correspondence, 1960–1966 and newspaper clippings, 1939–1975. Szappanos was active in the Szappanos Radio Ball. Some of the materials are in Hungarian. Note: The authors were unable to verify whether the Szappanos Radio Ball was a radio program.

2054. Inez Wallace and Frank Hubbell Papers, 1891–1969. Contains correspondence, writings, legal documents, clippings, scrapbooks, diaries, typescripts of Wallace's columns, magazine feature stories, unidentified radio and TV scripts, short stories and a novel. Also includes material on Wallace's script (media not identified) for the 1956 political commentary, "I'm Going to Scream Again."

2055. Leonard Levy Papers, 1936–1965. Contains clippings, correspondence, scripts for *Safety First, Your Town* and *You and Your Government* and other papers.

2056. Mutual Broadcasting System, Inc., White Paper, 1941. Prepared for the stockholders and affiliates of the MBS, the White Paper dealt with the FCC report on chain broadcasting and a May, 1941 agreement between Mutual and ASCAP. Mutual's second White Paper analyzing the FCC's revision of its chain broadcasting regulations is located in a separate file.

2057. *Ohio Story* Scripts, ca. 1947–1955. Radio and television scripts written by Frank Siedel. See related Anson F. Hardman collection on the development and production of the program. Sound recordings and films of the program are located in the Audio-Visual collection. The program was broadcast on WTAM.

2058. Payne Fund Inc. Records, 1924–1972. Records of a charitable fund focusing on children's literature, the effects of movies and radio on the values of children and the development of radio as an educational tool.

2059. *The Stark County Story.* Includes scripts on the cities, towns and villages of Stark County, OH as broadcast over WHBC. The broadcasts were launched by the Stark County Historical Society in cooperation with the Ohio Broadcasting Corp.

2060. Theodore Hall Papers, 1941–1945. Series I consists mainly of radio scripts written by Hall as an information specialist for the Cleveland Office of Civilian Defense during World War II. Recordings of the program are in the Audio Visual collection.

2061. United States Office of Civilian Defense. Includes scripts for *Sam At War* and *You Can't Do Business With Hitler.*

2062. Wade Hampton and Ruth Berry McKinney Papers. Includes papers relating to McKinney's one minute radio broadcasts, *Thot-O-Grams*, brief inspirational messages under the auspices of United Church Women of Cleveland.

Western Washington University
Center for Pacific Northwest Studies
Goltz-Murray Archives Building, Bellingham, WA 98225
(360) 650-7747; Fax: (360)650-3323
Contact: Elizabeth Joffrion; Elizabeth.Joffrion@wwu.edu
www.acadweb.wwu.edu/cpnws/collections.htm

2063. Bellingham Publishing Company, 1911–1963, bulk 1930–1938. Includes documents relating to the legal battle between the "Bellingham Herald" and KVOS, Inc., the first local radio station in Bellingham. The collection includes legal case transcripts of the Bellingham Publishing Company's attempt to prove that KVOS operated illegally by broadcasting "Herald" articles as KVOS news segments. The transcripts date from 1934 through the final decision of KVOS vs Associated Press was in 1936. Also includes legal depositions by the owner of KVOS, Rogan Jones, correspondence, plans, and brochures relating to the "Herald's" attempt to create a new radio station in Bellingham. See also Rogan Jones Collection below for related documents.

2064. Edward Block: Radio Heritage Collection. Includes correspondence, programming, scripts, and other records concerning International Good Music and KGMI radio. See also the Rogan Jones Collection below.

2065. Galen Biery Collection. Includes scrapbooks, newspapers, audio and visual materials, maps and photographs reflecting Biery's interest and research o n the history of Bellingham and Whatcom County, WA. Includes some material relating to early radio in the area.

2066. George and Anna McFarland Collection. Includes tapes from the 1970s of Edward R. Murrow radio broadcasts, recordings of news broadcasts, material regarding presidential politics and historical events, the *Reg Stone* show (organ music) and radio advertisements. Note: Check with repository on dates of non Murrow recordings.

2067. June and Farrar Burn Collection, 1888–1994, bulk 1930–1960. Collection chronicles the lives of homesteaders in the San Juan Islands and includes some radio transcripts.

2068. Rogan Jones Papers, mostly 1929–1970. Jones owned four stations in Washington: KXKO, Aberdeen, KGMI, Bellingham, KPQ, Wenatchee and KPCB, Seattle. Subject files include materials relating to the legal case, KVOS vs Associated Press concerning broadcasters' rights to access and present news information to their audience and Jones's conflicts with bodies such the American Society of Composers, Artists and Performers regarding the management, licensing and operation of his stations. In addition to business related papers, the collection contains a group of radio and oral history interviews that Jones and others recorded. Also includes a sound recording of KGMI's 40th anniversary show, November 15, 1967.

WGBH Education Foundation
Media Archives & Preservation Center
125 Western Avenue, Boston, MA 02134
(617) 300-2000; Fax: (617) 300-1026
mary_ide@wgbh.org; www.wgbh.org
Contact: Mary Ide

2069. Administrative Records of the Lowell Institute Cooperative Broadcasting Council (LICBC) and WGBH Educational Foundation, 1945–1994, bulk 1951–1991. Contains papers relating to the creation, broadcast and promotion of WGBH's programming and the development of related print and multimedia materials. The records also relate to the development of the LICBC and WGBH-FM/WGBH-TV and to some extent the development of public radio.

2070. WGBH Education Foundation, Records, 1945–1994. Includes papers, photographs and audio tapes of the Lowell Institute Cooperative Broadcasting Council & WGBH radio programming and related materials, 1951–present.

Wheaton College
Billy Graham Center
500 College Avenue, 3rd Floor, Wheaton, IL 60187
(630) 752-5910
www.wheaton.edu/bgc/archives/archhp1.html

General comments: The Center has an *extensive* collection of personal papers that contain material relating to evangelical broadcasting in the United States and elsewhere. The site includes a searchable database and for most collections there is a detailed list of the contents for each collection.

A keyword search for "radio program," for example, brings up an alphabetized list of radio programs from *Back to the Bible* through *Young People's Church of the Air* and within each program listing, specific personal and organizational collections that include materials about that program. Only one such program collection is noted below.

2071. Charles Edward Fuller Collection, 1940–1968. Includes clippings, sermons, radio logs, form letters to supporters, publicity materials and sound recordings of the *Old Fashioned Revival Hour.*

2072. National Religious Broadcasters Records, 1922, 1969–1989, 1991. Includes correspondence, reports, clippings, recordings and programs of the NAB which served as a professional association for persons involved in Protestant Christian radio and television broadcasting. There are very few files with information on the NBR prior to the mid-1960s.

Wichita State University
Library, Department of Special Collections
1845 Fairmount, Wichita, KS 67260
(316) 978-3590; Fax: (316) 978-3048
mary.nelson@wichita.edu; http://library.wichita.edu/
Contact: Mary Nelson

2073. Television and Radio Scripts of Kathleen Hite. Includes scripts for *Gunsmoke* (radio and television), 1957–1965, and other unidentified radio scripts. The catalog listing notes that Hite wrote for the following radio programs but it is not clear if scripts for any of the programs are included in the collection: *Fort Laramie, Rogers of the Gazette, Romance, The Ghost Walks, Night Beat, The Modern Adventures of Casanova, State Fair, The Perfect Crime, Will Rogers Country Editor* and the *Lux Summer Theatre.* Check unpublished finding aid for more information on the unidentified scripts.

Will Rogers Memorial Museum
1720 Will Rogers Boulevard, Claremore, OK 74018
(918) 341-0719
wrinfo@willrogers.com; www.willrogers.com

2074. Will Rogers Papers, 1880–1940. Contains correspondence, speeches, motion pictures, videocassettes, radio and movie scripts, telegrams, manuscripts, articles, contracts, recollections, books, maps, invitations, audio tapes, scrapbooks and photos relating to Rogers's career.

Williams College
Archives and Special Collections
Stetson Hall, Williamstown, MA 01267
(413) 597-2568; Fax: (413) 597-3931
archives@williams.edu
www.williams.edu/library/archives/pwc/pwc1.html

2075. Paul Whiteman Collection. Comprises some 4,000 arrangements of orchestral jazz dating from the 1920s to the 1940s as well as contemporary recordings, clippings files and small collections of photographs and artifacts. See extensive online finding aid for details.

Wisconsin Historical Society
816 State Street, Madison, WI 53706
(608) 264-6460; Fax: (608) 264-6486
http://arcat.library.wisc.edu

General comments: The vast majority of the individual special collections listed below are part of the Mass Communications History Collections (MCHC) and the collections in the Wisconsin Center for Film and Theater Research. Together, the two archives are a rich source of material relating to the Golden Age of Radio. The contents of both collections can be searched via a single integrated user friendly online catalog and extensive online finding aids.

The MCHC focuses on the importance of the mass media in twentieth century American life and holds the papers of hundreds of important individuals, corporations and professional organizations in the fields of journalism, broadcasting, advertising and public relations.

The Wisconsin Center for Film and Theater Research maintains over three hundred manuscript collections from outstanding playwrights, television and motion picture writers, producers, actors, designers, directors and production companies. In addition to the paper records, materials preserved include fifteen thousand motion pictures, television shows and videotapes, two million still photographs and promotional graphics and several thousand sound recordings.

2076. Agnes Moorehead Papers, 1923–1974. Papers relating to her work in radio, television, motion pictures and theater. Over half the collection is comprised of scrapbooks, 1928–1973, containing correspondence and fan mail, clippings, programs, photographs and memorabilia. Included are materials on her frequent radio appearances on *Cavalcade of America* and *Ceiling Unlimited*.

2077. Albert Lyman Warner Papers, 1923–1969. Papers of a capital reporter and radio commentator, including correspondence, biographical material and writings for publication and broadcast. Includes CBS scripts of general news and scripts for *Army Hour* for which Warner was a regular commentator. Includes recordings of *Army Hour* and *Three Star Extra*.

2078. Alice Keith Papers, 1906–1962. Papers of the founder of the National Academy of Broadcasting, Inc. and a teacher of music in schools and on the radio. Includes correspondence, articles and addresses, scrapbooks, press releases, printed materials, scripts and sound recordings. The correspondence is largely of a personal nature but letters written during the 1930s occasionally display her efforts to become recognized as a pioneer in educational broadcasting. Scripts and teachers' manuals relate to her position as broadcasting director for CBS's *American School of the Air*. Also includes scripts and recordings for several radio series used to promote NAOB as well as other instructional materials such as "How to Speak and Write for Radio," 1944, which she developed to teach broadcasting techniques.

2079. Aline W. Hazard Papers, 1938–1965. Papers of a broadcaster associated with WHA, Madison, WI relating chiefly to the *Homemaker Program* which she supervised. Includes listener correspondence, annual reports, committee minutes, 1938–1955, and a subject file containing scripts, circulars and information on program content.

2080. Allen Miller Papers, 1926–1949 and 1963. Papers relate to the beginnings of educational radio broadcasting. Includes minutes, 1926–1938, of the University of Chicago Radio Committee and papers on the Rocky Mountain Radio Council, Denver, 1945–1949, the University Broadcasting Council, Chicago, 1935–1938, and the *University of Chicago Roundtable*, 1938–1963.

2081. Alvin Boretz Papers, 1942–1998. Papers of a writer of dramatic series, specials and quiz programs for radio and television. Includes scripts and drafts for *Big Town* and some television programs. Also includes script for "Summer is Forever" aired on the *Children's Hour*.

2082. American Federation of Labor Records, 1888–1955. Includes three transcription discs for *The Labor Parade* issued by the Radio Division of the American Federation of Labor, 1938. It is likely these recordings were distributed to local unions.

2083. Av Westin Papers, 1945–1970. Papers of a news producer and executive with CBS, 1947–1967, and other stations. Radio related information includes CBS files containing correspondence and office memoranda to and from Fred W. Friendly, Richard S. Salant and others, news scripts, program ideas and clippings and news releases about Westin, programs he produced and CBS in general. Two scrapbooks pertain to radio programs on which he worked as a field reporter: *The People Act* and *Nation's Nightmare* of which there are 20 recorded episodes.

2084. *The Big News*, 1957–1958. Two promotional sound recordings of major news stories covered by CBS correspondents in 1957 and 1958. Among the correspondents featured are Walter Cronkite, Eric Sevareid, Robert Pierpoint, Edward R. Murrow, Daniel Schorr and Howard K. Smith. Other subjects or voices include Frank Zeidler, Milwaukee Braves, Dwight Eisenhower, Richard Nixon, Charles De Gaulle, the Cold War and changes in the Russian leadership, integration and Little Rock and Middle Eastern events.

2085. Bill Gavin Reports, 1958–1976. Reports on music trends prepared by a radio program consultant for use by program managers and disc jockeys in programming. Includes bi-weekly reports, chiefly 1958–1971, record evaluations and recommended playlists, information on personnel changes among local San Francisco Bay Area radio stations and Gavin's comments on radio programming and the music industry.

2086. Broadcast Music, Inc. Records, 1951–1966. Educational radio scripts distributed to local stations by a music-licensing corporation. Includes sample scripts for *Book Parade*, *The World of the Mind*, and *The American Story*. Also includes the complete run of the sub-series *A. Lincoln, 1809–1865* written by Bruce Catton, Allen Nevins, Carl Sandburg and other Lincoln scholars and some promotional materials for *The World of the Mind*.

2087. Bryson B. Rash Papers, 1956–1973. Papers of an award-winning news broadcaster with WRC/WRC-TV in Washington, DC consisting chiefly of scripts of human interest stories broadcast on *Emphasis*, *Monitor* and other NBC network radio news programs and television editorials on local, national, and international news events.

2088. C. E. Hooper, Inc. Records, 1936–1951. Records of the market research firm specializing in radio and television audience measurement. The collection consists primarily of *Hooperatings*, reports on radio listening on major network stations in selected U.S. cities, 1936–1947. Also includes newsletters, pamphlets and related material produced by the firm for its subscribers.

2089. C. Everett Kemp Papers, 1930–1954. Papers of an actor, producer and writer of *Happy Hollow*, a CBS dramatic serial which originated at KMBC, Kansas City, MO. Includes two 1936 scripts and promotional materials.

2090. C. Nielsen Company Reports, 1943–1957. Reports of the market research firm (1923–) best known for its ratings of network radio and television programs. Consists primarily of Nielsen Radio Indexes, 1943–1957, and Nielsen Television Indexes, 1951–1953, which summarize and analyze Nielsen's bi-weekly reports and includes several types of audience measurements. Also includes miscellaneous reports on CBS sustaining programs, 1943, D-Day listening, 1944, and the purchasing habits of television viewers, 1957.

2091. Carlton E. Morse Scripts, 1936–1959. Scripts for *One Man's Family* on seven reels of microfilm.

2092. *Cavalcade of America* Broadcasts, n.d. Twenty one recordings of selected episodes of *Cavalcade of America*. The discs were distributed by the National Association of High School Principals.

2093. CBS News Parodies, n.d. Sound recording of four parodies of CBS news figures and operations by Ham O'Hara. Spoofed is Walter Cronkite's D-Day re-visited interview with Dwight Eisenhower (featuring Mel Brooks), *The Bird,* an international satellite broadcast, *I've Got a Secret,* and Harry Reasoner's narration of a version of "The Night Before Christmas" entitled "Cronkiter's Christmas Carol."

2094. Cecil Brown Papers, 1907–1987. Contains mostly scripts for various radio and television programs, 1940–1967, including scripts of his news programs broadcast over the MBS. Also contains some manuscripts, diaries, scrapbooks, audio recordings, photographs and correspondence, including letters dealing with Brown's difficulties with networks and sponsors.

2095. Charles Collingwood Papers, 1943–1985. Includes personal and biographical files, professional and audience correspondence, speeches and writings, background material and scripts for *Edward R. Murrow and the News, Report to the West* and other CBS television news programs.

2096. Chet Huntley Papers, 1957–1974. With the exception of his farewell remarks broadcast on the *Huntley-Brinkley Report,* the holdings relate entirely to radio. The two series for which coverage is most complete are his daily five-minute editorials, *Perspective on the News* and *Emphasis: Plain Talk.* The tape recordings consist of editorials prepared under the auspices of Horizon Communications Corporation following his retirement from NBC.

2097. Chicago, Milwaukee, St. Paul and Pacific Railroad Company. Four anniversary recordings made at WTMJ, Milwaukee, WI of the program celebrating the ninetieth anniversary of the Chicago, Milwaukee, St. Paul and Pacific Railroad, November 20, 1940.

2098. Clifton M. Utley Papers, 1930–1960. The bulk of the collection consists of scripts, both radio and television, 1930–1960, with only three scripts prior to 1935. Includes scripts for special programs such as *The War That Must Not Come,* April 16, 1946, and for occasions on which Utley substituted for other commentators such as H. V. Kaltenborn and Joseph Harsch. Also includes scripts for dramatizations in which Utley participated or which he moderated such as the historical series entitled *We Came This Way,* 1944–1945, and *Quiz Kids,* 1946. Also includes fan mail and other correspondence. Utley broadcast his news reports and commentary over several Chicago stations, but the majority of the work originated from the NBC stations WMAQ and WNBQ, either for local or network broadcast.

2099. Columbia Broadcasting System, Inc. Records, 1958–1971. Miscellaneous material, consisting of recordings of *We Take You Back,* a 1958 radio program with excerpts from World War II news reports and commentary by Robert Trout and Edward R. Murrow and of *Calendar Days,* a 1962 tribute to radio with interviews of Murrow and Hans V. Kaltenborn by Harry Reasoner.

2100. Columbia University Oral History Research Office, 1950–1951. Microfilm copies of interviews of Phillips Carlin, Hans V. Kaltenborn, Raymond F. Guy, Mark Woods and William S. Hedges compiled by the Radio Unit of the Oral History Collection of Columbia University.

2101. Cooperative Analysis of Broadcasting, Inc., Reports, 1932–1946. Reports on radio listening by Crossley, Inc., a market research firm known for its "Crossley Ratings." The reports concern network programming, advertising in selected cities and audience composition and behavior.

2102. Dane County (Wis.) Labor Defense Council Records, 1938–1952. Consists mainly of radio scripts, 1941–1944, for broadcasts sponsored by a labor group organized during World War II and reactivated during the Korean War to coordinate union aid to government war programs. Topics covered in the scripts include war profits, overtime duty, the draft, workers' education and labor's attitude toward the national war effort.

2103. Dane County (Wis.) Bar Association Records, 1858, 1879–1994. Includes scripts of a weekly public service radio program, 1947–1948.

2104. David Brinkley Papers, 1960–1969, bulk 1965–1969. Consists mostly of mail from television viewers and radio listeners. Contains reactions to particular broadcasts of the *Huntley-Brinkley Report, David Brinkley's Journal* and other programs. Also includes papers relating to two radio programs: *Emphasis* and *On The Hour.*

2105. David P. Harmon Papers, 1941–1964. Consists entirely of annotated script material for radio and television series, including, for radio, *America on the Air, Cavalcade of America, Gang Busters* and *Now Hear This.*

2106. David Victor Papers, 1938–1964. Consists entirely of scripts and related production information for numerous radio and television series and pilots. The majority of the scripts, many of which are annotated, pertain to the radio series *The Hedda Hopper Show, The Mel Blanc Show* and *Let George Do It.*

2107. Dwight Woodward Interview Recording, 1953. Tape recorded interview with Dwight "Woody" Woodward, May 15, 1953, broadcast on WKOW, Sextonville, WI concerning the reconstruction and flight of a 1916 Morse Scout World War I fighter airplane recorded at Truax Field in Madison, WI and broadcast live as part of the series *The Old and the New at Truax Field.*

2108. E. P. H. (Edgar Percy Horace) James Papers, 1922–1976. Papers of an advertising and public relations executive instrumental in the establishment of advertising policy for radio and television. Includes correspondence, speeches and writings and a variety of advertising material, the bulk of which relates to James's employment at NBC as sales and promotion manager, 1927–1941, at MBS as vice-president in charge of advertising, promotion and research, 1946–1949, and at the A. C. Nielsen Company as vice-president in charge of new services, 1954–1971.

2109. Earl Wilson Papers, 1936–1964. Includes scattered radio scripts and recordings of *The Earl Wilson Show,* 1945–

1950, and *It Happened Last Night* and photographs.

2110. Ed Sullivan Papers, 1920–1974. Radio materials consist of scripts for *Ed Sullivan Entertains, Summer Silver Theatre* and various other programs and benefits.

2111. Edgar B. Gordon Papers, 1906–1961. Papers of a music professor at the University of Wisconsin and pioneer in radio education. Contains correspondence, articles and addresses, books, reminiscences and biographical material. Includes papers relating to *Journey in Music Land*, a program Gordon developed and directed for WHA, 1931–1955.

2112. Edward Montague Kirby Reminiscences, 1964. Reminiscences concerning radio broadcasting during World War II by a chief of the Radio Branch of the War Department's Public Relations Bureau, 1941–1945. The recollections encompass mobilization, the Armed Forces Radio Service and a review of programs produced by the commercial networks under army auspices.

2113. Edward P. Morgan Papers, 1923-1986. The bulk of the collection consists of annotated scripts for *Edward P. Morgan and the News*. Also includes opening and closing messages which reflect the views of the AFL-CIO, Morgan's sponsor, correspondence and over 100 recordings.

2114. Edward R. Murrow Recording, 1958. Recording of *We Take You Back*, March 13, 1958. The recording consists of excerpts from commentators' reports made from around the world on outstanding news events, ca. 1938–ca. 1945, with commentaries by Robert Trout and Murrow.

2115. Edward Tomlinson Papers, 1911–1972. Papers of an author, journalist and radio broadcaster who specialized in coverage of Latin American affairs. The bulk of the collection consists of radio scripts and writings, many in draft form, for magazines and newspapers. The radio scripts pertain to *Three Star Extra, The Other Americas, Paths to Prosperity* and news broadcasts.

2116. Elizabeth A. Charles and Charles E. Kading Papers, 1893-1976. Papers of a Wisconsin Congressman, including correspondence about the Federal Radio Commission.

2117. Ernest Kinoy Papers, 1948–1987. Papers of a journalist and writer for radio, television and theater. Majority of collection consists of scripts for radio and television. Among the best represented radio series are *Best Plays, Doctor Six-Gun, Five Star Matinee, Hollywood Love Story, The Marriage, My Secret Story, NBC Theatre, NBC University Theatre, Nick Carter, Woman in Love,* and *X Minus One.*

2118. Esther Van Wagoner Tufty Papers, 1910–1986. Collection documents Tufty's newspaper career and her work in radio and television broadcasting with her own programs as well as appearances as a guest on numerous other programs and activities in several professional organizations, including the American Women in Radio and Television, the American Newspaper Women's Club and the Women's National Press Club. Contains scripts of *Headlines From Washington, Tufty Topics, Panning the Press, Home* and others. Also includes tape and disc recordings of her programs and other broadcasts plus personal reminiscences, biographical interviews and memorabilia.

2119. *Fibber McGee and Molly* Scripts, 1935–1950. Microfilm of sponsor's corrected copies of scripts, including commercials, preserved by Johnson's Wax, a client of the advertising agency Needham, Harper and Steers. Also includes scripts for the series *Hap Hazard, 1941.*

2120. Florence Cornell Gomme Papers, 1932–1966. Includes scripts for *Adventures of a Modern Mother*, a dramatic series broadcast by NBC, 1940–1941, which was written by Gomme. Also includes a folder of photocopied memorabilia and correspondence.

2121. Frank E. Mason Papers, 1931–1945. Papers of a NBC vice-president in charge of Information. Contains correspondence, telephone logs, appointment books, speeches and reports. Includes letters and memoranda relating to NBC's development of short wave facilities, international broadcasting and planning for wartime broadcasting. Also includes speeches on newspaper-radio relations, short wave broadcasting and propaganda.

2122. Frank J. Young Papers, 1889–1968. Fragmentary personal and professional papers of a New York publicist and journalist. Contains correspondence, resumes, press releases, drafts of public relations projects, newspaper clippings about his career, including press releases for NBC, 1951–1952, and station and public relations records for WNEW, 1959–1962.

2123. Fred Coe Papers, 1949–1985. Papers document Coe's work as a producer and director in the theatre, television and film. However, the collection does include recordings of the radio detective series *Yours Truly, Johnny Dollar* in which Coe was not involved.

2124. Frederick W. Ford Papers, 1940–1982, bulk 1958-1968. Papers of an attorney, career government employee and former FCC member and chairman. Includes speeches, writings, correspondence, biographical clippings and subject files relating to equal time and political broadcasting, the fairness doctrine, UHF/VHF allocations, the Legislative Oversight Subcommittee's investigations of the FCC during the 1950s and other topics.

2125. Friends of Vic and Sade Newsletters, 1972–1988. Newsletters from an organization of collectors and fans of *Vic and Sade* containing news about members, collectibles and information on the program's scripts and productions.

2126. Gerald A. Bartell Papers, 1958–1977. A Wisconsin broadcasting executive, the 1958–1969 portion of the collection includes correspondence and subject files relating to Bartell's personal business ventures in the field of radio and TV. Includes some unidentified sound recordings, possibly of Bartell's radio scripts, n.d.

2127. Gillette Rubber Company Scripts, 1934–1935. Includes scripts for the *Morning Cheer, Bear* and *Magic Number* programs sponsored by the Gillette Rubber Company and broadcast over WTAQ, Eau Claire, WI. Scripts include advertising for the Gillette Rubber Company, jokes, humorous sketches, and stories. Also includes a folder containing historical information about WTAQ.

2128. *Great Gildersleeve* Scripts, 1942–1954. Microfilm of sponsor's corrected copies of scripts, including commercials.

2129. Gunnar Back Papers, 1931–1966. Fragmentary papers of radio and television news broadcaster Gunnar Back, including biographical clippings, scripts and other writings, publicity, photographs, sound and video recordings and correspondence. Because of the fragmentary nature of the papers, the value of the collection lies primarily in the events Back covered rather than its biographical information. Includes news and entertainment scripts Back wrote for KFAB/KFOR, Lincoln, NE , WJSV, Washington, DC and for *Whatever Happened To*, broadcast on WTOP. Also includes recorded transcripts of *Crossfire*, the ABC news interview program, transcripts of *Congress Today, America's Town Meeting of the Air* and *Americans At Work* and recordings of *The Lonesome Road*, a radio documentary about alcoholism as well as raw tape interviews apparently used in editing the broadcast. Also includes transcripts for a *Lonesome Road* program dealing with venereal disease. Photographs are primarily snapshots of Back broadcasting; most are unidentified, but there are snapshots of him with some people prominent in politics and entertainment and also of Back at WJNO, FL. Also includes material related to the *Officers Conference,* an interview program about world affairs that was aired by the military broadcast network (AFRS ?) in the 1950s.

2130. Hans V. Kaltenborn Papers, 1883–1964. Papers of the "Dean of American Radio Commentators" who introduced editorial analysis to radio news broadcasting. The bulk of the collection is made up of correspondence, scripts and recordings but there are also business and professional papers, book and article manuscripts, notes and scrapbooks. Radio scripts comprise a virtually complete record of his prepared broadcasts for *Kaltenborn Edits the News* and for a number of other series and specials. Supplementing the papers are more than 500 sound recordings of his regularly scheduled news broadcasts, chiefly 1940–1948, and other programs in which he was a participant. Correspondence includes Kaltenborn's involvement with the Association of Radio Television News Analysts, the Broadcast Pioneers, the Overseas Press Club, the Radio-Television Committee of the American Civil Liberties Union and the Kaltenborn Foundation.

2131. Hal Kanter Papers, 1941–1977. Papers of a writer, producer and director of numerous television comedies. Catalog listing notes that the collection includes "scripts for radio programs" but only identifies the *Beulah Show.* Other papers may only deal with television. Check with repository for more information.

2132. Harold A. Engel Papers, 1922–1968. Papers of an educational broadcaster associated with WHA and WHA-TV, Madison, WI, 1931–1968. Engel was an assistant director in charge of legislative and public relations. The collection deals exclusively with educational broadcasting and contains articles, clippings, surveys and reports. Most documentation concerns the development of WHA, particularly its early history. The balance deals with Engel's other activities in educational broadcasting with the Wisconsin Broadcasters Association, the National Association of FM Broadcasters, the University of Wisconsin Radio and Television Committee and other Wisconsin educational stations.

2133. Harold B. McCarty Papers, 1933–1986. Papers of a man who began his career with WHA in 1929 and was appointed the station's program director in 1931. McCarty originated the *Wisconsin School of the Air* program. For 36 years he was director of the Wisconsin State Broadcasting System

and executive director of the Wisconsin Radio and Television Council. Papers include correspondence, reports, newspaper clippings, magazine articles, budget material, scripts, listener letters, newsletters, organizational material for WHA-TV, State Radio Council meetings, minutes and reports, National Association for Educational Broadcasters newsletters and reports, program schedules for various educational stations and personnel files. Note: Additional collections include material relating to WHA.

2134. Harry Sosnik Papers, 1920–1995. Papers, primarily comprised of musical scores and parts, of a composer, arranger and conductor for radio and television and vice-president in charge of music for ABC. Also includes non radio sound recordings.

2135. Harry W. Flannery Papers, 1927–1968. Papers of a foreign correspondent, news analyst, author and AFL-CIO radio coordinator consisting chiefly of books, articles, World War II communiques, plays, scripts for films and radio programs, speeches and over 700 tapes. Radio programs represented in the collection include *John Vandercook and the News, Labor Answers Your Questions, Labor Reports to the Nation, Washington Reports to the Nation* and *As We See It.* Also includes extensive script files for programs broadcast by the CBS West Coast Network and KMOX, St. Louis. Papers involving listener mail from the late 1940s are noteworthy for their concern with alleged communist influence in California.

2136. Harry Walter Sova Compilation. An indexed compendium of important events in radio broadcasting which took place during 1927 and were reported in "The New York Times."

2137. Henry Cassidy Papers, 1934–1985. A newspaper, radio and television journalist, Cassidy spent most of his career as a foreign correspondent and executive for the Associated Press, NBC and Radio Free Europe. His radio scripts form the bulk of the collection and include scripts written in Paris, 1945–1950, for *Report on Europe* and those written in the United States, 1953–1955, for *Heart of the News, News of the World, World News Roundup* and other programs.

2138. Hilmar Robert Baukhage Papers, 1906–1962. Papers of a writer, newspaperman and Washington news commentator for NBC and ABC. Contains scripts, journals, speeches and recordings. Scripts and discs relate almost exclusively to Baukhage's regularly scheduled ABC program *Baukhage Talking.* Among the news events covered in the scripts are World War II, the 1944 political conventions, President Roosevelt's death, Truman's inauguration, the Nuremberg trials, the Cold War and the Berlin crisis.

2139. Howard K. (Howard Kingsbury) Smith Papers, 1941–1963. Papers consist of material on Smith's career with both the ABC and CBS networks. CBS radio scripts pertain to his work as a World War II correspondent and to his postwar commentaries.

2140. Howard Rodman Papers, 1942–1977. Collection documents the entire span of Rodman's career from his early days as a writer of short stories to a script writer for the broadcast media and a creator of television series. Best coverage of his broadcasting work is provided by files on United Nations Radio. Includes some unidentified tape recordings.

2141. Howard Teichmann Papers, 1939–1972. Papers of a

playwright, writer and educator, primarily comprised of scripts for radio and plays. Radio materials include *Cavalcade of America, Treasury Hour, Ford Theater, Theatre U.S.A.* and soap operas such as *Road of Life* and *Valiant Lady.*

2142. Hugh Carlson Recordings, 1939–1944. Dubbed tape recordings of four *Fibber McGee and Molly* shows, 1939, including segments with guest ZaSu Pitts and Harold Peary and of 24 *Vic and Sade* programs, November, 1943 and September, 1944.

2143. Irna Phillips Papers, 1931–1968. Papers of a creator and writer of radio and television soap operas. Includes scripts by Phillips herself and by Radio Scripts, Inc., to which she was a consultant, including outlines, advertising copy and correspondence with listeners, viewers, networks and advertising agencies. Includes *Another World, Brighter Day, The Guiding Light, Right to Happiness, Road of Life, Today's Children, Woman in White* and many other daytime serials.

2144. Isabel H. Baumann Interview, 1980. Sound recording of an interview conducted in April, 1980 by Dale Treleven of the Historical Society with Isabel Baumann, a Dane County, WI farm organization activist. Includes a discussion of Baumann's work with the series, *We Say What We Think Club.*

2145. Jane Crusinberry Papers, 1933–1960, 1983. Papers of the author of the radio serial *The Story of Mary Marlin.* Includes a complete run of scripts of the original show, 1934–1945, of an Australian version, 1959–1960, character sketches, show music, outlines, publicity, commercials, reference material, scenarios, story summaries and synopses. Also includes personal and business papers and correspondence with substitute authors, advertising agencies, networks, lawyers and Procter and Gamble, the show's sponsor.

2146. John Charles Daly Papers, 1935–1967. The collection is best for the years 1956–1967 and includes a wide variety of materials pertaining to his association with ABC as a newsman and vice-president of news, special events and public affairs, 1953–1967. Fragmentary early material includes a scrapbook on events covered by Daly as White House correspondent for WJSV, Washington, DC, 1938–1939, correspondence and scripts for *CBS Is There* (later known as *You Are There), The Front Page,* his coverage of the Italian theater during World War II and "The Sangamon," an Edgar Lee Masters radio play. There are no scripts dating from the later period covered but there are office memos, fan mail and publicity for Daly's television programs. Additional files pertain to ABC news administration and operation, outside speaking engagements, involvement with professional groups such as the National Association of Radio and Television Broadcasters and coverage of political conventions. Collection includes three disc recordings and 53 photographs.

2147. John K. M. McCaffery Recordings, 1956–1962. Recordings of a broadcaster and editor consisting mainly of *Books and Voices,* a radio series moderated for Westinghouse Broadcasting Co., 1956–1957, and *Progress,* a series of public service interviews prepared for General Electric, 1961–1962.

2148. John MacVane Papers, 1935-1977. Papers of a radio and television news broadcaster noted for his coverage of World War II and the United Nations. The bulk of the collection consists of scripts written for NBC, ABC, NET, CBC and the Voice of America plus speeches and writings. The scripts chiefly concern the North African theater during World War II and the development of the United Nations, 1950–1977, and were written for such programs as *ABC Evening News, Issues and Answers, News Around the World, United or Not?* and *Army Hour.* Written material is supplemented by films and recordings. There are also some letters relating to MacVane's presidency of the Association of Radio and Television News Analysts and the United Nations Correspondents Association.

2149. John Stanley Penn Papers, 1922–1953. Correspondence collected by Penn, a broadcast historian, concerning the early history of WHA, the radio station of the University of Wisconsin-Madison, and the work of physicist Earl M. Terry. Also includes an address by Terry, ca. 1925, a WHA program log, 1922–1925, and a history of the station by Harold A. Engel.

2150. John Wingate Interviews, 1957. Audio recording of interviews conducted by Wingate, October 8–11, 1957, on *Night Beat* on WABD with Arthur V. Crowley, J. Bracken Lee, Victor Riesel, Buff Donelli, Robert Elliot Fitch, Stuart Davis, John D. Odom and Helen Sobell dealing chiefly with labor and politics.

2151. Johnny and Penny Olson Papers, 1927–1997. Papers document the personal and professional activities of two radio and television personalities. Johnny Olson worked as an announcer at WTMJ, Milwaukee, 1933–1944, and WJZ, New York, 1944, before going on to emcee, with Penny as hostess, a number of radio shows, including *Ladies Be Seated* and *Rumpus Room.* Papers include scripts, correspondence, gag material and audience letters and response cards relating to Olson's radio career. The collection also includes unprocessed sound recordings of Olson's early radio program *The Price Is Right.*

2152. Joseph C. Harsch Papers, 1947–1960. Includes radio and television scripts, 1940s–1970, aired on NBC, CBS and BBC, including *Background, Meaning of the News* and *Report from Washington.* Also includes correspondence. Material reflects Harsch's varying assignments from coverage of the Harlan trial in Kentucky to the London Naval Conference, Germany and the Pacific theater during World War II and post-war foreign affairs responsibilities in London and Washington, D.C.

2153. Joseph Jastrow Papers, 1883–1942. Papers of an experimental and developmental psychologist best known for his NBC program *Keeping Mentally Fit* and newspaper columns on psychology for the lay person.

2154. Judith Waller Interview, 1951. Transcript of an interview with a public affairs director for WMAQ, the NBC owned station in Chicago. Topics discussed include the history of the station during its ownership by the "Chicago Daily News," CBS and NBC plus instructional and public service programming such as the *University of Chicago Roundtable.* Also covers other programs originating in Chicago such as *Amos 'n' Andy.*

2155. Kenyon Nicholson Papers, 1915–1960. Papers of a playwright, screenwriter and editor consisting chiefly of synopses, treatments, scenarios and scripts for Nicholson's work in theater, motion pictures and radio. Includes scripts for *Cavalcade of America* which Nicholson produced and *Theatre Guild on the Air*, a.k.a. *United States Steel Hour*.

2156. Kirk Douglas Papers, 1945–1969. The Radio files date from the late 1940s and include scripts and correspondence regarding plays and radio broadcasts on which Douglas appeared, including *Prudential Family Hour of Stars, Escape* and *Suspense*. Also includes radio adaptations of two of Douglas's films, "The Strange Love of Martha Ivers" and "The Champion."

2157. M. C. Batsel Papers, 1921–1923. Papers of an RCA engineer consisting of a 1921 catalog of Westinghouse Electric and Manufacturing Co. equipment, a booklet issued on the first anniversary of KDKA, a lecture service pamphlet on radio by S. M. Kintner, a Westinghouse engineer and several speeches by Westinghouse executives and engineers, including one by H. P. Davis, "the father of radio broadcasting."

2158. *March of Minnesota* Broadcast Recording, n.d. Transcription discs of "Austin," an episode of the radio series *March of Minnesota* apparently broadcast on WCCO, Minneapolis. Program was a dramatized history of Austin stressing the role of the meatpacking industry and includes studio interviews with four Austin residents followed by music by the Minnesota Symphony.

2159. Margaret S. Harding Scripts, 1930. Scripts for *Author's Nights* sponsored by the University of Minnesota Press, January 8–22, 1930, based on the book "America in the Forties."

2160. Martin Codel Papers. Collection consists of bound and unbound trade journals and clipping scrapbooks relating to the history and development of the radio and television broadcasting industry. Includes bound "Yearbooks of Broadcasting" magazine, 1961–1962 and 1964. Also includes papers relating to the daily radio column that Codel wrote for the Radio News Bureau and which appeared in a number of newspapers across the country.

2161. Mass Communications Ephemera Collection, 1930–1980. Collection includes a wide variety of printed ephemera (e.g. pamphlets, bulletins, newsletters, publicity and promotional materials, programs, directories, reports, studies and related materials) separated from the manuscript collections covering different aspects of broadcasting. Includes recordings of *Dr. Crane's Radio Talks,* Volume I, 1948, a collection of broadcasts by Dr. Crane, a Northwestern University psychologist, on topics concerning applied psychology for the lay person.

2162. Max Simon Ehrlich Papers, 1939–1964. Includes scripts and drafts for *The Crime Cases of Warden Lawes, Big Town* and *Big Story* on radio, scripts for some television programs and other papers.

2163. Melvyn Douglas Papers, 1892–1983. A portion of the collection includes scripts and recordings of various radio plays and documentation pertaining to various commercial recordings in which Douglas was featured.

2164. Merrill Mueller Papers, 1935–1976. Papers documenting Mueller's news reporting for NBC, 1944–1968. Includes radio scripts and sound recordings.

2165. Millard Lampell Papers, 1936-1997. Radio files contain scripts for *Green Valley, U.S.A, It's the Navy, The Long Way Home, Men, Machines, and Victory, On the Beam, First in the Air* and various United Nations Radio and public service programs. Also contains sound recordings for several of the programs and some general correspondence concerning Lampell's wartime broadcasting for the Army Air Force.

2166. Milwaukee Civic Broadcasting Association, Inc. Contract, 1924. Operating agreement establishing WCAY, the first commercial radio station in Milwaukee.

2167. Monona Broadcasting Company Records, 1945–1968. Business records of Monona Broadcasting which operated the ABC affiliate WKOW, Madison, WI, 1945–1960. Papers document the corporation's organization and operation, as well as its liquidation and sale to Midcontinent Broadcasting Company in 1960.

2168. Morris S. Novik Papers, 1950-1969. Contains scripts and films collected by a radio and television executive who served as media consultant for the AFL and the AFL-CIO. Included are opening and closing radio continuities, 1950–1952, for *Frank Edwards and the News* which states organized labor's position on the Cold War, communist subversion, the elections of 1950 and 1952 and other issues.

2169. Moss Hart and Kitty Carlisle Papers, 1922–1988. Contains correspondence, manuscripts, diaries, scripts, photographs and scrapbooks.

2170. Nat Hinken Papers, 1932–1968. The Radio files contain scripts from Hinken's early career in radio, including *The Grouch Club* and *The Magnificent Montague* as well as extensive scripts and production information for the *Fred Allen Show* for which Hinken was head writer for seven years and the *Milton Berle Show* with which he was associated, 1946–1949. Also includes a sound recording of the November 25, 1945 performance of the Berle show. Bulk of collection pertains to Hinken's work in television.

2171. National Association of Broadcasters Records, 1938–1982. Although most NAB activities concern the establishment of broadcasting codes and support of the industry in matters relating to government regulation, the bulk of the collection pertains to the association's research function. Includes materials on studies and surveys by the Broadcast Measurement Bureau of radio audiences and the National Opinion Research Center on public attitudes toward radio in the 1940s.

2172. National Association of Educational Broadcasters Records, 1925–1977, bulk 1950–1970. Includes correspondence, reports, clippings, speeches of president William G. Harley, files of the Office of Research and Development and of National Educational Radio (a division of the NAEB), a newsletter and a small publication file. The largest part of the collection is a subject file which documents the NAEB's board of directors, committees, conventions, conferences, seminars and workshops. Includes photographs relating to two radio programs, *World Neighbors* and *Report From Europe,* and tape recordings.

2173. National Broadcasting Company Records, 1921–1969. The collection offers representative coverage of operations in advertising, public relations, research, sales, news and public affairs broadcasting from the 1930s through the 1950s. Includes correspondence, memoranda, reports, logs, scripts, promotional material, publications, scenic designs, photographs, a few production files and a library of scripts and recordings. Limited legal and financial records. The finding aid has been split into 15 smaller documents. To get all fifteen, search for "National Broadcasting Company" as a Collection Author. Most radio program information is in Part 4 for which there is a detailed online finding aid. At the very end of the finding aid, there is an index of correspondents and of scripts. The scripts are arranged by genre and include the program name, dates, and box and folder number in which they appear. One of the categories is "commemorative programs" Most, but not all, of the programs are represented by single scripts.

2174. National Broadcasting Company, Inc, 1956 and 1957 Radio Broadcasts. Listed as two separate collections, the first collection features *Salute to Radio*, a review of the highlights in radio broadcasting history, narrated by H. V. Kaltenborn, broadcast May 15, 1956, on NBC's *Recollections at 30* series celebrating the network's 30th anniversary. The second collection, done for the same Series, includes H. V. Kaltenborn's 35th anniversary in radio, April 3, 1957, and other highlights of early radio programs and personalities such as Rudy Vallee, Clark and McCulla, Lum and Abner, Al Jolson, Frances Langford, Fred Allen and Portland Hoffa, Tom Cokely, Fanny Brice, Joe Penner, Ginger Rogers, Mickey Rooney, Bob Hope, Brenda and Cobina, Bob Burns and Judy Garland.

2175. Ned Calmer Papers, 1928–1965. Includes CBS radio scripts of his coverage of World War II in Europe, post-war documentaries and transcripts from the CBS Rome news bureau, 1951–1953, and from *The World Tonight*, 1961–1965. Also includes other papers.

2176. Newton N. Minow Papers, 1954–1965. Papers include Minow's tenure as chairman of the FCC, 1961–1963.

2177. Orestes H. Caldwell Papers, 1927–1955. One of the original commissioners of the Federal Radio Commission, the papers include scripts for Caldwell's weekly program *Radio Magic*, 1939–1942, and other broadcasts.

2178. Orson Welles Papers, 1938–1941. A very small collection containing some papers, scripts and recordings. The only radio related item is a recording of the "War of the Worlds," *Mercury Theatre of the Air* program.

2179. Pacifica Foundation Records, 1949–1976. Papers of the Foundation's four FM stations: KPFA, Berkeley, CA, KPFK, Los Angeles, CA, WBAI, New York City and KPFT, Houston, TX. Coverage is best for programming and operations of the individual stations. The files include a fairly comprehensive collection of program guides for KPFA, KPFK and WBAI and operational material chiefly for KPFA and KPFK. Although the remainder of the collection pertains to Pacifica in general, there is little documentation on overall policymaking. One box contains correspondence, memos, a printed history, personnel lists, financial information, program and station guidelines, newsletters, minutes of national meetings and general information on affiliates and tape sales. Another half box concerns investigations of Pacifica by the U.S. Senate and the FCC over alleged communist infiltration

and the use of obscenity on the air.

2180. Paddy Chayefsky Papers, 1937–1972. Papers of a writer for stage, screen, radio and television. Includes scripts for two radio plays: "The Meanest Man in the World," broadcast January 8, 1952 on *Theatre Guild on the Air* and "The Spectacle Lady" broadcast on May 5, 1952 on *Cavalcade of America.*

2181. Pat Weaver Papers, 1922–1989. The bulk of the papers pertains to Weaver's professional career, beginning with his employment as an advertising executive at Young & Rubicam in the late 1940s. His subsequent years at NBC are also represented although the majority of the collection relates to Weaver's various endeavors after resigning as chairman of the network.

2182. Patrick H. Barnes Papers, 1918–1969. Papers, including a transcript of an oral history interview primarily concerning Barnes's experiences at WGN and WGT and some audio recordings. Also includes some television related material

2183. Patrick Hayes Papers, 1942–1981. Papers of a Washington, DC, cultural impresario consisting chiefly of scripts for *People and Events in the World of Music*, a cultural affairs program aired by WGMS. Also includes correspondence and other papers.

2184. Paul Rhymer Papers, 1928–1988. Papers of the radio and television writer best known for *Vic and Sade*. Scripts for this radio program comprise the bulk of the collection but there are also materials pertaining to *Keystone Chronicles, The Public Life of Cliff Norton* and other programs which Rhymer wrote either as an NBC staff member or as a freelance writer. Also includes a few recordings of *Vic and Sade*, general correspondence, articles about Rhymer and Mrs. Rhymer's book about the *Vic and Sade* program.

2185. Perry Miller Adato Papers, 1940–1974. Includes papers dealing with *The 40's: The Great Radio Comedians*, a television documentary Adato produced and directed in 1972. Includes progressive script drafts and transcripts of interviews with Jack Benny, Edgar Bergen, George Burns, Bing Crosby, Jim Jordan and Arch Oboler.

2186. Perry Wolff Papers, 1945–1989. Papers relating to Wolff's career as a writer and producer of award-winning television documentaries best known for his work for CBS News. Also includes some WBBM scripts and material on documentary radio programs.

2187. Peter Lyon Papers, 1884–1998. Papers of a freelance writer of books, articles and radio scripts. The radio section contains correspondence and scripts for *Cavalcade of America, The Court of Missing Heirs, The Eternal Light, Labor for Victory, The March of Time, Win the War* and other programs and specials.

2188. Quincy Howe Papers, 1957–1958. Preliminary report on public service broadcasting by William Costello prepared for the Association of Radio Television News Analysts, 1957, together with a commentary on the same subject by news analyst Howe, then president of ARTNA.

2189. Radio Advertising Bureau Papers, 1951–1956. Records of an association of radio stations, networks and sales representatives founded in 1951 as the Broadcast Advertising Bureau, Inc. to promote the use of radio as an advertising medium. The collection consists of reports, lists, reprints of articles, radio spot announcements, summaries of research findings and some RAB publications. In addition, there are by-laws, minutes of an early membership meeting and a report on operations in 1951. The material illustrates the attempts to maintain the attraction of radio as an advertising medium in competition with newspapers, magazines and television. Particularly noteworthy are the files on car radio listening entitled "Listeners on Wheels," the files on television, and the series of twelve reports on the cumulative audience of advertising. There are also files on such targets of radio advertising as women and businessmen. Newsletters cover a wide variety of topics on radio advertising, from general promotion of the medium to specific advice on how to increase advertising effectiveness.

2190. Ralph Bellamy Papers, 1924–1988. Contains biographical materials, an oral history interview transcript, awards and certificates, newspaper clippings and reviews, correspondence, several programs scripts and other papers regarding plays, motion pictures, television mini-series and other papers. May not include any radio related material.

2191. Raymond Z. Henle Papers, 1883–1973. Papers of an NBC news commentator and newspaper journalist, consisting chiefly of material for his program *Three Star Extra* which was sponsored by the Sun Oil Company. Includes microfilmed scripts largely dating from January, 1956–May 26, 1965 and some editorials. For the period prior to 1955 the collection includes only a few scattered scripts but over 100 sound recordings. Also includes a small quantity of documentation relating to his broadcasting career with ABC and WOL.

2192. Rex Howell Broadcast Recording, 1953. *Yucca Flats Documentary,* a radio documentary made in 1953 by Reed Hixon and Howell, president of KREX/KREX-TV, Grand Junction, CO about the effectiveness and results of the first atomic bomb tests at Yucca Flats, NV.

2193. Robert Doyle Papers, 1935–1974, 1995. Papers and audio recordings of "Milwaukee Journal" reporter Bob Doyle, consisting of his programs broadcast over WTMJ, Milwaukee, WI during World War II about his experiences covering Wisconsin troops in the 32nd Division. Collection includes transcripts of programs and other papers.

2194. Robert E. Lee Papers, 1953–1981. Papers of a member of the FCC, including speeches and articles, correspondence, docket and subject files concerning obscenity in broadcasting, the development of UHF broadcasting, the Committee for the Full Development of All-Channel Television, congressional relations, the Catholic Apostolate of Mass Media which Lee helped found and other topics.

2195. Robert Edward Gard Papers, 1946–1976. Papers of an educator, writer, and founder-director of the Wisconsin Idea Theatre of the University of Wisconsin. The processed portion of the collection consists entirely of plays based on Wisconsin history and folklore which were written or narrated by Gard for the *Wisconsin College of the Air* and the *Wisconsin Idea Radio Theatre,* two series broadcast by WHA. One *College of the Air* production, "Lost Lady Elgin," is available on tape.

2196. Robert Goralski Papers, 1953–1986. Papers of a Washington, DC, correspondent for NBC and public relations director for the Gulf Oil Corporation. News scripts, 1961–1975, comprise the majority of the collection. Contents include scripts for *News on the Hour, Monitor, Today in Washington,* and *World News Roundup* plus scripts for Voice of America and television.

2197. Robert H. Fleming Papers, 1935–1966. Papers of a "Milwaukee Journal" reporter, ABC news broadcaster, and government official. Includes scripts for Fleming's appearances on *Edward P. Morgan and the News.* Of particular interest are files on Fleming's involvement with the National Association of Broadcasters and the Radio Television News Directors Association dealing with freedom of the press issues.

2198. Robert H. Segal Papers, 1945-1971. Scripts for radio dramas written, directed or produced by a cantor at Temple Beth-El in Cedarhurst, NY together with collected files on other religious broadcasts sponsored by various Jewish organizations such as the Jewish Theological Seminary and the American Zionist Council. Most extensively documented is *The Eternal Light* on which Segal was frequently featured as cantor.

2199. Robert K. McCormick Papers, 1941-1968. Consists of correspondence, an oral history interview, scripts for *Monitor, News on the Hour, Today in Washington, Weekend Report* and *World News Roundup* and subject files for NBC special and background reports.

2200. Robert Pierpoint Papers, 1943–1982. Papers and some sound recordings of the CBS news broadcaster. Note: Online information does not provide any details about the radio related portions of the collection.

2201. Robert R. Brown Papers, 1948–1958. Publicity material relating to Brown, considered the dean of religious broadcasting, whose weekly program, *Radio Chapel Service,* was broadcast from WOW, Omaha, NE.

2202. Rod Serling Papers, 1943–1971. Includes correspondence, scripts, speeches, articles, reports, press releases and clippings. Half of the collection consists of files on his produced and unproduced writings for television, motion pictures, radio and the theater. Note: As of 2005, the online description for the partially processed collection did not include any specific radio related information.

2203. Rogan Jones Letter, 1957. Letter, August 7, 1957, from Jones, a broadcast executive, describing his part in the litigation between the Associated Press and KVOS, Bellingham, WA which dealt with the right of radio stations to access and present news information to their audiences.

2204. Rudolph J. Topinka Papers, 1936–1991. A radio and television announcer, talk radio host and newspaper columnist best known for his association with WSAU and WSAU-TV, Wausau, WI. Collection consists of examples of his writings and scripts, clippings about his career and some listener mail. Audio recordings include examples of *55 Feedback,* early radio broadcasts, news, national and local musical performances and 1940 interviews with players for the Green Bay Packers recorded at WTAQ.

2205. Sig Mickelson Papers, 1947–1975. Professional papers include Mickelson's employment with CBS News, 1943–1961. Also contains personal papers.

2206. *Song of Liberty*, **1951.** Script from a dramatization of the Peshtigo Fire of 1871 broadcast on the Don Lee Broadcasting System, Hollywood, CA.

2207. Stanley I. (Stanislaus I.) Nastal Papers, 1922, 1934–1954. Papers of Nastal, a pioneer Milwaukee Polish-language radio broadcaster, and of his son, Stanley H., who succeeded him in 1947. The collection documents ethnic programming from the 1930s through the 1950s and includes biographical information, a copy of Nastal's reminiscences of service with Polish Volunteer Forces of the Canadian Army during World War I, advertising contracts, program logs and scripts. The logs, in English, are from *Our Polish Hour*, 1947–1954. The scripts, in Polish, are from *Theater of the Air* and daily serialized sketches. Also contains eleven tape recordings of broadcasts, primarily *Our Polish Hour*, ca. 1942–1947.

2208. State Historical Society of Wisconsin Recordings, 1946–1948. Forty eight transcription discs of the State Historical Society of Wisconsin broadcasts, including *Wisconsin Cavalcade*, broadcast by WKOW, WHA, WIBA and other stations.

2209. Susan Taylor White Papers, 1937–1979. A script writer for radio. The bulk of the collection consists of the scripts she wrote between 1943–1978, including *Merlin the Storyteller, Eye Witness, Cavalcade of America* and *Let's Meet the Ladies*. Some of the scripts include notes, research or memos relating to them. Also includes personal papers and tape recordings of some of the programs.

2210. *Theatre Guild on the Air* **Playbills, 1945–1947.** Playbills for several plays broadcast on the program.

2211. Theodore S. Delay: "An Historical Study of the Armed Forces Radio Service to 1946, 1951." Ph.D. dissertation done at the University of Southern California which incorporates an additional research study of *Command Performance*.

2212. Thomas L. Stix Papers, 1917–1974. Papers of a writer, storyteller and radio, television and literary talent agent. Stix conceived the idea of a talent agency for radio news commentators in the early 1940s and formed a company with CBS newsman John G. Gude. Their clients eventually included Eleanor Roosevelt, Raymond Gram Swing, Joseph C. Harsch, Fannie Hurst, William L. Shirer and Edward R. Murrow among others.

2213. *Town Meeting of the Air* **Broadcasts, 1954.** Two broadcasts of the program recorded in Madison, WI and sponsored by the State Historical Society of Wisconsin. Reel 1 contains "La Follette Liberalism: In Retrospect," June 26, 1954 (broadcast June 29th). Reel 2 contains 'The Role of Businessmen in American History," September 14, 1954.

2214. Victor C. Diehm Reminiscences, 1958. Brief recollections of a broadcasting executive, primarily concerning sports broadcasting by WRAW, Reading, PA in 1929 by means of Western Union wire reports.

2215. Wade Barnes Scripts, 1938–1941. Scripts for music, public service and dramatic programs prepared for presentation on the NBC-owned station WTAM, Cleveland, OH.

2216. Wakelin McNeel Papers, 1926–1951. Papers of a 4-H Club and conservation leader on the staff of the University of Wisconsin Extension Service. Includes mail pertaining to *Afield With Ranger Mac*, an educational program which McNeel conducted for WHA for 20 years.

2217. WCBS/WCBS-TV Records, 1965–1978. Although outside the general time frame for the Golden Age of Radio, of possible interest to researchers are the transcripts in this collection of the program *WCBS Radio Looks at Television* which featured interviews with such prominent media personalities and critics as Goodman Ace, Roone Arledge, Kenneth A. Cox, Walter Cronkite, Fred W. Friendly, Mark Goodson, Ernest Kinoy, Millard Lampell, Lee Loevinger, Elmer W. Lower, Richard A. R. Pinkham, Hubbell Robinson, Jr., Morley Safer, Ed Sullivan, David Susskind, Harriet Van Horne, Sylvester L. Weaver, Jr., John F. White, Perry Wolff and David L. Wolper. The collection also includes two interviews with Susskind.

2218. Wendell Hall Papers, 1915–1962, 1967. Papers of an early radio performer who was most famous for his composition "It Ain't Gonna Rain No Mo." The collection consists of biographical material and microfilmed scrapbooks, fan mail, miscellaneous printed matter and recordings, including one with Milton Berle.

2219. WHA Radio and Television Station Records, 1920–1989. Only a small portion of the sound recordings in the collection have been processed. These include recordings of "The First 50 Years of University of Wisconsin Broadcasting, 1919–1969" and coverage of the John F. Kennedy assassination. Paper records dealing with the station's history are also available in the University of Wisconsin Archives.

2220. WIBA Records, ca. 1950–1960. Records and audio recordings, including William Evjue's "Hello Wisconsin" speeches by prominent people and commercials.

2221. William M. Mandel Papers, 1942–1995. Collection of this expert on the Soviet Union includes general correspondence, transcripts of hearings and remarks, newsclippings and scripts of his program *Soviet Press and Periodicals* aired on KPFA, Berkeley, CA.

2222. William Saxby Hedges Papers, 1918–1962. Papers of an NBC broadcasting executive who served as vice-president in charge of its stations, planning and development and integrated services departments. Correspondence, 1926–1962, chiefly concerns Broadcast Pioneers, the National Association of Broadcasters, the "Chicago Daily News" and WMAQ. The limited NBC material is best for the inception of television during the late 1940s. Also includes speeches and articles, clippings, memorabilia, a transcript of an oral history interview and a number of NBC reports, including some by Hedges. Material pertaining to Broadcast Pioneers includes minutes, printed matter, issues of the group's in-house organ and material on its history project. Of special interest is Hedges's interview with John F. Royal and the inventories of the project's collection. Information on the NAB, of which Hedges was a founding member, includes a constitution and by-laws, a proposed code of fair competition, convention programs and a handbook. Photographs document a group of journalists, including Hedges, on *Broadcasters' Mission to Europe*, 1945.

2223. William Spier and June Havoc Papers, 1931–1963. Papers of a radio and television producer-director and his actress-wife. Radio material, which is the most complete aspect of the collection, includes files of annotated scripts and correspondence for *The Adventures of Sam Spade, Philip Morris Playhouse, Suspense* and other series which Spier produced and directed for CBS.

2224. William Waldo Bauer Papers, 1925–1967. Papers and audio recordings of a director of the American Medical Association's Bureau of Health Education. Consists primarily of radio and television scripts and recordings. The scripts, which were produced under Dr. Bauer's supervision, relate to programs broadcast over the NBC, ABC and CBS networks as well as to numerous programs prepared for local stations. Among the titles represented are NBC's *Doctors at War, Doctors at Work,* and *To America's Schools—Your Health,* ABC's *Medical Horizons* and CBS's *Stephen Graham, Family Doctor.* There are also scripts, 1931, written for WRJN, Racine, WI and scripts written by Mrs. Bauer for the Wisconsin State Medical Society and produced on WHA.

2225. Wilson Hall Papers, 1959–1973. Papers of a former NBC foreign correspondent relating to both his radio and television work.

2226. Wisconsin Communities Radio Broadcasts, 1951. Tape recordings and transcriptions of a series of documentary programs produced in 1951 by WHA concerning various communities in Wisconsin, including interviews with residents, historical background and profiles of the current communities.

2227. WJR Sound Recording, ca. 1957. A recording of selected events, personalities and a music broadcast by WJR, "The Goodwill Station," 1922–1957.

2228. "WLS Family Album," 1930–1957, 1967. Annual reports, heavily illustrated, published annually by the Chicago radio station. See separate listing below for collection of the "WLS Standby" magazine.

2229. "WLS Standby," 1935–1938. Copies of the weekly publication for listeners of the Chicago radio station. See separate listing above for collection of "WLS Family Album."

2230. Writers Guild of America, West Records, 1943–1962. Fragmentary records of the labor union which represented motion picture, television and radio writers and of its predecessor, the Screen Writers Guild. Records consist of agreements negotiated between members and the television industry, a constitution, by-laws, a code of working rules and a bulletin of credits for 1949.

2231. WTAM, WTAM-FM History, 1923–1955. Papers, including pamphlets, bulletins and newsletters, publicity and promotional materials, programs, directories, reports and studies and related material relating to the history of WTAM-AM and WTAM-FM, an NBC-owned stations in Cleveland, OH. See the catalog entry for information on possible additional materials and shelf locations.

WNYC Radio Archives

One Centre Street, 24th Floor, New York, NY 10007
(212) 669-7800; Fax: (212) 669-3312
alanset@wnyc.org; Contact: Andy Lanset
www.wnyc.org/about/preservation_intro.html

2232. Archives for WNYC, New York, NY, a City Owned Station From 1922–1997. Archive includes thousands of audio recordings, photographs, memorabilia, reports, news items, program guides, institutional records and promotional materials. Among its holdings are more than 50,000 recordings in a variety of formats, from early lacquer and acetate discs, to reel-to-reel tapes, digital audio tapes and compact discs. Note: This collection is distinct from the WNYC records in the New York City Municipal Archives; the material may or may not be duplicative.

Yale University

Beinecke Rare Book and Manuscript Library
New Haven, CT 06520
(203) 432-8127; Fax: (203) 432-4047
kathleen.burns@yale.edu; www.library.yale.edu/beinecke/
Contact: Kathleen Burns

General comments: See Addendum for brief descriptions of unprocessed collections.

2233. Adele Gutman Nathan Theatrical Collection. Includes radio scripts, (Box 10, folder 311; Box 11, folder 334) for many of Nathan's productions, 1930s–1940s, including interviews done for the *Catholic Charities Fund Appeal,* 1943, *Beyond the Call of Duty* for the Young Men's Christian Association, *Comrade Borozova,* n.d., *Flashbacks by Paddy,* n.d., *How Things Started,* n.d., *It's A Man's World,* 1941, *New Frontiers,* 1938?, *One Hundred Years With Youth,* n.d., the panel discussion program *Opinion Requested,* 1945, for the Army-Air Force broadcast on WOR, *Report From the Front,* 1944, the instructional series *The Story of Us All,* 1940, broadcast on WEAF, *That's News,* n.d., *They Chose to Die,* 1941, *Today's News For Tomorrow's Citizens,* 1944, *Your Rights and Mine,* 1940–1941, and *We've Got Something,* n.d.

2234. Cleanth Brooks Papers. Includes two undated, untitled radio scripts.

2235. David Low Papers. Includes radio scripts for single and serial programs on a variety of subjects, 1923–1959. Also includes non radio related materials

2236. Glenway Westcott Papers. Includes scripts for *Invitation To Learning,* war bond broadcasts and *Success Magazine.*

2237. George Harmon Coxe Papers. Contains personal and professional papers, newspaper clippings, outlines for possible television series, memorabilia and other papers. Includes some material relating to Coxe's pulp character, Flashgun Casey, Crime Photographer, which later became a radio series, *Casey, Crime Photographer.*

2238. Max Lerner Papers, 1927–1992. Consists of correspondence, speeches, writings, radio and television tapes, photographs, memorabilia and other printed materials.

2239. Richard Wright Papers. Includes two undated scripts with titles but no indication of what program/s they might have aired on.

2240. Steven H. Scheuer Collection of Television (and Radio ?) Scripts, ca. 1953–1963. Includes scripts for many radio programs that moved to television. See online finding aid for list of scripts. Scripts donated after 1964 may not be listed. Note: On different pages of the University's web site, this collection is listed as "television scripts" and "radio and tele vision scripts." The latter reference notes that there are 5,000 scripts in the collection and that only a portion of the collection has been indexed.

2241. Theatre Guild Survey. Includes radio and television scripts for *Theatre Guild on the Air* (a.k.a. *U.S. Steel Hour*), plus correspondence and other papers. Also includes non radio related Theatre Guild papers. Scripts are stored in 125 boxes, arranged alphabetically by title. Correspondence is arranged alphabetically. Note: Sound recordings of the programs are in the Music Library. See listing below.

Drama Library
225 York Street, Box 208244, New Haven, CT 06520
(203) 432-1554
drama.library@yale.edu; www.library.yale.edu/drama

2242. *Listener's Theatre* **Scripts, 1938–1940.** Collection of 46 scripts for the program broadcast on WICC. The programs were extra-curricular productions that were written and acted by students of the Department of Drama, Yale University.

Manuscripts and Archives
PO Box 208240, New Haven, CT 06520
(203) 432-1744; Fax. (203) 432-7441
mssa.assist@yale.edu; www.library.yale.edu

2243. Records of WYBC, Yale University. 1941–1984. Includes correspondence, programming and administration records for the university radio station.

Music Library
PO Box 208240, New Haven, CT 06520
(203) 432-1795
Contact: Richard Warren; richard.warren@yale.edu
www.library.yale.edu/musiclib/info.htm

2244. Benny Goodman Papers. Includes tapes, arrangements, photographs, scrapbooks, clippings and memorabilia. Contact library for more information about any radio related material in the collection.

2245. Deems Taylor Papers. Includes research notes for Taylor's New York Philharmonic Orchestra intermission commentaries.

2246. Historical Sound Recordings. Collection includes an unknown quantity of recorded radio broadcasts. Other than a complete run of the *Theatre Guild on the Air* there is no catalog of the collection that can be accessed by the public. Library staff will, however, respond to written or email inquiries regarding the availability of specific programs or performers. Inquiries should be as specific as possible, noting that it is easier for the library to search by performer than by program.

2247. Kurt Weill and Lotte Lenya Papers, 1890–1984. Contains manuscript scores and sketches of Weill's music, correspondence, programs, photographs, clippings and personal documents.

2248. Ted Lewis Collection. Contains scrapbooks, manuscript arrangements, numerous commercial recordings and 27 half-hour radio programs that, according to the library web site, were never aired and have not yet been cataloged.

Yiddish Radio Project
www.yiddishradioproject.org

2249. Collection. An oral history of Yiddish radio, 1930s–1950s, produced by the NPR program *All Things Considered* and available on 2 CDs. Also available in many libraries or can be purchased through the web site.

YIVO Institute for Jewish Research
15 West 16th Street, New York, NY 10011
(212) 294-6169; Fax: (917) 606-8289
lsklamberg@yivo.cjh.org; www.yivoinstitute.org

2250. Louis Gross Papers, 1937–1958. Papers of a journalist, radio commentator and producer of Yiddish radio programs in Philadelphia and Miami, 1952–1958. The collection includes scripts of his radio talks, commentaries and other appearances, clippings from Yiddish newspapers about the radio programs, correspondence and sound recordings of Jewish folk music, theater music and cantorial music.

2251. Radio Programs. Principal collection consists of over 200 recordings of Yiddish music, comedy, soap operas, news, commercials, poetry and drama spanning the years 1936–1955. The majority represent programming from New York-based stations, including WEVD, WBBS, WHN and WMCA (all cataloged). Represented in these recordings are the Barry Sisters, Jan Bart, Moishe Oysher, Nahum Stutchkoff and Dave Tarras. Collection also includes recordings of radio material up to the present day, including programs featuring Molly Picon, and a collection of over 900 WEVD programs spanning the 1970s–1980s.

Youngstown State University
William F. Maag Jr. Library
One University Plaza, Youngstown, OH 44555
(330) 941-3675; Fax: (330) 941-3734
www.maag.ysu.edu/

2252. Andrew Foos Interview, 1975. Foos discusses his personal experiences as host of the program *Musical Milestones* broadcast on WHHH.

2253. Ralph Bell Interview. Transcript of interview with Bell taped on November 24, 1975 in which he discusses his disc jockey experience.

2254. Warren P. Williamson Interview, 1975. Transcript of interview with Williamson taped on December 10, 1975 in which he discusses his experience with WKBN. A separate interview includes a biography of Williamson.

2255. WFMJ Radio Project, 1975. Transcript of interview with Bill Crooks taped on December 1, 1975 in which he discusses WFMJ in the 1940s.

2256. WYSU Oral History. Transcript of interview taped on December 7, 1990 on the history of Youngstown State University's radio station WYSU as told by Donald Elser who helped start the station.

(More special collections listings continued on the next page)

ADDENDUM

Archives of Iowa Broadcasting

Wartburg College
100 Warburg Boulevard, Waverly, IA 50677
(319) 352-8534
www.iowabroadcasting.com;   jeff.stein@wartburg.edu
Contact: Jeff Stein

General comments: On the archive's web site, the visitor can find stations by city and call letters. Additional information will be added to the web site sometime after 2005.

3739. Archives. Includes hundreds of transcription discs dating from the 1930s and reel-to-reel tapes of WHO programs, including many wartime broadcasts by Jack Shelley and Herb Plambeck, and hundreds of sporting events called by Jim Zabel. Note: Prof. Stein, the administrator of the Archives, has written a book about Iowa radio, "Making Waves: The People and Places of Iowa Broadcasting" (Wdg Communications, 2004.)

Bob Burns Museum

813 Min Street, Old Frisco Depot, Van Buren, AR 72956
(479) 474-6164; Contact: Stacy Cook
vanburen@vanburen.org

3740. Collection. Consists mostly of photographs. Museum is open Monday-Friday 8:30-5 and Saturday 9-5, except closed Saturday during winter months.

Boston Public Library (Additional collections)

Music Department
700 Boylston Street, Boston, MA 02134
(617) 536-5400, ext. 2285 Fax: (617) 536-7758
music@bpl.org; Contact: Diane Ota

3742. Koussevitzky Collection. Contains sound recordings, some from broadcasts during his tenure as conductor of the Boston Symphony Orchestra, 1924-1949. Also contains recordings of programs about Koussevitzky broadcast in the 1960s and 1970s.

3743. Victor Young Collection. Contains Victor's own music as well as arrangements that he made and some scripts. Young had his own radio show, ca. 1934, and was either the conductor and/or the composer-arranger for several radio programs, including the *Carnation Contented Hour*, May, 1950–December, 1951, *Texaco Star Theatre*, Westinghouse radio programs, ca. 1938-1945, and the *Woolworth Radio Hour*.

The Broadcast ARTS Library

PO Box 9828, Fort Worth, TX 76147
(310) 288-6511; www.broadcastartslibrary.com
Contact: Fuller French

3744. Script Collection. A privately held collection of radio and television scripts. Radio scripts are mostly comedy. Contact the owner for more information.

Title	Dates	#
Abbott and Costello Show	1942-1949	1
Adventures of Maisie (a.k.a. Maisie)	1945-1948	1
Alan Young Show	1944-19494	2
Aldrich Family	1939-1953	4
Americans, Speak Up!	1954	134
The Amos 'n' Andy Show	1929-1954	3
At Home With the Kirkwoods		2
The Big Show	1950-1953	51
Bill Squirrel	1940	63
Bing Crosby Show (Philco Radio Time)	1946-1956	3
Blondie	1939-1950	1
Bob and Ray Show	1946-1953	1
Bob Hope Show (Pepsodent Program)	1938-1955	45
Broadway Bandbox	1943	1
California Theatre	1924	14
Camel Caravan (Camel Program)	1933-1943	4
Cavalcade of America	1939-1953	1
Charlie McCarthy Show	1937-1955	2
(Chase and Sanborn Hour; Edgar Bergen and Charlie McCarthy Show)		
Charlotte Greenwood Show	1944-1946	3
Children's Theatre of the Air		
Comedy Writers' Show	1948	3
Command Performance	1942-1949	3
Danny Kaye Show	1945-1946	1
Danny Thomas Show	1947-	13
(Sanka Coffee Show)		
Dimension X	1950-1951	1
Dinah Shore Show	1939-1948	
Dorothy Lamour Show	1948-1949	1
(Sealtest Variety Theatre)		
Duffy's Tavern	1941-1951	1
Durante-Moore Show	1943-1947	5
Easy Aces (Mr. Ace and Jane)	1948-1949	50
Ed Wynn Show (Fire Chief)	1932-1947	10
Eddie Cantor Show (Texaco Town)	1931-1949	3
Family Theater	1947-1963	2
Father Goose Comes to Town	1939	9
Fibber McGee and Molly	1935-1956	3
Frank Sinatra Show	1944-1945	33
Gold and Silver Minstrels	1946	12
Gunsmoke	1952-1961	13
Hammerstein's Music Hall	1934-1938	2
Have Gun – Will Travel	1958-1960	1
Heart's Desire	1946-1948	1
Henry Morgan Show	1940-1950	6
Hollywood Barn Dance	1943-1948	2
Jack Benny Show (Jell-O Program)	1932-1958	96
Jack Carson Show	1943-1956	79
(Campbell's Soup Program)		
Jack Kirkwood Show (Drene Show)	1944-	1
Jack Oakie's College	1936-1938	2
Jim Backus Show	1947-1948	1
Johnny Mercer's Music Shop	1943-1945	2
Johnson Wax Program (Summer)	1942-	1
Judy, Jill, 'N' Johnny	1946-1947	8
Kate Smith's A&P Bandwagon	1936-1938	12
Kraft Music Hall	1933-1949	2
Laugh Liner	1938	4
Let Yourself Go	1944-1945	1
Lincoln Highway	1940-1942	2
Little Show	1947-	25
Lux Radio Theatre	1934-1954	7
Mail Call	1942-1950	1
Marlin Hurt and Beulah Show	1945-1946	3
Martin and Lewis Show	1949-1953	14
Maxwell House Coffee Time	1940-1944	1
Meet Corliss Archer	1943-1956	1
Meet Millie	1951-1954	2
Meet Your Match	1952-1953	1

Title	Dates	#
Mr. President	1947-1953	7
Nothing but the Truth		
Ohio Story	1948-1951	58
Old Gold Program	1942-1948	1
Our Miss Brooks	1948-1957	6
Pepper Young's Family	1936-1959	1
Phil Baker Show	1931-1939	4
Phil Harris/Alice Faye Show	1948-1954	185
Philco Radio Hall of Fame	1943-1946	4
Prudential Family Hour of Stars	1948-1950	2
Quiz Kids	1940-1953	52
Railroad Hour	1948-1954	144
Ransom Sherman Show	1939-1942	11
Rate Your Mate	1950-1951	1
Red Skelton Show	1939-1953	7
(Raleigh Cigarette Program)		
Request Performance	1945-1946	1
Rogue's Gallery	1945-1951	24
Rookies	1941	13
Rounding Up the World	1945-1946	60
Rudy Vallee Program	1936-1947	31
Screen Directors' Playhouse	1949-1951	1
(NBC Theatre)		
Screen Guild Players	1939-1951	4
(Gulf Screen Guild Theatre; Lady Esther Screen		
Guild Players)		
Sea Scouter	1935-1936	55
Sealtest Village Store (Village Store)	1943-1948	86
Silver Theatre (a.k.a. Silvertown Theatre)	1937-1944	3
Summer Stars	1937	4
Suspense	1942-1962	3
That's Rich (The Stan Freberg Show)	1954	21
This Woman's World	1940	44
Three Pages	1944-1947	128
Three Ring Time	1941-1943	4
Through a Woman's Eyes	1945?	1
Time to Smile	1940	1
To Your Industrial Health	1947-1951?	57
Tony Martin Show	1947-1948	21
Tuesday Night Party	1939	4
Vaughn Monroe Show	1946-1954	1
Vera Vague Show	1949	10
You're in the Navy Now	1942	4

Buffalo State College

E. H. Butler Library, BL 135, Archives and Special Collections
1300 Elmwood Avenue, Buffalo, NY 14222
(716) 878-6308; Fax: (716) 878-3134
blarchives@buffalostate.edu;
www.buffalostate.edu/library/archives

3745. E. H. Butler Family Correspondence, 1880-1975. Contains personal correspondence and related documents of members of the E. H. Butler family, owners of the "Buffalo Evening News" and founders of WBEN. Includes some items related to WBEN which was owned by the Butler family through the late 1970s.

3746. Joseph Haeffner Collection. Contains personal and business correspondence, office memos, photographs, news clips, a few radio scripts and other miscellaneous items from WBEN, Buffalo, NY and WBEN-TV from the late 1920s to late 1970s. Most of the radio scripts are incomplete. Also

includes miscellaneous information about the "Buffalo Evening News" which owned the station. Haeffner worked with E. H. Butler Jr., owner of the newspaper, in the establishment of the radio station. A detailed inventory of the collection is available.

3747. Lance Zavitz Collection. Contains transcripts of the weekly news/news analysis program entitled either The *Week in Review* or *The News in Review* broadcast January, 1935–May, 1940 on either WBEN or WEBR, Buffalo, NY. The program was hosted by Zavitz who also wrote the scripts. Also includes miscellaneous correspondence and newspaper clippings, 1933–1949.

Catholic University of America

American Catholic History Research Center and University Archives
101 Life Cycle Institute, Washington, DC 20064
(202) 319-5065; Fax: (202) 319-6554
meagher@cua.edu; Contact: Timothy J. Meagher
http://libraries.cua.edu/achrcua/index.html

3748. Catholic Interracial Council of the District of Columbia Series. Includes correspondence, schedules and clippings dealing with *Faith of Millions*, 1956–1963.

3749. John A. Ryan Papers, 1892–1945.. A strong opponent of Father Charles E. Coughlin, the audio visual series of the collection includes Ryan's address, "Roosevelt Safeguards America" in which he urged Catholics to repudiate Coughlin and support the New Deal and Roosevelt. The address was broadcast on national radio on October 8, 1936

3750. National Catholic Welfare Conference. Contains materials relating to *The Catholic Hour*, including scripts, transcripts, recordings and photographs.

3751. Paul Philips Cooke Papers. Includes scripts for *Faith of Millions*, 1953–1954 broadcast on WOOK.

3752. "Social Justice" Collection, 1936–1941. Includes a partial run of loose issues of "Social Justice" published by the National Union for Social Justice, the political vehicle for Father Coughlin.

Detroit Symphony

Max M Fisher Music Center
3711 Woodward Avenue, Detroit, MI 48201
(313) 576-5126; Contact: Jill Woodward

3753. Archive. Includes numerous recordings of its radio broadcasts in different formats. Check with archives regarding dates.

J. David Goldin

PO Box 542, Newtown, CT 06470
(203) 426-2524 (Call after 12 noon)
www.radiogoldindex.com

3754. Audio Collection. A privately held collection of approximately 86,000 hours of programming of mixed genres ranging from the 1920s to the present. The collection is searchable online at www.radiogoldindex.com.

Herbert Hoover Presidential Library & Museum

210 Parkside Drive, West Branch, IA 52358
(319) 643-5301; Fax: (319) 643-6045
www.hoover.archives.gov

3755. Collection: Includes papers relating to Hoover's involvement in regulating radio as Secretary of Commerce, 1921–1928. The library is operated by the National Archives.

Iowa State University (Additional collections)
Special Collections Department
403 Parks Library, Ames, IA 50011
(515) 294-6672; Fax: (515) 294-5525
archives@iastate.edu; www.lib.iastate.edu/spcl/index.html
Contact: Tanya Zanish-Belcher

3756. Clair B. Heyer Papers, ca. 1910–1990. Includes scrapbooks and photographs from Heyer's radio advertising work and his work with Armour & Company.

3757. John D. "Jack" Shelley Papers, 1944–1996. The bulk of the collection deals with Shelley's time as a war correspondent for WHO, Des Moines, 1944–1945, and includes correspondence, newsclippings, telegrams, broadcast schedules and recordings of broadcasts. Also includes a small biographical file. Shelley was one of the founders of the Iowa Broadcast News Association.

3758. John C. Baker Papers, 1922–1980. Includes farm radio directories, newsclippings, correspondence and materials assembled for his book, "Farm Broadcasting: The First Sixty Years" (1981).

3759. William E. Drips Papers, 1924–1964. Includes biographical information, photographs, scripts, newsclippings, materials on the 25th anniversary of NBC's *National Farm and Home Hour*, correspondence and scrapbooks. Drips was a farm broadcaster for NBC, 1934–1950.

Jot 'Em Down Store and Museum
4562 Highway 88, General Delivery, Pine Ridge, AR 71966
(870) 326-4442; nlstrucker@earthlink.net
www.lum-abner.com
Contact: Lon & Kathryn Stucker

3760. Lum and Abner Collection. A combination store and museum, the collection includes audio material, 1931–1955, two scripts from 1937, premiums, correspondence and other memorabilia. See web site for store hours. Appointments to view collection can be made during off season.

Museum of Television & Radio (Additional collection)
25 West 52nd Street, New York, NY 10019, (212) 621-6600
465 N. Beverly Dr, Beverly Hills, CA 90210, (310) 786-1000
www.mtr.org

3761. Boxing Broadcast Collection. Approximately 75 broadcasts, spanning 1934–1979, from the collection of boxing manager Bill Cayton. As of 2005, the collection was uncataloged but researchers may be able to access the broadcasts with the assistance of the Museum's library staff.

Northwestern University
Library
1970 Campus Drive, Evanston, IL 60208
www.library.northwestern.edu

Periodicals/Newspaper Reading Room
(847) 491-7680

3762. "The Making and Use of Recordings in Broadcasting Before 1936." A Ph.D. thesis by Michael Biel, 1977, Northwestern University, 1977.

Special Collections
(847) 491-3635

3763. Father Charles Edward Coughlin Collection. Consists of materials collected by Sheldon Marcus, Coughlin's biographer, and includes Marcus's typescript, interviews with people who knew Coughlin, a tape of one of his broadcasts and correspondence.

University Archives
(847) 491-3354

3764. Radio/Television/Film Department Scripts and Production Reports, 1937–1964. Includes student written scripts for *Radio Playshop*, 1939–1953, and adaptations of literary classics for *Radio Guild*, 1946–1948, and other dramatic, public service and documentary series broadcast over the university station, WNUR.

3765. WNUR-FM Records, 1953–1994. Includes general policy statements, correspondence, operating and play list logs arranged chronologically by date and materials relating to the station's public activities.

Radio Historical Association of Colorado (RHAC)
PO Box 1908, Englewood, CO 80150
(303) 761-4139; Contact: Maletha King
www.rhac.org

3766. Collection: A non profit group of old time radio collectors. The organization has a set of radio historian John Dunning's interviews of radio personalties (about 50+ interviews), approximately 100 scripts of mixed genre, including *Escape, First Nighters, Gunsmoke* and *The Whistler,* a collection of 1,200 16" transcription discs of mixed genre, including big bands, AFRS and World War II bond drives that are being transferred to CDs as of 2005 and a lending library of cassettes.

Roger Rittner's "Minds Eye Theatre"
2148 Lambert Drive, Pasadena, CA 91107
(626 792-5449; Contact: Roger Rittner

3767. Audio collection. A privately held collection of approximately 26,000 programs with an emphasis on comedy and mystery. Highlights include AFRS programs such as *Command Performance, Mail Call, G.I. Journal* and *Jubilee, The Lone Ranger,* 1938–1948, news broadcasts, primarily from World War II, *Fibber McGee and Molly, Our Miss Brooks, Phil Harris/Alice Faye, Philo Vance, Let George Do It* and *Boston Blackie.*

Schenectady Museum (Additional collections)
Nott Terrace Heights, Schenectady, NY 12308
(518) 382-7890; Contact: Chris Hunter
schdymuse@schenectadymuseum.org
www.schenectadymuseum.org

3768. Al Zink Collection. Contains papers and photographs of a 1930s WGY staff announcer who later became program manger of WRGB.

3769. Charles Huntley Scripts, 1930s–1940s. Includes original scripts for *Your Home Town,* an historical drama, and some World War II related dramas and other programs. Huntley was a writer, announcer and performer on WGY.

3770. Delores Carrara Papers. Collection documents Carrara's career on WRGB in the 1940s on a variety of programs, including fashion shows, commercials and dramas.

3771. Dorothy Sweeney Scripts. Includes scripts for *FBI In*

Action, FM Playhouse and *Chick Carter, Boy Detective*. Sweeney was a sound effects person on WGY during World War II and the scripts include her handwritten notes regarding the sound effects for the programs.

3772. Edward and Irene Dahlstedt Papers. Collection documents the careers of the Dahlstedts who performed on WGY and WRGB in the 1940s, including on *FBI in Action*.

3773. *Excursions in Science*. A collection of recordings of the program aired on WGY that featured scientists discussing both their work and also popular science.

3774. GE Photograph Collection. Includes more than 40,000 photographs relating to radio and television, including equipment, receivers and programming.

3775. Grant Van Patten Papers. Contains scripts, production logs and information about Van Patten's career as a director, writer and on-air host at WRGB, 1951–1970s. In the 1960s Van Patten created documentaries about the harmful effects of gambling and teenage drinking.

3776. Howard Tupper Collection. Papers include photographs and radio and television scripts. Tupper ("Tup") was a broadcaster on WGY and WRGB, 1937–1984.

3777. Pallophotophone Reels. A dozen reels of NBC programs, 1927, 1929, that were "recorded" onto an experimental sound-on-film format that led to the development of the RCA Photophone system. The programs include Walter Damrosch conducting the GE Symphony Orchestra.

3778. Radio and Television Advertisements, 1930s–1950s. Includes ads featuring many radio personalities, including Jack Benny, Lucille Ball, Groucho Marx, Frank Sinatra and Judy Garland.

3779. WRGB Papers. Includes press releases, program schedules and promotional booklets dating to the founding of the station in 1928.

The Society for the Preservation of Variety Arts
7001 Franklin Avenue, Hollywood, CA 90068
(323) 851-3443; Conact: Milt Larsen

General comments: A non profit organization that is a repository for both sound and print research material and memorabilia associated with the variety theater (music hall, vaudeville and burlesque) and the performers that moved from these venues to radio and early television.

3780. Audio collection. Includes a complete run of the *Texaco Star Theatre*, 1935–1949, a large collection of AFRS programs from the 1960s, including AFRS versions of *Gunsmoke, Walk Softly Peter Troy* and *Radio Novels*, interviews with variety and radio artists conducted by Bob Dwan and miscellaneous other programs, including *Behind the Story* and *Biography in Sound*.

3781. Print Collection. Includes Eddie Cantor's joke file, a Milton Geiger script collection, miscellaneous joke files and scripts for other radio comedians.

State Historical Society of Iowa (Additional collections)
State Historical Building
600 East Locust, Des Moines, IA 50319
www.iowahistory.org

Museum
(515) 281-3295
Contact: Jodi Evans; jodi.evans@iowa.gov

3782. FW Fitch Company Collection. In addition to a large number of artifacts from the company, the collection includes eight cassettes of the *Fitch Bandwagon*, March, 1945–May, 1945 and 18 issues of the monthly newsletter, "Bandwagon News."

Library
(515) 281-8976
Contact: Becki Plunkett; becki.plunkett@iowa.gov

3783. George and Edith Webber Papers, 1940s–1960s. Includes scripts for *Have You Heard*, written by Edith Webber in the 1940s for WHO, Des Moines. The program included book reviews and commentary about fashion, music, historical figures, etc. Also includes material relating to George Webber's career as the founder of KWDM-AM in 1948 which became KWKY in 1959 after it was sold to 3M. George Webber also started KWDM-FM in 1964.

3784. Photograph Collection. Includes 30 photographs of KSO, Des Moines personalities, events and broadcasting, 1940–1960.

3785. Wayne Ackley Papers, ca. 1935–1943. Contains papers relating to Ackley's career with KSO and KRNT, Des Moines owned by the Iowa Broadcasting Co. Ackely was a newscaster and master of ceremonies for special programming, transcriptionist and music director. Includes scripts, ephemera, a scrapbook and photographs.

3786. WHO Radio and Television Records, 1927–1966. Includes newsletters, souvenir programs, newsclippings, files on WHO, Des Moines radio and television history, information about the station's founder, B. J. Palmer, and scrapbooks.

University of California at Davis
Department of Special Collections
Shields Library, Department of Special Collections
100 N.W. Quad, Davis, CA 95616-5292
(530) 752-1621; Fax (530) 754-5758
http://www.lib.ucdavis.edu/dept/specol/

3787. *"The NBC Symphony Orchestra*. "A Ph.D. thesis by Donald Carl Meyer, University of California, Davis, 1994.

University of Florida
George A. Smathers Libraries
Department of Special and Area Studies Collections, Belknap Collection for the Performing Arts
PO Box 117007, Gainesville, FL 32611-7007
(352) 392-9075 ext.202
jimlive@mail.uflib.ufl.edu; Contact Jim Liversidge
www.uflib.ufl.edu/spec/belknap/tvradio/radiotv.htm

3788. Audio Collection (The Sound of Radio and Television). A collection of approximately 500 themes and related audio material on $33^{1}/_{3}$ rpm records. Includes compilations and specific broadcasts of mixed genre. See online finding aid for detailed listing of contents.

3789. Preston Wood Script Collection. Includes papers relating to the operation of WRUF, Gainesville, FL, 1942–1943 and scripts for the *Little Show*, 1947, including background information about Robert Q. Lewis and the *Kraft Music Hall*,

1947, with dates and names of guests. For details see online finding aid. Collection also includes an extensive collection of television scripts.

Yale University (Additional collections)
Beinecke Rare Book and Manuscript Library
New Haven, CT 06520
(203) 432-8127; Fax: (203) 432-4047
kathleen.burns@yale.edu. Contact: Kathleen Burns
http://beinecke.library.yale.edu/acqwww/default.htm

Uncataloged Acquisitions

General comments: The catalog listings on this web site contain a limited amount of information about unprocessed collections. In response to a keyword search for "radio," 32 hits were generated. Given the limited information about the collections, only some could be identified as falling within the general parameters for this volume. The titles of the collections as they are listed below are based on the author of the collection, the program title or the station.

3790. Amelia Earhart. Contains a copy of a 78rpm recording that includes the speech Miss Earhart made over a transatlantic radio hookup the day after she landed in Ireland, May, 1932.

3791. Christopher Sykes. Includes papers, possibly scripts, for radio broadcasts, 1961–1964.

3792. Joseph Carl Breil. Vocal score for a song (possibly the theme song) used on the *Pepsodent Hour*.

3793. Max Wilk. Includes three radio scripts, n.d., by Wilk written for the MBS.

3794. Texas Oil Radio. "Broadcasting to the world the latest information from the oil fields of Texas, Arkansas and the Great Southwest," March 26, 1923. Note: This may be a transcript of a broadcast.

3795. *University of Chicago Roundtable*. Contains the July 18, 1954 broadcast that includes the poetry of Dylan Thomas and a discussion by Reuel N. Denny, Elder J. Olson and Alan Simpson. Note: Description was unclear as to whether the material was a sound recording or a transcript.

3796. WCCO, Minneapolis, MN. Typescripts for WCCO programs No. 1–6, June–July 1947.

3797. William McFee. Contains a condensation of the book read by McFee on WJZ, Newark, NJ on Sunday, December 24 1922. Includes a printed notice of the broadcast which may have been sponsored by the United Fruit Company.

Chapter 3: Bibliography

How to use the Bibliography

The information in this section has been compiled from several sources, including more than a thousand titles in the personal collection of one of the co-authors who has been collecting books about the Golden Age of Radio for over 40 years.

While the Bibliography is probably the most comprehensive one in print today on the subject of the old time radio, the authors recognize that no bibliography on as broad a subject as this can ever be considered complete. What is presented here is a "starting point" that should lead to many additional titles, a number of which include bibliographies.

It should also be noted that while new books about the Golden Age of Radio are being written each year, the vast majority of the books listed below are out-of-print and may only be available in libraries and/or by contacting used book dealers. One such dealer with a specialty in radio is Bequaert Old Books in Fitzwilliam, NH, www.beqbooks.com.

What is included in the Bibliography

As with the Special Collections listings in Chapter 2, the Bibliography deals with the people and programming aspects of the Golden Age of Radio in the United States and does not include books relating to the technical side of radio, i.e., books dealing with radio equipment, transmission, reception, etc. Also excluded are books dealing with United States radio broadcasts aired overseas such as *Radio Free Europe* or *Radio Liberty*.

The Bibliography also includes books about individuals who may be known primarily for their non-radio careers but who, nonetheless, also performed on radio. Examples of such books would be biographies of the singer Frank Sinatra or the famous magician Dunninger who had a radio program of his own. Also, because researchers may be interested in a "comprehensive" portrait of a person, the Bibliography includes non radio related books by radio personalities. Examples in this category include Gracie Allen's "How To Become President," many of Bob Hope's books and a book about police departments by Jack Webb of *Dragnet* fame.

Again, for the researcher who is a completist, the Bibliography also includes some novels and plays that later became popular radio shows such as "Stella Dallas" by Olive Higgins Prouty and "Abie's Irish Rose" by Anne Nicholas.

While a considerable amount of radio related ephemera survives today, given the many issues associated with locating specific pieces of ephemera, the Bibliography does not, as a general rule, include printed material that falls into this category. Researchers are advised, however, that when contacting libraries for books or special collections, they should also inquire about their ephemera collection. Ephemeral materials are especially valuable when researching station histories.

The Bibliography also does not include program logs for specific radio shows although many of the books about specific programs listed in the Bibliography do contain logs. For more information on where to find other program logs, researchers should check the Internet Resources section of this volume.

Comic books with tie-ins to radio programs such as the *Dick Tracy* or *Jungle Jim* programs are also not included. For more information on this subject, researchers should check the many comic related sites on the Internet or the Lackmann reference book dealing with comics and radio that is listed in the "Genre: Children's" section of the Bibliography because of its general subject matter.

How the Bibliography is organized

The Bibliography is divided into 54 categories and subcategories ranging from Advertising and Biography/Autobiography to World War II. Within each section, the books are listed alphabetically by author and then by title. To assist the reader, certain category headings, e.g, "Reference" or "History: Informal," are followed by brief descriptions of the types of books included in the category.

Each entry in the Bibliography has been assigned a unique number for purposes of identifying the book in the Index.

Because many of the books cover more than one subject area or more than one person, assigning them to specific categories has not always been easy. While a biography of Mary Margaret McBride clearly belongs in the biography section, books by McBride that deal more with her programs than with her personal life are more appropriately grouped in the "Genre: Talk Show" section. A book about *Jubilee*, a popular World War II era music program featuring black performers could be listed in three sections: "Music," "Ethnic-African American," and "World War II." In the Index, the book is listed under four different subject headings: Music, Armed Forces Radio Service, Ethnic-African American and *Jubilee*.

The placement of biographies and autobiographies creates a different set of problems. Does a book about the sports broadcaster Ted Husing belong in the "Biography" section or the "Sports" section? The same question can be asked of biographies of Father Coughlin: do they belong in the "Biography" or "Religion" sections? As a general rule, the authors have listed most biographies and autobiographies in the "Biography/Autobiography" section — but in the Index, these books are listed under the name of the individual and, where appropriate, the name of the program the person was associated with or the type of program..

Biographies that include more than one person are listed in the "Biography/Mixed" section and are listed again in the Index under the heading "Biography-mixed" and, where appropriate, under other subject headings.

Books about news broadcasts, news broadcasts relating to

World War II and books by and about newscasters are grouped in several sections: Books about broadcasts dealing with World War II have been placed in the "World War II" section, while books about news broadcasting in general are in "Genre: News." Biographies of news broadcasters are in the "Biography/Autobiography" section and books by newscasters that are general commentaries are in the "Miscellaneous" section. Where appropriate, books in many of these four categories are cross referenced in the Index. Some examples: "World War II On The Air: Edward R. Murrow and the Broadcasts That Riveted a Nation" is listed in the Bibliography in the "World War II" section, but in the Index it is also listed under "World War II-news broadcasts" and "Murrow, Edward R." Elmer Davis's book, "But We Were Born Free," a general commentary on the times, is listed in the Bibliography in the "Miscellaneous" section and indexed under "Davis, Elmer." And finally, H.V. Kaltenborn's book, "Kaltenborn Edits the News" is listed in the Bibliography under "Genre-News" but is indexed under both "News" and "Kaltenborn, H.V."

For the best results in locating books about specific persons, programs or specific aspects of radio history, the authors strongly recommend that researchers use the Index in conjunction with this Bibliography.

Bibliographpy

Advertising

2260. American Tobacco Company. Sold American: The First 50 Years. American Tobacco Co., 1954.

2261. Arnold, Frank A. Broadcast Advertising: The Fourth Dimension. New York, John Wiley & Sons, 1931.

2262. Burt, F. Allen. American Advertising Agencies: An In quiry into Their Origin, Growth, Functions and Future. New York, Harper & Brothers, 1940.

2263. Day, Enid. Radio Broadcasting For Retailers. New York, Fairchild Publishing Company, 1947.

2264. Diehl, Lorraine B. and Marianne Hadart. The Automat: The History. Recipes and Allure of Horn & Hardart's Masterpiece. New York, Clarkson Potter Publishers, 2002.

2265. Felix, Edgar H. Using Radio in Sales Promotions. New York, McGraw Hill, 1927.

2266. Garver, Robert I. Successful Radio Advertising With Sponsor Participation Programs. New York, Prentice-Hall, 1949.

2267. Hepner, Harry Walker. Effective Advertising. New York, McGraw-Hill, 1941.

2268. Kleppner, Otto. Advertising Procedure. Englewood Cliffs, NJ, Prentice-Hall, 1959.

2269. Lewine. Harris. Good-bye To All That. New York, McGraw Hill. 1970.

2270. Lief, Alfred. The Firestone Story. New York, Whittlesey House, 1951.

2271. Marquette, Arthur F. Brands, Trademarks And Good Will: The Story of the Quaker Oats Company. New York, McGraw Hill. 1967.

2272. Midgley, Ned. The Advertising And Business Side Of Radio. New York, Prentice-Hall, 1949.

2273. Morell, Peter. Poisons, Potions And Profits: The Antidote To Radio Advertising. New York, Knight Publishers, 1937.

2274. NBC. Broadcast Advertising (2 vols.). New York, NBC. 1929.

2275. Rehder, Denny. The Shampoo King: F.W. Fitch and His Company. Des Moines, IA, Waukon & Mississippi, 1981.

2276. Rosenberg, Manuel, ed. The Advertiser's Sketch Book, 1937.

2277. Ross, Wallace A., ed. Best TV & Radio Commercials. New York, Hastings House, 1968.

2278. Sandage, C. H. Radio Advertising For Retailers. Cambridge, MA, Harvard University Press, 1945.

2279. Schisgall, Oscar. Eyes On Tomorrow: The Evolution of Procter & Gamble. Chicago, Ferguson, 1961.

2280. Seehafer, E. F. and J. W. Laemmar. Successful Radio And Television Advertising. New York, McGraw-Hill, 1951.

2281. Smith, Mickey C. Pharmacy And Medicine On The Air. Metuchen, NJ, Scarecrow, 1989.

2282. Swasy, Alicia. Soap Opera: The Inside Story Of Procter & Gamble. New York, Random House, 1993.

2283. Taishoff, Sol, ed. Broadcasting And Broadcast Advertising, 1935 Yearbook. Washington, DC, Broadcasting Publications Inc.

2284. Wolfe, Charles Hull. Modern Radio Advertising. New York, Funk & Wagnalls, 1949.

2285. Wood, James Playsted. The Story Of Advertising. New York, Ronald Press, 1958.

2286. Wyman, Carolyn. Jell-O: A Biography. San Diego, CA, Harcourt, 2001.

Biography/Autobiography

2287. Aadamson, Joe. Groucho, Harpo, Chico And Sometimes Zeppo. New York, Touchstone, 1973.

2288. Adams, Samuel Hopkins. A. Woollcott: His Life And His World. New York, Reynal & Hitchcock, 1945.

2289. Adler, Irene. I Remember Jimmy. New York, Arlington House, 1980.

2290. Allen, Fred. Much Ado About Me. Boston, Little, Brown and Company, 1956.

2291. _____. Treadmill To Oblivion. Boston, Little, Brown and Company, 1954.

2292 Allen, Steve. Bigger Than A Breadbox. Garden City, NY, Doubleday, 1967.

2293. _____. Mark It And Strike It. New York, Holt, Rinehart & Winston, 1960.

2294. Andrews, Robert Hardy. A Corner Of Chicago. Boston, Little, Brown and Company, 1963.

2295. Ansbro, George. I Have A Lady In The Balcony: Memoirs of a Broadcaster. Jefferson, NC, McFarland, 2000.

2296. Arce, Hector. Groucho. New York, G. P. Putnam's Sons, 1979.

2297. Arden, Eve. Three Phases Of Eve: An Autobiography. New York, St. Martin's Press, 1985.

2298. Atkinson, Carroll. I Knew The Voice Of Experience. Boston, Meador Publishing, 1944.

2299. Autry, Gene. Back In The Saddle Again. Garden City, NY, Doubleday, 1978.

2300. Bacall, Lauren. Lauren Bacall By Myself. New York, Ballantine, 1980.

2301. Backus, Henny and Jim. Backus Strikes Back. New York, Stein And Day, 1984.

2302. _____. What Are You Doing After The Orgy? The hilarious adventures of a pair of not-too-innocents abroad. Englewood Cliffs, NJ, Prentice-Hall, 1962.

2303. Backus, Jim. Rocks On The Roof: The hilarious, midstream memoir of a gaily checkered career in entertainment. New York, G. P. Putnam's Sons, 1958.

2304. Bain, Donald. The Control Of Candy Jones: A famous and beautiful woman's mind-shattering ordeal. Chicago, Playboy Press, 1976.

2305. _____. Donald. Long John Nebel: Radio Talk King, Master Salesman, Magnificent Charlatan. New York, Macmillan, 1974.

2306. Bakish, David. Jimmy Durante: His Show Business Career. Jefferson, NC, McFarland. 1995.

2307. Bankhead, Tallulah. Tallulah: My Autobiography. New York, Harper & Brothers, 1952.

2308. Bannerman, R. Leroy. Norman Corwin And Radio: The Golden Years. University, AL, University of Alabama Press, 1986.

2309. _____. On A Note Of Triumph: Norman Corwin and the Golden Years of Radio. New York, Lyle Stuart, 1986.

2310. Bannister, Harry. The Education Of A Broadcaster. New York, Simon & Schuster, 1965.

2311. Barber, Red and Robert Creamer. Rhubarb In The Catbird Seat, Red Barber: A Biography of America's Great Sportscaster. Garden City, NY, Doubleday, 1968.

2312. Barnes, Ken. The Crosby Years. New York, St. Martin's Press, 1980.

2313. Beals, Dick. Think Big. 1992.

2314. Benny, Jack and Joan. Sunday Nights At Seven. New York, Warner, 1990.

2315. Berg, Gertrude. Molly And Me. New York, McGraw Hill, 1961.

2316. Bergen, Candice. Knock Wood. New York, Simon & Schuster, 1984.

2317. Bergreen, Laurence. As Thousands Cheer: The Life Of Irving Berlin. New York, Viking, 1990.

2318. Berle, Milton. Milton Berle: An Autobiography. New York, Dell, 1975.

2319. Bickel, Mary E. Geo. W. Trendle. New York, Exposition Press, 1971

2320. Bilby, Kenneth. The General: David Sarnoff and the Rise of the Communications Industry. New York, Harper & Row, 1986.

2321. Blanc, Mel. That's Not All Folks! New York, Warner Books, 1988.

2322. Blythe, Cheryl and Susan Sackett. Say Goodnight, Gracie! New York, E. P. Dutton, 1986.

2323. Bogue, Merwyn. Ish Kabibble: An Autobiography of Merwyn Bogue. Baton Rouge, Louisiana State University Press, 1989.

2324. Bowen, Norman R., ed. Lowell Thomas: The Stranger Everyone Knows. Garden City, NY, Doubleday, 1968.

2325. Brady, Frank. Citizen Welles. New York, Scribners, 1989.

2326. Brian, Denis. Tallulah, Darling: A Biography of Tallulah Bankhead. New York, Macmillan, 1980.

2327. Brokenshire, Norman. This Is Norman Brokenshire. New York, David McKay, 1954.

2328. Brown. Cecil. Suez To Singapore: Cecil Brown's Story. New York, Random House, 1942.

2329. Burke, Billie. With A Feather On My Nose: The story of the gay redhead who became a famous actress and married Flo Ziegfeld. New York, Appleton-Century-Crofts, 1949.

2330. Burlingame, Roger. Don't Let Them Scare You: The Life & Times of Elmer Davis. New York, J.B. Lippincott, 1961.

2331. Burns, George. Dear George. New York, G. P. Putnam's Sons, 1985.

2332. Burns, George. Gracie, A Love Story. New York, G. P. Putnam's Sons, 1988.

2333. _____. I Love Her, That's Why! New York, Simon & Schuster, 1955.

2334. _____. The Third Time Around. New York, G. P. Putnam's Sons, 1980.

2335. Cahn, William. Good Night, Mrs. Calabash. New York, Duell, Sloan & Pearce, 1963.

2336. Callow, Simon. Orson Welles: The Road To Xanadu. New York, Viking, 1995.

2337. Cantor, Eddie. As I Remember Them. New York, Duell, Sloan & Pearce, 1963.

2338. _____. Caught Short! New York, Simon & Schuster, 1929.

2339. _____. My Life Is In Your Hands. New York, Harper, 1928.

2340. _____. Take My Life. Garden City, NY, Doubleday, 1957.

2341. _____. The Way I See It. Englewood Cliffs, NJ, Prentice-Hall, 1959.

2342. Carey, MacDonald. Days Of My Life. New York, St. Martins, 1991.

2343. Carrilo, Leo. The California I Love. Englewood Cliffs, NJ, Prentice Hall, 1961.

2344. Carroll, Carroll. None Of Your Business or My Life With J. Walter Thompson (Confessions of a Renegade Radio Writer). New York, Cowles, 1970.

2345. Carry, Harry and Verdi. Holy Cow! Berkely, 1990.

2346. Carson, Gerald. The Roguish World Of Doctor Brinkley. New York, Rinehart & Company, 1960.

2347. Cassiday. Bruce. Dinah! A Biography. New York, Franklin Watts, 1979.

2348. Cavett, Dick. Cavett. New York, Harcourt, Brace, Jovanovich, 1974.

2349. Chandler, Charlotte. Hello, I Must Be Going: Groucho And His Friends. Garden City, NY, Doubleday, 1978.

2350. Chase, Ilka. Past Imperfect. Garden City, NY, Doubleday, 1942.

2351. Cheerio. The Story Of Cheerio. New York, Garden City Publishing, 1936.

2352. Clements, Cynthia and Sandra Weber. George Burns And Gracie Allen: A Bio Biography. Westport, CT, Greenwood Press, 1996.

2353. Cline, Beverly Fink. The Lombardo Story: The Music, the People, the Pleasure. Don Mills, Ontario, Musson Books, 1979.

2354. Coe, Douglas. Marconi: Pioneer Of Radio. New York, Julian Messner, 1959.

2355. Colman, Juliet Benita. Ronald Colman: A Very Private Person. New York, William Morrow & Company, 1975.

2356. Colonna, Jerry. Who Threw That Coconut! McCombs Publications, 1945.

2357. Considine, Bob. Ripley, The Modern Marco Polo: The Life and Times of the Creator of "Believe It Or Not." Garden City, NY, Doubleday, 1961.

2358. Corwin, Norman. Years Of The Electric Ear: An Oral History. Metuchen, NJ, Scarecrow, 1994.

2359. Costello, Chris. Lou's On First. New York, St. Martin's Press, 1981.

2360. Crabb, Richard. Radio's Beautiful Day: An Account of the First Five Decades of Broadcasting in America Based on the Experience of Everett Mitchell. Chicago, North Plains Press, 1983.

2361. Crichton, Kyle. The Marx Brothers. Garden City, NY, Doubleday, 1950.

2362. Crosby, Bing. Call Me Lucky: Bing Crosby's Own Story. New York, Simon & Schuster, 1953.

2363. Crosby, Gary. Going My Own Way. Garden City, NY, Doubleday, 1983.

2364. Crosby, Ted. The Story Of Bing Crosby. Cleveland, World Publishing, 1946.

2365. Croy, Homer. Our Will Rogers. New York, Duell, Sloan & Pearce, 1953.

2366. DeCamp, Rosemary. Rosemary DeCamp Tigers in My Cap. Baltimore, Midnight Marquee, 2000.

2367. DeForest, Lee. Father Of Radio: The Autobiography Of Lee de Forest. Chicago, Wilcox & Follett, 1950.

2368. DeHaven, Bob. 55 Years Before the Mike. Minneapolis, James D. Thueson Publishers, 1985.

2369. DeLong, Thomas A. Pops: Paul Whiteman, King Of Jazz. Piscataway, NJ, New Century Publisher, 1983.

2370. DeMille, Cecil B. The Autobiography Of Cecil B. De Mille. Englewood Cliffs, NJ, Prentice-Hall, 1959.

2371. Dragonette, Jessica. Faith Is A Song. New York, David McKay, 1951.

2372. Dreher, Carl. Sarnoff: An American Success. New York, Quadrangle, 1977.

2373. Duke Of Paducah (Ben Ford). These Shoes Are Killing Me: The Duke of Paducah, Comedy of Grand Ole Opry. New York, Radco Publishers, 1947.

2374. Dwan, Robert. As Long As They're Laughing. Baltimore, Midnight Marquee, 2000.

2375. Edwards, Frank. My First Ten Million Sponsors: The famous commentator's own story of 30 years with the great, the near-great and the notorious. New York, Ballantine, 1956.

2376. Elliott, Bob and Ray Goulding. The New Improved Bob And Ray Book. New York, G. P. Putnam's Sons, 1985.

2377. Emery, Ralph. Memories: The Autobiography of Ralph Emery. New York, Macmillan, 1991.

2378. Faith, William Robert. Bob Hope: A Life In Comedy. New York, G. P. Putnam's Sons, 1982.

2379. Falkenburg, Jinx. Jinx. New York, Duell, Sloan & Pearce, 1951.

2380. Farrell, Eileen. Can't Help Singing: The Life of Eileen Farrell. Boston, Northeastern University Press, 1999.

2381. Fein, Irving A.. Jack Benny: An Intimate Biography. New York, Pocket Books, 1977.

2382. Ferguson, Max. And Now Here's Max: A funny kind of autobiography. New York, McGraw Hill, 1967.

2383. Fields, Ronald J., ed. W. C. Fields By Himself. Englewood Cliff, NJ, Prentice-Hall, 1973.

2384. Fisher, James. Eddie Cantor: A Bio Bibliography. Westport, CT, Greenwood Press, 1997.

2385. Ford, Tennessee Ernie. This Is My Story-This Is My Song. Englewood Cliffs, NJ, Prentice-Hall, 1963.

2386. Fowler, Gene. Good Night, Sweet Prince. Philadelphia, Blakiston, 1945.

2387. _____. Schnozzola. New York, Perma Book, 1953.

2388. Francis, Arlene. Arlene Francis, A Memoir. New York, Simon & Schuster, 1978.

2389. Francis, Anne. Voice From Home: An Inner Journey. Millbrae, CA, Celestial Arts, 1982.

2390. Frank, Sam. Ronald Colman: A Bio-Bibliography. Westport, CT, Greenwood Press, 1997.

2391. Freberg, Stan. It Only Hurts When I Laugh. New York, Times Books. 1988.

2392. Freedland, Michael. Irving Berlin. New York, Stein & Day, 1974.

2393. _____. Michael. Jolson: The Life and Times of the World's Greatest Entertainer. New York, Warner, 1973.

2394. Fuller, Daniel. Give the Winds a Mighty Voice: The Story of Charles E. Fuller. Waco, TX, Word Books. 1972.

2395. Gabler, Neal. Winchell: Gossip, Power and the Culture of Celebrity. New York, Alfred A Knopf, 1994.

2396. Gambling, John. Rambling With Gambling. Englewood Cliffs, NJ, Prentice-Hall, 1972.

2397. Garay, Ronald. Gordon McLendon. Westport, CT, Greenwood, 1992.

2398. Gargiulo, Suzanne. Hans Conried: A Biography; with a Filmography and a Listing of Radio, Television, Stage and Voice Work. Jefferson, NC, McFarland, 2002.

2399. Gehring, Wes D. Irene Dunne: First Lady of Hollywood. Metuchen, NJ, Scarecrow, 2003.

2400. Gibbons, Edward. Floyd Gibbons: Your Headline Hunter. New York, Exposition Press, 1953.

2401. Gilbert, Douglas. Floyd Gibbons: Knight Of The Air. New York, Robert M. McBride, 1930.

2402. Godfrey, Jean And Kathy. Genius In The Family. New York, G. P. Putnam's Sons, 1962.

2403. Goldman, Herbert G. Banjo Eyes: Eddie Cantor and the Birth of Modern Stardom. New York, Oxford University Press, 1997.

2404. _____. Fanny Brice, The Original Funny Girl. New York, Oxford University Press, 1992.

2405. Goldman, Herbert G. Jolson: The Legend Comes To Life. New York, Oxford University Press, 1988.

2406. Gowdy, Curt. Cowboy At The Mike: The Autobiography of a Great Sports Announcer. Garden City, NY, Doubleday, 1966.

2407. Graham, Virginia and Jean Libman Block. There Goes What's Her Name: The Continuing Saga of Virginia Graham. Englewood Cliffs, NJ, Prentice-Hall, 1965.

2408. Gray, Barry. My Night People: 10,001 Nights in Broadcasting. New York, Simon & Schuster, 1975.

2409. Griffin, Merv. Merv, An Autobiography. New York, Simon & Schuster, 1980.

2410. Grossman, Barbara W. Funny Woman: The Life And Times Of Fanny Brice. Bloomington, IN, Indiana University Press, 1991.

2411. Gunther, John. Taken At The Flood: The Story of Albert D. Lasker. New York, Popular Library, 1961.

2412. Hardman, Benedict E. Everybody Called Him Cedric. Minneapolis, Twin City Federal Savings & Loan Assoc., 1970.

2413. Harper, Laurie. Don Sherwood: The Life & Times Of World's Greatest Disc Jockey. Rocklin, CA, Prima Publishing & Communications, 1989.

2414. Havig, Alan. Fred Allen's Radio Comedy. Philadelphia, Temple University Press, 1990.

2415. Hayde, Michael J. My Name's Friday. Nashville, Cummerland House, 2001.

2416. Hayes, Richard K. Kate Smith. Jefferson, NC, McFarland, 1995.

2417. Heatter, Gabriel. There's Good News Tonight: The true story of a man who found the good with the bad. Garden City, NY, Doubleday, 1960.

2418. Helburn, Theresa. A Wayward Quest: The spirited memoir of a dynamic personality in the American Theater. Boston, Little, Brown and Company. 1960.

2419. Higham, Charles. Cecil B. DeMille: A Biography of the Most Successful Film Maker of Them All. New York, Charles Scribner's, 1973.

2420. _____. Orson Wells: The Rise And Fall Of An American Genius. New York, St. Martin's Press, 1985.

2421. Hildegarde. Over 50 - So What! Garden City, NY, Doubleday, 1963.

2422. Hill, Ona L. Raymond Burr: A Film, Radio and Television Biography. Jefferson, NC, McFarland, 1994.

2423. Hope, Bob. Don't Shoot, It's Only Me. New York, G.P. Putnam's Sons, 1990.

2424. _____. Five Women I Love: Bob Hope's Vietnam Story. New York, Avon, 1967.

2425. _____. Have Tux, Will Travel. New York, Simon & Schuster, 1954.

2426. _____.The Last Christmas Show. Garden City, Doubleday, 1974.

2427. _____. So This Is Peace. New York, Simon & Schuster, 1946.

2428. _____. They Got Me Covered. Hollywood, Bob Hope, 1941.

2429. _____. This Is On Me. London, Frederick Muller. 1954.

2430. Hopper, Hedda. From Under My Hat. Garden City, NY, Doubleday, 1952.

2431. Houseman, John. Final Dress: 1954-1974. New York, Touchstone, 1983.

2432. _____. Front and Center: 1942-1955. New York, Simon & Schuster, 1979.

2433. _____. Run Through: 1902-1941. New York, Simon & Schuster, 1972.

2434. Hoyt, Edwin. Alexander Woollcott: The Man Who Came To Dinner. London, Abelard-Schuman, 1968.

2435. Huntley, Chet. The Generous Years: Remembrances of a Frontier Boyhood. Greenwich, CT, Fawcett, 1970.

2436. Husing, Ted. My Eyes Are In My Heart. New York, Random House, 1959.

2437. _____. Ten Years Before The Mike. New York, Farrar & Rinehart, 1935.

2438. Hutchins, Ralph. Minabelle: The First Glamorous Soap Opera Queen. Piqua, OH, Ralph Hutchins, 1986.

2439. Isman, Felix. Weber And Fields: Their Tribulations, Triumphs and Their Associates. New York, Boni & Liveright, 1924.

2440. Israel, Lee. Kilgallen: An Intimate Biography of Dorothy Kilgallen. New York, Dell, 1980.

2441. _____. Miss Tallulah Bankhead. New York, Berkely, 1980.

2442. Jackson, Carlton. Hattie: The Life Of Hattie McDaniel. New York, Madison Books, 1990.

2443. Jessel, George. So Help Me. Cleveland, World Publishing, 1944.

2444. Jolson, Harry. Mistah Jolson. Hollywood, House-Warven Publishers, 1951.

2445. Julian, Joseph. This Was Radio: A Personal Memoir. New York, Viking, 1975.

2446. Kanter, Hal. So Far, So Funny. Jefferson, NC, McFarland. 1999.

2447. Katkov, Norman. Fabulous Fanny: The Story Of Fanny Brice. New York, Alfred A. Knopf, 1953.

2448. Keiter, Les. Fifty Years Behind The Microphone: The Les Keiter Story. Honolulu, University of Hawaii Press, 1991.

2449. Kendrick, Alexander. Prime Time: The Life of Edward R. Murrow. Boston, Little, Brown and Company, 1969.

2450. Ketchum, Richard. Will Rogers: The Man And His Times. New York, American Heritage Publishing Co., 1973.

2451. Kilgallen, Dorothy. Girl Around The World. Philadelphia, David MacKay, 1936.

2452. Kiner, Larry. Al Jolson Discography. Westport, CT, Greenwood Press, 1983.

2453. _____. Nelson Eddy: A Bio-Discography. Metuchen, NJ, Scarecrow, 1992.

2454. _____. The Rudy Vallee Discography. Westport, CT, Greenwood Press, 1985.

2455. Kirby, Durwood. My Life: Those Wonderful Years. Charlotte Harbor, FL, Tabby House Books, 1992.

2456. Kluckhohn, Frank and Jay Franklin. The Drew Pearson Story. Chicago, Chas. Hallberg, 1967.

2457. Klurfeld, Herman. Winchell: His Life And Times. New York, Praeger, 1952.

2458. Koseluk, Gregory. Eddie Cantor, A Life In Show Business. Jefferson, NC, McFarland. 1995.

2459. Kurth, Peter. American Cassandra: The Life of Dorothy Thompson. Boston, Little, Brown and Company, 1990.

2460. Lackmann, Ron. Mercedes McCambridge. Jefferson, NC, McFarland, 2005.

2461. Langguth, A. J., ed. Norman Corwin's Letters. New York, Barricade Books, 1994.

2462. Leaming, Barbara. Orson Welles. New York, Viking. 1985.

2463. Leonard, Bill. In The Eye Of The Storm: A Lifetime at CBS. New York, G. P. Putnam's Sons, 1987.

2464. Levant, Oscar. A Smattering Of Ignorance. New York, Garden City Publishing, 1942.

2465. _____. The Memoirs Of An Amnesiac. New York, G. P. Putnam's Sons, 1965.

2466. Lewis. Roger. The Life And Death Of Peter Sellers. New York, Applause, 1997.

2467. Linkletter, Art. Confessions Of A Happy Man: Art Linkletter's Own Story. New York, Random House, 1960.

2468. _____. Hobo On The Way To Heaven: An Autobiography. Elgin, IL, David C. Cook Publishing, 1980.

2469. _____. I Didn't Do It Alone: The Autobiography of Art Linkletter. Ottawa, IL, Caroline House, 1980.

2470. Livingston, Mary. Jack Benny. Garden City, NY, Doubleday, 1978.

2471. Lombardo, Guy. Auld Acquaintance: An Autobiography. Garden City, NY, Doubleday, 1975.

2472. Lonstein, Albert L. and Vito R. Marino. Revised Compleat Sinatra Discography. Filmography, TV, Movie, Radio. Ellenvile, NY, Cameron Publications, 1979.

2473. Lopez, Vincent. Lopez Speaking: An Autobiography. New York, Citadel, 1960.

2474. Louvish, Simon. Man On The Flying Trapeze: The Life and Times of W.C. Fields. New York, W.W. Norton, 1997.

2475. Love, Paula McSpadden. The Will Rogers Book. Indianapolis, Bobbs Merrill Company, 1961.

2476. Lyons, Eugene. David Sarnoff: A Biography. New York, Harper & Row, 1966.

2477. MacFarlane, Malcolm. Day by Day. Metuchen, NJ, Scarecrow, 2001.

2478. Maier, Paul L. A Man Spoke, A World Listened: The Story of Walter A. Maier. New York, McGraw-Hill, 1963.

2479. Marcus, Sheldon. Father Coughlin: The Tumultuous Life of the Priest of the Little Flower. Boston, Little, Brown and Company, 1973.

2480. Marill, Alvin H. Mickey Rooney. Jefferson, NC, McFarland, 2005.

2481. Martin, George. Damrosch Dynasty: America's First Family of Music. Boston, Houghton, Mifflin Co. 1983.

2482. Marx, Arthur. Every Body Loves Somebody Sometime (Especially Himself). New York, Hawthorn Books, 1974.

2483. _____. Red Skelton. New York, E. P. Dutton, 1979.

2484. _____. The Secret Life Of Bob Hope. New York, Barricade Books, 1993.

2485. Marx, Groucho. Groucho And Me. New York, Bernard Geis Associates, 1959.

2486. _____. The Marx Brothers Scrapbook. New York, Warner, 1975.

2487. _____. Memoirs Of A Mangy Lover. New York, Manor Books, 1974.

2488. McBride, Mary Margaret. A Long Way From Missouri. New York, G. P. Putnam's Sons, 1959.

2489. _____. Out Of The Air. Garden City, Doubleday, 1960.

2490. McCambridge, Mercedes. The Quality Of Mercy: An Autobiography. New York, Times Books, 1981.

2491. McGovern, Jim. The 50,000 Watt Broadcast Barnum: A Book Noir of Stanley E. Hubbard, His Life and Times. Duchas Press, 1996.

2492. McKelway, St. Clair. Gossip: The Life and Times Of Walter Winchell. New York, Viking Press, 1940.

2493. McMahon, Ed. Here's Ed: From Midway To Midnight. New York, G. P. Putnam's Sons, 1976.

2494. Mehlman, Jeffrey. Walter Benjamin For Children: An Essay on His Radio Years. Chicago, University of Chicago Press, 1993.

2495. Mitchell, Glenn. The Marx Brothers Encyclopedia. London, B.T. Batsford Ltd., 1996.

2496. Mix, Paul E. The Life And Legend Of Tom Mix. New York, A. S. Barnes, 1972.

2497. Morella, Joe E. Lucy: The Bittersweet Life Of Lucille Ball. London, W. H. Allen, 1974.

2498. _____. and Edward Z. Epstein and Eleanor Clark. Amazing Careers Of Bob Hope, From Gags to Riches. Carlstadt, NJ, Rainbow Books, 1973.

2499. Morgan, Henry. Here's Morgan: The Original Bad Boy of Broadcasting. New York, Barricade Books, 1994.

2500. Moyer, Daniel and Eugene Alvarez. Just The Facts Ma'am. Santa Ana, CA, Seven Locks Press, 2001.

2501. Mulholland, Jim. The Abbott And Costello Book. New York, Popular Library, 1977.

2502. Murray, Ken. Life On A Pogo Stick: An Autobiography of a Comedian. Philadelphia, John C. Winston, 1960.

2503. Naremore, James. Magic World of Orson Welles. New York, Oxford University Press, 1978.

2504. Nelson, Ozzie. Ozzie, Englewood Cliffs, NJ, Prentice-Hall, 1973.

2505. Nimmo, H. Arlo. Andrew Sisters: A Biography and Career Record. Jefferson, NC, McFarland, 2004.

2506. Nollen, Scott Allen. Boris Karloff: A Gentleman's Life. Baltimore, Midnight Marquee. 1999.

2507. Norris, M. G. "Bud". The Tom Mix Book. Waynesville, NC, World Of Yesterday, 1989.

2508. Nye, Frank W. Hoop Of Hooperatings: The Man and His Work. Norwalk, CT, 1957.

2509. O'Brian, Jack. Godfrey The Great: The Life Story of Arthur Godfrey. New York, Cross Publications, 1951.

2510. O'Brien, P.J. Will Rogers, Ambassador of Good Will, Prince of Wit and Wisdom. Philadelphia, John C. Winston Company, 1935.

2511. Oberfirst, Robert. Al Jolson: You Ain't Heard Nothin' Yet! New York, A. S. Barnes, 1982.

2512. Ohmart, Ben. Welcome Foolish Mortals: The Life and Voices of Paul Frees. Boalsburg, PA, Bear Manor Media, 2004.

2513. _____. and Charles Stumpf. Walter Tetley For Corn's Sake. Boalsburg, PA, Bear Manor Media. 2003.

2514. Oppenheimer, Jess. Laughs, Luck...And Lucy How I Came To Create The Most Popular Sitcom of All Time. Syracuse, NY, Syracuse University Press, 1996.

2515. Oursler Fulton. Behold This Dreamer! An Autobiography. Boston, Little Brown and Company, 1964.

2516. Paar, Jack. P.S. Jack Paar, An Entertainment. Garden City, NY, Doubleday, 1983.

2517. Pairpoint, Lionel, ed. And Here's Bing. International Crosby Circle, 2000.

2518. Paley, William S. As It Happened: A Memoir by William S. Paley, Founder and Chairman, CBS. Garden City, NY, Doubleday, 1979.

2519. Paper, Lewis J. Empire: William S. Paley and the Making of CBS. New York, St. Martin's Press, 1987.

2520. Pearl, Minnie. Minnie Pearl: An Autobiography. New York, Simon & Schuster, 1980.

2521. Pearson, Drew. Diaries: 1949-1959. New York, Holt, Rinehart & Winston, 1974.

2522. Persico, Joseph E. Edward R, Murrow: An American Original. New York, Laurel, 1988.

2523. Peyton, Father Patrick. All For Her: The Autobiography of Father Patrick Peyton. Garden City, NY, Doubleday, 1967.

2524. Phillips, Robert W. Roy Rogers: A Biography, Radio History, Television and Bibliography. Jefferson, NC, McFarland, 1995.

2525. Pilat, Oliver. Drew Pearson: An Unauthorized Biography. New York, Pocket Books, 1973.

2526. Pitts, Michael R. Kate Smith, A Bio Bibliography. Westport, CT, Greenwood, 1998.

2527. Powers, Tom. Life Studies: A Collection of New Monologues. New York, Samuel French, 1939.

2528. Quirk, Lawrence J. Bob Hope: The Road Well Travelled. New York, Applause, 1998.

2529. Raby, Ormand. Radio's First Voice: The Story of Reginald Fessenden. New York, Macmillan, 1970.

2530. Randall, Tony. Which Reminds Me. New York, Delacorte Press, 1989.

2531. RCA. Biographical Sketch Of Brigadier General David Sarnoff. New York, RCA. 1950.

2532. Reynolds, Quentin. By Quentin Reynolds. New York, McGraw-Hill, 1963.

2533. _____. The Curtain Rises. New York, Random House, 1944.

2534. Richmam, Harry. A Hell Of A Life. New York, Duell, Sloan & Pearce, 1966.

2535. Robbins, Jhan. Inka Dinka Doo: The Life Of Jimmy Durante. New York, Paragon House, 1991.

2536. Robinson, Edward G. All My Yesterdays: An Autobiography. New York, Hawthorn Books, 1973.

2537. Rogers, Roy and Dale Evans. Happy Trails. Carmel, NY, Guideposts, 1979.

2538. Rogers, Will. The Autobiography of Will Rogers. New York, Avon, 1975.

2539. Rosenfield, Joe, Jr. The Happiest Man In The World. Garden City, NY, Doubleday, 1955.

2540. Sander, Gordon F. Serling: The Rise And Twilight of Television's Last Angry Man. New York, Dutton, 1992.

2541. Schaffner, Franklin J.(Interviewer). Worthington Miner: Interviewed by Franklin J. Schaffner. Metuchen, NJ, Scarecrow, 1985.

2542. Schroth, Raymond A. The American Journey Of Eric Sevareid. South Royalton, VT, Steerforth Press, 1995.

2543. Sevareid, Eric. Not So Wild A Dream. New York, Alfred A. Knopf, 1946.

2544. Sforza, John. Swing It: The Andrew Sisters Story. Lexington, KY, University Press Of Kentucky, 2000.

2545. Shayon, Robert Lewis. Odyssey in Prime Time: A Life in Twentieth Century Media. Philadelphia, Waymark Press, 2001.

2546. Shepherd, Donald and Robert F. Slatzer. Bing Crosby: The Hollow Man. New York, St. Martin's Press, 1981.

2547. Shiels, Michael. J. P. McCarthy: Just Don't Tell 'Em Where I Am. Chelsea, MI, Sleeping Bear Press, 1997.

2548. Shilkret, Nathaniel. Nathaniel Shilkret: Sixty Years in the Music Business. Metuchen, NJ, Scarcrow, 2005.

2549. Shirer, William L. The Nightmare Years, 1930-1940: A Memoir of a Life and the Times. Boston, Little, Brown and Company, 1984.

2550. Singer, Arthur J. Arthur Godfrey: The Adventures of an American Broadcaster. Jefferson, NC, McFarland, 2000.

2551. Smith, Kate. Living In A Great Big Way. New York, Blue Ribbon Books, 1938.

2552. Smith, Sally Bedell. In All His Glory: The Life & Times Of William S. Paley. New York, Simon & Schuster, 1990.

2553. Smith, Steven C. A Heart At Fire's Center. Berkeley, University Of California Press, 1991.

2554. Smith, Wilber. A Voice For God: The Life of Charles E. Fuller, the Originator of The Old Fashioned Revival Hour. Boston, W. A. Wilde, 1949.

2555. Sperber, A. M. Murrow, His Life And Times. New York, Freundlich, 1986.

2556. Stagg, Jerry. A Half Century of Show Business and the Fabulous Empire of the Brothers Shubert. New York, Ballantine Books, 1969.

2557. Steiner, Rodney and Thomas A. Delong. Frank Munn, A Biodiscography Of The Golden Voice Of Radio. Southport, CT, Sasco Associates, 1993.

2558. Sterling, Bryan, ed. The Will Rogers Scrapbook. New York, Grosset & Dunlap, 1976.

2559. Stern, Bill. The Taste Of Ashes. New York, Hillman, 1961.

2560. Stilson, Kenneth L. Ezra Stone: A Theatrical Biography. Jefferson, NC, McFarland, 1995.

2561. Stone, Hal (Harlan). Aw Relax Archie, Re-laxx: When radio was "king" I was once a "prince But ended up a "Jughead." Sedona, AZ, Bygone Days Press, 2003.

2562. Striker, Fran, Jr. His Typewriter Grew Spurs: A Biography of Fran Striker–Writer. Lansdale, PA, Questco, 1983.

2563. Stuart, Lyle. The Secret Life Of Walter Winchell. New York, Boar's Head Books, 1953.

2564. Swallow, John W. Midwife To An Octopus. Encino, CA, Garden House Press, 1964.

2565. Swanberg, W. A. Luce And His Empire. New York, Dell, 1973.

2566. Swing, Raymond Gram. Good Evening! A Professional Memoir. New York, Harcourt, Brace & World, 1964.

2567. Taylor, John Russell. Orson Welles, A Celebration. Boston, Little, Brown and Company, 1986.

2568. Taylor, Robert. Fred Allen, His Life And Wit. Boston, Little, Brown and Company, 1989.

2569. Taylor, Robert Lewis. W. C. Fields His Follies And Fortunes. Garden City, NY, Doubleday, 1949.

2570. Teichmann, Howard. George S. Kaufman: An Intimate Portrait. New York, Atheneum, 1972.

2571. _____. Smart Aleck: The Wit, World and Life Of Alexander Woollcott, New York, William Morrow, 1976.

2572. Thomas, Bob. Bud And Lou. New York, J. B. Lippincott, 1977.

2573. Thomas, Bob. The One And Only Bing. New York, Ace, 1977.

2574. _____. Winchell. Garden City, NY, Doubleday, 1971.

2575. Thomas, Danny. Make Room For Danny. New York, G. P. Putnam's Sons, 1991.

2576. Thomas, Lowell. Good Evening Everybody: From Cripple Creek To Samarkand. New York, Avon, 1977.

2577. Thomas, Lowell. So Long Until Tomorrow: From Quaker Hill To Katmandu. New York, William Morrow, 1977.

2578. Thompson, Charles. Bing: The Authorized Biography. New York, David McKay, 1976

2579. _____. Bob Hope: The Road From Eltham. London, Thames Methuen, 1981.

2580. Thomson, David. Rosebud. New York, Alfred Knopf, 1996.

2581. Tranberg, Charles. I Love the Illusion: The Life and Career of Agnes Moorehead. Boalsburg, PA, Bear Manor Media, 2005.

2582. Treadwell, Bill. Head, Heart and Heel. New York, Mayfair Books, 1958.

2583. Tucker, L.E. From Dust to Glory: The Story Of J.L. Tucker, Founder "The Quiet Hour" Broadcast. Nashville, TN, Sceptre Book, 1979.

2584. Tucker, Sophie. Some Of These Days: The Autobiography of Sophie Tucker. New York, Garden City Publishing, 1945.

2585. Tull, Charles J. Father Coughlin & The New Deal. Syracuse, NY, Syracuse University Press, 1965.

2586. Ulanov, Barry. The Incredible Crosby. New York, McGraw-Hill, 1948.

2587. Vallee, Rudy. Let The Chips Fall: Unrestrained Reminiscences. Harrisburg, PA, Stackpole, 1975.

2588. _____. My Time Is Your Time: The Story of Rudy Vallee. New York, Ivan Obolensky, 1962.

2589. _____. Vagabond Dreams Come True. New York, E. P. Dutton, 1930.

2590. Wallace, Mike. Close Encounters: Mike Wallace's Own Story. New York, Berkely, 1985.

2591. Ward, Louis B. Father Charles E. Coughlin, An Authorized Biography. Detroit, Tower Publications, 1933.

2592. Waring, Virginia. Fred Waring And The Pennsylvanians. Urbana, IL, University of Illinois Press, 1997.

2593. Warren, Donald. Radio Priest: Charles Coughlin The Father of Hate Radio. New York, Free Press, 1996.

2594. Weaver, Pat. The Best Seat In The House: The Golden Years of Radio and Television. New York, Alfred A. Knopf, 1994.

2595. Weiner, Ed. Let's Go To Press: A Profile of Walter Winchell. New York, G. P. Putnam's Sons, 1955.

2596. Welk, Lawrence. Ah-One, Ah-Two! Life with My Musical Family. Englewood Cliffs, NJ, Prentice-Hall, 1974.

2597. _____. Wunnerful, Wunnerful! The Autobiography of Lawrence Welk. New York, Bantam, 1973.

2598. Welles, Orson and Peter Bogdanovich. Ed. Jonathan Rosenbaum. This Is Orson Welles. New York, Harper Collins, 1992.

2599. Wells, Jeff. Jeff Chandler. Jefferson, NC, McFarland, 2005.

2600. Wile, Frederic William. News Is Where You Find It: Forty Years' Reporting at Home and Abroad. Indianapolis, Bobbs-Merrill, 1939.

2601. Willson, Meredith. And There I Stood With My Piccolo. Garden City, NY, Doubleday, 1948.

2602. Wilson, Earl. Sinatra. New York, Macmillan, 1976.

2603. Winchell, Walter. Winchell Exclusive: Things That Happened to Me-And Me to Them. Englewood Cliffs, NJ, Prentice-Hall, 1975.

2604. Wolfman Jack and Byron Laursen. Have Mercy: Confessions of the Original Rock 'n' Animal. New York, Warner Books, 1995.

2605. Wood, Bret. Orson Welles, A Bio-Bibliography. Westport, CT, Greenwood, 1990.

2606. Youngkin, Stephen D. The Lost One: A Life of Peter Lorre. Univeristy Press of Kentucky, 2005.

2607. Zimmerman, Paul D. and Burt Goldblatt. The Marx Brothers At The Movies. New York, Signet, 1970.

Biography/Mixed

2608. Agan, Patrick. Is That Who You Think It Is. Vol. 1-3. New York, Ace, 1975 & 1976.

2609. Auerbach, Arnold M. Funny Men Don't Laugh. Garden City, NY, Doubleday, 1965.

2610. Cahn, William. A Pictorial History Of The Great Comedians. New York, Grosset & Dunlap, 1970.

2611. _____. The Laugh Makers. New York, G. P. Putnam's Sons, 1957.

2612. De Long. Thomas A. Radio Stars. Jefferson, NC, McFarland, 1996.

2613. Dunn, Helen, ed. People! Places! and Parties! Helen Dunn Associates,1973.

2614. Eells, George. Hedda And Louella. New York, G.P. Putnam's Sons, 1972.

2615. Eichberg, Robert. Radio Stars Of Today: Or Behind the Scenes in Broadcasting. Boston, L.C. Page, 1937.

2616. Gurman, Joseph and Myron Slager. Radio Round-Ups: Intimate Glimpses of the Radio Stars. Boston, Lothrop, Lee & Shepard, 1932.

2617. Henderson, Amy. On The Air: Pioneers of American Broadcasting. Washington, DC, Smithsonian Institution Press, 1988.

2618. Lamparski, Richard. Lamparski's Hidden Hollywood: Where the Stars Lived, Loved and Died. New York, Simon and Schuster, 1981.

2619. _____. Whatever Became Of? Series of 11 volumes. Published at different times by Crown, Bantam and Ace publishers, 1970-1989.

2620. Lentz,III, Harris M. Obituaries in the Performing Arts, 2004. Jefferson, NC, McFarland, 2005.

2621. Martin, Linda and Kerry Segrave. Women In Comedy. New York, Citadel. 1986.

2622. Marx, Samuel. Broadway Portraits. New York, Donald Flamm, 1929.

2623. Radio Publications Co. Who's Who In Radio: A Quarterly Review of American Broadcasting Personalities. New York, Radio Publications Co, 1935.

2624. Rockwell, Don, ed. Radio Personalities: A Pictorial and Biographical Annual. New York, Press Bureau, 1936.

2625. Skutch. Ira, ed. Five Directors: A Directors Guild of America Oral History. Metuchen, NJ, Scarecrow, 1998.

2626. Slide, Anthony. Eccentrics of Comedy. Metuchen, NJ, Scarecrow, 1998.

2627. Slide, Anthony. Great Radio Personalities In Historic Photographs. New York, Dover, 1982.

2628. Smith, Bill. The Vaudevillians. New York, Macmillan, 1976.

2629. Zolotow, Maurice. No People Like Show People. New York, Random House, 1947.

Broadcasting & Broadcasting Technqiues

Broadcasting: General
(See also History and Station Operation)

2630. Skornia, H. J., Robert H. Lee and Fred A. Brewer. Creative Broadcasting. Englewood Cliffs, NJ, Prentice Hall, 1950.

2631. Taylor, Sherril W., ed. Radio Programming In Action. New York, Hastings House, 1967.

2632. Willis, Edgar E. Foundations in Broadcasting: Radio and Television. New York, Oxford University Press, 1951.

Broadcasting: Acting

2633. Duerr, Edwin. Radio And Television Acting: Criticism, Theory and Practice. New York, Rinehart, 1950.

Broadcasting: Announcing and Speaking

2634. Barnhard, Lyle D. Radio And Television Announcing. Englewood Cliffs, NJ, Prentice-Hall, 1958.

2635. Bender, James F., ed. NBC Handbook Of Pronunciation. New York, Thomas Y. Crowell, 1943.

2636. C.de Witt White Co. Radio Announcers: 1933. C. de Witt White, 1933.

2637. Carmen, Ruth. Radio Dramatics: Instruction Lectures. New York, John C. Yorston, 1937.

2638. Dragonette, Jessica. Your Voice And You. Emmaus, PA, Rodale Books, 1966.

2639. Dunlap, Orrin E. Talking On The Radio. New York, Greenberg, 1936.

2640. Gilmore, Art and Glenn Y. Middleton. Radio Announcing. Hollywood, Hollywood Radio Publishers, 1946.

2641. Gould, Samuel B. and Sidney A. Diamond. Training The Local Announcer. New York, Longmans, Green, 1950.

2642. Henneke, Ben G. The Radio Announcer's Handbook. New York, Rinehart, 1948.

2643. Kaufman, William I., ed. How To Announce For Radio And Television. New York, Hastings House, 1956.

2644. Keith, Alice. Microphone And You. National Academy Of Broadcasting, 1955.

2645. Keith, Michael C. Broadcast Voice Performance. Boston, Focal Press, 1989.

2646. Kleiser, Grenville, ed. Radio Broadcasting, How To Speak Convincingly. New York, Funk & Wagnalls, 1935.

2647. Lawton, Sherman Paxton. Radio Speech. Boston, Expression Co., 1932.

2648. Lent, Henry B. This Is Your Announcer. Ted Lane Breaks Into Radio. New York, Macmillan, 1945.

2649. McNamee, Graham and Robert Gordon Anderson. You're On The Air. New York, Harper, 1926.

2650. Pear, T. H. Voice And Personality. New York, John Wiley & Sons, 1931.

2651. Poindexter, Ray. Golden Throats And Silver Tongues. Conway, AR, River Road Press, 1978.

2652. West, Robert. So-o-o-o You're Going On The Air and The Radio Speech Primer. New York, Rodin Publishing, 1934.

Broadcasting: Direction and Production

2653. Carlile, John S. Production And Direction Of Radio Programs. Englewood Cliffs, NJ, Prentice Hall, 1946.

2654. Crews, Albert. Radio Production Directing. Boston, Houghton Mifflin, 1944.

2655. Hoffer, Jay. Radio Production Techniques. TAB Books, 1974.

2656. Krulevitch, Walter and Rome. Radio Drama Production: A Handbook. Rinehart, 1946

2657. McGill, Earle. Radio Directing. New York, McGraw Hill, 1940.

2658. Willis, Edgar E. A Radio Director's Manual: A Survey of Principles and Techniques with Sixty-One Production Exercises. Ann Arbor, MI, Campus Publishers, 1961.

Broadcasting: Sound Effects

2659. Arnheim, Rudolf. Radio, An Art Of Sound. New York, Da Capo Press, 1972.

2660. Creamer, Joseph and William B. Hoffman. Radio Sound Effects. New York, Ziff-Davis, 1945.

2661. Mott, Robert L. Radio Live! Television Live! Those Golden Days When Horses Were Coconuts. Jefferson, NC, McFarland, 2000.

2662. _____. Radio Sound Effects. Jefferson, NC, McFarland, 1993.

2663. Turnbull, Robert B. Radio & Television Sound Effects. New York, Rinehart & Co., 1951.

Broadcasting: Writing
(See also Genre: News)

2664. Barnow, Erik. Handbook Of Radio Writing. Boston, Little, Brown and Company, 1939.

2665. Cheuse, Alan and Caroline Marshall, eds. The Sound Of Writing: America's Short Story Magazine of the Air. New York, Anchor Books, 1991.

2666. Cowgill, Rome. Fundamentals Of Writing for Radio. New York, Rinehart, 1949.

2667. Crews, Albert. Professional Radio Writing. Boston, Houghton Mifflin, 1946.

2668. Dixon, Peter. Radio Sketches And How To Write Them. New York, Frederick A. Stokes, 1936.

2669. Dixon, Peter. Radio Writing. New York, Century, 1931.

2670. Field, Stanley. Television And Radio Writing. Boston, Houghton Mifflin, 1958.

2671. Gielgud, Val. How To Write Broadcast Plays. Hurst & Blackett, 1932.

2672. _____. The Right Way To Radio Writing. Right Way Books, ca. 1940.

2673. Hasty, Jack. Done With Mirrors: Admissions of a Freelance Writer. New York, Ives Washburn, 1943.

2674. Hilliard, Robert L. Writing For Television And Radio. New York, Hastings House, 1970.

2675. Keith, Alice. How To Speak And Write For Radio: A Manual of Broadcasting Technique. New York, Harper & Brothers, 1944.

2676. Lawrence, Jerome, ed. Off Mike: Radio Writing by the Nation's Top Radio Writers. New York, Essential Books, 1944.

2677. Mackey, David R. Drama On The Air. New York, Prentice Hall, 1951.

2678. Nagler, Frank. Writing For Radio. New York, Ronald Press, 1938.

2679. Niggli, Josephina. Pointers On Radio Writing. Boston, The Writers Inc. 1941?

2680. Rivers, William L. The Mass Media: Reporting, Writing, Editing. New York, Harper & Row, 1964.

2681. Rogers, Ralph. Dos And Don'ts Of Radio Writing. Boston, Associated Radio Writers, 1937.

2682. Seymour, Katherine and John T. W. Martin. Practical Radio Writing. New York, Longmans, Green, 1938.

2683. Straczynski, J. Michael. The Complete Book Of Script Writing. Cincinnati, OH, Writer's Digest Books, 1982.

2684. Weaver, Luther. The Technique Of Radio Writing. New York, Prentice-Hall, 1948.

2685. Whipple, James. How To Write For Radio. New York, McGraw-Hill, 1938.

2686. Whitaker-Wilson, C. Writing For Broadcasting. A. & C. Black, 1935.

2687. Willis, Edgar E. Writing Television and Radio Programs. New York, Holt, Rinehart & Winston, 1967.

2688. Wylie, Max. Radio And Television Writing. New York, Rinehart, 1952.

2689. _____. Radio Writing. New York, Rinehart, 1939.

Career Training

2690. Carlisle, Norman V. and Conrad C. Rice. Your Career In Radio. New York, E.P. Dutton, 1941.

2691. Cott, Ted. How To Audition For Radio: A Handbook for Actors. A Workbook for Students. New York, Greenberg, 1946.

2692. Ewing, Sam. You're On The Air. Blue Ridge Summit, PA, TAB Books, 1972.

2693. Hayes, John S. and Horace J. Gardner. Both Sides Of The Microphone: Training For Radio. Philadelphia, J.B. Lippincott, 1938.

2694. Jones, Charles Reed, ed. Your Career In Motion Pictures, Radio, Television. New York, Sheridan House, 1949.

2695. Lerch, John H., ed. Careers In Broadcasting. New York, Appleton-Century-Crofts, 1962.

2696. Lowell, Maurice. Listen In. New York, Dodge, 1937.

Ethnic Radio

Ethnic: African American

2697. Barlow, William. Voice Over: Making of Black Radio. Philadelphia, Temple University Press, 1999.

2698. Lotz, Rainer E. and Neuert Ulrich. AFRS *Jubilee* Transcription Programs, An Exploratory Discography. (2 vols.),Frankfurt, Germany, Norbert Ruecker, 1985.

2699. MacDonald, J. Fred, ed. Richard Durham's *Destination Freedom*: Scripts from Radio's Black Legacy, 1948-50. Westport, CT, Praeger, 1989.

2700. McCleelland, Doug. Blackface to Blacklist: Al Jolson, Larry Parks, and *The Jolson Story*. Metuchen, NJ, Scarecrow, 1987.

2701. Newman, Mark. Entrepreneurs of Profit and Pride: From Black-Appeal to Radio Soul. Westport, CT, Praeger, 1988.

2702. Ottley, Roi. New World A-Coming: Inside Black America. Cleveland, World Publishing, 1941.

2703. Sampson, Henry T. Swingin' on the Etherwaves: A Chronological History of African Americans in Radio and Television Broadcasting, 1925-1955. Metuchen, NJ, Scarecrow,2005.

2704. Savage, Barbara Dianne. Broadcasting Freedom: Radio, War, and the Politics of Race 1938-1948. Chapel Hill, NC, University of North Carolina Press, 1999.

2705. Watkins, Mel. On The Real Side. New York, Touchstone, 1994.

2706. Williams, Gilbert A. Legendary Pioneers Of Black Radio. Westport, CT, Praeger, 1998.

2707. Wright Sr. Major R. R. Radio Speeches. Harriet Beecher Stowe Wright Lemon, 1949.

Ethnic: Mixed

2708. Corenthal, Michael G. Cohen On The Telephone: A History of Jewish Recorded Humor and Popular Music 1892-1942. Milwaukee, Yesterday's Memories, 1984.

2709. Keith, Michael. Signals in the Air: Native Broadcasting in America. Westport, CT, Praeger, 1995.

2710. Migala, Joseph. Polish Radio Broadcasting in the United States. New York, Columbia University Press, 1987.

2711. U.S. Office of Education. Americans All, Immigrants All: A Handbook for Listeners and a Manual. 1942.

Genre Programming

Genre: Advice and Inspirational

2712. Alexander, A. L., ed. Poems That Touch The Heart. Garden City, NY, Doubleday, 1963.

2713. Anthony, John J. Marriage & Family Problems And How To Solve Them. New York, Doubleday, 1939.

2714. Cheerio. Cheerio's Book Of Days. New York, Garden City Publishing, 1940.

2715. Drake, Galen. This Is Galen Drake. Garden City, NY, Doubleday, 1950.

2716. _____. What You Can Do Today. New York, Random House, 1960.

2717. Kenyon, Doris. Doris Kenyon's Monologues. Philadelphia, Penn Publishing, 1929.

2718. Kirkham, Art. This And That on KOIN. Portland, OR, Metropolitan Printing, 1939.

2719. Lord, Phillips H. Seth Parker And His Jonesport Folks Way Back Home. Philadelphia, John C. Winston, 1932.

2720. _____. Seth Parker's Album. New York, Century, 1930.

2721. _____. Seth Parker's Hymnal. New York, Carl Fischer, 1931.

2722. _____. Seth Parker's Scrap Book. New York, Phillips H. Lord, 1935.

2723. Lowe, Dr. Frank. Holiday From Worry: A 20th Anniversary Volume of Timely and Typical Broadcasts. Frank Lowe, 1956.

2724. Magpie. The Wine Of Words. Los Angeles, Wetzel Publishing, 1930.

2725. Maxwell, Richard. Cheer And Comfort. Chicago, Rodeheaver, Hall-Mack, 1937.

2726. Mirandy. Breezes From Persimmon Holler. Hollywood, Oxford Press, 1943.

2727. Old Counsellor. Answers By The Old Counsellor, Vol. 1. Halsey, Stuart, 1928.

2728. Osgood, Charles. There's Nothing That I Wouldn't Do If You Would Be My POSSLQ*, New York, Holt, Rinehart & Winston, 1981.

2729. Rosenfield, Joe, Jr. Have No Fear. New York, Citadel Press, 1959.

2730. Voice of Experience. Making Molehills of Mountains. New York, Voice of Experience, 1936.

2731. _____. Stranger Than Fiction. New York, Dodd, Mead, 1935.

2732. _____. The Voice Of Experience. New York, Dodd, Mead, 1934.

Genre: Children's

2733. Anderson, Arthur. Let's Pretend and the Golden Age of Radio. Boalsburg, PA, Bear Manor Media,2004.

2734. _____. Let's Pretend: The History of Radio's Best Loved Children's Show By A Longtime Cast Member. Jefferson, NC, McFarland, 1994.

2735. Assorted. Big Little Books. Both the Saalfield Company, Akron, OH and Whitman Publishing, Racine, WI published "Big Little Books" related to children's radio programs such as *Jungle Jim, Buck Rogers, Terry and the Pirates*, etc. The books were part text, part comic. For a more complete listing of these books, see *Big Little Books: A Collector's Reference & Value Guide* by Larry Jacobs,

Collector Books, Paducah, KY and *Price Guide to Big Little Books*, L-W Book Sales, Gas City, IN.

2736. Benson, Sally. Junior Miss. New York, Random House, 1941.

2737. Boemer, Marilyn Lawrence. The Children's Hour: Radio Programs For Children, 1929-1956. Metuchen, NJ, Scarecrow Press, 1989.

2738. Claire, Malcolm. Tune-In Again: Uncle Mal's Second Story Book. New York, Grosset & Dunlap, 1940.

2739. _____. Tune-In Tales. New York, Grosset & Dunlap, 1939.

2740. Davis, Stephen. Say Kids! What Time Is It? Notes from the Peanut Gallery. Boston, Little Brown and Company, 1987.

2741. Dixon, Peter. Bobby Benson In The Tunnel Of Gold or Secret Of Nugget Creek. Hecker H-O Co., 1936.

2742. Elliott, Bob and Ray Goulding. Linda Lovely And The Fleebus. Dodd, Mead, 1960.

2743. Grandinetti, Fred M. Popeye. Jefferson, NC, McFarland, 1994.

2744. Grossman, Gary. Superman: Serial To Cereal. New York, Popular Library, 1977.

2745. Herbert, F. Hugh. Meet Corliss Archer. Garden City, NY, Sun Dial Press, 1944.

2746. Kallis, Stephen, Jr. Radio's Captain Midnight: The Wartime Biography. Jefferson, NC, McFarland, 2000.

2747. King, Fred L. Jack Armstrong Scrapbook.: A Study in Premium Advertising. Fred King, 1979.

2748. Lachmann, Ron. Comic Strips & Comic Books of Radio's Golden Age 1920s-1950s: A biography of all radio shows based on comics. Boalsburg, PA, Bear Manor Media, 2004.

2749. Robeson, Kenneth. The Incredible Radio Exploits Of Doc Savage. Greenwood, MA, Odyssey Publications, 1982

2750. _____. The Invincible Doc Savage. Greenwood, MA, Odyssey Publications, 1983.

2751. Schulkers, Robert F. The Cazanovia Treasure. Seckatary Hawkins, 1921.

2752. _____. The Ghost of Lake Tapahoe. Seckatary Hawkins, 1932.

2753. _____. Stoner's Boy. Seckatary Hawkins. 1926.

2754. Sergeant Preston. Sergeant Preston Of The Yukon. New York, Dell, 1955.

2755. Sherwood, Lorraine. Old Abe, American Eagle. New York, Charles Scribners, 1946.

2756. Uncle Don. Uncle Don's Book On Etiquette And Things. New York, Broadcast Publishing, 1930.

2757. Warner, Henry Edward. Uncle Ed And His Dream Children: A Complete Collection of Radio Verses. Baltimore, Press/R. L. Polk Printing, 1929.

2758. Wicker, Ireene. The Singing Lady's Favorite Stories (Vol. 1). Racine, WI, Whitman Publishing, 1934?.

Genre: Comedy

(See also Plays and Scripts)

2759. Ace, Goodman. Ladies And Gentleman-Easy Aces. Garden City, NY, Doubleday, 1970.

2760. Andrews, Bart and Ahrgus Julliard. Holy Mackerel! New York, E.P. Dutton, 1986.

2761. _____. The Story Of I Love Lucy. New York, Popular Library, 1977.

2762. Appleberg, Marilyn, ed. America: An Illustrated Diary of Its Most Exciting Years: The Golden Age of Comedy, Books One and Two. American Family Enterprises, 1973.

2763. Barson, Michael, ed. Flywheel, Shyster, And Flywheel: The Marx Brothers Lost Radio Show. New York, Pantheon Books, 1988.

2764. Berger, Phil. The Last Laugh. New York, Ballantine, 1976.

2765. Brecher, Irving. Life Of Riley. Waltham, MA, Waverly House, 1949.

2766. Cahn, Willian and Rhoda. The Great American Comedy Scene. New York, Monarch, 1978.

2767. Correll, Charles J. and Freeman F. Gosden. All About Amos 'n' Andy and Their Creators Correll and Gosden. New York, Rand McNally, 1929.

2768. _____. Here They Are Amos 'n' Andy. New York, Ray Long & Richard Smith, 1931.

2769. _____. Sam 'n' Henry. Chicago, Shrewesbury, 1926.

2770. Ely, Melvin Patrick. Adventures Of Amos N' Andy: A Social History of an American Phenomenon. New York, The Free Press, 1991.

2771. Eyles, Allen. Marx Brothers, Their World Of Comedy. New York, Paperback Library, 1971.

2772. Falk, Irving A. An Analysis Of The Radio Network Daytime Serial Drama Vic & Sade, 1932-1947. New York University Ph.D. Thesis, 1971.

2773. Feldman, Michael. Whad' Ya Know? New York, Harper Perennial, 1992.

2774. Firestone, Ross, ed. The Big Radio Comedy Program. Contemporary Books, 1978.

2775. Ford, Senator, Harry Hershfield and Joe Laurie, Jr. Can You Top This? Garden City, NY, Blue Ribbon, 1946.

2776. Franklin, Joe. Encyclopedia of Comedians. New York, Bell Publishing Company, 1979.

2777. Funt, Allen. Eavesdropper At Large: Adventures in Human Nature with Candid Mike and Candid Camera. New York, Vanguard Press, 1952.

2778. Gaver, Jack and Dave Stanley. There's Laughter In The Air. New York, Greenberg, 1945.

2779. Harmon, Jim. The Great Radio Comedians. Garden City, NY, Doubleday, 1970.

2780. Josefsbert, Milt. The Jack Benny Show. New York, Arlington House, 1977.

2781. Kelland, Clarence Budington. Scattergood Baines. New York, Harper & Brothers, 1921.

2782. Leff, Laura. 39 Forever, Vol 1. International Jack Benny Fan Club, 2004.

2783. Linkletter, Art. People Are Funny. New York, Pocket Books, 1960.

2784. Lum and Abner. Jot Em Down Store Catalogue, Calendar, Game & Party Book For 1939. New York, Blue Ribbon Books, 1939.

2785. Mack, Charles E. Two Black Crows In The A. E. F. New York, Grosset & Dunlap, 1928.

2786. Martin, Linda and Segrave, Kerry. Women in Comedy: The Funny Ladies from the Turn of the Century to the Present. Secaucus, NJ, Citadel Press, 1986.

2787. McCleod, Elizabeth. Original Amos 'n' Andy: Freedman Gosden, Charles Correll and the 1928-1943 Radio Serial. Jefferson, NC, McFarland, 2005.

2788. Museum of Broadcasting. Bob Hope, A Half Century Of

Radio And Television. New York, Museum Of Broadcasting, 1986.

2789. Museum of Television and Radio. Jack Benny: The Radio & Television Work. New York, Harper Perennial, 1991.

2790. Nachman, Gerald. Seriously Funny: The Rebel Comedians of the 1950s and 1960s. New York, Pantheon Books, 2003.

2791. Nichols, Anne. Abie's Irish Rose. New York, Grosset & Dunlap, 1927.

2792. Ohmart, Ben.The Bickersons. Boalsburg, PA, Bear Manor Media, 2004.

2793. Poole, Gary. Radio Comedy Diary. Jefferson, NC, McFarland,2001.

2794. Rapp, Phil. Bickerson Scripts: Vol. 1. Boalsburg, PA, Bear Mountain Media, 2003.

2795. _____. Bickerson Scripts: Vol. 2. Boalsburg, PA, Bear Manor Media, 2004.

2796. Rhymer, Mary Frances, ed. Vic And Sade: The Best Radio Plays of Paul Rhymer. New York, Seabury Press, 1976.

2797. _____. Mary Frances. The Small House Half-Way Up In The Next Block: Paul Rhymer's Vic and Sade. New York, McGraw-Hill, 1972.

2798. Rogers, Will. Radio Broadcasts Of Will Rogers. Stillwater, OK, Oklahoma State University Press, 1983.

2799. Roth, Philip. Ben Ohmart, ed. The Baby Snooks Show Scripts. Boalsburg, PA, Bear Manor Media.

2800. Stumpf, Charles and Ben Ohmart. The Great Gildersleeve. Boalsburg, PA, Bear Manor Media, 2002.

2801. _____. and Tom Price. Heavenly Days: The Story of Fibber McGee and Molly. Waynesville, NC, World Of Yesterday, 1987.

2802. Treadwell, Bill. 50 Years Of American Comedy. New York, Exposition Press. 1951.

2803. Unterbrink, Mary. Funny Women: American Comediennes, 1860-1985. Jefferson, NC, McFarland, 1987.

2804. Wertheim, Arthur Frank. Radio Comedy. New York, Oxford University Press, 1979.

2805. Wilde, Larry. The Great Comedians. New York, Citadel, 1973.

2806. Wilk, Max. The Wit And Wisdom Of Hollywood. New York, Warner, 1973.

2807. Young, Jordan R. Laugh Crafters, Beverly Hills, CA, Past Times Publishing, 1998.

Genre: Drama
(See Also Plays and Scripts)

2808. Billips, Connie and Arthur Pierce. Lux Presents Hollywood: A Show-by-Show History of the Lux Radio Theatre and the Lux Video Theatre, 1934-1957. Jefferson, NC, McFarland, 1995.

2809. Brand, Max. Calling Dr. Kildare. Triangle, 1944.

2810. Cantril, Hadley. The Invasion From Mars: A Study in the Psychology of Panic. Princeton, NJ, Princeton University Press, 1982.

2811. Crook, Tim. Radio Drama Theory and Practice. London, Routledge, 1999.

2812. Fitelson, H. William, ed.Theatre Guild on the Air. New York, Rinehart, 1947.

2813. Fox, Dixon Ryan and Arthur M. Schlesinger, ed. The Cavalcade Of America. Springfield, MA, Milton Bradley Company, 1937.

2814. Grams, Martin, Jr. History Of The Cavalcade Of America. Churchville, MD, OTR Publishing, 1998.

2815. Grams, Martin, Jr. Radio Drama: American Programs 1932-1962. Jefferson, NC, McFarland,2000.

2816. Knight, Ruth Adams. Doctor Christian's Office. Cleveland, World Publishing, 1946.

2817. Koch, Howard. The Panic Broadcast: The Whole Story of Orsonm Welles's Legendary Radio Show. New York, Avon, 1970.

2818. Runyon, Damon. Guys And Dolls, Money From Home and Blue Plate Special. Philadelphia, J.B. Lippincott.

Genre: Educational

2819. Callahan, Jennie Waugh. Radio Workshop For Children. New York, McGraw-Hill, 1948.

2820. Goodman, Robert. Masterpieces For Radio Declamation (2 vols.). Liberty Publishing, 1943.

2821. Grams, Martin, Jr. Invitation to Learning. Churchville, MD, OTR Publishing, 2002.

2822 Harrison, Margaret. Radio In The Classroom. Englewood Cliffs, NJ, Prentice Hall, 1937.

2823. Herzberg, Max J. Radio And English Teaching. New York, D. Appleton Century, 1941.

2824. Levenson, William B. Teaching Through Radio. New York, Farrar & Rinehart, 1945.

2825. Olson, O. Joe, ed. Education On The Air. Ohio State University, 1950.

2826. Perry, Armstrong. Radio in Education: The Ohio School of the Air and Other Experiments. New York, The Payne Fund. 1929.

2827. Stewart. Irvin. Local Broadcasts To Schools. Chicago, University Of Chicago Press, 1939.

2828. Van Doren, Mark, ed.New Invitation to learning. New York, New Home Library, 1944.

2829. Woelfeld, Norman and I. Keith Tyler, eds. Radio And The School. World Book Company, 1945.

Genre: Homemaking/Domestic

2830. Birkby, Evelyn. Neighboring On The Air: Cooking with the KMS Radio Homemakers. Ames, IA, University of Iowa Press, 1991.

2831. Broeg, Helois Parker. Grandma Sez. Silver Lake, MA, James Westway McCue, 1947.

2832. Mystery Chef (John Macpherson). Mystery Chef's Own Cook Book. Longmans, Green, 1943.

Genre: Horror/Suspense

2833. Cole, Alonzo Deen. David S. Siegel, ed. The Witch's Tale. Yorktown Heights, NY, Dunwich Press, 1998.

2834. Cox, J. Randolph. Man of Magic and Mystery: A Guide to the Work of Walter B. Gibson. Metuchen, NJ, Scarecrow, 1988.

2835. Grams, Martin, Jr. Official Guide to Inner Sanctum Mysteries: Behind the Creaking Door. Churchville, MD, OTR Publishing, 2003.

2836. _____. Suspense: Twenty Years of Thrills and Chills. Churchville, MD, OTR Publishing, 1997.

2837. Haining, Peter, ed. Dead Of Night. New York, Stein & Day, 1986.

2838. _____. Tune In For Fear. London, William Kimber, 1985.

2839. Hand, Richard J. Terror theAir!: Horror Radio inAmerica, 1931–1952. Jefferson, NC, McFarland, 2005.

2840. Stedman, Raymond W. The Serials: Suspense and Drama by Installment. Norman, OK, University of Oklahoma Press, 1977.

Genre: Miscellaneous and Mixed Genres

2841. Anonymous. This Is The Story. Morton Publishing, 1949.

2842. Baker, John C. Farm Broadcasting: The First Sixty Years. Ames, IA, Iowa State University Press.

2843. Blackington, Alton H. Yankee Yarns. New York, Dodd, Mead, 1954.

2844. Dunninger, Joseph. Dunninger's Complete Encyclopedia Of Magic. London, Spring Books,?

2845. _____. Dunninger's Secrets: An exciting probe into the mystery of magic. Secaucus, NJ, Lyle Stuart, 1974.

2846. _____. What's On Your Mind? Cleveland, World Publishing, 1944.

2847. Edwards, Frank. Strange World.

2848. Harmon, Jim. The Great Radio Heroes. New York, Ace, 1967.

2849. _____, ed. It's That TimeAgain: More New Stores of Old-Time Radio. Boalsburg, PA, Bear Manor Media, 2004.

2850. Hix, John. Strange As It Seems. New York, Sears Publishing, 1931.

2851. Hix. Elsie. Strange As It Seems. Garden City, NY, Hanover House, 1953.

2852. Lederle Laboratories. The Doctors Talk It Over: A Series of Radio Programs Broadcast to the Medical Profession, October 6, 1944 to March 30, 1945. New York, Lederle Laboratories, 1945,

2853. McDonagh, Richard. Land Of The Free. Catholic University, 1941.

2854. Ohmart, Ben, ed. It's That Time Again: The New Stories of Old-Time Radio. Boalsburg, PA, Bear Mountain Media, 2003.

2855. Silver, Stuart and Isidore Haiblum. Faster Than A Speeding Bullet: An Informal History and Quiz of Radio's Golden Age. Chicago, Playboy Paperbacks, 1980.

2856. Waters. F. The Court of Missing Heirs. New York, Modern Age Books, 1941.

Genre: Music–General

2857. Bindas, Kenneth J. All This Music Belongs to the Nation: The WPA's Federal Music Project and American Society 1935-1939. Knoxville, University of Tennessee Press, 1995.

2858. Chase, Gilbert, ed. Music in Radio Broadcasting. New York, McGraw Hill, 1946.

2859. Cooper, David. Bernard Herrmann's The Ghost and Mrs. Muir: A Film Score Guide. Metuchen, NJ, Scarecrow, 2005.

2860. Corenthal, Michael G. ed. Illustrated History Of Wisconsin Music: 1840-1990. Milwaukee, WI, MGC Publications, 1991.

2861. Cox, Jim. Music Radio: The Great Performers and Programs of the 1920s through early 1960. Jefferson, NC, McFarland, 2005.

2862. Damrosch, Walter. Instructor's Manual for Music Appreciation Hour. New York, NBC, 1930.

2863. De Long, Thomas A. Mighty Music Box: The Golden Age of Musical Radio. Los Angeles, New World Communications, 1980.

2864. Kear, Lynn. Kay Francis: A Passionate Life and Career. Jefferson, NC, McFarland, 2005.

2865. Kiner, Larry F. and Harry Mackenzie. Basic Musical Library. "P" Series, 1-1000. New York, Greenwood Press, 1990.

2866. Kinscella, Hazel Gertrude. Music On The Air. New York, Viking, 1934.

2867. La Prade, Ernest. Broadcasting Music. New York, Rinehart,1947.

2868. Lopez, Vincent. What's Ahead? A Musician's Prophecies of World Events. New York, David McKay, 1944.

2869. Lotz, Rainer E. The AFR&TS (Gold Label) Transcription Library: A Label Listing.Menden, Der Jazzfreund, 1978

2870. Mackenzie, Harry and Lothar Polomski. One Night Stand Series, 1-100l. New York, Greenwood Press. 1991.

2871. Malone, Bill C. and Judith Mc Culloh, eds. Stars Of Country Music: Uncle Dave Macon to Jimmy Rodriguez. Urbana, IL, University of Illinois Press, 1975.

2872. Norback, Peter and Craig, eds. Great Songs Of Madison Avenue. New York, Quadrangle/N Y Times Book Co.,1976.

2873. Scholes, Percy A. Everybody's Guide To Radio Music. New York, Oxford University Press, 1926.

2874. Simon, George T. and Friends. The Best Of The Music Makers. Garden City, NY, Doubleday, 1979.

2875. Smith, Kate. Upon My Lips A Song. New York, Funk & Wagnalls, 1960.

2876. Spaeth, Sigmund. Fun With Music. New York, Greenberg.

2877. Strom, Robert. Miss Peggy Lee: A Career Chronicle. Jefferson, NC, McFarland, 2005.

2878. Wier, Albert E., ed. Scribner Radio Music Library (8 vols.). New York, Charles Scribner's Sons, 1946.

2879. Williams, John R. This Was Your Hit Parade. Rockland, ME, Courier-Gazette, 1973.

2880. Young, Morris N. and John C. Stoltzfus. Radio Music Live: 1920-1950: A Pictorial Gamut. Florida, Rainbow Books, 1998.

Genre: Music–Big Bands

2881. Conner, D. Russell and Hicks, Warren W. B G On The Record, A Bio-Discography Of Benny Goodman. New Rochelle, NY, Arlington House, 1978.

2882. Daniels, George G. ed. The Swing Era, 1944-1945: The Golden Age Of Network Radio. New York, Time-Life, 1971.

2883. Edmiston, Fred W. The Coon-Sanders Nighthawks. Jefferson, NC, McFarland, 2003.

2884. Flower, John. Moonlight Serenade, Bio Discography Of Glenn Miller Civilian Band. New Rochelle, NY, Arlington House, 1972.

2885. McCarthy, Albert. The Dance Band Era: The Dancing Decades From Ragtime to Swing, 1910-1950. New York, Spring Books, 1971.

2886. Richman, Saul. Guy: The Life and Times of Guy Lombardo. New York, RichGuy Publishing, 1978.

2887. Sanford, Herb. Tommy and Jimmy: The Dorsey Years. New Rochelle, NY, Arlington House, 1972.

2888. Simon, George T. Simon Says: The Sights and Sounds of the Swing Era, 1935-1955. New York, Galahad Books, 1971.

2889. Simon, George T. The Big Bands. London, Macmillan, 1967.

2890. Walker, Leo. The Big Band Almanac. Hollywood, Vinewood Book, 1978.

2891. Walker, Leo. The Wonderful Era Of The Great Dance Bands. Garden City, NY, Doubleday, 1972.

2892. Wright, Wilbur. The Glenn Miller Burial File. Southampton, England, Wright Books, 1993.

2893. Young, Jordan R. Spike Jones And His City Slickers: An Illustrated Biography. Beverly Hills, CA, Disharmony Books, 1984.

Genre: Music–Classical

2894. Burnham, Bob. Listening Guide To Classic Radio Programs. Livonia, MI, Bob Burnham, 1986.

2895. Downes, Olin. Symphonic Broadcasts. New York, Dial Press, 1931.

2896. Emmons, Shirlee. Tristanissimo: The Authorized Biography of Heroic Tenor Lauritz Melchior. New York, Schirmer, 1990.

2897. Frank, Mortimer H. Arturo Toscanini: The NBC Years. Portland, OR, Amadeus Press, 2002.

2898. Jackson, Paul. Saturday Afternoons At The Met: The Metropolitan Opera Broadcasts, 1931-1950. Portland, OR, Amadeus Press, 1994.

2899. _____. Sign-Off For The Old Met: The Metropolitan Opera Broadcasts, 1950-1966. Portland, OR, Amadeus Press, 1997.

2900. Kaufman, Schima. Everybody's Music. New York, Thomas Y. Crowell Company, 1938.

2901. Museum of Broadcasting. The Metropolitan Opera: The Radio And Television Legacy. Museum of Broadcasting, 1986.

2902. _____. The Telephone Hour: A Retrospective. Museum of Broadcasting, 1990.

Genre: Music–Country and Western

2903. Barfus, Gerald. David Stone In Sunset Valley. Minneapolis, James D. Thueson, Publisher, 1983.

2904. Griffis, Ken. Hear My Song: The Story of the Celebrated Sons of the Pioneers. Northglenn, CO, Norken, 1994.

2905. Hagen, Chet. Grand Ole Opry: The Complete Story of a Great American Institution and Its Stars. New York, Henry Holt, 1989.

2906. Haslam, Gerald W., Alexandra Haslam Russell and Richard Chon. Workin' Man Blues: Country Music in California. Berkeley, CA, Univ. of California Press, 1999.

2907. Laird, Tracey E. W. Louisiana Hayride. New York, Oxford University Press, 2005.

2908. Logan, Horace and Bill Sloan. Elvis, Hank, And Me: Louisiana Hayride. New York, St. Martin's Press, 1998.

2909. Millard, Bob. Country Music: 70 Years Of America's Favorite Music. New York, Harper, Perennial, 1993.

2910. Shelton, Robert and Goldblatt, Burt. The Country Music Story: A Picture History of Country and Western Music. Secaucus, NJ, Castle Books, 1971.

2911. Stamper, Pete. It All Happened in Renfro Valley. Lexington , KY, University Press of Kentucky, 1999.

2912. Strobel, Jerry, ed. Grand Ole Opry: WSM Picture History Book, 50th Anniversary Issue. WSM, 1976.

2913. Tribe, Ivan. Mountaineer Jamboree: Country Music in West Virginia. University Press of Kentucky, 1984.

2914. Wolfe, Charles K. A Good Natured Riot: the Birth of the Grand Ole Opry. Nashville, TN, Vanderbilt University Press, 1999.

Genre: Music–Disc Jockeys

2915. Cavanaugh, Peter C. Local DJ: A Rock 'n Roll History. Xlibris, 2001.

2916. Fisher, Hal. How To Become A Radio Disc Jockey. Blue Ridge Summit, PA, TAB Books, 1974.

2917. Kaufman, Murray. Murray the K Tells It Like It Is, Baby. New York, Holt, Rinehart, 1966.

2918. Passman, Arnold. Deejays. New York, Macmillan, 1971.

2919. Salowitz, Stew. Chicago's Personality Radio: WLS DJ's of the Early 1960's. Salowitz, 1993.

2920. Smith, Wes. Pied Pipers Of Rock 'N' Roll: Radio Deejays of the 50's and 60's. Marietta, GA, Longstreet Press, 1989.

2921. Sorkin, Dan. Blabbermouths. New York, Citadel, 1960.

2922. Whittinghill, Dick. Did You Whittinghill This Morning? The Madcap Adventures of a Hollywood Disc Jockey. Chicago, Henry Regnery, 1976.

2923. _____. Let's Whittinghill Again (Like We Did Last Summer). Chicago, Contemporary Books, 1977.

Genre: Music–Jazz and Blues

2924. Chilton, John. Who's Who Of Jazz: Storyville to Swing Street. New York, Time-Life, 1978.

2925. Cohn, Lawrence. Nothing But The Blues: The Music and the Musicians. New York, Abbeville Press, 1993.

2926. Keepnews, Orrin and Bill Grauer, Jr. A Pictorial History Of Jazz: People and Places From New Orleans to Modern Jazz. New York, Crown Publishers, 1968.

Genre: Music–Rock 'n' Roll

2927. Morrow, Cousin Bruce and Laura Baudo. Cousin Brucie! My Life In Rock And Roll Radio. New York, Beech Tree Books, 1987.

2928. Sklar, Rick. Rocking America: An Insider's Story. New York, St. Martin's Press, 1984.

Genre: Mystery and Detective

2929. Barer, Burl. Saint, Complete History in Print, Radio, Film & Television. Jefferson, NC, McFarland, 1993.

2930. Boucher, Anthony and Denis Green. Joe R. Christopher, ed. The Casebook of Gregory Hood. Norfolk, VA, Crippen & Landru Publishers, 2006.

2931. Boyle, Jack. Boston Blackie. New York, A. L. Burt, 1919.

2932. Bunds, J. Dennis. Perry Mason: Authorship & Repro Of Popular Hero. Westport, CT, Greenwood Press, 1997.

2933. Brown, Hyman, ed. Strange Tales From CBS Radio Mystery Theater. New York, Popular Library, 1976.

2934. Brusic, L., J. Hubbs and W. Nadel. Edith Meiser and Her Adventures With Sherlock Holmes. Minneapolis, University of Minnesota, 1999.

2935. Carr, John Dickson. Douglas G. Greene, ed. Dead Sleep Lightly and other Mysteries From Radio's Golden Age. Garden City, NY, Doubleday, 1983.

2936. Collins, Frederick L. The FBI In Peace And War. New York, G.P. Putnam's Sons, 1943.

2937. Coville, Gary and Patrick Lucanio. Jack The Ripper. Jefferson, NC, McFarland, 1999.

2938. Cox, J. Randolph and David S. Siegel. Flashgun Casey, Casey Photographer: From the Pulps to Radio and Beyond. Yorktown Heights, NY, Book Hunter Press, 2005.

2939. Cox, Jim. Mr. Keen, Tracer of Lost Persons: A Complete History and Episdoe Log of Radio's Most Durable Detective. Jefferson, NC, McFarland, 2004.

2940. _____. Radio Crime Fighters: Over 300 Programs from the Gold Age. Jefferson, NC, McFarland, 2002.

2941. De Waal, Ronald Burt. The World Bibliography of Sherlock Holmes and Dr. Watson: A Classified and Annotated List of Materials Relating to Their Lives and Adventures. New York, Bramhall House, 1974.

2942. Ellery Queen. Queen: The Adventures of the Murdered Moth and Other Radio Mysteries. Norfolk, VA, Crippen & Landru Publishers, 2005.

2943. _____. The Tragedy of Errors and Others: Ellery Queen. Norfolk, VA, Crippen & Landru Publishers, 1999.

2944. Ellis, Kenneth M. The Trial Of Vivienne Ware. New York, Grosset & Dunlap, 1931.

2945. French, Jack. Private Eyelashes. Boalsburg, PA, Bear Manor Media, 2004.

2946. Gibson, Walter B. The Shadow Scrapbook. New York, Harcourt Brace Jovanovich, 1979.

2947. Grams, Martin, Jr. Gang Busters: The Crime Fighters of American Broadcasting. Churchville, MD, OTR Publishing, 2004.

2948. _____. I Love A Mystery Companion. Churchville, MD, OTR Publishing, 2003.

2947. _____.and Patrik Wikstrom. Alfred Hitchcock Presents Companion. Churchville, MD, OTR Publishing, 2001.

2950. Harmon, Jim. Radio Mystery And Adventure And Its Appearances In Film, TV, Etc. Jefferson, NC, McFarland, 1992.

2951. Hornung, E.W. The Crime Doctor. Indianapolis, Bobbs-Merrill, 1914.

2952. Kelley, Gordon E. Sherlock Holmes Screen And Sound Guide. Metuchen, NJ, Scarecrow, 1994.

2953. McCarty, John. Alfred Hitchcock Presents. New York, St. Martins, 1985.

2954. Morse, Carlton E. Stuff The Lady's Hatbox. Woodside, CA, Seven Stones Press, 1988.

2955. Murray, Will. The Duende History of The Shadow Magazine. Greenwood, MA, Odyssey Publications, 1980.

2956. Nevins. Francis M., Jr. and Ray Stanich. Sound Of Detection: Ellery Queen's Adventures In Radio. Madison, TN, Brownstone, 1983.

2957. _____.and Martin Grams, Jr. Sound Of Detection: Ellery Queen. Churchville, MD, OTR Publishing, 2002.

2958. Payton, Gordon and Martin Grams, Jr. The CBS Radio Mystery Theater: An Episode Guide and Handbook 1974-1982. Jefferson, NC, McFarland, 1999.

2959. Philbrick Herbert A. I Led Three Lives. Washington, DC, Capital Hill Press, 1973.

2960. Sapper, Herman Cyril Mc Neile. Bulldog Drummond. New York, Carrol & Graf, 1989.

2961. Shimeld, Thomas J. Walter B. Gibson and The Shadow. Jefferson, NC, McFarland, 2005.

2962. Treadwell, Lawrence P., Jr. The Bulldog Drummond Encyclopedia. Jefferson, NC, McFarland, 2001.

2963. Van Hise, James. The Green Hornet. New York, Schuster & Schuster, 1988.

2964. Webb, Jack. The Badge: The Inside Story of One of America's Great Police Departments. Englewood Cliffs, NJ, Prentice Hall, 1958.

Genre: News
(See Also World War II)

2965. Aurandt, Paul. More Of Paul Harvey's The Rest Of The Story. New York, Bantam, 1981.

2966. _____. Paul. Paul Harvey's The Rest Of The Story. New York, Bantam, 1981

2967. Ball, Rick. Meet The Press: 50 Years Of History In The Making. New York, McGraw-Hill, 1997.

2968. Brooks, William F. Radio News Writing. New York, McGraw-Hill, 1948.

2969. Bulman, David, ed. Molders Of Opinion. Milwaukee, Bruce Publishing, 1945.

2970. Carter, Boake. Philco Radio Time. New York, CBS, 1936.

2971. CBS. Crisis: A Report From the Columbia Broadcasting System. New York, Columbia Broadasting System, 1939.

2972. Charnley, Mitchell V. News By Radio. New York, Macmillan, 1948.

2973. Cloud, Stanley and Lynne Olson. The Murrow Boys: Pioneers on the Front Lines of Broadcast Journalism. Boston, Houghton Mifflin, 1996.

2974. Culbert, David Holbrook. News For Everyman: Radio and Foreign Affairs In Thirties America. Westport, CT, Greenwood, 1976.

2975. Cullinan, Howell. Pardon My Accent: A Radio News Announcer Apologizes. Norwood, MA, Plimpton Press, 1934.

2976. Fang, Irving E. Those Radio Commentators! Ames, IA, Iowa State University Press, 1977.

2977. Fielding, Raymond. March Of Time: 1935-1951, New York, Oxford University Press, 1978.

2978. Franklin, O. Thomas. Broadcasting The News: A Practical Handbook for the Radio Newsman. New York, Pageant Press, 1962.

2979. Friendly, Fred W. Due To Circumstances Beyond Our Control. New York, Random House, 1967.

2980. Gates, Gary Paul. Air Time: The Inside Story of CBS News. New York, Harper, 1978.

2981. Gordon, George N. and Irving A. Falk. On-The-Spot Reporting: Radio Records History. New York, Julian Messner, 1967.

2982. Herndon, Booton. Praised And Damned: The Story of Fulton Lewis, Jr. New York, Duell, Sloan & Pearce, 1954.

2983. Hill, Edwin C. The Human Side Of The News. New York, Walter J. Black, 1934.

2984. Hobler, Herbert W. And Now The News, 1945: A Momentous Year Comes Alive Through Daily Radio Newcasts. Princeton, NJ, Passport Communications, 1994.

2985. Hohenberg, John. Foreign Correspondence: The Great Reporters and Their Times. New York, Columbia University Press, 1964.

2986. Hosley, David H. As Good As Any: Foreign Correspondence On American Radio, 1930-1940. Westport, CT, Greenwood Press, 1984.

2987. Hotaling, Burton L. A Manual Of Radio News Writing. Milwaukee, Milwaukee Journal, 1947.

2988. Howe, Quincy. The News And How To Understand It. New York, Simon & Schuster, 1940.

2989. James, Doug. Walter Cronkite, His Life And Times. Brentwood, TN, JMP, 1991.

2990. Kaltenborn, H. V. Fifty Fabulous Years: 1900-1950: A Personal Review by H.V. Kaltenborn. New York, G.P. Putnam's Sons, 1950.

2991. _____. I Broadcast The Crisis. New York, Random House, 1938.

2992. _____. Kaltenborn Edits The News. New York, Modern Age Books, 1937.

2993. Man at the Microphone. Washington Broadcast. Garden City, NY, Doubleday, Doran, 1944.

2994. Mott, Frank Luther. News In America. Cambridge, MA, Harvard University Press, 1952.

2995. Murrow, Edward R. In Search Of Light: The Broadcasts 1938-1961. New York, Alfred A. Knopf, 1967.

2996. NBC, The Fourth Chime. New York, National Broadcasting Company, 1944.

2997. Saerchinger, Cesar. Hello America! Radio Adventures in Europe. Boston, Houghton Mifflin, 1938.

2998. Schechter, A. A. I Live On Air. New York, Frederick A. Stokes, 1941.

2999. Schieffer, Bob. Face The Nation: My Favorite Stories From the First 50 Years of the Award-Winning News Broadcast. New York, Simon & Schuster, 2004.

3000. Schoenbrun, David. On And Off The Air: An Informal History Of CBS News. New York, E.P. Dutton, 1989.

3001. Thomas, Lowell. History As You Heard It. Garden City, NY, Doubleday, 1957.

3002. Warren, Carl. Radio News Writing And Editing. New York, Harper & Brothers Publishers, 1947.

3003. White, Paul W. News On The Air. New York, Harcourt, Brace, 1947.

3004. Winfield, Betty Houchin and Lois B. DeFleur. The Edward R. Murrow Heritage: Challenge for the Future. Ames, IA, Iowa State University Press, 1986.

Genre: Poetry

3005. Anthology. Poems For Radio. Poetry House, 1945.

3006. Arnold, Gene. Favorite Poems. Chicago, Reilly & Lee, 1934.

3007. Barnes, Pat. Pick-Ups. Chicago, Pat Barnes, WHT, 1927.

3008. Bowes, Major Edward, ed. Verses I Like. New York, Garden City Publishing, 1939.

3009. Guest, Edgar A. Edgar A. Guest Broadcasting. Chicago, Reilly & Lee, 1935.

3010. _____. It Can Be Done. Chicago, Reilly & Lee, 1938.

3011. Kaye, Sammy. Sunday Serenade. New York, Republic Music, 1942.

3012. Langworthy, Yolande. Poems From Arabesque. Walter J. Black. 1930,

3013. Lillenas, Haldor. Favorite Radio Songs And Poems. Lillenas, 1940.

3014. Malone, Ted. Adventures In Poetry. New York, William Morrow, 1946.

3015. _____. American Album Of Poetry. Chicago, Rodeheaver, Hall-Mack, 1938.

3016. _____. Between The Bookends, Volume Five. Camden, NJ, Bookmark Press, 1945.

3017. _____. Favorite Stories. Garden City, NY, Doubleday, 1950.

3018. _____. Listener's Aid To Pilgrimage Of Poetry. New York, NBC, 1940.

3019. _____. Pack Up Your Troubles. New York, Whittlesey House, 1942.

3020. _____. Ted. Scrapbook. Chicago, Rodeheaver, Hall-Mack, 1941.

3021. Rainey, Bud. Dreamtime. Traveller's Press, 1939.

3022. Ross, David. Poet's Gold. New York, Dial Press, 1945

3023. Village Rhymester. Cordially Yours, Nine Years Of Living. Chicago, Reilly & Lee, 1931.

3024. Wons, Tony. Tony's Scrap Book. Annual editions 1927-1945. Chicago, Reilly & Lee, 1935.

Genre: Public Affairs

3025. Bryson, Lyman. Time For Reason About Radio. New York, George W. Stewart, 1948.

3026. Cameron, W. J. The Ford Sunday Evening Hour Talks: Yearly bound copies of the weekly broadcasts. (1930's-1940's). Dearborn, MI, Ford Motor Company.

3027. Columbia Broadcasting System. Talks: 1936-1946. Eleven volumes of quarterly public affairs type talks. New York, CBS, 1936-1946.

3028. Geddes, Donald Porter, ed. Franklin Delano Roosevelt: A Memorial, New York, Pitman Publishing, 1945.

3029. Leys, James Farquharson. The Better Earth: Selected from the Broadcasts by James Farquaharson Leys. San Francisco, Olympic Press, 1940.

3030. Overstreet, Harry A. and Bonaro W. Town Meeting Comes To Town. New York, Harper & Brothers Publishers, 1938.

3031. Van Loon, Hendrik Willem. Air-Storming: A Collection of 40 Radio Talks. New York, Harcourt, Brace, 1935.

Genre: Quiz Shows

3032. Cox, Jim. The Great Radio Audience Participation Shows: Seventeen Programs from the 1940s and 1950s. Jefferson, NC, McFarland, 2001.

3033. De Long Thomas A. Quiz Craze: America's Infatuation With Game Shows. New York, Praeger, 1991.

3034. Fates, Gil. What's My Line? Englewood Cliffs, NJ, Prentice Hall, 1978.

3035. Feldman, Ruth Duskin. Whatever Happened To The Quiz Kids: Perils and Profits of Growing Up Gifted. Chicago, Chicago Review Press, 1982.

3036. Golenpaul, Dan, ed. Information, Please! (1939) 1st. New York, Simon & Schuster, 1939.

3037. _____. Information, Please! (1941 Edition). New York, Random House, 1940.

3038. Grams, Martin, Jr. Information Please. Boalsburg, PA, Bear Manor Media,2003.

3039. Hickok, Eliza Merrill. The Quiz Kids. Boston, Houghton Mifflin, 1947.

3040. Kieran, John. Not Under Oath: Recollections and Reflections. Boston, Houghton Mifflin, 1964.

3041. Mitchell, Albert. Here's The Answer. New York, Miles-Emmett, 1946.

3042. Quiz Kids. Questions And Answers. Akron, OH, Saalfield Publishing, 1941.

3043. _____. The Quiz Kids Blue Book: Entertaining Questions and Answers. Akron, OH, Saalfield Publishing, 1941.

3044. _____. The Quiz Kids Book of Stories & Poems. New York, Viking, 1947.

3045. _____. The Quiz Kids Questions and Answers. Akron, OH, Saalfield Publishing, 1941.

3046. _____. The Quiz Kids Red Book: Popular Questions and Answers. Akron, OH, Saalfield Publishing, 1941.

3047. Schwimmer Walter. The Tello-Test Game Book: Play Radio's First and Favorite Quiz Game. New York, Grosset & Dunlap, 1954.

3048. Smith, Carl W. Quiz Kids And The Crazy Question Mystery. Racine, WI, Whitman Publishing, 1946.

Genre: Religion

3049. Borders, William Holmes. Seven Minutes At The Mike In The Deep South. Atlanta, GA, Morris Brown College Press. 1943

3050. Cleveland, Denton E. Radio Heart Throbs. Yankton, SD, Gurney Seed & Nursery Co. 1929.

3051. Coughlin, Father Charles E. A Series of Lectures on Social Justice, Broadcast March, 1935. Royal Oak, MI, Radio League Of The Little Flower, 1935.

3052. _____. By The Sweat Of Thy Brow. Royal Oak, MI, Radio League Of The Little Flower. 1931.

3053. _____.Father Coughlin's Radio Discourses: 1931-1932. Royal Oak, MI, Radio League Of The Little Flower, 1932.

3054. _____. Father Coughlin's Radio Sermons: October, 1930 - April, 1931 Complete. Baltimore, Knox and O'Leary, 1931.

3055. Dorgan, Howard. The Airwaves Of Zion: Radio and Religion in Appalachia. Knoxville, TN, University of Tennessee Press, 1993.

3056. Ellens, J. Harold. Models Of Religious Broadcasting. William B. Eerdmans Publishing, 1974.

3057. Erickson, Hal. Religious Radio and Television in the United States, 1921-1991: The Program and Personalities, Jefferson, NC, McFarland, 1992.

3058. Forbes, Forrest. God Hath Chosen: The Story Of Jack Wyrtzen and the Word Of Life Hour. Grand Rapids, MI, Zondervan Publishing, 1948.

3059. Hangen, Tona J. Redeeming The Dial: Radio, Religion, & Popular Culture in America. Chapel Hill, University of North Carolina Press, 2002.

3060. Hill, George H. and Lenwood Davis. Religious Broadcasting: 1920-1983 A Selectively Annotated Bibliography. New York, Garland Reference Library. 1984.

3061. Jones, Clarence. Radio: The New Missionary. Chicago, Moody Press, 1946.

3062. Lamplighter (Rabbi Jacob Tarshish). Little Journeys. Columbus, OH, F.J. Heer, 1935.

3063. _____. Prelude To Happiness. Columbus, OH, F.J. Heer, 1937.

3064. Lee, Alfred McClung and Elizabeth Bryant, eds. The Fine Art Of Propaganda: A Study of Father Coughlin's Speeches. New York, Harcourt, Brace, 1939.

3065. Maier, Walter A. The Lutheran Hour: Winged Words to Modern America, Broadcast in the Coast-to-Coast Radio Crusade for Christ. St. Louis, Concordia Publishing, 1931.

3066. _____. Radio for Christ. St. Louis, Concordia Press, 1939.

3067. Parker, Everett C., David W. Barry and Dallas W. Smythe. The Television-Radio Audience and Religion. New York, Harper & Brothers, 1955.

3068. _____, Elinor Inmann and Ross Snyder. Religious Radio: What To Do And How. New York, Harper & Brothers, 1948.

3069. Segal, Eli. The Eternal Light. Newtown, CT, Yesteryear Press, 2005.

3070. Smith, Copeland. Straight Answers to Life Questions. Chicago, Willett, Clark & Colby, 1928.

3071. Sockman, Ralph. Now To Live! New York, Abingdon-Cokesbury Press, 1946.

3072. Spivak, John L. Shrine Of The Silver Dollar. New York, Modern Age Books, 1940.

3073. Talmage, James E. Sunday Night Talks By Radio: A Series of Radio Addresses relating to Doctrines of the Church of Jesus Christ of Latter-day Saints. Salt Lake City, UT, Mormon Church, 1931.

3074. Tarshish, Rabbi Jacob. Half Hours With Rabbi Jacob Tarshish. Columbus, OH, F.J. Heer,?.

3075. Winsett, R.E., ed. Radio and Revival Special: Fine Hymns and Evangelistic Songs. Dayton, TN, R.E. Winsett, 1939.

3075. Wishengrad, Morton. The Eternal Light: 26 radio plays from the famous Eternal Light program. New York, Crown, 1947.

3077. Wright, J. Elwin. The Old Fashioned Revival Hour and the Broadcasters. Boston, Fellowship, 1940.

Genre: Science Fiction

3078. Widner, James F. and Meade Frierson III. Science Fiction On Radio: A Revised Look at 1950-1975. Birmingham, AL, AFAB. 1996.

Genre: Soap Opera

3079. Allen, Robert C. Speaking Of Soap Operas. Chapel Hill, NC, University of North Carolina Press, 1988.

3080. Anonymous. Just Plain Bill: His Story. New York, David McCay, 1935.

3081. ____. Today's Children: A Story of Modern American Life. Minneapolis, Pillsbury Flour Mills, 1937.

3082. Berg, Gertrude. The Rise Of The Goldbergs. New York, Barse, 1931.

3083. Blair, Cornelia. The Nora Drake Story. New York, NY, Duel, Sloan & Pearce, 1950.

3084. Buckman, Peter. All For Love: A Study In Soap Opera. Salem, NH, Salem House, 1985.

3085. Cantor, Muriel G. and Suzanne Pingree. The Soap Opera. Beverly Hills, CA, Sage Publications, 1983.

3086. Carrington, Elaine. Red Davis. Engel-van Wiseman, 1935.

3087. Chambers, Robert W.. The Tracer Of Lost Persons. New York, D. Appleton-Century-Crofts, 1906.

3088. Clugston, Katherine and Richard Stevenson. Wilderness Road. New York, Blue Ribbon Books, 1937.

3089. Cox, Jim. Frank And Anne Hummert's Radio Factory: The Programs and Personalities of Broadcasting's Most Prolific Producers. Jefferson, NC, McFarland, 2003.

3090. ____. The Great Radio Soap Operas. Jefferson, NC, McFarland, 1999.

3091. ____. Historical Dictionary of American Radio Soap Operas. Metuchen, NJ, Scarecrow, 2005.

3092. Edmondson, Madeleine and David Rounds. The Soaps: Daytime Serials of Radio and TV. New York, Stein & Day, 1973.

3093. Flynn, Bess. Bachelor's Children: A Synopsis of the Radio Program. Chicago, Old Dutch Cleanser, 1939.

3094. Frentz, Suzanne, ed. Staying Tuned: Contemporary Soap Opera Criticism. Bowling Green, OH, Bowling Green State University Popular Press, 1992.

3095. Higby, Mary Jane. Tune In Tomorrow. New York, Cowles, 1968.

3096. LaGuardia, Robert. From Ma Perkins To Mary Hartman: Illustrated History of Soap Operas. New York, Ballantine, 1977

3097. ____. Soap World. New York, Arbor House, 1983.

3098. Mary and Bob. Prize True Story Dramas Of The Air. New York, Macfadden, 1931.

3099. ____. True Story Book. New York, Macfadden, 1930.

3100. Museum of Television and Radio. Worlds Without End: The Art and History of the Soap Opera. New York, Harry N. Abrams, 1997.

3101. Prouty, Olive Higgins. Stella Dallas: A Story of Mother Love. New York, Grosset & Dunlap, 1923.

3102. Ruthledge, Dr. John. The Guiding Light. Chicago, Guiding Light Publishing, 1938.

3103. Schemering. Christopher. Guiding Light: A 50th Anniversary Celebration. New York, Ballantine Books, 1986.

3104. Wakefield, Dan. All Her Children: The real life story of America's favorite soap opera. Garden City, NY, Doubleday, 1976.

3105. Westcott Edward Noyes. David Harum. New York, D. Appleton-Century-Crofts, 1899.

3106. Williams, Carol Traynor. It's Time For My Story: Soap Opera Sources, Structure and Response. Westport, CT, Praeger, 1992.

Genre: Sports

3107. Allen, Maury. Voices Of Sport. New York, Grosset & Dunlap, 1971.

3108. Barber, Red. The Broadcasters. New York, Dial Press, 1970.

3109. Brickhouse, Jack and Jack Rosenberg and Ned Colletti. Thanks For Listening. South Bend, IN, Diamond Communications, 1986.

3110. Buck, Jack and Bob Rains and Bob Broeg. That's A Winner. Champaign, IL, Sagamore Publishing, 1997.

3111. Cosell, Howard and Mickey Herskowitz. Cosell. Chicago, Playboy Press, 1973.

3112. Dean, Jerome H. (Dizzy). Dizzy Baseball: A Gay and Amusing Glossary of Baseball Terms Used by Radio Broadcasters. New York, Greenberg, 1952.

3113. Dunphy, Don. Don Dunphy At Ringside. New York, Henry Holt, 1988.

3114. Edwards, Bob. Friday's With Red: A Radio Friendship. New York, Simon & Schuster, 1993.

3115. Halberstram, David J. Sports On New York Radio: A Play-by-Play History. Chicago, Masters Press, 1999.

3116. Nelson, Lindsey. Hello Everybody, I'm Lindsey Nelson. New York, Beech Tree Books, 1985.

3117. Oriard, Michael. King Football: Sport and Spectacle in the Golden Age of Radio and Newsreels, Movies and Magazines, the Weekly and the Daily Press. chapel Hill, NC. University of North Carolina Press, 2002.

3118. Rice, Grantland. Tumult And The Shouting' "My Life in Sport." New York, A. S. Barnes, 1954.

3119. Smith, Curt. Voices Of The Game: The First Full-Scale Overview of Baseball Broadcasting, 1921 to the Present. South Bend, IN, Diamond Communications, 1987.

3120. Stern, Bill. Favorite Boxing Stories. New York, Pocket Books, 1948.

3121. ____. Favorite Sport Stories. New York, Pocket Books. 1947.

3122. ____. and David Ormont. Bill Stern's Sports Quiz Book. New York, Julian Messner, 1950.

Genre: Talk Shows

3123. Bergmann, Eugene B. Excelsior You Fatheads: The Art and Enigma of Jean Shepherd. New York, Applause, 2005.

3124. Doolittle, John. Don McNeill and His Breakfast Club. Notre Dame, IN, University Of Notre Dame Press, 2001.

3125. Elliott, Bob and Ray Goulding. From Approximately Coast To Coast...It's The Bob And Ray Show. New York, Atheneum, 1983.

3126. ____. Write If You Get Work: The Best Of Bob And Ray. New York, Random House, 1975.

3127. Farber, Barry. Making People Talk. New York, William Morrow, 1987.

3128. Franklin, Joe. Up Late With Joe Franklin. New York, Scribner, 1995.

3129. Harden, Frank and Jackson Weaver. On The Radio With Harden And Weaver. New York, William Morrow, 1983.

3130. Hopper, Hedda. The Whole Truth And Nothing But. Garden City, NY, Doubleday, 1963.

3131. Klavan, Gene. Turn That Damned Thing Off. Indianapolis, Bobbs Merrill, 1972.

3132. _____. We Die At Dawn. Garden City, Doubleday, 1964.

3133. Lieberman, Philip A. Radio's Morning Show Personalities: Early Hour Broadcasters and Deejays from the 1920's to the 1990's. Jefferson, NC, McFarland, 1996.

3134. McBride, Mary Margaret. America For Me. New York, Macmillan, 1941.

3135. _____. Here's Martha Deane. New York, Garden City Publishing, 1936.

3136. _____. Tune In For Elizabeth. New York, Dodd, Mead, 1946.

3137. McNeill, Don. The Breakfast Club Family Album. Chicago, Don McNeill, 1942.

3138. Nebel, Long John. The Way Out World. Englewood Cliffs, NJ, Prentice-Hall, 1961.

3139. Nightingale, Earl. This Is Earl Nightingale. Garden City, NY, J.G. Ferguson, 1969.

3140. Parsons, Louella O. Tell It To Louella. New York, Lancer, 1963.

3141. _____. The Gay Illiterate. Garden City, NY, Doubleday, Doran, 1944.

3142. Phillips, Wally. The Wally Phillips People Book: 1,762,913 Heads Are Better Than One. Ottawa, IL, Caroline House.

3143. Revell, Nellie. Right Off The Chest. New York, George H. Doran, 1923.

3144. Rose, Hilly. But That's Not What I Called About. Chicago, Contemporary Books, 1978.

3145. Sterling, Jack. So Early In The Morning: Or My Topsy Turvy Day. New York, Thomas Y. Crowell, 1958.

3146. Ware, Susan. It's One O'Clock And Here Is Mary Margaret McBride. New York, NYU Press, 2004.

3147. Wilson, Earl. I Am Gazing Into My 8-Ball. Garden City, NY, Doubleday, Doran, 1945.

Genre: Westerns

3148. Barabas, Suzanne and Gabor. Gunsmoke: A Complete History. Jefferson, NC, McFarland, 1990.

3149. Drew, Bernard A. The Hopalong Cassidy Show. Boalsburg, PA, Bear Manor Media.

3150. Felbinger, Lee J. The Lone Ranger Pictorial Scrapbook. Green Lane, PA, Countryside Advertising, 1979.

3151. Grams, Martin, Jr. and Les Rayburn. The Have Gun–Will Travel Companion. Churchville, MD, OTR Publishing, 2000.

3152. Heide, Robert and John Gilman. Box-Office Buckaroos: The Cowboy Hero from the Wild West Show to the Silver Screen. New York, Abbeville Press, 1982.

3153. Holland, Dave. From Out Of The Past: A Pictorial History Of The Lone Ranger. Holland House, 1988.

3154. Jones, Reginald M., Jr. Mystery Of The Masked Man's Music: A search for the music used on The Lone Ranger radio program, 1933-1954. Metuchen, NJ, Scarecrow, 1987.

3155. Rothel, David. Who Was That Masked Man? The Story of the Lone Ranger. New York, A. S. Barnes, 1981.

3156. Striker, Fran. Lone Ranger Books. (Many), New York, Grosset & Dunlap, Multiple years.

3157. Van Hise, James. The Story Of The Lone Ranger: Who Was That Masked Man? Las Vegas, NV, Pioneer Books, 1990.

History

History: General

3158. Anthology. Radio Industry: The Story of Its Development. As told by leaders of the industry to the students of the Graduate School of Business Administration at Harvard University. Chicago, A. W. Shaw, 1928.

3159. Archer, Gleason L. Big Business And Radio. New York, American Historical Company, 1939.

3160. _____. History Of Radio to 1926. New York, American Historical Society, 1938.

3161. Balk, Alfred. The Evolution of American Broadcasting: Broadcasting from Marconi through the Golden Age. Jefferson, NC, McFarland, 2005.

3162. Barnard, Stephen. Studying Radio. New York, Oxford University Press, 2000.

3163. Barnouw, Erik. A Tower In Babel: A History of Broadcasting in the United States to 1933. Vol I. New York, Oxford University Press, 1966.

3164. _____. The Golden Web: A History of Broadcasting in the United States 1933-1953. Vol II. New York, Oxford University Press, 1968.

3165. _____. The Image Empire: The History of Broadcasting in the United States from 1953. Vol III. New York, Oxford University Press, 1970.

3166. _____. Mass Communication, Television, Radio, Film, Press. New York, Rinehart, 1960.

3167. Beaumont, Charles. Remember? Remember? New York, Macmillan, 1963.

3168. Bergreen, Laurence. Look Now, Pay Later: The Rise of Network Broadcasting. New York, Mentor, 1981.

3169. Brindze, Ruth. Not To Be Broadcast: The Truth About Radio. New York, Vanguard, 1937.

3170. Broadcasting Publications. The First 50 Years of Broadcasting: The Running Story of the Fifth Estate. Washington, DC, Broadcasting Publications, 1982.

3171. Campbell, Robert. The Golden Years Of Broadcasting: A Celebration of the First 50 Years of Radio and TV on NBC. New York, Scribners, 1976.

3172. Carothers, Diane Foxhill. Radio Broadcasting from 1920–1990. New York, Garland Publishing, 1991.

3173. CBS. The Sound Of Your Life: A record of radio's first generation. New York, Columbia Broadcasting System, 1950.

3174. Chester, Girard and Garnet R. Garrison. Radio And Television: An Introduction. New York, Appleton-Century-Crofts, 1950.

3175. Codel, Martin, ed. Radio and It's Future. New York, Harper & Brothers, 1930.

3176. Cox, Jim. Say Goodnight, Gracie: The Last Years of Network Radio. Jefferson, NC, McFarland, 2002.

3177. Craig, Douglas B. Fireside Politics: Radio and Political Culture in the United States, 1920–1940. Baltimore, The Johns Hopkins University Press, 2005.

3178. Douglas, George H. The Early Days of Radio Broadcasting. Jefferson, NC, McFarland, 1987.

3179. Douglas, Susan J. Inventing American Broadcasting 1899-1922. Baltimore, Johns Hopkins University Press, 1989.

3180. _____. Listening in: Radio and the American Imagination, from Amos 'N" Andy and Edward R. Murrow to Wolfman Jack and Howard Stern. New York, Times Books, 1999.

3181. Dunlap, Orrin E. The Story Of Radio. New York, Dial Press, 1937.

3182. Emery, Walter B. National And International Systems of Broadcasting. East Lansing, MI, Michigan State University Press, 1969.

3183. Finkelstein, Norman H. Sounds In The Air: The Golden Age of Radio. New York, Scribners, 1993.

3184. Firth, Major Ivan and Glady Shaw Erskine. Gateway To Radio. New York, Macauley, 1934.

3185. Foster, Eugene S. Understanding Broadcasting. Reading, MA, Addison-Wesley, 1978.

3186. Greenfield, Thomas Allen. Radio: A Reference Guide. Westport, CT, Greenwood, 1989.

3187. Gutterman, Leon, ed. The Wisdom Of Sarnoff and the World Of RCA. Wisdom Society for the Advancement Of Knowledge, 1968.

3188. Hall, Claude and Barbara. This Business Of Radio Programming. New York, Billboard Book, 1977.

3189. Hasling, John. Fundamentals Of Radio Broadcasting. New York, McGraw Hill, 1980.

3190. Head, Sydney W. Broadcasting In America: A Survey of Television and Radio. Boston, Houghton Mifflin, 1972.

3191. Hilliard, Robert L. and Michael C. Keith. The Broadcast Century: A Biography of American Broadcasting, 4th Ed. Focal Press, 2004.

3192. Hilmes, Michele. Hollywood And Broadcasting: From Radio to Cable. Urbana, IL, University of Illinois Press, 1990.

3193. _____. Only Connect: A Cultural History of Broadcasting in the United States. Belmont, CA, Wadsworth, 2002.

3194. Huth, Arno. Radio Today: The Present State of Broadcasting. New York, Arno Press, 1971.

3195. Inglis, Andrew F. Behind the Tube: A History of Broadcasting Technology and Business. Boston, Focal Press, 1990.

3196. Jackaway, Gwenyth L. Media at War: Radio's Challenge to the Newspapers, 1924-1939. Westport, CT, Praeger, 1995.

3197. Jensen, Peter L. The Great Voice. Richardson, TX, Havilah Press, 1975.

3198. Journal of Popular Culture. In-Depth Radio, Vol XII: 2. Bowling Green, KY, Bowling Green State University, 1978.

3199. Kahn, Frank J. ed. Documents Of American Broadcasting. New York, Appleton-Century-Crofts, 1973.

3200. Landry, Robert J. This Fascinating Radio Business. Indianapolis, Bobbs-Merrill, 1946.

3201. Lawton, Sherman Paxton. Radio Continuity Types. Boston, Expression Company, 1938.

3202. Lewis, Tom. Empire Of The Air: The Men Who Made Radio. New York, Edward Burlingame Books, 1991.

3203. Lichty, Lawrence and Malachi C. Topping. American Broadcasting: A Source Book on the History of Radio and Television. New York, Hastings House. 1975.

3204. Loviglio, Jason. Radio's Intimate Public: Network Broadcasting and Mass-Mediated Democracy. Minneapolis, University of Minnesota Press, 2005.

3205. MacDonald, J. Fred. Don't Touch That Dial! Radio Programming In American Life, 1920 to 1960. Chicago, Nelson-Hall, 1980.

3206. Maltin, Leonard. Great American Broadcast. New York, Dutton, 1997.

3207. McChesney, Robert W. Telecommunications, Mass Media, and Democracy: The Battle for the Control of U.S. Broadcasting, 1928-1935. New York, Oxford University Press, 1993.

3208. McNicol, Donald. Radio's Conquest Of Space. New York, Murray Hill Books, 1946.

3209. Merz, Charles. Great American Bandwagon: A Study Of Exaggerations. New York, Literary Guild Of America, 1928.

3210. Metz, Robert. CBS: Reflections In A Bloodshot Eye. New York, Signet, 1976.

3211. Milam, Lorenzo Wilson. Radio Papers From KRAB to KCHU: Essays on the Art and Practice of Radio Transmission. San Diego, CA, MHO & MHO Works, 1986.

3212. Mitchell, Curtis. Cavalcade Of Broadcasting. Chicago, Follett, 1970.

3213. National Association of Broadcasters. Management in the Public Interest: A Picture History of Radio. Washington, DC, NAB, 1945.

3214. National Broadcasting Company. Broadcasting: 4 volumes, New York, NBC, 1935.

3215. Nye, Russel B. The Unembarrassed Muse: The Popular Arts in America. New York, Dial Press, 1970.

3216. Quinlan, Sterling. Inside ABC: American Broadcasting Company's Rise to Power. New York, Hastings House, 1979.

3217. Radio Corporation of America. Radio Enters The Home. Vestal, NY, Vestal Press, 1922.

3218. RCA. The Radio Decade. New York, Marchbanks Press, 1930.

3219. Rhoads, Eric B. Blast From The Past: A Pictorial History Of Radio's First 75 Years. West Palm Beach, FL, Streamline Press, 1995.

3220. Rose, C.B., Jr. National Policy For Radio Broadcasting. New York, Harper & Brothers, 1948.

3221. Rothafel, Samuel L. and Raymond Francis Yates. Broadcasting: Its New Day. New York, Arno Press, 1971.

3222. Sarnoff, David. Looking Ahead: The Papers Of David Sarnoff. New York, McGraw-Hill, 1968.

3223. Seldes, Gilbert. The Great Audience. New York, Viking, 1950.

3224. _____. The Public Arts: A report on the movies, radio and television and on what the shift from the printed word to the electronic tube means to the American people. New York, Simon & Schuster, 1956.

3225. Sennett, Ted. The Old-Time Radio Book. New York, Pyramid, 1976.

3226. Settel, Irving. A Pictorial History Of Radio. New York, Citadel, 1960.

3227. Shurick, E.P.J. The First Quarter Century Of American Broadcasting. Kansas City, Midland Publishing, 1946.

3228. Siepmann, Charles A. Radio's Second Chance. Boston, Little, Brown and Company, 1946.

3229. Skornia, Harry J. and Jack William Kitson. Problems And Controversies In Television And Radio: Basic Readings. Palo Alto, CA, Pacific Books, 1968.

3230. Slater, Robert. This Is CBS: A Chronicle Of 60 Years. Englewood Cliffs, NJ, Prentice Hall, 1988.

3231. Slide, Anthony, ed. Selected Radio & Television Criticism. Metuchen, NJ, Scarecrow, 1987.

3232. Smulyan, Susan. Selling Radio: The Commercialization Of American Broadcasting 1920-1934. Washington, DC, Smithsonian Institution Press, 1994.

3233. Sobel, Robert. RCA. New York, Stein and Day, 1986.

3234. Soley, Lawrence C. and John C. Nichols. Clandestine Radio Broadcasting: A Study of Revolutionary and Counterrevolutionary Electronic Communication. Westport, CT, Praeger, 1986.

3235. St. John, Robert. Encyclopedia Of Radio And Television Broadcasting: The Man Behind the Microphone. Milwaukee, Cathedral Square Publishing,1970.

3236. _____. Encyclopedia of Radio and Television Broadcasting: The men behind the microphone. Milwaukee, Cathedral Square, 1970.

3237. Sterling, Christopher H., ed. Electronic Media: A Guide to Trends in Broadcasting and Newer Technologies. New York, Praeger, 1984.

3238. _____.and John M. Kittross. Stay Tuned: A Concise History of American Broadcasting. Belmont, CA, Wadsworth Publishing, 1978.

3239. Summers, Harrison B. and Robert E. Broadcasting And The Public. Belmont, CA, Wadsworth Publishing, 1966.

3240. Thomas, Lowell. Magic Dials: The Story of Radio and Television. Polygraphic Co. Of America, 1939.

3241. Tyler, Poyntz, ed. Television And Radio. New York, H. W. Wilson, 1961.

3242. Walker Jesse. Rebels On The Air. New York, NYU Press, 2001.

3243. Woodfin, Jane. Of Mikes and Men: The Humorous Inside Story of Early Radio. New York, McGraw-Hill, 1951.

History: Blacklisting and Censorship

3244. Faulk, John Henry. Fear On Trial. New York, Simon & Schuster, 1964.

3245. Miller, Merle. The Judges And The Judged: The report on black-listing in radio and television. Garden City, NY, Doubleday, 1952.

3246. Summers. H.B., ed. Radio Censorship. New York, H.W. Wilson Co.,1939.

History: Economic and Social

3247. Allen, Frederick Lewis. The Big Change. New York, Bantam, 1961.

3248. _____. Only Yesterday. New York, Bantam, 1950.

3249. _____. Since Yesterday. New York, Bantam, 1961.

3250. Barnouw, Erik. The Sponsor: Notes on a Modern Potentate. New York, Oxford University Press, 1978.

3251. Brown, Robert J. Manipulating the Ether: The Power of Broadcast Radio in Thirties America. Jefferson, NC, McFarland, 1998.

3252. Cantril, Hadley and Gordon W. Allport. The Psychology Of Radio. New York, Peter Smith, 1941.

3253. Capsuto, Steven. Alternate Channels: The Uncensored Story of Gay and Lesbian Images on Radio and Television: 1930s to the Present. New York, Ballantine Books, 2000.

3254. Connah, Douglas Duff. How To Build The Radio Audience. New York, Harper & Brothers, 1938.

3255. Czitrom, Daniel J. Media And The American Mind: From Morse To McLuhan. Chapel Hill, University of North Carolina Press, 1982.

3256. DeForest, Tim. Storytelling In The Pulps, Comics & Radio: How Technology Changed Popular Fiction In America. Jefferson, NC, McFarland, 2004.

3257. Fornatale, Peter and Joshua E. Mills. Radio In The Television Age. Woodstock, NY, Overlook Press, 1984.

3258. Frost, S.E., Jr. Is American Radio Democratic? Chicago, University of Chicago Press, 1937.

3259. Halper, Donna L. Invisible Stars: A Social History of Women In American Broadcasting. Armonk, NY, M.E. Sharpe, 2001.

3260. Harvey, Rita Morley. Those Wonderful, Terrible Years: George Heller and the American Federation of Television and Radio Artists. Carbondale, IL, Southern Illinois University Press, 1996.

3261. Hill, Frank Ernest and W. E. Williams. Radio's Listening Groups: The United States and Great Britain. New York, Columbia University Press, 1941.

3262. Hilmes, Michele & Jason Loviglio, eds. Radio Reader: Essays in the Cultural History of Radio. New York, Routledge, 2002.

3263. Hilmes, Michele. Radio Voices: American Broadcasting 1922-1952. Minneapolis, University of Minnesota Press, 1997.

3264. Johnson, Phyllis A. and Michael C. Keith. Queer Airwaves: The Story of Gay and Lesbian Broadcasting. Armonk, NY, M.E. Sharpe, 2001.

3265. Jones, Gerard. Honey, I'm Home: Sitcoms Selling the American Dream. New York, St. Martin's Press. 1992.

3266. Landry, Robert J. Who, What, Why is Radio? New York, George W. Stewart, 1942.

3267. Lynes, Russell. The Lively Audience: A Social History of the Visual and Performing Arts in America 1980-1950. New York, Harper & Row, 1985.

3268. Meany, Anthony B. America Handcuffed By Radio C-H-A-I-N-S: Our Radio Revolution Prosperity's Flight Through the Air. New York, Ryerson, 1942.

3269. Schiffer, Michael Brian. The Portable Radio In American Life. University Of Arizona Press, 1991.

3270. Schwoch, James. American Radio Industry and Its Latin American Activities, 1900-1939. Urbana, IL, University Of Illinois Press, 1990.

3271. Shayon, Robert Lewis. Open To Criticism. Boston, Beacon, 1971.

3272. Siepmann, Charles A. Radio, Television, and Society. New York, Oxford University Press, 1950.

3273. West, Robert. The Rape Of Radio. New York, Rodin Publishing, 1941.

3274. White, Llewellyn. The American Radio: Report from the Commission of Freedom of the Press. Chicago, University of Chicago Press, 1947.

3275. Williams, Albert N. Listening: A Collection of Critical Articles on Radio. Denver, Univ. Of Denver Press, 1948.

History: Informal
(Includes memoirs, reflections, anecdotes, etc.)

3276. Barfield, Ray. Listening To Radio, 1920-1950. Westport, CT, Praeger, 1996.

3277. Carroll, Renee. In Your Hat. New York, Macaulay, 1933.

3278. Castleman, Harry andWalter J. Podrazik. 505 Radio Questions Your Friends Can't Answer. New York, Walker, 1983.

3279. Chase, Francis, Jr. Sound And Fury: An Informal History of Broadcasting. New York, Harper & Brothers, 1942.

3280. Crosby, John. Out OfThe Blue: A BookAbout RadioAnd Television. New York, Simon & Schuster, 1952.

3281. Downs, Hugh.Yours Truly...Hugh Downs. New York Holt, Rinehart and Winston, 1960.

3282. Eskenazi, Gerald.I HId Under the Sheets: Growing Up with Radio. Columbia, MO, University of Missouri Press, 2005.

3283. Floherty, John J. BehindThe Microphone. New York, J.B. Lippincott, 1944.

3284. Franklin, Joe. A Gift For People. New York, M. Evans & Company, 1978.

3285. Garner, Joe.We Interupt This Broadcast. Naperville, IL, Sourcebooks, 1998.

3286. Goldsmith, Alfred N. and Austin C. Lescarboura. This Thing Called Broadcasting: A simple tale of an idea, an experiment, a mighty industry, a daily habit, and a basic influence in our modern civilization. New York, Henry Holt, 1930.

3287. Gross, Ben. I Looked And I Listened. New Rochelle, NY, Arlington House, 1970.

3288. Harris, Credo Fitch. Microphone Memoirs of the Horse and Buggy Days of Radio. Indianapolis, Bobbs-Merrill, 1937.

3289. Houseman, John. Entertainers and the Entertained: Essays on the theater, film and television. New York, Simon and Schuster, 1986.

3290. Kupcinet, Irv. Kup's Chicago: A many-faceted and affectionate portrait of Chicago. Cleveland, World Publishing, 1962.

3291. Lackmann, Ron. Remember Radio. New York, G.P. Putnam's Sons, 1970.

3292. _____. This Was Radio. Great American Audio, 2000.

3293. Levant, Oscar. The Unimportance Of Being Oscar. New York, Pocket Books, 1969.

3294. McMahon, Morgan E.A Flick OfThe Switch, 1930-1950. Palos Verdes, CA, Vintage Radio, 1976.

3295. Morris, Lloyd. Not So Long Ago. New York, Random House, 1949.

3296. Nachman, Gerald. Raised On Radio. NewYork, Pantheon, 1998.

3297. Peet, Creighton.AllAbout Broadcasting. NewYork,Alfred A. Knopf, 1942.

3298. Pomeroy, Owens L. The Other Side Of The Microphone: A Radio Buff Remembers. Baltimore, O.L. Pomeroy, 1986.

3299. Poteet, G. Howard. Radio! Dayton, OH, Pflaum Publishing, 1975.

3300. Ranson, Jo and Richard Pack. Quiz Book Of The Seven Arts: More Than OneThousand Questions andAnswers. New York, Summit Press, 1946.

3301. Reck, Franklin M. Radio From Start To Finish. New York, Thomas Y. Crowell, 1942.

3302. Schaden, Chuck. Speaking of Radio: Chuck Schaden's Conversations with the Stars of the Golden Age of Radio.

3303. Simons, Mel. Old Time Radio Trivia Book. Boalsburg, PA, Bear Manor Media.

3304. Sioussat, Helen. Mike's Don't Bite. New York, L. B. Fischer, 1943.

3305. Slate, Sam J. and Joe Cook. It Sounds Impossible: The hilarious story of radio broadcasting from the beginning to the future. New York, Macmillan, 1963.

3306. Stumpf, Charles. Ma Perkins, Little Orphan Annie And Heigh Ho Silver! New York, Carlton Press, 1971.

3307. Taylor, Glenhall. Before Television: The RadioYears. New York, A. S. Barnes, 1979.

3308. Wilson, Earl. The NBC Book Of Stars. New York, Pocket Books, 1957.

3309. Woolley, Lynn. The Last Great Days Of Radio. Plano, TX, Republic Of Texas Press, 1994.

History: Legislation and Regulation

3310. Bensman, Marvin. Beginning Of Broadcast Regulation In The 20th Century. Jefferson, NC, McFarland, 2000.

3311. Emery, Walter B. BroadcastingAnd Government: Responsibilities and Regulations. Michigan State University Press, 1971.

3312. Robinson, Thomas Porter. Radio Networks And The Federal Government. NewYork, Columbia University Press, 1943.

3313. Rosen, Philip T. The Modern Stentors: Radio Broadcasters and the Federal Government, 1920-1934. Westport, CT, Greenwood, 1980.

3314. Spring, Samuel. Risks And Rights In Publishing Television, Radio, Motion Pictures, Advertising and the Theater. New York, W.W. Norton, 1952.

History: Propaganda

3315. Hale, Julian. Radio Power: Propaganda and International Broadcasting. Philadelphia, Temple Univ. Press, 1975.

History: Research

3316. Audience Research. Continuing Audit Of Radio Personalities, Fall-Winter 1948-49/No 4. Princeton, NY, Audience Research Inc. ,1949.

3317. CBS. TheThird Study Of Radio Network Popularity. New York, CBS, 1932.

3318. Chappell, Matthew N. and C. E. Hooper. Radio Audience Measurement. New York, Stephen Daye, 1944.

3319. Goode, Kenneth M.WhatAbout Radio? New York, Harper & Brothers, 1937.

3320. Hettinger, Herman S. A Decade Of Radio Advertising. Chicago, University of Chicago Press, 1933.

3321. Lazarsfeld, Paul F. The People LookAt Radio: Report on a survey conducted by The National Opinion Research Center. Chapel Hill, NC, University Of North Carolina Press, 1946.

3322. _____. Radio And The Printed Page. New York, Duell, Sloan & Pearce, 1940.

3323. _____ and Frank N. Stanton, eds. Radio Research, 1942-1943. New York, Duell, Sloan & Pearce, 1944.

3324. _____.and Patricia L. Kendall. Radio Listening In America: The People Look at Radio - Again. New York, Prentice-Hall, 1948.

3325. Lumley, Frederick H. Measurement In Radio. Columbus, OH, Ohio State University, 1934.

3326. NBC, Young People As Radio Listeners And Customers. NBC, 1948.

3327. Routt, Edd and James B. McGrath and Fredric A. Weiss. The Radio Format Conundrum. New York, Hastings House. 1978.

Humor

(Includes, in part, non radio related humor
book by radio personalities.)

3328. Ace, Goodman. Better Of Goodman Ace. New York, Doubleday, 1971.

3329. _____. Book Of Little Knowledge. New York, Simon & Schuster, 1955.

3330. Adams, Cedric. Poor Cedric's Almanac. Garden City, NY, Doubleday, 1952.

3331. Adams, Joey. Here's To The Friars. New York, Crown, 1976.

3332. Allen, Gracie. How To Become President. New York, Duell, Sloan & Pearce, 1940.

3333. Allen, Steve. The Funny Men. New York, Simon & Schuster, 1956.

3334. _____. Funny People. New York, Stein & Day, 1984.

3335. _____. Make 'Em Laugh. New York, Prometheus Books, 1993.

3336. _____. More Funny People. New York, Stein And Day, 1982.

3337. Anobile, Richard J. Drat. New York, Signet, 1969.

3338. Arquette, Cliff. Charley Weaver's Family Album. Philadelphia, John C. Winston, 1960.

3339. _____. Cliff. Charley Weaver's Letters From Mamma. Philadelphia, John C. Winston, 1959.

3340. Barnes, Pat. Sketches Of Life. Chicago, Reilly & Lee, 1932.

3341. Berle, Milton. B.S. I Love You: Sixty Funny Years with the Famous and the Infamous. New York, McGraw-Hill, 1988.

3342. _____. Out of My Trunk. Garden City, NY, Blue Ribbon Books, 1945.

3343. Burns, George. All My Best Friends. New York, G.P. Putnam's Sons. 1989.

3344. _____. Dr. Burns' Prescription For Happiness: Buy 2 Books & Call Me In. New York, G.P. Putnam's Sons, 1984.

3345. _____. Living It Up or They Still Love Me In Altoona! New York, G. P. Putnam, 1976.

3346. Cantor, Eddie. An Hour With You. Racine, WI, Whitman Publishing, 1934.

3347. _____. Between The Acts. New York, Simon & Schuster, 1930.

3348. _____. World's Book of Best Jokes. Cleveland, World Publishing Company, 1943.

3349. _____. Yoo-Hoo Prosperity! (5 Year Plan). New York, Simon & Schuster, 1931.

3350. _____. Your Next President. Ray Long & Richard Smith, 1932.

3351. Day. Donald, ed. Will Rogers On How We Elect Our Presidents. Boston, Little, Brown and Company, 1952.

3352. Ford, Ben (Duke Of Paducah). These Shoes Are Killing Me. New York, Radco, 1947.

3353. _____. My Home Town. New York, Howell, Soskin, 1945.

3354. _____, Harry Hershfield and Joe Laurie Jr. Cream Of The Crop. New York, Didier, 1947.

3355. Godfrey, Arthur. Stories I Like To Tell. New York, Simon & Schuster, 1952.

3356. Hample, Stuart, ed. All the Sincerity In Hollywood: Selections from the writings of radio's legendary comedian Fred Allen. Golden, CO, Fulcrum, 2001.

3357. Hay, Peter. Canned Laughter. New York, Oxford University Press, 1992.

3358. Hershfield, Harry. Laugh Louder, Live Longer. New York, Grayson Publishing, 1959.

3359. _____. Now I'll Tell One. New York, Greenberg, 1938.

3360. Hope, Bob. I Never Left Home. New York, Simon & Schuster, 1944.

3361. _____. I Owe Russia $1200. Garden City, NY, Doubleday, 1963.

3362. Hubbard, Kin. Abe Martin's Broadcast: Kin Hubbard Announcing. Indianapolis, Bobbs-Merrill, 1930.

3363. Jessel, George. Elegy In Manhattan. New York, Holt, Rinehart And Winston, 1961.

3364. Jessel, George. Halo Over Hollywood. Van Nuys, CA, Toastmaster Publishing, 1963.

3365. _____. George. Hello, Momma. Cleveland, World Publishing, 1946.

3366. _____. Jessel, Anyone? Englewood Cliffs, NJ, Prentice-Hall, 1960.

3367. _____. This Way, Miss. New York, Henry Holt, 1955.

3368. _____. The Toastmaster General's Favorite Jokes. Secaucus, NJ, Castle Books, 1973.

3369. _____. The World I Lived In. Chicago, Henry Regnery Company, 1975.

3370. _____. You Too Can Make A Speech. New York, Grayson Publishing, 1956.

3371. Lee, Hap. Radio Joke Book. Philadelphia, David McKay Company, 1935.

3372. Lehr, Lew, Cal Tinney and Roger Bower. Stop Me If You've Heard This One. Garden City, NY, Halcyon House, 1948.

3373. Linkletter, Art. Kids Say The Darndest Things! Englewood Cliffs, NJ, Prentice-Hall, 1958.

3374. _____. Oops! Or, Life's Awful Moments. Garden City, NY, Doubleday, 1967.

3375. _____. Women Are My Favorite People: Stories gleaned from Art's years of experience. Garden City, NY, Doubleday, 1974.

3376. Lyons, Jimmy. Mirth Of A Nation. New York, Vantage Press, 1953.

3377. Marx, Groucho. Many Happy Returns, An Unofficial Guide to Your Income Tax Problems, New York, Simon and Schuster, 1942.

3378. _____. Beds. Indianapolis, The Bobbs-Merrill Company, 1976.

3379. _____. The Groucho Letters. New York, Manor Books, 1974.

3380. _____. The Secret Word Is Groucho. New York, G.P. Putnam's Sons, 1976.

3381. _____. What Groucho Says. New York, Harper & Brothers, 1930.

3382. McCarthy, Joe, ed. Fred Allen's Letters. Garden City, NY, Doubleday, 1965.

3383. Morgan, Henry. And Now A Word From Our Sponsor. New York, The Citadel Press, 1960.

3384. Oliver, Donald, ed. The Greatest Review Sketches. New York, Avon, 1982.

3385. Paar, Jack. I Kid You Not. Boston, Little, Brown and Company, 1960.

3386. _____. My Saber Is Bent. New York, Simon & Schuster, 1961.

3387. _____. P.S. Jack Paar. Garden City, NY, Doubleday, 1983.

3388. Pearl, Jack. Detective Baron Munchausen. Goldsmith, 1934.

3389. Porch, Ludlow. The Cornbread Chronicles. Atlanta, Peachtree Publishers, 1983.

3390. Revell, Nellie. The Funny Side Out. New York, George H. Doran, 1925.

3391. Schafer, Kermit. All Time Great Bloopers. New York, Avenel, 1973.

3392. Schafer, Kermit. Blunderful World Of Bloopers. New York, Bounty Books, 1973.

3393. Schafer, Kermit. Super Duper Bloopers! New York, Avenel, 1975.

3394. _____. Your Slip Is Showing: A Collection of Radio and TV's Most Hilarious Boners. New York, Grayson, 1953.

3395. _____. Best Of Bloopers. New York, Avenel, 1973.

3396. Singer, Spizz. Forty Years Behind the Mike in Lincolnland: Wit, Wisdom and Fascinating Facts. Springfield, Il, 1968.

3397. Steele, Bob. Bob Steele: A Man And His Humor. Hartford, CT, Spoonwood Press, 1980.

3398. Sterling, Bryan. The Best Of Will Rogers. New York, Crown Publishers, 1979.

3399. Stewart, Cal. Uncle Josh Weathersby's "Punkin Centre" Stories. Chicago, Punkin Centre, 1903.

3400. Stone, Ezra and Weldon Melick. Coming, Major! New York, J.B. Lippincott, 1944.

3401. Stoopnagle, Colonel Lemuel Q. (Chase Taylor). My Back To The Soil: Or Farewell To Farms. Howell, Soskin, Publishers, 1947.

3402. _____. My Tale Is Twisted! New York, M. S. Mill, 1946.

3403. _____. You Wouldn't Know Me From Adam. New York, McGraw-Hill, 1944.

3404. Thomas, Lowell. Fan Mail. New York, Dodge Publishing. 1935.

3405. Woollcott, Alexander. Long, Long Ago. New York, Viking, 1943.

3406. Wynn, Ed. Fire Chief Ed Wynn And His Old Fire Horse. Goldsmith Publishing, 1934.

Miscellaneous

(Includes, in part, non radio related writings
by people associated with radio.)

3407. Anthology. Thirteen For Corwin. University of Southern California, 1985.

3408. Berg, Jerome S. On The Short Waves, 1923-1945. Jefferson, NC, McFarland, 1999.

3409. Carter, Boake. I Talk As I Like. New York, Dodge Publishing, 1937.

3410. _____. Johnny Q. Public Speaks: The Nation Appraises the New Deal. New York, Dodge Publishing, 1936.

3411. _____. This Is Life. New York, Dodge Publishing, 1937.

3412. Corwin, Norman. Holes In A Stained Glass Window: Selected New Writings. Secaucus, NJ, Lyle Stuart, 1978.

3413. Davis, Elmer. But We Were Born Free. Indianapolis, Bobbs-Merrill, 1954.

3414. _____. Show Window. New York, John Day, 1927.

3415. _____. Two Minutes To Midnight. Indianapolis, Bobbs-Merrill, 1955.

3416. Edwards, Frank. Strange People, ,

3417. Faulk, John Henry. The Uncensored John Henry Faulk. Austin, TX, Texas Monthly Press, 1985.

3418. Green, Stanley. The Great Clowns Of Broadway. New York, Oxford University Press, 1984.

3419. Harmon, Jim. Radio And TV Premiums. Krause, 1997.

3420. Harvey, Paul. Autumn Of Liberty. Garden City, NY, Hanover House, 1954.

3421. _____. Remember These Things. Chicago, Heritage Foundation, 1952.

3422. Heatter, Gabriel. Faith: A Selection of Essays and Editorials. Unknown, 1936.

3423. Hepner, Arthur W., ed. The Best Of Emphasis: Opinions and Insights by the World NBC News Staff. Westminster, MD, Newman Press, 1962.

3424. Herr, Michael. Walter Winchell: A Novel. New York, Alfred A. Knopf. 1990.

3425. Herzog, David Alan. Collecting Today for Tomorrow. New York, Arco Publishing, 1980.

3426. Kaltenborn, H. V.. It Seems Like Yesterday. New York, G.P. Putnam's Sons, 1956.

3427. Kassel, Michael B. America's Favorite Radio Station, WKRP in Cincinnati. Bowling Green, OH, Bowling Green State University Popular Press, 1993.

3428. Malone, Ted. Mansion's Of Imagination Album. New York, Columbia University Press, 1941.

3429. Malone, Ted. Should Old Acquaintance. Bookmark Press, 1943.

3430. Morgan, Edward P. Clearing The Air. Washington, DC, Robert B. Luce, 1963.

3431. Murrow, Edward R. This I Believe. New York, Simon & Schuster, 1954.

3432. Oral Hygiene Committee of Greater New York. Radio Manual: A Guide To Broadcasting For Mouth Health Education. Oral Hygiene Committee Of Greater New York, 1947.

3433. Reasoner, Harry. The Reasoner Report. Garden City, NY, Doubleday, Garden City, 1966.

3434. Schechter, A. A. Go Ahead Garrison. New York, Dodd, Mead, 1944.

3435. Sevareid, Eric. In One Ear: 107 Snapshots of men and events which make a far-reaching panorama of the American situation at midcentury. New York, Knopf, 1952.

3436. _____. Small Sounds In The Night: A collection of capsule commentaries on the American scene. New York, Knopf, 1956.

3437. Swing, Raymond Gram. How War Came. New York, W.W. Norton, 1939.

3438.   _____. Preview Of History. Garden City, NY, Doubleday, Doran, 1943.

3439.   _____, ed. This I Believe: The Personal Philosophies of 100 Thoughtful Men and Women. New York, Simon & Schuster, 1954.

3440.   _____. Watchman, What Of The Night? Grabhorn Press, 1945.

3441.   Thomas, Lowell. Back To Mandalay. New York, Greystone, 1951.

3442.   Wons, Tony. 'R' You Listenin? Tony's Own Philosophy. Chicago, Reilly & Lee, 1931.

Plays

(See also Scripts)

3443.   Bacher, William A., ed. Treasury Star Parade: 27 Radio Plays. New York, Farrar & Rinehart, 1942.

3444.   Barnouw, Erik, ed. Radio Drama In Action: Twenty-Five Plays Of A Changing World. New York, Farrar & Rinehart, 1945.

3445.   Benet, Stephen Vincent. They Burned The Books. New York, Farrar & Rinehart, 1942.

3446.   _____. We Stand United And Other Radio Scripts. New York, Farrar & Rinehart, 1945.

3447.   Boyd, James, ed. The Free Company Presents: A Collection of Plays About the Meaning of America. New York, Dodd, Mead and Company, 1941.

3448.   Bristol, Stephen. Crime Photographer: A Thrilling Mystery Comedy in Three Acts. New York, Samuel French, 1950.

3449.   Brodkin, Sylvia Z. and Elizabeth J. Pearson, eds. On The Air: A Collection Of Radio and TV Plays. New York, Charles Scribner's Sons, 1977.

3450.   Burack, A. S., ed. Four Star Radio Plays For Teen-Agers: A collection of royalty free radio dramas adapted from great literature. Boston, Plays Inc. 1959.

3451.   Burr, Jane. Fourteen Radio Plays. Hollywood, CA, Highland Press, 1945.

3452.   Carr, John Dickson. Speak of the Devil. Norfolk, VA, Crippen & Landru, 1994.

3453.   _____. Douglas G. Greene, ed. The Door To Doom And Other Detections. London, Hamish Hamilton, 1981.

3454.   Clark, Perry and R.J. Mann. Our Miss Brooks: A Comedy in Three Acts. Chicago, Dramatic Publishing, 1950.

3455.   Connery, Robert H., ed. The Land Of The Free: Six Radio Plays. Washington, DC, The Catholic University, 1941.

3456.   Corwin, Norman. More By Corwin: 16 Radio Dramas. New York, Henry Holt, 1944.

3457.   _____. On A Note Of Triumph. New York, Simon & Schuster, 1945.

3458.   _____. They Fly Through The Air With The Greatest Of Ease. Weston, VT, Vrest Orton, 1939.

3459.   _____. Thirteen By Corwin. New York, Henry Holt, 1942.

3460.   _____. Untitled And Other Radio Dramas. New York, Henry Holt, 1947.

3461.   _____. We Hold These Truths: The drama of our Bill of Rights with an address by Franklin D. Roosevelt. Howell, Soskin Publishers, 1942.

3462.   Coulter, Douglas, ed. Columbia Workshop Plays: Fourteen Radio Dramas. New York, McGraw-Hill, 1939.

3463.   Davis, Blevins. National Broadcasting Company Offers Great Plays: Drama guide, 1940–1941. New York, Columbia University Press, 1940.

3464.   Feigenbaum, Lawrence H. ed. Radio And Television Plays. New York, Globe Book, 1956.

3465.   Fletcher, Lucille. Sorry, Wrong Number and The Hitch-Hiker. New York, Dramatists Play Service, 1952.

3466.   Gorman, Herbert. World's Great Novels: Handbook, Vol. II, 1946. New York, Columbia University Press. 1946.

3467.   Hackett, Walter. Radio Plays For Young People: Fifteen Great Stories Adapted for Royalty-Free Performance. Boston, Plays, 1950.

3468.   Henry, Robert D. and James Lynch Jr. History Makers: Eight Radio Plays. Row, Peterson, 1941.

3469.   Kozlenko, William, ed. One Hundred Non-Royalty Radio Plays. New York, Greenberg, 1941.

3470.   Lampell, Millard. The Long Way Home. New York, Julian Messner, 1946.

3471.   Lass, A. H., Earle L. McGill and Donald Axelrod, eds. Plays From Radio. Cambridge, MA, Houghton, Mifflin, 1948.

3472.   Leverton, Garrett H. On The Air: Fifteen Radio Plays for Broadcast and for Classroom Use. New York, Samuel French, 1944.

3473.   Liss, Joseph, ed. Radio's Best Plays. New York, Greenberg, 1947.

3474.   MacLeish, Archibald. The American Story: Ten Broadcasts. New York, Duell, Sloan and Pearce, 1944.

3475.   _____. The Fall Of The City. New York, Farrar & Rinehart, 1937.

3476.   _____. Six Plays. Boston, Houghton Mifflin, 1980.

3477.   Morris, James M. Radio Workshop Plays. New York, H. W. Wilson, 1943.

3478.   Oboler, Arch. Fourteen Radio Plays. New York, Random House, 1940.

3479.   _____. House On Fire. London, Bartholomew House, 1969.

3480.   _____. Ivory Tower And Other Radio Plays. Chicago, William Targ, 1940.

3481.   _____. Night Of The Auk. New York, Horizon, 1958.

3482.   _____. Oboler Omnibus: Radio Plays and Personalities. New York, Duell, Sloan & Pearce, 1945.

3483.   _____. Plays For Americans: 13 New Non-Royalty Radio Plays. New York, Farrar & Rinehart, 1942.

3484.   _____. This Freedom: Thirteen New Radio Plays. New York, Random House, 1942.

3485.   _____. and Stephen Longstreet, eds. Free World Theater: Nineteen New Radio Plays. New York, Random House, 1944.

3486.   Olfson, Lewy. Radio Plays From Shakespeare. Boston, Plays, Inc. ,1958.

3487.   _____. Radio Plays Of Famous Stories. Boston, Plays, Inc. ,1956.

3488.   Thorne, Sylvia and Marion Norris Gleason. Pied Piper Broadcasts: Radio Plays For Children. New York, H. W. Wilson, 1943.

3489.   United States Office of Education. Let Freedom Ring! 13 scripts by Harold G. Calhoun and Dorothy Calhoun. U.S. Government Printing Office, 1938.

3490.   Watson, Katherine Williams, ed. Radio Plays For Children. New York, H.W. Wilson, 1947.

3491. Weiser, Norman S., ed. The Writer's Radio Theater: 1940-1941 Outstanding Plays of the Year. New York, Harper, 1941.

3492. ____. The Writer's Radio Theater: 1941 Outstanding Plays of the Year. New York, Harper & Brothers, 1942.

3493. White, James Roberts. Let's Broadcast! Twelve One-Act Plays. New York, Harper & Brothers, 1939.

3494. Writers Guild of America. Prize Plays Of Television And Radio, 1956. New York, Random House, 1957.

Reference

(Includes program listings, annual yearbooks and program summaries.)

3495. Alicoate, Jack, ed. Radio Annual: Published yearly 1938-1965. (Title changed to Radio Annual: Television Yearbook in 1950.) Radio Daily.

3496. Bresee, Frank and Bobb Lynes. Radio's Golden Years: A Visual Guide to the Shows & the Stars. Frank Bresee Productions, 1998.

3497. Buxton, Frank and Bill Owen. The Big Broadcast: 1920-1950. New York, Viking, 1972.

3498. ____. Radio's Golden Age: The Programs & the Personalities. Easton Valley Press, 1967.

3499. Corenthal, Michael G. Iconography Of Recorded Sound: 1886-1986. Milwaukee, Yesterday's Memories, 1986.

3500. Dunning, John. On The Air: The Encyclopedia Of Old Time Radio. New York, Oxford University Press, 1998.

3501. ____. Tune In Yesterday, Encyclopedia Of Old Time Radio 1925-1976. Englewood Cliffs, Prentice Hall, 1976.

3502. Godfrey, Donald G. and Frederic A. Leigh, eds. Historical Dictionary Of American Radio. Westport, CT, Greenwood Press, 1998.

3503. Goldin, J. David. Golden Age Of Radio. Sandy Hook, CT, Radio Yesteryear, 1998.

3504. Grunwald, Edgar A., ed. Variety Radio Directory. Annual. 1937-38; 1938-39; 1939-40; 1940-41. Variety.

3505. Hayden, Terese and Paul L. Ross, eds. Players' Guide, sponsored by Actors' Equity Association and American Federation of Television and Radio Artists. New York, Actors' Equity Association, 1944.

3506. Hickerson, Jay. The Ultimate History of Network Radio of Programming and Guide to All Circulating Shows, 3rd Ed. Hamden, CT, Jay Hickerson, 2005.

3507. Lackmann, Ron. Same Time...Same Station: An A-Z Guide to Radio from Jack Benny to Howard Stern. New York, Facts On File, 1996.

3508. Mackenzie, Harry. Directory Of Armed Forces Radio Services Series. Westport, CT, Greenwood, 1999.

3509. McCavitt, William E., ed. Radio And Television: A Selected, Annotated Bibliography. Metuchen, NJ, Scarecrow, 1978.

3510. Paulson, Roger G. Archives of the Airwaves. Boalsburg, PA, Bear Manor Media. Vol 1 & 2, 2005. Additional volumes due out in 2006.

3511. Pitts, Michael R. Radio Soundtracks: A Reference Guide. Metuchen, NJ, Scarecrow Press, 1976.

3512. Price, Tom. Radio Program Time Lines: 1920-1980: A Charted Cross-Reference of American Radio Broadcasting Displaying Program Titles, Broadcasting Timelines, Sponsorship, and Network Affiliation. Tom Price, 1980.

3513. Shapiro, Mildred. Radio Network Prime Time Programming, 1926-1967. Jefferson, NC, McFarland, 2002.

3514. Sies, Leora and Luther. Encyclopedia Of Women In Radio, 1920-1960. Jefferson, NC, McFarland, 2003.

3515. Sies, Luther E. Encyclopedia of American Radio 1920-1960. Jefferson, NC, McFarland, 2000.

3516. Slide, Anthony. International Film, Radio, and Television Journals. Westport, CT, Greenwood, 1985.

3517. Smart, James R., ed. Radio Broadcasts In The Library Of Congress: 1924-1941: A Catalog of Recordings. Washington, DC, Library Of Congress, 1982.

3518. Sterling, Christopher H., ed. Encyclopedia of Radio. New York, Fitzroy Dearborn, 2004.

3519. Summers, Harrison B., ed. A Thirty-Year History Of Radio Programs 1926-1956. Salem, NH, Ayer, 1958.

3520. Swartz, Jon D. and Robert C. Reinehr. Handbook of Old-Time-Radio: A Comprehensive Guide to Golden Age Radio Listening and Collecting. Metuchen, NJ, Scarecrow, 1993.

3521. Terrace, Vincent. Radio Programs Openings and Closings: 1931-1972. Jefferson, NC, McFarland, 2003.

3522. ____. Radio's Golden Years: Encyclopedia Of Radio Programs 1930-1960. New York, A. S. Barnes, 1981.

Scripts

(See also Plays and Genre Listings)

3523. Berard, Jeanette M. and Klaudia Englund. Radio Series Scripts, 1930-2001. Jefferson, NC, McFarland, 2006.

3524. Cohen, Diana and Irene Burns Hoeflinger, eds. The Shadow Knows. Glenview, IL, Scott, Foresman & Co., 1977.

3525. Cuthbert, Margaret, ed. Adventure In Radio. Howell, Soskin. 1945.

3526. Poteet, G. Howard. Published Radio, Television And Film Scripts. A Bibliography. Troy, NY, Whitston Publishing, 1975.

3527. Rapp, Philip. Ben Ohmart, ed. The Baby Snooks Scripts. Cranston, RI, The Writer's Collective, 2003.

3528. Wylie, Max, ed. Best Broadcasts Of 1938-1939. New York, McGraw-Hill, 1939.

3529. ____. Best Broadcasts Of 1939-1940. New York, Whittlesey House, 1940.

3530. ____. Best Broadcasts Of 1940-1941. New York, Whittlesey House, 1942.

Show Business

3531. Andacht, Sandra. Joe Franklin's Show Biz Memorabilia. Wallace Homestead, 1985.

3532. Burrows, Abe. Honest, Abe: Is There Really No Business Like Show Business? Boston, Little, Brown and Company, 1980.

3533. Csida, Joseph and June Bundy. American Entertainment. Billboard, 1978.

3534. Dimeglio, John. Vaudeville U. S. A. Bowling Green, OH, Bowling Green University Popular Press, 1973.

3535. Durante, Jimmy and Jack Kofoed. Night Clubs. New York, Alfred A. Knopf. 1931.

3536. Green, Abel and Joe Laurie, Jr. Show Biz From Vaude To Video. New York, Henry Holt, 1951.

3537. ____, ed. Spice Of Variety. New York, Henry Holt, 1952.

3538. Laurie, Joe, Jr. Vaudeville: From The Honky-Tonks To The Palace. New York, Henry Holt, 1953.

3539. Lyons, Ruth. Remember With Me. Garden City, NY, Doubleday, 1969.

3540. Minksy, Morton and Milt Machlin. Minsky's Burlesque: A Fast and Funny Look at America's Bawdiest Era. New York, Arbor House, 1986.

3541. Mosedale, John. The Men Who Invented Broadway: Damon Runyon, Walter Winchell & Their World. New York, Richard Marek Publishers, 1981.

3542. Murray, Lynn. Musician, A Hollywood Journal of Wives, Women, Writers, Lawyers, Directors, Producers and Music. Secaucus, NJ, Lyle Stuart, 1987.

3543. Paskman, Daily. Gentleman Be Seated. New York, Clarkson N. Potter/Crown. 1976.

3544. Rubin, Benny. Come Backstage With Me. Bowling Green, OH, Bowling Green University Popular Press, ?

3545. Sobel, Bernard. A Pictorial History Of Vaudeville. New York, Bonanza Books, 1961.

3546. Spitzer, Marian. The Palace. New York, Atheneum, 1969.

3547. Toll, Robert C. Entertainment Machine. New York, Oxford University Press, 1982.

Station History

3548. Alderman, Virginia. Fifty Years of Broadcasting at WWVA, Wheeling, W.Va. Wheeling, WWVA Radio Station.

3549. Allen, Gene. Voice on the Wind: Early Radio in Oklahoma. Oklahoma Heritage Association (Western Heritage Books), 1993.

3550. Banning, William Peck. Commercial Broadcasting Pioneer: The WEAF Experiment 1922-1926. Cambridge, MA, Harvard University Press, 1946.

3551. Becker, Martha Jane and Marilyn Fletcher. Broadasting in West Virginia: A History. S. Charleston, WV, West Virginia Broadcasters Assc., 1989.

3552. Birkby, Robert. KMA Radio, The First Sixty Years. Shenandoah, IA, May Broadcasting,1985.

3553. Bloch, Louis M., Jr. Gas Pipe Networks, History Of College Radio 1936-1946. Cleveland, Bloch & Co., 1980.

3554. Brawley, Harry. Twenty Years on an Oasis in the Vast Wasteland. Charleston, WV, Education Foundtion, 1981.

3555. Brouder, Edward W., Jr. Granite and Ether: A Chronicle Of New Hampshire Broadcasting. Bedford, NH, New Hampshire Association of Broadcasters, 1993.

3556. Cantor, Louis. Wheelin' On Beale: WDIA, Memphis. New York, Pharos Books, 1992.

3557. Chasan, Daniel Jack. On The Air: The King Broadcasting Story. Anacortes, WA, Island Publishers, 1996.

3558. Detroit News, Radio Staff. WWJ - The Detroit News. Detroit, Evening News Association, 1922.

3559. Doll, Bob. Sparks Out of The Plowed Ground: The History of America's Small Town Radio Stations. West Palm Beach, FL, Streamline Publishing, 1996.

3560. Doubleday, Robert. Deacon, The Deacon Speakin: Up Country Comin' Down City. Sherburne, NY, Heritage Press, 1966.

3561. Earl, Bill. Dream House, KRLA: The Complete 30 Year History of a Major West Coast Radio Station. Desert Rose, 1967.

3562. Eberly, Philip K. Susquehanna Radio: The First Fifty Years. York, PA, Susquehanna Radio Corp., 1992.

3563. Evans, James F. Prairie Farmer and WLS: The Burridge Butler Years. Urbana, IL, Univ. Of Illinois Press, 1969.

3564. Fink, John. WGN, A Pictorial History. Chicago, WGN, 1961.

3565. Fowler, Gene and Bill Crawford. Border Radio: Quacks, Yodelers, Pitchmen, Psychics, and Other Amazing Broadcasters of the American Airwaves. Texas, Limelight Editions, 2002.

3566. Friedersdorf, Burk. From Crystal To Color WFBM. Indianapolis, IN, WFBM, 1964.

3567. Heath, Horton. NBC: A History. New York, NBC, 1965.

3568. Jaker, Bill and Frank Sulek and Peter Kanze. Airwaves Of New York. Jefferson, NC, McFarland, 1998.

3569. Kneitel, Tom. Radio Station Treasury: 1900-1946. Commack, NY, CRB Research, 1986.

3570. Kruse, Len. Unforgettable Radio: A Program Chronicle of WKBB 1933-1941. Len Kruse, 1993.

3571. Lasar, Matthew. Pacifica Radio: The Rise of an Alternative Network. Philadelphia, Temple University Press, 1999.

3572. Macy, Marianne. WOR Radio 1922-1982: The First Sixty Years. New York, Nightengale Gordon, 1982.

3573. McDonald, C. Howard. Voices In The Big Sky: The History of Montana Broadcasting. Bozeman, MT, Big M Broadcast Services, 1996.

3574. McKinney, Eleonore (ed). The Exacting Ear: The story of listener-sponsored radio, and an anthology of programs from KPFA, KPFK, and WBAI. New York, Random House, 1966.

3575. McRaney, Bob Sr. The History of Radio in Mississippi.

3576. Nightingale Gordon. WNEW Where The Melody Lingers On (1934-1984). New York, Nightengale Gordon, 1984.

3577. Osgood, Dick. WYXIE Wonderland (An Unauthorized 50 Year Diary Of WXYZ Detroit. Bowling Green, OH, Bowling Green University Press, 1981.

3578. Perry, Dick. Not Just A Sound: The Story Of WLW. Englewood Cliffs, NJ, Prentice Hall, 1971

3579. Peterson, James D. A History of KLTZ: 'Kilts' Radio. Wolf Point, MT, James D. Peterson, 1991.

3580. Poindexter, Ray. Arkansas Airwaves. Cassville, MO, Litho Printers, 1974.

3581. Richardson, David. Puget Sounds: A Nostalgic Review of Radio and TV in the Great Northwest. Seattle, WA, Superior Publishers, 1981.

3582. Sanger, Elliot M. Rebel In Radio: The Story Of WQXR. New York, Hastings House, 1973.

3583. Sarjeant, Charles F. ed. The First Forty: The Story Of WCCO Radio. Minneapolis, MN, T.S. Denison, 1964.

3584. Schaden, Chuck. WBBM Radio, Yesterday & Today. Chicago, WBBM, 1988.

3585. Schroeder, Richard. Texas Signs On: The Early Days of Radio and Television. College Station, TX, Texas A & M University Press, 1998.

3586. Thompson, Ellie. The History Of Broadcasting In Maine: The First Fifty Years. Augusta, ME, Maine Association Of Broadcasters, 1990.

3587. Velia, Ann M. KOB: Goddard's Magic Mast, 50 Years Of Pioneer Broadcasting. New Mexico State University,1972

3588. WFAA. WFAA: Counting Stars And Kilocycles: 25th Anniversary. Dallas, TX, WFAA, 1947.

3589. WHEC,The Story of WHEC. Rochester, NY, WHEC. 1951

3590. Yoder. Andrew R. Pirate Radio Stations. Blue Ridge Summit, PA, TAB Books, 1990.

Station Operation

3591. Abbot, Waldo. Handbook Of Broadcasting. New York, McGraw-Hill, 1941

3592. Barnouw, Erik. Handbook Of Radio Production. Boston, Little, Brown and Company, 1949.

3593. Ennes, Harold E. Broadcast Operator's Handbook. New York, John F. Rider, 1951.

3594. Ewbank, Henry L. and Sherman Lawton. Broadcasting: Radio And Television,New York, Harper & Brothers, 1952.

3595. Floherty, John J. On The Air: The Story of Radio. Garden City, NY, Doubleday, Doran, 1937.

3596. Hilliard, Robert L. ed. Radio Broadcasting: An Introduction to the Sound Medium. New York, Hastings House, 1982.

3597. Keith, Michael C. and Joseph M. Krause. The Radio Station. Boston, Focal Press, 1986.

3598. NBC. NBC And You: An account of the Organization, Operation and Employee-Company Policies. New York, NBC. 1944.

3599. Reinsch, J. Leonard. Radio Station Management. New York, Harper, 1948.

3600. Reinsch, J. Leonard and Elmo Israel Ellis. Radio Station Management. New York, Harper & Brothers, 1960.

3601. Sill, Jerome. The Radio Station: Management, Function, Future. New York, George W. Stewart, 1946.

3602. Tyler, Kingdon S. Modern Radio. New York, Harcourt, Brace, 1944.

3603. Waller, Judith C. Radio: The Fifth Estate. Boston, Houghton, Mifflin, 1946.

World War II

3604. Andrews, Maxine and Bill Gilbert. Over Here, Over There: The Andrew Sisters and USO Stars in World War II. New York, Zebra Books, 1993.

3605. Bergmeier, Horst and Rainer Lotz. Hitler's Airwaves: The Inside Story of Nazi Radio Broadcasting and Propaganda Swing. New Haven, CT, Yale Univ. Press, 1997.

3606. Bernstein, Mark and Alex Lubertozzi. World War II On The Air: Edward R. Murrow and the Broadcasts That Riveted a Nation. Naperville, IL, Sourcebooks, 2003.

3607. Blue, Howard. Words At War: World War II Radio Drama and the Postwar Broadcasting Industry Blacklist.

Metuchen, NJ, Scarecrow, 2002.

3608. CBS. From D-Day Through Victory In Europe: The Eye-Witness Story as Told by War Correspondents on the Air. New York, CBS, 1945.

3609. Christman, Trent. Brass Button Broadcasters: A Light-hearted Look at 50 Years of Military Broadcasting. Paducah, KY, Turner Publishing, 1992.

3610. Corwin, Norman, ed. This Is War! A Collection of Plays About America on the March. New York, Dodd, Mead & Co. ,1942.

3611. Delmer, Sefton. Black Boomerang. New York, Viking Press, 1962.

3612. Dryer, Sherman H. Radio In Wartime. New York, Greenberg, 1942.

3613. Dunn, William J. Pacific Microphone. College Station, TX, Texas A & M University Press, 1988.

3614. Edwards, John Carver. Berlin Calling: American Broadcasters in Service to the Third Reich. New York, Praeger, 1991.

3615. Fawkes, Richard. Fighting For A Laugh: Entertaining the British and American Armed Forces 1939-1946. London, MacDonald And Jane's, 1978.

3616. Hoopes. Roy. When The Stars Went To War: Hollywood and World War II. New York, Random House, 1994.

3617. Kirby, Edward M. and Jack W. Harris. Star-Spangled Radio: Radio's Part in World War II. Chicago, Ziff-Davis, 1948.

3618. Lingerman, Richard R. Don't You Know There's A War On: The American Homefront, 1941-1945. New York, G. P. Putnam's Sons, 1970.

3619. Mackenzie, Harry. AFRS Downbeat Series: A Working Draft. Joyce Record Club, 1986.

3620. Mackenzie, Harry, Compiler. Command Performance, USA! A Discography. Westport, CT, Greenwood, 1996.

3621. MacVane, John. On The Air In World War II. New York, William Morrow, 1979.

3622. Morley, Patrick. This is the American Forces Network: The Anglo-American Battle of the Air Waves in World War II. Westport, CT, Praeger, 2001.

3623. Murrow, Edward R. This Is London. New York, Schocken, 1985.

3624. Rolo, Charles J.. Radio Goes To War: The 'Fourth Front. New York, G. P. Putnam's Sons, 1942.

3625. Ryan, Milo. History In Sound: A Descriptive Listing of the KIRO-CBS Collection of Broadcasts of the World War II Years and After in the Phonoarchives of the University of Washington. Seattle, WA, University Of Washington Press, 1963.

3626. Shirer, William L. Berlin Diary. New York, Popular Library, 1961.

3627. _____. The Rise And Fall Of The Third Reich. New York, Simon & Shuster, 1960

3628. _____. This Is Berlin: Radio Broadcasts from Nazi Germany. Woodstock, NY, Overlook Press, 1999.

3629. Soley, Lawrence C. Radio Warfare: OSS and CIA Subversive Propaganda. New York, Praeger, 1989.

3630. Sproat, Iain. Wodehouse At War: The extraordinary truth about P.G. Wodehouse's broadcasts on Nazi radio. London, Milner & Co. ,1981.

3631. Sweeney, Michael S. Secrets of Victory: The Office of Censorship and the American Press and Radio in World

War II. University of North Carolina Press, 2001.

3632. Thompson, Dorothy. Listen, Hans: New and constructive thinking about the war. Boston, Houghton, Miflin, 1942.

3633. Tillich, Paul. Ronald H. Stone and Matthew Lon Weaver, Eds. Against The Third Reich: Paul Tillich's Wartime Radio Broadcasts Into Nazi Germany. Louisville, KY, Westminster John Knox Press, 1998.

3634. Voss, Frederick S. Reporting The War: The Journalistic Coverage of World War II. Washington, DC, Smithsonian Institute, 1994.

3635. Radio Magazines

The following is a list of consumer oriented radio magazines published between the 1920s–1950s. Beginning and ending dates for the publication are shown where the information is known.

Additional information about radio magazines and journals may be available in: International Film, Radio and Television Journals by Anthony Slide (Westport, CT, Greenwood Press, 1985).

Broadcast Listener, (Formerly The Radio Listener), Monthly, beginning 1926.

Broadcast Weekly, ca. 1928/1929–at least 1930

Broadcasting, Weekly, 1931–1937

Listener's Digest, 1939–.

Major Bowes Amateur Magazine, 1936–.

Microphone, 1932–at least 1938.

National Radio News, 1924–at least 1935.

News Digest, 1941 (?)–at least 1944.

Popular Song 1934–at least 1935.

Radio Album, 1942–1950.

Radio and Entertainment in and Around St. Louis, 1931–1932

Radio and Television Best, 1948–at least 1950.

Radio Art (Blue Book of the Air.), 1932–.

Radio Best (See Radio and Television Best), 1947–1948.

Radio Digest, 1922–1933.

Radio Digest (Different from earlier magazine of same name.), 1939–.

Radio Doings, (The Red Book of Radio), ca. 1922–at least 1928.

Radio Fanfare, (Continuation of Radio Digest above.), 1993–.

Radio Guide (Became Movie-Radio Guide), 1931–1940.

Radio Hit Songs, 1941–.

Radio Home Makers Magazine of the Air, 1929–at least 1930.

Radio Index, 1923?–at least 1929.

Radio Life, 1940–at least 1947.

Radio Mirror, 1933–at least 1971.

Radio News, 1919?

Radio Parade, 1941–.

Radio Program Weekly, 1927–.

Radio Row, 1946–at least 1947.

Radio Stars and Television, 1948–at least 1949.

Radio Stars, 1932–1938.

Radio Times, 1923–present.

Radio Varieties, 1938–at least 1941.

Radio Weekly, 1938?–.

Radio World, 1922–at least 1924.

Radioland, 1933–at least 1935.

Rural Radio, 1938–1938?

Stand By, 1935–at least 1938.

Tower Radio, 1934–at least 1935.

Tune In, 1943–at least 1946.

Voice of Experience, 1935–.

What's On The Air, 1929–at least 1931.

Chapter 4: Internet Resources

Researching the Internet

Challenges and choices

Deciding what Internet sites to include in this section presented the authors with both challenges and choices. The major challenge was deciding if indeed it was feasible to undertake the task of meticulously researching millions of potential web sites containing material about thousands of potential people, programs or subjects. Some of the choices included deciding what people and programs to include or exclude in this section of the Resource Guide and, considering the many different types of sites dealing with old time radio, determining what types should be included or excluded. For example, should this chapter include sites that offered the visitor a chance to listen to a program, acquire a program, access a database with historical information about a program or read articles about a program?

Google, Yahoo and other Internet search engines have revolutionized the way research is conducted online; they have made it both easier for researchers to "find" information, especially on often obscure subjects, but at the same time, they have inundated researchers with an almost impossible number of sites to "check out."

A Google search for "'Fred Allen' AND Radio" brought up 66,800 listings while the number of listings for "'Jack Benny' AND Radio" jumped to 225,000. Searching for specific programs, especially the more popular ones, was similarly daunting. A search for "'old time radio' AND Suspense" generated 69,400 listings and about half that number, 39,400, for "'old time radio' AND 'Fibber McGee.'"

What is included in this section

Ultimately, in deciding which listings to include in this section of the Resource Guide, the authors narrowed the focus of the chapter to include a limited but select list of sites that contain information of interest to researchers and which are not exclusively or primarily designed to be listened to, downloaded or for the purpose of marketing recordings of old time radio programs.

Web sites that are already listed in the Special Collections chapter such as the web pages for the NUCMC (National Union Catalog of Manuscript Collections) or the repositories with significant radio related collections are not repeated in this section.

The sites that have been selected for inclusion in this chapter fall into the following four categories:

1. Sites generally not associated with the Golden Age of Radio but which *may* lead to additional information about the subject such as links to state historical societies.
2. Old time radio sites that include large databases of programs such as RadioGoldindex.com which contains information on more than 86,000 program listings.
3. Sites that include links to other radio related sites such as Jeff Miller's site that contains links to many station history sites.
4. Sites that provide a general historical overview of the Golden Age of Radio such as Barry Mishkind's site which contains articles and links on different aspects of radio history.

The web pages selected for inclusion on the following pages are not meant to be a definitive listing of research oriented sites but only the *beginning* of the Internet search process. As anyone familiar with online searches knows, sometimes, all that is necessary is one link; the rest follows.

In contrast to the listings in the Special Collections and Bibliography sections of the Resource Guide which are designed to assist researchers locate information about specific people and programs, with a few exceptions, the Internet section does not include sites that deal primarily or exclusively with specific programs or personalities. The rational for this seemingly apparent omission relates back to the overall goal of the Guide: to assist researchers to identify *hard-to-find* sources of information about the Golden Age of Radio and not simply to repeat, in a new format, information that is already available elsewhere and easy to access.

Before the authors set out to research special collections with radio related material in repositories throughout the United States, little if any information existed that documented the existence or whereabouts of these primary sources of information. Also, while there are some bibliographies of the Golden Age of Radio, most are appendices in books about radio and they are not included in an Index that can be searched by name, program or subject. In sharp contrast to these two resources, information available on the Internet is accessible to anyone with a computer or access to one.

This point is best exemplified by the *Amos 'n' Andy* program. The Resource Guide Index lists 16 separate entries for the program, including ten in the Special Collections section, six with scripts, one each with audio, photographs, music and a discussion about the program, and six in the Bibliography section, including three books about the program and three books by Charles Correll and Freeman Gosden, the creators of the program. But, the Internet section does not include *any* of the 39,800 listings that were generated by a Google search for "'Amos and Andy' AND radio" or the 70,400 listings generated when the search parameters were changed to "'Amos 'n' Andy' AND radio," including the site of the widely respected *Amos 'n' Andy* scholar Elizabeth McLeod whose web site includes summaries of many early *Amos 'n' Andy* scripts as well as a lengthy article about the early origins of the program and its creators.

How this section is organized

In organizing the listings in this section, the authors used many of the same general category and subcategory headings that are used in the Bibliography section such as Religion-Catholic, Religion-Evangelical and Religion-Judaism.

Individual listings include the title of the Internet page as it appears at the top of the computer browser screen, the Internet address (URL) and, where appropriate, additional information about the content of the site. If the page title or URL is self explanatory, such as "State Archives & Historical Societies," no additional descriptive text was added to the listing.

It should be noted that the page title that appears on the top of the browser screen is the page title assigned by the owner of the site and that in many cases the title may not be indicative of the contents of the page. Readers are advised, therefore, that the key parts of each listing on the following pages are the URL and the site description.

In listing the Internet address (URL), if the address includes a "www," the beginning "http://" was omitted.

Some web sites were listed in more than one section because they contain sub pages with different types of content. The full web address for each listing is, however, slightly different.

Program Logs

The "Program Log" section of this chapter only includes sites that contain logs to many different programs. Researchers looking for logs for specific programs are advised to do a program specific Internet search as well as check the Bibliography section as many program specific books such as "Lux Presents Hollywood: A Show-By-Show History of the Lux Radio Theatre and the Lux Video Theatre, 1934–1957" by Connie Billips and Arthur Pierce include detailed logs. Researchers should also note that for some programs, multiple logs compiled by different people may exist and there may be differences in each of the logs.

Tips on searching

This is not the place for a general discussion on how to search the Internet. Nonetheless, what follows are some general suggestions relating to searching for Golden Age of Radio material.

1. When searching for radio material about a person or a program that also appeared in other media such as movies or television, add the word "radio" or "broadcasting" to the search, e.g., "'Al Jolson' AND radio."

2. Narrow the search by adding the phrases "old time radio" or "golden age of radio."

3. When researching specific programs, adding the words "scripts," "logs," "shows" or "programs" may be helpful.

4. To further narrow the search, add additional relevant terms, e.g., the sponsor, network, a year or the name of a person associated with the show.

Some cautionary notes

Internet sites come and go and, over time, are subject to changes of address, with and without links to their new addresses. While all the initial links included in the following pages were active as of November, 2005, there may be links on the individual pages that are no longer active.

It should also be noted that while the Internet provides a gateway to a wealth of information, it can also be a source of misinformation. In listing sites with historical information, the authors have selected sites that are generally well respected within the old time radio community. However, because they have not personally verified the content of each site, the authors suggest that researchers verify the online information with at least a second source.

Internet Resources

Archival Resources

Archives: General

3636. ArchivesUSA
http://archives.chadwyck.com
Access to holdings and contact information of more than 5,480 repositories with listings 132,396 special collections. Access is via subscription. Check with local libraries and/or other repositories for access.

3637. Corporate Archives
www.hunterinformation.com/corporat.htm
Online directory of corporate archives in the United States and Canada. The site is maintained by the Business Section of the Society of American Archivists.

3638. Historical Societies
www.ohiohistory.org/textonly/links/arch_hs.html
State Archives & Historical Societies

3639. OAC: List of Contributing Institutions
www.oac.cdlib.org/institutions/
Links to the online finding aids of a wide range of California repositories participating in the OAC (Online Archive of California), including public libraries, college and university libraries, including all campuses of the University of California, private museums, historical societies and more. Site can be searched for finding aids in all the included repositories.

3640. Proquest: Proquest Historical Newspapers
www.il.proquest.com/proquest
Access to the historical databases of "The New York Times" and many other newspapers dating back to the 19th century. Access is by subscription. Check with local libraries and/or other repositories for access.

3641. Northwest Digital Archives
http://nwda.wsulibs.wsu.edu/
As of 2005, the regional Archives provides information about collections at nineteen archives in Washington, Oregon, Idaho, and Montana.

3642. Repositories of Primary Sources
www.uidaho.edu/special-collections/Other.Repositories.html
A listing of over 5,000 web sites describing holdings of manuscripts, archives, rare books and historical photographs in the United States and overseas.

3643. Rigler and Deutsch Index
http://www.loc.gov/coll/nucmc/
An index to 78rpm recordings held in five libraries, including the Library of Congress and the New York Public Library for the Performing Arts, Rodgers and Hammerstein Sound Archive. Includes commercial recordings of all kinds of music and the spoken word. Access to the Index from the Library of Congress's web site is through the RLG/NUCMC web site, www.loc.gov/coll/nucmc/rlinsearch.html.

3644. Texas Archival Resources Online
www.lib.utexas.edu/taro/about.html
Searchable database of finding aids for libraries, museums and other repositories of archival materials in Texas.

3645. UMI: Dissertation Services
www.il.proquest.com/umi/dissertations/
A comprehensive database of Ph.D. dissertations. Copies can be purchased.

Archives: Chicago

3646. Chicago Area Archivists Online Repository
http://libsys.lib.uic.edu:591/CAA
Information about repositories and collections in the Chicago metropolitan area, including Cook, DuPage, Kane, Lake, McHenry and Will counties in Illinois and Lake and Porter counties in northwest Indiana. Site can be searched by keyword. A list of participating archives can be downloaded. Repositories include businesses, academic institutions, ethnic groups and other categories of institutions.

Archives: Educational/Public Broadcasting

3647. Collections in Other Repositories
www.lib.umd.edu/NPBA/other/list.html
Includes collections that are NOT in the National Public Broadcasting Archives but which are relevant to educational and public broadcasting.

Archives: Ethnic–African American

3648. African American Music and Culture Links
www.indiana.edu/~aaamc/links.html
Music links are divided by category. Additional links include history, art, media and publications.

Archives: Ethnic–Croatian

3649. History of Croatian American Radio Club
www.midwest-croatians.org/archives/croamrad.html
A Chicago based organization founded in 1935.

Archives: Ethnic–Mixed

3650. Index of The Immigration History Research Center: A Guide to Collections
www.loc.gov/catdir/toc/becites/genealogy/immigrant/91016262.idx.html
An exhaustive list of collections relating to various ethnic groups.

Archives: Ethnic–Polish

3651. Polish Archival Collections in the USA and Canada
www.piasa.org/polisharchivesinamerica.html#anchor18932
Maintained by The Polish Institute of Arts & Sciences of America. Also lists PISSA special collections.

Archives: Music–General

3652. Special Collections of Music
www.lib.washington.edu/Music/special.html

Archives: Music–Jazz

3653. Jazz/Blues Archives
www.lib.uchicago.edu/e/su/cja/jazzarch.html
An alphabetical listing arranged by state. Includes links to specific archives, e.g., Black Archives Research Center and the Archives of Folk Culture as well as links to the collections of individual musicians, e.g., Johnny Mercer and Duke Ellington.

Archives: Performing Arts

3654. SIMBA's International Directory of Performing Arts Collections and Institutions
www.sibmas.org/idpac/index.html
A searchable online database of special collections relating to the performing arts, including theatre, opera, music, ballet, film, circus, radio, television, cabaret and pantomime in over 7,000 international repositories. The database can be searched by name of institution, name of collection or location of institution but not by subject keyword, e.g., radio.

Archives: Religion–Catholic

3655. Catholic Archives, United States
www.catholiclinks.org/archivesenglish.htm

Archives: Religion–Evangelical

3656. Selected Other Archives with Material of Interest
www.wheaton.edu/bgc/archives/nonwarch.html
Maintained by the Billy Graham Center Archives.

Archives: Religion–Judaism

3657. Judaica Libraries and Archives on the Web
www.bibliomaven.com/judaica.html

3658. Libraries and Archives with Jewish Music Collections
www.jmwc.org/jmwc_libraries.html

Audio Preservation

3659. Audio preservation and restoration
www.lib.washington.edu/Music/preservation.html
Links to many organizations involved in audio preservation and restoration and a discussion of relevant issues. Includes different audio formats.

Bibliographies

3660. Radio Theory Site
www.kent.ac.uk/sdfva/rsn/
Additional radio related books, including many published outside the United States.

3661. Old Time Radio Bibliography and Book Reviews
www.old-time.com/bookreview/index.html
A downloadable file in a zip format of radio related books in the Library of Congress catalog based on keyword searches for radio history, broadcasting, radio and radio program.

Databases of Old Time Radio Programs

3662. Humongous Old-Time Radio Database Search Engine
www.old-time.com/humongousdb
As of 2005, the database contained about 86,000 shows and can be searched by program name, episode title or broadcast date.

3663. Otter Project
www.otterprojectonline.info/Otter_index.htm
As of 2005, the site contained a database of 1,369 series with over 135,000 episodes. Database is not searchable online but can be downloaded.

3664. RadioGoldindex
www.radiogoldindex.com
A comprehensive database with more than 86,000 program listings as of October, 2005. Searchable by program, artist and date. Includes general program content.

Databases of Old Time Radio Web Sites

3665. The Original Old Time Radio (OTR) Web Pages
www.old-time.com
A good starting page for many searches. The site indexes a wide array of radio related material on the Internet and contains a "google-like" search page where a keyword or phrase can be entered. A search for "Gracie Allen," for example, brought up pages that included references to her in articles and in audio recordings of programs.

3666. Radio Days
Otr.com
An extensive, user friendly list of links in a database searchable by keyword.

Music

(See also   Archives section)

Music: Big Bands

3667. Big Bands Database
www.nfo.net

Music: Country

3668. Music in the Digital Library of Appalachia
www.aca-dla.org/DLAMUSIC/dlamusic.html
Includes non-commercial sound recordings that document much of Appalachian music's geographic, ethnic, vocal and instrumental diversity.

Music: Radio Themes

3669. Old-Time Radio Music Theme List
w w w . c l a s s i c t h e m e s . c o m / o l d T i m e R a d i o T h e m e s /
radioThemeList.html
Music themes for U.S. old time radio series. Listed by both program and themes.

3670. Old Time Radio Theme Music
www.old-time.com/themes.html
Alphabetical list of programs with name of the theme music.

Miscellaneous

3671. California Radio Historical Society
www.californiahistoricalradio.com/community.html
Links to other radio history sites dealing primarily with the technical aspect of radio but also to other aspects of radio such as history, station history and more.

3672. Call Letter Origins: The List
www.oldradio.com/archives/nelson/origins.call-list.html
Includes a list of call letters with state and city locations. Note: Because the list is in alphabetical order, it begins with Canadian call letters.

3673. Old Time Radio (OTR) Internet Mailing List
www.lofcom.com/nostalgia/maillist.phtml
The oldest and largest Internet mailing list dedicated to Old Time Radio.

3674. OTR Articles
http://www.otrsite.com/articles/index.html
A collection of articles by various authors on a wide range of topics dealing with the Golden Age of Radio, including specific programs, the old time radio hobby, programming genres and radio personalities.

3675. OTR Researchers Group
http://groups.yahoo.com/group/OldTimeRadioResearchersGroup/
Mailing list for OTR collectors interested in sharing collections.

Programs

Programs: General

3676. The Nostalgia Pages Phorums
www.lofcom.com/nostalgia/phorums/index.php?f=23
Includes forums (phorums) for specific programs or personalities such as Jack Benny, Arthur Godfrey, the Great Gildersleeve, Sherlock Holmes, etc.

3677. Radio Days
www.otr.com
Includes pages dealing with specific programming genre, e.g., news broadcasts, mystery, science fiction , plus articles, a history timeline and also a database of other Internet sites.

Programs: Logs

3678. Armed Forces Radio Services Broadcasts
www.kcmetro.cc.mo.us/pennvalley/biology/lewis/crosby/afrs.htm
Includes *Command Performance, Mail Call* and *GI Journal.*

3679. Log List Index: Audio Classics Archive
www.audio-classics.com/1logalphalist.html
Logs can be downloaded without charge.

3680. OTR Database Logs
www.old-time.com/otrlogs2, or
www.old-time.com/otrlogs2/dbaselog.html
Logs can be downloaded in a zipped database ("dbf") format for a select list of programs.

3681. OTR Plot Summaries
www.geocities.com/sittingduck_1313
As of 2005, contained summaries of over 1,500 programs. Site lists program names and the number of summaries for each program.

3682. Old Time Radio Logs and Reviews
www.old-time.com/otrlogs2/index.html
As of 2005, contains about 160 logs.

3683. Radio and Audio (Thrilling Detective Web Site)
www.thrillingdetective.com/radio.html
Includes program information for dozens of radio detective programs.

3684. Vintage Radio Logs
www.otrsite.com/radiolog/index.html
Over 500 logs with episodic listings for several thousand programs that can be downloaded without cost. Also lists commercial sites that sell logs.

Programs: Ratings

3685. A.C. Nielsen Company
www.museum.tv/archives/etv/A/htmlA/acnielsen/acnielsen.htm
Part of the web page of the Museum of Broadcast Communications, the site features a series of articles about the company and its system of ratings. Includes a bibliography.

3686. Ratings Main Menu
http://www.dg125.com/Gazette/BestOfTheBest/RATINGSMAINMENU.htm
Includes information on Nielson and Hooper ratings for popular radio shows during the Golden Age of Radio.

Programs: Scripts

3687. Generic Radio Workshop OTR Script Library
www.genericradio.com
As of 2005, lists 108 scripts.

3688. Simply Radio Scripts
www.simplyscripts.com/radio_gz.html
Links to separate web pages with lists of available scripts. Many of the scripts are also listed on the Generic Radio Workshop site cited above.

3689. Tobacco Documents Online
www.Tobaccodocuments.org
The site contains scans of hundreds of scripts for programs that were sponsored by tobacco companies. The site can be searched for specific programs, e.g., *Big Story, Your Hit Parade* or *Lucky Strike Radio Hour* or for ALL radio scripts. To search for the latter, type the words "radio continuity" in the search box. The result will be 251 separate "hits" with each hit containing more than one script for the specific program. To maximize the number of possible hits, the search should be for "all collections," e.g., for all tobacco companies. Site can also be searched from a more user friendly site: http://dlxs.ckm.ucsf.edu.

Radio History

3690. Airchecks: Radio: Reelradio Reel Top 40 Radio Repository
www.reelradio.com
Links to Top 40 Radio sites and personalities, most from 1960s and later.

3691. The Broadcast Archive
www.oldradio.com
Hosted by Barry Mishkind, the site has links to different aspects of radio history including both the technical and programing components of radio. Sections dealing with the programing aspects of radio include general history, the people who built broadcasting, history of local and network programming, station histories and what the author calls "war stories from deep in the trenches of broadcast history." Also includes a discussion of station call letters and links to other sites.

3692. Broadcast History Resource Links
www.midcoast.com/~lizmcl/intro.html
Hosted by radio historian Elizabeth McLeod, this site includes several articles on early radio history by McLeod and links to other general radio history sites.

3693. The Broadcast Legends Home Page
www.broadcastlegends.com/links.html
Includes links to other organizations and sites of legendary broadcast figures.

3694. GAOR-WTIC (Golden Age of Radio)
www.goldenage-wtic.info/index.html
Audio recordings of 87 interviews conducted over seven years with noted radio personalities, including actors, writers, producers, engineers and others. A list of the interviews and the dates they were done is shown on the web site. Check the web site for information on how to obtain copies of specific interviews.

3695. Halper's History of Radio
www.old-time.com/halper/index.html
Hosted by Donna Halper, a broadcast historian at Emerson College, the site includes a series of articles by Halper on early radio history. The articles are organized by year and range from 1931 to 1947.

3696. History and Old-Time Radio
www.old-time.com/otrhx.html
Links to various aspects of radio history, from articles on sound effects and Tom Mix to chronologies of programs.

3697. History of American Broadcasting
http://members.aol.com/jeff560/jeff.html
Hosted by Jeff Miller, the radio portion of the site is divided between AM and FM history. The site includes articles by different authors on different aspects of radio history, including station history, the history of specific stations, call letter lists by year for both AM and FM stations, articles about specific radio broadcasts such as the "War of the Worlds" broadcast, the broadcast of the Hindenburg disaster and more.

3698. History of Radio
http://history.acusd.edu/gen/recording/radio.html
Includes a timeline beginning with the invention of radio and the starting year for many of the most popular programs from 1927 to 1950. Includes a comparative grid of network programming by genre for 1930 and 1940. For the period 1935–1950, it highlights key events in radio programing history. Has some additional history related links.

3699. OTR-The Golden Years
www.old-time.com/golden_age/index.html
Includes a series of tables, by year, showing the year selected programs started and the last year they were heard.

3700. Pacifica Radio Archives
http://www.pacificaradioarchives.org/
History of Pacifica's four listener supported stations.

3701. Radio Days
http://radio.barkis.net/links.html
Includes links to radio and television history sites, radio stations and radio station databases.

3702. United States Early Radio History
http://earlyradiohistory.us
Maintained by Thomas H. White, the site includes articles and extracts about early radio and related technologies concentrating on the United States in the period from 1897–1927. Includes articles relating to regulation, financing, building the broadcast band, history of early stations and lots more.

Radio Museums

3703. AWA (American Wireless Association) Selected Web Links-Museums
www.antiquewireless.org/links02.htm
Also includes links to radio (technical) clubs.

3704. Radio Magazine
http://beradio.com/industrylinks/
A list of radio museums, most but not all, dealing with the technical side of radio. Also includes a list of radio associations, also mostly, but not exclusively, with a technical orientation.

Reference

3705. Birth and Death Dates
http://mywebpage.netscape.com/bogusotr/instant/taz.html
List of over 3,800 radio personalities.

3706. Media-related Abbreviations
www.terramedia.co.uk/reference/abbreviations.htm

Station History

Station History: Individual Stations

Notes: What follows are just a few of the many web sites highlighting the history of specific stations. Links to additional stations can be found on the city and state Internet pages below.

This section is organized alphabetically by call letters or city without regard for the "title" of the web page.

3707. KDKA (Pittsburgh, PA)
http://kdkaradio.com/history.shtml
http://members.aol.com/jeff560/kdka.html

3708. KPFA (Berkeley, CA)
www.kpfa.org

3709. KQV (Pittsburgh, PA)
http://user.pa.net/~ejjeff/history.html

3710. Pacifica Radio (KPFA, KPFK, KPFT, WBAI)
www.pacificaradioarchives.org

3711. WCEN (Mount Pleasant, MI)
http://radio.barkis.net/wcen.html

3712. WGM (Chicago, IL)
wgmgold.com

3713. WLS (Chicago, IL)
wlshistory.com

3714. WLW (Cincinnati, OH)
www.fybush.com/site-020109.html
http://members.aol.com/jeff1070/wlw.html

3715. WMTE (Manistee, MI)
http://radio.barkis.net/wmte.html

3716. WTAE (Pittsburgh, PA)
http://user.pa.net/~ejjeff/taehist.html

3717. WTIC (Hartford, CT)
http://wticalumni.home.comcast.net

3718. WXYZ (Detroit, MI)
http://www.wxyz.com/wxyz/station_history/article/
0,2132,WXYZ_15941_3629658,00.html

Station History: Individual Cities

3719. Boston
www.tangentsunset.com/radioboston.htm
www.bostonradio.org

3720. Chicago
www.richsamuels.com/index1.html

3721. Cincinnati
www.oldradio.com/archives/stations/cinc.htm

3722. Cleveland
www.cleve-radio.com

3723. Denver
www.ad-mkt-review.com/public_html/docs/fs046.html

3724. Philadelphia
www.broadcastpioneers.com
http://members.aol.com/philaradio

3725. San Francisco
http://users.adams.net/~jfs/

3726. Washington, DC
www.dcrtv.org/mediaw4.html

Station History: Multiple Locations

3727. American Radio History
www.tangentsunset.com/usradiohistory.htm
Links to individual cities, e.g., Cleveland, Dallas, Detroit, Kansas City, Los Angeles, etc.

3728. History of U. S. Broadcasting by City
www.oldradio.com/archives/stations
As of 2005, includes links to 21 cities.

3729. Radio History links
http://users.adams.net/~jfs/links.htm
Links to other area histories, e.g., St. Louis, Chicago, etc.

Station History: States

3730. Florida (South) Radio History
www.univox.com/radio/wradioh.html
From 1923–present.

3731. Michiguide.com: History of Michigan AM Broadcasting
www.michiguide.com/history/am.html

3732. New Jersey AM Radio History
www.angelfire.com/nj2/piratejim/njamhistory7.html

3733. Texas: A History of Radio in North Texas, 1920s–1965
www.dfwradioarchives.com/origins1.htm

3734. West Virginia Broadcasting History Page
http://members.aol.com/jeff99500

Station History: Networks

3735. Amalgamated Broadcasting System
http://pcasacs.org/SPC/spcissues/25.1/Ward.htm
"The Quest to Form a Third Radio Network in the Early 1930s."
An article by Richard Ward in *Studies in Popular Culture,* 25:1

3736. Mutual Broadcasting System
http://oldradio.com/archives/prog/mbs.htm
An article about MBS by James Snyder.

3737. Network Histories
www.oldradio.com/archives/prog/nets.htm
Histories for various networks, from major ones to special interest, e.g., Metropolitan Opera, agriculture, etc.

3738. RKO, Mutual and General Teleradio Chronology
www.ketupa.net/rko2.htm
Includes NBC, RCA, ABC and more.

Chapter 5: Combined Index

How to Use the Index

Most indexes are straight forward and usually do not require an explanation. However, because of the special nature of the material in the Resource Guide, the authors believe that a few clarifying notes will assist the reader make the maximum possible use of this Index and the Guide.

How to use the Index

The Index includes the listings that appear in all three sections of the Guide: Special Collections (1–2256, 3739–3797), Bibliography (2260–3635) and Internet (3636–3738)

Program titles are italicized and titles of individual scripts or publications are in quotation marks. The beginning article "The" is not included in the listing. In titles that begin with an "A," the article is either dropped or placed at the end of the title.

Because many of the programs were known over the years by different names, every effort has been made to consolidate the listings under one heading with appropriate cross referencing. All the listing for *The Jack Benny Program*, for example, are shown under that listing with cross references listed under the *Jello-O Program, Canada Dry Ginger Ale Program* and the *General Tire Program*. In some instances, a program's alternate name/s is shown in parenthesis after the primary name, also with a cross reference.

The consolidation of titles becomes more problematic, however, when dealing with programs that kept the same sponsor and name such as the *Chase and Sanborn Hour* but over the years changed format and hosts. As a result, when a catalog description contains scripts for the *Chase and Sanborn* program it is not always clear which specific version of the program the script is for. If and when the date/s of the program are available, the reader can check the dates in a standard reference book such as Dunning's "On The Air: The Encyclopedia of Old-Time Radio" to determine which personality hosted the program during that time period.

When sufficient information was not available to safely consolidate similar but slightly different listings such as *The Drene Show* and *The Drene Shampoo Show* that *could or could not be* the same program, the Index lists each program separately.

Programs identified by the person's name, e.g., the *Danny Kaye Show*, are generally shown both under the program name and the performer's name, e.g., *Danny Kaye Show* and Kaye, Danny. However, in at least one large script collection where some programs are identified only by the name of the main performer, e.g., *Paul Whiteman*, and that person was known to have hosted many different programs, the Index entry is the person's name, e.g., Whiteman, Paul.

Entries that are cross referenced are shown either as "See also" or by repeating the appropriate entry number in both listings.

Given the above caveats and qualifications, researchers looking for specific programs or about specific personalities are advised to check the Index by both the program title *and*

the names of any of the people who may have been associated with the program such as supporting actors, writers, directors, producers and others.

Genre listings

A special feature of the Index is the grouping of programs into genre categories. This feature should be particularly helpful for identifying less well known programs.

Programs are listed under specific genre headings only when sufficient information about their content was known based on a description of the program in the Guide listing, on information in reference materials or because the name of the program was obvious, e.g., the *Children's Bookshelf*. However, it should be noted that some titles can be deceiving; the program listed simply as the *Rumpus Room* initially "sounded" like a children's program but upon further investigation turned out to be a musical variety show whose full name was *Johnny Olsen's Rumpus Room*.

As a general rule, a program title is listed only once under the appropriate genre heading although there may be multiple entries about the program throughout the Guide. For example, the *Cavalcade of America* is listed once under the "Drama" genre heading but under the *Cavalcade of America* listing, there are 22 separate entries for the program.

Placing programs into genre headings is a subjective process and the authors note that even well respected reference books on old time radio often assign the same program to different genre categories. The *Kate Smith Hour*, for example, could be considered both a music program and a variety program. Also, many programs can legitimately be placed in more than one category, e.g., *Fashions With Rations* dealt with fashion but because it dealt with wartime rationing it can also be considered a World War II program and *Amos 'n' Andy* is listed under both the "Comedy" and "Ethnic-African American" headings.

What follows is a brief description of the major genre headings used in the Index with examples of the types of programs assigned to each genre. The Index also includes many additional genre and subject oriented references such as agricultural, civil rights, consumer issues, gossip, libraries, soap operas, talk shows, temperance, westerns, weather, etc. that are self explanatory. All genre and subject oriented headings are shown in bold.

Selected Headings

Adaptations: Listings of specific plays, books or movies that have been adapted for radio.

Advertising: Includes listings about people involved in the advertising aspects of radio, scripts for advertisements and recordings of commercials. When a specific product or company is identified, they are listed separately in the Index.

Advice and inspirational: General advice, such as John J. Anthony's *Goodwill Hour*, "feel good" programs like *Cheerio* and inspirational programs like the *Voice of Experience.*

Biography-assorted: Includes special collections and books that contain information about more than one person.

Broadcasting techniques: Follows the general sub headings used in the Bibliography section as most of the entries in the Index are from this section of the Guide.

Business: Includes business oriented programs like *Wall Street Reports* or *Caravan of Industry* as well as listings dealing with general business issues and the business side of radio.

Cold War and communism: Includes news broadcasts, discussion programs and series such as *I Led Three Lives* and *I Was a Communist for the FBI.*

Comedy: Includes programs such as the *Aldrich Family, Lum and Abner* and the *Milton Berle Show.*

Drama: Includes "anthology" type programs such as *Cavalcade of America* and "historic" drama programs such as *Gallant American Women.*

Educational: Self explanatory, although this section may also include programs with a science content.

Gossip: Programs such as *Hedda Hopper's Hollywood.*

Health and medicine: Includes regularly scheduled programs such as *Voice of Chiropractic* as well as individual talks on health issues.

History of radio: Divided into three sub headings: General, which is self explanatory, Informal, which includes reminiscences, anecdotes, etc. and Economic and Social, which includes material that focuses on these aspects of radio history.

Homemaking: Self explanatory. This section overlaps Consumer issues, Fashion and Women's programs

Human interest: A small but hard-to-define category that includes a few programs that did not neatly fit into any other category such as the Ripley's *Believe It Or Not* or *Strange As It Seems.*

Husband and wife: Programs hosted by husbands and wives such as *Breakfast With Dorothy and Dick.* This section overhaps "Morning programs."

Labor: Divided into three sub headings. General, which includes material about labor or labor issues, Performing art's unions, which includes groups such as AFTRA and the Screen Writers Guild and Use of radio which includes programs created by or sponsored by labor unions or broadcast on union-owned stations.

Music: Divided into several sub headings based on the type of music, e.g., country and western, classical, jazz, etc. Music programs that could not be identified as to "type" are listed in the general Music heading. Note. As there may be an overlap between "Music" and "Variety" programs, researchers are advised to check both genre headings.

Mystery/Crime/Adventure: A broadly defined heading that includes programs such as *Gang Busters, Casey Crime Photographer* and *FBI In Peace and War.*

News broadcasts: Includes commentary and analysis programs by reporters and journalists but does not include entries for large audio collections that may also include some news broadcasts. News broadcasts relating specifically to World War II are indexed under "World War II-News broadcasts."

Politics and government: Generally includes entries about political figures e.g., Alfred M. Landon, programs by lawmakers "to the folks back home," programs about government or politics such as *Your County Government Report* and collections of political speeches. Programs on political issues or current events are generally listed under the "Public affairs" heading. Also, some large audio collections may also contain political speeches.

Public affairs: A broadly defined heading that includes programs dealing with current events, political issues and community affairs such as *America's Town Meeting of the Air, Americans All, Immigrants All* and *Minority Report.*

Public service: Includes Advertising Council campaigns, messages about the Red Cross or March of Dimes and reports about natural disasters.

Quiz and game programs: Self explanatory, except there can be an overlap between comedy and quiz shows as well educational programs and quiz shows.

Reference: Generally includes books and Internet sites that contain information about many programs and/or personalities such as annual yearbooks or John Dunning's "On the Air."

Religion: Subdivided into denominational sub headings such as Catholic, Evangelical, Methodist, etc. Listings dealing with religious programming in general or about programs that could not be identified by denomination are listed under the "Religion-general" heading.

Science: Self explanatory, except that some science programs of an educational nature may also be listed under the "Educational" heading.

Show business: Generally includes material about show business in general or other non radio aspects of show business. Vaudeville and minstrel shows are listed separately.

State, regional and local: Subdivided alphabetically by state, these listings include programs of local, regional or state interest such as centennial celebrations, local personalities, local historic events, etc.

Station history: Listings are grouped under three sub headings: by call letter, by city and by state. As a general rule, when the listing contains historical information about a station or notes that a particular program was aired on a specific station, or that a person was associated with a specific station, the listing is indexed under the station call letters. When the entry includes significant historical data about the station, it is also included in the state section.

Women's Programs: Many programs "appear" to fall into this category based on their names but only when the content was known were they placed in this genre category.

World War II listings: Divided into the following sub headings: General: Anything that does not fit into the other categories, Government agencies: Listings that involved work for a war related agency such of the Office of War Information (AFRS is listed under its own heading), Home front: A broadly defined category that includes the GI Wives Club of Minneapolis, scrap metal drives and building support for the war, News broadcasts and Programs and scripts: Self explanatory, except that many programs that "appeared" to deal with the war such as *Doctors at War* are not included unless additional confirming information about the program was available

Combined Index

About the Authors

The Siegels have been collaborating as authors since 1992, combining their knowledge, experience, interests and diverse skills.

A collector of Golden Age of Radio broadcasts, books and ephemera for over 40 years, David is the editor of *The Witch's Tale*, an anthology of scripts from the pioneering 1930s horror program of the same name and the co-author of *Flashgun Casey, Crime Photographer: From the Pulps to Radio and Beyond,* an in-depth look at the varied media career of a popular pulp hero. He has also written articles about the Golden Age of Radio for other publications, provided resource material to numerous authors for their books on different aspects of old time radio and made audio material of hard-to-find broadcasts available to film and documentary makers.

Although Susan's involvement in old time radio is more recent (only the past 15 years), her interest in researching the whereabouts of radio related special collections is an outgrowth of her ongoing conversations with old time radio authors and enthusiasts about the difficulty of finding source material scattered in libraries throughout the United States.

The Siegels alternate their time between radio and used books and are the authors of the *Used Book Lover's Guides*, a series of seven guidebooks to 8,000 used book dealers in the United States and Canada. The guidebooks are continually updated on the Book Hunter Press main web site, www.bookhunterpress.com.

Prior to embarking on a career as authors and publishers, David was a Superintendent of Schools and Susan was a public relations professional.

www.ingramcontent.com/pod-product-compliance
Lightning Source LLC
Chambersburg PA
CBHW050412110426
42812CB00006BA/1870